AMERICAN DECADES

1950 - 1959

AmericaN DecadeS

1950-1959

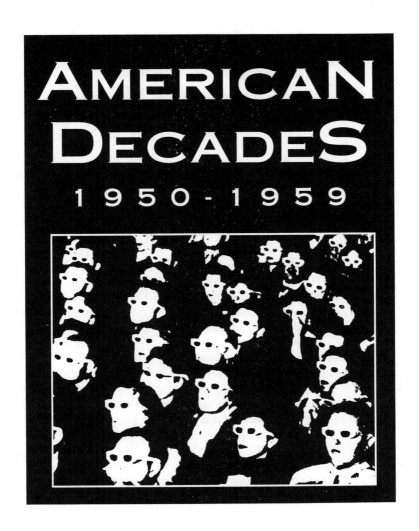

Edited by
Richard Layman

Associate Editors
James W. Hipp and Dennis Lynch

A MANLY, INC. BOOK

Gale Research Inc. • DETROIT • WASHINGTON, D.C. • LONDON

AMERICAN DECADES
1950-1959

Matthew J. Bruccoli and Richard Layman, *Editorial Directors*

Printed in the United States of America

Published simultaneously in the United Kingdom
by Gale Research International Limited
(An affiliated company of Gale Research Inc.)

Library of Congress Catalog Card Number 93-40732
ISBN 0-8103-5727-5

The trademark **ITP** is used under license.
10 9 8 7 6 5 4 3

CONTENTS

INTRODUCTION

The Danger of Generalization. It is always tempting to oversimplify history; even so, no American decade in the twentieth century lends itself more readily to facile summation than the 1950s. It is clear that there was a sweeping change in American life after World War II. It is equally clear that generalizations about the decade must be carefully considered and applied only with caution. The American people constitute a very large topic. In 1950 there were more than 151 million Americans, and the population increased at what some thought to be the alarming rate of 19 percent over the decade. There were, on average, some 100 million voting-age adults in America during the 1950s, and, being Americans, they tended to blaze their own paths, even if there are certain patterns recognizable in hindsight.

Innovation. To make history palatable, popular historians tend to label periods for convenience. Labels come easily to the 1950s — so easily that it is difficult to choose a suitable name among them for the busy decade. It was a time of unparalleled innovation: nationally broadcast television, commercial jet transport, microwave ovens, turnpikes, rock 'n' roll, commercial hotel chains, fast food, polio and measles vaccinations, and birth control pills were all introduced during the 1950s, though in many cases their major impact came later.

In Search of a Label. Portable radios the size of a hardbound dictionary were plugged into a wall outlet or alternatively ran on a handful of D-cell batteries in 1950; battery-operated radios the size of cigarette packs were available by 1960. Records were, for the most part, 78 RPM and were played on raspy, single-speaker sets in 1950; by 1960, 45 RPM records and long-playing albums were played on high-quality, low-cost stereophonic sound systems. Many of the nation's public schools, particularly in the South, were segregated in 1950; by 1960 the federal government had taken an active and effective role in school desegregation. Children were killed or incapacitated by polio and a host of other infectious diseases in 1950; by 1960 polio was all but eradicated, and vaccinations had been developed for the most threatening childhood diseases.

Big Science. To some the 1950s were the age of big science. The success of the war effort triggered an explosive release of technological creativity in the postwar era and provided the stimulus for an unparalleled period of scientific discovery. With the success of the Manhattan Project, which developed the atom bomb, attitudes toward science changed. Scientists were no longer viewed as daydreaming eggheads who engaged in experiments out of simple curiosity. They were problem solvers. They no longer worked in benign isolation; teams of scientists shared their expertise to achieve practical goals. Top scientists no longer worked in makeshift laboratories or in underfunded university departments where they checked on experiments between classes; they had access to such expensive scientific tools as electron microscopes and atomic accelerators in well-funded research facilities. When America needed military might to win World War II, science came to the rescue by providing practical applications for complicated principles. The performance was so impressive that it suggested a method for solving almost any problem: bring together the best scientific minds in a field and provide them with unlimited resources.

Big Results. This method was called "big science," big because it cost a lot of money and because the results were astonishing. Big science cured polio, produced the computer, introduced the space age, and created the television generation by inventing the medium of obsession. Big science redefined American commerce because it created huge industries, such as the health-care industry and what President Dwight D. Eisenhower called the military-industrial complex. Big science provided the technology for thousands of new products that businesses became prosperous selling and that consumers worked, saved, and borrowed to buy.

Cold War. To some the 1950s were the age of the cold war, when American leaders defined their role in international diplomacy and thus molded the American personality. By demonstrating the concept of weapons so awesome that they could destroy civilization, military leaders convinced a generation of Americans that a responsibility of government was to ensure military superiority. Strong government required a strong military, people were convinced; and the military must not only be strong, it must be unequaled. In atomic warfare losing was a permanent condition. The high-stakes arms race with the Soviet Union that resulted had repercussions that extended into schoolrooms and suburban neighborhoods, as American anxiety about the encroaching enemy seeking to subvert the government and spy on American ingenuity approached hysteria. Political careers were made on the promise of revealing the level of Communist infiltration into American life; lives were ruined by charges of Communist sympathizing; and the average American's view of the world was affected by the cold-war spectacle known as McCarthyism.

Atomic Dread. In world politics, America undertook the role of policeman for the world, beginning with a three-year military action in Korea to prevent "the forcible absorption of free peoples into an aggressive despotism," in the words of Secretary of State Dean Acheson. The cost was 33,629 American soldiers killed in battle. Halting or at least containing the spread of communism was excuse enough for military intervention, or, preferably, the threat of intervention, at trouble spots around the world. The result was a decade of tension as annihilation by ever-more-powerful weapons seemed always possible and too-often imminent. That aura of dread had curious effects. Some people were unable to confront their own mortality. They built fallout shelters, sought refuge in extremist political organizations, and found comfort in the paternalistic arms of religious groups, both traditional and evangelistic. Others were liberated by atomic dread. In the arts, movements espousing fiercely independent modes of free expression attracted an enthusiastic following, and the commercial fallout from atomic research offered appealing diversions for people seeking relief from the tensions of the day.

Education. To some, the 1950s were the decade of education, when the priorities of the nation shifted markedly from brawn to brains. Hard work was still the American virtue, but Americans recognized that hard work alone was insufficient to ensure success in the postwar world. The nation came to recognize that intelligence and knowledge are key elements of strength and that they must be nurtured. The availability and the quality of education, from kindergarten through graduate school and even self-teaching — was a national concern during the 1950s. Americans recognized that only by thoughtful instruction, including vocational training, would their children grow up with the skills necessary to compete. Attracted by dreams of prosperity and by urban values that promoted communal action, families moved in unprecedented numbers from rural America to the cities, where, in one way or another, either wittingly or not, they confronted life in a world more sophisticated than the one their fathers and mothers inhabited.

Integration. To some, the 1950s were the decade of integration, a time when Americans had to confront the image of a World Series championship baseball team with three black players, contrasted with the image of a black schoolgirl being turned away from the schoolhouse door in Little Rock, Arkansas; the image of their daughters dancing suggestively to the rock 'n' roll sounds of lusty black performers singing about sex, contrasted with the image of two white men in Mississippi bragging after they were found innocent by an all-white jury of mutilating and drowning a fourteen-year-old black boy for whistling at a white woman. Integration was pioneered, as so many innovations in the 1950s were, by the military. In the name of constitutional rights and human decency integration was forced during the 1950s on a white society often unwilling to make a place in the workforce and in its neighborhoods for people considered socially, if not physiologically, inferior. The civil rights struggle was sometimes violent; more often it was soul wrenching and agonizing, as people struggled with their consciences, weighing deeply etched convention against moral rectitude.

Broad Inequities. Civil rights was more than a social issue. It was economic at its roots. Black men wanted more than the right to sit in the front of public buses and drink at the same water fountains as whites. They wanted the right to work alongside white men and to earn the same pay. So did white women. The consideration of equal rights for blacks suggested inevitably that other elements of society might have been subjected to inequitable treatment by an insensitive social system dominated by white males. Women, in particular, having been forced by the war to the workplace and forced by the war's end back to domestic service, began to see a commonality between their lack of economic opportunity and that of blacks.

Rock 'n' Roll. To many, the 1950s were the age of rock 'n' roll, a time when the nation's youth asserted themselves through a music that was distinctly theirs. The message the music delivered was more complex than it was given credit for during the decade. The message of rock 'n' roll was clearly racial. The dominant influence on rock 'n' roll came from black rhythm and blues music, and after the color barrier was cracked in the mid 1950s, black groups were at least as popular among white audiences as white groups; and black superstars, such as Chuck Berry, Ray Charles, and Fats Domino, commanded huge audiences. The message of rock 'n' roll was hedonistic. The music was about sex, good times, freedom from parental control, and expressions of love. Parents worried that the music undermined traditional values, and they were on the right track. The music did not undermine values, but it did announce that these values were under revision by a new generation. The message of rock 'n' roll was libertine. Rock 'n' roll was the music of a generation announcing its independence. It was blamed for a perceived rise in juvenile crime, teen marriage, and adolescent incorrigibility. Elders mistook the symptom for the cause. The message of rock 'n' roll was commercial. The exploding music industry demonstrated the financial clout wielded by the children of the 1950s. They possessed the stuff of real power in a capitalist society — money.

Spontaneity. To some, the 1950s were the decade of spontaneity. The arts took on qualities after the war that disturbed traditionalists. Abstract expressionist artists turned their backs on representation, even representation of the subconscious mind. They embraced instead a theory of spontaneity in which art was defined as the enduring record of an event, recording the frenzy of motion of an artist's swinging arms and feet at some moment or, in layers, some set of moments. In jazz, improvisation was held in higher regard than studied composition. As jazzmen became more skilled in the uses of atonal harmonies and syncopated rhythms, pioneers in the field introduced musical forms that shunned standard melodic structures and rhythm altogether, so that music became purely expressive without any of the strictures of form. The Beats explored similarly liberating techniques in literature. Truly spontaneous prose was considered the pinnacle of creative expression by some, to the dismay of careful writers who believed that art required craft, by definition.

These and More. The 1950s were the decade of miniaturization, when the development of the transistor coupled with people's concerns about the use of space made the word *compact* a staple of consumerism. The 1950s were the decade of the tail fin, when cars came to symbolize the futuristic spirit of the postwar age, representing speed, independence, conspicuous consumption, and technical superiority. The 1950s were the decade of lost innocence, the decade of communication, the decade of exploration and discovery. All of these and more.

PLAN OF THIS VOLUME

This is the first of nine volumes in the *American Decades* series. Each volume will chronicle a single twentieth-century decade from thirteen separate perspectives, broadly covering American life. The volumes begin with a chronology of world events outside of America, which provides a context for American experience. Following are chapters, arranged in alphabetical order, on thirteen categories of American endeavor ranging from business to medicine, from the arts to sports. Each of these chapters contains the following elements: first, a table of contents for the chapter; second, a chronology of significant events in the field; third, Topics in the News, a series, beginning with an overview, of short essays describing current events; fourth, anecdotal sidebars of interesting and entertaining, though not necessarily important, information; fifth, Headline Makers, short biographical accounts of key people during the decade; sixth, People in the News, brief notices of significant accomplishments by people who mattered; seventh, Awards of note in the field (where applicable); eighth, Deaths during the decade of people in the field; and ninth, a list of Publications during or specifically about the decade in the field. In addition, there is a general bibliography at the end of this volume, followed by an index of photographs and an index of subjects.

ACKNOWLEDGMENTS

This book was produced by Manly Inc.

Photography editors are Edward Scott and Timothy C. Lundy. Layout and graphics supervisor is Penney L. Haughton. Copyediting supervisor is Bill Adams. Typesetting supervisor is Kathleen M. Flanagan. Julie E. Frick is an editorial associate. Systems manager is George F. Dodge. The production staff includes Phyllis Avant, Joseph Matthew Bruccoli, Ann M. Cheschi, Patricia Coate, Denise Edwards, Sarah A. Estes, Joyce Fowler, Laurel Gladden, Jolyon M. Helterman, Ellen McCracken, Rebecca Mayo, Kathy Lawler Merlette, Sean Moriarty, Pamela D. Norton, Thomas J. Pickett, Patricia Salisbury, Maxine K. Smalls, William L. Thomas, Jr., and Wilma Weant.

Robert S. McConnell was lead library researcher. Walter W. Ross and Deborah M. Chasteen did library research. They were assisted by the following librarians at the Thomas Cooper Library of the University of South Carolina: Linda Holderfield and the interlibrary-loan staff; reference librarians Gwen Baxter, Daniel Boice, Faye Chadwell, Cathy Eckman, Gary Geer, Qun "Gerry" Jiao, Jean Rhyne, Carol Tobin, Carolyn Tyler, Virginia Weathers, Elizabeth Whiznant, and Connie Widney; circulation-department head Thomas Marcil; and acquisitions-searching supervisor David Haggard.

AMERICAN DECADES

1950 · 1959

WORLD EVENTS: SELECTED OCCURENCES OUTSIDE THE UNITED STATES

1950

- Thor Heyerdahl's book *Kon-Tiki* is published.
- Marc Chagall's painting *King David* is exhibited.
- Alberto Giacometti's sculpture *Seven Figures and a Head* is exhibited.
- Max Ophüls's film *La Ronde* premieres.
- Akira Kurosawa's film *Rashomon* premieres.
- Australia retains Davis cup in tennis, winning finals against United States.

18 Jan. Christopher Fry's play *Venus Observed* opens at Saint James Theatre, London.

21 Jan. T. S. Eliot's play *The Cocktail Party* opens at New York's Henry Miller Theater.

29 Jan. The Vatican recognizes baptisms in the Presbyterian, Congregational, Baptist, Methodist, and Disciples of Christ faiths.

24 Feb. The executive committee of the World Council of Churches in Bossey, Switzerland, appeals for a world peace initiative.

7 Feb. Great Britain and the United States recognize the Vietnamese government of Bao Dai.

1 Mar. Chiang Kai-shek assumes the presidency of Nationalist China on the island of Formosa (Taiwan).

27 Apr. Marshal Tito is reelected premier of Yugoslavia.

8 May President Harry S Truman initiates the U.S. military mission to Vietnam.

11 May Eugène Ionesco's play *The Bald Soprano* opens at Paris's Théâtre des Noctamules.

25 June North Korea invades South Korea.

30 June U.S. combat troops enter the Korean War.

22 July Leopold III, exiled king of Belgium, returns to his country and is met by socialist demonstrations protesting his arrival.

1 Aug. Leopold III reluctantly abdicates the throne of Belgium in favor of his son Baudouin.

3 Aug.	Pope Pius XII declares abstract art and "art for art's sake" immoral.
25 Oct.	Jean Anouilh's play *The Rehearsal* opens at Paris's Théâtre Marigny.
1 Nov.	Pope Pius XII publicly proclaims the bodily assumption of the Virgin Mary into heaven.
5 Nov.	The London *Sunday Times* awards £1000 to T. S. Eliot, naming his play *The Cocktail Party* the year's outstanding contribution to English literature.
30 Nov.	The Soviet Union vetoes a UN ultimatum demanding Chinese Communists withdraw from Korea.
19 Dec.	Gen. Dwight D. Eisenhower is named supreme commander of Allied Forces in Western Europe by NATO.
23 Dec.	The Vatican confirms the discovery of Saint Peter's tomb beneath Saint Peter's Basilica.
28 Dec.	The *Time* magazine choice for "Man of the Year" is the "U.S. Fighting Man," the first time the magazine has selected a symbol instead of an individual.

1951

- The Chemise Lacoste is exported to the United States for the first time by the Izod Company.
- In September Great Britain's first supermarket chain opens.
- Albert Camus's novel *L'Homme révolté* (The Rebel) is published.
- Max Ophüls's film *Le Plaisir* premieres.
- Jean Anouilh's play *Colombe* opens.
- Salvador Dalí's painting *Christ of St. John of the Cross* is exhibited.
- Pablo Picasso's painting *Massacre in Korea* is exhibited.
- Australia retains Davis cup in tennis, winning finals against the United States.

11 Jan.	The Vatican newspaper publishes a decree prohibiting Roman Catholic priests from membership in Rotary clubs, which, the church says, are connected with the Masons and are, therefore, anti-Catholic.
12 Jan.	The United Nations Convention on Prevention and Punishment of Genocide goes into effect.
14 Feb.	Moscow's Communist youth newspaper *Komosomolskaya Pravda* describes the successful heart and lung transplant from one dog to another.
19 Mar.	The European Coal and Steel Community is established by France, West Germany, Italy, Belgium, Holland, and Luxembourg.
11 Apr.	Three unidentifed men return the stolen Stone of Scone to Westminster Abbey after it was stolen the previous Christmas by Scottish Nationalists.
20 Apr.	*Miracle in Milan* and *Julie* win the Cannes Film Festival's Grand Prize; Michael Redgrave wins best actor, and Bette Davis wins best actress.
21 Apr.	Iranian Parliament nationalizes the country's oil industry.

13 June   The Roman Catholic church beatifies Pope Pius XII after a church investigation declares his recovery from two tumors as miraculous.

5 Aug.   Five hundred thousand youths participate in the Communist-sponsored World Youth Festival in East Berlin.

8 Sept.   Japan signs a treaty with forty-eight non-Communist countries, formally ending World War II.

25 Oct.   Winston Churchill wins reelection as Great Britain's prime minister.

26 Nov.   In response to criticism, Pope Pius XII retracts his earlier statement against abortion when the mother's life is endangered.

27 Nov.   The United Nations and North Korean negotiators agree on a cease-fire line and begin discussing truce enforcement proposals.

27 Dec.   Peace negotiators fail to agree on an armistice by midnight, consequently voiding the 27 November cease-fire in Korea.

1952

- Doris Lessing's *Martha Quest,* the first volume of her five-novel sequence *The Children of Violence,* is published.
- Evelyn Waugh's novel *Men at Arms* is published.
- Angus Wilson's novel *Hemlock and After* is published.
- Samuel Beckett's play *Waiting for Godot* opens.
- Marc Chagall's artwork *The Green Night* is exhibited.
- Raoul Dufy's painting *The Pink Violin* is exhibited.
- Georges Rouault's artwork *End of Autumn* is exhibited.
- Vittoria de Sica's film *Umberto D* opens.
- At the Olympic Games in Helsinki, the United States wins forty-three gold medals to twenty-two for the Soviet Union and twenty-two for Hungary.

12 Feb.   The Civil Aeronautics Board limits transatlantic air service to regularly scheduled lines.

6 Feb.   Princess Elizabeth becomes Queen of England on the death of her father, King George VI.

10 Mar.   Former Cuban president Fulgencia Batista y Zaldívar becomes dictator after overthrowing President Prio Soccaras in a military coup.

14 Mar.   The UN's Economic and Social Council's Subcommittee on Freedom of Information issues a draft of an international code of ethics for journalists.

16 Mar.   Roman Catholic bishop auxilliary Fulton J. Sheen declares that American Catholics do not want an established church and will obey a government that "comes from God."

5 Apr.   At the International Economic Conference the Soviet Union offers to buy $7.5–$10 billion worth of goods from the West in the next two to three years.

22 Mar.	Pope Pius XII reaffirms the right of the church to interpret divine law in regard to public, economic, and social life.
29 Apr.	New York's Lever House opens and becomes the example for energy-wasting architecture throughout the world.
30 Apr.	President Tito announces that Yugoslavia will not join NATO.
6 May	King Farouk I of Egypt proclams he is a direct descendant of Prophet Mohammed, assuming the title of El Sayed.
10 May	The Cannes International Film Festival awards Orson Welles's *Othello* best film honors and Marlon Brando best actor for his role in *Viva Zapata.*
12 May	The International Press Institute says that an increasing number of governments are imposing more restrictions on legitimate news-gathering organizations.
26 May	The Church of England rejects the idea of easing divorce laws and also recommends outlawing artificial insemination.
3 June	Nguyen Van Tam is appointed premier of Vietnam, replacing Tran Van Huu.
26 July	King Farouk I abdicates after Gen. Mohammed Naguik leads a successful anti-corruption coup.
22 Aug.	West German movie theaters show the movie *The Desert Fox,* a sympathetic depiction of German World War II general Erwin Rommel, after a ten-month delay caused by American objections.
27 Aug.	Nonwhites are removed from electoral rolls in South Africa.
28 Aug.	The Third World Conference on Faith and Order in Lund, Sweden, closes without reaching agreement on uniting Christian religions.
18 Sept.	The Soviet Union vetoes UN admission for Japan.
22 Sept.	Sears, Roebuck and Company forms a partnership with the Toronto mail-order house Simpson, Ltd.
22 Oct.	The American Biblical Encyclopedia Society publishes the Torah in English for the first time.
4 Nov.	Dwight D. Eisenhower is elected president of the United States.
15 Dec.	Communist China rejects the UN's Korean truce plan.

1953

- Denmark enacts a new constitution lowering the nation's voting age to twenty-three.

- The U.S. Justice Department informs Charlie Chaplin he will not be allowed into the United States until he can satisfy the Immigration and Naturalization Office that he is not "a dangerous and unwholesome character" (that is, a Communist).

- Christian Dior creates an uproar when he announces his 1953 fall hemlines will measure sixteen inches from the ground.

- The coronation of Queen Elizabeth influences fashion, making jeweled tiaras the year's most popular accessory for evening gowns.

- British Overseas Airways (BOAC) begins operational use of the Rolls-Royce turboprop-powered Vickers *Viscount* passenger aircraft.

- German chemist Karl Ziegler uses atmospheric pressure instead of a more difficult pressure method in a new catalytic process for producing polyethylene.

- Researchers in Basel, Switzerland, synthesize carotene, the provitamin of vitamin A, from acetone and acetylene.

- Australian Ken Rosewall wins the French and Australian tennis singles titles.

- Australia retains the Davis cup in tennis, winning in finals against the United States.

- Maureen Connally wins tennis "Grand Slam" by winning the Australian, French, English, and U.S. women's singles titles.

- Ben Hogan wins the British Open.

- Marc Chagall's painting *Eiffel Tower* is exhibited.

- Henri Mattisse's painting *The Snail* is exhibited

- Heinrich Böll's novel *Acquainted with the Night* is published.

1 Jan.	Ernest Bloch's musical *Suite Hebraique* is performed in Chicago.
1 Feb.	Japan's first television station begins broadcasting.
14 Feb.	Hollywood's Foreign Press Association announces that in 1952 Susan Hayward and John Wayne were the most popular stars according to a poll of fans in fifty countries.
25 Feb.	President Dwight Eisenhower says that he favors the reciprocal trade agreement but it should include an escape clause because of cheap foreign-labor competition.
4 Mar.	Iranian premier Mohammad Mossadegh retains power after four days of fighting by Nationalists, Royalists, Communists, and religious groups.
5 Mar.	Soviet premier Joseph Stalin dies.
6 Mar.	Georgy Malenkov becomes Soviet premier.
26 Mar.	Jean Anouilh's play *Medea* opens at Paris's Théâtre de l'Atelier.
2 June	Queen Elizabeth II is coronated.
6 June	Darius Milhaud's Fifth Symphony is broadcast on radio from Turin.
7 June	Vietnamese premier Nguyen Van Tam demands that France give his government a say in foreign affairs.
27 July	The Korean War ends.
22 Aug.	Shah Mohammad Reza Pahlevi returns to power as Prime Minister Mossadegh is ousted from the Iranian government.
25 Aug.	The British Trades Union Congress recommends a cautious approach to continuing the nationalization of British industry.
13 Sept.	Nikita Khrushchev is named first secretary of the Soviet Communist party's Central Committee.

26 Sept.	Pope Pius XII proclaims 1954 a Marian Year to celebrate the one hundredth anniversary of the definition of Immaculate Conception as Catholic dogma.
12 Oct.	Six thousand sugar workers strike in British Guiana (Guyana).
5 Nov.	Terrence Rattigan's play *The Sleeping Prince* opens at London's Phoenix Theater, with Laurence Olivier and Vivien Leigh.
6 Nov.	Masao Oki's *Atomic Bomb* symphonic fantasy is performed in Tokyo.
20 Nov.	U.S. Roman Catholics issue a statement condemning Communist efforts to suppress religion as "the bitterest, the bloodiest persecution in all history."
1 Dec.	AT&T announces it will lay the first telephone cable across the Atlantic.
17 Dec.	Dmitry Shostakovich's Tenth Symphony performed in Leningrad.
22 Dec.	Friedrich Dürrenmatt's play *Ein Engel Kommt nach Babylon* (An Angel Comes to Babylon) opens at Munich's Kammerspiele.

1954

- Ilya Grigorovich Ehrenburg's *The Thaw* is the first Russian novel to criticize the Stalin regime in the Soviet Union; "The Thaw" is taken as the name of the post-Stalin liberalization of Soviet literature.

- Thomas Mann's novel *Felix Krull* is published.

- Heinrich Böll's novel *The Unguarded House* is published.

- William Golding's novel *Lord of the Flies* is published.

- Salvador Dalí's painting *Crucifixion* is exhibited.

- Pablo Picasso's painting *Sylvette* is exhibited.

- Marc Chagall's painting *The Red Roofs* is exhibited.

- Akira Kurosawa's film *The Seven Samurai* premieres.

- Ingmar Bergman's film *Smiles of a Summer* premieres.

- Jean Renoir's film *French Can Can* premieres.

- Gabrielle "Coco" Chanel brings her famed Chanel Look back into haute couture after a fifteen-year absence.

- Montreal physicians Heinz Lehmann and G. E. Hanrahan report success in treating psychotic patients with the French drug chlorpromazine. Philadelphia pharmaceutical company Smith, Kline, and French market it as Thorazine, a brand-name drug for schizophrenic patients.

- Britain permits antibiotic feed supplements for farm animals. United States livestock farmers purchase $50 million worth of these supplements.

- Mercedes introduces the first fuel-injection system for automobiles on its Mercedes 300 SL.

- West Germany defeats Hungary for the World Cup Soccer championship 3 to 2 at Bern's Wanddorf Stadium.

19 Jan.	Costa Rica's demand for a 50 percent share of United Fruit Company's profits is rejected by the company.
12 Feb.	*The Legend of the Stone Flower,* a ballet, is performed at Moscow's Bolshoi Theater, with music by the late Sergey Prokofiev.
13 Mar.	French forces are attacked by Vietminh combat troops at Dien Bien Phu in northern Vietnam.
12 Mar.	*Moses and Aaron,* an opera by the late Arnold Schoenberg, is performed at Hamburg's Musikhalle.
23 Apr.	The United States lends $100 million to the European Coal and Steel Community to revive the European capital market.
30 Apr.	Darius Milhaud's Fourth Piano Concerto performed at Haifa, Israel.
5 Apr.	President Dwight D. Eisenhower announces that the United States will not strike first with the hydrogen bomb.
6 May	Roger Bannister of Great Britain runs the mile in three minutes, 59.4 seconds at Oxford, the first runner to break the four-minute mile.
29 May	Pope Pius XII proclaims the late Pope Pius X a saint of the Roman Catholic church.
6 July	The evangelist Billy Graham returns from a five-month tour during which he preached at three hundred meetings in Great Britain and Western Europe.
21 July	Vietnam is divided into North and South Vietnam at the 17th parallel by the Geneva Accord.
1 Aug.	Egypt ends its economic blockade of the Suez Canal Zone.
17 Aug.	Roman Catholic clergy are given the option to use English in administering the sacraments of baptism, matrimony, and extreme unction.
30 Aug.	The World Council of Churches calls for abolition of all mass destruction weapons and reduction of conventional arms as a step to ending war.
8 Sept.	The Manila Pact establishes the Southeast Treaty Organization (SEATO).
12 Sept.	The three hundredth anniversary of the first Jewish settlement in North America is celebrated.
14 Sept.	Benjamin Britten's opera *Turn of the Screw,* with libretto adapted from Henry James's work, is first performed.
22 Sept.	Terence Rattigan's plays *Separate Tables* and *Table Number Seven* open at London's Saint James's Theatre with Eric Portman.
27 Sept.	Mao Tse-tung is reelected chairman of the People's Republic of China.
1 Oct.	Yugoslavia and the Soviet Union settle their first trade agreement since 1948, involving the exchange of nonstrategic goods.
22 Oct.	West Germany is admitted to NATO.
6 Nov.	The General Agreement on Trade and Tariffs members approve a Danish resolution censuring the United States for maintaining quantitative import restrictions on dairy products.

1955

- Ross and Norris McWhirter publish *The Guinness Book of World Records*, which sells twenty-four million copies.

- Graham Greene's novel *The Quiet American* is published.

- J. R. R. Tolkien's novel *Lord of the Rings* is published.

- Philip Larkin's poetry volume *The Less Deceived* is published.

- Pablo Picasso's painting *The Women of Algiers* is exhibited.

- Salvador Dalí's painting *The Lord's Supper* is exhibited.

- Giorgio De Chirico's painting *Italian Square* is exhibited.

- Bernard Buffet's painting *Double Portrait of Birdie* is exhibited.

- The Vienna State Opera House reopens after having been almost completely destroyed by wartime bombing and shelling.

- France's Notre Dame du Haut at Ronchamp is completed by Le Corbusier.

- British biochemist Dorothy Hodgkins discovers vitamin B-12 (cyanocobalamin). Vitamin B-12 can be used to treat pernicious anemia and other deficiency diseases.

- Volkswagen introduces the Kharmann-Ghia two-seat sportscar. The Kharmann company of Osnabrück produced the body while Ghia of Italy designed the car.

5 Jan.	The World Bank expels Czechoslovakia for nonpayment of dues and for not furnishing required trade and economic information.
13 Feb.	Four Dead Sea Scrolls are purchased by the Israeli government from the Syrian Archbishop Metropolitan.
6 Apr.	Anthony Eden becomes Great Britain's prime minister upon the retirement of Winston Churchill.
14 May	The Soviet Union, Albania, Bulgaria, Czechoslovakia, East Germany, Hungary, Poland, and Romania form a unified military command under the Warsaw Pact.
30 May	Fifteen South American coffee producers establish an International Coffee Bureau to stabilize coffee prices.
5 June	Billy Graham opens a crusade in Paris, his first visit into a non-English-speaking and predominantly Catholic city.
25 July	Yugoslavian president Tito says his country is willing to resume relations with the Soviet Communist party.
28 Aug.	Israel and Egypt continue skirmishes along the Gaza Strip.
13 Sept.	West Germany and the Soviet Union establish diplomatic relations.
26 Oct.	Ngo Dinh Diem proclaims South Vietnam a republic and names himself premier.
16 Nov.	Israel requests military aid from the United States to counteract the Soviet aid Egypt is receiving.
29 Dec.	West Germany passes Great Britain as the major West European steel producer.

1956

- Erich Fromm's book *The Art of Loving* is published.

- Albert Camus's novel *La Chute* (The Fall) is published.

- Françoise Sagan's novel *Un Certain Sourine* (A Certain Smile) is published.

- Cecil Day-Lewis's novel *A Tangled Webb* is published.

- Eugenio Montale's novel *La farfalla di Dinard* (The Butterfly of Dinard) is published.

- Yevgeny Yevtushenko's poetry volume *Zima Junction* is published.

- Salvatore Quasimodo's poetry volume *The False and the True Green* is published.

- Léopold Sédar Senghor's poetry volume *Chaka* is published.

- Kathleen Raine's *Collected Poems* is published.

- Ingmar Bergman's film *The Seventh Seal* premieres.

- Laurence Olivier's film *Richard the Third*, with Olivier, Sir John Gielgud, Ralph Richardson, and Claire Bloom, premieres.

- Albert Lamorisse's film *The Red Balloon*, with Lamorisse's son Pascal, premieres.

- Kenji Mizoguchi's film *Street of Shame* premieres.

- Great Britain creates the Clean Air Act as a systematic ban on burning of soft coal and other smoky fuels.

- The Olympic Games are held in Melbourne with 3,539 contestants from sixty-seven nations. The Soviet Union wins in the medal count for the first time in history.

- Brazilian soccer player Edson Arantes "Pele" do Nacimento signs with Brazil's Santos team to begin an eighteen-year career of 1,253 games in which he will score 1,216 goals.

29 Jan.   Friederich Dürrenmatt's play *Der Besuch der alten Dame* (The Visit of the Old Lady) premieres at Zurich's Schauspielhaus.

25 Feb.   Soviet first secretary denounces former leader Stalin as a dictator who misruled and committed many crimes.

2 Apr.   Peter Ustinov's play *Romanoff and Juliet* opens at England's Manchester Opera House.

4 Apr.   Enid Bagnold's play *The Chalk Garden* opens at London's Theatre Royal.

5 Apr.   The Vatican announces the discovery of a catacomb containing fourth-century murals of Christian scenes at a construction site in Rome.

11 Apr.   The Korean peace treaty is broken by North Korean forces attacking UN forces on the cease-fire line.

14 May   Pope Pius XII approves on moral grounds the transplanting of corneas from a dead person to restore sight but disapproves transplantation of organs from a living person.

24 May   Israel and Egypt agree on the establishment of UN truce observation posts on the Gaza Strip border.

24 May   Brendan Behan's play *The Quare Fellow* opens at Stratford's London Theatre Royale.

8 May   John Osborne's play *Look Back in Anger* opens at London's Royal Court Theatre, with Kenneth Haigh, Mary Ure, and Alan Bates.

17 June   Israeli labor minister Goldie Myerson (Golda Meir) is appointed foreign minister.

19 June   Biblical scrolls said to contain the books of Genesis, Exodus, Leviticus, Numbers, and Deuteronomy are found in a cave near the site of the Dead Sea Scrolls.

25 June   One hundred thousand members of Peru's Private Employees Central Union strike in a wage dispute with the International Petroleum Company.

16 July   Federico Fellini's film *La Strada,* starring Anthony Quinn, premieres in New York.

4 Aug.   The World Council of Churches central committee approves efforts to bring the Moscow Patriarchate of the Russian Orthodox church into the organization.

30 Aug.   Egyptian president Gamal Abdel Nasser declares the Suez Canal not an international waterway.

15 Sept.   An Aeroflot Tupolev-104 airliner takes off from Moscow, making the first scheduled passenger flight from Moscow to Irkutsk.

14 Oct.   Two hundred fifty thousand untouchables convert to Buddhism in India in what is believed to be the largest mass conversion in history.

17 Oct.   England's Calder Hall is the first full-scale commercial nuclear power plant. It produces ninety thousand kilowatts of power and plutonium for nuclear weapons.

23 Oct.   The Hungarian uprising against the Soviet Union begins.

1 Nov.   Hungary leaves the Warsaw Pact.

4 Nov.   Soviets forces attack Hungary.

4 Nov.   Hungarian Communist party first secretary János Kádár replaces Imre Nagy as premier after the Soviet invasion.

1957

- Boris Pasternak's novel *Doctor Zhivago* is published.
- Alain Robbe-Grillet's novel *La Jalousie* (Jealousy) is published.
- Claude Simon's novel *Le Vent* (The Wind) is published.
- Mordecai Richler's novels *A Choice of Enemies* and *The Apprenticeship of Duddy Kravitz* are published.
- Octavio Paz's novel *Piedra de Sol* is published.
- Ingmar Bergman's film *Wild Strawberries* premieres.
- Federico Fellini's film *Nights of Cabiria* premieres.
- Satyajit Ray's film *Aprajito* premieres.
- David Lean's film *Bridge on the River Kwai*, with William Holden, Alec Guinness, Jack Hawkins, and Sessue Hayakawa, premieres.

- Akira Kurosawa's film *Throne of Blood* premieres.

- The chemise is introduced at the late-summer Paris and Rome couturière showings.

- Italy develops the antibiotic rifampian, which is used to cure patients of tuberculosis.

- In Germany nitrite poisoning from meat causes a scandal. German butchers have been using sodium nitrate to make meat look fresh, exposing consumers to methemoglobinemia, a reduction of blood hemoglobin by intestinal bacteria. Nitrite can be produced from nitrates by the bacteria which then convert hemoglobin in the bloodstream to methemoglobin, which cannot carry oxygen.

- German engineer Fritz Wankel designs the Wankel Rotary Engine at Lindau on Lake Constance. The Wankel has only two moving parts, making it lighter, less expensive, smoother in its motion, and easier to maintain than conventional piston engines, although it is slightly less fuel-efficient.

16 Jan.   The U.S. State Department supports a free-trade zone and European common market.

15 Feb.   Andrei Gromyko is named Soviet foreign minister.

24 Feb.   The *New York Times* reports guerrilla warfare being waged by rebel leader Fidel Castro in Cuba.

22 Mar.   Pope Pius XII decrees that required fasting before receiving Holy Communion be reduced to three hours.

10 Apr.   John Osborne's play *The Entertainer* opens at London's Royal Court Theatre, with music by John Addison.

14 Apr.   The U.S. Trade Fair, with exhibits from fifty-nine nations, opens in New York.

10 May   Dmitry Shostakovich's Piano Concerto, with soloist Maxim Shostakovich, is performed in Moscow.

25 June   The United Church of Christ is formed by merging the Congregational Christian General Council and the Evangelical and Reformed church.

3 July   Soviet first secretary Khrushchev removes several members of the Central Committee after they unsuccessfully try to remove him from power.

11 Aug.   *Die Harmonie der Welt* (The Harmony of the World) is performed in Munich, with music by Paul Hindemith.

6 Oct.   Pierre Boulez's Polyphonie X for 17 Solo Instruments is performed at the Donaueschippu Festival of Contemporary Music.

19 Oct.   Gian Carlo Menotti's *Apocalypse* (symphonic poem) is performed in Pittsburgh.

30 Oct.   Dmitry Shostakovich's Eleventh Symphony (1905) is performed in Moscow.

7 Nov.   Heitor Villa-Lobos's *Erosion, or the Origin of the Amazon River* (symphonic poem) is performed in Louisville.

23 Dec.   NATO discloses that U.S. delivery of missiles to Western Europe will not begin for two years.

1958

- Evelyn Waugh's novel *The Ordeal of Gilbert Pinfield* is published.

- Pablo Picasso's painting *Peace* is exhibited.

- Gian Carlo Menotti founds the Spoleto Festival, which has its first season ninety miles north of Rome, Italy.

- Jacques Tati's film *Mon Oncle* (My Uncle) premieres.

- Akira Kurosawa's film *The Hidden Fortress* premieres.

- The first parking meters appear in London.

- The last debutantes are presented at the British court.

- Pan Am and BOAC (British Overseas Airways) begin transatlantic jet passenger flights.

- Brazil wins its first World Cup soccer championship, defeating Sweden 5 to 2. Pele scores two goals for Brazil.

1 Jan. Prime Minister David Ben-Gurion agrees to establish a new Israeli government.

Feb. Yves St.-Laurent, a young designer and protégé of Christian Dior, makes his debut with his Trapeze line.

11 Feb. John Osborne and Anthony Creighton's play *Epitaph for George Dillon* opens at London's Royal Court Theatre.

27 Mar. Nikita Khrushchev becomes premier of the Soviet Union, consolidating Soviet party and state leadership.

29 Mar. Max Frisch's play *Biedermann und die Brandstifter* (Biedermann and the Firebugs) opens at Zurich's Schauspielhaus.

4 Apr. Eugène Ionesco's play *Tueur sans gages* (The Killer) opens at Darmstadt's Landestheater.

24 Apr. The tenth anniversary of the founding of the Jewish state in Palestine is celebrated in Jerusalem.

28 Apr. Harold Pinter's play *The Birthday Party* opens at the Arts Theatre, Cambridge, England.

8 May Terence Rattigan's play *Variations on a Theme* opens at London's Globe Theatre.

10 May Dmitry Shostakovich's Second Piano Concerto is performed in Moscow.

31 May Gen. Charles de Gaulle accepts the premiership of France.

18 June The opera *Noye's Fludde* (Noah's Flood) is performed at Oxford Church, Suffolk, with music by Benjamin Britten and the libretto from the fourteenth-century *Chester Miracle Play.*

24 June Premier Charles de Gaulle states France's desire to exert a greater influence on NATO.

7 July The Soviet Union and East Germany link their two countries' heavy industries with an economic agreement.

17 July Peter Shaffer's play *Five Finger Exercise* opens at London's Comedy Theatre.

28 Sept. French voters approve Premier de Gaulle's constitution establishing a strong presidency by an 80 percent margin.

14 Oct.	Brendan Behan's play *The Hostage* opens at London's Theatre Royale, Stratford, England.
16 Oct.	The *Nocturne* song cycle for tenor and small orchestra by Benjamin Britten opens in Leeds.
26 Oct.	Pan American World Airways begins daily New York–Paris service.
10 Nov.	Bertolt Brecht's play *Der aufhaltsame Aufstieg des Arturo Ui* (The Resistable Rise of Arturo Ui) opens in Stuttgart, Germany.
17 Dec.	Mao Tse-tung retires as leader of Communist China.
21 Dec.	Charles de Gaulle is elected president of France's Fifth Republic.

1959

- Ian Fleming's novel *Goldfinger* is published.
- Marc Chagall's painting *Le Champ de Mars* is exhibited.
- Alain Resnais's film *Hiroshima, Mon Amour*, with Emmuelle Rosa, premieres.
- Marcel Camus's film *Black Orpheus* premieres.
- François Truffaut's film *The 400 Blows* premieres.
- Jean-Luc Goddard's film *Breathless*, with Jean-Paul Belmondo and Jean Seaberg, premieres.
- Michelangelo Antonioni's film *L'Avventura* premieres.
- Alexei Batalov's film *The Overcoat* premieres.
- Kon Ichakawa's film *Fires on the Plain* premieres.
- West German clinics observe births of children with the physical deformity phocomelia, which has not appeared in the past five years.
- The Nikon F 35-mm Single Lens Reflex camera is manufactured by Nippon Kogaku.
- Russian archeologist Tatiana Proskeuriakov finds an important pattern of dates in the lives of certain Mayan individuals in the Yucatán. This discovery allows scholars to decipher the glyph symbols depicting the periods in which certain rulers reigned.
- Christopher Sydney Cockerell, a pioneer in hovercrafts, demonstrates his SRN-1 hovercraft by crossing the English Channel.

2 Jan.	Fidel Castro assumes control of Cuba.
5 Jan.	*Time* magazine selects Premier Charles de Gaulle of France as man of the year.
10 Feb.	Shelagh Delaney's play *A Taste of Honey* opens at London's Wyndham Theatre, directed by Joan Littlewood.
16 Feb.	Fidel Castro is sworn in as premier of Cuba.
5 Mar.	Indonesia announces nationalization of 270 Dutch-owned enterprises.

27 Mar.	Pope John XXIII withdraws references to Jews as "perfidious" from Good Friday services.
23 Apr.	The first Arab Petroleum Congress ends with nine countries calling for an increase in Arab participation in all aspects of the oil industry.
26 June	Swedish boxer Ingemar Johansson wins the world heavyweight crown by knocking out Floyd Patterson in third round of a title fight in New York.
5 July	Prime Minister Ben-Gurion of Israel resigns after cabinet opposition on the sale of arms to West Germany.
17 July	Cuban president Lleo resigns because of disagreement with Premier Castro's policy on land reform and the death penalty for counterrevolutionaries.
8 Aug.	President Nasser of Egypt declares that Israel will not be allowed to use the Suez Canal.
3 Sept.	Vatican radio states that representatives of the Roman Catholic and Eastern Orthodox churches will meet to discuss possible reunification.
15 Sept.	Soviet premier Khrushchev begins a two-week visit to the United States.
29 Sept.	Premier Khrushchev leaves for Peking to celebrate Communist China's tenth anniversary.
4 Oct.	Dmitry Shostakovich's Concerto in E-flat for Violoncello and Orchestra is performed at Leningrad with solo by Mstislau Rostropovich.
22 Oct.	John Arden's play *Sergeant Musgrave's Dance* opens at London's Royal Court Theatre.
26 Oct.	Fidel Castro accuses the United States of dropping anticommunist material from airplanes flying over Cuba.
3 Nov.	President de Gaulle announces his plan for France to withdraw from NATO.
10 Nov.	A Soviet-U.S. film exchange begins with simultaneous premieres of the Soviet film *The Cranes Are Flying* in Washington, D.C., and the U.S. film *Marty* in Moscow.
19 Nov.	U.S. Roman Catholic bishops assert their opposition to the use of public money to promote "artificial birth prevention for economically underdeveloped countries."

CHAPTER TWO
THE ARTS

by RICHARD LAYMAN

CONTENTS

Sidebars and tables are listed in italics.

1950

Movies   *Sunset Boulevard*, starring Gloria Swanson and William Holden; *All about Eve*, starring Bette Davis and Anne Baxter.

Fiction   Ray Bradbury, *The Martian Chronicles;* Budd Schulberg, *The Disenchanted;* Ernest Hemingway, *Across the River and Into the Trees.*

Popular Songs   Bing Crosby, "Dear Hearts and Gentle People"; Red Foley, "Chattanoogie Shoe Shine Boy"; Eileen Barton, "If I Knew You Were Comin' I'd've Baked a Cake"; Billy Eckstine, "My Foolish Heart"; Bill Snyder and His Orchestra, "Bewitched, Bothered, and Bewildered"; Nat "King" Cole, "Mona Lisa"; Sammy Kaye and His Orchestra, "Harbor Lights"; Betty Hutton and Perry Como, "A Bushel and a Peck."

- Musical festivals in the United States and abroad commemorate the bicentenary death of Johann Sebastian Bach. Notable among them are the yearlong Bach series of the University of California School of Music and the augmented program in the annual Bach series at the Berkshire Music Festival.

- *Basquet-Banquet* by Karl Knaths wins the thirty-five-hundred-dollar first prize in the New York Metropolitan Museum of Art exhibit "American Painting Today — 1950."

- Marilyn Monroe, twenty-four, makes her debut in John Huston's film *The Asphalt Jungle.*

Jan.   Alto saxophonist Charlie ("Yardbird") Parker and his quintet end a monthlong series of perfomances begun on 15 December 1949 at Birdland, opening the jazz nightclub named for Parker located at 52nd St. and Broadway in Manhattan.

5 Jan.   Carson McCullers's dramatization of her novel *The Member of the Wedding* opens at New York's Empire Theatre, beginning a run of 501 performances.

Mar.   Roberta Peters, a twenty-year-old opera singer from the Bronx, debuts with the Metropolitan Opera as a stand-in for Nadine O'Connor in Wolfgang Amadeus Mozart's *Don Giovanni.*

Mar.   The Boston Institute of Contemporary Art in conjunction with the New York Metropolitan Museum and the Whitney Museum issue a joint Statement on Modern Art opposing "any attempt to make art or opinion about art conform to a single point of view."

31 May   Edward Johnson retires after fifteen years as manager of the Metropolitan Opera. His successor is Rudolph Bing.

14 Nov.   The fiftieth birthday of composer Aaron Copland is celebrated by the League of Composers with a concert of his works.

24 Nov.   *Guys and Dolls,* with music and lyrics by Frank Loesser, opens at the 46th Street Theater. It is one of the longest-running and most popular Broadway musicals ever staged.

10 Dec.   The novelist William Faulkner receives the 1949 Nobel Prize in literature; no literature prize had been given in 1949, so both the 1949 and 1950 prizes are awarded in 1950. He is the fourth American to win the prize.

1951

Movies   *The African Queen,* starring Humphrey Bogart and Katharine Hepburn; *An American in Paris,* starring Gene Kelly and Leslie Caron; *Strangers on a Train,* directed by Alfred Hitchcock and starring Robert Walker; *A Streetcar Named Desire,* starring Karl Malden, Vivien Leigh, Kim Hunter, and Marlon Brando; *Cinderella,* Walt Disney animation.

Fiction   James Jones, *From Here to Eternity;* Carson McCullers, *The Ballad of the Sad Cafe;* William Styron, *Lie Down in Darkness;* Herman Wouk, *The Caine Mutiny;* J. D. Salinger, *The Catcher in The Rye.*

Popular Songs   Patti Page, "Tennessee Waltz"; Perry Como, "If"; The Weavers with Terry Gilkyson's Choir and Vic Schoen's Orchestra, "On Top of Old Smoky"; Nat "King" Cole, "Too Young"; Tony Bennett, "Because of You"; The Four Aces, "Sin."

- There are 691 orchestras in America, of which 32 are professional. The rest are college and community orchestras.

- United Artists, a leading film studio in the silent-film era now losing one hundred thousand dollars a week, is taken over from surviving partners Charlie Chaplin and Mary Pickford by two New York lawyers under the condition that they make it profitable by 1954.

- Hank Williams's "Cold, Cold Heart" is number one on the country-music charts; as sung by Tony Bennett, it is also number one on pop-music charts.

Jan.   President Harry S Truman requests that the congressional Commission of Fine Arts begin a survey of the "activities of the Federal Government in the field of art."

Summer   NBC televises a series of concerts from the National Gallery of Art in Washington. During intermissions, artworks are discussed.

25 Oct.–16 Dec.   The sixtieth annual American Exhibition at Art Institute of Chicago takes place. Willem de Kooning's *Excavation* wins the one-thousand-dollar first prize.

Nov.   The twenty-fifth anniversary issue of *Art Digest* is published; *Art News* celebrates its fiftieth annniversary.

1–15 Nov.   Orchestras and operas "receiving substantial support from voluntary contributions" are exempted from the 20 percent federal admissions tax; price controls are lifted from such organizations.

1952

Movies   *High Noon,* starring Gary Cooper and Grace Kelly; *The Greatest Show on Earth,* starring Betty Hutton and Charlton Heston; *Viva Zapata!,* starring Anthony Quinn, Marlon Brando, and Jean Peters; *The Quiet Man,* starring John Wayne and Maureen O'Hara; *Come Back, Little Sheba,* starring Shirley Booth and Burt Lancaster.

Fiction   Ralph Ellison, *The Invisible Man;* Shelby Foote, *Shiloh;* Bernard Malamud, *The Natural;* Flannery O'Connor, *Wise Blood;* John Steinbeck, *East of Eden;* Ernest Hemingway, *The Old Man and the Sea;* Kurt Vonnegut, *Player Piano;* E. B. White, *Charlotte's Web.*

Popular Songs

Pee Wee King with Redd Stewart, "Slow Poke"; Johnnie Ray, "Cry"; Kay Starr, "Wheel of Fortune"; Georgia Gibbs, "Kiss of Fire"; Johnnie Ray, "Walkin' My Baby Back Home"; Vera Lynn, "Auf Wiederseh'n, Sweetheart"; The Mills Brothers, "The Glow Worm"; Joni James, "Why Don't You Believe Me?"

Jan.

"American Bandstand," a popular-music show hosted by Dick Clark, debuts on ABC television.

July

The House Judiciary Committee recommends amending the U.S. copyright law to provide for payment of royalties to the copyright owner for jukebox play of music.

Sept.

Ernest Hemingway's short novel *The Old Man and the Sea* is first printed in *Life* magazine (1 September, 5 million copies), as September co–main selection by the Book-of-the-Month Club (153,000 copies), and then for the trade by Scribners (50,000 copies).

Nov.

Bwana Devil, the first 3-D movie, is released.

Dec.

The art critic Harold Rosenberg coins the term *action painting* to describe the work of the abstract expressionists.

1953

Movies

From Here to Eternity, starring Burt Lancaster, Deborah Kerr, and Frank Sinatra; *Stalag 17*, starring William Holden; *Roman Holiday*, starring Audrey Hepburn and Gregory Peck.

Fiction

James Baldwin, *Go Tell It on the Mountain*; Saul Bellow, *The Adventures of Augie March*; Raymond Chandler, *The Long Goodbye*; Louis L'Amour, *Hondo*; J. D. Salinger, *Nine Stories*; Leon Uris, *Battle Cry*; William S. Burroughs, *Junkie*.

Popular Songs

Perry Como with Mitchell Ayres's Orchestra, "Don't Let the Stars Get in Your Eyes"; Teresa Brewer with Jack Pleis's Orchestra, "Till I Waltz Again With You"; Frankie Laine, "I Believe"; Pattie Page, "The Doggie in the Window"; Nat "King" Cole with the Nelson Riddle Orchestra, "Pretend"; Percy Faith and His Orchestra, "The Song From *Moulin Rouge* (Where Is Your Heart?)"; Les Paul and Mary Ford, "Vaya Con Dios (May God Be With You)"; the Ames Brothers with Hugo Winhalter and His Orchestra, "You, You, You"; Frank Chacksfield and His Orchestra, "Ebb Tide."

- The National Music Council reports that of 1,834 performances by major symphony orchestras in the United States only 7.5 percent were of works by American composers.

- Doubleday Anchor Books, a new line of quality paperbacks, is introduced.

- Henry Koster's *The Robe*, starring Richard Burton, was the first film in CinemaScope, which used wider screens and stereophonic sound; the technique was designed to counter the popularity of television by attracting viewers to the big screen once again.

- Former Harvard *Lampoon* editor George Plimpton begins publication of the *Paris Review*.

19 Feb.   William Inge's play *Picnic,* starring Paul Newman, opens a run of 477 performances at the Music Box Theatre in New York.

16 Mar.–
11 Apr.   Willem de Kooning's *Paintings on the Theme of Woman* is exhibited at the Sidney Janis Gallery in New York City.

Aug.   The Commission of Fine Arts recommends that a music center be established in Washington, D.C., and that federal funds be appropriated for an auditorium to stage productions of operas, symphonies, and ballets.

Oct.   A survey by the Metropolitan Opera Guild indicates that 744 performances of seventy-three contemporary operas, about half of which were by professional companies, were produced in the United States between October 1951 and October 1952.

- The Broadway production of Arthur Miller's *The Crucible,* dramatizing the 1692 Salem witch trials, served as a parallel to the persecution of alleged Communist sympathizers in the United States.

1954

Movies   *On the Waterfront,* starring Marlon Brando and Karl Malden; *Rear Window,* starring James Stewart and Grace Kelly; *Country Girl,* starring Bing Crosby, Grace Kelly, and William Holden; *A Star is Born,* starring Judy Garland.

Fiction   William Faulkner, *A Fable;* Evan Hunter, *The Blackboard Jungle.*

Popular
Songs   Roy Hamilton, "Ebb Tide"; Tony Bennett with the Percy Faith Orchestra, "Stranger in Paradise"; Frank Sinatra with the Nelson Riddle Orchestra, "Young at Heart"; Perry Como with the Hugo Winterhalter Orchestra, "Wanted"; Kitty Kallen with the Jack Pleis Orchestra, "Little Things Mean a Lot"; Archie Bleyer and His Orchestra, "Hernando's Hideaway"; Rosemary Clooney, "Hey, There"; Doris Day, "If I Give My Heart to You"; The Chordettes with Archie Bleyer's Orchestra, "Mister Sandman."

- The Whitney Museum in New York is moved from quarters in Greenwich Village to a building adjoining the Museum of Modern Art.

- The International Congress of Art Historians and Museologists estimates that there are ten million amateur artists in the United States.

- Alfred Hitchcock's *Dial M for Murder* is the first serious film to be released in 3-D; when it fails to reach as many viewers as Hitchcock is used to, he re-releases the movie in a standard version.

31 Mar.   Howard Hughes, criticized for capricious business practices in running RKO film studios, in which he has held controlling interest since 1948, buys the outstanding RKO stock for $23.5 million.

4 Apr.   Arturo Toscanini conducts the last broadcast concert of the NBC Orchestra at Carnegie Hall.

July   The first Newport Jazz Festival is held in Newport, Rhode Island.

1955

19 July	Nineteen-year-old Elvis Presley's first professional record, "That's All Right, Mama" and "Blue Moon of Kentucky," is released on Sun Records (#219).
28 Oct.	Ernest Hemingway wins the Nobel Prize in literature.

Movies
Marty, starring Ernest Borgnine; *The Seven Year Itch,* starring Marilyn Monroe and Tom Ewell; *Mister Roberts,* starring Henry Fonda, James Cagney, William Powell, and Jack Lemmon; *The Rose Tattoo,* starring Anna Magnani and Burt Lancaster; *East of Eden,* starring James Dean, Julie Harris, Raymond Massey, Burl Ives, and Jo van Fleet.

Fiction
Herman Wouk, *Marjorie Morningstar;* Sloan Wilson, *The Man in the Gray Flannel Suit;* MacKinley Kantor, *Andersonville;* Norman Mailer, *The Deer Park;* Flannery O'Connor, *A Good Man is Hard to Find;* John O'Hara, *Ten North Frederick;* Wright Morris, *Field of Vision.*

Popular Songs
Joan Weber, "Let Me Go Lover"; Fontaine Sisters, "Hearts of Stone"; McGuire Sisters, "Sincerely"; Bill Hayes, "The Ballad of Davy Crockett"; Perez Prado, "Cherry Pink and Apple Blosson White"; Bill Haley and His Comets, "Rock Around the Clock"; Tennessee Ernie Ford, "Sixteen Tons."

- The American Shakespeare Theatre has its first season at Stratford, Connecticut, which was founded in 1623 by settlers from Stratford-Upon-Avon.

Jan.	The contralto Marian Anderson is the first black singer to appear at the Metropolitan Opera; the performance is Giuseppe Verdi's *Un Ballo in maschera,* conducted by Dimitri Mitropoulos.
24 Mar.	Tennessee Williams's *Cat on a Hot Tin Roof,* starring Barbara Bel Geddes and Burl Ives, opens a 694-performance run at New York's Morosco Theater.
July	Howard Hughes sells RKO Corporation, the motion-picture subsidiary of RKO Pictures, to General Tire and Rubber Company for $25 million.
20 Aug.	Chuck Berry gains immediate success with his first release, "Maybellene," which he follows with many other hits including "Roll Over Beethoven" (1956), "School Day" (1957), and "Johnny B. Goode" (1958).
30 Sept.	Actor James Dean, twenty-four, is killed when he crashes his Porsche roadster.
Oct.	Leopold Stopowski begins a three-year engagement as conductor of the Houston Symphony Orchestra.
13 Oct.	Poet Allen Ginsberg gives the first reading of his controversial poem-in-progress, "Howl."
16 Nov.	The option owned by Sam Phillips of Sun Records on Elvis Presley's recording contract is purchased by the RCA Record Company for thirty-five thousand dollars.
5 Dec.	Thornton Wilder's *The Matchmaker,* a revision of *The Merchant of Yonkers* (1938), opens a 486-performance run at the Royal Theatre in New York. The play is the basis for the 1965 hit musical *Hello, Dolly.*

1956

Movies	*The King And I,* starring Yul Brynner and Deborah Kerr; *Lust for Life,* starring Anthony Quinn and Kirk Douglas; *Anastasia,* starring Ingrid Bergman and Yul Brynner; *Giant,* starring Elizabeth Taylor, Rock Hudson, and James Dean; *Around the World in Eighty Days,* starring David Niven and Shirley MacLaine.
Fiction	Nelson Algren, *A Walk on the Wild Side;* John Barth, *The Floating Opera;* Saul Bellow, *Seize the Day;* Edwin O'Connor, *The Last Hurrah;* Grace Metallious, *Peyton Place;* William Brinkley, *Don't Go Near the Water;* Patrick Dennis, *Auntie Mame.*
Popular Songs	Dean Martin, "Memories Are made of This"; Platters, "The Great Pretender"; Kay Starr, "Rock and Roll Waltz"; Elvis Presley, "Heartbreak Hotel"; Perry Como, "Hot Diggity"; Morris Stoloff, "Moonglow" and the "Theme from *Picnic.*"

- Rock 'n' roll disc jockey Alan Freed stars in three movies: *Rock around the Clock; Rock, Rock, Rock;* and *Don't Knock the Rock.*

- The North Carolina Museum of Art in Raleigh opens; it is the first museum in the United States to use state-voted public funds to purchase artworks.

- Construction begins on the Solomon R. Guggenheim Museum in Manhattan, designed by Frank Lloyd Wright.

- The Joffrey Ballet Company is founded by dancer-choreographer Robert Joffrey.

- Elvis Presley makes his film debut in *Love Me Tender.*

20 Apr.	T. S. Eliot attracts an audience of fourteen thousand to a baseball stadium at the University of Minnesota to hear him speak on "The Frontiers of Criticism," a lecture on literary criticism.
10 Aug.	Jackson Pollock and one of his passengers are killed when he crashes his Oldsmobile convertible while drunk.
20 Oct.	At age twenty-four, country singer Johnny Cash releases "I Walk the Line," which makes the Billboard Top 40. As a result, he begins appearing on "Grand Ole Opry" and comes to be ranked as one of the top three male vocalists of the country charts.
29 Oct.	Soprano Maria Callas makes her New York debut at the Metropolitan Opera in *Norma.*
11 Oct.	The National Broadcasting Company of singers begins its first season with a fifty-performance tour in forty-seven cities in the East, Southeast, and Midwest.
7 Nov.	*A Long Day's Journey Into Night,* an autobiographical play by the late playwright Eugene O'Neill, opens at New York's Helen Hayes Theater.

1957

Movies   *The Bridge on the River Kwai,* starring William Holden and Alec Guinness; *Twelve Angry Men,* starring Henry Fonda and Lee J. Cobb; *Love in the Afternoon,* starring Gary Cooper, Audrey Hepburn, and Maurice Chevalier; *Sayonara,* starring Marlon Brando, Miyoshi Umeki, and Red Buttons; *The Three Faces of Eve,* starring Joanne Woodward and Lee J. Cobb.

Fiction   James Agee, *A Death in the Family;* James Gould Cozzens, *By Love Possessed;* William Faulkner, *The Town;* Jack Kerouac, *On the Road.*

Popular Songs   Pat Boone, "Don't Forbid Me" and "April Love"; Elvis Presley, "Too Much," "All Shook Up," "Let Me Be Your Teddy Bear," and "Jailhouse Rock"; Sonny James, "Young Love"; Buddy Knox, "Party Doll"; Debbie Reynolds, "Tammy"; Johnny Mathis, "Chances Are"; and Sam Cooke, "You Send Me."

- *The Cat in the Hat,* by Dr. Seuss, is wildly popular with children learning to read, and becomes the first in a series of rhyming, entertainingly fanciful beginners' readers. The book is translated into many foreign languages and sells eight to nine million copies over the next twenty years.

- Motown Corporation is founded by thirty-year-old entrepreneur Berry Gordy, Jr., who invests seven hundred dollars to start the recording company that helps define black popular music over the next two decades.

21 May   City Lights Bookshop owner and publisher Lawrence Ferlinghetti is charged with selling lewd and indecent materials when San Francisco undercover police buy a copy of Allen Ginsberg's *Howl.* Later in the year Ferlinghetti is found innocent.

26 Sept.   *West Side Story,* a modern-day adaptation of William Shakespeare's *Romeo and Juliet,* premieres at the Winter Garden Theater with music by Leonard Bernstein.

1958

Movies   *Gigi,* starring Leslie Caron and Maurice Chevalier; *Cat on a Hot Tin Roof,* starring Elizabeth Taylor, Paul Newman, and Burl Ives; *Marjorie Morningstar,* starring Gene Kelly and Natalie Wood; *Separate Tables,* starring Burt Lancaster, Rita Hayworth, David Niven, and Wendy Hiller; *I Want to Live!,* starring Susan Hayward.

Fiction   Truman Capote, *Breakfast at Tiffany's;* John O'Hara, *From the Terrace;* Bernard Malamud, *The Magic Barrel.*

Popular Songs   Danny and the Juniors, "At the Hop"; Elvis Presley, "Don't" and "Hard-Headed Woman"; McGuire Sisters, "Sugartime"; Silhouettes, "Get a Job"; Champs, "Tequila"; Everly Brothers, "All I Have to Do Is Dream" and "Bird Dog"; Platters, "Twilight Time"; Perry Como, "Catch a Falling Star"; and Laurie London, "He's Got the Whole World in His Hands."

- Seventy percent of all records sold are bought by teenagers.

- Alan Freed is arrested in Boston for inciting a riot at a rock 'n' roll show he had staged.

- Robert Rauschenberg pioneers "pop art" by creating a "semiabstraction" with a hole into which he has inserted four Coca-Cola bottles.

- The first Grammy Award is presented by the National Academy of Recording Arts and Sciences to the song "Volare" by Italian composer Dominic Modugno, with English lyrics by Mitchell Paris; the award is widely criticized for favoring older, more conservative white artists over youth-oriented pop artists.

13 Apr. American pianist Van Cliburn wins the Tchaikovsky International Competition in Moscow.

29 July Fifteen-year-old Paul Anka becomes an instant success with his first release, "Diana"; he has three more hits within a year and is a millionaire by the time he is seventeen.

2 Oct. Leonard Bernstein begins his first season as director of the New York Philharmonic Orchestra by introducing "previews," in which he comments on works being played.

1959

Movies *Anatomy of a Murder,* starring James Stewart and Lee Remick; *Ben Hur,* starring Charlton Heston; *The Diary of Anne Frank,* starring Millie Perkins and Joseph Schildkraut.

Fiction William S. Burroughs, *The Naked Lunch;* William Faulkner, *The Mansion;* Shirley Jackson, *The Haunting of Hill House;* Philip Roth, *Goodbye, Columbus.*

Popular Songs Platters, "Smoke Gets in Your Eyes"; Lloyd Price, "Stagger Lee"; Frankie Avalon, "Venus"; Fleetwoods, "Come Softly to Me"; Dave "Baby" Cortez, "The Happy Organ"; Wilbert Harrison, "Kansas City"; Bobby Darin, "Mack the Knife."

- E. B. White's revision of *The Elements of Style,* by his Cornell teacher, the late William Strunk, Jr., is published.

3 Feb. Buddy Holly, Richie Valens, and J. P. Richardson are killed in a plane crash near Clear Lake, Iowa. They are the first rock 'n' roll stars to die.

11 Mar. Lorraine Hansberry's play *Raisin in the Sun,* starring Sidney Poitier, opens a 530-performance run at the Ethel Barrymore Theatre in New York.

21 July The U. S. Post Office ban on distributing the 1928 novel *Lady Chatterley's Lover,* by D. H. Lawrence, is lifted by a federal district court. Judge Frederick van Pelt Bryan rules that the postmaster general is not qualified to judge obscenity of material to be sent through the mail.

21 Oct. New York's Solomon R. Guggenheim Museum, designed by architect Frank Lloyd Wright, opens to mixed reviews.

7 Oct. One hundred eight musicians in the Philadelphia Orchestra accept a contract after a strike that caused cancellation of the first three concerts of the season; the new contract stipulates a minimum wage of $170 per week for instumentalists.

16 Nov. The long-running Rodgers and Hammerstein musical *The Sound of Music* opens at New York's Lunt-Fontanne Theater.

OVERVIEW

A Quiet Rebellion. It may not have been clear at the time, but American society, which seemed so stable and prosperous on the surface, was being urged toward revolution in the wake of World War II by a brash generation of artists using bold works to test their ideas. As rebels always are, these young rebels were bitterly opposed by their elders. But as the 1950s progressed, the rebellion seemed to grow increasingly determined, and it became more threatening than it had ever been before.

Cold War Response. The cold war set the tone for the arts of the decade. Americans enjoyed their image as the most prosperous people in the most powerful nation in the world. Yet they dreaded the centralization of power and the impersonality of life in the atomic age. *Nineteen Eighty-Four* (1949), British novelist George Orwell's novel about a totalitarian government that imposed absolute uniformity of thought and action, was read as a warning about the future. "Big Brother is watching you," a refrain from the novel, became a slogan for people who feared the effect of a social organization so powerful that it could control thought and stifle creativity. The 1950s are remembered as a time of complacency. It was also the time when shrill, profane, and menacing voices of individualism and dissidence were raised — Elvis Presley, Jack Kerouac, Thelonious Monk, and Jackson Pollock; rock 'n' roll, the Beats, bebop, and abstract-expressionist art.

Alienation. Perhaps in reaction to cold-war tensions, perhaps in rebellion against the anxious conformity of a generation trying to settle into the comforts of middle-class life, American artists restlessly and aggressively defined themselves as outsiders. In 1950 the Boston Institute of Contemporary Art, the New York Museum of Modern Art, and the Whitney Museum of American Art issued a manifesto called "Statement on Modern Art" opposing "any attempt to make art or opinion about art conform to a single point of view" and deploring "the reckless and ignorant use of political or moral terms in attacking modern art." Novelist Norman Mailer observed in 1952 that although "this period smacks of healthy manifestos . . . I wonder if there has been a time in the last fifty years when the American artist has felt more alienated." In 1955 and 1956 Carl Perkins and then Pre-

sley shouted their independence in separate hit recordings of a rock 'n' roll song that warned "You can do anything but lay off of my blue suede shoes."

Abstract Expressionism. In the art world the rebellion against conformity took the name *abstract expressionism*. It was led by a group of painters and sculptors called the New York School, who sought to move away from the propagandist art of the 1930s. The bomb, government control, and greed seemed the most compelling issues confronting postwar Americans. The New York School reacted by emphasizing individual emotion and by presenting their emotive art with as little inhibition and as much confrontation as possible. They rebelled against restrictions.

A New Image. Avant-garde artists of the period redefined their roles. They defied the image of the crafter sitting at an easel and painting with a brush on a canvas designed for wall display. They painted on huge canvases, when they used canvas at all — just as often they worked with papier-mâché or in sculpture; they employed unconventional tools — sticks, trowels, spray cans; they incorporated whatever media was at hand in their art — sand, glass, toilet seats, garbage.

Confrontation/Response. Artists of the 1950s were not content with declaring their individuality; they wanted a response. Pollock's drip paintings, also called "the art of obliteration" because during one period they consisted of recognizable forms almost completely covered by random paint drippings, symbolized the spirit of the time: negate the past with spontaneous action in the present. Larry Rivers said his 1953 painting *George Washington Crossing the Delaware* was conceived as a "disgusting, dead, and absurd" painting of "a national cliche" calculated to outrage viewers. In the mid 1950s Robert Rauschenberg introduced his "combines" — artworks that incorporate everyday objects such as beds, umbrellas, and tires — designed to "fill the gap between art and life." Claes Oldenburg opened his first one-man show in 1959 by walking through the streets of New York in a papier-mâché elephant mask, taking his art into the streets "to invite public action and involvement."

Audience Response. To the dismay of the angry young artists, critics and viewers responded enthusiasti-

In February 1952 playwright Lillian Hellman was subpoenaed to testify before the House Un-American Activities Committee about her Communist activities and affiliations. By that time, the Hollywood Ten had already gone to jail and served their terms for contempt of Congress after refusing to testify before the committee. They were Hollywood, and Hellman was pure Broadway. No one knew better how to steal a stage than Lillian Hellman.

Before her scheduled appearance, she sent a letter to the committee. The letter read, in part, "I am not willing, now or in the future, to bring bad trouble to people who, in my past association with them, were completely innocent of any talk or any action that was disloyal or subversive. I do not like subversion or disloyalty in any form and if I had ever seen any I would have considered it my duty to have reported it to the proper authorities. But to hurt innocent people whom I knew many years ago in order to save myself is, to me, inhuman and indecent and dishonorable. I cannot and will not cut my conscience to fit this year's fashions, even though I long ago came to the conclusion that I was not a political person and could have no comfortable place in any political group." She so informed the committee that she would willingly testify about her own activities, but she would not rat on her friends. In fact, she did nei-

ther, pleading protection under the Fifth Amendment to most questions.

When she was called to testify, she asked the committee to consider her written request that she not be asked to answer questions about others. With that, her counsel began passing out copies of the letter to the press, and the matter was before the bar of public opinion. Hellman remembers that someone in the gallery called out, "Thank God somebody finally had the guts to do it." No one else in the room seems to have heard the comment, but the press had the letter, and when it was published Hellman's act was complete. She was, for the public, a martyr to the cause of righteousness.

In fact, several people had had the guts to take the no-rat position since the early days of the committee's investigation, most notably Hollywood writer and producer Sidney Buchman eight months before Hellman appeared. The difference was that most witnesses took their stances in pre-hearing conferences, and the committee chose not to call them to avoid just the sort of embarrassment Hellman caused. Hellman, on the other hand, played her role perfectly, timing her statement so that it was too late for the committee to back down.

Source: William Wright, *Lillian Hellman: The Image, the Woman* (New York: Simon & Schuster, 1986)

---

cally if with some bewilderment. One of Pollock's paintings sold for $13,600 in 1950; after his death in 1956, prices soared. A Mark Rothko painting brought $8,950 in 1950, a time when the standard price for a contemporary painting was $500, and in 1959 Rothko was commissioned to do a painting to hang in the posh Four Seasons restaurant in Manhattan. But even the successful rebels found reason for complaint. Both Pollock and Rothko were members of a group called "The Irascibles" whose 1951 boycott of a juried competition for eighty-five hundred dollars in prizes at the Metropolitan Museum of Art was their declaration of war on the art-world establishment. The Irascibles complained that in the early 1950s the Met spent about four hundred thousand dollars each year on acquisitions, of which only about ten thousand went for contemporary art — not enough to buy a Pollock or a Willem de Kooning or a John Marin, who was by a vote of museum directors the most accomplished living artist in 1952.

Art for the People. Prosperity brings an appetite for culture, and during the 1950s Americans were hungry. They wanted to understand and appreciate art, particularly American art. A chain of New Jersey supermarkets attempted (with mixed success) to sell paintings by young American artists for prices ranging from $10 to $100. The Art Rental Gallery in Chicago loaned the work of local artists at fees a worker's family could afford. In Richmond, Virginia, local funds supported an artmobile to take art to the people. American audiences were almost as determined to understand and appreciate art as contemporary artists were to demonstrate contempt for them.

Music. The music world was in much the same situation, but the revolt took a different form. The music revolution was popular rather than elitist, and it signaled a social rather than an intellectual rebellion. A young untrained country singer and guitar player named Hank Williams captured the spirit of the time for what was called the hillbilly audience (rural and blue-collar) with

JAMES GOULD COZZENS

Before publication of *By Love Possessed* in August 1957 James Gould Cozzens was the least-celebrated living major American novelist. Despite 12 novels published since 1924 and a Pulitzer Prize for *Guard of Honor* (1948), Cozzens had achieved neither wide readership nor substantial critical recognition. His best novels including *The Last Adam, Men and Brethren,* and *The Just and the Unjust* which scrutinized professional figures (doctors, lawyers, clergy, soldiers) in a restricted time frame were stringently anti-sentimental and tightly structured. Moreover, he was a private man who did not participate in the literary life. *By Love Possessed* focuses on 49 hours in the life of Arthur Winner, Jr., a fifty-four-year-old lawyer in a Delaware Valley town. The principal action is his discovery that his senior partner has embezzled large amounts from the   law firm. Cozzens provided a description of his novel that was not used on the dust jacket: "He ends face to face with the fact of this life—the underlying, everlasting opposition of thinking and feeling, with life's simple disaster of passion and reason, self-division's cause." The novel was a pre-publication literary event. Cozzens was the subject of a *Time* cover story which portrayed him as a reclusive eccentric. The novel was a best-seller, a Book-of-the-Month Club main selection, and even a Reader's Digest Condensed Books selection. The initial critical response was laudatory; John Fischer, editor of *Harper's,* headed his review "Nomination for a Nobel Prize," and the *Saturday Review* ran Cozzens's photo on the cover with a receptive review by Whitney Balliett. A counter-response ensued. Cozzens's style was condemned as too dense and his vocabulary as too difficult. Cozzens was variously denounced as bigoted, reactionary, misogynistic, misanthropic, undemocratic, and aristocratic. His initial admirers mostly pusillanimously retreated from the counter-attack. Although there was a record paperback deal ($101,505) and a big-budget movie, *By Love Possessed* was gradually neglected. Cozzens published one more novel, *Morning Noon and Night* (1968), which failed to find readers or admiring reviews. At the time of his death in 1978 James Gould Cozzens was the least-celebrated major American novelist.

Source: Matthew J. Bruccoli, *James Gould Cozzens* (New York, San Diego & London: Harcourt Brace Jovanovich, 1983).

---

his lonesome, lovesick wails about life gone sour. Despite being the first nationally popular country singer, hailed as a master of soulful expression, he was banned from the Grand Old Opry because of his hell-raising and womanizing — because he lived the songs he sang. Wil-

liams died of a drug overdose in the back seat of his Cadillac on the way to a performance in 1953. He was twenty-nine. Ernest Tubb, Jim Reeves, Porter Waggoner, and a housepainter turned singer named George Jones took up where Williams had left off.

Jazz. In big-city nightclubs, black musicians played bebop, a syncopated, dissonant music that sounded far different but expressed the same stubborn individualism as hillbilly soul. Miles Davis, Dizzy Gillespie, Monk, Sonny Rollins, and John Coltrane were reacting against the traditional harmonies, predictable rhythms, and sentimentality of the swing era in small-group sessions that emphasized the improvisational abilities of the soloist and an appreciation for the unorthodox. Bebop was the music of isolation, black isolation in particular. Not unlike Pollock's drip paintings, it was a "music of obliteration" that frequently reinterpreted standard songs in a way that infuriated outsiders and delighted the closed bebop audience, which grew larger as the decade progressed — driving the bebop musicians to new levels of atonality and arrhythmia to maintain their separateness.

Classical. Even the classical music world reacted to the spirit of the time. A young conductor of unquestionable talent named Leonard Bernstein shocked purists when he wrote the music for *West Side Story,* a Broadway musical about gang life. The show directly confronted one of the most pervasive domestic fears of the time — juvenile delinquency and gangland violence — in a medium that rarely addressed social problems. *West Side Story* was a record-breaking hit, and two years later, in 1959, Bernstein was appointed to the most prestigious conductor's job in America as head of the New York Philharmonic. His first move was to try to broaden the Philharmonic's audience by appealing directly to a mass audience that wanted to know how to appreciate music properly. He became the most influential conductor in America as he alternately sponsored innovation for aficionados and spoon-fed the classics to untutored audiences. At the other extreme, composer John Cage seemed indifferent to the opinions of his audiences. He attracted more attention with his theories about music as pure sound and silence, the stuff of real life, than with his compositions, which emphasized random and chance occurrence of sounds. One of his pieces involves playing twelve radios tuned to various stations.

Rock 'n' Roll. The music that dominated the decade was called rock 'n' roll. It was music about sex, rebellion, and plain hip-shaking good times, introduced by young white musicians showing a distinctly black blues influence. Presley was the undisputed King of Rock 'n' Roll. No musician in American history had been so popular. Six months after his first nationally distributed record, *Heartbreak Hotel,* was released it had sold 8 million copies, and that was only the beginning. In the next two years twenty of his records sold over a million copies each, his total record sales were over 28 million, and his income was said to be more than $10 million a year. In his wake came hundreds of rock performers. Some, such as the piano-banging singer Jerry Lee Lewis, were more untamed on stage than Elvis himself; others, such as the Everly Brothers and Buddy Holly, relied exclusively on music to express their feelings about adolescent life, love, and isolation.

Musical Integration. With the popularity of rock 'n' roll came an acceptance of black performers who had provided its inspiration. Fats Domino, Chuck Berry, Little Richard, and Ray Charles gained popularity playing more or less traditional rhythm and blues (R&B) music. Black singing groups, such as the Coasters and the Drifters, brought to rock 'n' roll the sassy, sensual sound of urbanized black folk music. To the parents of rock 'n' roll fans, they brought the intemperate fear that their sons were being corrupted by rhythms communicating low values and that their daughters were being seduced by dark men with smooth voices.

Literature. American literary elders were accorded unprecedented international respect, while young writers adopted alienation as their theme and disdain for accepted social values as their attitude. Young writers after World War II reacted in much the same way as did artists and musicians, selling themselves against the dominant figures of the decade — writers past their primes being recognized for prewar achievements. William Faulkner won the Nobel Prize in 1950 and the Pulitzer Prize in 1954 for his novel *A Fable,* a symbol-laden story of a wartime separate peace that baffled readers and critics alike. He finished his ambitious Snopes trilogy with *The Town* (1957) and *The Mansion* (1959), but it was widely held that they did not live up to the promise of *The Hamlet* (1940). Ernest Hemingway won the Nobel Prize in 1954 and enjoyed the status of the preeminent literary figure of the time. He wrote *The Old Man and the Sea* (1952) to prove he was not through as a writer, he told his editor. Though it was arguably the most popular literary novel of the decade — previewed memorably before book publication in *Life* magazine and on the best-seller list for half a year — critics agree that it lacks the substance of Hemingway's novels a quarter-century earlier.

The Elders. John Steinbeck did not receive his Nobel Prize until 1962, but his reputation and his bank account flourished in the 1950s. To critics, his *East of Eden* (1952), a multigenerational study of the biblical forces of good and evil, was his first major novel since *The Grapes of Wrath* (1936). To the average American it was a 1955 movie adapted from the novel starring James Dean, who was killed in a car crash just before the movie was released. John O'Hara routinely wrote a book a year and produced an admirable portrayal of life among the socially privileged in the East during the first half of the twentieth century. His *Ten North Frederick* (1955) won a Pulitzer Prize, and *From the Terrace* (1958) was widely praised.

War Response. Those who expected that World War II would be a stimulating literary theme, as World War I had been, were disappointed. Norman Mailer was hailed as the most important young writer after the war when *The Naked and the Dead* was published with great fanfare in 1948, but the subsequent status derived more from his reputation than from his achievement. What he did do better than any other writer of the decade was to promote himself as literary spokesman and he-man artist-intellectual. His reputation soared based not on his literary achievement but on his ability to claim more convincingly than anyone else that he was the leading writer of the time. Irwin Shaw's *The Young Lions* (1948) and James Jones's *From Here to Eternity* (1951) were also important novels about World War II that achieved critical and popular success, and throughout the decade they were considered among the most promising literary talents in America. Jones failed to deliver over the long term though, and Shaw succumbed to the forces of commercialism, many thought.

Young Writers. There was a wealth of young writers who chose to write about subjects other than war. Flannery O'Connor produced *Wise Blood* (1952), a southern-gothic tale about the narrow boundary between religious excess and the damnation of madness. William Styron was hailed as one of the brightest young writers in the country upon the publication of his first novel, *Lie Down in Darkness* (1951), which preached the moral that white-middle-class life could be thoroughly degenerate. The fulfillment of his promise was at least a decade away, though. John Cheever had been writing short stories for the *New Yorker* for twenty years before his first novel, *The Wapshot Chronicle* (1957), was published. The novel charts the development of two sons in an eccentric New England family as they make their own places in the world.

Jewish Writers. Mailer led an impressive group of Jewish authors who came to prominence during the 1950s, writing out of a sense of cultural urgency and religious identity. Saul Bellow's first two novels were published before the decade began, but *The Adventures of Augie March* (1953), *Seize the Day* (1956), and *Henderson the Rain King* (1959) established him as a major novelist. Bernard Malamud's *The Natural* (1952) and *The Assistant* (1957) and Philip Roth's *Goodbye, Columbus* (1959) marked the beginnings of distinguished careers.

Salinger. The most influential novel of the decade, for young readers at least, was J. D. Salinger's *The Catcher in the Rye* (1951), a coming-of-age novel that uncompromisingly takes the side of the adolescent hero frustrated by the hypocrisy of adult values. Holden Caulfield was the spokesman for a generation trying to resist the corruption that age and experience seemed inevitably to bring.

Cozzens. If Salinger spoke for the young and innocent, James Gould Cozzens was the voice of adult re-

R&B

1. PLEDGING MY LOVE (Johnny Ace, Duke)
2. AIN'T THAT A SHAME (Fats Domino, Imperial)
3. MAYBELLENE (Chuck Berry, Chess)
4. EARTH ANGEL (Penguins, Dootone)
5. I'VE GOT A WOMAN (Ray Charles, Atlantic)
6. WALLFLOWER (Etta James, Modern)
7. ONLY YOU (Platters, Mercury)
8. MY BABE (Little Walter, Chess)
9. SINCERELY* (Moonglows, Chess)
10. UNCHAINED MELODY* (Roy Hamilton, Epic)
11. HEARTS OF STONE* (Charms, DeLuxe)
12. TWEEDLE DEE (L. Baker, Atlantic)
13. EVERYDAY (Count Basie, Clef)
14. I'TS LOVE, BABY (L. Brooks, Excello)
15. FLIP, FLOP AND FLY (J. Turner, Atlantic)
16. DON'T BE ANGRY (N. Brown, Savoy)
17. BO DIDDLEY (Bo Diddley, Checker)
18. WHAT'CHA GONNA DO? (Drifters, Atlantic)
19. UNCHAINED MELODY (Al Hibbler, Decca)
20. STORY UNTOLD (Nutmegs, Herald)
21. SOLDIER BOY (Four Fellows, Glory)
22. I HEAR YOU KNOCKIN' (Smiley Lewis, Imperial)
23. FOOL FOR YOU (Ray Charles, Atlantic)
24. AT MY FRONT DOOR (El Dorados, Vee Jay)
25. ALL BY MYSELF (Fats Domino, Imperial)

C&W

1. IN THE JAILHOUSE NOW (Webb Pierce, Decca)
2. MAKING BELIEVE (Kitty Wells, Decca)
3. I DON'T CARE (Webb Pierce, Decca)
4. LOOSE TALK* (Carl Smith, Columbia)
5. SATISFIED MIND (P. Wagoner, Victor)
6. CATTLE CALL (Eddy Arnold & Hugo Winterhalter, Victor)
7. LIVE FAST, LOVE HARD AND DIE YOUNG (Faron Young, Capitol)
8. IF YOU AIN'T LOVIN '* (Faron Young, Capitol)
9. YELLOW ROSES (Hank Snow, Victor)
10. I'VE BEEN THINKING (Eddy Arnold, Victor)
11. MORE AND MORE* (Webb Pierce, Decca)
12. LOVE, LOVE, LOVE (Webb Pierce, Decca)
13. SATISFIED MIND (Red & Betty Foley, Decca)
14. BALLAD OF DAVY CROCKETT (Tennessee Ernie, Capitol)
15. JUST CALL ME LONESOME (Eddy Arnold, Victor)
16. THERE SHE GOES (Carl Smith, Columbia)
17. ARE YOU MINE* (Ginny Wright & Tom Tall, Fabor)

18. SATISFIED MIND (J. Shepard, Capitol)
19. LET ME GO, LOVER* (Hank Snow, Victor)
20. ALL RIGHT (Faron Young, Capitol)
21. SIXTEEN TONS (Tennessee Ernie, Capitol)
22. SMOKE DON'T LIE (Carl Smith, Columbia)
23. HEARTS OF STONE (Red Foley, Decca)
24. THE OLD HOUSE (Stuart Hamblen, Victor)
25. KENTUCKIAN SONG (Eddy Arnold, Victor)

POP

1. CHERRY PINK AND APPLE BLOSSOM WHITE (P. Prado, Victor)
2. ROCK AROUND THE CLOCK (Bill Haley, Decca)
3. YELLOW ROSE OF TEXAS (Mitch Miller, Columbia)
4. AUTUMN LEAVES (Roger Williams, Kapp)
5. UNCHAINED MELODY (L. Baxter, Capitol)
6. BALLAD OF DAVY CROCKETT (Bill Hayes, Cadenos)
7. LOVE IS A MANY-SPLENDORED THING (Four Acres, Decca)
8. SINCERELY (McGuire Sisters, Coral)
9. AIN'T THAT A SHAME (P. Boone, Dot)
10. DANCE WITH ME, HENRY (G. Gibbs, Mercury)
11. CRAZY OTTO MEDLEY I & II (Crazy Otto, Decca)
12. MELODY OF LOVE (Billy Vaughn, Dot)
13. SIXTEEN TONS (Tennessee Ernie, Capitol)
14. LEARNIN' THE BLUES (Frank Sinatra, Capitol)
15. HEARTS OF STONE (Fontane Sisters, Dot)
16. TWEEDLE DEE (G. Gibbs, Mercury)
17. MOMENTS TO REMEMBER (Four Lads, Columbia)
18. MR. SANDMAN* (Chorlettes, Cadence)
19. LET ME GO LOVER* (Joan Weber, Columbia)
20. BLOSSOM FELL (Nat "King" Cole, Capitol)
21. UNCHAINED MELODY (A. Hibbler, Decca)
22. BALLAD OF DAVY CROCKETT (Fess Parker, Columbia)
23. HONEY BABE (A. Mooney, M-G-M)
24. BALLAD OF DAVY CROCKETT (Tennessee Ernie, Capitol)
25. KO KO MO (Perry Como, Victor)
26. NAUGHTY LADY OF SHADY LANE* (Ames Brothers, Victor)
27. HARD TO GET (G. MacKenzie, X)
28. THAT'S ALL I WANT FROM YOU* (Jaye P. Morgan, Victor)
29. ONLY YOU (Platters, Mercury)
30. IT'S A SIN TO TELL A LIE (Somthin' Smith & the Redheads, Epic)

Source: *Billboard,* 7 January 1956

sponsibility. His dense, meticulous prose was the talk of the literary world in 1957, the year *By Love Possessed* was published. No serious novel during the decade received more popular attention, and no author reacted to celebrity with more disdain.

The Beats. As rich as the writing of the 1950s was, the dominant literary group is remembered not so much for its talent as for its message, which was bitterly critical of American society. Allen Ginsberg complained in his 1956 poem *Howl* that he "saw the best minds of his generation destroyed by madness" "with the absolute heart of the poem of life butchered out of their bodies." When the poem was published by San Francisco poet and publisher Lawrence Ferlinghetti, it prompted charges of obscenity. In a show trial, Ferlinghetti was found innocent.

Spontaneous Writing. Ginsberg's friends Jack Kerouac, William S. Burroughs, Ferlinghetti, and Gregory Corso were the most visible members of the Beats. Like the abstract expressionists, they wanted to bridge the gap between art and life, and they took to the roads in search of raw experience, to see for themselves what the country was like. Their hero was a fast-talking, free-living, nonwriting rogue named Neal Cassady, who ex-

emplified the freedom of spirit they admired. Kerouac's *On the Road* (1957) was the defining work of the movement, whose philosophy can be reduced to one word: spontaneity. Individualism was cherished above all by the Beats, who clung to a simple reduction of the existentialist philosophy current among such French intellectuals as Jean-Paul Sartre and Albert Camus: every person should seize the freedom to determine who he or she is and then act accordingly.

Freedom of Expression. In 1952 Lionel Trilling observed that "for the first time in the history of the modern American intellectual, America is not to be conceived of as *a priori* the vulgarest and stupidest nation of the world. And this is not only because other nations are exercising as never before the inalienable right of nations to be stupid and vulgar." As the military and diplomatic power of the nation was accepted worldwide, creative people looked to America for an interpretation of what that power meant and how it affected life. The responses took various forms, but in the 1950s they reduced to a common theme: people are more important than nations; individuals are more precious than weapons; freedom of expression is the basic right, and it can be maintained only if it is exercised.

TOPICS IN THE NEWS

ABSTRACT EXPRESSIONISM

Action Painters. The abstract expressionists — also called "Action Painters" because their blobs, drips, whorls, and scribbles express the process of painting, which they considered the essence of art — were too abstract for untutored American art lovers in the 1950s. The major young American artists of the day were redefining art and revolutionizing the aesthetic principles on which it was based, the public be damned. Such painters as Hans Hofmann, Willem de Kooning, Jackson Pollock, Lee Krasner, Robert Motherwell, and Mark Rothko drew their inspiration from the Western European movements cubism and surrealism, from the publicly sponsored artists' programs of the Works Progress Administration (WPA) of the 1930s, and from an unrelentingly threatening world political situation. The result was the first distinctly American art movement to have international influence.

Background. With the upheaval of Western Europe during the 1930s and the military threat of the Nazis beginning in 1939, an influential group of artists migrated to New York: André Breton, Salvador Dalí, Max Ernst, Piet Mondrian, Fernand Léger, Marc Chagall, and others. They were among the most respected modern artists in the world, and by the time of World War II their influence was concentrated in Manhattan. Meanwhile a generation of talented American artists had just emerged from the federally sponsored WPA, painting murals, contemplating the purposes of art in society, and benefiting from federal support providing the freedom to develop their talents and ideas.

American Roots. Beginning in the 1940s with the work of Hofmann and de Kooning, both immigrants who had settled permanently in New York City, a new attitude toward art began to evolve. Providing an American perspective on surrealism (art that attempts to portray experience beyond the realm of conscious perception),

Willem de Kooning and *Merritt Parkway*

this new movement rejected all boundaries — those of form, shape, color, and medium. The artworks tended to be large, more suited to display in warehouses than on living-room walls or in traditional exhibit spaces. Materials were those at hand — house paint (more suitable for dripping than oils), tar, glue and whatever would stick to it, anything that would make a mark.

Theory. Frames were too restrictive and traditional shapes and forms too limiting for the abstract expressionists. The composition of these new artworks was intended to reflect spontaneous motion. Rather than re-creating some perception on a canvas, the abstract expressionists recorded action: a splatter of paint, a series of random movements of some object attached to a marker, a mixture of colors producing the random arrangement of various colored objects. De Kooning painted a series of figures of women, departing progressively from realistic portrayals until he reached the point of complete obliteration of form. In fact, it seems that the primary point of representing a figure in his paintings of the 1950s was to distort it and to blur its similarity to a living figure.

Pollock. Pollock liked busy canvases. During the 1950s he developed the technique of drip painting, which was the flinging of paint of different colors onto a surface.

The paint drippings recorded the motion of the artist's arm as he worked; the accumulation of sets of these drippings compressed time as the motion of one moment was layered over the motion of another. The drippings also had the effect of obliterating whatever was underneath them, and so the painterly actions of more-recent moments obscured those of earlier sessions, suggesting a philosophy akin to nihilism.

Obscurantists. Such artists as Franz Kline and Motherwell went a step further with their obscurantist tendencies: they obscured everything, so all that was left in their artworks was a nearly blank surface that, in the case of Kline, might have a single line across it or, in the case of Motherwell, might resemble an inkblot.

The Critics. Such aesthetic principles led to puzzling art that can be difficult to view. Moreover, the art enthusiast who turned to art critics for clarification found the explanations more baffling than the art itself. *New Republic* quoted an example of what it called " 'advanced' criticism" from *Art News*. The subject of the comments is a white canvas by Kline with horizontal, broad, uneven black lines across it (a description that applies to several of his works): "In the past two years, there has been a change in [Kline's] style. Not a drastic one; white and black forms still soar, tumble and stand in as permanent a state of instability as ever. But . . . the white paint is whiter, bluer, more snow-like. The black pigments differentiate themselves as fat and lean pigments. He endows the absence of totality of refraction with the range of the spectrum. This is achieved by an emotional intensity that seems to burn all the color out of art."

The Audience. The casual museum-goer was confused to the point of annoyance by the art, by its explanation, and by the attention it received. By the mid 1950s works of what was referred to generically as modern art were being routinely sold for over ten thousand dollars. *New Republic* summarized the opinion of a generation of art lovers lagging slightly behind the avant-garde in its observation that "uninhibited daubing has recognized educational value for children in early grades and as a therapeutic device in certain instances of adult mental disorder. . . . We part company [with advocates of modern art] . . . when the talk turns to 'masterpieces' and when abstract expressionism is held aloft as the apogee of contemporary creativeness."

Sources:

Robert Carleton Hobbs and Gail Levin, *Abstract Expressionism: The Formative Years* (New York: Cornell University, Herbert F. Johnson Museum of Art / New York: Whitney Museum of American Art, 1978);

Robert Myron and Abner Sundell, *Modern Art in America* (New York: Crowell-Collier / London: Collier-Macmillan, 1971);

"Mystique of the Drip," *New Republic*, 140 (5 June 1959): 6-7;

Frank O'Hara, *Art Chronicles 1954-1966* (New York: Braziller, 1975).

ART CRITICS

The Spokesmen. In the art world of the 1950s, critics had an exaggerated importance. The art itself was new and difficult to understand, so art lovers, even artists themselves, turned to the critics for direction. Two men, representing different theories of abstract art, dominated avant-garde art criticism of the day. They were Clement Greenberg, art critic for the *Nation* from 1945 to 1950 and associate editor of *Commentary* from 1945 to 1957, and Harold Rosenberg, a regular contributor to *Art News* (and reputed creator of Smokey the Bear for the national campaign against forest fires). They not only represented different views of art, they championed different celebrity artists. Rosenberg considered Willem de Kooning to be the preeminent artist of the day. Greenberg championed Jackson Pollock. Between them they popularized — even commercialized — an art form that was introspective above all and seemed a most unlikely subject for general interest.

Clement Greenberg. Greenberg was considered the bully of the art world. He was dogmatic, irreverent, and overbearing. He was also successful in championing the cause of abstract art as the only defensible artistic form of the age — a historical inevitability, he called it. He observed that art in America after World War II had no coherent philosophy, and he set out to provide one. He argued that American artists should forsake the early modern obsession with spatial planes and focus on what he called a flat surface. He insisted that the surrealists were "too literary" and that American art ought not refer the viewer to images or ideas outside the scope of the work itself. He talked about quality of line and paint as if he were quoting from some master rule book. Because Greenberg seemed so sure of himself and communicated his seemingly simplified view of abstract art so effectively, he was able to convince museum curators, gallery owners, magazine editors, and the reading public that he was teaching them truths about art that they needed to know — and buy. He, more than anyone else, was responsible for the popularization of abstract art in the 1950s.

Harold Rosenberg. Rosenberg considered Greenberg to be a simplistic philistine. Of the two, most people in the art world conceded that Rosenberg was better equipped intellectually, had a better understanding of the concepts that drove American abstract artists, and was more sympathetic to their art. Rosenberg explained abstract art as the record of an event — an encounter between the artist and, for painters, the canvas. The purpose of art was uninhibited, sincere self-expression, and the quality of the artwork was measured by the degree of creativity it exhibited. The artist who accepted rules or preconceptions about how and what to paint compromised his creativity. By these ground rules such concepts as subject, form, composition, and shape were simply types of limitations on the artist's self-expression. Rosenberg expressed his ideas forcefully, but his prose style was almost as abstract as the painting he described. Many inhabitants of the art world complained that they had no idea what he was saying — except that it seemed clear that he was excluding Pollock from the gallery of serious abstract artists and Greenberg from the audience of perceptive critics.

Greenberg and Pollock. Greenberg was a promoter. In 1949 he announced that Pollock was the greatest painter in America, a statement that attracted attention because it seemed so outrageous at the time. As a result, in August *Life* magazine published a tongue-in-cheek pictorial essay on the artist, "Jackson Pollock: Is He the Greatest Living Painter in the United States?" In November 1949 Pollock showed his paintings at a small, overflowing gallery in Manhattan and made his first substantial sales. His career was launched, and Greenberg laid claim to the title greatest living art critic in the United States.

Rosenberg's Attack. Rosenberg disputed the claim. In the December 1952 *Art News,* he published "The American Action Painters," calculated to discredit Greenberg and Pollock. His forum drew the attention of

---

KLINE ON ART CRITICS

Excerpt from an interview with Franz Kline, 1958:

Then of course there are reviewers. I read reviews because they are a facet of someone's mind which has been brought to bear on the work. Although if someone's against it, they act as if the guy had spent his life doing something worthless.

Someone can paint *not* from his own time, not even from himself. Then the reviewer cannot like it, maybe. But just to review, like a shopper, I saw one this, one that, good, awful, is terrible. Or he may be hopelessly uninterested in what it is anyway, but writes about it. I read Leonard Lyons in the john the other day and he said every other country picked out the best art for the Venice Biennale, but we didn't. Then someone in the government went to Brussels and said painters should have to get a license for buying brushes. Lyons went on to say that there will be a day when abstractions are not supposed to be made for a child's playroom.

Criticism must come from those who are around it, who are not shocked that someone should be doing it at all. It should be exciting, and in a way that excitement comes from, in looking at it, that it's *not* that autumn scene you love, its *not* that portrait of your grandmother.

Source: Frank O'Hara, *Art Chronicles 1954–1966* (New York: Braziller, 1975).

Harold Rosenberg

the art world rather than the general public, to whom Greenberg took his argument, but Rosenberg was nonetheless brilliant in attacking Greenberg's ideas about art. Rosenberg insisted that any critic who goes about declaring art movements is promoting values that are not shared by the best artists.

Synthesis. It took both a Greenberg and a Rosenberg to accomplish the acceptance of abstract art that occurred in the 1950s — Greenberg to make the pitch and to create a celebrity artist to represent the movement, Rosenberg to provide an intellectual justification. They were antagonists, and they spoke to different audiences, but together promoted the public awareness of a body of art that may well have gone unappreciated without their attention.

Sources:

Clement Greenberg, *Art and Culture: Critical Essays* (Boston: Beacon, 1961);

Steven Naifeh and Gregory White Smith, *Jackson Pollock: An American Saga* (New York: Clarkson Potter, 1989);

Harold Rosenberg, "The American Action Painters," *Art News*, 51 (December 1952): 22–23, 48–50.

THE BEAT MOVEMENT

A Literary Protest. The Beats were members of an artistic protest movement in the mid 1950s in which a small group of writers declared themselves disaffected nonconformists and were elevated by the media to the status of antiheroes. *GO!* (1952), by John Clellon Holmes, is said to be the first Beat novel because it is a lightly disguised account of the lives of key Beat figures — Jack Kerouac, Neal Cassady, and Allen Ginsberg. In the novel, as in real life, they consider themselves to be moral pioneers, turning their backs on materialism, and the values that support it, in favor of adventuresome lives given purpose by the search for meaning. *GO!* is valued much more highly by literary historians, who consider it documentary evidence of the early days of the movement, than by contemporary audiences, who were largely uninterested, if sales are a gauge.

Definition. The meaning of *Beat* has always been vague. Kerouac, who is said to have coined the term *Beat Generation*, seems to have been suggesting that he and his friends were "beaten" down in frustration at the difficulty of individual expression in an era of conformity. At another time he claimed that "beat" was a derivation from "beatific," suggesting that the Beats had earned a kind of intellectual grace through the aesthetic purity of their lives. Ginsberg construed the term to refer to people looking at society from the "*underside*" and thus avoiding the distortion of commonly held values.

A Square's View. *Life* magazine, which took the lead in the print media among social commentators seeking to characterize the Beats, described them in 1959 as "sick little bums" and "hostile little females" who were unwashed, uneducated, unmotivated, unprincipled, and lived in the cold-water flats in Greenwich Village in lower Manhattan. The popular media coined the term *beatniks* and established the stereotype of the man, generically referred to as "daddy-o," in an untrimmed goatee, sandals, soiled sweatshirt, and blue jeans, and the woman, called a "chick," in black leotard, short skirt, black eye

Clement Greenberg

shadow, and pale lipstick, sitting lazily in a coffeehouse listening to jazz and muttering phrases that included the words *hip, far out,* and *groovy.* Sexual freedom and alcohol and drugs, particularly amphetamines and marijuana, were staples of Beat life, giving further impetus to establishment attacks. There was a fear that the Beat lifestyle would spread from New York City and North Beach in San Francisco to infect Middle America.

The Literary View. The literary establishment was no more receptive to the Beat movement than the popular media. Beat literature was uniformly dismissed as adolescent and uninteresting. Even Ginsberg's *Howl* (1956) and Kerouac's *On the Road* (1957), the two major works of the movement, which produced few enduring pieces of literature, were far more widely denounced than praised by critics. Even in retrospect, literary historians tend to dismiss the Beat movement as having been notable more for its social significance than for its literary contributions.

Ginsberg. The poet Ginsberg was the most credible literary figure among the Beats. Like Kerouac he was at Columbia University after World War II, but, unlike most of the other noteworthy Beats, he graduated, having studied with Mark Van Doren and Lionel Trilling. As a result, Ginsberg had more of a literary tradition on which to draw and his work was given more-serious consideration by critics and academics. He was angrier in his response to the conformity of the time and more flamboyant than any of the Beats except, perhaps, for Cassady.

Howl. Ginsberg produced only one book during the 1950s, but it galvanized the Beat movement. *Howl and Other Poems* was dedicated to Kerouac, Cassady, William S. Burroughs, Jr., a hipster father figure to the Beats, and Lucien Carr, who killed an obsessed homosexual lover in an incident that caused both Kerouac and Ginsberg to be

A HAPPENING AT BLACK MOUNTAIN

An account from the diary of Francine du Plessix, 1952, a summer student at Black Mountain College, of a recital by composer John Cage:

"At 8:30 tonight John Cage mounted a stepladder and until 10:30, he talked of the relation of music to Zen Buddhism, while a movie was shown, dogs barked, Merce [Cunningham] danced, a prepared piano was played, whistles blew, babies screamed, coffee was served by four boys dressed in white and Edith Piaf records were played double-speed on a turn-of-the-century machine. At 10:30 the recital ended and Cage grinned while [Charles] Olson [director of the college] talked to him again about Zen Buddhism, Stefan Wolpe bitched, two boys in white waltzed together, [David] Tudor played the piano, and the professors' wives licked popsicles."

Source: Martin Duberman, *Black Mountain: An Exploration in Community* (New York: Dutton, 1972).

Beats Allen Ginsberg and Peter Orlovsky in their Greenwich Village "pad"

indicted as accessories; Carr's name was removed from the dedication page in the second printing. The book was published in October 1956 by City Lights Press, owned by San Francisco Beat poet, publisher, and bookseller Lawrence Ferlinghetti. The small volume was seized by U.S. Customs officials and the juvenile division of the San Francisco Police Department as obscene material, and a highly publicized obscenity trial in August 1957 served to focus attention on Ginsberg's messianic situation report about the deplorable state of American culture. Ten thousand copies were sold by the end of the trial and over a quarter of a million by 1980. *Howl* is among the best-selling volumes of American verse ever published.

Kerouac. Kerouac's second novel, *On the Road,* was published in September 1957, the month after the *Howl* obscenity trial, and it was declared by influential critics to be the definitive fictional statement of Beat tenets. The novel is about essentially the same group and some of the same incidents that provided the material for *GO!* The timing was better for Kerouac, though, because Ginsberg and Ferlinghetti had drawn national attention to the social dissatisfaction of some college students as they looked uneasily to the prospect of graduation without confidence in the values of the marketplace. Kerouac gave voice to their uncertainty and discontent in his depiction of the Beats, who left convention behind as they headed west from New York City to explore the frontiers of freedom.

Cassady. Kerouac chose a rambler, not a writer, as the embodiment of spontaneity, the primary virtue of the Beat Generation. Cassady was born in 1926 on the road and raised from the age of six in the slums of Denver, where he received his education on skid row. By the age of fifteen he was a prostitute and petty thief; by eighteen he was in jail. The combination of Cassady's street savvy, eclectic education, intelligence, restlessness, and sexual energy attracted Kerouac when they met at in the neighborhood around Columbia University in spring 1945. Cassady's rapid-fire, free-association speech pattern reminded Kerouac of jazz improvisation and provided a model for his fictional technique. With *On the Road* Kerouac made Cassady into a symbol of Beat virtue, a romantic rogue who blazed his own trail without regard for social precept, civil ordinance, or criminal statute.

Fading Voices. By the end of the 1950s the Beats had made their literary and social statement. Lesser voices continued to promote the spirit of the movement, but they were redundant. Ginsberg and Kerouac had become interested in Eastern religions, which Kerouac wrote about in *The Dharma Bums* (1958) and subsequent novels, though it was a subject that failed to attract many Beat disciples. Kerouac gradually faded from the literary scene; Ginsberg and Ferlinghetti moved on energetically to other interests and remained major figures in the avant-garde of the 1960s and 1970s; Cassady became a sort of mascot of the hippie movement of the 1960s and 1970s, serving most notably as driver of the bus "Further" for Ken Kesey's Merry Pranksters.

Sources:
Ann Charters, "Jack Kerouac," *Dictionary of Literary Biography: Documentary Series*, vol. 3 (Detroit: Gale, 1983), pp. 71–122;

Charters, ed. *Dictionary of Literary Biography,* vol. 16: *The Beats* (Detroit: Gale, 1983);

Bruce Cook, *The Beat Generation* (New York: Scribners, 1971);

Paul O'Neil, "The Only Rebellion Around," *Life* (30 November 1959): 114–130;

"Squaresville U.S.A. vs. Beatsville," *Life* (21 September 1959).

THE DAY THE MUSIC DIED

Buddy Holly. At the end of January 1959 Buddy Holly was at the peak of his career. It had been three years since the young rock 'n' roll singer and guitar player had begun recording his music, and he had enjoyed a handful of hits: "That'll be the Day," "Oh Boy!," and "Peggy Sue," which had been in the top ten rock 'n' roll songs in both the United States and Great Britain. Holly had recently left his hometown band and fired his business manager in an attempt to capitalize fully on his success, with the help of his new wife.

The Tour. Despite his hit records, he needed money in winter 1958–1959. His wife was pregnant, and he was building his career, so he signed up to tour with the Winter Dance Party, a rock 'n' roll show scheduled to play in remote locations throughout the Midwest. The attractions, in addition to Holly, were two acts that had just enjoyed their first hits: Ritchie Valens, whose "Donna" reached number two on the rock charts, had just recorded "La Bamba"; and the Big Bopper (J. P. Richardson), whose "Chantilly Lace" had sold over one million copies, a performance he hoped his new record, "Big Bopper's Wedding," would duplicate.

The Problems. The tour began poorly. Before the musicians made it to the stage, their bus broke down and Holly's drummer was hospitalized with frostbite. Subsequent engagements proceeded so shakily that Holly considered going home. The severe winter weather caused a succession of delays, and as a result he was unable to do his laundry regularly. Because he was repeatedly forced to perform tired and disheveled, he feared the tour would damage his reputation.

The Plane. On Monday 2 February Holly desperately sought relief. He chartered a plane to take him and two of his sidemen from Clear Lake, Iowa, where they were scheduled to play that night, to the next stop on the tour, Moorhead, North Dakota, a distance of some four hundred miles. The benefit was a night in a hotel instead of the tour bus.

The Crash. When Valens and Richardson found out about Holly's plan, they managed to appropriate the seats of Holly's sidemen, Tommy Allsup and bass player Waylon Jennings. That night the Winter Dance Party played to an audience of eleven hundred at the Surf Ballroom in Clear Lake. Just after midnight the plane took off in light snow and heavy fog. Within ten minutes it had crashed, killing the pilot and all three passengers.

The Shock. No rock 'n' roll star had ever tragically lost his life before. The day 3 February 1959 has come to be known as "the day the music died," after the phrase in Don McLean's hit song of another decade, "American Pie."

Source:
John Tobler, *The Buddy Holly Story* (New York: Beaufort Books, 1979).

Front page *New York Daily Mirror,* 4 February 1959

45 RPM RECORDS

Background. Until June 1948, home listening to recorded music required a forgiving ear and a vivid imagination. The records were all ten or twelve inches in diameter and made of shellac. They cost about $1.50 each and played for about four minutes per side at 78 revolutions per minute. They broke easily, scratched at the slightest touch, and wore quickly with repeated play. The sound quality of the recording was terrible by today's standard, and, as a result, more energy went into improving record-player cabinets than in enhancing the quality of their sound reproduction. Even so, Americans bought about 350 million records in 1947 and owned 16 million record players, all of which ran at a single speed, because only 78-RPM records were available.

More Music Per Disc. New technology reformed the industry. There were two major record manufacturers, RCA-Victor and Columbia, vying with one another for dominance. Columbia took the first step, introducing

In 1950 the music industry recognized three major types of popular music: mainstream pop, country pop, and R&B (black) pop. They constituted 50 percent, 13 percent, and 6 percent, respectively, of popular-music record sales. *Billboard* and *Cash Box* magazines tracked record sales in all three fields, monitored by reports from designated retail outlets, and published them weekly. Radio play by disc jockeys was related to sales, and it was also reported.

An important precursor of rock 'n' roll was the erosion of the boundaries between markets that began in about 1950. What were called crossover hits — songs that appeared on more than one pop chart, usually by different musicians — began to appear with increasing frequency. In 1950, for example, "Goodnight Irene" by Gordon Jenkins and the Weavers was number one on the mainstream pop chart in June 1950. The same song by Ernest Tubb and Red Foley was number one on the country chart in August 1950. As performed by Paul Gayton, "Goodnight Irene" made it to number six on the R&B chart in September. The same song was also recorded in 1950 by Frank Sinatra, Jo Stafford, Dennis Day, and Moon Mullican, and each of these versions made it into the top thirty in its category (all mainstream except for Mullican's version, which was country).

"Mona Lisa," as recorded by Nat King Cole, was number one on both the mainstream (June 1951) and R&B (July 1951) charts, and "Chatanoogie Shoe Shine Boy" by Red Foley was number one on both the mainstream and country charts in January 1950. In all, there were six songs in 1950 that appeared in the top thirty of all three pop charts and twenty-five that appeared in the top thirty of two pop charts. At first it was much easier for songs to cross over than for performers to do so. Elvis changed that. In the late 1950s he had an average of nine records per year on the mainstream pop charts (which by then were predominantly rock 'n' roll) and five per year on both the country and R&B charts.

Source: Philip H. Ennis, *The Seventh Stream: The Emergence of Rocknroll in American Popular Music* (Hanover & London: Wesleyan University Press, 1992).

industry standard. The price was about four or five dollars per record.

Too Many Sizes. On 31 March 1949 RCA-Victor countered with 6 7/8–inch discs that played at 45 RPM. They offered lower price, about seventy-nine cents, and improved quality. RCA-Victor relied on reports that 90 percent of record listeners preferred popular music, which almost always fit nicely into the three and one-half minutes of playing time that 45s, as they were called, offered. The 45s could claim better sound reproduction — though most listeners could not tell the difference on their home players — because the grooves that reproduced the music ran only a couple of inches from the outside edge of the record and thus were more uniform in their configuration. There was also a hole 1 1/2 inches in diameter in the center of 45s to accommodate the player spindle that further distinguished them from 78s and LPs, which had quarter-inch spindle holes.

What To Do with the Old Player. The result of the record-format wars was that sixteen million 78-RPM record players became obsolete in the last eighteen months of the 1940s. Both RCA-Victor and Columbia offered mechanical attachments to 78-RPM players that would allow them to accommodate the new records, but consumers, already angry and confused by the new technology, refused to buy them. Accordingly, record sales fell to two hundred million in 1949. At the same time, though, records became easier and cheaper to make, so as the industry bottomed out, it became easier for new companies to get into the recording business.

45 RPM records and player

unbreakable, scratch-resistant (but far from scratch-proof) vinylite records in ten-inch and twelve-inch versions that played at 33 1/3 RPM. The twelve-inch records, called long-playing (or LPs), could hold twenty-five minutes worth of music on a side, and in time they became the

A Revitalized Industry. It was not until 1952 that the industry recovered, and the recovery was booming. Player sales, which had been 830,000 in 1950, jumped to nearly 1.5 million in 1952 and doubled again before the end of the decade, reaching $200 million in annual sales by 1957. The term *hi-fi,* short for high-fidelity sound, came into common usage as listeners insisted on quality sound reproduction, even though the cost of the player increased. In 1950 a standard portable record player cost about thirty-five dollars. By the end of the decade hi-fi sets commonly cost several hundred dollars, and discriminating listeners were acquiring new components capable of playing stereophonic sound recordings, introduced in 1958. Stereo equipment gave the illusion of live performance by transmitting slightly different tracks, captured on specially prepared LP records, to two different speakers that were ideally placed several feet from one another. New-stereo owners could be identified by their ownership of records playing train noises, street sounds, or bird calls that demonstrated the effectiveness of their systems.

The Long-lived LP. The LP won out in the long run, but the 45 was the standard medium for popular music during the decade, and it allowed the continued development of what came to be a cultural icon — the jukebox. Though jukeboxes were hardly new inventions, the 45s made them more practical and increased their use at casual food-serving establishments and a necessary piece of equipment in teen gathering places. Because of their durability, space-saving size, and popularity among teen audiences due to their low price, 45s were ideal for jukebox use. A typical jukebox held as many as 150 records — 300 sides — that could be played for five cents a song or three plays for a dime.

Sources:

Lawrence C. Goldsmith, "War in Three Speeds," *Nation,* 168 (7 May 1949): 523–525;

Ann M. Lingg, "Record Rumpus," *Reader's Digest,* 55 (December 1949): 139–142;

William J. Temple, "Which Playback?," *Senior Scholastic,* 58 (4 April 1951): 26–T, 40–T.

GATHINGS COMMITTEE

A Congressman's Indignation. On 16 June 1952 Congressman Ezekiel Candler Gathings went to war against obscenity as chairman of the House Select Committee on Current Pornographic Materials. He had been upset about newsstand titillation since he had come to Washington, D.C.: "Everytime I went to the drugstore to get cigars there would be a long line at the bookstand looking at the lewd covers. . . . I thought, what is this country coming to if we are distributing this type of thing to the youth of the land. Then, to follow it through, these kids seem to have the idea that one must go out and commit rape."

The Investigation. Representative Gathings established his credentials by sponsoring a congressional inquiry on radio and television during which he admitted that he did not know the difference between a good and a bad television program. Then Speaker Rayburn appointed him chairman of a special committee to investigate "Immoral, obscene, or otherwise offensive matter" in print. He and eight congressional colleagues, aided by two lawyers, two investigators, and a budget of twenty-five thousand dollars, studied an array of some one hundred exhibits with such single-minded zeal that they were ridiculed in the press. Seeking to reassure people uncertain about his motives, Gathings reassured them: "We are interested only in the extreme type of publication of pornographic material. . . . Only what's available at the corner drugstore or what you can order through the mails."

The Report. The committee's report was released early in 1953, coinciding roughly with publication of the first issue of *Playboy.* The report alleged that there were 70 million comic-book readers in the United States who bought 100 million comics a month, 30 percent of which contained objectionable material. The committee charged that millions of girlie magazines are published in America and that one in ten Americans reads them, or at least turns the pages. Over half the report was reserved for the subject of lurid paperbacks, which, the committee charged, deserved most of the blame for the "trash and obscenity" being circulated in print form. Paperback publishers took objection, pointing out that 90 percent of paperbacks are reprints of hardcover books and that it is unfair to characterize all paperbacks on the basis of a small and selective sampling.

Rep. Ezekiel Gathings

The Indifference. The Gathings Committee prompted little response aside from polite criticism. Books were defended against the conclusions of the report by two of the committee's own members, who prepared a minority dissent arguing that books promote knowledge and freedom of expression and thus deserve protection. Representative Gathings, annoyed by the criticism his efforts attracted, withdrew into the legislative shadows until his retirement in 1969.

Sources:

"No Witch Hunt," *Newsweek* (7 July 1952): 80;

W. W. Wade, "Libraries and Intellectual Freedom," in *Collier's 1954 Yearbook* (New York: Collier, 1954), p. 334.

HOWL OBSCENITY TRIAL

A Dirty Book in San Francisco. *Howl and Other Poems* (1956), the first book by Beat poet Allen Ginsberg, had been for sale at the City Lights bookshop in San Francisco for eight months when, on 21 May 1957, local city and county police officers Russell Woods and Thomas Pagee were sent by their boss, Capt. William Hanrahan, chief of the Juvenile Bureau, to purchase a copy of the book and swear out a warrant for the arrest of the salesclerk and Lawrence Ferlinghetti, the shop owner. Ferlinghetti's City Lights Books had also published the volume. The book was variously described as "a howl of pain" caused by "Mr. Ginsberg's personal view of a segment of life he has experienced . . . colored by exposure to jazz, to Columbia, a university, to a liberal and Bohemian education, to a great deal of traveling on the road, to a certain amount of what we call bumming around" (by Luther Nichols, a San Francisco reviewer) or as "a lot of sensitive bullshit," in the words of the prosecutor. The defendants pleaded not guilty to charges of selling lewd and indecent writings, and a highly publicized trial followed in San Francisco Municipal Court, the lowest ranking California court. The circuslike court proceedings were reported nationwide, though from a legal perspective the ultimate outcome was a foregone conclusion of dubious significance.

To Trial. Ferlinghetti (charges against his clerk were dismissed) was defended free of charge by Jake Ehrlich, who had achieved legal celebrity by defending murderer Caryl Chessman and exotic dancer Sally Rand, among others. He faced Ralph McIntosh, an aging assistant district attorney who specialized in prosecuting pornographers. The issue was whether a work could be judged obscene because it contained individual words that might be considered offensive without regard to context. The court found Ferlinghetti not guilty and, presumably, staved off a wave of indictments in San Francisco against publishers and sellers of books with obscene words in them.

The Issue. The *Howl* trial was less about law than about exposure. Ginsberg and Ferlinghetti received hundreds of thousands of dollars worth of free publicity that made Ginsberg a celebrity and his book publishing legend. As of 1993 it was in its forty-first printing, and some 850,000 copies had sold. The author and publisher were portrayed as libertarian spokesmen, symbols of First Amendment rights, and crusaders against ignorance and censorship. A spotlight was cast on professional literary criticism as well when Ehrlich called a parade of writers and critics as witnesses to elucidate the literary qualities of the book. They prompted less enthusiasm than the other principles, though.

Witnesses for the Defense. Among the critics, Mark Schorer led off, followed by Walter Van Tilburg Clark, Kenneth Rexroth, and six others. Professor Schorer, a highly respected author and scholar, stated that poetic expression could not be reduced to the level of common language, and thus he could not say what lines in the poem mean; poet, teacher, and critic Rexroth proclaimed *Howl* "probably the most remarkable single poem, published by a young man since the second war"; and Clark, critic and author of *The Ox-Bow Incident* (1940), was warned to avoid lecturing the court and the prosecutor when he described the difficulty of defining literary merit and questioned its relevance to the case at hand.

Witnesses for the Prosecution. The prosecution's witnesses were an assistant professor teaching freshman

THE SCREEN EXPLODES WITH SEX

In 1953 the big news in Hollywood was not who would win the Academy Awards but Otto Preminger's defiance of the movie morality codes. He produced a movie adaptation of the racy Broadway play *The Moon Is Blue*, by F. Hugh Herbert, about a woman who flaunts her virginity. Officials at the Breen office, the enforcers of the Motion Picture Production Code (MPPC), bristled at the language in the script: the lady might flaunt her virginity, but she better watch her language. Unless Preminger omitted the words *virgin* and *pregnant* from the script, the Breen office ruled, it would withhold the MPPC seal of approval.

Preminger made a rude comment and proceeded to distribute the movie without the seal. The Catholic Church was aghast. The official church paper gave the movie a "Condemned" rating, which meant that practicing Catholics sinned grievously if they watched it. One church movie reviewer had failed to read his paper, though. He described the movie as "irresistible." Secular audiences agreed. The movie was a box-office hit.

Source: Mason Wiley and Damien Bona, *Inside Oscar: The Unofficial History of the Academy Awards* (New York: Ballantine, 1986).

Howl obscenity trial. Lawrence Ferlinghetti is in the forefront on the left, with his hand in his coat pocket.

English and engineering English at the University of San Francisco who was working on his Ph.D. and a college instructor and writer who had rewritten *Faust* (incorporating forty versions of the story, she said) and *Everyman,* among other works. The first witness attempted to define the literary shortcomings of *Howl:* "It is really just a weak imitation of a form that was used 80 or 90 years ago by Walt Whitman"; "The statement of the idea of the poem was relatively clear, but it has little validity, and, therefore, the theme has a negative value, no value at all"; and "this poem is apparently dedicated to a long-dead movement — 'Dadaism' and some late followers of Dadaism. And therefore the opportunity is long past for any significant literary contribution of this poem." The second witness complained that "you feel like you are going through the gutter when you have to read that stuff. I didn't linger on it too long, I assure you."

The Verdict. After due consideration, the Honorable Clayton W. Horn found the defendant not guilty, because isolated words cannot be considered obscene, the effect of the work was not "erotic or aphrodisiac," and he found the poem to have redeeming value. He concluded his decision with the motto of the highest order of English knighthood: "In considering material claimed to be obscene it is well to remember the motto: 'Honi soit qui mal y pense' (Evil to him who evil thinks)."

As of 1993, *Howl* sells some twenty thousand copies each year.

Sources:
Jake W. Ehrlich, ed., *Howl of the Censor* (San Carlos, Cal.: Nourse, 1956);

David Perlman, "How Captain Hanrahan Made 'Howl' a Best-Seller," *Reporter,* 17 (12 December 1957), pp. 37–39.

MOVIES

Pressure from Television. As television became an increasingly popular entertainment medium throughout the 1950s, the movie industry did everything within its power to pull people away from the box in the living room and into the theaters. *Bigger* became the byword for the movies. Wide-screen techniques such as CinemaScope and VistaVision were used to add a panoramic effect to spectacles, swashbucklers, musicals, and otherwise splashy movies with big-name stars, big casts, big sets, and big budgets. Although hard-hitting social dramas on both small and large scales had an impact, they were overshadowed at the box office by the melodramatic woman's picture. Science-fiction and horror movies proved more commercially viable than ever, and some were filmed in the short-lived 3-D process.

Spectacle. Historical epics with huge casts were a mainstay of the 1950s. Many of them drew on the Bible: *The Robe* (1953) was the first movie filmed in the CinemaScope process. *David and Bathsheba* (1951) and *Solomon and Sheba* (1959) were big grossers during their respective years of release. *Ben-Hur* (1959), the most expensive movie up to that time, won an Academy Award for Best Picture. *Quo Vadis?* (1951), set during the reign of the Roman emperor Nero, was one of the largest-scale productions of the decade.

More Spectacle. Lavishly produced costume pictures featuring swashbucklers also flourished. *Ivanhoe* (1952), *Scaramouche* (1952), and *Beau Brummel* (1954) were among the most popular of them. Cecil B. DeMille, the master of cinema spectacle since the 1920s, not only produced and directed *The Ten Commandments* (1956) but also the circus spectacular *The Greatest Show on Earth* (1952), which won an Academy Award for Best Picture. At the beginning of the 1950s *Gone With the Wind* (1939) was the top-grossing movie of all time, and it remained so throughout the decade. *The Greatest Show on Earth* became the second-top-grossing movie of all time but was replaced in that spot by *The Ten Commandments* and then *Ben-Hur*.

Drama. Social commentary persisted in film dramas during the 1950s. It had begun to take root in such post–World War II movies of the 1940s as *The Lost Weekend* (1945), concerning alcoholism, and *The Snake Pit* (1948), dealing with mental illness. In the 1950s many movies approached the subjects of teenagers' delinquency, angst, and love, the most famous being *Rebel Without a Cause* (1955), which explores all three. *The Blackboard Jungle* (1955), about troubled high-school

Elvis Presley in *Jailhouse Rock* (1957)

youths in New York City, was one of the first movies with a rock 'n' roll score. *The Wild One* (1954) starred Marlon Brando as a motorcycle-gang leader.

Giant. The epic-proportioned *Giant* (1956), one of the most famous movies of the 1950s, features three of the decade's biggest stars: Rock Hudson, Elizabeth Taylor, and James Dean. *Giant* is filled with many memorable scenes, but one in particular has become a classic of social commentary. When the American Indian daughter-in-law of Hudson's character is refused service in a Texas diner, he starts a brawl with the manager. The two slam into a jukebox, and a recording of "The Yellow Rose of Texas" begins blaring while the fight continues.

Award Winners. Some small-scale, black-and-white dramas, such as Paddy Chayefsky's *Marty* (1955), about a Bronx butcher, and his *The Catered Affair* (1956), about a Bronx housewife planning her daughter's wedding, did well commercially and gained much critical praise. *Marty* won three Academy Awards, including one for best picture. Some large-scale, black-and-white dramas enthralled both moviegoers and critics. *All About Eve* (1950), written and directed by Herman Mankiewicz, offers some of the wittiest dialogue ever written for the screen; it garnered six Academy Awards. *From Here to Eternity* (1953), concerning servicemen and their loves in Hawaii before the bombing of Pearl Harbor, received

---

TRUMBO BREAKS THE BLACKLIST

Like several of the blacklisted screenwriters during the 1950s, Dalton Trumbo assumed a pseudonym after he was sentenced to jail for contempt of Congress, and continued to write as before. But with the use of his name denied him, he went from being the highest-paid screenwriter in Hollywood to accepting the pay of a drudge. Then, in 1956, as if to generalize from Anita Loos's observation that the harder she worked, the luckier she got, Trumbo got lucky. His screenplay for *The Bold and the Brave*, written under the pseudonym Robert Rich, won an Oscar for the best screenplay of the year.

After enjoying speculation that Robert Flaherty, Orson Welles, Jesse Laskey, Jr., Willis O'Brien, or Paul Tader was the real Robert Rich, Trumbo revealed his identity in 1959. Never one to pass up an opportunity to resist authority, Otto Preminger announced that Trumbo would be asked to write his next movie. But Kirk Douglas got to Trumbo first. Douglas was executive producer and star of the epic *Spartacus*, and he hired Trumbo to write the screenplay under his own name. The movie won three Oscars, for cinematography, art direction, and supporting actor (Peter Ustinov). Despite Hedda Hopper's opinion that the movie "was one of the worst pictures I've ever seen and the script was written by Dalton Trumbo," *Spartacus* was widely acclaimed, and after its success, the blacklist was defeated.

Sources: Stefan Kanfer, *Journal of the Plague Years* (New York: Atheneum, 1973);

Mason Wiley and Damien Bona, *Inside Oscar* (New York: Ballantine, 1986).

eight Academy Awards. *On the Waterfront* (1954), a gritty portrayal of New York City labor unions, also won eight Academy Awards, including a best-actor Oscar for Brando.

Censorship. Censorship of movies began to lighten by the end of the decade. The romantic comedy *The Moon Is Blue* (1953) was banned in many cities for its use of the word "virgin". However, in *A Summer Place* (1959) Sandra Dee is dragged to a doctor by her mother to make sure Dee's virginity is intact after a night on the beach with Troy Donahue.

The Woman's Picture. In *Sleepless in Seattle* (1993), which features allusions to and scenes from *An Affair to Remember* (1957), Tom Hanks's character refers to the latter movie as a "chick's picture." In the 1950s such a movie was known as a woman's picture. The melo-dramatic movie love story reached a pinnacle during the 1950s, rescuing the careers of such 1940s favorites as Lana Turner, Jane Wyman, and June Allyson, who was the top female star of the mid 1950s. Allyson teamed with James Stewart in *The Glenn Miller Story* (1954) and *Strategic Air Command* (1955). Wyman paired with Hudson for *Magnificent Obsession* (1954) and *All That Heaven Allows* (1955). Turner followed *Peyton Place* (1957) with the hugely successful *Imitation of Life* (1959), a glossy remake of the 1934 movie based on Fannie Hurst's tear-jerking story about an interracial friendship between two women. In the mid 1980s viewers of cable television's superstation Turner Broadcasting Service selected the 1959 *Imitation of Life* as their favorite movie.

Star Actresses. Marilyn Monroe, Taylor, Audrey Hepburn, Doris Day, Debbie Reynolds, and Grace Kelly became popular movie stars of the 1950s because they appealed to a vast audience of women who looked to them as trendsetters. Kelly's movie career spanned the years from 1950 to 1956, when she left Hollywood to marry Prince Rainier of Monaco. She starred in such Alfred Hitchcock–directed classics as *Dial M for Murder* (1954), *To Catch a Thief* (1955), and *Rear Window* (1954), which was rereleased theatrically in 1983.

Musicals. A slew of Broadway musicals made it to the big screen during the 1950s. *Annie Get Your Gun* (1950), *Show Boat* (1951; the third film version of the Jerome Kern/Oscar Hammerstein musical), *Kiss Me Kate* (1953), *Call Me Madam* (1953), *Brigadoon* (1954), *Oklahoma!* (1955), *The King and I* (1956), and *South Pacific* (1958) were enormously popular. Monroe and Jane Russell were marvelous in *Gentlemen Prefer Blondes* (1953), also adapted from a Broadway musical. Monroe donned a strapless hot-pink gown with a huge bow for the popular "Diamonds Are a Girl's Best Friend" number.

M-G-M Musicals. M-G-M produced a new round of its highly popular musicals, including *Singin' in the Rain* (1952), *The Band Wagon* (1953), and *Seven Brides for Seven Brothers* (1954). The studio's *Gigi* (1958) — Alan Jay Lerner and Frederick Loewe's adaptation of a story by

Marilyn Monroe in her film debut, *Asphalt Jungle* (1950)

Colette — won nine Academy Awards. Judy Garland, the queen of the M-G-M musical in the 1940s, teamed with James Mason for the 1954 CinemaScope musical remake of the 1937 drama *A Star Is Born*. The star-studded premiere party was broadcast live on national television. *Time* magazine (25 October 1954) hailed the movie as "just about the greatest one-woman show in modern movie history." It was rereleased theatrically in 1983 with restored footage cut soon after the premiere.

Science Fiction and Horror. Although many grade-Z science-fiction and horror movies were released during the 1950s, some superior efforts in these genres were produced. *The Day the Earth Stood Still* (1951), *The Thing from Another World* (1951), *War of the Worlds* (1953), *Forbidden Planet* (1956), and *Invasion of the Body Snatchers* (1956) are among the stellar examples of the decade's science-fiction movies.

Invaders. Youth-oriented horror movies such as *The Blob* (1958), starring Steve McQueen, and *I Was a Teenage Werewolf* (1957), starring Michael Landon, have become cult, if not critical, favorites. Horror blends with science fiction in a host of atomic-age movies in which insects and arachnids take on gargantuan proportions after a nuclear nudge. *Them!* (1954), about giant ants, and *Tarantula* (1955) are undoubtedly the best of the lot. *The Fly* (1958), another insect-oriented science-fiction/horror movie, features Vincent Price in one of his best efforts. Price also appeared in the 3-D horror classic

M-G-M COLLECTION

Paul Newman and Elizabeth Taylor in *Cat on a Hot Tin Roof* (1958)

House of Wax (1953). *It Came from Outer Space* (1953) and *Creature from the Black Lagoon* (1954) were also filmed in this process, which was soon abandoned because of the nuisance of wearing the special glasses required to view it.

Sex and Technology. As the battle between movies and television raged on into the 1960s, developments in film technology continued, resulting in seventy-millimeter film stock for wide-screen projection. However, movies turned increasingly to controversial subjects, violence, and sex and nudity in order to lure patrons into the theaters. Gone were the days when a film would be banned because one of its characters uttered the word "virgin."

Sources:

Pauline Kael, *5001 Nights at the Movies: A Guide from A to Z* (New York: Holt, Rinehart & Winston, 1982);

David Shipman, *The Great Movie Stars: The International Years* (New York: St. Martin's Press, 1972);

Ken Wlaschin, *The Illustrated Encyclopedia of the World's Great Movie Stars and Their Films* (New York: Harmony, 1979).

NEWPORT JAZZ FESTIVAL

Respectability. Jazz was traditionally a music too closely associated with sin and race to attract an establishment following. Born in southern whorehouses and barrooms and developed by black musicians with a reputa-

tion for intemperance and licentiousness, its pulsating rhythms and libertine melodies had the right degree of naughtiness for a young dance crowd, but most people felt it was inappropriate for the concert stage and quite likely immoral in a nightclub setting. It was therefore mildly scandalous when social scions Elaine and Louis L. Lorillard of Newport, Rhode Island, announced plans to stage the first annual Newport Jazz Festival in mid July 1954 at the seventy-five-year-old Newport Casino, an exclusive open-air club founded by Mr. Lorillard's great-grandfather Pierre, the tobacco baron.

Six Thousand Fans. *Time* magazine reported that "Newport's narrow streets were thronged with loud-shirted bookie types from Broadway, young intellectuals in need of haircuts, crew-cut Ivy Leaguers, sailors, Harlem girls with extravagant hairdos, and high-school girls in shorts." Six thousand jazz fans paid three, four, or five dollars for a ticket to the two-day program that included jazz traditionalists such as Eddie Condon, Pee Wee Russell, and Wild Bill Davison, as well as modernists such as Dizzy Gillespie, Oscar Peterson, and Gerry Mulligan. To keep the event in perspective, the festival ended with an intellectual forum about the origins of jazz and its significance.

The Second Year. In 1955 the board of governors of the casino refused to lease the facility to Lorillard and festival producer George Wein for the second festival. The grass tennis courts had been nearly ruined by the 1954 crowd, and sanitary facilities were inadequate, they complained. Elaine Lorillard pronounced festival opponents "socially insecure"; Lorillard announced a new venue. For $22,500 he bought Belcourt, the huge but

HIGH SCHOOL STUDENT MUSIC PREFERENCES IN 1957		
Favorite Type of Music	**Boys %**	**Girls %**
Rock 'n' Roll	55	53
Pop	19	31
Country & Western	7	4
Jazz	11	6
Favorite Singer		
Pat Boone	4	45
Elvis Presley	22	18
Tommy Sands	8	11
Perry Como	11	10
Frank Sinatra	5	7
Harry Belafonte	10	9

Source: James S. Coleman, *The Adolescent Society* (New York: Free Press, 1961), as reprinted in Philip H. Ennis, *The Seventh Stream* (Hanover & London: Wesleyan University Press, 1992).

Pee Wee Russell, Gerry Mulligan, and Eddie Condon at first Newport Jazz Festival, 1954

run-down Newport estate of Oliver Hazard Perry Belmont, who had himself shocked the blue bloods half a century earlier when he married the divorced wife of William K. Vanderbilt. When Belcourt neighbors complained about the prospect of loud music and rambunctious crowds, a compromise was struck: performances would be held at the city-owned baseball field, Freebody Park, and Belcourt would be reserved for festival-related lectures and forums.

The Happy Sounds Festival. The 1955 festival brought twenty-six thousand jazz fans and two hundred musicians to Newport for a three-day program. The festival was opened by Rhode Island's Sen. Theodore Green and closed by Count Basie's band in a session that, according to Whitney Balliett, "tore at its jazz so hard one felt as though he had been literally banged in the chest."

The Curse of Success. By 1957 the Newport Jazz Festival had established itself firmly, drawing crowds of some forty-five thousand and operating on a self-sustaining financial basis. But for established musicians the festival was beginning to lose its luster. They complained about the inferior sound system, the lack of intimacy in a ballpark setting, and the restricted stage time — twenty-five minutes for headliners in 1957.

Jazz Supermarket. Louis Armstrong responded rudely, most thought, to a fifty-seventh-birthday celebration arranged for him, refusing to vary the program of songs that he had played without alteration for the two previous years. He even abruptly terminated his performance after he was presented a birthday cake and informed that the festival had instituted a scholarship in his honor. Miles Davis called the festival a jazz supermarket, and Paul Desmond, alto saxophonist for the Dave Brubeck Quartet, said in 1958, "Next year maybe they could arrange to have Eisenhower," since everybody else of note seemed to be present. Elaine Lorillard responded, "We see no point in jazz being private and ingrown."

Resolution. Jazzmen did, however, and by the end of the decade the Newport Jazz Festival was on its way to being reserved for young performers who needed exposure, senior musicians resting on their laurels, and journeymen down on their luck.

Sources:

Whitney Balliett, "Jazz at Newport: 1955," *Saturday Review*, 38 (30 July 1955): 48–49;

"Cats by the Sea," *Time*, 64 (August 1954): 43;

Nat Hentoff, "The Newport Festival Blues," *Saturday Review*, 40 (20 July 1957): 29, 31;

"Jam in Newport," *Time*, 66 (25 July 1955): 65;

"Jazz on the Plush," *Mademoiselle*, 44 (July 1955): 92–93;

"Jazz Supermarket," *Time*, 72 (14 July 1958): 40;

"Trumpets are for Extroverts," *Time*, 70 (15 July 1957): 50;

Dan Wakefield, "Jazzmakers' Showcase," *Nation*, 185 (20 July 1957): 31–32.

PAPERBACK PUBLISHING

An Industry in Decline. At the beginning of the 1950s book publishing seemed to be in trouble. Sales were in decline, and readers seemed to be showing less and less interest in hardcover books. Brentano's Book Store in New York City, which carried about a one-thousand-title stock, reported that 50 percent of its annual sales came at Christmas, when gift buyers were searching desperately for presents. *Fortune* reported an unnamed major publisher's estimate that 60 percent of its annual sales were institutional — that is, to libraries and schools. Book clubs selling hardcover books were doing as badly. Between 1947 and 1952 Book-of-the-Month Club membership fell from nine hundred thousand to five hundred thousand. The book-buying public seemed to be dwindling.

Causes. Reasons for the apparent decline in readership were publicly debated. Television was the culprit of choice, though there was spotty evidence to back up the belief that potential readers spent too much time watching their new televisions to buy books. Price was blamed by others. Trade books (those sold in bookstores), which averaged $3.50 per title and ranged from $2.50 to $6.00 in 1953, were too expensive, some said.

Price. Some credence was given the price argument by the success of paperbacks, which typically cost 25¢ or 35¢ in the early 1950s (though some were as costly as 75¢). In 1953, 35 percent of all book purchases were paperbacks. That year 295 million paperbacks from sixteen publishers were sold, bringing total sales since Pocket Books introduced trade paperbacks in 1939 to over 1.75 billion copies.

Distribution. There were important reasons for the success of paperbacks other than price. Availability was one. In 1953 there were about three thousand bookstores in America, and hardcover books rarely sold elsewhere. There were one hundred thousand retail outlets for paperbacks, which were distributed to retailers much as magazines were by about one thousand independent distributors, roughly one third of which belonged to the powerful American News Group, which had a virtual monopoly over newsstands in large cities.

Material. Conservative observers argued that the success of the paperback publishers was the result of the material they published. Paperbacks, like the pulp magazines and dime novels that preceded them, pandered to a low audience attracted by lurid covers and sex-oriented topics, critics charged. There was no denying the criticism, but it was an oversimplification. It is true that in 1952 Mickey Spillane's novels accounted for about one-fourth of all paperback sales, but the titles of other top sellers are significant. The British firm Penguin, which set up its American branch in Baltimore, reported Geoffrey Chaucer's *Canterbury Tales* and Dante's *Inferno* among their best-selling titles. *The Pocket Book of Baby and Child Care* sold 5 million copies early in the 1950s,

SALES OF MAJOR PAPERBACK BOOK PUBLISHERS, 1952			
PUBLISHERS	EST. COPIES SOLD (MIL)	TOTAL SALES (MIL)	NO. OF TITLES
Pocket Books	46	14	109
New American Library	42	12	80
Bantam	35	9.5	94
Dell	26	6.5	105
Avon	22	6	102
Popular Library	21	5.5	85
Gold Medal	21	5.5	86
Permabooks	10	4	52
Pyramid	7	2	30
Lion	7	2	42
Others	6	2	45
Total	243	69	830

Source: "The Boom in Paper Bound Books," *Fortune*, 48 (September 1953).

Webster's Pocket Dictionary 4.5 million, Homer's *Iliad* and *Odyssey* 800,000 each, and Ruth Benedict's *Patterns of Culture* 400,000 copies.

Generic Reads. Paperbacks did so well during the early 1950s that some publishers suspected that titles did not matter — anything would sell; but they made the mistake of underestimating the American reader. By 1953, 25 million copies of one hundred titles a month were being sent to distributors. The market was glutted, and publishers paid the price for their cynicism. Books were sold to retailers with return privileges, allowing the return of unsold copies for full credit. At the start of the decade hardback publishers reported average returns of 8.5 percent for trade books, and paperback publishers reported 10 percent returns. By the middle of the decade paperback returns had risen to about 35 percent, with some publishers admitting 50 percent returns. It was a serious problem that had to be addressed.

Support for Hardback Publishers. Even with their problems, the paperback industry provided a much-needed financial boost to hardcover publishers. The economics of paperback publishing is based on slim margins of profit. The publishers saved on printing costs by using cheap materials and printing large quantities. Gold Medal reported that it never printed fewer than 200,000

A selection of 1950s paperback covers

copies, for example. Paperback publishers paid reduced royalties. On a 25¢ book, Gold Medal paid 1¢ on the first 150,000 copies, 1.5¢ thereafter; other paperback publishers paid royalties of about 7.5 percent of the retail price.

Economics. Paperback publishers did not advertise, saving about 10 percent of the retail price, the amount customarily reserved by hardback publishers for promotion. Paperback publishers looked to hardcover houses to introduce a book so it could be effectively distributed, and they paid the hardback publisher for reprint rights, an amount that often made the difference between profit and loss on an average hardcover book. Half the paperback income went to the author, half to the publisher. As the decade progressed, advances went up to what some thought were disastrous heights. When New American Library paid $101,000 for reprint rights to James Jones's *From Here to Eternity,* some insiders thought it was a move toward bankruptcy. The book, which sold 240,000 copies in hardcover, sold 6 million copies in paperback. New American Library grossed about $2.5 million on the book.

Sources:

Sam Boal, "Everyone's Got a Book," *Nation's Business,* 40 (October 1952): 96–98;

Harvey Breit, "The New Books," *Harper's,* 215 (September 1957): 90–94;

"The Boom in Paper Bound Books," *Fortune,* 48 (September 1953): 123–125, 144, 146, 148;

"But Paperbacks' Success Comes High," *Business Week* (31 July 1954): 40, 44;

Piet Schreuders, *Paperbacks, U.S.A.: A Graphic History, 1939–1959* (San Diego: Blue Dolphin Enterprises, 1984);

Lovell Thompson, " ' New Daring Possibility,' " *Saturday Review,* 35 (21 June 1952): 14, 15, 46.

ROCK 'N' ROLL

Restless Blood and Jungle Rhythms. At a time when America's most serious domestic problem in the minds of many people was the integration of schools, when federal integration laws were being defied across the nation, when angry parents were rioting in the streets to protest being forced to share public facilities with blacks, American teenagers became infected in epidemic proportions with an insatiable urge to dance to what their parents called jungle rhythms. Rock 'n' roll was a musical revolution in which young people, white and black, united in spirit, if not in person, outside segregated schoolhouses to adopt a criterion for musical judgment that had never been widely accepted before. Emotive expression laid over an insistent backbeat were the primary elements of the music they danced to — not pleasing melodies, clever lyrics, or even virtuosity.

Soul. If a performer had soul — the ability to experience and express deep feeling — other qualities in his music were incidental. Thus, a not particularly talented white prerock singer named Johnny Ray who writhed, agonized, fell to the floor, and cried what seemed to be real tears was hailed for his raw talent because he sang from the heart. An extremely animated, gaudily dressed black singer named Little Richard, whose talent lay in barely controlling a series of musical yells and screams, became a star because he was able to communicate his ecstatic emanations with unusual effectiveness and his rhythm never faltered.

Turn Me Loose. Rock 'n' roll was an expression of independence by adolescents socially secure enough to reject their parents' musical tastes, which valued songs in which primal impulses had been refined beyond recognition. Vic Damone, Peggy Lee, Pat Boone, Perry Como, Frank Sinatra, even Nat King Cole sang songs that lacked relevance to young listeners. It was too inhibited, too class-conscious, and too slow. The young audience of the 1950s responded to basic musical expression that they could understand and that they could even perform, if so moved. Most of all it had to be music with a dance beat — not a foxtrot, closer to a jitterbug.

"Got a Backbeat, You Can't Lose It." The formula was simple. As Ray Charles observed, "When they get a couple of guitars together with a backbeat, that's rock and roll." Elaborate instrumentation was not required — only a singer, a rhythm guitar, a bass guitar, and, most important, drums — overstated rhythm was the foundation. Simple were mandatory. The music had to be loud, and a little distortion was acceptable, but it had to sound authentic, unlike highly rehearsed, clean sounding popular music. The quality of the singer's voice and his articulation were secondary to soulful expression. The words did not matter; the feeling did. The music was reduced to elemental values: basic chords, simple melodies, uncomplicated arrangements. One did not have to be practiced to become a rock 'n' roll musician.

R&B. Rock 'n' roll sprang from a southern blues tradition that came in two forms — white and black. Black blues and its city brother rhythm and blues, or R&B, had their roots in slavery, borrowed their rhythms from the church, and took their vitality from the intensity with which people who endured hard lives enjoyed good times. Black blues in America was nearly as old as the nation itself, yet in the 1950s it was still classified as race music and was sold and broadcast narrowly to black audiences.

The King of Rock 'n' Roll

In the South that meant that it reached poor, white audiences as well, because the towns were small and segregation had almost as much to do with social class as with race.

Hillbilly Music. White blues was called hillbilly music. It was songs of grief, loneliness, and sometimes rough-edged humor by rural musicians closely in touch with folk traditions. It was the music of poor rural people, who sang and played soulfully on the instruments at hand. Hillbilly music was crude, simple, rhythm-bound, and cloyingly sentimental, so much so that when country fans moved to the city, they were quick to turn their backs on that unsophisticated music associated with heartache and failure.

Sun Records. In the early 1950s record producer Sam Phillips remarked that all he needed to become a millionaire was a white country boy to sing black music. Young black R&B musicians were innovative and energetic, and their music had a strong rhythmic base and an aura of sensuality that he knew would appeal to young audiences. At the time, black blues and R&B records were not sold in white record stores, available on jukeboxes in white restaurants, or played on white radio stations. Of nearly eleven thousand disc jockeys in the country, only seven hundred played R&B. However attractive ethnic black music was, it could not be sold outside the black commu-

---

EL DORADOS' TOUR

Late in 1955 the five-man rock 'n' roll band El Dorados went on a fifteen-city tour that lasted two months. They began in South Bend, Indiana, on 6 November and ended in Detroit the day after Christmas. In between they played, in order, Boston, Washington, Baltimore, Gary, Pittsburgh, Ypsilanti, Atlanta, Newark, Newport News, Philadelphia, Canton, Lima, and Flint. Over the course of the tour they grossed a total of $4186.80, of which the agent took 10 percent. Their nightly earnings ranged from $150 for the concert in Boston to $800 for the date in Philadelphia.

By the end of the tour each band member had earned $753.62. The agent maintained a drawing account for expenses on the road. On 31 December the account balance was $132.62: each musician had $26.52 to show for his work.

Source: Philip Ennis, *The Seventh Stream: The Emergence of Rocknroll in American Popular Music* (Hanover & London: Wesleyan University Press, 1992).

Alan Freed

much of the resources of the record and entertainment industries were devoted to rock 'n' roll, and radio found its salvation in rock music at a time when traditional programming was being challenged by television. Rock 'n' roll was the music of youth and the music of the future. By 1959 it was also very big business.

SCIENCE FICTION

Atomic Age Literature. Science fiction gained respectability after World War II. As the nation came to terms with the atomic age and began to speculate about the possibility of space travel, fictional accounts of alien creatures in stellar worlds became plausible enough to interest general readers. Before the war, science fiction was written according to standard genre formulas for plot and character, distinguished only by galactic settings. Nine science-fiction magazines published virtually all of the new work in the field, and, as a result, short stories dominated the genre. When science-fiction novels were published, they were either serialized in magazines or presented in paperback format and marketed to what was regarded as an undiscriminating audience.

Popular Demand. After the war, science fiction matured as it attracted the attention of big business. Hollywood led the way with films that exploited Americans'

nity. So Phillips determined to find a white band that could perform with its own intensity, rhythmic drive, and honesty of expression.

City Rock. Meanwhile, a disc jockey named Alan Freed was experimenting in Cleveland and New York with the concept of what he called rhythm reviews, in which a program of black R&B groups played for white audiences. The reaction was surprisingly enthusiastic. He drew crowds of three times capacity and thus even had to turn fans away. He also began broadcasting a late-night radio program in New York in which he played race music with an unorthodox presentation. The program was popular, and Freed was encouraged to find a way to bring R&B to a wider audience. The solution was clear to him when he heard Elvis Presley and saw the sales of a sanitized version of "Shake, Rattle, and Roll" by a white country-roots band called Bill Haley and his Comets soar after release of the 1955 movie *Blackboard Jungle* in which they played the song: Freed understood that his audience would respond to a variation on the black music he had been promoting. He turned to what he called rock 'n' roll, which was two parts rhythm and blues, one part country, and one part pure performance.

"Gotta Be Rock 'n' Roll Music. . . . " After Elvis a wave of rock 'n' roll musicians overwhelmed the industry. The success of such stars as Buddy Holly from Texas, Jerry Lee Lewis from Memphis, and Eddie Cochran from Nashville opened the way for presentation of black groups to white audiences. Chuck Berry, Chubby Checker, Lloyd Price, Wilson Pickett, Otis Redding, and a series of singing groups, both white and black, took over the airways and elbowed their way to the frontstage of the entertainment industry. By the end of the decade

Front cover for science-fiction pulp magazine, January 1953

fear of invasion. *The Thing* (1951), *The Day the Earth Stood Still* (1951), *When Worlds Collide* (1951), and *War of the Worlds* (1953) were successful movies with budgets exceeding one million dollars each. They exposed large audiences to plots based on speculative fiction. ABC spent twelve thousand dollars per episode to attract established actors and talented writers for the television series *Tales of Tomorrow*, prompting CBS to follow with *Out There* and NBC to search for an entry into the science-fiction market. With the debut of Rod Serling's *The Twilight Zone* in 1959, science-fiction television drama captured the imagination of a huge and loyal audience. The number of science-fiction magazines increased from 9 in 1945 to 53 in 1953, led by *Galaxy* (begun in October 1950), which paid three to five cents a word for stories (as compared to the standard rate of one cent a word for pulp fiction). *Business Week* estimated the total science-fiction magazine readership to be about three hundred thousand. In addition there were some 250 fanzines, cheaply produced periodicals in which fans traded comments with one another on such topics as their favorite works, and 10 new science-fiction comic books introduced in 1950 and 1951.

Paperbacks. The success of science-fiction magazines prompted paperback houses, led by Ace and Ballantine, to develop aggressive science-fiction publishing programs. In the beginning, the paperback publishers concentrated on anthologies composed of magazine fiction, but as talented novelists with enthusiastic fans emerged, the paperback houses began to promote single-author works. New American Library reported that individual science-fiction novels sold over two hundred thousand each in 1951, and hardcover anthologies sold as many as thirty-five thousand copies.

Fans. Science-fiction fans were distinguished by their eccentricity and their devotion. They viewed being a fan as an active pursuit. Fans arranged half a dozen conferences a year, sometimes referred to as "fanferences," at which they dressed as their favorite science-fiction characters, traded memorabilia, shared ideas, and gave awards both to their favorite authors and to one another. The best known of the awards were the Hugos, named for Hugo Gernsback, who founded the first science-fiction magazine, *Amazing Stories*, in 1926. Instituted in 1953 by the organizers of the Worldcon in Philadelphia, Hugos were awarded in several categories (that changed from year to year) upon the vote of registered attendees of the conference. In 1953 there were seven categories; Alfred Bester won the best-novel award for *The Demolished Man*, and Forrest J. Ackerman was named "Number 1 Fan Personality."

Literary Celebrities. *Life* reported in 1951 that there were twenty thousand or so hard-core American science-fiction fans, though participation at the conventions tended to be measured in hundreds rather than thousands. The objects of the fans' attention were such writers as Isaac Asimov, Alfred Bester, Ray Bradbury, Lester del Rey, Robert A. Heinlein, Murray Leinster, Walter M. Miller, Frederik Pohl, Theodore Sturgeon, Clifford D. Simak, A. E. Van Vogt, and — despite his protestations that he was not a genre writer — Kurt Vonnegut, Jr. By the end of the decade these names commanded the attention, and often the respect as well, of a still-growing readership and eager publishing, television, and movie-making industries.

Sources:

David Cowart and Thomas L. Wymer, eds., *Dictionary of Literary Biography, vol. 8: Twentieth-Century American Science Fiction Writers* (Detroit: Gale, 1981);

Fletcher Pratt, "Time, Space & Literature," *Saturday Review*, 34 (28 July 1951): 16–17;

Winthrop Sargeant, "Through the Interstellar Looking Glass," *Life*, 30 (21 May 1951): 127–130;

"Science Fiction Rockets Into Big Time," *Business Week* (20 October 1951): 82–84, 89.

SUN RECORDS

Sam Phillips and the Record Business. In January 1950 a disc jockey named Sam Phillips opened the Memphis Recording Service, the first professional recording studio in the city. It had a clearly defined purpose — to scout talent and produce black R&B record masters that could be distributed under a partnership agreement with such specialist labels as Chess and Dot. At the time, 95 percent of the record business was controlled by the major companies. The rest was open to small independents, like Phillips, who appealed to special markets.

Yellow Sun Records. "My aim was to try and record the blues and other music I liked and to prove whether I was right or wrong about this music. I knew, or I *felt* I knew, that there was a bigger audience for blues than just the black man of the mid-South," Phillips remembered. He soon found that if he wanted his business to be profitable, he would have to form his own record label and handle his own distribution. In 1952, after a false start with a label called The Phillips,' he founded Sun Records, which served as a launching pad for the rock 'n' roll revolution that began in 1955.

Black Blues. By 1954 Phillips had recorded some of the finest blues musicians in the South: Riley "B. B." (for Black Boy) King, Chester Burnett (who called himself Howlin' Wolf), Ike Turner, James Cotton, "Little Junior" Parker, and "Little Walter" Jacobs. The Prisonaires were transported under guard from the Tennessee State Penitentiary in Nashville to record their classic performance of "Just Walkin' in the Rain," for which phrasing was suggested by a kid named Elvis Presley, who hung around the studio waiting for his chance to try for a hit record.

White Blues. The music was inspiring, but sales were not. Good music was not enough, Phillips concluded: "The base wasn't broad enough because of racial prejudice. When the jukebox operators would come by the distributor for their weekly supply of records, and . . .

Sam Phillips at the Sun Records console

when the smaller retail outlets would come by, I'd be there. They'd tell me, 'These people [blacks] are ruining our children' . . . so I knew what I had to do to broaden the base of acceptance." He began promoting white performers who could perform R&B music.

Rockabilly. After 1954 Sun Records concentrated on what was called rockabilly, a combination of country music and R&B driven by a dominant rhythm section and sung with uninhibited expression. Rockabilly was white musicians' interpretations of the black music Phillips had recorded since he opened his studio. It attracted an audience of young people eager for songs more lively than those their parents enjoyed; it was sellable; and there was plenty of talent to draw upon. Between 1954 and 1956, Sun released debut records by Carl Perkins, Johnny Cash, Roy Orbison, Jerry Lee Lewis, and Elvis Presley. It was a stunning performance by a small independent record producer.

Paydirt. Elvis Presley was, of course, the discovery that earned Phillips lasting distinction as a talent scout. Elvis had hung around the Sun studio for a year and had made two private recordings for his own use before Phillips asked him to make a record for sale in May or June 1954. "That's All Right, Mama" and "Blue Moon of Kentucky" were released on 19 July 1954. *Billboard* called Presley "a strong new talent," and he began to attract a following. The record sold sixty-three hundred copies in

the first three weeks, some twenty-five thousand by the end of the year. Elvis recorded eight more songs that were released in the next thirteen months, and by that time he was well on his way to national recognition, out of Sun's league. As of 31 October 1955 Phillips had sold all recording rights to works by Elvis Presley for thirty-five thousand dollars, five thousand of which he owed Presley in back royalties.

After Elvis. Sun released 182 records in the next twelve years, but as Phillips soon recognized, with the rights to Elvis he sold his corner on a type of music that was too much in demand for a small company like his to compete. He was uninterested in releasing his music on long-playing albums instead of on 45-RPM records because he did not see the potential of the market, and he lacked the capital to promote his records as aggressively as the established companies did. As a result, his stars left for better contracts, and new talent in the field was harder to attract.

Sunset. Sun continued to record rockabilly music, and it continued to be among the most interesting of the independent recording companies, but by the late 1950s Phillips had lost interest in the record business. He could afford to rest on his laurels, and, partly as a result of his 1952 investment in the new Holiday Inn started by his Memphis friend Kemmons Wilson, Phillips did not need the money.

Source:
Colin Escott with Martin Hawkins, *Good Rockin' Tonight: Sun Records and the Birth of Rock 'n' Roll* (New York: St. Martin's Press, 1991).

ARTURO TOSCANINI'S FAREWELL

The Maestro. In the early 1950s "Maestro" referred to only one conductor: Arturo Toscanini, the fiery symphony conductor whose pursuit of perfection without compromise, unparalleled musical intelligence, and mastery of scores astonished professional musicians throughout his long career. When he retired in 1954 at the age of eighty-seven he had been a professional musician and conductor for seventy-eight years and a key figure in the American music world since 1908, when he became conductor of the Metropolitan Opera in New York City.

The NBC Symphony Orchestra. American audiences were so enamored of Toscanini that when he resigned as conductor of the New York Philharmonic-Symphony Orchestra in 1937 at the age of seventy to return to his native city of Milan, NBC made him an irresistible offer. He was already the highest-paid symphony conductor in the world, and his records on the RCA Victor label sold more than those of any other classical musician. So NBC offered him the largest live audience a performer of serious music had ever known. They formed specifically for him an orchestra of internationally acclaimed musicians who performed weekly concerts at Carnegie Hall in New York City under the direction of the Maestro for live national radio broadcast. The broadcast reached two

Arturo Toscanini's last concert

having performed the piece for years. Midway through the last act Toscanini stopped the music and scolded the soprano for singing a B when she should have sung B-flat. She argued, pointing to her score, which clearly signified a B; the Maestro must be wrong, she insisted. In fact, the score was wrong, and no other conductor over the years had noticed the error.

The Farewell Concert. The most dramatic moment in Toscanini's career came on Sunday, 4 April 1954. It was the final broadcast of the NBC Symphony for the 1953–1954 season, and it took place less than two weeks after the Maestro's eighty-seventh birthday. Few in the audience knew that he had resigned and that this was his last broadcast with the NBC Symphony. The program was *Tannhäuser,* by Toscanini's favorite composer, Richard Wagner. At the beginning of the performance he looked frail as he was assisted onto the Carnegie Hall stage, but he shook off his helpers and walked unassisted to the podium. He began brilliantly as ever; then, perhaps overcome by emotion, he and the orchestra faltered. He clutched the baton fiercely with his right hand and pressed his forehead with his left: Toscanini had forgotten the score. His protégé directed the radio engineers to cut the broadcast, and for thirty-eight seconds radio listeners heard only silence. Then Toscanini composed himself, organized the orchestra, and resumed the performance brilliantly enough to earn a standing ovation. But he would have none of it. He was in tears when he left the stage. He dropped his baton beside the podium and never returned.

Toscanini died in New York City on 16 January 1957, two months before his ninetieth birthday.

hundred stations, and Toscanini had absolute, unquestioned musical control. The cost over the seventeen years of the NBC Symphony's existence was more than fifteen million dollars.

Genius. At age eighty-seven Toscanini still managed to astonish musicians with his talent and intimidate them with his demanding standards. He tirelessly conducted three-and-a-half hour rehearsals without missing a note, and when the music did not please him, he yelled savagely, it was reported, "They play like that in hell — not in paradise." When soprano Herva Nelli came to rehearsals for a recording of Giuseppe Verdi's opera *Un Ballo in Maschera* with the NBC Symphony, she was confident,

Sources:
"After Toscanini," *Time,* 63 (5 April 1954): 71;

George Marek, "87 Candles," *Good Housekeeping,* 138 (March 1954): 138;

"The Podium Stood Bare," *Time,* 43 (12 April 1954): 68;

Winthrop Sargeant, "The Maestro," *New Yorker,* (15 May 1954): 127–129.

HEADLINE MAKERS

LEONARD BERNSTEIN
1918-1990

SYMPHONY CONDUCTOR, COMPOSER

Career Launched. Leonard Bernstein's career was launched on 14 November 1943. He was twenty-five, four years out of Harvard, a recent graduate of the Curtis Institute of Music in Philadelphia, an assistant conductor at the New York Symphony Orchestra, and otherwise undistinguished except for his energy, his good looks, and a vaguely defined artistic potential. Bruno Walter, director of the New York Symphony, was stricken with stomach cramps on 13 November, and the musical director was out of town, so the next day's conducting chores fell to Bernstein by default. His performance was so impressive that the *New York Times* praised his brilliance in an editorial.

Movies and Plays. During the 1950s Bernstein was a very busy man. He was a conductor, a concert pianist, a composer, and an impresario. He wrote the musical score for the movie *On the Waterfront* (1954), starring Marlon Brando; he collaborated with Lillian Hellman and Richard Wilbur on the Broadway stage production of *Candide* (1956); he recorded music, as a conductor and as a pianist, at a furious pace; he wrote the hit Broadway musical *West Side Story* (1957); and he became director of the New York Philharmonic in 1958. It was a spectacular decade for Bernstein, who was applauded as much for his charm as for his genius. He had the ability to make classical music appealing and enjoyable to large audiences, and he exploited that talent fully.

Critics. Throughout the decade critics found fault with Bernstein's performances while always taking care to note his potential. In 1952 Irving Kolodin wrote in the *Saturday Review* that "his [Bernstein's] piano playing is hardly good enough to be imposed on us," and *Time* speculated that perhaps he would be better off concentrating on one of his many skills rather than attempting to develop them all. In 1955 Winthrop Sargeant wrote in the *New Yorker* that Bernstein's con-

ducting style "suggested he was enacting the stellar role in a public crucifixion" but then admitted that his stage presence added interest to the evening.

New York Philharmonic. When Bernstein took over the New York Philharmonic his performance was so energetic that the critics were unanimously supportive. He instituted a lecture/performance format for many of the orchestra's presentations that was extremely successful. His Young People's Concerts, designed to attract youthful listeners, were so popular that clubs were formed in cities where the concerts were televised so that groups could watch together. The Saturday-evening telecasts of Philharmonic programs had been carried by 130 stations nationwide before Bernstein; in his first year the number of those stations doubled. Donations increased, and requests were received for transcripts of Bernstein's remarks to the audience before performances: for the first time in its history the orchestra began to hope for an operating profit.

International Tour. Bernstein's greatest success of the decade came with the Philharmonic's seventeen-nation European tour, culminating with eighteen concerts in the Soviet Union. It was unheard of in the Soviet Union for a conductor to speak to his audience, but Bernstein ignored tradition and introduced each of the works the orchestra performed, via a translator. The response in Moscow was so enthusiastic that the audience insisted that a Charles Ives piece be played twice so that they could appreciate what Bernstein had told them about the music. Throughout Europe audiences reacted as if they had witnessed a once-in-a-lifetime event. "A new god has come to Athens," a Greek lady was reported to have exclaimed after his performance.

Appeal. Harold C. Schonberg, writing in *Harper's,* summed up Bernstein's appeal. It was due to three attributes, he argued: first, Bernstein was an American, and serious-music audiences were hungry for one of their own to appreciate; second, he had an academic background that allowed him to explain lucidly the music he played; and finally, he was a formidable public figure — a personality. The mix went over well in a decade in which the concept of good public relations dominated. Bernstein was hardly the successor to Arturo Toscanini in terms of talent, but he had a measure of the Maestro's appeal.

Sources:
Irving Kolodin, *Saturday Review*, 35 (29 March 1952): 30;

"Lennie's Brainchild," *Time*, 59 (23 June 1952): 44–46;

David Lindsay, "The Remarkable, Musical Mr. Bernstein," *Coronet*, 41 (January 1957): 145–148;

Winthrop Sargeant, "Home Grown," *New Yorker*, 30 (29 January 1955): 69–70;

Harold C. Schonberg, "What Bernstein Is Doing to the Philharmonic," *Harper's*, 218 (May 1959): 43–48.

MARLON BRANDO
1924-
ACTOR

The Look. Before James Dean, Marlon Brando popularized the jeans-and-T-shirt look, with and without leather jacket, as a movie idol during the early 1950s. The theatrically trained actor began to turn away from his youth-oriented persona with such movie roles as Mark Antony in *Julius Caesar* (1953). After winning an Academy Award for Best Actor for *On the Waterfront* (1954), he portrayed a wide variety of characters on-screen, garnering popular acclaim and critical consensus as one of the greatest cinema actors of the late twentieth century.

Background. Brando was born in Omaha, Nebraska, on 3 April 1924. After expulsion from a military academy he dug ditches until his father offered to finance his education. Brando moved to New York to study with acting coach Stella Adler and at Lee Strasberg's Actors' Studio. While at the Actors' Studio, Brando adopted the Method approach, which emphasizes characters' motivations for actions. He made his Broadway debut in John Van Druten's sentimental *I Remember Mama* (1944). New York theater critics voted him Broadway's Most Promising Actor for his performance in *Truckline Cafe* (1946). In 1947 he played his greatest stage role, Stanley Kowalski — the brute who rapes his sister-in-law, the fragile Blanche du Bois — in Tennessee Williams's *A Streetcar Named Desire*.

Early Career. Hollywood beckoned to Brando, and he made his movie debut as a paraplegic World War II veteran in *The Men* (1950). Although he did not cooperate with the Hollywood publicity machine, he went on to play Kowalski in the 1951 film version of *A Streetcar Named Desire*, a popular and critical success that earned four Academy Awards. His next movie, *Viva Zapata!* (1952), with a script by John Steinbeck, traces Emiliano Zapata's rise from peasant to revolutionary to president of Mexico. Brando followed that with *Julius Caesar* and then *The Wild One* (1954), in which he played a motorcycle-gang leader in all his

leather-jacketedglory. Next came his Academy Award–winning role as a longshoreman fighting the system in *On the Waterfront*, a hard-hitting look at New York City labor unions.

Pinnacle. During the rest of the decade Brando's screen roles ranged from Napoleon Bonaparte in *Désirée* (1954), to Sky Masterson in *Guys and Dolls* (1955, in which he sang and danced), to a Nazi soldier in *The Young Lions* (1958). From 1955 to 1958 movie exhibitors voted him one of the top ten box-office draws in the nation. During the 1960s, however, his career had more downs than ups, especially after M-G-M's disastrous 1962 remake of *Mutiny on the Bounty*, which failed to recoup even half of its enormous budget. Brando portrayed Fletcher Christian, Clark Gable's role in the 1935 original.

Later career. Brando's career was reborn with his depiction of Mafia chieftain Don Corleone in *The Godfather* (1972), for which he refused his Academy Award for Best Actor. He proceeded to the highly controversial yet highly acclaimed *Last Tango in Paris* (1973), which was rated X. Since then Brando has received huge salaries for playing small parts in such movies as *Superman* (1978) and *Apocalypse Now* (1979). He was nominated for an Academy Award for Best Supporting Actor for *A Dry White Season* (1989).

Sources:
Gary Cary, *Marlon Brando: The Only Contender* (London: Robson, 1985);

Christopher Nickens, *Brando: A Biography in Pictures* (Garden City, N.Y.: Doubleday, 1987);

Richard Schickel, *Brando: A Life in Our Times* (New York: Atheneum, 1991).

JAMES DEAN
1931-1955
ACTOR

The Look. Few personalities are more tied to the 1950s than James Dean. His look — piercing eyes, thick shock of combed-back hair, jeans, and jacket worn open over a T-shirt — is still popular in the 1990s. What makes his influence even more remarkable is that he starred in only three movies: *East of Eden* (1955), *Rebel Without a Cause* (1955), and *Giant* (1956). He had small parts in three others: *Sailor Beware* (1951), *Fixed Bayonets* (1951), and *Has Anybody Seen My Gal?* (1952).

Background. Dean was born on 8 February 1931 in Marion, Indiana. His mother died when he was nine years old, and he was raised by an aunt and uncle. He won the Indiana State Dramatic Contest while in high school and then attended the University of California, Los Angeles. He worked with a group of actors instructed by

James Whitmore, and that association led to the brief appearances in his three early movies.

Stage. With Whitmore's encouragement Dean moved on to study at the Actors' Studio in New York City, where he worked as an extra in television programs. He also had roles in two Broadway plays, *See the Jaguar* (1952) and *The Immoralist* (1954). His appearance in the latter attracted the attention of director Elia Kazan, who cast him as Cal in *East of Eden*, based on the 1952 novel by John Steinbeck. Dean received critical praise for his role as one of the brothers in this family-oriented drama with a Cain-and-Abel theme.

Stardom. Dean is most closely associated with his next movie, *Rebel Without a Cause*, in which he played Jim Stark, an angst-ridden teenager at odds with his parents, leather-jacketed gangs, police, and the world in general. *Rebel Without a Cause* influenced a generation of youthful Americans who shared similar feelings and faced the same conflicts as Dean's character. His last role was Jet Rink, the wildcatter-turned-tycoon in *Giant,* a sprawling, multigenerational saga of Texas oilmen adapted from the 1952 novel by Edna Ferber. The part required him to age from about twenty to about sixty-five, and his climactic confrontation with Rock Hudson in the liquor storeroom of a posh hotel is a memorable scene.

Death. The day after he finished work on *Giant,* 30 September 1955, Dean struck another car in his new Porsche at 115 MPH and was killed instantly. *Rebel Without a Cause* was released on 26 October. A year after his death, his studio, Warner Bros., was receiving more than five thousand fan letters a week for him. Hundreds of James Dean Appreciation Societies were formed, and Warner Bros. produced a documentary, *The James Dean Story* (1957).

Sources:

Leith Adams and Keith Burns, eds., *James Dean: Behind the Scenes* (New York: Birch Lane, 1990);

David Dalton, *James Dean: The Mutant King,* revised edition (New York: St. Martin's Press, 1983);

Joe Hyams, with Jay Hyams, *James Dean: Little Boy Lost* (New York: Warner, 1992).

WILLEM DE KOONING

1904-

ABSTRACT EXPRESSIONIST ARTIST

W. AUERBACH

Recognition. In 1954 when the Museum of Modern Art mounted the exhibit for the American Pavilion at the Venice Biennale, the most prestigious world display of contemporary art, only two artists were included: Ben Shahn, a proletarian painter and poster-art innovator, and Willem de Kooning.

It was the second of three times during the 1950s that de Kooning's works had been included in the Venice Biennale, and it was a recognition of his preeminent place among contemporary American artists. In New York his works were included in the Whitney Museum Annual Exhibition of Contemporary American Painting every year during the decade except for 1955, 1957, and 1958; his works were at the center of the influential Young American Painters exhibit at the Guggenheim Museum; and his three one-man shows at the Sidney Janis Gallery in Manhattan were among the most influential of the decade. No living American artist commanded more critical attention than de Kooning — not even his competitive friend Jackson Pollock.

Apprenticeship. De Kooning was born in Holland and studied at the Rotterdam Academy of Fine Arts and Techniques before moving to New York in 1926. He was a housepainter briefly before moving to Greenwich Village in New York, where he took a job as a commercial artist to support himself while he attempted more serious work on his own time. He joined the Federal Arts Project in 1935 and decided soon thereafter to abandon his work designing window displays for shoe stores and painting public murals to concentrate on a new kind of art called abstract expressionism (see entry). By 1950 he was the acknowledged master of this controversial art form, producing paintings that in the words of a *Time* reviewer "look like scribbles any kid could do" and selling them to museums and private collectors for several thousand dollars per scribbled-upon canvas.

Woman. In 1950 de Kooning began a work he called *Woman I.* Over a two-year period he painted daily and washed away images on the same canvas, never able to satisfy his vision. Then in June 1952 he finished his work and for the remainder of the year produced a series of increasingly grotesque and decreasingly recognizable paintings of women that was exhibited with great fanfare in March 1953 at the Sidney Janis Gallery. Critic Harry Gaugh referred to the works as a "coven of sympathetic witches."

Critics. The art world was divided in its response to de Kooning's new works. He was praised by the more conservative critics, who were struggling for a vocabulary to discuss abstract expressionism and were thankful to be able to discern a vaguely recognizable image in his works. More-devoted adherents of abstract expressionism criticized de Kooning for a lack of commitment to abstraction. Robert Coates in the *New Yorker* noted that de Kooning fails in his Woman series of paintings to "commit himself to either their representational or their abstract possibilities but hesitates constantly between the two, and the result is a splashy and confused muddle of pigment that obscures as much as it reveals of the subject."

Freedom of Abstraction. Two years before, in a lecture at the Museum of Modern Art, De Kooning had answered those who criticized his paintings for their references to recognizable objects. He observed that when the abstractionists of the turn of the century came to prominence they brought with them a theory of what art should be that had negative qualities — it dictated what could not be included in art: "The question, as they saw it, was not so much what you *could* paint but rather what you could *not* paint. You could *not* paint a house or a tree or a mountain. It was then that subject matter came into existence as something you ought *not* to have."

Landscapes. After his Woman series de Kooning turned to trees and mountains as his subjects in a series of abstract landscapes, beginning with a 1955 painting called *Woman as Landscape*. That year Hurricane Diane hit the East Coast, causing 184 deaths and a record amount of damage, and de Kooning appropriated the event as a metaphor for his art. His transition paintings had a chaotic appearance, and they marked his movement by the end of the decade into pure abstraction.

Reputation. Among his contemporaries de Kooning was admired for his honesty, intensity, and dedication to his art. He established himself as a spokesman for and representative of the abstract-expressionist values, and he became so powerful a personage that he was accused by the end of the decade of dominating the profession and thus stifling the creativity of younger artists. Influential art critic Clement Greenberg attacked de Kooning for his respect of traditional values and for the lack of spontaneity in his paintings. De Kooning's response was that he had to think about his paintings, and it took intense concentration and often several attempts to achieve the effect he sought. His integrity won out. As Stevan Naifeh and Gregory White Smith point out in their biography of de Kooning's friend Pollock, "No artist was more respected or better liked . . . [de Kooning] was the embodiment of culture."

Sources:

Robert Coates, "The Art Galleries," *New Yorker* (4 April 1953): 94–96;

Harry F. Gaugh, *De Kooning* (New York: Abbeville Press, 1983);

Irving Sandler, *The New York School: The Painters and Sculptors of the Fifties* (New York: Icon / Harper & Row, 1978).

WILLIAM FAULKNER

1897-1962
WRITER

Awards. A self-described Mississippi farmer was hailed as one of the world's greatest writers in 1950. In June the American Academy of Arts and Letters awarded William Faulkner the Howells Medal, their highest honor to a senior writer, and in November Faulkner was named winner of the 1949 Nobel Prize for literature, which the Swedish Academy had withheld the previous year. In America the choice was roundly criticized. Faulkner was variously described in the popular press as depraved, obscure, insignificant, and irrelevant. As recently as 1945 none of Faulkner's seventeen books had been in print, and his two new novels of the early 1950s, *A Requiem for a Nun* (1951) and *A Fable* (1954), did little in the minds of most readers to justify the American Academy's and the Swedish Academy's judgments.

A Requiem for a Nun. It was unclear to most readers whether *A Requiem for a Nun* was a play or a novel. It had elements of each and was criticized with equal vehemence when presented in either form. Faulkner clarified by explaining that the work was a novel in the form of a play. Even setting aside confusion about the form, readers in the 1950s were offended by the plot, which recalls brutal rape and abandonment in the context of a murder trial for infanticide that results in the death sentence of a mad, drug-addicted maid. The *Times* reviewer likened Faulkner's novel to the type of farming or lumber cutting that left the land denuded.

A Fable. *A Fable* created further controversy. It was a sort of Christian allegory played out during a privately declared armistice on the battlefields of France during World War I. Such highbrow reviewers as Maxwell Geismar and Leslie Fiedler tended to agree with Faulkner that *A Fable* was his best novel. That was, however, the minority opinion. Gilbert Highet in *Harper's* wrote that if *A Fable* had been sent to him without the author's name indicated, "It would have scarcely seemed possible that it was the work of a sane man who had lived through both world wars, still less that it was a major novel by a winner of the Nobel Prize." Opinions about Faulkner's greatness were so divided that *Atlantic* magazine ran an article in 1951 by critic Harvey Breit that promised to "make Mr. Faulkner's work more meaningful for those who wish to make up for lost time" because Faulkner had "never received the thorough reading he deserved from his own countrymen."

Public Service. Faulkner was an intensely private man, and he made the mistake after winning the Nobel Prize of assuming responsibility as a spokesman on certain public issues. He learned soon enough that literary talent does not necessarily arm one to practice the art of politics. The Cultural Services Office of the State Department asked Faulkner to participate in several events abroad, notably in Japan in 1955, where he was greeted warmly. During the decade he spent some eight months in various countries discharging his duties as a world citizen.

Controversy. It was in America that his efforts at diplomacy created controversy. Race relations was a chief domestic issue of the time, and the State Department looked to Faulkner to provide guidance. He took a position too liberal for segregationists, too conservative for integrationists, and too philosophical for pragmatists, angering almost everyone. At the request of President Eisenhower, in 1956 Faulkner joined with novelist John Steinbeck and poet Donald Hall in a government program called People to People to promote American values in Communist nations. After a frustrating three months Faulkner quit. In a letter to the *New York Times* on 13 October 1957, he observed that "white people and Negroes do not like and trust each other and perhaps never can," suggesting a cleavage that liberals construed to be bordering on racism. But, he continued, it may not be necessary for us to like one another; we must simply federate. He concluded that "because of the good luck of our still unspent and yet unexhausted past" the country might still prevail over its problem as people see the necessity of dedicating themselves to "the proposition that a community of individual free men not merely must endure, but can endure." *Harper's* magazine commented that the statement was "clearly and explicitly meaningless."

Return to Writing. By the end of the decade Faulkner had returned to what he did best — writing and talking, when he talked, about his work. In 1956 he accepted a temporary position as writer in residence at the University of Virginia that was renewed annually. Nonetheless, Faulkner enjoyed the university setting and turned his attentions back to literature. On 1 May 1957 *The Town*, the second volume of his highly acclaimed Snopes Trilogy, was published, and on 13 November 1959 the third volume, *The Mansion*, appeared. They were hailed as works worthy of a writer of his stature.

Sources:

Joseph Blotner, *Faulkner: A Biography* (New York: Random House, 1974);

Harvey Breit, "William Faulkner," *Atlantic*, 188 (October 1951): 53–56;

Madeleine Chapsal, "A Lion in the Garden," *Reporter*, 13 (3 November 1955): 40;

Leslie Fiedler, "Stone Grotesques," *New Republic*, 131 (23 August 1954): 18–19;

Maxwell Geismar, "Latter-Day Christ Story," *Saturday Review*, 37 (31 July 1954): 11–12;

Brendan Gill, "Fifth Gospel," *New Yorker*, 30 (28 August 1954): 78–80;

Michel Gresset, *A Faulkner Chronology* (Jackson: University of Mississippi Press, 1985);

Gilbert Highet, "Sound and Fury," *Harper's*, 209 (September 1954): 98–104;

"Mr. Faulkner Exhausts the Future," *Nation*, 185 (26 October 1957): 274–275;

"No Sanctuary," *Newsweek*, 38 (24 September 1951): 90–92.

ERNEST HEMINGWAY
1899-1961
WRITER

Celebrity. No literary figure during the 1950s, or any other decade in American history, achieved a degree of literary celebrity equal to that of Ernest Hemingway. Tough, experienced, independent-minded, action-seeking, hard-drinking, and photogenic, he represented the full romance of authorship for readers of the time.

Fading Reputation. To many literary critics, though, he seemed through as a writer at the beginning of the decade, and if there was any suspicion that he still might have a spark of creative genius left, his novel *Across the River and Into the Trees* (1950) dispelled it. He had, it seemed, entered the phase of his life given over to accepting awards for past achievements.

The Old Man and the Sea. Then came *The Old Man and the Sea* (1952), Hemingway's twenty-seven-thousand-word short novel (one-third to one-half the length of the average novel) about an old fisherman struggling against bad times. It is arguable that more readers were exposed to *The Old Man and the Sea* in the month of its publication than any novel ever before. *Life* magazine devoted twenty pages of its 1 September issue to publication of the full text one week before book publication; 5 million copies of the magazine were printed in anticipation of the unusual interest Hemingway's new work would attract. The Book-of-the-Month Club chose *The Old Man and the Sea* as part of a dual feature selection for September 1952 and printed 153,000 copies. Scribners, the trade publisher, published a first printing of 50,000 copies and reprinted frequently, as the novel remained on best-seller lists for a year and a half.

Critical Response. Critics competed with one another to offer the highest praise to Hemingway and his work. Mark Schorer, a professor of English, novelist, short-story writer, and regular reviewer in the *New York Times Book Review*, expressed the majority view: "Everywhere the book is being called a classic," he wrote, and he went on to proclaim Hemingway "unquestionably the greatest craftsman in the American novel in this century." The novel won a Pulitzer Prize for Fiction in 1953 — Hemingway's first — and reaffirmed his candidacy for the Nobel Prize.

Career Assessment. *The Old Man and the Sea* was Hemingway's last novel published during his lifetime. It seemed in 1952 that the time had come to assess his achievement. He was approached by an English professor who wanted to write his biography. Hemingway responded angrily and forcefully: "The writing published in books is what I stand on and I would like people to leave my private life the hell alone. What right has anyone to go into it? I say no right at all." Nonetheless, the incident that culminated the Hemingway legend in 1954, the year in which his literary greatness was proclaimed all over the world, had nothing to do with writing.

Report of Death. The year began with the reports of his death. In September 1953 the Hemingways began a five-month, highly publicized African safari, his second. *Look* magazine sent along a photographer to do a feature story. After the safari was over, the Hemingways were on a three-day sight-seeing tour of the Belgian Congo when their plane crashed on 23 January 1954. They and the pilot crawled to safety, leaving the wreckage behind, but rescue teams that discovered the crash site assumed the worst and informed news sources that the Hemingways had been killed. The next day a riverboat picked up the survivors, and a local pilot agreed to fly them out of the wild. The second plane crashed, too, and this time Hemingway was seriously injured. His skull was fractured, a kidney and his spleen were ruptured, and he suffered burns on his arms and face crawling through burning brush. Newspapers that had failed to carry reports of the first crash now joined those already carrying Hemingway's obituary on the front page. He was declared dead around the world before the error was discovered. Two months later a photo of the solemn writer, head battered, waving his hand so that the scars of the crash were visible, was widely published. He was a hero, declaring his toughness to the world.

Nobel Prize. On his return to the United States in March 1954, Hemingway received the Award of Merit from the American Academy of Arts and Letters. In July he received the highest honor Cuba could grant, and in November he became the sixth American to win the Nobel Prize for Literature. Unable to attend the presentation ceremony due to illness, he sent a characteristically terse acceptance statement: "A writer should write what he has to say and not speak it."

Last years. Hemingway's last years were troubled. He was ill — physically and mentally — much of the time. He participated in the filming of *The Old Man and the Sea,* followed a dramatic series of bullfights in Spain, about which he wrote, and wrote a long account of his trip to Africa, but all his projects of the period were marked by frustration that drove him deeper into depression. By the end of the decade there were undeniable signs of the mental torment that drove him to suicide on 2 July 1961.

Sources:

Carlos Baker, *Ernest Hemingway: A Life Story* (New York: Scribners, 1969);

Jeffrey Meyers, *Hemingway* (New York: Harper & Row, 1985);

Michael Reynolds, *Hemingway: An Annotated Chronology* (Detroit: Manly/Omnigraphics, 1991).

JACK KEROUAC
1922-1969

Beat Novelist

GALE PORTRAIT GALLERY

The Right Time. Jack Kerouac was a writer who earned his place in cultural history because of timing more than literary merit. In his books, most notably *On the Road* (1957), he expresses the spirit of the 1950s for an audience aimlessly seeking a suitable mode of expression. Kerouac's depiction of a band of free spirits discovering themselves as they improvised their way across America in what was intended to be a real-life analogue to a jazz-ensemble improvisation struck a chord with young iconoclastic readers. Kerouac became a representative figure, the king of the Beats.

Background. When his father died in 1948, Kerouac's future looked dismal. He had done nothing so consistently as fail. He had attended Columbia University between 1940 and 1942 and hoped to play football, but, because of an injury and a characteristic lack of resolve, he quit the team. Academically he did no better, though he did show a promising interest in creative writing. After dropping out of college, he joined the U.S. Navy in 1943. Within six months he had been discharged for mental instability and had returned to upper Manhattan, where he took up with a group of equally unstable Columbia students, including poet Allen Ginsberg and novelist William S. Burroughs, who introduced him to drugs and a bohemian lifestyle.

Hit the Road. In 1944 Kerouac was indicted as an accomplice when a friend killed a man in a fight. When Leo Kerouac refused to pay his son's bail, Jack Kerouac got married so his new wife's grandfather could be induced to pay. The marriage was shorter than his stint in the navy. Kerouac left his wife and took to the road on his own, deciding somewhere along the way to become a professional writer like his Beat friends Ginsberg and Burroughs.

Literary Career. Kerouac's first novel, *The Town & the City,* was published in 1950, when he was twenty-eight. He wrote it after his father died, in hopes of earning enough to provide for his mother's support. The novel, based on personal experience, is about a young man who splits with his family and his town to strike out for the city in a quest for identity and fulfillment. It stakes out his literary territory and his creative method. His subject is what he called the Beat Generation, by which he meant restless hipsters like himself, receptive to the values implied by spontaneity and unwilling to accept the stultification of conformity. His literary method was constituted by the use of emotive realism in which he refused to censor his feelings. "Godamn it, FEELING is what I like in art, not CRAFTINESS and the hiding of feelings," he explained to a *Paris Review* interviewer in 1967.

On the Road. Kerouac's second novel, *On the Road,* was written in the early 1950s. When it was published in 1957, the Beat Generation adopted it as their bible. The novel was touted as an example of a new form, "spontaneous prose," and was rumored to have been typed in a single amphetamine-driven burst of inspiration on a roll of tele-type paper chosen so Kerouac would not have to suffer the interruptions of moving from one piece of typewriter paper to another. That story bore only passing resemblance to the truth (in fact, researchers have found that the novel was written, edited, and rewritten), but the point is valid. The novel is about striking out, exploring the limits of freedom, appreciating beauty, making new acquaintances, coming to know what you believe — spontaneity.

Critics. Reviews were generally hostile, with the notable exception of the *New York Times.* Gilbert Millstein (stand-in reviewer for the staid Orville Prescott, who hated the book) announced that publication of *On the Road* was a historic occasion and named Kerouac as the spokesman and exemplar of the Beat Generation. Dan Wakefield recalls in *New York in the Fifties* (1992), "You had to read, or at least try to read, *On the Road,* in the fall of 1957, simply to be able to express your dislike of it with authority at the bars and coffeehouses where such things were discussed." Nat Hentoff of the *Village Voice* said, "After that Millstein review in the *Times,* if you didn't read it, you were a square."

Aftermath. For the rest of his life Kerouac lived off the reputation of his second novel. He produced books at the rate of more than one a year until his death, but none has had the impact of *On the Road.* His most successful subsequent novels were *Subterraneans* (1958), read as an exposé of beatnik life, and *Dharma Bums* (1958), a wander novel that grew out of his interest in Buddhism. But even these sold on the basis of Kerouac's reputation.

The End. By the late 1950s Kerouac had little creative to offer. He had become a pitiful, reclusive, intolerant figure whose mind had been damaged and whose health had been destroyed by drugs and alcohol. In his last years he complained about the youthful spirit of the 1960s that some said his work had inspired. He died having clearly outlived his time at the age of forty-seven in 1969.

MARILYN MONROE
1926-1962

ACTRESS

Reputation. Marilyn Monroe is one of the most popular stars the movies have ever produced. When she stood over a subway grate in *The Seven Year Itch* (1955), her white pleated dress billowing above her waist, and squealed, "Isn't it delicious?," she created a legendary image. Yet she was far more than a face and a voluptuous body, although those were her major assets to a flesh-conscious industry. She was a superb comedienne, a honey-toned singer, and a dramatic actress of above-average range, as witnessed by her chilling portrayal of a villainess in *Niagara* (1953), her role as a down-and-out divorcée in *The Misfits* (1961), and her evocation of a honky-tonk performer in *Bus Stop* (1956). Acclaimed stage and screen director Joshua Logan, who worked with her on *Bus Stop,* called her "the most completely realized and authentic film actress since [Greta] Garbo."

Background. Monroe was born Norma Jeane Mortenson (later changed to Norma Jean Baker) on 1 June 1926 in Los Angeles. Her unwed mother, a film editor, thereafter spent most of her life in mental institutions, and Monroe was haunted throughout her adult life by the fear that she, too, might lose her sanity. She grew up in foster homes and orphanages. At age eight she was raped by a lodger in a house where she was residing. She escaped the chaos of her early life by marrying James Dougherty, a twenty-one-year-old aircraft-plant worker, when she was sixteen.

Early Career. During World War II Monroe worked at the Radioplane Company factory in Burbank, California. She began modeling and posing for pinups at this time. By 1946 photographs of her were appearing in national magazines. Then 20th Century–Fox signed her, but her career went nowhere during her first stint with that studio. She worked in B movies at Columbia Pictures until she befriended agent Johnny Hyde, who negotiated small but important roles for her in such A movies as *The Asphalt Jungle* (1950) and *All About Eve* (1950).

Sex Symbol. Before his death in 1950 Hyde secured a six-month contract for Monroe at 20th Century–Fox. After she enchanted movie exhibitors at a studio dinner, Fox extended her contract to seven years. The studio, however, did not know quite what to do with her. Meanwhile she made herself available for interviews and public appearances. The press adored her, and her cheesecake photos were served up almost everywhere. When nude shots of her from a 1949 calendar popped up again in 1951, her fame spread.

Early Movies. In 1953 20th Century–Fox released three movies starring Monroe: *Niagara, Gentlemen Prefer Blondes,* and *How to Marry a Millionaire.* Movie exhibitors voted her one of the top ten box-office draws for that year. In 1954 she became an even bigger celebrity through marriage to baseball star Joe DiMaggio. Also that year she sang for the troops in Korea, wearing a sleeveless dress in subzero weather.

Dispute. After completing *The Seven Year Itch* Monroe left Hollywood over a dispute with 20th Century–Fox about the bland roles being offered her. She studied at the Actors' Studio in New York and was then lured back with a new contract stipulating one hundred thousand dollars per picture plus director approval. Her next movie, *Bus Stop,* an adaptation of William Inge's Broadway play, provided her with her greatest role. "My name is Che-RIE, and I'm a chan-TEUSE," she proclaims. Her expert blend of humor and heartbreak showed audiences the breadth of her range.

Arthur Miller. In 1956 Monroe married playwright Arthur Miller. Their marriage was upended by her rumored affairs with John and Robert Kennedy, and it broke apart during filming of *The Misfits,* which Miller wrote for her. It was to be her last movie. She died of an overdose of barbiturates on 5 August 1962, two months after being suspended from the production of "Something's Got to Give." A 1991 documentary on that failed project includes most of the footage of Monroe that was shot for the movie, showing her as luminous as ever.

Death. A week before her death Monroe told *Life* magazine, "A sex symbol becomes a thing — I just hate to be a thing. But if I'm going to be a symbol of something, I'd rather have it sex." Monroe has passed from symbol to phenomenon. Each year a new spate of books, articles, calendars, and other merchandise keeps her firmly in the public eye, and it is not unusual to see her on magazine covers. There have been dozens of plays, movies, and television programs concerning her life, and even a 1993 opera.

Sources:

James Haspiel, *Marilyn: The Ultimate Look at the Legend* (New York: Holt, 1991);

Norman Mailer, *Marilyn: A Biography* (New York: Grosset & Dunlap, 1973).

CHARLIE PARKER
1920-1955
JAZZ ALTO SAXOPHONIST

RAY WHITTER

Reputation. It is the consensus of jazz critics that no modern jazz musician played with the brilliance of alto saxophonist Charlie Parker. His professional career lasted half his life — some seventeen years — and he left as his legacy about one hundred records made during his last decade. They preserve examples of the melodic bursts and rhythmic innovations that earned him his nickname, "Bird" or "Yardbird," because his inspiration and the purity of his music was considered birdlike. According to Dizzy Gillespie, Parker invented bebop, the jazz sound of the postwar period. He was so highly regarded that in 1949, when he was twenty-nine years old, a jazz club on Broadway in Manhattan was renamed Birdland in his honor.

Drugs and Despair. Charlie Parker was a legend before his death at the age of thirty-five. A man of huge appetites, he overindulged frequently. He was a neurotic, hospitalized twice for mental breakdowns, and he was a drug addict whose habit caused him to misbehave flamboyantly. In February 1954 his two-and-a-half-year-old daughter Pree died of pneumonia. After that Parker was through. He was unable to reconcile himself to her death, and what had been a dangerous drug habit became a suicidal plunge into despair.

Birdland. In August 1954 he was booked to play Birdland with singer Dinah Washington. Both she and Parker had August birthdays and legendary capacities for alcohol. They got drunk, and he was unable to perform as contracted. The manager had a camera girl take Parker's picture for posterity and then fired him from the club named in his honor. Parker went home, argued with his common-law wife Chan, and attempted suicide by drinking a bottle of iodine. He was committed to Bellevue Hospital in Manhattan, where he stayed, except for a two-week trial release, until mid October. Two weeks later he played Town Hall in New York City, followed by a succession of grueling and demeaning club dates that only deepened his depression.

Last Performance. Charlie Parker's last public appearance was at Birdland on 5 March 1955, and the show was as stormy as in 1954. After a Saturday evening of unprofessional bickering with his sidemen, he stormed off the stage and was banished from Birdland again. Before he left, he told his bass player, "Mingus, I'm going someplace, pretty soon, where I'm not going to bother anybody."

Death. The following Wednesday he began vomiting blood while visiting his friend Baroness Pannonica de Koenigswarter, aristocratic jazz connoisseur and patroness, at her suite in the Stanhope Hotel in Manhattan. She called her doctor, who ordered Parker to bed. The baroness agreed to care for him in her apartment. That Saturday he collapsed while watching the Tommy Dorsey variety show on television. He died from a heart attack induced, apparently, by bleeding ulcers and cirrhosis of the liver.

Memorial. Parker died broke. A benefit concert for his son and wife at Carnegie Hall on 2 April sold out, raising about $5,740. At 3:40 A.M. police closed down the show, which had begun at midnight, and the musicians who had not yet had an opportunity to play their tribute to Parker created a scene. Gillespie, Art Blakey, Thelonious Monk, Billie Holiday, Stan Getz, Oscar Pettiford, Lester Young, and Horace Silver were among the musicians who appeared on the stage in front of an audience of 2,760 jazz fans that night. It was a fitting tribute to the greatest of all bebop saxophonists, who found perfection in his music and bitter disappointment in the rest of his life.

Sources:

Lawrence O. Koch, *Yardbird Suite: A Compendium of the Music and Life of Charlie Parker* (Bowling Green: Bowling Green University Popular Press, 1988);

Robert George Reisner, *Bird: The Legend of Charlie Parker* (New York: Da Capo Press, 1975).

JACKSON POLLOCK

1912-1956

ABSTRACT EXPRESSIONIST ARTIST

WILFRED ZOGBAUM

Notorious Celebrity. Jackson Pollock was the art world's most notorious celebrity during the 1950s. Despite a long apprenticeship he came to prominence suddenly late in 1949, largely as a result of the advocacy of *Nation* art critic Clement Greenberg, who declared Pollock's greatness. In response to what many thought was an outrageous claim, *Life* magazine published a feature story titled "Jackson Pollock: Is He the Greatest Living Painter in the United States?" The article featured photographs of Pollock's huge drip paintings that consist of layers of multicolored paint spatters and quoted the artist as saying that when he painted he had to get "in" his paintings and "When I am *in* my painting I'm not aware of what I'm doing."

"Jack the Dripper." Pollock made many enemies, among whom he was known as "Jack the Dripper." During the 1950s the Cedar Tavern in Greenwich Village, New York, was as significant a place in his life as his art studio. Pollock drank heavily and was abusive when he was drunk. He was a Tuesday-night regular at the Cedar, an artists' hangout, and his appearance came to be dreaded because he was so rude and contentious. As his fame as an artist grew, so did his reputation as a nasty drunk, profane, insulting, and slovenly. Artist Larry Rivers, looking back some fifteen years, remembered, "What was obviously gorgeous in his work was becoming infused with a mindlessness impossible to separate from his social personality."

Background. Pollock was born in Los Angeles and moved to New York in 1932 at the age of twenty to study art with Thomas Hart Benton at the Art Students League. Like many of the abstract expressionists (see entry), Pollock worked for the WPA art program during the war. After he was terminated early in 1943, he decorated ties and lipstick cases at the Museum of Non-Objective Painting in New York City. He made his first drip paintings in the winter of 1946, and that style dominated his work until his death a decade later.

Success. No American artist of the time, abstract or otherwise, attracted the popular attention Pollock did. His studio in East Hamption, Long Island, was repeatedly visited by art-features writers; his work habits were described by critics; his demeanor was commented on by colleagues. By the early 1950s he was the most successful of abstract painters, selling individual drip paintings for twice the price of a new Cadillac. But the personal toll was steep. His wife, artist Lee Krasner, was finally driven away by his violent drinking episodes and his promiscuous sexual behavior. Though she still appreciated and defended his artistic talent, she could no longer abide his destructive behavior.

Death. One Tuesday night in spring 1956 Pollock met Ruth Kligman, an art student who wanted to spend some time with the best American artists. They became friendly, and in August he invited her for a weekend visit to his home in East Hampton, after his wife had moved out. She brought a friend, Edith Metzger, and on Friday, 10 August, the three of them went out to eat and drink, Pollock driving in his Oldsmobile convertible. At one point Pollock passed out behind the wheel, and a patrolman stopped to investigate. When Pollock told him he was OK, the patrolman left, and the three went to a bar in East Hampton so that Pollock could steady his nerves with a drink. When he was ready to go, Edith Metzger refused to get into the car because she thought him too drunk to drive. Pollock flew into a rage, and with Kligman's help they forced her into the car. Pollock raced off recklessly. Within minutes he and Edith Metzger were dead, killed when the car veered off the winding road.

Reputation. With his death, Pollock's reputation was crystallized. He was eulogized as America's greatest artist, answering the question posed in *Life* seven years earlier. He was buried at Green River Cemetery in East Hampton, a location that subsequently became so popular as an artists' burial ground that the sylvan setting around Pollock's natural-rock gravestone had to be disturbed to make more burial space. Sixteen years after his death the Australian government paid $2 million for *Blue Poles,* a painting begun in a drunken suicidal fit. It set an all-time-record price for an artwork by an American.

Source:
Steven Naifeh and Gregory White Smith, *Jackson Pollock: An American Saga* (New York: Clarkson N. Potter, 1989).

ELVIS PRESLEY

1935-1977

ROCK 'N' ROLL SINGER

A Revolutionized Industry. In 1956 the Record Industry Association of America reported a 43 percent increase in sales — $100 million — to $331 million per year. The average annual growth in sales over the previous year had been about 4 percent a year. The reason was that teenagers, stimulated by new stars, had begun buying records, the most exciting of which was Elvis Presley.

Birth. Elvis Aron Presley was born at home in a two-room shack on North Saltillo road in Tupelo, Mississippi, on 8 January 1935. His twin brother was stillborn. Not since Union general A. J. Smith defeated Nathan Forest there on 14 July 1864 had Tupelo witnessed such a portentous event. By the time he was twenty-one the boy, so famous that like kings and queens he was known by his first name only, would have an impact on American culture without parallel among entertainers in the history of America.

Old Shep. When Elvis was thirteen his family moved to Memphis, where the boy entered L. C. Humes High School. He was an indifferent student who demonstrated little potential and almost no talent, most teachers agreed, until his senior year. That was when Elvis sang "Old Shep" onstage and discovered the effect he could have on an audience.

Early Career. While he was still in school Elvis began hanging around the only professional recording studio in town, Sam Phillips's Sun Records. In 1954 he recorded a birthday song for his mother, and he helped out around the studio as much as he was allowed. That summer Phillips, who had been trying to find a white singer for black music, asked the boy to record a cover (a white version) of a song by black blues singer Arthur Crudup. The result was "That's All Right Mama," a rocking song for hip-hop dancers. For marketing reasons, Phillips suggested a country song for the flip side, so Elvis sang bluegrass originator Bill Monroe's "Blue Moon over Kentucky." Sun released the record and sent nineteen-year-old Elvis on the road to promote the country song. By September, Elvis had earned a spot on the Grand Ole Opry, the top live show in the South for country musicians. The manager was incensed by his performance of "Good Rockin' Tonight": "We don't do that nigger music around here. If I were you, I'd go back to driving a truck," he told Elvis.

Gabriel Parker. But there was no stopping Elvis Presley: he had audience appeal. Within a year he was on tour with country star Hank Snow playing for as many as fourteen thousand people a night at $250 a show. Then Elvis attracted the attention of Colonel Tom Parker, a flamboyant promoter in search of a client, and his life took a new direction. By November 1955 Parker had formally become Elvis's agent and had negotiated a deal with RCA to purchase Presley's recording and publishing contract from Sun Records. Within months RCA was selling seventy-five thousand copies of Elvis's records a day.

Spoils of Stardom. In 1956, RCA sold 10 million singles (forty-five RPM records) by Elvis, the largest annual sale ever of records by a single performer, and he earned $1 million in royalties alone. That same year Parker negotiated a three-movie film contract that brought Elvis $100,000 for the first movie, $150,000 for the second, and $200,000 for the third. In addition, he negotiated eighteen separate licenses for Elvis merchandise — including fan magazines, books, stuffed teddy bears and

hound dogs — which grossed $55 million in 1956. Of that $55 million, Elvis got between 4 and 11 percent, depending on the product, and Colonel Parker got 50 percent. There had never been a star of Elvis's magnitude, and he was only twenty-one.

Ed Sullivan Show. In September 1956 Elvis played the "Ed Sullivan Show." His contract was for three performances at $50,000 each. Before the first performance people had heard of Elvis Presley, but they knew him only by reputation. That reputation was so strong that 82.6 percent of the viewing audience tuned in to see what the fuss was about, a record audience for Sullivan that stood until he presented the Beatles in 1964. By the third show Elvis was too popular to deny, but older viewers had begun to complain about the suggestiveness of his hip-shaking performance. When television cameras were forbidden to show Elvis's pelvic gyrations, the Sullivan show demonstrated the principle that what is not seen is often sexier than full exposure. By that time he was the undisputed king of rock 'n' roll.

Acting. As an actor, Elvis ranged from bad to barely mediocre; as a screen idol, he was hard to match. During the 1950s he starred in four movies: *Love Me Tender* (1956), *Jailhouse Rock* (1957), *Loving You* (1957), and *King Creole* (1958). He played singing roles in all of these movies, of course, and the theaters were filled with his fans.

Memorable Tour. It was estimated that Elvis's income topped $10 million in 1957, and his stock seemed to be on the rise. Late in August 1957 Elvis began a twenty-performance tour of the West. Onstage he wore a ten thousand dollar outfit in gold and rhinestone, and he played before audiences of as many as 10,000 fans. It was a successful tour. Earnings were $375,000, a pittance by Elvis's standards, but the fans counted themselves fortunate for the rest of the decade. They saw Elvis on his last live concert tour until the 1970s.

Drafted. On 24 March 1958 Elvis was drafted. Army barbers cut his long hair, and he turned in his flashy clothes for uniforms of olive drab. He was in the army, and he followed army rules: no performances, no publicity, no exceptions. Within seven months he was in Germany, where he quietly served his two-year obligation. When he returned, the decade was over, and while he continued to achieve unmatched heights of celebrity and earned more money than any performer of his time, he was changed — more mature, more cautious, more cynical, less spontaneous, and flabbier. He had changed with the times.

Sources:

Marc Eliot, *Rockonomics: The Money Behind the Music* (New York: Watts, 1989);

Philip Ennis, *The Seventh Stream: The Emergence of Rocknroll in American Popular Music* (Hanover & London: Wesleyan University Press, 1992);

Albert Goldman, *Elvis* (New York: McGraw-Hill, 1981).

J. D. SALINGER
1919-
FICTION WRITER

Adolescent Point of View. In 1959 critic Arthur Mizener wrote that J. D. Salinger "is probably the most avidly read author of any serious pretensions in his generation." Salinger attracted his admiring readership, which was concentrated on college campuses, with one novel, *The Catcher in the Rye* (1951), and one volume of short stories, *Nine Stories* (1953), most of which had originally appeared in the *New Yorker.* Salinger's reputation as a serious writer was difficult for some members of the literary establishment to swallow, because it was based on what was considered to be an adolescent readership. Salinger wrote about and appealed to young people. A *Time* magazine reviewer observed that he could "understand an adolescent mind without displaying one."

Writings. Salinger's literary output during the 1950s consisted of *The Catcher in the Rye,* a first-person narrative by Holden Caulfield, a troubled sixteen-year-old boy seeking to minimize the scars of his own experience and searching for a way to save the innocence of children, and of seven stories about the very intelligent children of the Glass family as they face the responsibility of growth and maturity. Salinger's writing is marked by its direct language, its unsolicitous sympathy for adolescent characters, and an element of spiritual sensitivity, especially in the Glass stories.

Celebrity. His literary celebrity owes as much to his eccentricity as to his talent. Salinger proved that one way to interest the press was to shun it. When he learned that the dust jacket of his first novel included a photograph of him on the back, he insisted that it be replaced. His publishers dutifully withdrew the photograph dust jacket and replaced it with a jacket that has a blank back. He also made his publishers promise not to send him any reviews of the book or any publicity notices because he feared that he might come to believe them.

Retreat. Soon after *The Catcher in the Rye* was published, Salinger moved to Cornish, New Hampshire, got married, and became the most determined literary recluse in America. By 1953 he was refusing all contacts with strangers and had cut off all but necessary relationships with the world outside his home, where he lived without electricity or running water and grew much of his own food organically.

Best-seller. *The Catcher in the Rye* was a publishing success from the beginning. It reached number four on the *New York Times* best-seller list and remained in the top ten for seven months, a considerable achievement for an author's first book. It was not until it was published in paperback, however, that it reached its most appreciative audience, which was students. By 1968 the novel was counted among the twenty-five American best-sellers of the previous seventy-five years.

Reputation. By the late 1950s Salinger's reputation was among the highest of all living writers, which included Ernest Hemingway, William Faulkner, and John Steinbeck. Granville Hicks, writing in the *Saturday Review,* observed that "there are, I am convinced, millions of young Americans who feel closer to Salinger than to any other writer." Frederick Gwynn and Joseph Blotner, in the first critical volume about Salinger's work, named him the only postwar writer whose fiction was "unanimously approved by contemporary literate American youth." In 1951 Salinger told a *Time* reporter, "Some of my best friends are children . . . in fact, all of my best friends are children." He was also their literary spokesman.

Sources:

Donald Barr, "Saints, Pilgrims and Artists," *Commonweal,* 67 (25 October 1957): 8–9;

Ian Hamilton, *In Search of J. D. Salinger* (New York: Random House, 1988);

Arthur Mizener, "The Love Song of J. D. Salinger," *Harper's,* 218 (February 1959): 83–90;

George Steiner, "The Salinger Industry," *Nation,* 189 (14 November 1959): 360–363.

HANK WILLIAMS
1924-1953
COUNTRY MUSIC SINGER

"King of the Hillbillies." Hank Williams's promoters called him "King of the Hillbillies." He was an illiterate country-music songwriter and guitar player who was more popular than any musician in his field had ever been. He rarely failed to have at least one record on the list of top-ten hits in its category during the last two years of his life — such songs as "Your Cheatin' Heart," "I'm So Lonesome I Could Cry," "Lovesick Blues," and "I'll Never Get Out of This World Alive" — and they all reflected his torment. Singing them night after night was more than he could endure. He was twenty-nine years old when he died on New Year's Day 1953.

Background. A psychiatrist called Hank Williams "the most lonesome, the saddest, most tortured and frustrated of individuals." He had learned to play guitar at age six from a black street singer named Teetot whom he had met while working as a shoeshine boy in Georgiana, Alabama, and at age twelve he was playing and singing in honky-tonks. By the late 1940s he was a regular on the nation's, which is to say the South's, two most popular country radio shows — first "Louisiana Hayride," broadcast from Shreveport, Louisiana, and then the Grand Ole Opry, in Nashville, Tennessee — whose performers were acknowledged as the field's brightest stars.

Dr. Feelgood. In 1951 Hank Williams earned some $175,000 a year making personal appearances all over the South five nights a week and returning to Nashville for the Grand Ole Opry on Saturday, but the pace was deadly, and he needed help. So, for $300 a week, he engaged a personal physician, an ex-con named Tony Marshal who had bought a mail-order medical degree, to provide him with drugs to wake him up in the morning and put him to sleep at night.

Losing Control. In 1952 he was more popular than ever, and his earnings soared to over $200,000, but his behavior became so erratic that many thought his career was in danger. On New Year's Day he left his wife (whom he had married at seventeen), his son, his fleet of Cadillacs, and his lavish Nashville home for another woman. He began wearing a gun in his belt and used it to shoot up hotel rooms in fits of fury. He sometimes appeared on stage, announced that he was too drunk to perform, and cursed the audience. He threw wads of money onto the ground and stomped them with uncontrollable anger. In September the Grand Ole Opry banned him from its stage for erratic behavior.

Death. On New Year's Day 1953 he was scheduled to perform in Canton, Ohio. On New Year's Eve bad weather had grounded his flight in Knoxville, Tennessee, and Williams sought a physician to provide drugs to help him sleep and a driver to take him by car to Canton. He died en route in the back seat of the car. The coroner said the cause of death was heart failure.

Memorial. The next evening in Canton, promoters announced Hank Williams's death, a spotlight was trained on the center of the empty stage, and Williams's band the Drifting Cowboys led the audience in a singing of Williams's favorite hymn, "I Saw the Light." He was buried in Montgomery, Alabama. Twenty thousand fans showed up to pay homage, jamming the area around City Auditorium, where the funeral was held. A two-ton truck was required to bring flowers from Nashville alone.

Reputation. Hank Williams's life, like his music, had poignant significance for his fans. It signified loneliness, self-destruction, and exploitation by people more powerful, all expressed in the language of uncensored emotions. His songs were about the heartaches suffered by simple people who lived reckless lives, and his own life exemplified his music.

Sources:
"Sadly the Troubadour," *Newsweek,* 41 (19 January 1953): 55;

Eli Waldron, "Country Music: I. The Death of Country Music; II. The *Squaya Dansu* from Nashville," *Reporter,* 12 (19 May 1955): 35–37; (2 June 1955): 39–42;

Waldron, "The Life and Death of a Country Singer," *Coronet,* 39 (January 1956): 40–44.

PEOPLE IN THE NEWS

Film rights to *Don't Go Near the Water,* by **William Brinkley,** reportedly sold for four hundred thousand dollars in summer 1956 despite bad reviews of the novel.

Nobel Prize–winning novelist **Pearl S. Buck,** poet **Leonard Bacon,** and composer **Douglas Moore** were named members of the American Academy of Arts and Letters on 30 November 1951.

In 1950 New American Library claimed that *God's Little Acre,* by **Erskine Caldwell,** was the all-time best-selling twenty-five-cent paperback, having sold 5 million copies. New American Library reported that it had sold 18 million copies of Caldwell's books.

On 2 January 1958 soprano **Maria Callas** walked out during an opening-night performance at the Opera House in Rome, nearly prompting a riot; eleven months later **Rudolf Bing** fired her from the Metropolitan Opera when she refused to perform as contracted.

Singer **Sammy Davis, Jr.,** lost the sight in his left eye in an auto accident on 19 November 1954.

In April 1953 **Bethsabée de Rothschild,** daughter of Baron de Rothschild, underwrote "American Dance," a two-week presentation of modern dance at the Alvin Theater in New York City. She chose the choreographers **Merce Cunningham, Nina Fonaroff, Pearl Lang, Helen McGehee,** and **May O'Donnell.**

In 1953 **John Dos Passos** noted the lack of common understanding Americans had of their language, which left them with little common culture except possibly comic books.

Swedish-born actress **Greta Garbo** became a United States citizen on 9 February 1951.

Erroll Garner, winner in the pianist category of *Downbeat* magazine's Jazz Critics' Poll, played one of his own works with the Cleveland Symphony in summer 1957. Performances were chaotic because of inaccuracies in the score. Garner, who did not read music, attempted a form of musical dictation.

Jazz tenor saxophonist **Stan Getz** was sentenced on 18 February 1954 to 180 days in jail for drug violations.

In February 1952 **Thor Johnson,** director of the Cincinnati Symphony Orchestra, conducted the first uncut version of Arnold Schoenberg's *Gurre-Lieder,* requiring six soloists, a 147-piece orchestra, and a 349-voice chorus. The estimated cost of the performance was twenty thousand dollars.

In October 1958 New York art dealer **Georges Keller** paid $616,000 for *Garçon au Gillet Rouge,* the highest price ever paid for a painting.

Soprano **Lotte Lehmann** announced her retirement on 16 February 1951.

Liberace sued the *London Daily Mirror* in 1959 for reporting that he was homosexual. He was awarded $22,400 in damages.

Author **Grace Metalious** was sued for libel in 1958 because her novel *Peyton Place* included characters too close to real-life models. The suit was settled out of court.

Playwright **Arthur Miller** was granted a temporary passport in July 1956 after admitting to Communist associations. He requested permission to travel to London on his honeymoon with Marilyn Monroe.

Marianne Moore received the Bollingen Prize for her *Collected Poems* in January 1952 and the Gold Medal of the National Institute of Arts and Letters in April 1953.

At the Camera Club in New York City, photographer **Arnold Newman** staged an acclaimed exhibit of his pictures of creative artists in February 1951.

Actor **Paul Newman** was arrested on Long Island in July 1956 after knocking over a fire hydrant and challenging the patrolman who stopped him to a fight. Newman, whose new film was *Somebody Up There Likes Me,* about middleweight champion Rocky Graziano, was charged with running a red light.

In 1953 the top three orchestras in America were the Philadelphia Orchestra, conducted by **Eugene Ormandy**; the Boston Symphony, conducted by **Charles Munch**; and the New York Philharmonic-Symphony, conducted by **Dimitri Mitropoulos**.

Actor **Ronald Reagan** married actress **Nancy Davis** on 4 March 1952. It was his second marriage, her first.

In 1953 **Fritz Reiner** became the third director in the history of the Chicago Symphony Orchestra. His predecessor **Frederick Stock** served for thirty-eight years.

On 13 March 1950 black singer **Paul Robeson** was barred by NBC from appearing on Eleanor Roosevelt's television program because of his leftist activities.

Dore Schary replaced **Louis B. Mayer** as head of M-G-M on 16 July 1951.

Violinist **Isaac Stern** performed in Moscow's Grand Conservatory Hall, the first appearance by an American musician in Moscow in ten years.

Eighteen-year-old actress **Elizabeth Taylor** divorced hotel heir **Conrad Hilton** on 29 January 1951.

Writers **Robert Penn Warren** and **Eleanor Clark** were married on 7 December 1952.

Eudora Welty and **Tennessee Williams** were awarded membership in the National Institute of Arts and Letters.

AWARDS

PULITZER PRIZES

1950

Fiction: *The Way West*, by **A. B. Guthrie, Jr.**

Drama: *South Pacific*, by **Richard Rodgers, Oscar Hammerstein II**, and **Joshua Logan**

Poetry: *Annie Allen*, by **Gwendolyn Brooks**

Music: *The Consul*, by **Gian Carlo Menotti**

1951

Fiction: *The Town*, by **Conrad Richter**

Drama: no award

Poetry: *Complete Poems*, by **Carl Sandburg**

Music: *Giants in the Earth*, by **Douglas Moore**

1952

Fiction: *The Caine Mutiny*, by **Herman Wouk**

Drama: *The Shrike*, by **Joseph Kramm**

Poetry: *Collected Poems*, by **Marianne Moore**

Music: *Symphony Concertante*, by **Gail Kubik**

1953

Fiction: *The Old Man and the Sea*, by **Ernest Hemingway**

Drama: *Picnic*, by **William Inge**

Poetry: *Collected Poems 1917–1952*, by **Archibald MacLeish**

Music: no award

1954

Fiction: no award

Drama: *The Teahouse of the August Moon*, by **John Patrick**

Poetry: *The Waking*, by **Theodore Roethke**

Music: *Concerto for Two Pianos and Orchestra*, by **Quincy Porter**

1955

Fiction: *A Fable*, by **William Faulkner**

Drama: *Cat on a Hot Tin Roof*, by **Tennessee Williams**

Poetry: *Collected Poems*, by **Wallace Stevens**

Music: *The Saint of Bleecker Street*, by **Gian Carlo Menotti**

1956

Fiction: *Andersonville*, by **MacKinlay Kantor**

Drama: *Diary of Anne Frank*, by **Albert Hackett** and **Frances Goodrich**

Poetry: *Poems — North & South*, by **Elizabeth Bishop**

Music: *Symphony No. 3*, by **Ernest Toch**

1957

Fiction: no award

Drama: *Long Day's Journey into Night*, by **Eugene O'Neill**

Poetry: *Things of This World*, by **Richard Wilbur**

Music: *Meditations on Ecclesiastes*, by **Norman Dello Joio**

1958

Fiction: *A Death in the Family*, by **James Agee**

Drama: *Look Homeward, Angel*, by **Ketti Frings**

Poetry: *Promises: Poems 1954–1956*, by **Robert Penn Warren**

Music: *Vanessa*, by **Samuel Barber**

1959

Fiction: *The Travels of Jaimie Mcpheeters*, by **Robert Lewis Taylor**

Drama: *J. B.*, by **Archibald MacLeish**

Poetry: *Selected Poems 1928–1958*, by **Stanley Kunitz**

Music: *Concerto for Piano and Orchestra*, by **John La Montaine**

THE AMERICAN THEATRE WING ANTOINETTE PERRY AWARDS. TONY AWARDS.

1950

Play: *The Cocktail Party,* **T. S. Eliot**

Actor, Dramatic Star: **Sidney Blackmer,** *Come Back, Little Sheba*

Actress, Dramatic Star: **Shirley Booth,** *Come Back, Little Sheba*

Musical: *South Pacific*

Actor, Musical Star: **Ezio Pinza,** *South Pacific*

Actress, Musical Star: **Mary Martin,** *South Pacific*

1951

Play: *The Rose Tattoo,* **Tennessee Williams**

Actor, Dramatic Star: **Claude Rains,** *Darkness at Noon*

Actress, Dramatic Star: **Uta Hagen,** *The Country Girl*

Musical: *Guys and Dolls*

Actor, Musical Star: **Robert Alda,** *Guys and Dolls*

Actress, Musical Star: **Ethel Merman,** *Call Me Madam*

1952

Play: *The Fourposter,* by **Jan de Hartog**

Actor, Dramatic Star: **Jose Ferrer,** *The Shrike*

Actress, Dramatic Star: **Julie Harris,** *I Am a Camera*

Musical: *The King and I*

Actor, Musical Star: **Phil Silvers,** *Top Banana*

Actress, Musical Star: **Gertrude Lawrence,** *The King and I*

1953

Play: *The Crucible,* **Arthur Miller**

Actor, Dramatic Star: **Tom Ewell,** *The Seven Year Itch*

Actress, Dramatic Star: **Shirley Booth,** *Time of the Cuckoo*

Musical: *Wonderful Town*

Actor, Musical Star: **Thomas Mitchell,** *Hazel Flagg*

Actress, Musical Star: **Rosalind Russell,** *Wonderful Town*

1954

Play: *The Teahouse of the August Moon,* **John Patrick Googan**

Actor, Dramatic Star: **David Wayne,** *The Teahouse of the August Moon*

Actress, Dramatic Star: **Audrey Hepburn,** *Ondine*

Musical: *Kismet*

Actor, Musical Star: **Alfred Drake,** *Kismet*

Actress, Musical Star: **Dolores Gray,** *Carnival in Flanders*

1955

Play: *The Desperate Hours,* **Joseph Arnold Hayes**

Actor, Dramatic Star: **Alfred Lunt,** *Quadrille*

Actress, Dramatic Star: **Nancy Kelly,** *The Bad Seed*

Musical: *The Pajama Game*

Actor, Musical Star: **Walter Slezak,** *Fanny*

Actress, Musical Star: **Mary Martin,** *Peter Pan*

1956

Play: *The Diary of Anne Frank*

Actor, Dramatic Star: **Paul Muni,** *Inherit the Wind*

Actress, Dramatic Star: **Julie Harris,** *The Lark*

Musical: *Damn Yankees*

Actor, Musical Star: **Ray Walston,** *Damn Yankees*

Actress, Musical Star: **Gwen Verdon,** *Damn Yankees*

1957

Play: *Long Day's Journey into Night,* **Eugene O'Neill**

Actor, Dramatic Star: **Frederic March,** *Long Day's Journey into Night*

Actress, Dramatic Star: **Margaret Leighton,** *Separate Tables*

Musical: *My Fair Lady*

Actor, Musical Star: **Rex Harrison,** *My Fair Lady*

Actress, Musical Star: **Judy Holliday,** *The Bells Are Ringing*

1958

Play: *Sunrise at Campobello,* **Dore Schary**

Actor, Dramatic Star: **Ralph Bellamy,** *Sunrise at Campobello*

Actress, Dramatic Star: **Helen Hayes,** *Time Remembered*

Musical: *The Music Man*

Actor, Musical Star: **Robert Preston,** *The Music Man*

Actress, Musical Star: **Thelma Ritter,** *New Girl in Town*

Gwen Verdon, *New Girl in Town*

1959

Play: *J. B.,* **Archibald MacLeish**

Actor, Dramatic Star: **Jason Robards, Jr.,** *The Disenchanted*

Actress, Dramatic Star: **Gertrude Berg,** *A Majority of One*

Musical: *Redhead*

Actor, Musical Star: **Richard Kiley,** *Redhead*

Actress, Musical Star: **Gwen Verdon,** *Redhead*

ACADEMY OF MOTION PICTURE ARTS AND SCIENCES AWARDS. THE OSCARS.

1950
Actor: **Jose Ferrer**, *Cyrano De Bergerac*

Actress: **Judy Holliday**, *Born Yesterday*

Picture: *All About Eve*, **20th Century–Fox**

1951
Actor: **Humphrey Bogart**, *The African Queen*

Actress: **Vivien Leigh**, *A Streetcar Named Desire*

Picture: *An American in Paris*, **M-G-M**

1952
Actor: **Gary Cooper**, *High Noon*

Actress: **Shirley Booth**, *Come Back, Little Sheba*

Picture: *Greatest Show on Earth*, **Cecil B. DeMille, Paramount**

1953
Actor: **William Holden**, *Stalag 17*

Actress: **Audrey Hepburn**, *Roman Holiday*

Picture: *From Here to Eternity*, **Columbia**

1954
Actor: **Marlon Brando**, *On the Waterfront*

Actress: **Grace Kelly**, *The Country Girl*

Picture: *On the Waterfront*, **Horizon-American, Columbia**

1955
Actor: **Ernest Borgnine**, *Marty*

Actress: **Anna Magnani**, *The Rose Tattoo*

Picture: *Marty*, **Hecht and Lancaster's Steven Prods., United Artists**

1956
Actor: **Yul Brynner**, *The King and I*

Actress: **Ingrid Bergman**, *Anastasia*

Picture: *Around the World in 80 Days*, **Michael Todd, United Artists**

1957
Actor: **Alec Guinness**, *The Bridge on the River Kwai*

Actress: **Joanne Woodward**, *The Three Faces of Eve*

Picture: *The Bridge on the River Kwai*, **Columbia**

1958
Actor: **David Niven**, *Separate Tables*

Actress: **Susan Hayward**, *I Want to Live*

Picture: *Gigi*, **Arthur Freed Production, M-G-M**

1959
Actor: **Charlton Heston**, *Ben-Hur*

Actress: **Simone Signoret**, *Room at the Top*

Picture: *Ben-Hur*, **M-G-M**

DEATHS

Irving Addison Bacheller, 90, novelist, 24 February 1950.

Fred E. Ahlert, 61, popular-song writer ("I'll Get By," "Walkin' My Baby Back Home"), president (1948–1952) of American Society of Composers, Authors and Publishers (ASCAP), 20 October 1953.

Zoë Akins, 72, playwright, poet, novelist, and 1935 Pulitzer Prize winner for her dramatization of *The Old Maid*, 29 October 1958.

Fred Allen (John Florence Sullivan), 61, comedian, 17 March 1956.

Frederick Lewis Allen, 63, author (*Only Yesterday, Since Yesterday*), editor in chief of *Harper's Magazine* (1941–1953), 13 February 1954.

Paul Hastings Allen, 68, composer of operas and symphonies, winner of the 1910 Paderewski Prize, 28 September 1952.

Maxwell Anderson, 70, playwright (*Winterset, High Tor, Both Your Houses*) who popularized the use of blank verse in modern drama, 28 February 1959.

Henry W. Armstrong, 71, song composer ("Sweet Adeline," "Eyes of Blue"), 28 February 1951.

Edward Arnold (Guenther Schneider), 66, motion-picture actor (*Diamond Jim Brady, Command Decision, All That Money Can Buy*), 26 April 1956.

Sholem Asch, 76, Polish-born Yiddish novelist (*Three Cities, Mottke the Thief, The Nazarene, The Apostle*) 10 July 1957.

Nathaniel (Nat) Davis Ayer, 65, songwriter ("Oh, You Beautiful Doll"), 19 September 1952.

Leonard Bacon, 66, poet, winner of the Pulitzer Prize in 1941, 1 January 1954.

Irene Temple Bailey, 80?, novelist, 6 July 1953.

Mildred Bailey, 48, blues singer, 12 December 1950.

Ethel Barrymore, 79, actress of stage, motion pictures, and television, whose career spanned sixty years and who had a New York theater named after her, 18 June 1959.

Lionel Barrymore, 76, stage, motion-picture, and radio actor, 15 November 1954.

Evelyn Beatrice Longman Batchelder, 79, sculptress, the first woman elected to the National Academy of Design, 10 March 1954.

Warner Baxter, 58, film actor, winner of 1929 Motion Picture Academy Award, 7 May 1951.

Chester Beach, 75, sculptor (*Fountain of Waters, Torch Race*) and medalist, noted for his fluid, impressionistic style, 6 August 1956.

Sidney Bechet, 70, New Orleans–style jazz soprano saxophonist and clarinetist, 14 May 1959.

William Rose Benét, 64, poet, critic, novelist, and editor, winner of the 1941 Pulitzer Prize for poetry, 4 May 1950.

Ernest Bloch, 78, composer and conductor of music based on Jewish themes, 15 July 1959.

Maxwell Bodenheim, 63, Greenwich Village poet and novelist of the 1920s, 7 February 1954.

Humphrey Bogart, 57, motion-picture actor, starred in some seventy-five films (*The Petrified Forest, The Maltese Falcon, The African Queen*), Best Actor Academy Award (1951), 14 January 1957.

Paul Breisach, 56, conductor of the San Francisco Opera Association and former New York Metropolitan Opera conductor, 26 December 1952.

Fanny Brice (Fannie Borach), 59, stage, motion-picture, and radio comedienne and singer, 29 May 1951.

Louis Bromfield, 59, Pulitzer Prize–winning novelist (*Early Autumn, The Green Bay Tree, The Rains Came, Malabar Farm*), 18 March 1956.

Lew Brown (Louis Brownstein), 64, songwriter of many popular hits ("Black Bottom," "Don't Sit Under the Apple Tree"), 5 February 1958.

Margaret Wise Brown, 42, writer of children's books, 13 November 1952.

Nigel Bruce, 58, actor, best known as Dr. Watson in *Sherlock Holmes,* 8 October 1953.

Katharine Brush, 49, novelist (*Young Man of Manhattan, Red-headed Woman*), 10 June 1952.

Gelett Burgess, 85, illustrator, humorist, famed for verse about the "purple cow," 18 September 1951.

John Horne Burns, 37, novelist (*The Gallery*), 11 August 1953.

Robert Elliot Burns, 64, author (*I Was a Fugitive from a Georgia Chain Gang*), 5 June 1955.

Edgar Rice Burroughs, 74, author (creator of Tarzan), 19 March 1950.

Adolf Georg Wilhelm Busch, 60, violinist, founder of the Busch String Quartet, 9 June 1952.

James Branch Cabell, 79, author (*Jurgen, The Way of Ecben, The Rivet in Grandfather's Neck*), 5 May 1958.

Louis Calhern (Carl Henry Vogt), 61, actor on the stage (*Dinner at Eight, Golden Boy, King Lear*) and in motion pictures (*Magnificent Yankee, Executive Suite, Asphalt Jungle*), 12 May 1956.

Dale Carnegie, 66, teacher of public speaking, author of the best-selling *How to Win Friends and Influence People,* 1 November 1955.

Edward Childs Carpenter, 78, novelist and playwright, 7 October 1950.

Mady Christians, 51, Broadway star, 28 October 1951.

Robert Peter Tristram Coffin, 62, poet, winner of the Pulitzer Prize in 1935 for *Strange Holiness,* 20 January 1955.

Octavus Roy Cohen, 67, author of books, plays, and motion-picture screenplays, best known for his dialect stories about African-Americans in the South, 6 January 1959.

Constance Collier (Laura Constance Hardie), 75, actress, 25 April 1955.

Ronald Colman, 67, star of stage and motion pictures (*Kismet, A Tale of Two Cities, Bulldog Drummond, Lost Horizon, Beau Geste, A Double Life*) who won the 1948 Best Actor Academy Award, 19 May 1958.

Jack Conway, 65, motion-picture star, director, and producer (*A Tale of Two Cities, Viva Villa, Boom Town, The Hucksters*), 11 October 1952.

Madison Cooper, 62, novelist, author of *Sironia, Texas,* the longest American novel ever published (seventeen hundred pages), 28 September 1956.

Lou Costello, 52, comedian of motion pictures and television, partner in the comedy team of Abbott and Costello, which broke up in 1957, 3 March 1959.

Jane Cowl, 65, actress, famous for her role as Juliet, 22 June 1950.

Rachel Crothers, 79, playwright (*Susan and God, When Ladies Meet*), 5 July 1958.

Walter Johannes Damrosch, 88, conductor, composer, and pianist, conductor of the New York Symphony Orchestra for forty-one years, 22 December 1950.

Jo Davidson, 68, sculptor, 2 January 1952.

Owen Davis, 82, Pulitzer Prize–winning playwright (*Icebound, Nellie, Jezebel, Mr. and Mrs. North, No Way Out*), 14 October 1956.

James Dean, 24, motion-picture actor (*East of Eden, Rebel Without a Cause*), 30 September 1955.

Cecil B. DeMille, 77, motion-picture pioneer, producer of multimillion-dollar spectacles (*The Greatest Show on Earth, The Ten Commandments, Samson and Delilah*), 21 January 1959.

Peter De Rose, 53, songwriter ("Wagon Wheels," "Deep Purple"), 23 April 1953.

George Gard ("Buddy") De Sylva, 54, songwriter ("Sonny Boy," "April Showers") and stage and motion-picture producer, 11 July 1950.

Clarence Derwent, 75, actor in more than five hundred plays on the London and New York stages, president of the American National Theatre and Academy (1952–1959), 6 August 1959.

William Hunt Diederich, 69, sculptor, 14 May 1953.

Jimmy Dorsey, 53, dance-band leader, saxophonist, and clarinetist, 12 June 1957.

Tommy Dorsey, 51, trombonist and bandleader, 26 November 1956.

Lloyd Cassel Douglas, 73, novelist (*Magnificent Obsession, The Robe*), 13 February 1951.

Olin (Edwin) Downes, 69, music critic for the *New York Times* since 1924, 22 August 1955.

Ruth Draper, 72, monologuist, famed for her one-woman shows, 30 December 1956.

Katherine Drier, 75, painter and writer, 20 March 1952.

Edwin (Eddy) Frank Duchin, 41, dance-orchestra leader, 9 February 1951.

Rosetta Duncan, 58, stage star, one of the famed vaudeville comedy team of the Duncan sisters, 4 December 1959.

Emma Eames, 84, New York Metropolitan Opera soprano (1891–1909), 13 June 1952.

Paul Eisler, 76, composer, conductor of New York Metropolitan Opera (1904–1929), 16 October 1951.

Gertrude Elliott, 76, actress, 24 December 1950.

Sir Jacob Epstein, 78, American-born sculptor whose stormy career in modern art was eventually crowned by worldwide recognition and knighthood, 19 August 1959.

Philip G. Epstein, 42, film-scenario writer (*Casablanca, The Man Who Came to Dinner, The Male Animal, Arsenic and Old Lace*), 7 February 1952.

John Erskine, 71, novelist (*The Private Life of Helen of Troy*), pianist, president of the Juilliard School of Music (1928–1937), 2 June 1951.

Janet Ayer Fairbank, 73, novelist (*The Smiths, Rich Man–Poor Man*), 28 December 1951.

William Farnum, 76, motion-picture actor (highest paid in the silent era), 5 June 1953.

Dorothy Canfield Fisher, 79, author, educator, and authority on Vermont, 9 November 1958.

John Gould Fletcher, 64, writer, winner of the Pulitzer Prize for poetry in 1939, 10 May 1950.

Anne Crawford Flexner, 80, playwright (*Mrs. Wiggs of the Cabbage Patch, Marriage Game*), 11 January 1955.

Errol Flynn, 50, motion-picture actor whose swashbuckling roles put him among the top ten moneymaking stars in the industry, 14 October 1959.

William Fox, 73, motion-picture pioneer, founder of Fox Film Corporation, which he lost in the Depression, 8 May 1952.

Richard S. ("Skeets") Gallagher, 64, stage and motion-picture comedian, 22 May 1955.

Albert Eugene Gallatin, 70, painter, art collector, and author, 15 June 1952.

John Garfield (Julius Garfinkle), 39, stage and motion-picture star, 21 May 1952.

Robert Garland, 60, drama critic of the *New York Journal–American* (1943–1951), 27 December 1955.

Eleanor Gates, 75, novelist, playwright (*The Poor Little Rich Girl*), 7 March 1951.

Norman Bel Geddes, 65, stage and industrial designer, noted for the 1939 New York World's Fair Futurama, 8 May 1958.

Charles William Goddard, 71, writer of popular movie serial *Perils of Pauline,* 11 January 1951.

John Golden, 80, Broadway producer of over 150 plays, a founder of ASCAP, 17 June 1955.

Charles Grapewin, 86, motion-picture character actor (*Tobacco Road, Grapes of Wrath*), 2 February 1956.

Gilda Gray (Marianne Michalski), 58, singer and dancer who created the "shimmy" dance of the Roaring Twenties, 22 December 1959.

Maria Grever, 57, composer ("What a Difference a Day Makes," "Besame"), 15 December 1951.

Edmund Gwenn, 83, actor of stage and motion pictures, 1948 Academy Award winner for his supporting role in *Miracle on 34th Street,* 6 September 1959.

James Norman Hall, 64, novelist, co-author with Charles B. Nordhoff of *Mutiny on the Bounty,* 5 July 1951.

Walter Hampden (Walter Dougherty), 75, actor noted for Shakespearean roles, 11 June 1955.

W. C. Handy (William Christopher), 84, composer of "St. Louis Blues" and called "father of the blues," 28 March 1958.

Oliver Hardy, 65, motion-picture actor, comedy partner of Stan Laurel, 7 October 1957.

Fletcher H. Henderson, 55, jazz bandleader, arranger, pianist, and composer, 29 December 1952.

Hugh Herbert, 66, motion-picture comedian, 12 March 1952.

Joseph Hergesheimer, 74, author (*Three Black Pennys, Java Head*), 25 April 1954.

Jean Hersholt, 69, motion-picture actor (*Greed, Stella Dallas, The Mask of Fu Manchu*), creator of the film and radio role of Dr. Christian, 2 June 1956.

Billie Holiday (Eleanora Fagan McKay), 44, blues singer, 17 July 1959.

Buddy Holly, 22, rock 'n' roll musician, in a plane crash, 3 February 1959.

Charles R. Hopkins, 69, theatrical producer, director, and actor, 1 January 1953.

Edna Wallace Hopper, 85(?), actress, star of *Floradora* and other hits of the early 1900s, who prided herself on her perpetual youth, 14 December 1959.

Tom Howard, 69, radio, television, and motion-picture comedian, 27 February 1955.

Rupert Hughes, 84, author and historian (noted for his often-misunderstood biography of George Washington), playwright, screenwriter, and historical novelist, 9 September 1956.

Josephine Hull, 71, actress (*Arsenic and Old Lace, Harvey, The Solid Gold Cadillac*) and 1951 Academy Award winner as supporting actress, 12 March 1957.

Doris Humphrey, 63, dancer and choreographer, winner of the 1954 Capezio award, 29 December 1958.

Walter Huston, 66, stage and motion-picture actor, 7 April 1950.

Rex Ingram, 58, motion-picture director, 21 July 1950.

Charles Edward Ives, 79, composer whose *Third Symphony* won a Pulitzer Prize in 1947, 19 May 1954.

Dr. Herbert Eugene Ives, 71, pioneer in research on television and 3-D movies, 13 November 1953.

Emil Jannings, 63, motion-picture actor, winner of the Motion Picture Academy's first "Oscar," 2 January 1950.

Charles Jehlinger, 86, actor, dean of the American Academy of Dramatic Arts, 29 July 1952.

James Price Johnson, 61, jazz pianist and composer ("Charleston"), 17 November 1955.

Owen McMahon Johnson, 73, novelist (*Stover at Yale*) and playwright, 27 January 1952.

Al Jolson (Asa Yoelson), 67, stage, motion-picture, and radio singer, 23 October 1950.

Margo Jones, 42, Broadway producer and founder of the Theatre in the Round in Dallas, Texas, 24 July 1955.

Robert Edmond Jones, 67, stage designer, noted for his sets for many of Eugene O'Neill's plays and the New York Metropolitan Opera, 26 November 1954.

William Kapell, 31, concert pianist, 29 October 1953.

Guy Bridges Kibbee, 74, motion-picture actor (*Babbitt, Captain Blood, Power of the Press, Scattergood Baines* series), 24 May 1956.

Fiske Kimball, 66, director of the Philadelphia Museum of Art (1925–1955), 14 August 1955.

Erich W. Korngold, 60, Austrian-born composer, winner of an Academy Award in 1936 for the *Anthony Adverse* score and in 1938 for *Adventures of Robin Hood* score, 29 November 1957.

Yasuo Kuniyoshi, 59, Japanese-born American artist, 15 May 1953.

Howard Kyle (Kyle Anderson Vandergrift), 89, actor, 1 December 1950.

Jacquin Leonard ("Jack") Lait, 71, editor of the *New York Mirror* since 1936, playwright, and author (with Lee Mortimer of the *Confidential* series on New York, Chicago, the United States, and so on), 1 April 1954.

Mario Lanza, 38, singer, motion-picture star (*The Great Caruso*), and recording artist ("Be My Love"), 7 October 1959.

Canada Lee (Leonard Lionel Cornelius Canegatao), 45, African-American actor, 9 May 1952.

Lewis C. ("Lew") Lehr, 54, motion-picture comedian, 6 March 1950.

Sinclair Lewis, 65, novelist (*Main Street, Babbitt, Elmer Gantry*), first American winner of the 1930 Nobel Prize for Literature, 10 January 1951.

Ludwig Lewisohn, 72, author (*The Case of Mr. Crump, The Island Within, Mid-Channel*), 31 December 1955.

Elmo Lincoln (Otto E. Linkenhelt), 63, motion-picture actor, the screen's first Tarzan, 27 June 1952.

Stanley Logan, 67, stage and motion-picture actor, producer, and director, 30 January 1953.

Walter H. Long, 70, motion-picture actor, 5 July 1952.

Pauline Lord, 60, actress, 11 October 1950.

Bela Lugosi, 71, stage and motion-picture actor (*Dracula*), 16 August 1956.

Charles G. MacArthur, 60, playwright, screenwriter, and co-author with Ben Hecht of *Front Page* (1928) and other plays, 21 April 1956.

Betty MacDonald, 49, novelist whose *The Egg and I* became a record-breaking best-seller and was made into a film, 7 February 1958.

Edward Madden, 75, songwriter ("By the Light of the Silvery Moon," "Moonlight Bay"), 11 March 1952.

Herman J. Mankiewicz, 55, screenwriter, film producer, and playwright, 5 March 1953.

John Marin, 80, watercolor artist, 1 October 1953.

Julia Marlowe (Sarah Frances Frost), 85, Shakespearean actress, 12 November 1950.

Reginald Marsh, 56, painter who specialized in New York scenes, 3 July 1954.

Riccardo Martin, 77, opera and concert tenor, first American tenor to sing at the New York Metropolitan Opera, 11 August 1952.

Edgar Lee Masters, 81, poet (*Spoon River Anthology*), 5 March 1950.

Louis B. Mayer, 72, Russian-born movie producer (*Ben Hur, Dinner at Eight, Grand Hotel*) and vice-president of M-G-M, 29 October 1957.

Hattie McDaniel, 57, African-American actress, winner of an Academy Award for best supporting actress (1940) for her role in *Gone With the Wind,* starred as Beulah on radio and television, 26 October 1952.

John McNulty, 60, writer of short stories and articles for *New Yorker* and other magazines, 29 July 1956.

Henry Louis Mencken, 75, author, editor, lexicographer, and critic (*The American Language*), 29 January 1956.

Gaetano Merola, 72, founder and director of the San Francisco Opera Company, 30 August 1953.

Edna St. Vincent Millay, 58, poet, Pulitzer Prize winner for poetry in 1923, 19 October 1950.

Hortense Monath, 52, concert pianist, program director for the *New Friends of Music* (1936–1952), 21 May 1956.

Harry Moore, 70, comedian, best known for his role as Kingfish on the "Amos 'n Andy" television show, 13 December 1958.

Polly Moran (Pauline Therese Moran), 78, motion-picture comedienne, 24 January 1952.

Harry Mountfort, 79, actor, playwright, and editor of *Vanity Fair,* 4 June 1950.

Gerald Nailor, 36, Navajo artist whose murals decorate the Interior Building in Washington, D.C., 12 August 1952.

Florence Nash, 60, comedienne, 2 April 1950.

George Jean Nathan, 76, drama critic and magazine editor, 8 April 1958.

Spencer Baird Nichols, 75, muralist and portrait painter, 27 August 1950.

Eugene Gladstone O'Neill, 65, American playwright, 27 November 1953.

Helen Fuller Orton, 82, author of children's books (*Cloverdale Farm*), 16 February 1955.

Charles Fulton Oursler, 59, editor and author (*The Greatest Story Ever Told, The Greatest Book Ever Written*), 24 May 1952.

Oran ("Hot Lips") Page, 46, jazz trumpeter, 5 November 1954.

Frank A. Panella, 75, bandleader, composer of "The Old Gray Mare" and other songs, 10 May 1953.

Brock Pemberton, 64, New York theatrical producer, 11 March 1950.

Ezio Pinza, 64, Italian-born singer, left New York Metropolitan Opera in 1948 for Broadway musicals, died 9 May 1957.

Walter Boughton Pitkin, 74, author (*Life Begins at Forty*), 25 January 1953.

Jackson Pollock, 44, abstract-expressionist painter, 11 August 1956.

Ernest Poole, 69, author and correspondent, winner of the first Pulitzer Prize for fiction (*His Family*, 1918), 10 January 1950.

Tyrone Power, 44, actor of stage and motion pictures, 15 November 1958.

George Palmer Putnam, 63, publisher and author, husband of the late Amelia Earhart, 4 January 1950.

Samuel Putnam, 57, author, critic, and founder-editor of the *New Review*, 15 January 1950.

Marjorie Kinnan Rawlings, 57, novelist (*The Yearling*), winner of the 1939 Pulitzer Prize for literature, 14 December 1953.

Irving Reis, 47, motion-picture director (*The Fourposter, All My Sons*), 3 July 1953.

J. P. Richardson, rock 'n' roll musician, killed in a plane crash, 3 February 1959.

Lynn Riggs, 54, playwright (*Green Grow the Lilacs*, which was adapted as the popular musical *Oklahoma!*), 30 June 1954.

Mary Roberts Rinehart, 82, mystery novelist, 23 September 1958.

Artur Rodzinski, 64, conductor who assembled the New York Philharmonic and directed, among other orchestras, the Cleveland Orchestra and the Chicago Symphony, 27 November 1958.

Sigmund Romberg, 64, composer of musicals and operettas (*The Student Prince, Blossom Time*), 9 November 1951.

Jerry Ross (Jerold Rosenberg), 29, songwriter ("Pajama Game," "Damn Yankees"), 11 November 1955.

Léon Rothier, 76, opera star, a leading bass at the New York Metropolitan Opera (1910–1942), 6 December 1951.

Homer S. Saint-Gaudens, 79, art authority and stage director (*What Every Woman Knows, Beyond the Horizon*), 8 December 1958.

Lawrence Schwab, 57, theatrical producer, 29 May 1951.

Edward Seiler, 40, lyricist ("When the Lights Go On Again All over the World," "I Don't Want to Set the World on Fire"), 1 January 1952.

John J. Sheehan, 66, stage and motion-picture actor, 15 February 1952.

Ruth Shepley, 59, Broadway theatrical star, 15 October 1951.

Harry Sherman, 67, producer of original *Hopalong Cassidy* movies, 25 September 1952.

Robert Emmet Sherwood, 59, playwright and author, 14 November 1955.

Lawrence James Shields, 60, pioneer jazz musician, co-writer of "Tiger Rag," 21 November 1953.

Lee Shubert, 78?, prominent theater owner and producer; Shubert Alley, in New York's theater district, is named for him and his brother; 25 December 1953.

John Sloan, 80, painter, 8 September 1951.

Albert Spalding, 64, violinist, 26 May 1953.

Andrew B. Sterlin, 80, songwriter ("Wait Till the Sun Shines," "Nellie," "When My Baby Smiles at Me," "Meet Me in St. Louis"), 11 August 1955.

Wallace Stevens, 75, poet, winner of the 1955 Pulitzer Prize in poetry, 2 August 1955.

Belle Stoddard (Mrs. Paul M. Johnstone), 81, stage and motion-picture actress, 13 December 1950.

Fred Stone, 85, actor, onetime vaudeville comedian of the team of Montgomery and Stone, best known as creator of the Scarecrow role in *The Wizard of Oz* (1903), 6 March 1959.

Michael Strange (Blanche Marie Louise Oelrichs), 60, author and actress, wife of John Barrymore (1920–1928), 5 November 1950.

Erich von Stroheim, 71, Austrian-born motion-picture actor and director, 12 May 1957.

Austin Strong, 71, playwright (*Seventh Heaven, Three Wise Fools*), 17 September 1952.

Preston Sturges, 60, motion-picture director and producer who won a 1940 Oscar for writing and directing *The Great McGinty*, 6 August 1959.

Norma Talmadge, 60, silent-film actress (*The Dixie Mother, The Battle Cry of Peace, Kiki*), 24 December, 1957.

Art Tatum, 46, jazz pianist, 5 November 1956.

Francis Henry Taylor, 54, director of the Metropolitan Museum of Art in New York (1939–1954) and director of the Worcester Art Museum, 22 November 1957.

Michael Todd (Avrom Hirsch Goldbogen), 50, theatrical and motion-picture producer (*Around the World in 80 Days*), 22 March 1958.

Ridgely Torrence, 75, poet, winner of the Shelley Memorial Award in 1941, 25 December 1950.

Arturo Toscanini, 89, Italian conductor, former music director of La Scala Opera, the New York Metropolitan Opera, the New York Philharmonic Orchestra, the NBC Symphony Orchestra, 16 January 1957.

Lamar Trotti, 54, film-scenario writer and producer (*Wilson, The Ox Bow Incident*), 28 August 1952.

Ritchie Valens, rock 'n' roll musician, in a plane crash, 3 February 1959.

Egbert Van Alstyne, 73, composer of more than five hundred popular songs, 9 July 1951.

Carl Van Doren, 64, literary figure and educator, winner of the 1938 Pulitzer Prize for biography (*Benjamin Franklin*), 18 July 1950.

Albert (Gumm) Von Tilzer, 78, songwriter ("Take Me Out to the Ball Game," "Put Your Arms Around Me Honey," "I'll Be with You in Apple Blossom Time"), 1 October 1956.

Robert Walker, 32, motion-picture star, 28 August 1951.

Edwin Walter, 81, actor who performed over twenty-six hundred times in *Tobacco Road*, 23 November 1953.

Harry M. Warner, 76, motion-picture pioneer and cofounder with his two brothers of Warner Bros. film studio, 25 July 1958.

Percival Wilde, 66, playwright, novelist, 19 September 1953.

Ben Ames Williams, 63, novelist (*House Divided, The Strange Woman*), 4 February 1953.

Frances Williams, 57, musical-comedy actress, blues singer, and dancer who is credited with having introduced the Charleston in the 1920s, 27 January 1959.

Hank Williams, 29, hillbilly singer and composer ("Cold, Cold Heart," "Jambalaya"), 1 January 1953.

Frank H. Wilson, 70, actor (*Porgy, The Green Pastures*) 16 February 1956.

Clement Wood, 62, poet, 26 October 1950.

William E. Woodward, 75, novelist, biographer, and historian, creator of the word *debunk*, 27 September 19

Frank Lloyd Wright, 89, architect, author, teacher, and pioneer in functional and organic architecture, 9 April 1959.

PUBLICATIONS

Leo Lowenthal, *Literature, Popular Culture, and Society* (Englewood Cliffs, N.J.: Prentice-Hall, 1961);

Bernard Rosenberg and David Manning White, eds., *Mass Culture: Popular Arts in America* (Glencoe, Ill.: Free Press, 1957).

Movies

George Bluestone, *Novels into Film* (Berkeley: University of California Press, 1957);

George N. Fenin and William K. Everson, *The Western* (New York: Orion, 1962);

Penelope Houston, *The Contemporary Cinema, 1945–1963* (Baltimore: Penguin, 1963);

Houston, *Introduction to the Art of the Movies* (New York: Noonday Press, 1960);

Siegfried Kracauer, *Theory of Film* (New York: Oxford University Press, 1960);

Film Culture, periodical;

Photoplay, periodical.

Music

Whitney Balliett, *The Sound of Surprise: 46 Pieces on Jazz* (New York: E. P. Dutton, 1959);

Rudi Blesh, *Shining Trumpets: A History of Jazz* second edition (New York: Knopf, 1958);

Steve Chapie, *Rock 'n' Roll is Here to Pay* (Chicago: Nelson-Hall, 1977);

Samuel B. Charters and Leonard Kunstadt, *Jazz: A History of the New York Scene* (Garden City, N.Y.: Doubleday, 1962);

Charters, *Jazz, New Orleans, 1885–1963*. Rev. ed. (New York: Oak, 1963);

Charters and Kunstadt, *The New Edition of the Encyclopedia of Jazz* (New York: Horizon Press, 1960);

Jonathan Eisen, *The Age of Rock: Sounds of the American Cultural Revolution: A Reader* (New York: Random House, 1969);

Colin Escott *Good Rockin' Tonight: Sun Records and the Birth of Rock 'n' Roll* (New York: St. Martin's, 1991).

David Ewan, *The Complete Book of 20th Century Music* (Englewood Clifs, N.J.: Prentice Hall, 1959);

Ewan, *History of Popular Music* (New York: Barnes and Noble, 1961);

Ewan, *The New Book of Modern Composers*, (New York: Knopf, 1961);

Andre Hodeir, *Jazz: Its Evolution and Essence* (New York: Grove Press, 1956);

Orrin Keepnews and Bill Grauer, Jr., *A Pictoral History of Jazz* second revised edition (New York: Crown, 1966);

Neil Leonard, *Jazz and the White Americans: The Acceptance of a New Art Form* (Chicago: University of Chicago Press, 1962);

Alan P. Merriam and Robert J. Benford, *A Bibliography of Jazz* 1954. Reprint. (New York: Da Capo Press, 1970);

Henry Pleasants, *The Agony of Modern* (New York: Simon & Schuster, 1955);

Joseph Machlis, *Introduction to Contemporary Music* (New York: Norton, 1961);

Russell Sanjet, *From Print to Plastic: Publishing and Promoting America's Popular Music 1900–1980* (Brooklyn, N.Y.: Institute for Studies in American Music, 1983);

Gilbert Seldes, *The Public Arts* (New York: Simon and Schuster, 1956);

Country Song Roundup, periodical;

Down Beat, periodical;

Hit Parader, periodical;

Opera News, periodical;

Jazz, periodical.

Literature

Gene Feldman and Max Gartenberg,eds., *The Beat Generation and the Angry Young Men* (New York: Citadel, 1958);

Leslie Fiedler, *An End To Innocence* (Boston: Beacon, 1955);

Anne Lyon Haight, *Banned Books* (New York: Bowker, 1955);

Alfred Kazin, *Bright Book of Life*, (Boston: Little Brown, 1973);

Lawrence Lipton, *The Holy Barbarians* (New York: Messner, 1959);

Frederick Karl, *American Fictions, 1940-1980: A Comprehensive History and Critical Evaluation* (New York: Harper, 1983);

Dan Wakefield, *New York in the Fifties* (Boston: Houghton Miflin/Seymour Lawrence, 1992);

Publishers Weekly, periodical

Art

Frank O'Hara, *Art Chronicles, 1954-1966* (New York: Braziller, 1975);

Serge Guibaut, *How New York Stole the Idea of Modern Art: Abstract Expressionism, Freedom, and the Cold War*, trans. Arthur Goldhammer (Chicago & London: University of Chicago Press, 1983);

Irving Sandler, *The New York School: The Painters and Sculptors of the Fifties* (New York: Harper & Row, 1978);

Artnews, periodical;

Art in America, periodical.

Teenagers dancing on "American Bandstand" 1958

CHAPTER THREE

BUSINESS AND THE ECONOMY

by LARRY SCHWEIKART

CONTENTS

Sidebars and tables are listed in italics.

1950

- The gross national product (GNP) reaches $284.6 billion, up from $100.6 billion in 1940.

- Du Pont introduces Orlon commercially and approves plans to spend $50 million on constuction of research and development facilities.

- The Celler-Kefauver Amendment strengthens the antimerger section of the Clayton Antitrust Act by prohibiting corporate acquisitions that reduce competition.

- The first Xerox copy machine is produced.

11 Jan.– 5 Mar.   The U.S. coal industry suffers from massive strikes.

22 Jan.   Auto inventor Preston Tucker is cleared of securities and fraud charges related to the failure of his attempt to build an innovative automobile.

8–9 Feb.   Government antitrust efforts succeed as major film companies are ordered to separate their production and distribution activities.

29 Mar.   RCA demonstrates the first single electronic color-television tube.

20 June   The housing industry reports housing starts rose 52 percent over the same period in 1949.

June–Sept.   The outbreak of the Korean War sends stock prices tumbling and commodities prices soaring.

25 Aug.   President Harry S Truman orders the U.S. Army to seize and operate the nation's railroads to avert a strike threatened by railroad unions.

1951

- Prices rise with the onset of the Korean War; price controls are put in place on food and critical materials.

- Du Pont introduces Dacron commercially and licenses nylon to other companies under pressure from the government antitrust division.

12 Jan.   President Truman demands higher taxes to put the U.S. military on a "pay-as-you-go basis."

9 Apr.   The Federal Communications Commission (FCC) approves an agreement by American Telephone & Telegraph (AT&T) and Western Union to stay out of each other's communications field.

15 May   AT&T becomes the first American corporation with one million stockholders.

23 June   A Newport News shipbuilding company launches the SS *United States*, the biggest and fastest ocean liner ever built in the United States.

25 June   CBS debuts color television in a one-hour broadcast.

1952

- The U.S. GNP reaches a record $346.1 billion, up from the 1951 total of $328.2 billion.

- General Dynamics Corporation is founded.

4 Mar.	One hundred eighty-six members of the Du Pont family are named in an anti-trust suit for their ownership of controlling interest in General Motors, U.S. Rubber, and E. I. Du Pont de Nemours & Company.
27 Mar.	The Federal Reserve Board votes to dissolve the A. P. Giannini banking empire, headed by Transamerica Corporation, which controls the nation's largest bank, Bank of America.
8 Apr.	President Truman orders Commerce Secretary Charles Sawyer to seize the nation's $7 billion steel industry to avert a walkout of 650,000 steelworkers.
May –25 July	The steel strike ends, but when the U.S. Supreme Court rules Truman's seizure unconstitutional, workers walk out again. A final agreement ends the impasse on 25 July.
23 July	Movie industry box-office totals for 1951 reach $1.6 billion; professional football franchises earn $9 million.
23 Sept.	Howard Hughes sells his controlling stock in RKO Radio Pictures.

1953

- The annual income of an average American family reaches $4,011.
- The first IBM computer, the 701, is introduced.
- The Small Business Administration Act is passed.

12 Mar.	The last price curbs from the Korean War, on coffee, beer, and home-heating oil, are removed.
Mar.	General Motors reports earnings of $558 million for 1952; General Electric tops $151 million; Standard Oil of New Jersey, $518 million.
3 –28 Sept.	The aerospace industry rides a roller coaster as Air Force Secretary Harold E. Talbott announces a cut of 147 Boeing bombers then reverses the government's position to order expanded production of Boeing's B-52s.
26 Nov.	U.S. economic growth continues to soar, rising 5 percent ($368 billion) above 1952 levels.

1954

- The government's share of the GNP reaches 12 percent.
- The silicon transistor is developed.
- Top tax rates rise to 67 percent on incomes of $100,000, up from 16 percent on the same incomes in 1929.
- Swanson Foods introduces the first frozen "TV Dinners."

1 Jan.	Federal income tax rates are reduced, bringing the U.S. out of recession.
9 Mar.	General Motors leads all U.S. companies in income, reporting sales of $10.2 billion.
22 June	The Studebaker and Packard auto manufacturers announce their merger.
8 Aug.	Hilton Hotels purchases 49 percent of Statler Hotels Corporation's stock.

Sept.– Oct.   The recession ends as consumer credit rises for six straight months; personal income also rises.

23 Nov.   General Motors produces its fifty millionth motor vehicle since its formation in 1916

21 Dec.   Eastman-Kodak settles its government antitrust suits, agreeing to sell color film to amateur photographers without first requiring advance charges for processing the negatives.

1955

- Consumer credit reaches an all-time high of $32.5 billion.

- The number of families owning their own homes increases by 6.5 million since 1948.

- The U.S. GNP hits a record annual level equivalent of $392 billion during the July–September period.

- Small corporations earn $1.233 billion before taxes, a $290 million increase over 1954 earnings.

- IBM introduces the first business computer, the 752.

4 Jan.   The Federal Reserve Board raises the required down payment for purchasing stock to 60 percent to dampen speculation.

9 Jan.   The U.S. Atomic Energy Commission invites private companies to submit proposals for construction of private experimental atomic power plants.

13 Jan.   Directors of the Chase National Bank and the Bank of the Manhattan Company announce the merger of their institutions into the nation's second-largest bank.

2 Feb.   The American Federation of Labor (AFL) and the Congress of Industrial Organizations (CIO) agree to merge.

1 Mar.   National City Bank and First National City Bank announce their merger into the nation's third-largest bank.

2–6 May   U.S. steel companies set a one-week record by producing 2.32 million net tons of ingots and casting.

6 –13 June   Ford and General Motors agree to provide unemployment benefits for laid-off workers for up to twenty-six weeks.

1 July   The Civil Aeronautics Board revokes the license of North American Airlines, the largest nonscheduled airline in the United States.

17 July   Disneyland opens.

30 July   Congress raises American workers' minimum wage to one dollar an hour.

14 Oct.   The Commerce Department reports that the U.S. national income rose to an annual record level equivalent of $321 billion in the April – June period; the Securities and Exchange Commission reports U.S. corporations' working assets had risen to $100.6 billion as of 30 June.

1956

- Treasury Secretary George M. Humphrey predicts a U.S. budget surplus of $230 million. The actual surplus comes to $1.754 billion.

- Retail sales total $191 billion, a 3 percent increase over 1955.

- Congress funds the National System of Interstate and Defense Highways, a forty-one-thousand-mile national system of expressways.

20 Mar. The AFL-CIO and Westinghouse settle their labor dispute, ending a 156-day strike at the electric plants.

**4 May –
28 June** The Atomic Energy Commission issues permits to Consolidated Edison to begin construction in Illinois of the nation's first large-scale, privately run atomic power plant.

**30 June –
27 July** The United Steelworkers of America's 650,000 members strike one hundred companies. The strike is settled on 27 July.

4 Nov. Personal income reaches a record annual rate of $330.5 billion.

1957

- Ford introduces its new car, the Edsel, to an unfavorable public response.

- Percent of income received by the top one-fifth of U.S. families falls to a new low (45.3 percent); the middle three-fifths now accounts for 49.9 percent.

20 May The AFL-CIO expels Dave Beck, the president of the International Brotherhood of Teamsters, for misuse of union funds.

25 July William Zeckendorf of Webb & Knapp announces the biggest deal in New York real-estate history, selling 75 percent control of the Chrysler Building and its annex for $66 million.

7 Oct. Farm real-estate value rises 8 percent to a record $112 million over the same period the previous year.

20 Oct. *New York Times Magazine* lists oilman H. L. Hunt of Dallas as the richest American, with a fortune of $400–700 million.

2 Dec. The first full-scale civilian atomic power plant, built by Westinghouse at a cost of $110 million, goes into operation in Shippingport, Pennsylvania.

20 Dec. The jury cannot reach a verdict in the trial of Jimmy Hoffa on charges that he wiretapped Teamster telephones.

1958

- John Kenneth Galbraith's *The Affluent Society* is published.

- By the beginning of the year, fringe benefits for American employees rise from an average of $819 in 1955 to $981.

- Du Pont employs three-tenths as many chemists as are employed in academia.

- The United States enters the sharpest recession since the 1930s.

23 Jan.	President Eisenhower recommends legislation to end labor racketeering.
16 Mar.	Ford produces the company's fifty millionth vehicle.
16 Apr.	The Federal Aid Highway Act of 1958 is signed into law, providing a $1.8 billion increase in federal spending on interstate roads.
30 June	International Ladies Garment Workers Union leader David Dubinsky claims that racketeers control 10 percent of New York's dress industry — down from 25 percent in the 1930s.
16 July	Congress creates the National Aeronautics and Space Administration, ensuring employment opportunities for civilians in the aerospace industry.
25 Nov.	Lloyd's Register of Shipping ranks the U.S. merchant fleet the largest in the world at 25.5 million tons.
27 Dec.	Sales go up and failures go down: department stores report a $10 million sales increase over 1957 levels, and business failures fall over the same period.

1959

- The federal government reports a "modest surplus" of $70 million.

- Unemployment dips to less than 5 percent for the first time since 1957, signaling the end of the recession.

- Corporate income-tax revenues fell in fiscal 1959 by $1.4 billion despite continued higher rates.

- Annual personal income is on a record level ($376 billion).

- Expenditures on goods and services related to the military fall to 10 percent of the GNP (compared to 34 percent in 1945).

- Private pension funds top $44 million (compared to $11 million in 1950).

19 Jan.	President Eisenhower recommends continuation of a 52 percent tax rate on corporate profits.
May	Monthly steel output rises to a record 11.6 million tons. For the first half of 1959 total steel output is at a record 64.2 million tons.
15 July–31 Dec.	The United Steelworkers of America strike twenty-eight companies that produce 90 percent of American steel; the decade ends without a settlement, despite intervention by President Eisenhower.
22 July	The consumer price index reaches a new peak (124 percent of the 1947–1949 average).
29 Sept.	The tobacco industry thrives as 47 percent of all Americans over the age of fourteen smoke.
1 Oct.	Consumer credit rises to a record $47.2 billion.
19 Nov.	Ford announces the end of Edsel production, which has lost the automaker $350 million.

OVERVIEW

Importance of the Economy. By 1950 people generally recognized that the nation's economy — the financial performance of its businesses — affects every American personally. The security of our jobs and how much we earn doing them, the cost of the goods we buy, the price we pay to borrow money, and the interest we get by saving it are all directly related to the health of the economy. During the 1950s the American economy was the strongest in the world.

Biggest in the World. A nation's prosperity is measured by its national income — the value of all the goods and services it produces, also called the gross national product (GNP). By that measure, as by many others, the United States was the unquestioned world leader after World War II. In 1950 the U.S. GNP was $284.6 billion, and by the end of the 1950s it had increased to $482.7 billion. American exports reached all-time highs as they steadily increased during the decade, and the amount by which the value of exports exceeds the value of imports, called the trade surplus by economists, had never been higher in peacetime. People all over the world were willing to buy the products American workers produced; automobiles, electronics, furniture, chemicals, glass, metals — anything bearing a tag that read "Made in the U.S.A." — were respected internationally for their quality and reliability.

Confidence of Business. There was also an undeniable sense of confidence within the business community that almost any problem could be solved quickly, often in cooperation with a federal government that seemed in most respects to be probusiness. Congress imposed price controls on commonly used goods to slow quickly rising costs and passed antitrust regulations to prevent corporate takeovers from strangling competition in the marketplace. When energy shortages were predicted, government and business acted together to harness the atom and exploit natural resources more energetically. With increased government involvement in the business affairs of the nation, however, there was a price to pay — most immediately in the form of higher taxes and often in rising prices, called inflation.

Role of Government. Government did not merely set the rules by which the economy would operate; it became a major participant in the economy as a consumer of goods and services. A healthy corporate sector supplied the government's growing appetite for funds, which it acquired in part by taxes. In 1950 the Internal Revenue Service reported receiving $39.4 billion in tax revenues; by 1959 tax revenues had soared to $79.7 billion. Corporations, which paid taxes at a rate as high as 67 percent during the decade, faced a particularly heavy burden (underscoring the definition of taxing as "burdensome"). With companies such as General Motors reporting high annual earnings ($558 million in 1952), the federal government received unprecedented income.

Labor Unions. Government had to keep labor happy but was afraid to let the unions become corrupt or infested with Communists. During the decade Congress, with the approval of the executive and judicial branches, passed laws to allow management to get rid of Communists in the labor movement. Unions could also not be allowed to become too powerful, lest they shut down critical U.S. industries. President Harry S Truman, therefore, did not hesitate to call in troops in 1952 to run the country's steel mills in the face of a steelworkers-union strike, and President Dwight D. Eisenhower used the same tactic to break a steel strike at the decade's end. As a result, the government's share of the GNP steadily crept upward in the 1950s, beginning in 1954 when its share of the economy (that is, the amount of total labor and capital consumed by the government) passed 12 percent. Under Eisenhower, often viewed as a "small government" president, the total government share of the GNP exploded to exceed 28.7 percent; after that it grew dramatically, reaching more than 33 percent a decade later.

TOPICS IN THE NEWS

ADVERTISING IN THE 1950S

Irrational Buying. During the 1950s American businessmen began to suspect that consumers could not be trusted to know what products they wanted to buy. Makers of everything from cars to catsup regularly lost money when they offered Americans what they said they wanted. A survey revealed that most beer drinkers would prefer a "light, dry" beer; but when questioned further, no one could explain how a "dry" beer would taste. Further, as U.S. companies produced goods in increasing amounts, it was in their interest to stimulate demand — that is, to convince consumers that they wanted (or, better yet, *needed*) products that otherwise would begin stacking up in warehouses. In 1955 the religious magazine *Christianity and Crisis* lamented the pressure on Americans to "consume, consume and consume, whether we need or even desire the products almost forced upon us." That same year advertisers were spending approximately fifty-three dollars per man, woman, and child in the country to hawk products. The key to sales success, advertisers believed, was reaching the irrational side of people that seemed to control their buying habits as much as their rational side did.

The Hidden Persuaders. Vance Packard's 1957 bestseller *The Hidden Persuaders* offered people an eye-opening account of business's use of motivational research (MR) to determine the psychological reasons behind American buying habits. In the marketplace, Packard explained, consumers frequently had to choose among a wide variety of competitors offering essentially the same product. There was little reason to prefer one detergent or brand of peanut butter to another. Motivational researchers — experts in human behavior such as psychologists and sociologists — were consulted to dis-

A psychologist, right, discusses old and new Lipton soup packages with a panel of housewives.

Lucille Ball and Desi Arnaz advertise Philip Morris cigarettes, the sponsor of "I Love Lucy."

offending potential consumers. Writers for the show "Man Against Crime," for example, followed specific guidelines established by the show's sponsor, Camel cigarettes. No criminals could be shown smoking, and the hero could not investigate an arson case because viewers might be reminded of fires caused by cigarettes. When playwright Reginald Rose proposed *Thunder on Sycamore Street* — a script about racial intolerance in an Illinois suburb — to CBS's "Studio One," the network and the show's sponsor approved the script only on the condition that Rose made the black family "something else." Otherwise, southern audiences might be offended. Advertisers generally disliked drama series such as "Studio One" because they presented, as playwright Paddy Chayefsky put it, "the marvelous world of the ordinary"; realistic portrayals of life's problems ran counter to advertisers' commercials, which claimed that all problems had easy answers.

Sources:
Erik Barnouw, *Tube of Plenty*, second revised edition (New York: Oxford University Press, 1990);

Vance Packard, *The Hidden Persuaders* (New York: McKay, 1957).

cover hidden sources of appeal that advertisers could exploit. On the advice of MR experts companies redesigned packages to take into consideration the psychological effects of color; and they changed their advertising to include appeals to such powerful subconscious motivators as sexual desire, the fear of death, and the need for security. Packard quoted one advertising executive: "The cosmetic manufacturers are not selling lanolin, they are selling hope. . . . We no longer buy oranges, we buy vitality. We do not just buy an auto, we buy prestige."

A New Medium. The sophisticated research into the psychology of consumers was only one indication of American business's emphasis on advertising during the decade. Another was the amount of money advertisers spent. Annual spending on advertising rose from $5.7 billion in 1950 to nearly $12 billion in 1960. Much of this increase was due to the discovery of the advertising potential of television. By 1960 advertisers could use television commercials to reach almost 90 percent of American homes. Companies spent more of their advertising dollars on the new medium each year of the decade, and by 1955 it was already business's preferred promotional tool. Advertisers benefited from endorsements by television celebrities, from Ronald Reagan for General Electric to Howdy Doody for Wonder Bread. Companies also sponsored entire series, with the company name featured prominently in the show's title — "Ford Star Jubilee," "Kraft Television Theatre," and the "Lux Show Starring Rosemary Clooney," for example. By the end of the decade advertisers had a stranglehold on American television. Out of every ten minutes of broadcasting, two were devoted to advertising.

No Offense. Sponsors also exerted considerable influence over the content of programming, out of fear of

THE AFL-CIO

A Year of Change. Events in 1952 had profound effects on the American Federation of Labor (AFL) and the Congress of Industrial Organizations (CIO), the country's two large federations of labor unions, which together represented 14.5 million of American workers. The election of President Eisenhower in November of that year brought an end to twenty years of Democratic, prolabor control of the national government. Within a

---

THE AMERICAN WORKER IN THE 1950S

Most Americans had moved off of the farm by 1950. Nonagricultural workers, numbering almost 52 million, constituted 83 percent of the workforce. Manufacturing led the nonfarm employers, with more than 15 million laborers. Wholesale and retail trade exceeded 9 million to hold second place. Average earnings in manufacturing in 1957 climbed above $2 per hour, almost double the 1945 level. The average family income reached $5,976 by the end of the decade. Worker productivity rose 48 percent between 1950 and 1960. More women than ever worked, with 23.2 million in the labor force in 1960. The number of married women in the workforce also increased by 2 million.

Source: U.S. Department of Commerce, *Historical Statistics of the United States* (Washington, D.C.: GPO, 1975).

George Meany, left, of the American Federation of Labor, clasps hands with Walter Reuther of the Congress of Industrial Organizations at the AFL-CIO merger convention on 5 December 1955.

month labor also experienced a change in leadership when the longtime leaders of both the AFL and the CIO died. The AFL's secretary-treasurer, George Meany, became its president, and United Auto Workers president Walter Reuther was elected head of the CIO.

An End to Rivalry. Meany and Reuther almost immediately began discussions on merging the two federations. Doing so would mean overcoming the long-standing and sometimes bitter rivalry between industrial unions (CIO) and craft unions (AFL), which had prompted eleven unions to split from the AFL and form the CIO in 1935. In the changing political climate of 1953, however, the rivalry began to seem less important than working together to protect labor's interests. "There's too much effort wasted in competition between unions," Meany said in an interview six days after his election.

Unity. Although many in labor thought the union was desirable, it was not going to be easy. "Raiding" — when a CIO union attempted to steal membership from an AFL union, or vice versa — had created some bad feelings between the two federations. Jurisdictional disputes between local chapters of AFL and CIO unions had complicated matters further. Reuther was concerned that the AFL, the larger and more conservative of the two unions, would dominate the merger. To resolve the various conflicts, a unity committee, made up of leaders from both federations, was formed in April 1953. Over two years the committee drafted the charter of the AFL-CIO. Raiding was forbidden; jurisdictional disputes would be settled fairly; the tradition of autonomy — each affiliate union controlling its own internal affairs — was maintained; and craft workers and industrial workers were recognized as equally important to American industry. At the AFL-CIO's first convention, in December 1955, Meany was elected president and Reuther vice-president.

Cleaning House. One of the chief priorities of the new federation was to rid itself of corrupt elements. The leaders of several AFL unions — most notably the powerful International Brotherhood of Teamsters, the trucking union — had well-publicized relationships with known criminals and lived luxuriously off of stolen union funds. Their improprieties threatened to tarnish the reputation of organized labor in general. In a break from the tradition of autonomy, an AFL-CIO ethics committee adopted a set of guidelines for union officials in 1956; unions whose officers were corrupt could be expelled from the federation. When the Senate's McClellan committee began its investigation of labor racketeering in 1957, the AFL-CIO cooperated fully. Based on the committee's revelations of corruption within the Teamsters union, the federation first suspended Teamsters president Dave Beck and then voted at its 1957 convention to expel the trucking union completely. The decision was not a painless one: losing the Teamsters cost the federation almost two million members.

A Significant Defeat. The AFL-CIO's attempts to police itself were not enough to satisfy labor's congressional opponents. A coalition of Republicans and conservative southern Democrats passed the Landrum-Griffin Act over the federation's objections in April 1959. The act was designed not only to eliminate labor corruption but also to place new restrictions on organizing and picketing. The federation protested that labor's enemies had taken the opportunity to weaken all unions, honest as well as crooked. Passage of the Landrum-Griffin Act was a significant political defeat for the AFL-CIO, the worst for labor since the Taft-Hartley Act of 1947.

New-Membership Drives. Nor did the federation make the membership gains it had hoped for. At the first AFL-CIO convention Reuther had set a goal of doubling the federation's membership in ten years. Labor leaders hoped that a united federation could support stronger organizing drives in the South, for example, which was traditionally antiunion, and among white-collar workers. But by the end of its first decade the AFL-CIO's membership had actually declined, from 15 million in 1955 to 13.5 million in 1964. Although the expulsion of the Teamsters accounted for much of the loss, industrial unions were also losing membership as workers migrated to the less unionized "sun belt."

Sources:
Arthur J. Goldberg, *AFL-CIO: Labor United* (New York: McGraw-Hill, 1956);

Archie Robinson, *George Meany and His Times: A Biography* (New York: Simon & Schuster, 1981).

AIR TRAVEL IN THE 1950S

Coach Class. In the 1950s the American aviation industry grew dramatically. Airline companies had gradually adopted the technological improvements of World War II for their civilian planes, and commercial air travel became faster and more comfortable. It also became cheaper as new planes accommodating more people were introduced. Airlines began to offer "air coach class" seating, priced to compete with railroad's "coach" business. By paying coach fares, passengers could fly almost anywhere in the country for about one hundred dollars, one-third less than airfares of the late 1940s. "For the first time the ordinary man began to fly with us," observed Juan Trippe, longtime head of Pan American. By 1955 more Americans were traveling by air than by railroad.

Traffic Jams in the Sky. So many ordinary people began to fly that the industry had to struggle to serve them. Boardings more than doubled from 17.3 million in 1950 to 38 million in 1958. The nation's airports had to expand to accommodate heavy air traffic: ports built to handle hundreds of passengers were faced with thousands, even tens of thousands. With the crush of passengers, waiting became an unpleasant fact of air travel — waiting for baggage, in traffic on the congested roads to the airport, and in the air. A foggy day in New York City, 14 September 1954, became known as "Black Wednesday" after some three hundred airliners were stacked in holding patterns over the city, waiting to land one by one. The airborne traffic jam delayed forty-five thousand passengers by as much as twenty-four hours.

JET LAG

Unexpectedly, Americans discovered that rapid transit across several time zones took a physical toll on them. Air travelers often complained of physical and mental exhaustion for days after a long flight. In 1958 researchers at the University of Minnesota attributed this malady to the temporary disruption of the body's "circadian rhythms" — fluctuations in heart rate, temperature, and other bodily processes that correspond to the cycle of day and night. Since a plane flight from one time zone to another distorted the length of its passengers' day, it also threw their metabolisms out of whack. During the 1960s this phenomenon came to be called "jet lag."

Source: "Travels of the Jet-Age Traveler," *Popular Science*, 172 (May 1958): 93.

Disaster. With the number of aircraft in the skies growing from 960 in 1950 to 1,647 in 1959, new safety regulations were needed. The first major airline to install radar aboard its fleet was United, in 1955. Without radar pilots had only a general idea of the location of their planes in relation to the others around them. In good weather they relied on eye contact to avoid each other, but commercial airliners flew far too fast for pilots to avoid collisions that way. On 30 June 1956 the deadliest air disaster to that date occurred when a TWA liner collided with a United DC-7 over the Grand Canyon, killing 128. The federal government responded by requiring that all air traffic be monitored by radar at all times; and Congress passed the Federal Aviation Act of 1958, which created the Federal Aviation Administration (FAA) to oversee all matters of air safety.

The Race to Europe. Though some thirty commercial domestic airlines operated during the decade, four major carriers — United, American, Trans World Airways (TWA), and Eastern (which merged with Colonial in 1956) — divided most of the passenger traffic. A fifth airline, Delta, started to make a move to join the front-runners, and Pan American held many of the U.S. overseas routes. Each airline tried to gain competitive advantage over the others by flying passengers farther, faster, and cheaper than the rest. In 1953 TWA scored a coup by offering the first nonstop air service from New York to California. After that the race was to cross the Atlantic nonstop. In the early 1950s TWA advertised the "fastest trips to Europe," but its planes still had to stop to refuel. In 1957 Pan Am introduced the first true transatlantic liner, the DC-7C, and regained the lead in transatlantic service from TWA.

Miraculous Flights. Transcontinental and transatlantic flights offered Americans what seemed to be nearly miraculous opportunities to travel to distant places quickly. Passengers regularly flew across the country in hours and across oceans in less than a day. Thanks to the development of the pressurized cabin during the decade, planes could also fly at higher altitudes, offering travelers a smooth flight. Still, mass-transit flying offered fewer of the luxuries that air passengers had enjoyed before the war. Seats were packed closely together to increase capacity, so that passengers had little room for their knees and elbows. Dinners were served on longer flights, but airlines were still a decade from producing enjoyable meals. Bernard DeVoto wrote in 1956 that he preferred the sandwiches airlines used to serve: "They ran an excellent lunch counter in those days; they run a poor restaurant now. I have seldom had even a mediocre meal at it; most are definitely bad." There was some solace for uncomfortable passengers, however: airlines began serving in-flight cocktails during the 1950s.

Source:
Carl Solberg, *Conquest of the Skies: A History of Commercial Aviation in America* (Boston: Little, Brown, 1979).

ALCOA, ALUMINUM, AND THE END OF A MONOPOLY

Government Creates Competition. The production of commercial aluminum was a twentieth-century industry. A natural oxide found in bauxite mined directly from the earth's crust, aluminum was made by running an electric current through molten bauxite to remove ferric ore and silica. The metal was lightweight and highly tensile, a strong, cheap alternative to steel. For the first half of the century aluminum production was monopolized by Alcoa (Aluminum Company of America). During World War II, however, the government's enormous demand for aluminum exceeded Alcoa's ability to produce it. To make up for the shortfall, the government encouraged smaller competitors such as Reynolds Metals and Kaiser Aluminum and Chemical to increase their output; it also funded new production facilities, which Alcoa built and operated. After the war, in 1946, the government's War Surplus Properties Board, under the supervision of Stuart Symington, sold its plants to Alcoa's competitors, specifically to break the company's monopoly and create a competitive situation.

Alcoa Expands. Spurred by the Korean War, the aluminum oligopoly thrived. Despite the presence of new competition, Alcoa found itself hardly worse for wear: between 1946 and 1958 the company's gross revenues grew threefold, to $869 million. Net income reached a high of $89.6 million in 1958 — more than 10 percent of gross sales. By 1958 Alcoa had four times the production capability that it had in 1939. Even after a drop in aluminum prices, the company still made strong profits. It was able to expand its production into other light metals and building materials. Alcoa even sponsored television series, such as "See It Now," which ran from 1951 to 1955. On a September 1954 broadcast of the series host Edward R. Murrow made his famous denunciation of Communist-witch-hunter Sen. Joseph R. McCarthy. Much of Alcoa's success during the decade could be attributed to Irving "Chief" Wilson (whom the American public called "Mr. Aluminum"), a shrewd businessman with a knack for public relations. But the company also benefited from the presence on its board of R. K. "General" Mellon of the powerful Pittsburgh Mellon family.

The "Splendid Retreat." By 1960 Alcoa turned out 853 million short tons of aluminum per year, 34.6 percent of the U.S. total. Reynolds followed with 701 million tons, and Kaiser produced 609 million tons. All of the production by rival companies had been made possible by Alcoa's "splendid retreat" (as *Fortune* magazine called it in October 1955) from monopoly status, showing that competition enriched everyone, even the former monopolist.

Sources:

Aluminum Company of America, *Aluminum on the Skyline* (Pittsburgh, 1953);

George David Smith, *From Monopoly to Competition* (Cambridge: Cambridge University Press, 1988).

BANK OF AMERICA LEADS A FINANCIAL EXPANSION

Branching Out. In the 1950s America's banking structure remained regulated at two levels, federal and state. The states retained the authority to permit a bank to open additional offices, or "branches," but in 1960 most states still had restrictions against branch banking. Few states had unfettered branch laws, and no banks could branch across state lines. Led by such giants as the Bank of America in California, branching expanded in the Southwest and South. States such as Arizona, with tiny amounts of capital compared to other states, could boast several banks in the top one hundred in the nation in terms of size and one in the top thirty. Yet unit banking still remained the norm. In 1960 the number of banks exceeded branches (13,472 to 10,472), the last decade that such a relationship would exist.

A GOOD NIGHT'S SLEEP

When Tennessee architect-builder Kemmons Wilson took his family on vacations across the country, he always had the same complaints: the motels were dirty, the rooms were too small, children were charged the same as adults, there was not enough bathroom space, and so on. He decided to do something about it: he would open his own motel chain. First, however, Wilson took his family on a cross-country trip, staying at dozens of motels, taking meticulous notes on room dimensions, service quality, conveniences at the front desks and rooms, and, of course, price.

Upon his return, Wilson determined from his research the "optimal" room for a family of four — size, facilities, and "extras." Most significantly, he decided that children would stay free in his motel. In 1954 Wilson opened the first Holiday Inn of America outside Memphis. By 1962 there were 280 of the green and gold motels in thirty-five states — thirty thousand rooms all based on Wilson's design. Some Holiday Inns, such as those in cold regions such as Alexandria, Minnesota, featured the "Holidome," which enclosed the pool and game area for use in any weather. Others adhered to theme motifs. Interviewed in the 1970s on a special "Merv Griffin Show" on "Self-Made Millionaires," Wilson pointed out that money had never been a concern when he started his motels. Rather, he wanted to provide America with a place where a person could get a good night's sleep and families would not be penalized for bringing their kids on vacation.

Source: Kemmons Wilson, *The Holiday Inn Story* (New York: Newcomen Society of North America, 1968).

B of A Growth. Aided by branch banking, the Bank of America became the nation's largest bank, with 534 branches in 1954. "B of A," as it was called, achieved that position with a merger among four of its top eastern rivals (Chase National Bank, Bank of the Manhattan Company, First National Bank, and National City Bank). California's diversified economy provided fertile investment fields for Bank of America to exploit through branches. When a particular sector suffered from a depression, the bank could shore it up with funds from other sectors doing better. Branches in every city brought a flood of deposits to B of A and ensured loyal customers who remembered the bank when it came time to borrow. A. P. Giannini, who built Bank of America in the 1920s, focused his entire banking strategy on the small depositor. He frequently loaned to farmers whom others rejected. When Kaiser-Frazer auto company made its foray into auto manufacturing, B of A gave it some of its largest loans.

Level Playing Field. The rise of trust companies, holding companies, insurance funds, and other financial intermediaries concerned commercial bankers, who saw those institutions as immune to the tight federal and state regulations under which the bankers operated. Multibank holding companies purchased new banks in communities, circumventing antibranch banking laws. Other holding companies simply had one bank and several unrelated businesses. Competition from "nonbank banks" led the American Bankers Association to lobby for an "equal playing field," resulting in the Bank Holding Company Act of 1956. That law forced banks to choose between banking and other businesses. It restricted multibank holding companies from engaging in unrelated activities. However, it did not act on the one-bank holding companies that had other activities. Those institutions proliferated in the 1960s.

Prosperity. For all their complaining, bankers had a good decade. Although the number of commercial banks had fallen from 15,076 in 1940 to 14,676 in 1950, the number of branches had grown. In 1957 the nation's banks had 8,000 branches; by 1965 the number was 16,000. By 1960, although the number of banks had shrunk to 14,019, assets had risen by $103 billion to $282 billion.

Sources:

Marquis James, *Biography of a Bank* (New York: Harper, 1954);

Moira Johnston, *Roller Coaster: The Bank of America and the Future of American Banking* (New York: Ticknor & Fields, 1990).

BIG VS. SMALL BUSINESSES

Land of the Giants. Clearly big business reigned supreme in the United States. In 1951 AT&T became the first American corporation to have one million stockholders. In 1957 the largest real-estate deal in U.S. history, a $66 million sale of William Zeckendorf's share of the Chrysler Building, occurred. Chemical giant DuPont employed more than one-third as many chemists as all of academia. Large corporations made their share of crucial technological breakthroughs: IBM introduced new computers; NBC and CBS pioneered color television broadcasts; and airlines introduced jet aircraft service.

Small Successes. Despite the dominance of big business in American industry (General Motors was the largest company in the world, Bank of America the largest financial institution), the 1950s also witnessed a boom in small businesses, many of which became well known. Companies such as Baskin-Robbins Ice Cream, McDonald's, Church's Fried Chicken, Stouffer's Frozen Food, Oscar Meyer, Culligan, Gerber Baby Foods, Bic, TRW, and Holiday Inn all started, made significant business surges, or introduced product breakthroughs during the 1950s. Other small businesses verged on tremendous technological successes, from Bill Lear's small, six- to eight-seat private jet to the introduction of the silicon chip by numerous small computer companies. The Small Business Administration was established in 1953, reflecting the growing political clout of small-business owners.

CREATING THE COMPUTER

The "Automatic Calculator." Americans of the 1950s witnessed the dawn of the information age. During the decade the computer developed from its earliest models — hundreds of square feet of flashing neon bulbs, dials,

Kemmons Wilson, founder of Holiday Inn, at the Holiday Inn headquarters in Memphis, Tennessee

The IBM 702, the first IBM computer for business users, on display in 1955 at IBM headquarters in New York City

cables, and clicking switches — to relatively small units that were widely affordable by the academic and business communities. In 1950 there were twenty computers in the United States, with a total worth of one million dollars. No two of these machines were the same; they were all refinements of the ENIAC (Electronic Numerical Integrator and Computer), the first real computer, which had been developed by scientists at the University of Pennsylvania for the government during World War II. The "automatic calculator," which weighed thirty tons and occupied eighteen hundred square feet, was first demonstrated to the public in 1946.

Early Successors. As the first electronic machine that could solve mathematical problems quickly, ENIAC was a marvel of the time. The scientists who created the computer were aware of its flaws, however, and immediately began work on a better machine. Reprogramming the huge computer was a complicated process of changing dial settings and rewiring cables. What the ENIAC lacked was stored memory, that is, the ability to save and retrieve previous instructions or calculations. In the late 1940s several different groups of researchers offered new computers, each one a slight improvement over ENIAC: EDVAC (Electronic Discrete Variable Automatic Computer), BINAC (Binary Automatic Computer), and, from England, the Mark I and Mark II. In these years the development of computers split into two branches: business machines, which processed great volumes of data and could provide great volumes of output; and scientific machines, which completed long, complex calculations with only small amounts of data. The business machines came to dominate the computer market — scientific computers evolved into pocket calculators. Early customers for the machines included the U.S. Census Bureau, several large insurance companies, and Northrop Aircraft. The early machines were built on commission, at a cost to the customer of between $100,000 and $150,000.

UNIVAC. In 1951 ENIAC's original designers — now working for Remington-Rand, an office-supply company — debuted UNIVAC I, the best computer yet. UNIVAC was one-tenth the size of ENIAC, much easier to program, and capable of storing information on magnetic tape. It became the first computer to capture widespread public attention when the CBS television network used it during coverage of the 1952 presidential election. Based on the data it was given, UNIVAC contradicted the political experts and predicted a landslide Republican victory. At first UNIVAC's operators were skeptical and tried to manipulate its program to get it to change its answer. As the election results came in, however, it was clear that UNIVAC had performed well: with only 7 percent of the votes tallied, the computer had predicted that Eisenhower would win 438 electoral votes. He actually won 442.

A Giant Enters the Market. Unfortunately for Remington-Rand, the success of UNIVAC awakened a sleeping giant. IBM, the leader in the office-equipment field, had hesitated to enter the computer market because the company's president, Thomas Watson, Sr., did not anticipate a future in the machines. His son Thomas, Jr., did, though; and when the younger Watson succeeded his father as IBM's president in 1952, he pushed the company into the competition. In 1953–1954 IBM introduced the 700 series — the 701 and 702, which were soon followed by their successors, the 704 and 705. The 700-series machines were technologically inferior to UNIVAC, but IBM's excellent sales force stole the market from the poorly run Remington-Rand.

IBM and the Seven Dwarfs. Within five years of its entrance into the market IBM was selling more than half of the computers in America. By 1957 people were describing the industry as "IBM and the Seven Dwarfs." Remington-Rand (now called Sperry Rand) was the first of the dwarfs, a distant second to IBM with 10 percent of the market. Several of the dwarfs, such as General Electric and RCA, were considerably larger than IBM but only dabbled in making computers. Other dwarfs made superior machines by utilizing smaller, more stable transistors instead of vacuum tubes to run the machines. But IBM, its sales, service, and marketing staffs second to none, continued to dominate at the end of the decade.

Sources:

William Rodgers, *Think: A Biography of the Watsons and IBM* (New York: Stein & Day, 1969);

Joel N. Shurkin, *Engines of the Mind: A History of the Computer* (New York: Norton, 1984).

Signs advertising the availability of charge accounts and financing, and encouraging customers to buy on credit

CREDIT, INFLATION, AND PRICE CONTROLS

"Buying on Time." During the 1950s "buying on time" — paying for a large purchase in monthly installments — became acceptable as a regular practice, not just in time of need. Americans used credit to purchase new cars, electronic equipment, household goods, and appliances at a record pace. (Of course, age generally determined whether you were a borrower or a saver: people forty years old or older saved far more and borrowed less than younger people.) During the 1920s, the last time consumers had any real purchasing power, banks were reluctant to grant personal loans for consumer spending. But the late 1940s saw a sharp increase in the number of new families, many of whom were furnishing their new households. Banks recognized a large pool of potential loan customers and encouraged consumers to finance their auto purchases. By 1956 nearly 20 percent of the nation's commercial bank loans were to individual consumers. Banks profited by collecting interest on the loans, between 6 and 12 percent annually. By 1960 consumer loans had risen to more than $47 billion.

"Horsemeat Harry." The increase in money circulating in the economy due to the credit boom, higher em-

ployment and rising wages, and increasing consumer spending brought with it inflation. In August 1952 the government reported that retail food prices had soared to 235.1 percent of the 1935–1939 average. Inflated prices on such items as meat brought genuine hardship: by the late 1940s some housewives had substituted horse meat at meals for beef and chicken due to its lower cost; but they did not like it. During the 1948 presidential campaign disgruntled consumers referred to President Truman as "Horsemeat Harry." With the onset of the Korean War in June 1950, the government's determination to control inflation increased, and price ceilings were established for war goods and many necessities. The Federal Reserve Board boosted bank reserve requirements in 1951 to slow banking's newfound enthusiasm for consumer lending. Banks passed along their higher expenses to borrowers, and interest rates rose accordingly.

An End to Price Controls. Though inflation continued to afflict the economy — food prices rose 15 percent between June 1950 and August 1952 — price controls were lifted completely by March 1953. Truman's successor, President Eisenhower, wanted to retain "stand-by" powers to freeze wages and prices and requested authority to extend rent controls. A recession in 1953–1954, however, slowed the pace of rising prices. Afterward the nation started a long period of prosperity accompanied by only moderate price increases.

In 1950 the Diners Club in New York pioneered a charge card for meals, heralding the arrival of "plastic money," a credit account that the user paid off, with interest, at the end of each month. Eight years later American Express Company developed a card used for goods and services at member establishments across the country, again with the provision that the borrower pay the total balance monthly.

The Bank of America pioneered the first true domestic "revolving" credit card used nationally when it introduced the BankAmericard in 1959. The "revolving" concept meant that the card's user could make a minimum monthly payment and the balance would "revolve" to the next month's bill, with interest. Partly due to the large number of depositors at Bank of America and the fact that it was the nation's largest bank at the time, its credit card soared in popularity. In 1966 Bank of America created its own service corporation to handle the BankAmericard franchisees. To appeal to a national and international consumer base in 1977 the name of the card was changed to VISA.

Source: "Not So Clubby: Diners' Club," *Newsweek*, 53 (19 January 1959): 66+.

ENERGY

A Reliance on Oil. Aside from the relatively new atomic energy, the United States relied on crude oil (in refined form) to run its automobiles, to produce electricity in power plants, and for lubricants. Oil use exceeded that of coal or natural gas. In 1953 the United States imported more oil than it exported for the first time. Congress attempted to protect domestic producers of oil with a quota system on imports, initiated in 1959.

The Appliance Boom. Electrical-energy production stood at 329 billion kilowatts in 1950, 232 percent more than the 142 billion in 1940, with the cost per kilowatt steadily declining. Soon after the end of World War II a vast array of new electrical devices made its way into households, including dishwashers, freezers, dryers, vacuum cleaners, ranges and ovens, and refrigerators. The availability of smaller items such as vacuum cleaners increased through door-to-door sales, and larger items benefited from another institution to emerge in the 1950s, the shopping mall. When combined with the new eagerness of banks to lend money for such items, an electric-appliance boom ensued, and with it a demand for more electricity. Production increased to meet the demand: by 1959 the United States generated 798 billion kilowatts.

Political power followed consumer demand: in 1953 the National Association of Electric Companies was the best-funded lobbying organization in the United States, with a $268,000 budget, ahead of the Association of American Railroads and even the U.S. Chamber of Commerce.

Energy from Atoms. Americans and the rest of the world had already been convinced that nuclear fission could generate enormous, and destructive, amounts of energy. But by the 1950s many individuals in government and business expected that atomic power could be adapted to peaceful, private industrial uses as well. They focused at first on producing electricity from atomic reactors. In 1956 the Atomic Energy Commission issued permits for construction of the first large-scale, privately run atomic-power plants to Consolidated Edison, which planned to build a $55 million plant capable of generating 140,000 kilowatts when running at full capacity in Indian Point, New York, and Commonwealth Edison of Chicago, which proposed a plant with a capacity of 180,000 kilowatts in Dresden, Illinois. Atomic energy was already being used to generate electricity at the Argonne National Laboratory, indicating its feasibility as a peacetime power source. The first peacetime plant to produce commercial power was at Shippingport, Pennsylvania, in 1957.

The "Atomic Airplane." Experiments with other uses of atomic power included the short-lived "Atomic Airplane," a project assigned to Lockheed Aircraft in 1956. Researchers reasoned that they could place an atomic reactor in an airplane frame. But the weight of reactors at the time proved prohibitive, and by the 1960s the Department of Defense had given up on the idea.

Sources:
Ronald Clark, *The Greatest Power on Earth: The Story of Nuclear Fission* (London: Sidgwick & Jackson, 1980);

William Laurence, *Men and Atoms: The Discovery, the Uses, and the Future of Atomic Energy* (New York: Simon & Schuster, 1959).

FARMING IN THE 1950S

"Agri-businessmen." American farmers continued to dwindle in number during the decade. In 1950 the farm population of 23 million stood at slightly more than 15 percent of the total population. Ten years later only 15.6 million farmers remained, constituting 8.7 percent of the total population. The American farmers of the 1950s did not necessarily resemble the gentleman farmers of Thomas Jefferson's day: they had become specialized and mechanized "agri-businessmen."

Leaps in Production. Despite the decline in the number of farmers, gross income from farming rose steadily from $32.3 billion in 1950 to $38.1 billion a decade later. Still, the cost of living increased faster than farm income. Between 1950 and 1960 total farm output rose 23 percent. Farm output per man-hour soared, increasing 157 percent during the decade. The staggering leaps in pro-

A self-propelled harvester-thresher

ductivity, coming at a time when European markets still needed U.S. food imports, were made possible by two primary factors, increased mechanization and the use of fertilizers and pesticides. Mechanical power and machinery use climbed by more than 15 percent, while fertilizer use rose by almost 70 percent. Farmers in 1950 made use of 3.3 million tractors, 2.2 million motortrucks, 714,000 grain combines, and 456,000 corn pickers. Ten years later they used 4.6 million tractors, 2.8 million trucks, 1 million grain combines, and 792,000 corn pickers. The advantages of such technological improvements were clear: for example, the installation of a "herringbone" milking machine enabled dairy farmers to milk sixty cows in an hour — a much more time-consuming and tiring job by hand.

Drops in Income. Because of equipment purchases, however, expenses for farmers rose faster than prices for farm goods. As a result, in the 1950s net farm income actually sagged, even though the farmers had increased their output per acre by more than 27 percent.

Sources:

Stewart Holbrook, *Machines of Plenty: Pioneering in American Agriculture* (New York: Macmillan, 1955);

Robert Howard, *The Vanishing Land* (New York: Villard, 1985).

HOUSING IN THE 1950S

New Families. At the end of World War II, soldiers returned home, took brides, and started families. These new families needed housing. With wartime controls lifted, consumer and mortgage lending rose. Using Veterans Administration (VA) and Federal Home Administration (FHA) loans, banks could insure their loans to qualified home buyers through the federal government: if the home buyer defaulted the government paid off the loan. Banks in the West, in particular, used huge savings pools accumulated by eastern insurance companies to fund new loans. By 1953 the number of Americans owning their own homes climbed to twenty-five million, up from eighteen million in 1948. Throughout the decade Congress provided greater opportunities for individuals to buy homes by lowering the down payments on FHA-insured loans and increasing the limit on purchases from other agencies or investment groups by the Federal National Mortgage Association on the second-mortgage market.

Housing Boom. The boom in home construction, especially in the newly developing West, came through a unique set of circumstances. Cheap water, made available by government water projects and dams, made land inexpensive to develop. At the same time, eastern sources of investment funds, particularly insurance companies and savings banks, suddenly had no outlet for their mortgage loans. As small a mortgage lender as the Arizona-based A. B. Robbs Trust Company (which could barely scrape together the $100,000 net worth the FHA required to make FHA-approved loans) quickly amassed $30 million worth of mortgages it processed each month. Whereas few eastern banks or savings and loans took the lead on FHA mortgages, the West had always recognized the value of such instruments: in the 1930s tiny Valley National Bank of Arizona was the eleventh largest FHA lender in the United States.

Expansion in the West. Growth in the housing market in Phoenix and Los Angeles reflected the West's expansion in general. Between 1954 and 1960 housing in Phoenix rose by five thousand single-unit dwellings — in 1958 Arizona ranked eleventh in the nation in new home starts, with sixteen thousand — while Los Angeles witnessed a sharp rise in the number of multiunit houses (an increase of thirty-three thousand between 1954 and 1959). California's savings and loans and its insurance companies accounted for most of the new residential lending by 1951, the banks already having been eclipsed. But the ultimate source of funds was the FHA guarantee that stood behind the loans: in 1951, 23 percent of the $677 million FHA and VA mortgages bought nationwide were linked to properties in the Golden State.

Rent Control. If FHA and VA loans allowed more Americans to own their own homes, large numbers still rented. In large cities rising rents for high-demand apartments led many policy makers to implement rent controls. As a result, a growing portion of the U.S. population lived in housing covered by federal rent control (19.8 million people, or 12 percent of the U.S. population as of July 1952). Although that marked a decline from the 1949 level (some 23 million), rent control had become a way of life in large cities. In eastern urban centers especially, rent control made it cheaper to rent than to own, and development in the East was stifled. The debate had

A tract-housing development in California, 1955

shifted from whether rent control was a proper policy to how far rent control should be implemented. Few saw the truly damaging aspects of rent control (as the cause of urban abandonment, for example) until the 1960s, by which time the entrenched special interests that benefited from rent control could outvote opponents systematically.

Sources:

Kenneth T. Jackson, *Crabgrass Frontier: The Suburbanization of America* (New York: Oxford University Press, 1985);

Gwendolyn Wright, *Building the Dream: A Social History of Housing in America* (New York: Pantheon, 1981).

LABOR IN THE 1950S

Labor Asserts Itself. American workers never had it so good as in the years after World War II. The postwar boom created a demand for consumer items of all sorts, from appliances to autos. Organized labor, which had gained power during the Great Depression, had consolidated its gains during the war. Yet by 1946 many unions felt that the nation owed their members for the sacrifices they had made during the war. Wages, for example, had been frozen. Postwar inflation cut into workers' paychecks for the first time in twenty years. Consequently, as the recession of 1948–1949 ended, labor was poised to reassert its interests.

New Benefits. The decade started well for the unions. Strikes of the coal industry and the Chrysler company's automotive plants led to the adoption of company-financed pension plans and health insurance. Such benefits soon became standards of American business. In May of that year a wage settlement between General Motors and the United Auto Workers also had a significant effect on industry. The GM contract entitled employees to pay raises based on increases in the cost of living and technological improvements which raised profits. Other unions were quick to work this wage system (called an "escalator arrangement") into their own negotiations. By the end of 1950 more than two million U.S. workers benefited from the GM wage formula.

The Strike. Labor's most potent weapon, of course, was the threat of strike, and unions throughout the decade did not hesitate to walk out. Strikes affected airlines, railroads, automakers, and, perhaps most dramatically, the steel industry. When the steelworkers union threatened to walk out in early 1952, during the Korean War, President Truman responded by "nationalizing" the industry, ordering the Department of Commerce to seize and operate the country's steel mills. Such an action was necessary, Truman claimed, because of the importance of steel production to the war effort. In May of that year, however, the U.S. Supreme Court ruled that Truman had exceeded his legal authority. Workers returned to their strike, reaching a settlement with management in July.

The Weapon Backfires. Strikes sometimes worked against the unions, however; the steel strike is one example: to many Americans the steelworkers seemed to be selfishly undermining the war effort. Union leadership also lost some of its authority in the face of the "wildcat" strikes such as the one that paralyzed the nation's coal mines in January 1950. Dissatisfied with the concessions granted to the mine owners by United Mine Workers (UMW) president John L. Lewis, 70,000 members of the union struck in protest. Ultimately the strike involved 370,000 miners who defied the orders of both Lewis and President Truman that they return to work. In early

An effigy of Teamsters president Dave Beck burning in protest of his alleged corruption

March, only after Lewis had signed a contract more acceptable to the miners, did they return to work. The strikes had slashed U.S. coal output by one-third compared to 1948 levels and left Americans wondering who was running the unions.

Left-Wingers and Criminals. Some suspected that organized labor was dominated by left-wingers and criminals. Early in the decade unions worked hard to distance themselves from any Communist associations. In 1949–1950 the Congress of Industrial Organizations (CIO) expelled eleven member unions, including the fifty-thousand-member Fur and Leather Workers Association and the ten-thousand-member American Communications Association, for their alleged Communist sympathies. Other member unions, such as the United Furniture Workers, conducted their own purges of left-wingers rather than face expulsion from the CIO.

Purges. Even after the war and the peak of McCarthyism, when the threat posed by subversives began to seem less urgent, the government kept pressure on the unions to get rid of suspected Communist elements. In 1955, for example, the Justice Department asked the Subversive Activities Control Board to declare the one-hundred-thousand-member United Electrical, Radio and Machine Workers a "Communist-infiltrated" union. Unions knew that if they did not act the government would, as it did in November 1956 when it charged fourteen officials of the International Union of Mine, Mill and Smelter Workers with fraud regarding their Communist activities.

Corruption among the Leadership. A more legitimate and persistent danger to the integrity of organized labor was corruption among its leadership. Thanks to highly publicized cases of fraud, graft, and associations with mobsters, union officials were frequently viewed with distrust by the American public and the workers they were "elected" (often under suspicious circumstances) to represent. In 1952 the American Federation of Labor (AFL) created a special ethics committee to clean out racketeers in the union. Two years later the AFL expelled the International Longshoreman's Association for refusing to rid itself of known criminal elements.

Too Little, Too Late. As far as the government was concerned, it was too little, too late. In 1957 the Senate Select Committee on Irregular Activities in the Labor-Management Field was formed to investigate labor corruption. The committee was better known as the McClellan committee, after its chairman, Arkansas senator John L. McClellan; the committee's chief counsel was Robert Kennedy, future U.S. attorney general and brother of John F. Kennedy. The McClellan committee was ostensibly concerned with all labor unions, but most of its time and energy was spent exposing the corrupt Teamsters' leadership, President Dave Beck and Vice-president Jimmy Hoffa. The improprieties of these and a few other labor leaders hurt the reputation of organized labor in general. As a result, by the end of the decade the country's unions were faced with stern new regulations governing their behavior.

Racketeer Johnny Dioguardi, better known as Johnny Dio, was a good example of the criminal element organized labor wanted to flush from its ranks during the decade. In 1952 his name came up in connection with International Ladies Garment Workers Union manager Sam Berger, who helped Dio get a charter to organize a local chapter of the American Federation of Labor's United Auto Workers (UAW). Dio then set up "paper," or fake, locals in New York City for the UAW and a variety of other unions. These locals had no actual membership, but as their official representative Dio could extort money from businesses with the threat of pickets and labor violence. Dio also helped corrupt labor leaders stay in power by lending them support from these phantom locals during union elections. At least seven of Dio's "locals" were chapters of the International Brotherhood of Teamsters, obtained from Teamsters vice-president Jimmy Hoffa. Hoffa was the union leader with whom Dio was most closely associated: when labor reporter Victor Riesel was blinded by an unknown assailant, it was believed (but never proven) that Dio planned the attack in order to curry favor with the powerful Teamster.

Dio continued his criminal activities until a conviction on bribery and conspiracy charges in 1957. By that time Hoffa stood next in line for the presidency of the Teamsters union, and Dio's knowledge of the union's activities potentially stood in Hoffa's way. The Senate Committee on Improper Activities in Labor-Management Relations (the McClellan committee) got Dio paroled from jail to testify. Dio, however, was an uncooperative witness, invoking the Fifth Amendment 146 times in refusing to answer questions. "It cannot be said . . . ," reported the committee, "that John Dioguardi was ever interested in bettering the lot of the working man." On 15 August 1957, a federal grand jury in New York indicted Dio on tax evasion charges. Hoffa, despite his illicit connections with the mobster, went on to assume the presidency of the Teamsters union, thanks in part to the support of paper locals such as the ones he had granted Dio.

Source: "Kindly Racketer," *Newsweek*, 50 (26 August 1957): 33.

Sources:
James R. Green, *The World of the Worker: Labor in Twentieth-Century America* (New York: Hill & Wang, 1980);

Archie Robinson, *George Meany and His Times* (New York: Simon & Schuster, 1981).

THE MERGER WAVE

If You Can't Beat 'em. American businesses merged with increasing frequency in the 1950s. By 1955, the year that marked the crest of this "merger wave," combinations ran at three times their 1949 rate. In 1955 Chase National Bank and Bank of the Manhattan Company merged to create Chase-Manhattan, the second largest bank in the nation, and First National City Bank, the nation's third largest, was formed from the union of National City Bank and First National City Bank. Within a few months in 1955 Remington-Rand merged with Sperry Corporation to form Sperry Rand; Childs Food Stores (Piggly Wiggly) was purchased by the Kroger Company; Neiman-Marcus of Dallas merged with Wolfman, Inc., of Houston; Stromberg-Carlson merged with General Dynamics; and Brown Shoe Company and G. R. Kinney Company announced a merger. Most of these combinations represented attempts by companies to expand their production or to increase their market share, as when Hilton Hotels gobbled up numerous other hotel companies over the course of the decade. Other mergers, such as Kaiser-Frazer with Willys-Overland, represented attempts by sick companies to get well, usually with unsuccessful results.

The Celler-Kefauver Act. Such business activity was closely scrutinized by the federal government throughout the 1950s. With the passage of the Celler-Kefauver Act in 1950, Congress gave the Federal Trade Commission (FTC) broad powers to block attempts by business to dominate a market or control prices. Thus Hilton Hotels found some of its attempts to acquire hotels rejected. Likewise, in August 1952 the FTC accused five U.S. oil companies of establishing a cartel to control the price of oil. Included were Standard Oil Company of New Jersey and Texas & Gulf. Along with Royal Dutch-Shell and the British-owned Anglo-Iranian Oil Company, those companies controlled 65 percent of the estimated world crude reserves by 1949.

Vertical Combinations. The government looked not only at businesses combining in similar operations (called "horizontal combinations") but also at "vertical combinations" — attempts by businesses to control a single product through all phases of its production and distribution. For example, in 1950 motion-picture manufacturers were forced to give up control of the theater chains they also owned. Similarly, in 1954 a flurry of antitrust suits made Eastman-Kodak cease their practice of requiring amateur photographers to pay for film developing before the company would sell them film.

Trust-Busting. Many in business felt abused by the government's trust-busting activities. In 1956 the Senate Commerce Committee heard testimony that the Columbia Broadcasting System (CBS) and the National Broadcasting Company (NBC) had profited unfairly from their "economic stranglehold" on the television-broadcast industry. (The two giants and their affiliate stations received 46 percent of the industry's income in 1954.) NBC president David Sarnoff scoffed at the notion: his company lost money five of its first nine years. Such cases convinced business leaders and some scholars and policy makers that the antitrust laws needed revision.

The Conglomerate Wave. By the end of the decade a new type of merger also appeared, in which unrelated companies joined in an organizational structure called a conglomerate. The conglomerate wave continued into the 1960s. A typical early conglomerate originated when Jimmy Ling of Dallas started an electrical-contracting business, then purchased other electrical-contracting companies, then finally positioned the company to buy, in 1960, the Temco Company, a producer of military aircraft and missiles. That same year he made his first overtures to purchase Chance-Vought Corporation, an aircraft manufacturer, although he did not complete that merger, which created Ling-Temco-Vought (LTV), until 1961.

THE MILITARY-INDUSTRIAL COMPLEX

No Profit in Peacetime. Cold-war politics dictated that the United States maintain a standing army, navy, and air force equipped with modern weapons. But no profit existed in making weapons during peacetime — even the purchases of the U.S. military proved too small to support many of the major defense companies. Manufacturers anticipated and planned for peacetime lulls in their production, but ultimately the government had to support defense contractors with constant new orders or subsidize them directly with cash payments. Reasoning that it never hurt to have state-of-the-art equipment, the government pursued the policy of continually developing and deploying new weapons systems. This policy also kept most of the major manufacturers' production lines primed in case of emergency. Near the end of his presidency, in 1961, Eisenhower cautioned Americans about the growth of this new sector of the economy, which he called the "military-industrial complex."

Missiles. Aircraft manufacturers such as Convair, Lockheed, and North American Aviation that were able to make the transition to missile production in the 1950s found a solid, if somewhat erratic, profit in defending the nation. In 1955 North American correctly anticipated significant gains in missile work and restructured into three divisions in order to meet the government's needs: Rocketdyne produced engines; Aeromatics produced guidance systems; and Atoms International produced warheads. Between 1956 and 1961 Convair's missile sales almost tripled, and Lockheed's nearly doubled. Aerospace manufacturers drew half their earnings from missiles and other defense-related production by the end of the decade.

The Gun Belt. This "defense boom" directly benefited the southwestern states and California, where most of the defense plants were located. Secluded desert areas and proximity to the Pacific Ocean made possible secret, safe testing of missiles and aircraft. The plants were also near such government research facilities as Edwards Air Force Base, the Western Development Division of the Air Research and Development Command, and the Ames Test Center. Clearly Texas, California, and the states between them — dubbed the "gun belt" — provided the most advantageous locations for defense contractors. East-coast aircraft manufacturers such as Grumman, Fairchild, and Curtiss-Wright were unable to keep up. Led by the growth of the defense industry, political and economic clout shifted somewhat by the end of the decade, from the Northeast to the South and Southwest.

Civilian Industry Benefits. The military-industrial complex also benefited nondefense industries by provid-

THE RISE OF TRW

Military interservice rivalries had much to do with the shift of defense business from the frost belt to the sun belt. The U.S. Air Force, freed from army control by the late 1940s, was the beneficiary of the Strategic Missiles Evaluation Committee (the "Teapot Committee"), which in 1954 recommended a six-year crash program for R&D in ballistic missiles. It proposed that the air force lead the new effort, based on the West Coast at Western Development Division (WDD), which was created in 1954 and located in Inglewood (Los Angeles).

Meanwhile two engineers in the Howard Hughes aircraft organization, Simon Ramo and Dean Wooldridge, had built up a huge scientific and engineering organization within Hughes. At one time they oversaw the work of four hundred scientists. Ramo and Wooldridge left the Hughes operation in 1953, joining with a Cleveland aircraft-engine firm called Thompson Products. They were given the green light to form a new California-based company "to apply creative science and technology both to military and nonmilitary applications." Although only Ramo, Wooldridge, and two other employees opened the business during its first days, the company had 220 contracts and thousands of subcontractors. In 1958 Thompson merged with Remo-Wooldridge to form TRW, which produced everything from engine parts to famous racing pistons. But the primary defense work went to California.

Source: "Teamwork Across 2,000 Miles," *Business Week* (29 November 1958): 52+.

---

later the secretary of the air force announced a cut of 147 B-52s produced by Boeing, then suddenly reversed himself to order expanded production of the bomber. In 1953 Congress suggested that contractors and the armed forces conspired to pad the Defense Department's budget. A House government operations subcommittee headed by Rep. R. Walter Riehlman (R-New York) demanded that the military punish those responsible for spending $3 million on "useless" navy forklifts, $45 million for "unsuitable" army overcoats, and $1 million for unnecessary air-force chain-link fences. The subcommittee demanded that Secretary of Defense Charles E. Wilson explain his plan to end "costly and wasteful" service loyalties and correct other "deficiencies" harming the purchase and distribution of supplies. Appropriately or not, however, the government continued to spend growing amounts on defense: by the end of the decade defense spending stood at $46.4 billion, a 38 percent increase over 1949 levels.

Sources:

Roger W. Lotchin, *Fortress California, 1910–1961: From Warfare to Welfare* (New York: Oxford University Press, 1992);

Ann R. Markusen, *The Rise of the Gunbelt: The Military Remapping of Industrial America* (New York: Oxford University Press, 1991).

THE NATIONAL HIGHWAY ACT AND THE AUTO INDUSTRY

New Highways. By the 1950s Americans had made a firm commitment to private cars over public mass transportation such as buses and trains, even though it meant higher personal expense, traffic jams, and occasional frustrations. The dominance of the transportation field by the automobile and trucking industries was assured when Congress passed the National Highway Act in 1958. America already had 1.68 million miles of surfaced road in 1950 — up from 1.34 million in 1940 — but the highway act promised a significant improvement over even those paved roads by funding the building of wider, safer, more-modern four- to eight-lane freeways. Justified as a defense measure to speed the transport of troops in an emergency, the new freeways benefited the average American, who could shave days off cross-country auto trips by avoiding the "backroads." Also as a result, once-legendary highways such as Route 66 were virtually abandoned in favor of the new freeways.

American Independence. Although frequently criticized as extravagant or wasteful, transportation by private autos gave Americans an independence that no other nation had. Drivers enjoyed greater safety and comfort than they could expect on subways or buses. For Americans their private means of transportation was part of their lives: in 1950 there was one passenger car for every 3.75 Americans, representing ownership of some forty million cars by 60 percent of the households in the United States.

A Profitable Decade. For Detroit's automakers, the National Highway Act proved a final topping to an already profitable decade. U.S. auto production in 1950

---

ing the basis for tremendous amounts of research and development (R&D) in the decade. Scholars still debate whether the computer or the jet passenger aircraft would have appeared when it did, without military R&D or subsidies. Inarguably, however, technology that had been designed for the military was also found to have civilian applications. The complex also benefited academic research: in 1956 Lockheed transferred its missile research division to Stanford University and built new labs at Palo Alto for military R&D.

A Strained Relationship. But the tight relationship between business and the military was still occasionally strained. In 1950, for example, the Defense Department's weapons-system-evaluation panels cleared the Convair B-36 bomber of charges that it was inadequate to U.S. needs, keeping intact an order for more than 60 of the bombers and saving hundreds of Convair jobs. Two years

A cloverleaf interstate-highway intersection

rose 1.4 million over 1949 totals to reach 6.7 million. As production increased, however, the number of competitors shrank. Down from hundreds of automakers before World War II, the industry was dominated by the "Big Three" — General Motors, Ford, and Chrysler — with a handful of other competitors hanging on by their nails, including Kaiser-Frazer, Nash, Hudson, Studebaker, and Willys-Overland. Preston Tucker's attempt to produce the "Tucker Torpedo," a departure from the offerings of the big automakers, ended when he went bankrupt in 1949. (Tucker died seven years later after being acquitted on charges of fraud.)

Growing Through Merger. Some of the smaller companies reacted by attempting to grow through merger. Nash and Hudson merged in 1954, then were absorbed by Chrysler. Kaiser-Frazer merged with Willys-Overland too late to save the merged company from bankruptcy. Packard and Studebaker's merger ended when Packard made its last car in 1958 and Studebaker produced its last auto in 1963.

The "Big Three." Even among the Big Three some companies were weaker than others: Chrysler's plants were old and could not keep up after the war. The automaker sank further into debt until it needed a government bailout in 1979 to return to health. Ford, which emerged as the second-leading automaker in 1952, found that to raise capital it had to sell its shares to the public beginning in 1955. It stayed healthy by offering new models, such as the Thunderbird, introduced in 1954,

which boosted its "youth" image (later continued with the introduction of the Mustang). General Motors by far was the giant, holding over 50 percent of the market by the mid 1950s. Chevrolet alone, by 1960, offered forty-six models, thirty-two engines, twenty transmissions, twenty-one colors, and more than four hundred accessories. American autos dominated the world market by the 1960s, even though storm clouds were on the horizon.

Sources:

James J. Flink, *The Car Culture* (Cambridge: MIT Press, 1975);

John B. Rae, *The American Automobile: A Brief History* (Chicago & London: University of Chicago Press, 1965).

THE RAILROAD AND ITS DECLINE

All But Obsolete. Due to the increasing popularity of air, auto, and truck transportation, the railroad industry during the 1950s became all but obsolete as a competitive form of passenger transportation. The railroads had to make massive new investments to keep up with its competition. By 1955 estimates placed the needed improvements at $3.3 billion, for twenty-one thousand new diesel locomotives alone. Track, rolling stock, and other capital improvements would be extra. That year the Interstate Commerce Commission chairman predicted the end of railroad passenger service without the help of increased government subsidies.

Congress Steps In. Shortly thereafter the famous B&O (Baltimore and Ohio) Railroad requested permission from the state public-service commissions of Maryland and New York to discontinue all service on its Baltimore–New York City run due to that route's "enormous deficit." State governments had the ability to force railroads to maintain a certain passenger route, no matter if the route lost money for its owners. Congress attempted to help the railroads by passing the Transportation Act of 1958, which gave the Interstate Commerce Commission the authority to approve discontinuation of passenger routes. As a result, many railroads gutted their passenger services by the end of the decade.

A Few Improvements. Railroads did make some improvements during the 1950s, however. During the decade trailers on flatcars (or TOFCs) were introduced, and although they were little used at first, they proved a boon during the oil crisis of the early 1970s. But positive signs were few and far between. Dining cars, by 1959, had lost $29 million. Total passengers carried by rail had fallen from 897 million in 1945 to only 413 million in 1957. The trucking industry made tremendous gains.

Sources:

George B. Abdill, *This Was Railroading* (Seattle: Superior, 1958);

George H. Douglas, *All Aboard!: The Railroad in American Life* (New York: Paragon House, 1992).

SHOPPING MALLS

The Largest in the Country. During the decade retailers discovered that while America's cities were growing, their stores were not necessarily gaining new customers. Cities expanded mostly outward, away from their traditional downtown shopping and business districts. Rex Allison, the manager of a Bon Marche department store in Seattle, Washington, used an aerial photographic map in 1946 to determine that a suburban branch of the store would be within twelve minutes' driving time from

WHAT IT COST TO RIDE THE RAILS

Eastern railroad fares on coach class rose significantly. If a passenger rode the train from New York westward in 1941, $18.50 would have taken him to Chicago. By 1950 the same fare would have gotten him only as far as Youngstown, Ohio. A first-class passenger on eastern routes would have paid 3.3 cents a mile in 1946, but by 1950 he would have paid 4.5 cents. A seventeen-hour coach trip on a railroad cost more than an express bus trip ($15), a nonscheduled airplane trip of four hours ($26), and almost as much as a scheduled air coach trip ($34).

Source: "Dying Passenger Train," *U.S. News and World Report*, 45 (3 October 1958): 36–39.

275,000 Seattle consumers who spent $500 million yearly. Allison proposed to Allied Stores Corporation, the owner of Bon Marche, that the company build a shopping mall, with Bon Marche as its cornerstone. In May 1950 Seattle's Northgate Mall, at the time the largest in the country, opened for business.

The Appeal of the Malls. Across the country retailers were making similar decisions. The new malls had obvious appeal for both shoppers and merchants. Parking was abundant and usually free, and shoppers could go from store to store without moving the car or worrying about the weather. Security was less of a problem for the owner of the enclosed stores, and smaller-store owners benefited from their association with more-prestigious department stores. By 1956 the United States had sixteen hundred shopping malls, six hundred of which opened that year. Mall owners were not content until they relieved their customers of the need to go anywhere else. Grocery stores, movie theaters, and restaurants were added. Northgate Mall was equipped with an office building in which it leased space to doctors and dentists. Malls even became community meeting places, hosting Christmas programs, Easter-egg hunts, and exhibits.

Strip Malls. The poor cousin to the larger mall was the "strip mall," which featured a row of connected stores but no enclosed walkway space. Strip malls were easier to construct than larger malls, but they had higher rates of failure because of the unpredictability of their business tenants. Low-cost jewelry, auto parts, and even adult bookstores might rent space. Strip malls became a common feature of the suburban landscape, but they never gained the prestige of the enclosed mall. As much as any other factor, the success of these malls sealed the doom of "downtown" as the shopping center for suburbanites.

Source:

William Kowinski, *The Malling of America: An Inside Look at the Great Consumer Paradise* (New York: Morrow, 1985).

THE STOCK MARKET AND INVESTMENT TRENDS

New Types of Investment. Stock prices rose during the 1950s. In 1954 the market passed a milestone of sorts, finally eclipsing the 1929 Dow Jones high of 381.17. Part of the growth occurred due to a new type of investment, the mutual fund, which made its appearance during the decade. Mutual funds expanded to 2.5 million shareholders by 1960. Mutual funds were mixtures of many different stocks managed by a brokerage firm or mutual-fund firm. For a small sum an investor could purchase a small "piece" of General Motors, IBM, Coca-Cola, or any of dozens of other companies. The flexibility of the fund reduced risk and encouraged small investors to get back into the market. Direct stock ownership remained in the hands of a small minority, however, as only 8 percent of Americans owned stock in 1955.

Aerial view of the Roosevelt Field Shopping Center on Long Island, New York

Massive Pools of Money. The rise of huge insurance companies, with their massive pools of money (assets of $56 billion by 1948), brought on another change in the capital markets. Insurance companies found they could subscribe to an entire issue of a security from the borrowing corporation in direct competition with investment bankers. That gave the insurance companies considerable influence in the business decisions of companies. Banks increasingly found their share of the investment market shrinking. By 1955 banks' share of the assets held by financial intermediaries fell to just half that held by insurance companies, savings-and-loan associations, and mutual savings banks. Meanwhile, pension funds, insurance companies, foundations, mutual funds, trusts, and other nonbank money pools, which held $9.5 billion in securities in 1949, started a dramatic expansion that by 1960 topped $70.5 billion. During the decade nonbank institutional holdings rose from 12.5 percent at the beginning of the decade to 20 percent of all equities by the end.

THE SUN BELT

The Frost Belt Peaks. The 1950s marked the peak of the northern-midwestern industrial axis as an economic power. In 1950 the midwestern, middle Atlantic, and New England regions combined to add 67.7 percent of the total value added to manufacturing. With only 8 percent of the nation's land area, the Northeast alone had 43 percent of the U.S. population and 68 percent of the manufacturing employment. Two of the three largest

banks in America were located in New York. The dense population of the Northeast gave it political power to match its economic clout: the Frost Belt (as the manufacturing belt was alternately called) carried 286 electoral votes in the presidential election of 1960, compared to 245 for the increasingly important Sun Belt.

Defense Leads the Way. The *Sun Belt* was the term used to describe the southern one-third of the United States, stretching from the southeastern states across to the Pacific coast, as far to the north as San Francisco. The migration of American business from the Frost Belt to the Sun Belt was led by defense industries. The open spaces and milder climate of the Southwest, in particular, provided the ideal environment in which to test missiles and aircraft. At the start of the Korean War, New York and Michigan accounted for 30 percent of prime defense contracts, but by 1962 California alone claimed almost 24 percent. Michigan's defense contracts had by then plummeted to less than 3 percent of the national total.

Missiles for Profit. The government's 1954 decision to commit to a national defense based on missiles prompted the geographic shift. Many of the nation's leading experts in the field had trained or taught in California schools. Researchers from Pasadena's California Institute of Technology, in fact, had been the first to confirm that a hydrogen bomb could fit into the nose cone of an ICBM (intercontinental ballistic missile), thus proving that nuclear missiles were feasible. With the military as their principal — sometimes their only — cus-

Research and development (R&D), a virtually ignored aspect of American entrepreneurship the turn of the century, became in the 1950s a critical element in American business's quest to offer new and higher-quality products at lower prices. By 1953, the first year national statistics were kept, total national R&D expenditures, of which the federal govenment supplied 53.7 percent, exceeded $8.7 billion. By 1960 national investment in R&D topped $19.6 billion; the federal government's share, 64.6 percent, had fallen sightly from its 1950s high of 65.1 percent.

Funding for basic research, an important component of all R&D, passed the $440-million mark in 1953. Industry put up $153 million, with universities and colleges kicking in $10 million. By 1960 total expenditures on basic research had reached $1.1 billion. At that time, colleges and universities had increased their contributions sevenfold, while industry had only doubled its investment.

Aerospace technology constituted a key area of research investment for industry in the 1950s: in 1950 American business spent $169 million on aerospace R&D, and in 1953, $576.5 million. After 1953, however, industry's contribution to aerospace R&D tailed off, until it stood at $478 million in 1960. That decline reflected the huge investment in aerospace R&D by the federal government, $2.4 billion by 1960, more than double its 1950 level of investment.

Source: U.S Department of Commerce, *Historical Statistics of the United States* (Washington, D.C.: GPO, 1975).

tomer, California companies continued to prosper and innovate, benefiting from their proximity to government facilities such as the RAND (Research and Development) Corporation, a military "think tank" established in Santa Monica in the mid 1940s, and Edwards Air Force Base.

The Clean Industries. The Sun Belt's position as the country's technological innovator tended to reinforce itself. Highly skilled white-collar workers left traditional northern industrial centers to take part in the technology "boom." Their expertise, in turn, led to further new developments. Possibly the most significant advance of the decade was the integrated circuit: the delicate silicon chips on which the circuits were built could be damaged by moisture in more-humid climates. Soon, such "clean" industries — industries which produced no pollution

during the manufacturing process — were further adding to the West Coast's prosperity.

Heavy Industry Migrates. Heavy industry also discovered the Sun Belt in the 1950s, although the shift was not as definitive as in defense contracting. The auto and steel industries were in their heyday during the decade, and virtually all of their factories were located in the Frost Belt. Du Pont, which pioneered Orlon and Dacron in the 1950s and initiated a revolution in textiles, also kept manufacturing thriving in the North. Increasingly, however, lower tax rates, antiunion attitudes, and a lower cost of living lured industry to choose locations in the South. A good example of southern manufacturing was John Fontaine's Truck Equipment Company in Birmingham, Alabama, which reported sales in 1958 of $2.75 million of its heavy-duty trailers and its patented "fifth wheels," the doughnut-shaped devices that attached semitrailers to the trucks.

Source:
Ann R. Markusen, *The Rise of the Gunbelt: The Military Remapping of Industrial America* (New York: Oxford University Press, 1991).

THE TELEVISION INDUSTRY

Two Thriving Industries. The "television industry" actually comprised two industries: one that manufactured television receiver sets, and one that manufactured the shows that people watched. Both of these industries developed quickly in the years after World War II, and both were thriving by the middle of the 1950s. The percentage of American homes with television sets rose dramatically throughout the decade, from slightly less than 20 percent in 1950 to nearly 90 percent in 1960. By then few aspects of American life remained untouched by the new medium.

A Long Infancy. Industry pioneers such as Sarnoff, president of the Radio Corporation of America (RCA), had waited several decades to offer television for mass consumption. Sarnoff had followed research on the broadcast of images since the mid 1920s. By the late 1930s several companies, including RCA, were broadcasting experimentally in large urban areas. In 1940 there were twenty-three stations in the country, offering limited schedules of sports, filmed stage plays, old cartoons, and government documentaries. That year RCA planned its first large-scale test of the medium, building twenty-five thousand sets for sale in New York City to receive broadcasts from RCA's transmitter in the Empire State Building. The Federal Communications Commission (FCC) gave approval for the test but then reversed itself, and RCA was suffered a substantial financial loss. In May 1940 President Franklin D. Roosevelt declared a state of national emergency as the United States edged toward entry into World War II. Further development of television took a backseat to military production.

Rival Networks. After the war ended production on television sets began in earnest. The "Model T" of televi-

Since Emmitt J. Culligan began his water softener firm in 1924 in Saint Paul, Minnesota, the company had suffered through long and expensive lawsuits and through the Great Depression, when no one wanted the two-hundred-to-four-hundred-dollar softener apparatus. The distraught entrepreneur took a job with National Aluminate Corporation in Illinois. There he found an answer to the problem of high cost: do not sell the softener, sell the service. When Culligan started his new, service-oriented business in 1936, he installed the water softening machines at no cost to customers who paid two dollars a month as a user fee. Under a "no deposit, no obligation" arrangement, customers could cancel the service at any time. By 1938 he started to franchise outside Illinois, and within ten years the Culligan dealer network serviced six hundred thousand subscribers at an average monthly fee of $2.75 to $3.00.

The 1950s brought another major hurdle, though. A change in consumer attitudes led to hesitation on the part of housewives to let Culligan dealers into their homes. The Culligan network had relied on in-home sales; but the "traveling salesman" was becoming obsolete. Culligan developed a successful advertising campaign in 1959, designed by Dassas Williams Productions of Los Angeles. The ads had a female voice call "Hey Culligan Man!" and suddenly the hostility toward home demonstrations by the Culligan dealers evaporated. Thanks in large part to the ad campaign, the Culligan company's sales had risen to $11.2 million by 1961.

sions, the RCA Victor, received a ten-inch, black-and-white image and sold for $375 in 1946. By 1950 the Sears, Roebuck catalogue offered Silvertone receivers for less than $150. Most families who owned sets lived in or near "television cities," such as New York or Los Angeles, where several different broadcasters were in operation. The National Broadcasting Company (a subsidiary of RCA) and the Columbia Broadcasting System, which had been rival radio networks, now competed in the television market. CBS and NBC each offered a nightly schedule of variety shows, comedy series, and drama series produced by the network.

The Industry's Structure. The network structure of television was established early. Broadcasters around the country applied to the FCC to be assigned a frequency, or channel, in their area. Approved stations then affiliated with companies such as NBC, agreeing to broadcast programs produced by the network in return for a share of the profits the networks made selling airtime to advertisers. Stations also produced their own local programming and sold time to local advertisers. But as competition in each television market grew, affiliates broadcast a greater share of the networks' more popular and profitable programming.

"Television Cities." In the years 1948 to 1952 television made its way into more and more American homes, from 6 to 42 percent of the nation's total. Television sets were bought as quickly as they were produced. Broadcasting was not yet available in all parts of the country, however. In 1948 the FCC froze the number of licensed stations at 108 until some of the medium's technical difficulties were resolved. The freeze was originally supposed to last six to nine months, but, because of general production restrictions on the industry during the Korean War, it remained in effect until the war ended in 1952. During this time "television cities" had full television service, but other large cities — Portland, Oregon, for example, or Little Rock, Arkansas — had no television at all. Where television was available, sets sold briskly, an average of 410,000 a month. Social observers who contrasted the television and nontelevision cities sensed that American life would soon change dramatically. In 1951 television cities experienced a 20 to 40 percent drop in movie attendance; in nontelevision cities attendance stayed the same or climbed. Attendance at sporting events declined in television cities, as did business in restaurants and nightclubs. Public libraries lost circulation, and bookstores reported falling sales.

UHF versus VHF. The freeze kept down competition in the developing industry. Most areas were served by one or two stations, and CBS and NBC dominated them. Only thirty-three areas were assigned three or more stations by the FCC, and only seven areas received four or more assignments. In this atmosphere companies such as Mutual and Philco abandoned plans to operate networks, and two smaller networks, the American Broadcasting Company (ABC) and the DuMont Network, struggled to hang on. One way to increase competition was to allow stations to broadcast on ultra-high frequencies (UHF) as well as very high frequencies (VHF), increasing every market's number of potential channels from 12 to more than 80. The FCC debated the merits of UHF and VHF during the freeze and in 1952 assigned 1,319 UHF channels as well as 276 additional VHF channels. Practically, however, UHF-stations were at a disadvantage. Since most television sets only received VHF signals (channels 2–13), UHF-station owners had a hard time convincing networks or advertisers that anyone was watching. Between 1952 and 1956 the FCC received and approved applications for only 363 of the 1,319 available UHF assignments. Of those, 151 never went on the air, and 56 went bankrupt. In 1961, with the passage of a federal law requiring that all new television sets be able to receive

UHF channels, the survival of UHF operators was finally assured.

Educational Television. Hoping that television would be used in the public interest as well as for profit, the FCC reserved some UHF channels for noncommercial, educational programming. Those stations faced even greater financial difficulties than commercial UHF operators. Much of their programming came from a production center called National Educational Television (NET), which made programs for distribution around the country. NET was founded in 1952 with a grant from the Ford Foundation. Even with the support of NET, noncommercial stations struggled. One such station on the VHF waveband, KQED (channel 9) in San Francisco, raised funds by holding an on-the-air auction in 1955. Other educational channels around the country tried KQED's idea, with some success.

The Birth of Color. Meanwhile CBS and NBC/RCA continued to compete for control of the commercial television industry. (ABC, through a fortunate merger with the United Paramount Theatres movie-house chain, found the capital it needed to survive its lean years. DuMont was not as lucky: the network ceased operations in 1955.) Controversy between the two industry leaders over color-television broadcasting began in 1946. That year CBS president William Paley introduced a successful color system; but the color set could not receive black-and-white broadcasts. Sarnoff ordered RCA's technicians to produce a "compatible" set in six months. Almost four years later RCA researchers finally demonstrated a usable system. In the meantime the FCC had ruled that the CBS color system should be the industry standard, a decision that was upheld by the Supreme Court in May 1951. Undaunted, RCA continued to refine its system.

RCA's Triumph. In 1953 the National Television System Committee (NTSC), a group of experts from all segments of the industry, endorsed the RCA system and petitioned the FCC to reverse itself. By that time even CBS executives did not seriously object to the committee's conclusions. Over half of all American homes had black-and-white sets; families could hardly be expected to own two televisions, one of which could only be used to watch the occasional color broadcast. The FCC accepted the NTSC's recommendation and approved the RCA color system as the industry standard in December 1953.

Expensive Sets. The first color-television receivers, offered to the public in 1954, were expensive: between nine hundred dollars and thirteen hundred dollars for a set with a fifteen-inch screen, four or five times the cost of a black-and-white set with a twenty-one-inch screen and about one-quarter of an average household's yearly income. Not surprisingly, the sets sold poorly. People found the screen too small and the price too large. Within a year sets were selling for slightly less than five hundred dollars, still a major expenditure for most Americans.

Color Spectaculars. Network executives tried to stimulate interest in the new product by offering viewers exciting color programming. The rivalry between CBS and NBC continued, each network attempting to outdo the other with spectacular, colorful productions featuring famous stars. In 1955, for example, when NBC produced a color version of Thornton Wilder's *Our Town* starring Frank Sinatra, ABC countered by offering a special with Judy Garland. Over the course of the decade, however, NBC made the strongest commitment to color broadcasting — perhaps because RCA had invested so much in the production of color sets. But the dominance of color television was still a decade away: black-and-white sets outsold color models until 1968.

The Biggest Casualty. Perhaps the biggest casualty in the growth of the television industry was radio. Production and ownership of radios continued to increase throughout the decade, but radio programming changed considerably. American families no longer thought of the radio as their main source for news or dramatic entertainment. Radio could not promise success stories like Hazel Bishop's: after advertising on television the cosmetic company's sales shot from fifty thousand dollars in 1950 to $4.5 million in 1952. Radio advertising rose from $605 million in 1950 to $618 million in 1957; by contrast, over the same period television gained over $1 billion in sponsors. Advertisers had abandoned radio like "bones at a barbecue," as comedian Fred Allen put it in 1952. Radio looked in new directions: some stations programmed "Negro music" stations aimed at African-American audiences. Panels on radio talk shows discussed issues more frankly than they ever could have during radio's golden age. Critics complained that television programs required more attention than radio programs, taking away from other pursuits. Some claimed that radio news programs covered events more thoroughly and insightfully than did television. Still, by the end of the decade television's dominance in both information and entertainment seemed assured.

Sources:
Erik Barnouw, *Tube of Plenty,* second revised edition (New York: Oxford University Press, 1990);

William Boddy, *Fifties Television: The Industry and Its Critics* (Urbana & Chicago: University of Illinois Press, 1990).

THE TURBULENT TEAMSTERS

Teamsters and Crime. Once a union that represented coach and wagon drivers, the Brotherhood of Teamsters dominated the trucking industry by the 1950s. Few industries were as vulnerable to under-the-table or illicit operations as was trucking. In the 1950s the connections between the Teamsters and gangsters became public and ultimately led to the ouster of the Teamsters union from the AFL-CIO.

Sen. John McClellan, left, chief counsel Robert F. Kennedy, center, and Sen. John F. Kennedy listening to testimony about alleged corruption involving Teamsters president Dave Beck

Suspicions Build. Trouble started when Teamsters president Dave Beck was accused by the AFL-CIO of abusing union funds. Such suspicions only brought the character of all union leadership into question. The first indication of the seriousness of Beck's activities, and its effect on the entire AFL-CIO, came in March 1957 when Labor Secretary James P. Marshall rejected George Meany's nomination of Beck to serve as a delegate to a committee of the United National International Labor Organization in Hamburg, Germany. On 9 April 1957 AFL-CIO president Meany attacked Beck without calling him by name, but the implication was clear: the Teamsters were a blot on organized labor.

The McClellan Committee. Beginning in May the Senate Select Committee on Labor-Management Relations, under Arkansas senator John McClellan, investigated the Teamsters and publicly accused Beck of misuse of funds. When called as a witness before the Senate committee, Beck invoked the Fifth Amendment more than two hundred times during his three-month testimony, lending credence to the committee's suspicion that he was "dirty." The AFL-CIO expelled Beck on 20 May; he was shortly thereafter indicted on grand-larceny charges, after which he decided not to run for reelection as Teamsters president. His vice-president and heir apparent, a pugnacious fireplug named James R. (Jimmy) Hoffa, had an equally suspicious background linked to racketeer Johnny Dio.

Hoffa Takes Charge. After Beck's expulsion the Teamsters promised to support him, charging that the AFL-CIO had acted outside its authority. Beck attempted, meanwhile, to move Hoffa in as a temporary president, which only brought stiffer opposition to Hoffa. The Senate committee again acted, calling Hoffa to testify in August 1957 on charges of misappropriation of funds. Like Beck, he took the Fifth Amendment repeatedly. On 4 October, despite Hoffa's troubles, in an election considered suspect by many and outright fraudulent by some, Hoffa was named the new Teamsters president. Polls showed that the rank and file opposed Hoffa three-to-one, and that 64 percent of the public opposed having him as Teamsters president. The AFL-CIO did not want the Teamsters' activities to taint it further, and it indicted the Teamsters for their operations. In September the Senate added new charges against Hoffa, and in October a federal judge barred Hoffa from assuming the presidency due to "election irregularities."

A Blank Check. The Teamsters stood by their choice of president, resisting all efforts at a cleanup. Hoffa escaped a wiretapping charge in June 1958 on a hung jury, but his predecessor was not as lucky: Beck was found guilty of grand larceny in November 1957, then in February 1959 found guilty of tax evasion. A Seattle, Washington, court also convicted Beck of embezzlement in December 1957. Hoffa finally assumed the full presidency of the union and even attempted to unite it with the Longshoreman's Union in an organization called the Conference on Transportation Unity. On 25 September 1958 the Teamsters thumbed their noses at the U.S. government, the AFL-CIO, and public opinion when it gave Hoffa a blank check to use union funds as he saw fit. Only after repeated efforts did Hoffa agree to government "reforms" in the union, but even those were half-hearted and seldom enforced.

Robert Kennedy's Crusade. The government was not through with Hoffa, however: in 1960 the new president of the United States, John F. Kennedy, appointed his brother, Robert, as U.S. attorney general. Robert made it a personal crusade to stamp out organized crime, and he pursued Hoffa as the most visible link between crime and the unions. He never convicted Hoffa, and, long after the assassinations of both Kennedys, Hoffa fended off federal authorities in the courts. Eventually, however, in 1964 the U.S. government convicted Hoffa on charges of jury tampering and jailed the Teamsters leader from 1967 to 1971. President Richard Nixon pardoned Hoffa in 1971 on the condition he resign as president of the Teamsters. Even so, Hoffa announced that he would make a new run at the Teamsters presidency and continued his efforts to gain the presidency in secret. Apparently he threatened some of the new union leaders who had come into power during his absence. After dinner with two members of organized crime at a Bloomfield Hills, Michigan, restaurant in 1975, Hoffa disappeared, probably murdered in a mob hit. He was declared "presumed dead" in 1982.

Source:
Steven Brill, *The Teamsters* (New York: Simon & Schuster, 1978).

HEADLINE MAKERS

JAMES R. HOFFA

1913-1975(?)

LABOR LEADER AND RACKETEER

Teamsters Hierarchy. At one time possibly the most powerful union leader in the United States, James R. (Jimmy) Hoffa had worked his way up through the ranks of the Teamsters union, the largest union in the nation. In 1952 he won election as international vice-president of the Teamsters behind president Dave Beck, who was already under investigation by federal agencies. Hoffa centralized the administration and bargaining procedures of the union in the international union office and succeeded in creating the first national freight-hauling agreement.

President. In 1957 Beck was summoned before the U.S. Senate's McClellan Committee, where he took the Fifth Amendment approximately two hundred times. When Beck finished his testimony, he had little credibility left as the Teamsters leader. Hoffa moved in. The election to put Hoffa in the presidency was disputed, and the government publicly emphasized Hoffa's connections with organized-crime figures. Nevertheless, Hoffa held on to the presidency and avoided jail for almost a decade.

Disappearance. During that time Hoffa became the target of U.S. Attorney General Robert F. Kennedy and Federal Bureau of Investigation director J. Edgar Hoover. The two, however, despised each other so much that they never worked together to put the Teamsters leader behind bars. Only after a barrage of charges did the government finally convict Hoffa in 1964 for jury tampering, fraud, and conspiracy. Hoffa remained president of the Teamsters while in jail, despite government orders that he resign. In 1971 President Richard Nixon pardoned Hoffa but stipulated that he could not hold union office until 1980. Hoffa fought the restriction in court and continued his political activities in secret. On 30 July 1975, following a dinner in Bloomfield Hills, Michigan, with two Mafia figures, Hoffa disappeared. He was declared "presumed dead" in 1982.

Sources:
Walter Sheridan, *The Fall and Rise of Jimmy Hoffa* (New York: Saturday Review Press, 1972);

Arthur A. Sloane, *Hoffa* (Cambridge: MIT Press, 1991).

RAYMOND A. KROC

1902-1984

FAST-FOOD MAGNATE

Early Career. Few millionaires begin a worldwide empire with a paper cup. But Raymond A. Kroc, who had sold Lily cups for almost twenty years, started just that way. Kroc spent much of his early life as a paper-cup salesman until, in 1941, he abandoned cups for the milkshakes that went in them. He joined the Mult-A-Mixer company, which produced multiple-milkshake mixers for restaurants. When he visited the McDonald Brothers hamburger stand owned by Dick and Mac McDonald in San Bernardino, California, in 1954, Kroc saw a mass-production operation — using his Mult-A-Mixers in sets — that no one else had developed. Kroc was impressed by the McDonalds' procedures for food preparation: "each step was stripped down to its essence and accomplished with a minimum of effort." Kroc reasoned that by combining the fast service offered at McDonald Brothers with his Mult-A-Mixers and disposable eating utensils (exemplified by his paper cups), a new type of restaurant could be created. He signed an agreement with the McDonalds, acquiring virtually all of their business, including their name. Kroc said "visions of McDonald's restaurants dotting crossroads all over the country paraded through my brain."

Franchising. The key, Kroc thought, to spreading McDonald's product to the American consumer lay in consistent recipes — which he had acquired with the McDonald's name in 1960 — and similar, predictable restaurants across the country. He could only guarantee that consistency by selling the rights to do business under the McDonald's name with the condition that the restaurant use McDonald's recipes, meet the company's standards, and utilize its national advertising and marketing. Kroc accomplished that through franchising, wherein the local owners pay a fee to the company for the use of the product (the burgers and french fries, in McDonald's case) and for its training, advertising, and corporate support. Franchising was not a new idea — A & W Root Beer and Howard Johnson's restaurants and motels had used franchising for years — but in the hands of Kroc led to a "burger boom" that took hold in the 1960s.

The Empire. From 1955 to 1977 Kroc created a vast empire of hamburger stands bearing the McDonald's name and featuring predictable fare at low prices. Kroc took making hamburgers and fries seriously: he established a "Hamburger University" to train managers and employees of McDonald's, demanding of his "burger flippers" a commitment to excellence. He ventured into sports ownership by purchasing the San Diego Padres baseball team and serving as its chairman from 1974 until his death ten years later. Kroc told his story in *Grinding It Out: The Making of McDonald's* (1977).

Sources:

Ray Kroc, *Grinding It Out: The Making of McDonald's* (Chicago: Regnery, 1977);

John F. Love, *McDonald's: Behind the Arches* (Toronto & New York: Bantam, 1986).

GEORGE MEANY
1894-1980
PRESIDENT OF THE AFL-CIO

GALE PICTURE GALLERY

Reunion of Labor. To many Americans in the 1950s, the term *organized labor* meant George Meany, president of the American Federation of Labor (AFL) after his election in 1952. Meany orchestrated the reunification of that union with the Congress of Industrial Organizations (CIO) in 1955. As president of the newly unified AFL-CIO, Meany led the campaign to rid the union of its gangster elements.

Early Career. Organized labor was a part of Meany's life since his childhood. His father had been the president of the Bronx's local chapter of the Plumbers International union. Young Meany regularly spent Sunday afternoons watching the informal union meetings that took place in his home. After he left school, and against his father's wishes, Meany became an apprentice plumber. Before long he also followed his father into union affairs, and in 1922 he won election to a full-time post as a union administrator in the local union his father had led.

Anticommunism. Meany quickly proved to be a natural leader: a tough, sensible negotiator who won over union members with his straightforward approach. In the 1930s he became involved successively in citywide and then statewide labor affairs. In 1935, when a group of craft unions within the AFL split to form the CIO, Meany was president of the New York State Federation of Labor. In 1936 he threw the support of the union

behind President Franklin Roosevelt's reelection bid, thus extending his influence into national issues. In 1940 he became national secretary-treasurer of the AFL. He was instrumental in coordinating labor's support of the war effort during World War II. Although Meany was a vocal anticommunist, he also deplored the tactics of McCarthyism and the U.S. support of right-wing dictators simply because of their anticommunist stance. By the 1950s he was known as an outspoken critic of any threat to freedom, from extremists on the Right or the Left.

Civil Rights. In the 1960s Meany aligned the unions with civil-rights causes, public housing, minimum wages, and national health insurance. He supported the U.S. involvement in Vietnam. A fervent Democrat, he joined the chorus of those calling for the impeachment of President Richard Nixon following the Watergate affair. Meany's support for conservative foreign policies and liberal domestic plans reflected the broader tensions within the labor movement itself, which during the 1950s still remained firmly linked to the Democratic party.

Source:

Archie Robinson, *George Meany and His Times* (New York: Simon & Schuster, 1981).

WALTER PHILLIP REUTHER
1907-1970
PRESIDENT OF THE CIO

GALE PICTURE GALLERY

Early Career. Walter Reuther, long associated with the United Auto Workers (UAW), established his legitimacy in a May 1937 leaflet distribution outside the River Rouge plant at Ford where he and several others were physically assaulted and hospitalized. His commitment to the labor cause, combined with his organizing skills, made him a natural leader, although early in his career he was an avowed Socialist. By 1938, however, Reuther had abandoned the Socialist party; even so, his close connections with Communists opened him to allegations from the Dies Committee, predecessor to the House Un-American Activities Committee (HUAC), that he was a Communist.

Anticommunism. When World War II came, Reuther helped to isolate and expose the Communists in the UAW, showing that they supported "the brutal dictatorships, and wars of aggression of the totalitarian governments. . . ." He devised a plan to adapt automobile mass-production methods to producing warplanes, but the head of the government's Office of Production Management, former General Motors president Bunkie Knudsen, thought the plan far-fetched. President Franklin Roosevelt never supported the plan, despite considerable public acclaim for it. Unlike some union leaders in the subsequent postwar period, Reuther's patriotism and strong anticommunism insulated him from charges of subversion. Business management could not use such accusations against him in negotiations or to influence relations with the federal government or the public. Reuther's anticommunist influence remained through the Vietnam War, when union workers, known as "hardhats," steadfastly supported Presidents Lyndon Johnson's and Richard Nixon's handling of the war, then through the 1980s when many voted for Republican Ronald Reagan, despite the endorsement of Democratic candidates by union officials, including Reuther.

Socialist Background. Nevertheless, in the 1950s Reuther's socialist background consistently led him to emphasize public coordination instead of private solutions, income distribution instead of wealth creation, and national planning as a way to maintain an economy free of business cycles. He supported a mix of auto sizes, including small cars, as early as 1949.

Split With the AFL-CIO. Reuther disagreed with AFL-CIO president George Meany on support for the war in Vietnam. In 1968 Reuther and the UAW board separated from the AFL-CIO over "fundamental trade union differences." Ironically, then, Reuther left a legacy of a union free from any hints of subversion, yet he also developed a membership base that frequently tended to support political candidates other than those the union endorsed. A union leader who had succeeded largely because of his determination to keep communism out of the unions, he left the AFL-CIO in a disagreement over a war against communism. Reuther died on 9 May 1970.

Source:
John Barnard, *Walter Reuther and the Rise of the Auto Workers* (Boston: Little, Brown, 1983).

THOMAS J. WATSON, JR.

1914-1993

PRESIDENT OF IBM

Succession. Taking over an industry giant is never easy, but replacing a legend is even more challenging. Thomas Watson, Jr., had to do both when he assumed command of IBM from his father in 1952. Watson, Sr., had been the company's president since 1915, bringing his experiences from his previous work as a corporate officer at the successful National Cash Register Corporation to IBM. He dominated IBM with his personality and infused it with a spirit exemplified by his one-word motto THINK. Under Watson, Sr., IBM rarely made the great technological breakthroughs but always caught up with or passed its competition with superior sales and service.

UNIVAC. When Thomas Watson, Jr., took over, IBM entered the computer market to compete with Remington-Rand's UNIVAC, a vacuum-tube technology computer. Watson allowed his competitors to develop new technologies, such as the transistorized computer, pioneered by Sperry Rand (Sperry Corporation and Remington-Rand merged in 1955) in the mid 1950s. Instead Watson remained true to his father's strategy, focusing on sales, service, and adaptation. Quickly IBM surpassed Sperry Rand and all other computer competitors, controlling an astounding 65 percent of the U.S. computer market by 1965 with gross revenues of $2.5 billion. By that time IBM's closest competitor, Sperry Rand, only held 12 percent of the market.

Antitrust. Watson led IBM through numerous bouts with the federal government over antitrust violations in the 1960s, and when he retired in 1973, IBM remained the leader in American computers.

Source:
William Rodgers, *Think: A Biography of the Watsons and IBM* (New York: Stein & Day, 1969).

CHARLES E. WILSON

1890-1961

PRESIDENT OF GENERAL MOTORS, SECRETARY OF DEFENSE
(1954-1957)

Controversy and Power. Charles Erwin Wilson, best known for a quotation he never uttered — "What's good for General Motors is good for the country" — played a key role in the development of General Motors Corporation (GM) and as secretary of defense during the Dwight D. Eisenhower administration. As the head of GM, Wilson had led the world's largest corporation; President Eisenhower wanted him to oversee the rapidly growing military and the developing "military-industrial complex." Wilson's association with the enormous automaker, however, made his cabinet appointment Eisenhower's most controversial.

Early Career. Trained as an electrical engineer, Wilson climbed steadily up GM's long corporate ladder, becoming chief executive of the conglomerate in 1946. As head of GM, Wilson successfully negotiated labor agreements with the United Auto Workers (UAW) in 1948 and 1950. In the 1948 contract he offered the innovative "escalator clause," which raised employee salaries to meet increases in the cost of living. During a new round of negotiations two years later, the union suggested a pension plan. Wilson was a strong proponent of a profit-sharing plan for GM workers even before the union included them as negotiating points. He proposed to invest the pension money in the stock market, whereby American workers would become owners of American businesses in a single generation: "Exactly what they should and must be," he said. According to one Wilson biographer, the 1948 and 1950 labor negotiations represented Wilson's "finest accomplishments during his career as the president of GM." The benefits granted to GM employees quickly became standards of American industry.

Secretary of Defense. When Eisenhower was elected president in 1952, he looked to the business community for most of his cabinet appointments. For the Department of Defense, in particular, he wanted a leader who was an effective, budget-conscious administrator. GM, under Wilson's direction, had been one of the military's chief suppliers during World War II, and Wilson and Eisenhower had exchanged friendly correspondence for years. The GM executive seemed the logical choice to head the Department of Defense.

Senate Reluctance. Members of the Senate Armed Services Committee were reluctant initially to confirm Wilson's appointment. Because GM was still a major defense contractor in the 1950s, Wilson could face a conflict of interest: he would have to spend public money in a way that might affect his private fortune. When Sen. Robert Hendrickson of New Jersey asked if he could separate the public welfare from that of GM, Wilson responded, "I cannot think of [such a conflict] because for years I thought that what was good for the country was good for General Motors, and vice versa." Wilson was expressing the GM philosophy that the company could only be prosperous if the nation were prosperous: he had publicly expressed the same sentiment on several previous occasions. In their reports of the hearings, the press distorted Wilson's remark. He was made to sound as if he put GM's interests before the country's. In order to win confirmation, he had to step down as GM's executive and sell his stock in the company, at a personal loss of $2 million.

Trimming Defense. Known as "Engine" Charlie Wilson (to differentiate him from "Electric" Charlie Wilson, the former head of General Electric who headed the Truman administration's mobilization effort in the Korean War), Wilson, as secretary of defense, trimmed $5 billion from the total defense budget in his first year. He reorganized the Department of Defense along the same lines as GM and created a staff of assistant secretaries of defense who served the same purposes as the vice-presidents at the auto giant. His tenure as secretary was the third longest in U.S. history. Under Wilson, the United States began research and development on ballistic missiles, added new jets to the air force, and oversaw the introduction of nuclear power to the U.S. Navy. Wilson died on 26 September 1961.

Source:
E. Bruce Geelhoed, *Charles E. Wilson and Controversy at the Pentagon, 1953 to 1957* (Detroit: Wayne State University Press, 1979).

PEOPLE IN THE NEWS

In January 1951 **Michael V. DiSalle,** director of the Office of Price Stabilization, endorsed a freeze on prices by saying it was like "bobbing a cat's tail": better to do it all at once close to the body; otherwise the result would be a mad cat and a sore tail.

On 7 October 1959 **Walter D. Facler,** assistant economic research director of the U.S. Chamber of Commerce, told a Senate committee that some unemployment could be a "positive economic good."

In 1959 **Harold Geneen,** executive vice-president of Raytheon, took over as president of International Telephone & Telegraph (IT&T).

In 1957 *Fortune* magazine listed **Jean Paul Getty,** with a fortune of $700 million to $1 billion in American and Arabian oil and real estate, as the richest American.

In 1959 **Milton J. Hammergren,** former vice-president of Rudolph Wurlitzer jukebox manufacturers, testifying before a Senate hearing on the $2-billion-a-year industry, admitted that his company found it difficult to sell jukeboxes until it started working with the underworld.

In 1959 **Stanley C. Hope,** president of the National Association of Manufacturers, urged Congress to outlaw industrywide collective bargaining.

In 1957 **Roy Hurley,** chairman of Studebaker-Packard Corporation, negotiated an agreement to become the exclusive distributor in the United States of German-made Mercedes-Benz autos.

On 15 May 1951 **Eric Johnston,** economic stability administrator, told the 1951 Industry-Armed Forces

Conference in Washington that he would "get tough" in keeping wages and prices down.

In 1959 **Henry J. Kaiser** tried, without success, to mediate the steel strike.

In 1954 **James J. Ling** founded Ling-Temco-Vought Corporation (LTV), one of the nation's first conglomerates.

In 1959 **Norman P. Mason,** Housing and Home Finance Agency administrator, assailed the omnibus housing bill passed on 23 June as too costly and "full of bonuses for the big people."

In 1952 **John J. McCloy,** former high commissioner to West Germany and later a member of the Warren Commission investigating the assassination of John F. Kennedy, was named president, with **David Rockefeller** named senior vice-president, of Chase National Bank.

On 11 December 1958 **George Meany,** president of the AFL-CIO, predicted that the labor movement would form its own political party if necessary "to lick the people who want to drag us back to the past."

In 1957 **Nancy C. Morse** and **Robert S. Weiss** of the University of Michigan's Institute for Social Research reported that most American men liked their jobs and would continue working even if they found themselves suddenly rich.

In 1958 **Richard Nixon,** vice-president of the United States, speaking at Harvard Business School Association, called for business tax cuts to create more jobs.

In 1952 **Franz Pick,** who published *Pick's 1951 Black Market Year Book,* estimated that about one hundred thousand people throughout the world earned their livings by transferring $10 billion worth of gold and currency on free or black markets every year. The United States currently had $6 billion to $7 billion of its $28 billion outstanding in U.S. currency abroad.

In 1953 **Simon Ramo** and **Dean Wooldridge** left Hughes Aircraft to form TRW Corporation.

On 15 June 1959 **Walter Reuther,** president of the AFL-CIO's United Auto Workers, proposed at the Industrial Relations Conference in Philadelphia that "some new mechanism" be created to bring labor, industry, the consumer, and other economic groups together for periodic conferences on common problems. Later that year Reuther proposed "international fair labor standards" to narrow the gap between workers of different countries.

In 1951 **Alfred P. Sloan,** chairman of General Motors, published "Big Business Must Help Our Colleges" in *Colliers,* signaling the start of large corporate contributions to universities. On 23 May 1956 **Sloan** retired as chairman of GM.

In 1957 U.S. atomic energy chairman **Lewis L. Strauss** said at the dedication of Pacific Gas & Electric Company's Vallecitos power plant that the United States has the "most comprehensive" atomic power development program in the world.

In 1951 Labor Secretary **Maurice J. Tobin** announced in a speech that white-collar workers average fifteen dollars weekly less than union factory workers and urged them to unionize.

In 1952 **Carl Wente** was named president of Bank of America.

DEATHS

Horatio M. Adams, 102, founder of Adams & Sons (later American Chicle Company), which secured the first U.S. patent for making chewing gum in 1872, 27 January 1956.

Vincent Astor, 67, board chairman of *Newsweek* and great-great-grandson of New York real-estate tycoon John Jacob Astor, 3 February 1959.

Walter C. Baker, 87, inventor of Baker Electric auto (1897) and auto-equipment manufacturer, 26 April 1955.

Cesare Barbieri, 78, the Italian-born inventor of auto antifreeze and machines to make paper cups, 25 May 1956.

Sailing P. Baruch, Jr., 53, president of Baruch Brothers and Company, an investment house, and nephew of Bernard M. Baruch, 9 February 1956.

Siegfried Bechhold, 55, German-born industrialist and former president of Armored Tank Corporation of New York, which developed the Sherman tank during World War II, 7 February 1956.

Lawrence Dale Bell, 62, founder and chairman of Bell Aircraft Corporation who aided in the design and construction of the Bell X-1 experimental jet (the first aircraft to surpass the speed of sound) and several other experimental aircraft, 20 October 1956.

Clarence Frank Birdseye, 69, who developed methods of freezing and dehydrating foods for preservation and founded Birdseye General Food Company. He also invented infrared-heat lamps for industrial use, 7 October 1956.

Alfred Cleveland Blumenthal, 66, wealthy realtor who bought and sold West Coast theaters for movie distributors; established Fox Theaters Corporation; produced Broadway shows; operated Mexican hotels and restaurants, 29 July 1957.

William E. Boeing, 74, aircraft-manufacturing pioneer who in 1916 founded Pacific Aero Products, which became Boeing Aircraft in 1929, 28 September 1956.

Joel M. Bowley, 70, president of Eagle-Picher Company, director of Cleveland Federal Reserve Bank, 23 August 1957.

Paul Braniff, 56, founder of Braniff Airways, 1 June 1954.

James Cardwell, 84, chairman of Cardwell Westinghouse Company and rail-equipment inventor, 8 December 1957.

Clyde V. Cessna, 74, pioneer aviator and inventor of private aircraft, 20 November 1954.

Malcolm Greene Chace, 80, New England industrialist (public utilities, banking, textiles) who maintained the largest independent tanker fleet in World War I and most of World War II, 16 July 1955.

Raymond E. Christie, 73, vice-president of Crucible Steel Company who advanced uses of stainless steel, 27 June 1956.

Robert Glass Cleland, 72, historian of American business, especially in the West, 3 September 1957.

Jack Cohn, 67, cofounder, with brother Harry, of Columbia Pictures in 1920 and the first to produce newsreels and animated cartoons, 8 December 1956.

Harry D. Collier, 83, president of Standard Oil Company of California and chairman of Arabian American Oil Company (ARAMCO), 30 January 1959.

Hugh Roy Cullen, 76, founder of South Texas Petroleum Company and Quintana Oil Company. He was also a philanthropist who donated $26 million to the University of Houston and $10 million to the Texas Medical Center; established the $160 million Cullen Foundation, 4 July 1957.

George H. Davis, 93, cofounder of Ford, Bacon and Davis, construction engineers who helped rebuild San Francisco after the 1906 earthquake, 3 May 1957.

Albert Blake Dick, Jr., 60, chairman of A. B. Dick Office Machine Company, 24 October 1954.

James Drummond Dole, 80, founder of Hawaiian pineapple industry with Hawaiian Pineapple Company in 1900, 14 May 1958.

George Terry Dunlap, 92, cofounder of Grosset and Dunlap book publishers, 27 June 1956.

Samuel Simeon Fels, 90, president of Fels Naptha Soap, 23 June 1950.

Homer Ferguson, 80, chairman of Newport News Shipbuilding and Drydock, 14 March 1953.

Marshall Field III, 63, publisher and philanthropist, heir to the Chicago department-store fortune and founder of the *Chicago Sun* newspaper; he also headed Field Enterprises (which included Simon and Schuster and Pocket Books), 8 November 1956.

Martin M. Foss, 74, president of McGraw-Hill Book Company, 13 January 1953.

Jack Frye, 54, president of TWA (1934–1947), president of General Anailine and Film Corporation (1947–1955), chairman of Frye Corporation (1955–1959) aircraft manufacturers, 3 February 1959.

Alfred Howard Fuller, 46, president of Fuller Brush Company, 9 May 1959.

Michael Gallagher, 87, Cleveland coal and shipping industrialist, 27 August 1957.

Frank Ernest Gannett, 81, founder of the Gannett chain of twenty-two newspapers and several television and radio stations, 3 December 1957.

Frank Gerber, 79, developer of canned baby foods, chairman of Gerber Products, 7 October 1952.

Lawrence Mario Giannini, 57, president of Bank of America, the largest bank in the United States, 19 August 1957.

Moses Ginsburg, 85, Polish-born shipowner, construction firm head, operator of the American-Foreign Steamship Company (American Star Line), 30 August 1959.

Truman Parker Handy, 69, chairman of Celluloid Corporation, 18 November 1959.

C. William Hazelett, 64, economist-author of business and economics books, 16 March 1956.

John Jay Hopkins, 63, chairman of General Dynamics Corporation, which built the *Nautilus* nuclear submarine, 3 May 1957.

Albert S. Howell, 71, cofounder and chairman of Bell and Howell Camera Company, credited with taking the flicker out of movies, 3 January 1951.

Rowland Robert Hughes, 61, U.S. Budget Director (1954–1955) and vice-president of First National City Bank of New York (1951–1953), 2 April 1957.

Paul W. Kesten, 58, pioneer in development of color television and vice-chairman of Columbia Broadcasting System (CBS), 4 December 1956.

Charles F. Kettering, 82, engineer and inventor of the automobile starter, the electric cash register, and safety glass and General Motors research director; cofounder with Alfred P. Sloan, Jr., of Sloan-Kettering Institute for Cancer Research, 25 November 1958.

Col. Evan Ewan Kimble, 87, founder of Kimble Glass Company and pioneer in manufacturing glass for scientific uses, 15 March 1956.

James Lewis Kraft, 78, former cheese salesman who founded Kraft Foods, 16 February 1953.

S. Ralph Lazarus, 61, president and cofounder of Benrus Watch Company, 4 September 1959.

Samuel A. Lerner, 72, founder of Lerner Stores, a women's apparel chain, 5 December 1956.

Harry Lundeberg, 56, Norweigan-born anticommunist maritime leader, president of the AFL-CIO Maritime Trades Department, 28 January 1957.

William C. Mack, 94, co-originator of Mack Trucks, 13 February 1953.

Herbert Marcus, Sr., 72, cofounder of Neiman Marcus and Company, 11 December 1950.

Clair Maxwell, 67, president and publisher of *Life* magazine before its 1936 sale to Henry Luce, 11 May 1959.

John H. McFadden, Jr., 65, international cotton dealer and president of the New York Cotton Exchange (1934–1936), 17 August 1955.

Andrew McNally, 67, chairman of Rand-McNally, 20 May 1954.

Charles E. Merrill, 70, founder in 1914 of Merrill Lynch, Pierce Fenner and Beane, investment bankers. Merrill pioneered the sales of securities to middle-class investors and foresaw the 1929 crash, saving his clients millions of dollars. He also started the *Family Circle* magazine and Safeway Stores, 6 October 1956.

Leeds Mitchell, 80, investment broker and head of Chicago Stock Exchange (1922–1923), 27 July 1957.

Mark Morton, 92, cofounder of Morton Salt Company, 25 June 1951.

Harry Morgan Moses, 59, president of the Bituminous Coal Operators Association, who negotiated three industrywide contracts with the United Mine Workers, 1 April 1956.

Arnold H. Munk, 69, president of Platt and Munk, publishers of children's stories, including "The Little Engine that Could," 6 August 1957.

Carrie Neiman, cofounder of Neiman-Marcus stores in Dallas, Texas, 6 March 1953.

Henry Nias, 76, head of Lily-Tulip Corporation, 22 August 1955.

Fred Pabst, 88, chairman of the board of Pabst Brewing Company and internationally known cattle breeder, 21 February 1958.

Herbert Pulitzer, 61, publisher of New York *World* newspapers before their sale to Scripps-Howard in 1931, 4 September 1957.

Lawson Valentine Pulsifer, 75, chemical engineer and president of Valspar Corporation, inventor of first waterproof varnish, 24 July 1957.

John W. Rath, 79, cofounder of Rath Packing Company, one of the largest U.S. meat packers, 22 December 1951.

William Neal Reynolds, 88, former president of R. J. Reynolds Tobacco Company, 10 September 1951.

O. Pomeroy Robinson, Jr., 64, vice-president of General Dynamics Corporation and submarine builder who helped develop the atomic submarine *Nautilus*, 26 February 1956.

Harry H. Rogers, 80, Oklahoma industrialist and president of Rotary International 1926–1927, 3 December 1957.

Alan Magee Scaife, 58, industrialist and vice-president of T. Mellon and Company, 24 July 1958.

Charles Scribner, 62, president of Charles Scribner's Sons publishers, 11 February 1952.

Harry Ford Sinclair, 80, founder of Sinclair Oil Corporation in 1916 after the first well he dug came in a gusher, 10 November 1956.

Gerald H. Smith, 42, president of Street and Smith Publications, 18 June 1955.

Thomas Lewis Smith, 79, president of Standard Brands (1937–1941), 5 March 1957.

Harry E. Soreff, 70, inventor of the laminated padlock and founder of Master Lock Company, 1 March 1957.

Otto Stahl, 85, German-born founder of Stahl-Meyer, Inc., meat packers, 27 January 1957.

Theodore Edwin Steinway, 73, president of Steinway and Sons piano manufacturers, 8 April 1957.

Gordon Stouffer, 51, chairman of the board of Stouffer restaurant chain, 6 June 1956.

Joseph F. Taylor, 67, chairman of the board of Bausch and Lomb Optical Company, 16 June 1956.

Myron Charles Taylor, 85, textile industrialist and chairman of U.S. Steel finance committee (1927–1934) who paid off the firm's $340 million debt in three years, 6 May 1959.

Dr. J. E. Walker, 78, chairman of Universal Life Insurance Company, 28 July 1958.

Harry Morris Warner, 76, founder, with brothers Albert and Jack, of Warner Bros. film company, 25 July 1958.

Thomas John Watson, 82, chairman of International Business Machines (IBM). He built a business-machine company that grossed $629 million at the time of his death and employed more than fifty-nine thousand, 19 June 1956.

John Philip Weyerhaeuser, Jr., 57, president of Weyerhaeuser Timber Company, 8 December 1956.

Clarence Mott Wolley, 92, industrialist and chairman of American Radiator Company, 18 July 1956.

PUBLICATIONS

Adolf A. Berle, *The 20th Century American Capitalist Revolution* (New York: Harcourt, Brace, 1954);

Edward Bursk, Donald T. Clark, and Ralph W. Hidy, *The World of Business* (New York: Simon & Schuster, 1962);

Richard Caves, *American Industry: Structure, Conduct, Performance* (Englewood Cliffs, N.J.: Prentice-Hall, 1964);

Caves, *Essays in Positive Economics* (Chicago: University of Chicago Press, 1953);

Peter F. Drucker, *The New Society* (New York: Harper, 1950);

Marriner S. Eccles, *Beckoning Frontiers* (New York: Knopf, 1951);

Milton Friedman and Rose Friedman, *Capitalism and Freedom* (Chicago: University of Chicago Press, 1962);

John K. Galbraith, *The Affluent Society* (Boston: Houghton Mifflin, 1958);

Galbraith, *American Capitalism: The Concept of Countervailing Power* (Boston: Houghton Mifflin, 1956);

Arthur J. Goldberg, *AFL-CIO: Labor United* (New York: McGraw-Hill, 1956);

Stewart Holbrook, *Machines of Plenty: Pioneering in American Agriculture* (New York: Macmillan, 1955);

Lewis Mumford, *The Myth of the Machine: The Pentagon of Power* (New York: Harcourt Brace, 1964);

Vance Packard, *The Hidden Persuaders* (New York: McKay, 1957);

Packard, *The Pyramid Climbers* (New York: McGraw-Hill, 1962);

David Reisman, Jr., Revel Denny, and Nathan Glazer, *The Lonely Crowd* (New Haven, Conn.: Yale University Press, 1950);

Herbert A. Simon, *The New Science of Management Decision* (New York: Harper & Row, 1960);

Henry William Speigel, *The Rise of American Economic Thought* (Philadelphia: Chilton, 1960);

William H. Whyte, Jr., *The Organization Man* (New York: Simon & Schuster, 1956);

Business Week, periodical;

Forbes, periodical.

EDUCATION

by JENNIFER DAVIS

CONTENTS

Sidebars and tables are listed in italics.

1950

- An estimated 29.828 million elementary and secondary students and 2.3 million college and professional-school students attend school.

- National Science Foundation Act is passed.

1 July　New Orleans Board of Education grants full privileges to married teachers, including the right to promotion (not granted since the Depression).

16 Oct.　New Jersey Supreme Court upholds the practice of reading of five verses of the Old Testament each day in all public schools.

1951

18 Aug.　The Associated Press reports college costs up 400 percent from fifty years ago. Average cost is $1,800.

18 Sept.　Pope Pius XII states his opposition to sex education in schools.

19 Oct.　Yale University celebrates its 250th anniversary.

1952

- Baby boomers enter school in record numbers.

- Nationally 20 percent of college and 10 percent of elementary- and secondary-school students are in desegregated classrooms.

2 Mar.　Supreme Court rules "subversives could be barred from teaching."

6 Apr.　University of Florida student honor court resigns over reinstatement of two hundred students, including several football players, accused of cheating.

29 Apr.　The University of Rochester ends a 107-year policy of separate colleges for men and women with the opening of a coeducational College of Arts and Sciences.

2 July　The Stevens Institute of Technology, Hoboken, New Jersey, begins installment financing for college educations.

1953

- The Department of Health, Education, and Welfare is created.

- National Education Association membership passes five hundred thousand.

14 Jan.　President Harry S Truman states that federal money for education has doubled since 1929.

9 Feb.　Williams College's Phi Delta Theta fraternity is suspended for pledging a Jewish student.

11 Feb.　National Council for Financial Aid to Education is formed to help colleges and universities obtain funds from business and industry.

3 Apr.　Fisk University, Nashville, Tennessee, establishes the first Phi Beta Kappa chapter at a black college.

11 June　Harvard University Law School confers its bachelor of law degree on women for the first time, eleven that year.

21 Aug. Due to a clause permitting government "disapproval" of faculty members, fourteen universities decline to renew contracts with the U.S. Armed Forces Institute for correspondence courses for the military.

6 Dec. National Educational Association (NEA) reports that American school children are less fit physically than Italian and Austrian children due to lack of exercise, particularly among students in cities.

1954

7 Jan. President Dwight D. Eisenhower calls for each state to hold a conference on education; nine hundred thousand dollars is appropriated for this purpose.

21 Feb. Columbia University reports that 10 percent of American public-school students suffer from emotional disturbances.

17 May *Brown* v. *Board of Education of Topeka, Kansas* overrules "separate but equal" doctrine for education and declares segregated public schools unconstitutional.

June NEA National Convention votes to endorse integration (Mississippi and South Carolina vote against the measure), stating, "All problems of integration . . . are capable of solution by citizens of intelligence, saneness and reasonableness working together. . . ."

19 Nov. Grants by philanthropic agencies for research and study fellowships are declared tax exempt by U.S. Tax Court.

1955

- First White House conference on education is held.

- National Merit Scholarship Corporation is formed.

- Advanced Placement Program comes under control of College Entrance Examination Board.

18 Jan. Harvard Divinity School announces the admission of women for fall 1955.

10 May New York City Board of Education reports an "end to social promotion." Pupils two years or more behind in reading will be held back.

2 Sept. Census Bureau reports that male college graduates can expect one hundred thousand dollars more in lifetime income than high-school graduates.

1956

- President Eisenhower calls for special attention to schools for American Indian children.

- Creation of president's Committee on Education Beyond the High School.

1 Feb. Civilian Conservation Corps school-lunch milk fund is raised to $60 million.

21 Sept. Twelve-year-old Fred Safier of Berkeley, California, enrolls in Harvard College to study physics.

3 Nov.   A U.S. Office of Education study of classroom-equipment requirements reports that 11 percent of the thirty three hundred students surveyed are left-handed.

26 Nov.   Study by the Fund for the Republic reveals blacks show no inherent inferiority to whites in intelligence tests.

1957

- Little Rock, Arkansas, segregation crisis.
- Nonpublic enrollments doubled since 1944.
- Soviet launch of *Sputnik* raises concern about the quality of American education.

4 Apr.   National Education Association celebrates its one hundredth anniversary.

7 Dec.   American workers average 11.8 years of schooling (9 percent completed college) compared to 9.3 years (6.4 percent completed college) in 1940.

1958

- Public Law 926 provides teachers and programs for mentally retarded students.

10 Mar.   The Vatican Sacred Congregation of Religious Studies calls for the separation of boys and girls in sports, study halls, and classrooms even in coeducational schools.

2 Sept.   Congress passes National Defense Education Act.

1 Dec.   Fire kills ninety students and three nuns at Our Lady of the Angels school in Chicago.

12 Dec.   President Eisenhower favors the addition of a year or two of junior college (or a similar program) to high-school curricula to combat deficiencies in American education.

1959

- An estimated 42.7 million elementary and secondary students and 3.4 million college and professional students attend school.

20 Oct.   One hundredth anniversary of birthday of John Dewey, distinguished philosopher and educator.

24 Oct.   The Department of Health, Education, and Welfare pledges to rid the United States of "college-degree mills," which grant degrees but do not require academic courses.

OVERVIEW

Even if some Americans in the 1950s still believed that "a little learnin' goes a long way," they became concerned during the decade that it took more than a little learning to face the challenges of the day. American education in the 1950s ran headlong into the social controversies that changed the nation. Racial problems, McCarthyism, the Cold War, and budget shortages all affected the world of education. The notion of education itself became more than the traditional training of reading, writing, and arithmetic for children. The social and cultural events of the decade had an immense impact on the way in which Americans defined education. Who should be trained to teach students, how should teachers perform their jobs, and what were the goals of education all were questions the country asked.

School Enrollments. School enrollments increased 30 percent over the decade as the baby boomers, born after World War II came of school age. Increases of more than 1.5 million elementary- and secondary-school students occurred in 1952, 1953, 1955, and 1958. A record 2 million new students entered school for the 1959–1960 school year. New-student populations increased at twice the growth rate of the general population. College enrollments showed a decline only in the early years of the decade (down 150,000 between 1950 and 1952) as the Korean War took young men to war and as the GI Bill for World War II veterans came to an end. The biggest college-enrollment increase occurred in 1956, with more than 450,000 new students (colleges would feel the full effect of the baby boomers during the 1960s and 1970s). Ten straight years of increased enrollment strained the physical capacity of aging school buildings and challenged the flexibility of outmoded curricula.

Teacher and School Shortages. In 1950 there were 166,473 existing elementary and secondary schools to educate over twenty-nine million students; by 1960 the student population had increased to over forty-one million children and the number of schools had decreased to 135,372. As the flood of children ages five to seventeen entered the country's school systems over the course of the decade, shortages in teachers and school resources led to frenetic attempts to meet the demand. In 1953 the Office of Education reported a shortage of 345,000 class-

rooms, which caused overcrowding in 60 percent of the nation's classrooms, and some 20 percent of students attended schools that failed to meet basic safety standards, such as fire protection. In addition, the Office of Education reported that 132,000 qualified teachers were needed to staff American classrooms adequately. Funding was sought, teacher recruitment soared, and construction began throughout the nation over the course of the decade. By 1959, after some $20.9 billion had been spent on new construction, the classroom deficit, although narrowing, was still present, and the number of people wanting an education still exceeded resources.

Desegregation of Education. The biggest event in education during the 1950s was the desegregation of the country's public schools. The highly publicized legal case *Brown* v. *the Board of Education of Topeka, Kansas,* which reached the United States Supreme Court, not only declared segregation unconstitutional in schools but prompted measures to end discrimination in other public institutions. The Court's decision in 1954 changed the course of education for states, educators, and, most important, America's students. Black families, who had been forced to send their children to generally poorly funded, black-only schools, could now legally demand that their children be able to attend the same schools as white students. This ruling came under heavy fire as the country wrestled with integration. Schools closed, and Health, Education, and Welfare Secretary Arthur Flemming stated in 1958 that immeasurable "social, economic, and psychological" harm was afflicting students and educators alike. However, states, mostly in the South, were slow to integrate their schools, and full desegregation took more than twenty years.

Public vs. Private. Debates about the funding of private education — pertaining for the most part to parochial schools — continued throughout the 1950s, as states debated over the separation of church and state. In 1950 over three million American students were in parochial elementary and secondary schools.

Religion in Schools. Religion in the classroom remained commonplace throughout the 1950s. Daily readings from the Bible and religious instruction of some sort continued to be part of public-school curricula. However, as the debate over funding and the separation of church and state intensified, states began to question the appropriateness of biblical instruction in public schools. In 1959 Pennsylvania outlawed Bible reading in public classrooms, foreshadowing the movement away from religious education in public schools in subsequent decades.

Effect of *Sputnik*. The launching of *Sputnik* in 1957 caused anxiety across the country. Not only were the Soviets the first in space, devastating the national pride and sense of security Americans felt, but symbolically the Soviet educational system had surpassed our own. Educators, parents, and government officials charged that U.S. education had become soft and oriented toward a comfort-based life. Science and mathematics came under close scrutiny, and efforts began to upgrade the educational system with renewed emphasis on the "hard" and applied sciences — physics, biology, chemistry, and engineering.

Federal Government in Education. The 1950s brought increased involvement in education by Uncle Sam. State and local school boards called for increased federal funding to meet the teacher and school shortages. Federal funding brought spending guidelines, such as bans on Communist teachers and the requirement to integrate schools. Restrictions on where and to whom the money went made the jobs of the state and local school boards even harder. Some chose not to accept the federal money because it meant giving up complete control over administration. In addition, before the federal money could even reach the state and local boards, members of Congress debated federal funding, and several funding bills for education did not pass because Congress tacked on amendments restricting the uses for funds. For all the help the federal money brought — more schools and teachers along with better curricula — the full effects of that involvement, some negative, would be felt in the coming decades.

TOPICS IN THE NEWS

ADULT EDUCATION

In an effort to rectify the problems of increased dropout rates, the importance of adult education increased during the 1950s. The average American worker had not completed high school. In 1950 only 58.2 percent of all fifth-graders would eventually graduate from high school.

An adult education class in Baltimore, Maryland

At a time when science and mathematics were becoming a matter of national defense, improving the quality of the adult population became a priority.

Vocational and life-skills training comprised the most common courses and most effective solutions available. Those courses, offered in home economics, trade and industry, agriculture, and health-related fields, provided Americans with practical training for employment. The students who would have left school or those who had left school could now be educated for the employment they sought. And those students would also increase their annual incomes: skilled workers earned an average of two thousand dollars more per year than their unskilled counterparts. All levels of government funded the programs ($129 million in 1950; $228 million in 1959), with the bulk of resources coming from local government. People recognized that only through a better-trained and better-educated adult population could the country compete in the growing international market and defense spheres which would follow in the coming decades. Schools offered courses at night and on weekends for working adults. A new type of student — the nontraditional student, as schools soon called them — became an important constituency for public schools.

Church vs. State

Funding Private Schools. Religious instruction for children was debated as the economy tightened. As calls for more federal funding increased, the government, educators, and parents questioned whether public federal funds should go toward the funding of a private-education system. In 1950 over three million children (or approximately 10 percent of the children enrolled in all schools) were in the Catholic education system. In the view of some people, parochial schools served a block of students substantial enough to warrant funding.

Buses. The push for federal funding of parochial schools originated over bus transportation. In March 1950 Representative John F. Kennedy, a Catholic Democrat from Massachusetts, failed to gain support from the House Labor Committee to allocate federal money for bus service to parochial-school children. Eleanor Roosevelt had spoken against the bill on 6 March, stating that she had sent her children to private schools and never expected "anyone to pay for it." A week later a $3.145-million Senate-approved aid-to-education bill was rejected by the House Labor Committee due to controversy over federal money for auxiliary services in parochial schools. The bill would have permitted each state to determine funding allocations.

States' Reactions. Signs from the states were mixed. In the predominantly Catholic state of Massachusetts, Governor Paul A. Dever ignored federal mandates and signed a bill 4 May 1950 allowing the use of federal funds for free busing for parochial students. Connecticut, in 1957, allowed local districts to decide whether or not to transport parochial students. In New Mexico, on the other hand, the state school board banned the distribution of free textbooks to parochial schools and transportation of parochial students in state-owned public-school buses in 1951. In addition, the board prohibited public-school teachers from wearing religious garb.

Teaching Nuns. In 1952 Wisconsin halted state aid to fourteen public schools that employed Roman Catholic nuns as teachers. Not only was funding to parochial schools cut, but public schools, already facing vast teacher shortages, could no longer employ church-based teachers. The National Education Association (NEA) offered no support for funding of church-based teachers. It opposed the use of federal funds for parochial schooling at its annual conventions throughout the decade. Indeed, the NEA assumed a strong antireligious stance that only grew stronger over the next thirty years.

A Dual System. Dr. James B. Conant, president of Harvard University, started a fresh controversy over private schools when he contended that they created a dual educational system harmful to democratic unity; only through one system could the nation maintain its social continuity, he argued. Several groups attacked Conant's statements, notably the National Catholic Educational Association. It countered that Catholics supported public schools and paid their taxes for public schools as a civic duty. Many expressed concern that two bases of support for children — church and school — were under attack.

Position of the Catholic Church. The Roman Catholic bishops issued a statement on the issue from their annual meeting in 1955. Stating that parochial and other private schools were an integral part of the U.S. educational system, the group said it was "unfair and discriminatory" to treat such schools as "less wholly dedicated to the public welfare" than public schools. Despite the commotion over funding a private education, religion was routinely taught in public schools during the decade.

Released-Time. "Released-time" programs were common during the 1950s. These programs excused children from public school for an hour a week to attend religious classes off school grounds. However, as the controversy over funding for parochial schools intensified, the issue of religious training and its effect on public schools resurfaced. Court cases involving the released-time programs were filed in several states. In April 1952 the U.S. Su-

---

GOD, MAN, AND BUCKLEY AT YALE

While a student at Yale, young William F. Buckley, Jr., began on a writing career that would span the next four decades and lead him to found *National Review* magazine in 1955. Buckley was appalled at the trends he saw in higher education at Yale: many of his professors espoused communism or socialism in economics and politics and atheism instead of religion. The senior found it particularly ironic that a once-religious school, such as Yale, promoted such views. He also detected more than a hint of anti-Americanism and a general disdain for "American values." With the help of conservative publisher Henry Regnery, Buckley in *God and Man at Yale* (1951) chronicled his journey through college, wittily exposing what he considered "leftist" ideas and professors by referring to their class lectures. "I believe the net influence of Yale economics," he wrote, "to be thoroughly collectivistic." He concluded, "Individualism is dying at Yale, and without a fight." Buckley never lost his suspicion of academics, once commenting that he would rather "be governed by the first 500 names in the Boston phone directory than the faculty of Harvard."

Sources:

Malcolm S. Knowles, *The Adult Education Movement in the United States* (New York: Holt, Rinehart & Winston, 1962);

Fritz Machlup, *The Production and Distribution of Knowledge in the United States* (Princeton, N.J.: Princeton University Press, 1962).

preme Court ruled on the question of whether released-time violated the constitutional guarantee of separation of church and state. The majority opinion held that the program constituted "free exercise" and that New York had maintained its neutrality by allowing all religious training to be included in the released-time. At the end of 1952 forty-six states had some form of released-time for students.

Bible Reading. A related issue — that of Bible reading in public education — came before the Supreme Court in 1952. Many American school systems had times during the school day when the Bible was read. The District of Columbia and twelve states required a daily Bible reading in public schools. Five other states permitted Bible reading, and Mississippi required instruction in the Ten Commandments. The Supreme Court case involved the New Jersey school system, which had reinstated its requirement of daily Bible readings in 1950. Supporters of public funding for parochial schools wanted to show a precedent for a state/church relationship in education. The Supreme Court, however, refused to rule on the issue.

Religious Beliefs vs. Classroom Curriculum. In New York, local school boards agreed to compromises with religious groups. In 1951 New York was one of ten states to excuse pupils from health instruction conflicting with their religious background. In addition, questions on the State Board of Regents examinations concerning germ theory were to be omitted from all biology examinations in deference to Christian Science beliefs that relied on prayer to cure diseases. After negotiations with Christian Science representatives in 1952, New York state officials returned germ theory to the high-school biology curricula and required students to attend instructions on germ theory and public health. However, students were allowed to omit examination questions that conflicted with their religious views and to request exemption from certain instruction forbidden by church leaders.

Sources:
J. Ronald Oakley, *God's Country: America in the Fifties* (New York: Dembner Books, 1986);

John M. Swamley, Jr., *Religion, the State & the Schools* (New York: Pegasus, 1968).

CURRICULA

Life Adjustment. Educational methods changed significantly during the 1950s as Americans started to reap the benefits of a strong economy, with a job waiting for almost every able-bodied adult. To face this new, prosperous world, schools changed curricula. Teaching students "life adjustment" took precedence over the traditional skills of math, science, and reading. Schools emphasized mental, physical, and emotional aspects of a child's life. The humanities and life skills became the new focus of educators. Home-economics classes and government classes attained record enrollments as citizenship and managing the home and family became high priori-

ties. Comprehensive high schools offered a wide variety of vocational training as well as numerous electives in such areas as photography, botanical care, and baby care. Audio-visual aids, modern laboratory equipment, and supplemental reference materials regularly enhanced education in the modern school system.

Higher Education. Universities and colleges, for the first time in decades, required philosophy as a general-education course to ensure a more liberal education. In March 1950 the *New York Times* reported that 34 percent of U.S. colleges required history, up from 18 percent in 1942. Science-based graduates decreased and home-economics graduates increased. Critics charged that the educational system had become soft and called for renewed emphasis on the hard sciences and mathematics.

Sputnik **Rocks the World.** In October 1957 the Soviet Union launched *Sputnik,* a small satellite that orbited the globe. *Sputnik* convinced Americans that Soviet scientific knowledge surpassed that of American scientists and that, as a result, the Soviet Union had developed the capacity to launch nuclear warheads at the United States from the Russian heartland. Suddenly, "life adjustment" took a backseat to national pride and security. Educators, government officials, and parents all laid the blame of "falling behind" on the quality of schools. The nation's educational system had become "too relaxed," "too lenient." It was now time to reverse the damage and return to the traditional studies of math, science, and reading. Quality education was perceived as vital to national defense. From all sides came demands for higher standards in schools and colleges, more training in science and mathematics, better provisions for gifted students, and more study required for all students. A strong curriculum-revision movement started in 1958 in the field of mathematics. Reformers also called for improved instruction in foreign languages as well as various revisions in curricula, teaching methods, and requirements. Educators suddenly found themselves facing a crisis.

Tracking. After stepping down as president of Harvard University, Conant, who had criticized the existence of a private school system earlier in the decade, devised a plan in 1958 to improve the nation's high schools. He developed a model school in which bright, average, and slow students all had specific educational "tracks" that they followed throughout their high-school careers. Each particular track would prepare students with similar abilities for a career. Through better planning and more parental involvement the education system, Conant contended, could be saved. Conant's plan closely resembled European models, in which students took periodic tests to advance. Failing a test condemned a student to a certain set of vocations, regardless of the student's personal wishes or professional aspirations.

Humanities. In 1952 the *New York Times* had reported a study that 90 percent of research funds at U.S. universities and colleges was being earmarked for physical and biological sciences. Educators expressed concerns about the lack of funding for the humanities and "soft" sciences. In 1956 the Council for Basic Education was founded to encourage the training of students in English, mathematics, science, history, and foreign languages. Those skills, the council contended, were undertaught. A year later educators reexamined those skills on a national scale, but, in the wake of *Sputnik,* humanities and social studies stood in line behind the sciences for support.

Meeting the Soviet Challenge. Noting the "Soviet challenge," President Dwight D. Eisenhower, during his 1958 state-of-the-union address, called for an expanded National Science Foundation program and new efforts by the Department of Health, Education, and Welfare to improve research and education in the sciences. A Gallup poll in April 1958 reported that high-school principals thought they were meeting the challenge and improving their schools' curricula.

Sources:

J. Ronald Oakley, *God's Country: America in the Fifties* (New York: Dembner Books, 1986);

Nathan M. Pusey, *American Higher Education, 1945–1970: A Personal Report* (Cambridge, Mass.: Harvard University Press, 1978).

DESEGREGATING EDUCATION

Social Revolution. Prior to the 1950s the uniform desegregation of the educational system had already begun at the university level. But it took nothing less than social revolution to force integregation of the nation's segregated elementary and secondary schools,

An anti-integration demonstration in Baltimore, Maryland, 1955

and the higher-education experience provided little help as the entire educational system grappled with the issue.

Sweatt v. *Painter.* In June 1950 the Supreme Court handed down two cases that affected Southern higher education. Heman Marion Sweatt, a black, had applied for admission to the University of Texas Law School in 1946. His application was rejected solely due to race, and he brought a case against the university that resulted in a separate law school being set up for blacks, with part-time faculty from the University of Texas. Sweatt refused to attend, and more litigation ensued. Finally the Supreme Court ruled that the University of Texas Law School must admit Sweatt because the separate law school was "not substantially equal to those available to white law students."

McLaurin v. *Oklahoma State Regents.* The other case involved G. W. McLaurin, a black doctoral student in education at the University of Oklahoma. The school had set aside special places for him to sit in classrooms, the cafeteria, and the library away from white students. The Court decided that McLaurin must "receive the same treatment at the hands of the state as students of other races."

Reaction. The effect of those two cases was profound. Some universities grudgingly admitted black students, while others planted their heels for a fight to the finish. Governor Herman Talmadge of Georgia declared, "As

NAACP lawyers who had argued for the plaintiff in *Brown* v. *Board of Education* stand outside the U.S. Supreme Court Building. Thurgood Marshall stands fourth from right.

long as I am governor, Negroes will not be admitted to white schools." The University of Virginia, the University of Tennessee (both in 1950), and the University of North Carolina (in 1951) joined in Georgia's stand and refused to admit blacks, despite a court ruling requiring them to do so.

Out-of-Court Concessions. Prior to the Supreme Court rulings blacks had won several desegregation battles. Dartmouth College students, in early 1950, voted by more than 80 percent to bar fraternities that practiced religious or racial discrimination. The University of Louisville reported in April that it would close the Louisville Municipal College, a black-only branch campus, and admit blacks to the main campus.

Elementary and Secondary Schools. Prompted by the successful ruling at the university level, the National Association for the Advancement of Colored People (NAACP) pushed on for desegregation of the public elementary and secondary schools. In South Carolina a court case calling for the integration of public schools in Clarendon County came before a special three-judge federal. Gov. James F. Byrnes applied pressure on the court by declaring that he would "reluctantly" close the schools before "mixing the races." The special panel brushed aside the issue, two to one, stating that it was a matter for local authorities to decide, because local control "is essential to the peace and happiness of the people in the communities as well as to strength and unity of the country as a whole." The NAACP promised to appeal.

By 1953 five school-segregation cases were pending before the Supreme Court. Black parents in five areas — Clarendon County, South Carolina; Prince Edward County, Virginia; Topeka, Kansas; Wilmington, Delaware; and Washington, D.C. — contended that separate schooling maintained by school boards violated the Fourteenth Amendment to the Constitution, which prohibited states from abridging constitutional rights of citizens. They also contended that the separate schools were unequal to those of their white counterparts in equipment

and resources. After calling for rearguments several times, the Supreme Court made its landmark decision 17 May 1954 in the case of *Brown* v. *the Board of Education of Topeka, Kansas.*

Brown* v. *the Board of Education of Topeka, Kansas. Setting aside the "separate but equal" doctrine established in *Plessy* v. *Ferguson* (1896) that had allowed states to maintain segregated schools as long as equal support services were provided for blacks and whites, the U.S. Supreme Court ruled unanimously that racial segregation in the public schools was unconstitutional. "In the field of public education," Chief Justice Earl Warren declared, "the doctrine of 'separate but equal' has no place. Separate educational facilities are inherently unequal. Therefore, we hold that the plaintiffs and others similarly situated . . . are . . . deprived of the equal protection of laws guaranteed by the Fourteenth Amendment."

The Effect of Segregation. Reformers made efforts throughout the first half of the decade to end the "separate but equal" doctrine, but the court hesitated to overturn precedent. Even in *Sweatt* v. *Painter,* which in effect outlawed segregation in higher education, the Court shied away from directly overturning *Plessy* v. *Ferguson.* However, in the *Brown* case the Court agreed that even if facilities, academic programs, and teacher qualifications were equal in black and white schools, the effects of segregation still had to be considered.

Prompt, Reasonable Desegregation. The Court discussed the detrimental effect of segregation on the black students. Segregation denoted the inferiority of the Negro race as a whole and had "a tendency to [retard] the educational and mental development of Negro children and to deprive them of some of the benefits they would receive in a racial[ly] integrated school system." The Court made no specific requirements about how quickly its landmark decision had to be implemented. It stipulated only that the nation's schools should be desegregated in a prompt and reasonable manner. That opening gave segregationists time to consolidate their position.

Upheaval. At the time of the ruling 40 percent of the public-school students lived in areas that required segregation by law. Mandatory-segregation laws were in effect in Alabama, Arkansas, Delaware, Florida, Georgia, Kentucky, Louisiana, Maryland, Mississippi, Missouri, North Carolina, Oklahoma, South Carolina, Tennessee, Texas, Virginia, West Virginia, and the District of Columbia. Permissive statutes existed in Arizona, Kansas, New Mexico, and Wyoming. (Phoenix had ended racial segregation in its public high schools through "permissive integration" in July 1953.) Delaware, Maryland, Missouri, West Virginia, and the District of Columbia took steps to integrate students while the remainder of the segregated states decided to wait and see what would occur next.

Reaction to the *Brown* Case. Heated reaction to *Brown,* especially in the South, came immediately. Sev-

Federalized Arkansas troops escort black students into Little Rock Central High School on 25 September 1957.

eral states defied the court decision. Louisiana and Georgia voters approved proposals to permit racially segregated education in November 1954. Louisiana requested a state constitutional amendment to provide such schooling under "police power." Georgia allowed for the allocation of public educational funds to individuals to start private segregated schools. Michigan voters followed suit in December when they approved, almost two to one, a state constitutional amendment to permit the abolition of public schools if there was no other way to avoid racial desegregation of school children. Such actions also occurred in Alabama, Mississippi, North Carolina, and South Carolina. Governor Byrnes of South Carolina contended that state school-building allocations were greater for black students by $168 for the 1954–1955 school year, and therefore these students were receiving a better education.

"Good Faith." The Supreme Court had requested arguments from both sides of the issue to decide when and how to have the *Brown* decision executed. This action culminated in the 31 May 1955 ruling which put the responsibility on lower federal courts and local school authorities. Although the Court gave no specific time frame, it urged "good faith" in the completion of integration.

Defiance and Violence in 1956. North Carolina voters approved a local-option plan for the closing of schools to avoid integration. Florida and Virginia (calling the *Brown* decision an error) adopted pupil-assignment systems in 1956 to avoid desegregation. These programs placed black students away from the white students based on district lines, which the school board could change

autonomously. Tennessee called in local troops and national guardsmen when violence erupted during efforts to integrate. Throughout the South, violence hindered progress in integration. Those black students who did try to attend white schools met with harassment and violence.

Little Rock. Five school districts in Arkansas had planned to integrate with the opening of the 1957–1958 school year. In one of those districts was Little Rock Central High School, scheduled to open 3 September. Five days before the planned opening Gov. Orval Faubus testified before a state chancery court that possible violence and bloodshed would accompany the integration of Central High. That prompted the court to order integration not to proceed, despite the support for integration by the school board. The following day the federal court overruled the lower court and called for no interference with the integration. Still opposing the integration, Faubus, in the name of "maintain[ing] or restor[ing] the peace and good order of this community," ordered the Arkansas National Guard to surround the school the night before it opened. The school year opened the next day with no black students attempting to enroll.

Arkansas National Guard. However, tensions rose as the Arkansas National Guardsmen blocked nine black students from entering the school on 4 September. President Eisenhower met with Governor Faubus on 14 September, and subsequently the governor withdrew the troops, replacing them with local and state police. The nine black students attempted to return to school on 23 September and were met by an angry mob. By noon school officials sent the nine home as the crowd turned

Based on *New York Times* survey, 15 September 1957 (school populations estimated)

Alabama — None (273,200 black; 471,900 white)

Arkansas — Integration in 8 of 228 districts; blocked in Little Rock (102,000 black, 316,700 white)

Delaware — Integration in and around Wilmington; segregation in rest of state (11,411 black, 53,904 white)

District of Columbia — Complete integration (73,723 black, 34,758 white)

Florida — None (165,957 black, 594,220 white)

Georgia — None (297,692 black, 644,378 white)

Kentucky — About 50 percent integrated (38,358 black, 551,771 white)

Louisiana — None (225,000 black, 375,000 white)

Maryland — Baltimore area integrated; considerable integration in western counties; areas with large black populations integrating slowly (109,720 black, 397,417 white)

Mississippi — None (268,216 black, 273,722 white)

Missouri — 95 percent of Negro students in some level of integrated schools (67,000 black, 677,500 white)

North Carolina — "Limited integration" in some schools (301,161 black, 724,302 white)

South Carolina — None (243,574 black, 319,670 white)

Tennessee — Some despite opposition (128,164 black, 626,781 white)

Texas — Proceeding slowly but nonviolently (248,532 black, 1,565,568 white)

Virginia — None (184,417 black, 566,596 white)

West Virginia — Integration started in all 43 counties with black population (23,806 black, 434,001 white)

threatening. Eisenhower then issued a proclamation ordering the mob to disperse and cease interfering with a court order. When a mob returned 24 September the president ordered the Arkansas National Guard into federal service and sent members of the 101st Airborne Division to enforce the integration of the school. (Those were the same guardsmen, now under federal, not state, control, who a few weeks earlier had been keeping the black students out.)

Enrolled at Last. With the protection of rifles and bayonets, the nine students returned to Central High on 25 September. A majority of the troops withdrew in November, but federalized state militia continued to protect the students throughout the school year. Although the situation fueled the segregationists' fire — for example, they charged the militia with misconduct (peeking in the girls' bathrooms) — eight of the original nine black students completed the school year, with one graduating.

The Court's Resolve. Efforts to halt any form of desegregation ensued during the summer of 1958. Cases brought before the Supreme Court, however, renewed the Court's resolve to see the nation's schools integrated. In the end, Governor Faubus effectively closed Central High for the 1958–1959 school year after the Supreme Court ordered the resumption of racial integration in September 1958. Students received makeshift educations in private schools sponsored by private organizations and churches, and Faubus announced a nationwide appeal for funds to support this private system in October of that year. Finally, the delays and continuances ran out, and the 1959–1960 school year opened with integrated classes.

Repercussions of Little Rock. The events in Little Rock shook the nation and rippled throughout the world. Propaganda from behind the iron curtain portrayed the U.S. educational system as racist and the violence as symptomatic of a permissive nation. Southern citizens felt oppressed by the federal government once again, dredging up comparisons to the occupation during Reconstruction. Only North Carolina, of the unintegrated states as of 1956, had moved toward real desegregation.

Virginia. Virginia watched closely the events in Arkansas as it strove to avoid the integration of its schools through "massive resistance." Pupil-placement systems were established, and many school districts closed in efforts to keep the races apart. By October 1958 Virginia had instituted a private educational system in the city of Norfolk, similar to that in Arkansas though some black students were admitted to the University of Virginia.

The Supreme Court Steps in Again. After several southern states had taken drastic steps to avoid integration, including closing their schools, the Supreme Court ruled in September 1958 that states could not use "evasive schemes," nor other direct or indirect methods, to perpetuate public-school segregation. The decision reiterated the requirement of state officials to obey the court decisions and called for states to take immediate measures toward desegregation.

The Breaking of Virginia's Resistance. Despite court orders and appeals by segregationists, the persistence of the integrationists paid off. In early 1959 Governor J. Lindsey Almond, Jr., stated that all efforts to maintain segregation had been "exhausted" and some integration would soon be "inevitable." The state repealed its compulsory-attendance laws, arguing it could not force students to attend integrated schools, and funds for tuition grants to private schools were increased. Efforts to resist the integration of Virginia's student population continued at the beginning of the 1959–1960 school year. However, black students slowly worked their way into the public schools and the program of "massive resistance" gradually broke down.

Student Attitudes. Critics and educators examined the effect on the students in Little Rock and Norfolk. Few doubted that the lost school time would adversely affect students. Department of Health, Education, and Welfare Secretary Arthur Flemming warned of immeasurable "social, economic and psychological" harm to the students. A study by *Life* magazine in 1958 revealed many students went to work stating they would not return to school if it reopened, and many married early; but the majority wanted to return to school even if it meant integration.

The North. The fight for desegregation was not strictly a Southern problem. Schools around the nation were affected; emotions ran high in all parts of the country. Four fraternities, Lambda Chi Alpha, Sigma Nu, Kappa Sigma, and Sigma Chi, at the University of Connecticut lost their national charters for breaking a university ban on racial and religious discrimination in 1951. New York City schools faced charges, not only of segregating blacks but of discrimination against Italian and Puerto Rican students as late as 1958.

Integration at the Close of the Decade. By the end of the 1950s, six school years after *Brown*, five states remained segregated — Alabama, Georgia, Louisiana, Mississippi, and South Carolina. Desegregation at the college level moved along, albeit slowly. Several all-black institutions accepted white students for the first time. Integration of the races had started but still had a long road ahead — the issue of discrimination continued to plague school boards well into the next decades.

Sources:

Jennifer L. Hochschild, *The New American Dilemma: Liberal Democracy and School Desegregation* (New Haven, Conn.: Yale University Press, 1984);

Lewis B. Mayhew, ed. *Higher Education in the Revolutionary Decades* (Berkeley, Cal.: McCutchan Publishing, 1967).

JOHN DEWEY AND PROGRESSIVE EDUCATION

John Dewey, the father of "progressive education," died in 1952. The founder and president of the American Association of University Professors, Dewey spent his life dealing with philosophy and education as they related to democracy. His work, *Democracy and Education* (1916), charged that education was an experimental science capable of guiding individual and community growth toward better democracy.

Progressive education, while not new in the 1950s, was a driving force in schools. Dewey challenged educators to concern themselves with such aspects of learning as conversation, curiosity, construction skills, and artistic expression. His view of education advocated learning by doing. Students were taught by "projects" wherein, for example, the study of milk could be related to science, math, reading, and so on. Critics, including the Council on Basic Education, charged that students under this program were lacking in basic skills. Despite this criticism, progressive education continued to affect teaching methods throughout the decade.

Source:

Daniel Tanner, *Crusade for Democracy* (Albany: State University of New York Press, 1991).

DRAFTING COLLEGE STUDENTS

The Korean War in the early 1950s resulted in an active draft of college-age males. In January 1951 Secretary of Defense George C. Marshall announced that male college students could finish their academic year, but then they had to enlist in the military branch of their choice or risk the draft. There was a 50 percent drop in spring-semester enrollments, due to panic enlistments by students who wanted to choose for themselves which branch of the military to enter.

Two months later, in March 1951, President Harry S Truman approved deferment of college students of superior scholastic standing or those who achieved high scores on national aptitude tests. In October 1951 it was reported that 37 percent of the 339,056 college students who took the aptitude tests, given on four different dates earlier in the year, had passed, earning deferment. Some local boards complained that college deferments made it difficult for them to meet quotas.

PARTING SHOT

Budget cuts "are making it impossible . . . to serve education in this country through this office."

— Earl J. McGrath resigning as U.S. commissioner of education, April 1953.

A soldier stationed overseas works to complete a college degree by correspondence.

In the South more college-age men escaped the draft because of illiteracy than scholastic potential. Draft boards in five southern states had the highest rejection rates in the nation of men educationally unfit to serve in the military: in South Carolina 58 percent of all persons aged twenty-five to thirty-five tested functionally illiterate, in Louisiana 48 percent; in Mississippi 45 percent; in Alabama 43 percent; and in Georgia, 36 percent.

After the war a debate began about educational benefits for the veterans. World War II veterans received eductional benefits under the Serviceman's Readjustment Act of 1944 (better known as the G.I. Bill of Rights). That act provided monthly allowances for books and living expenses as well as up to $500 paid directly to colleges for tuition. The Veterans Readjustment Assistance Act of 1952 provided Korean War veterans with $110–$160 monthly, but they had to pay their own tuition and expenses. The Association of American Colleges worked in 1954 for the equalization of benefits for all veterans, arguing that Korean veterans were not being treated fairly, but Congress was unsympathetic.

Source:
J. Ronald Oakley, *God's Country: America in the Fifties* (New York: Dembner Books, 1986).

FEDERAL FUNDING FOR EDUCATION

Federal funding for education was controversial during the 1950s. Social and political events shaped education and how it was financed. The U.S. Chamber of Commerce reported in 1950 that the annual cost of educating a pupil, adjusted for inflation, rose 37 percent over the previous decade (from $92 per pupil per year in 1940 to $232 in 1950 in dollars of the day; by 1960 per pupil expenditure for education rose to $433). The funding from all sources needed for pupil education during the 1950s reached over $15 billion by 1959. However, the percentage of national income spent on education had dropped from 15.31 percent in 1940 to 8.24 percent in

1950 and was predicted to drop more during the 1950s. (In fact, the percentage rose slightly during the decade.) Educators and social observers argued for more federal aid to education as a means of ensuring the ability of the nation to compete in the world economy and to keep pace in the age of technology.

Little attention was paid at the time, however, to the strings attached to federal funds. Few realized the potential for federal intrusion into education until 1954, when the federal government ordered desegregation. Although the U.S. Supreme Court did not apply the principle at the time, it later argued that even though the federal government provided only about 4.5 percent of the cost of educating a student in public elementary and secondary schools in 1956, the use of federal funds obligated a school or school system to comply with all federal "guidelines" (not statutes). States, which supplied nearly 40 percent of the cost of education, and local governments, which contributed more than the states, felt that their preferences should have precedence over those of the federal government. But their argument was ultimately rejected, and though federal funding increased modestly, most of the cost of education was raised from state and local taxes.

Source:
Erick L. Lindman, *The Federal Government and Public Schools* (Washington, D.C.: American Association of School Administrators, 1965).

GREAT BOOKS PROGRAM

The American Dream and Self-Education. The 1950s was a decade in which middle-class Americans sought to improve themselves through self-education. In this country the path of upward social mobility is clear-cut. First comes prosperity, then respectability, and one of the components of respectability is a liberal arts education. It was too late for newly prosperous adults to return to the classroom to get the knowledge they imagined they had missed the first time through, if they had been lucky enough to receive a college education: only about 6 percent of adults had college degrees in 1950. Self-education was the next best alternative, and it was offered through the highly touted Great Books program.

Bringing the Great Books to the Masses. The Great Books Foundation was started in 1947 by Robert M. Hutchins, president of the University of Chicago, "to provide the means of general liberal education to all adults." The foundation boasted a distinguished team of experts, including philosopher-historian Mortimer J. Adler. By 1950 there were some twelve hundred Great Books programs in four hundred cities with about twenty-five thousand participants. Adults ranging in occupation from cabdriver to clergyman met in classrooms, YMCAs, churches, and homes to discuss those works that the foundation had designated as "Great Books."

A 1952 poster advertising the Great Books program

Group Discussions. Each group had a trained leader who led the discussions. The group leader did not lecture, for the purpose of the program in Hutchins's words was to allow people to participate in the "Great Conversation" of world culture. Hutchins believed that through open discussion of the ideas presented in the books a kind of cultural vocabulary was formed, allowing the group to communicate in an enlightened way and to appreciate and advance their cultural traditions.

Publishing the Great Books. The curriculum of the Great Books program was traditional. It was heavy on ancient Greek and Roman writers and on Renaissance culture and, as some critics pointed out, was noticeably light on American literature. In 1952 the Encyclopaedia Britannica brought out a fifty-four-volume set called *Great Books of the Western World*, edited by Hutchins. The set sold for $249.50 and included the works of seventy-four authors from Homer to Sigmund Freud.

MIDCENTURY WHITE HOUSE CONFERENCE ON CHILDREN AND YOUTH

On 3–7 December 1950 the White House Conference on Youth and Children, held at the beginning of each decade, brought together over six thousand delegates and observers from the United States and abroad. The conference was the culmination of two years of preparation by 464 national organizations, including the National Education Association. The first attendance by children was in 1950.

The conference was a nonpartisan, nongovernmental project with only one-fifth of the funding coming from federal sources. The purpose was "to consider what we need to do in order to develop in children the mental, emotional, and spiritual qualities essential to individual happiness and responsible citizenship; and how the physical, economic, and social conditions of our society affect this great goal." A set of sixty-seven recommendations and a pledge to children resulted from the four days of panels and sessions. Among the many recommendations were several related to education including:

* That elementary, secondary, college and community education includes such appropriate experiences and studies of childhood and family life as will help young people to mature toward the role of parenthood.

* That further federal aid be provided to the states for educational services, in tax-supported public schools, without federal control, to help equalize educational opportunity; the issue of auxiliary services to be considered on its merits in separate legislation.

* That it be made possible for qualified youth to obtain college or university education which would otherwise be denied them because of inability to pay.

* Recognizing that knowledge and understanding of religious and ethical concepts are essential to the development of the moral and spiritual health of our nation and the work of religious education in our homes and families, and in our institutions of organized religion, we nevertheless strongly affirm the principle of separation of church and state which has been the keystone of our American democracy, and declare ourselves unalterably opposed to the use of the public schools, directly or indirectly, for religious educational purposes.

* That the Federal Communications Commission reserve television channels for noncommercial educational television stations so that some part of the limited number of frequencies to be allocated by the commission may be reserved for educational uses and purposes which contribute to healthy personality development.

* That local boards of education accept full responsibility for providing adequately for the education of children with physical and mental handicaps.

* That racial segregation in education be abolished.

* That school lunches be provided and that children unable to pay for their lunches be furnished them free.

NATIONAL DEFENSE EDUCATION ACT OF 1958

NDEA. By 1958 the Soviet threat grew more immediate; the Soviet Union had launched *Sputnik* in late 1957, suggesting the capability to launch offensive missiles at the United States. For the first time in the decade, the president recommended deferring plans for school

To You, our children, who hold within you our most cherished hopes, we the members of the Midcentury White House Conference on Children and Youth, relying on your full response, make this pledge:

"From your earliest infancy, we give you our love, so that you may grow with trust in yourself and in others.

We will recognize your worth as a person, and we will help you to strengthen your sense of belonging.

We will respect your right to be yourself and, at the same time, help you to understand the rights of others, so that you may experience cooperative living.

We will help you to develop initiative and imagination, so that you may have the opportunity freely to create.

We will encourage your curiosity and your pride in workmanship, so that you may have the satisfaction that comes from achievement.

We will provide the conditions for wholesome play that will add to your learning, to your social experience, and to your happiness.

We will illustrate by precept and example the value of integrity and the importance of moral courage.

We will encourage you always to seek the truth.

We will provide you will all opportunities possible to develop your own faith in God.

We will open the way for you to enjoy the arts and to use them for deepening your understanding of life.

We will work to rid ourselves of prejudice and disrimination, so that together we may achieve a truly democratic society.

We will work to lift the standard of living and to improve our economic practices, so that you may have the material basis for a full life.

We will provide you with rewarding educational opportunities, so that you may develop your talents and contribute to a better world.

We will protect you against exploitation and undue hazards and help you grow in health and strength.

We will work to conserve and improve family life and, as needed, to provide foster care according to your inherent rights.

We will intensify our search for new knowledge in order to guide you more effectively as you develop your potentials.

As you grow from child to youth to adult, establishing a family life of your own and accepting larger social responsibilities, we will work with you to improve conditions for all children and youth.

Aware that these promises to you cannot be fully met in a world at war, we ask you to join us in a firm dedication to the building of a world society based on freedom, justice, and mutual respect.

SO MAY YOU grow in joy, in faith in God and in man, and in those qualities of vision and of the spirit that will sustain us all and give us new hope for the future."

Unanimously adopted by the Midcentury White House Conference, December 7, 1950.

---

construction in favor of support for the sciences. The National Defense Education Act provided $887 million over four years for education that could support national security goals — especially training scientists. The act contained ten titles designed to improve the nation's schools:

Title I prohibited federal control over curriculum, administration, or personnel;

Title II provided federal assistance for low-interest loans to college students ($295 million);

Title III provided financial assistance for science, mathematics, and modern foreign-language instruction ($300 million);

Title IV created National Defense Fellowships for students entering teaching fields at universities or colleges;

Title V established grants for state educational agencies for guidance testing services ($88 million);

Title VI provided support for modern foreign language programs ($15.25 million);

Title VII provided for research and experimentation in effective uses for television, radio and other audiovisual mediums for educational purposes ($18 million);

Title VIII authorized grants for occupations necessary for the national defense ($60 million);

Title IX provided for the Science Information Service in the National Science Foundation;

Title X authorized federal grants for improvement of statistical services for state educational agencies.

No Strings. Controversy erupted in 1959 over two provisions of the act. Some twenty colleges and universities refused to accept loans because the act required loan recipients to pledge their loyalty to the United States and swear that they did not support attempts to overthrow the government. President Dwight D. Eisenhower stated he "deplored" the actions by the universities involved, and the requirement stayed. In another case, the Board of Education in Cincinnati, Ohio, refused to accept a grant, based on its desire to avoid any federal control of its system as a result of its acceptance of federal funding.

Sources:

Douglas M. Knight, ed., *The Federal Government and Higher Education* (prepared for the American Assembly, Columbia University (Englewood Cliffs, N. J.: Prentice-Hall, 1960);

Erick L. Lindman, *The Federal Government and Public Schools* (Washington, D.C.: American President's Committee on Education).

OFFICE OF EDUCATION AND DEPARTMENT OF HEALTH, EDUCATION, AND WELFARE (HEW)

Background. For almost a century the United States valued education enough to dedicate a special governmental office to it. The Office of Education was formed in 1867 in President Andrew Johnson's administration and was under the Department of the Interior. In 1939 the office came under the Federal Security Agency. Although the Office of Education had no direct administrative authority over the various state educational agencies, it did have specific tasks. The office conducted educational research and collected statistics and other facts about education; it administered federal grants-in-aid for vocational training in a variety of fields; and it helped in program planning with respect to school standards in administration, instruction, teacher training, and supervision. Its legal mandate was to "aid the people of the United States in the establishment and maintenance of efficient school systems, and otherwise promote the cause of education throughout the country."

Oveta Culp Hobby being sworn in as secretary of the newly created cabinet-level Department of Health, Education, and Welfare

A New Secretary. On 1 April 1953 President Eisenhower created the cabinet-level Department of Health, Education, and Welfare when he signed Joint Resolution 223. Sworn in on 11 April, Oveta Culp Hobby became the first secretary of HEW. During the decade she and two other secretaries dealt with a variety of crises in education.

Chaotic Year. During 1954 Hobby struggled to meet the demands of desegregation and shortages of both teachers and classrooms while struggling to distribute effectively the newly licensed Salk vaccine to protect the country's children from polio. It was a chaotic time for the new department, and Hobby resigned after a year. On 13 July 1955 President Eisenhower named Marion B. Folsom to replace her.

PRESIDENT'S COMMITTEE ON EDUCATION BEYOND THE HIGH SCHOOL

White House Conference on Education. In April 1956, as one result of the White House Conference on Education in 1955, the president created a thirty-three-member committee to study the problems of higher education. The committee examined four problems: the demand for post–high-school education now and in the next fifteen years; the resources to meet this demand; the proposals made for modification and improvement; and the appropriate relationships of the federal government to education beyond the high school.

Interim Report. The committee presented an interim report in November 1956 that called attention to the need for (1) state-by-state surveys of future enrollments, necessary facilities, and staff along with probable costs;

(2) a definite federal policy on aid to education beyond the high school; (3) expansion of sources for financial support; (4) a broader ranger of post–high-school educational opportunities; and (5) "many more able and qualified teachers than present efforts can provide."

Final Report. A final report, prepared in August 1957, called for emphasis on recruiting teachers, creation of a work-study program, income-tax deductions for college expenses, and long-range goal planning for college budgets, and long-range planning for college facilities. It concluded that in order to get the best, the government must support the best.

QUALITY IN EDUCATION?

A 1951 test by the California State Board of Education of eleven thousand Los Angeles high school juniors revealed startling facts about the nation's schools. Three percent of the students tested could not tell time; 18 percent did not know the number of months in a year; 9 percent did not know how many 3 cent stamps could be bought for 75 cents; and 16 percent did not know how many U.S. senators came from each state.

A *New York Times* survey, reported on 11 June 1951, revealed that college and university students showed a "shocking" lack of knowledge about U.S. and world geography. Less than 50 percent could estimate the U.S. population within 50 percent. Critics of the new "life-adjustment" curricula used the result to renew their calls for a return to basics.

FUNDING THE FUTURE THROUGH R AND D

Help for the Sciences. In 1950 the National Science Foundation began an annual survey of funding available from various sources for use in research and development, with a special emphasis, as one might expect, on funds available for scientific R and D. The results of the first survey, which covered the year 1953, showed research at the country's colleges and universities was big business but not big enough. In 1953 $334 million was expended at American institutions of higher education for R and D; the total national expenditure was $5.2 billion, of which 53 percent came from federal sources. By 1960 R and D expenditures had jumped to $825 million at universities as compared to a total of $13.7 billion of which 63.7 percent came from federal sources. In short, only about 6 percent of the nation's research and development was on college campuses, and the percentage of expended money that came from industry shrunk over the decade.

University Response. The lesson seemed clear. Universities could be called upon to produce scientists and mathematicians to meet the challenges of the future, but after they were trained, big business put them to work. Doctoral degrees in the hard sciences, mathematics, and education grew slightly over the decade as funding pro-

moted better programs. But universities did not respond well to the challenge of producing more scientists. What they did prove adept at was producing more teachers. In 1959 there were over 1,000 doctorates awarded in each of only two fields: education, 1,549, and chemistry, 1,054. The next highest total was in engineering, with 699.

Source:
Homer D. Babbidge, Jr., and Robert M. Rosenzweig, *The Federal Interest in Higher Education* (New York: McGraw-Hill, 1962).

THE "RED SCARE" IN EDUCATION

Hunting Communists. The "Red Scare" of the 1950s touched every aspect of people's lives, including education. The loyalty of educators, at all levels, came under scrutiny as people expressed their fears that subversive forces were seeking control of schools. In February 1950 the U.S. commissioner of education, Dr. Earl James McGrath, warned against Communists teaching in public school, and the National Education Association barred membership of Communists at its annual meeting in July 1950. School districts required loyalty oaths from their teachers and employees. Universities cleansed their staffs and faculties of suspected subversive personnel. Such purges came at a price. The New York City school districts found so may suspected subversives that they suffered teacher shortages due to dismissals.

New York Eight. In May 1950 eight teachers in New York City suspected of being Communists were suspended without pay, pending a board subcommittee trial. By mid December the eight were recommended for dismissal, although no specific proof could be found during a seven-month investigation that any of them had Com-

A crowd of students watches as the University of California board of regents debates the issue of requiring faculty members to sign a loyality oath.

RADICALISM ON CAMPUS

The student activism which would result in violence protest during the coming decades got its start in the late 1950s. Students, angered over segregation and political issues such as loyalty oaths, began to grumble starting in 1958. Colleges and universities which were seeking to produce a better "product" (that is, a better-trained adult population) also brought students a more-enlightened product. Students were finding their voices in a world where their sheer number was increasing. The "silent and apathetic" college atmosphere of the early 1950s evolved into the breeding ground for the student radicals of the 1960s and 1970s.

munist ties or sympathies. The subcommittee used as its strongest argument against the teachers a 30 November decision by the New York Court of Appeals, which upheld the controversial Feinberg law barring Communists or suspected Communists from teaching school. (The Supreme Court upheld the Feinberg law on 3 March 1952. The majority opinion held that "school authorities have the right and duty to screen" those who "shape the attitude of young minds toward the society in which they live. . . .") In February 1951 the eight suspected teachers were fired, and three more quit over the controversy. A year later eight more teachers and administrators were suspended for alleged Communist connections. In 1957 the New York State education commissioner reversed the suspension and rehired five of the teachers.

The Rest of the Nation. Other states felt the effect of these fears. In both Ohio and New Jersey the state Supreme Courts upheld the validity of requiring public school teachers to take a loyalty oath, and in 1951 Oklahoma's governor, Johnston Murray, signed a bill that required a statement of loyalty from teachers and government employees. In Philadelphia public schools suspended twenty-six teachers in 1953 after they pleaded the Fifth Amendment and refused to answer questions about Communist ties.

Burning Books. Educational materials used in the classrooms also came under scrutiny. In December 1951 the New York State Board of Regents commissioned three men to check on subversive material in public-school textbooks. Similar actions took place around the country and led to the censorship of reading materials in the schools and in the community libraries. In February 1952 Charles Hartman, vice president of the board of education in Sapulpa, Oklahoma, reported the burning of "5 or 6" books which dealt with "socialism and sex."

Higher Education. Educators and administrators at the university level also fell victim to the "Red Scare" in record numbers. Many were forced to sign loyalty oaths or answer interrogation-style questions. That posed a difficult problem for professors who objected to both the infringements of their academic freedom and their constitutional rights. Sen. Joseph McCarthy made it his personal goal to clean house of the "Communist thinkers" and subversive influences in colleges. Being a member of the Communist party constituted sure grounds for dismissal from schools, but at the college level even having communist or socialist ideas could get one fired.

Loyalty Oath in California. On 25 March 1949 the Board of Regents of the University of California proposed to require that faculty members sign a loyalty oath. Controversy ensued, and faculty members mourned the fate of their academic freedom. By the end of the year the opposing sides were stalemated. Then in February 1950 the University of California singled out and ordered 13.5 percent of its 11,000 faculty members to sign a loyalty oath or to resign. After more heated controversy the university dropped the mandatory oath in April and insisted instead that the faculty in question sign a constitutional loyalty oath, which the state of California already required state employees to sign. Over the late spring and summer, 15 percent of the faculty and staff members received their dismissals by the university after still refusing to sign. Because of the faculty shortages, forty-eight classes were then dropped from the fall semester in September. The winter semester opened with 15 new faculty members, hired to fill positions held by the 188 fired, who themselves refused to sign the state loyalty oath. By April 1951 the state court of appeals ruled the university's action unconstitutional and ordered it to reinstate 18 faculty members previously dismissed. In October 1952, the California Supreme Court, which declared the university oath unconstitutional but upheld the validity of the state oath, upheld the appeals court's ruling. Subsequently the 18 faculty members were reinstated.

AAUP Report. The loyalty oath issue came before the U.S. Supreme Court in late 1952. The court ruled that states could not deny employment to people "solely on the basis of organizational membership, regardless of their knowledge concerning the organization to which they had belonged." That essentially reinstated hundreds of university-level personnel across the country. Nonetheless, in March 1953 the American Association of University Professors released a report declaring that membership in the Communist party was sufficient to fire a faculty member because of the Communist code of conduct. However, the AAUP also denounced loyalty oaths, banning books, and the congressional investigations in its report.

Federal Intrusion. By 1954 the "Red Scare" had abated, but debates over the right of government to question the organizational ties of its citizens continued. Many felt local school boards should police their own teachers and that the federal government should stay out of local affairs. The fear of communism was soon replaced, for whites at least, by a more easily identifiable fear — of blacks in the schools — raising the argument about federal intrusion into local schools to a higher pitch.

Sources:

David Pierpont Gardner, *The California Oath Controversy* (Berkeley: University of California Press, 1967);

Charles Howard McCormick, *This Nest of Vipers: McCarthyism and Higher Education in the Mundel Affair, 1951–52* (Urbana: University of Illinois Press, 1989).

REPORT CARDS

SNUX. How students should be evaluated came under scrutiny during the 1950s. As curricula and teaching methods changed, so did the traditional method of grading: As, Bs, Cs, and so on. The newest fad in grading became known as SNUX, or Satisfactory or Unsatisfactory. The change affected all grade levels and brought about a revolt by the parents who grew up with the traditional method.

Comparing Students. Parents and critics of the new system contended that a former "C" student would be considered "Satisfactory," undistinguished from the former "A" student. Some educators feared a drop in the natural competition between students which fosters learning. In addition, the new system also increased the amount of work for teachers who had to rate a student's ability in science and math as well as evaluating him or her in such new categories as "Ability to communicate" and "Ability to not spread disease." Critics were unsuccessful, however, and the new grading system continued well into the coming decades, especially at the elementary-school level.

SCHOOL DROPOUTS

Who Had to Go. State laws defining compulsory school attendance varied widely during the 1950s. Children between the ages of fourteen and sixteen who had legal employment typically were allowed to quit school. In twenty-one states a student could leave only after reaching the eighth grade, and in twelve states only after reaching the sixth or seventh grade. In 1955 the NEA called for mandatory attendance until graduation from high school or age eighteen. But the issue fell under the states' control, so each state had to debate the issue and pass its own law.

Why Drop Out? A survey in 1950 of students who dropped out before completing high school reported that 36 percent preferred to work; 15 percent needed the money to help at home; 11 percent were not interested in school; and the remainder cited various reasons, such as failure, poor performance, ill health, or dislike of a subject or teacher. A majority of students called for more work-experience opportunities, specific vocational train-

ing, and smaller class sizes to provide increased individual attention. Those requests played into the hands of educators who stressed the life-adjustment curriculum.

SCHOOL SHORTAGES

Too Many Students. The baby boom after World War II traumatized the education system during the 1950s. School enrollment had been more or less unchanged from year to year from the 1930s until 1952, when the first wave of baby boomers hit. Every year thereafter elementary school population increased by 1.5 to 2 million students, and between 1950 and 1960 the number of students in elementary school had increased by 50 percent. Concerns over the supply of teachers and school buildings to educate those students began well before 1952. In February 1950 the U.S. Office of Education warned in its annual report that the nation's educational system had "shocking disorder and ineffectiveness." The report estimated that $10 billion would be needed to improve and build school buildings and increase the teacher supply; by 1951 estimates had increased to $14 billion. The nation needed to build approximately 270,000 new classrooms to meet enrollment increases.

Threatened Standards. As educators and government strived to increase the amount of money appropriated for schools, the U.S. Office of Education reported that expenditures for towns of more than twenty-five hundred dropped six dollars per pupil per year in 1950–1951. Commissioner of Education Earl J. McGrath called the drop "shocking" and stated "we cannot afford a further reduction in education standards."

Construction Needs. Several times a year during the decade Office of Education or NEA reports underscored the shortage of classrooms and schools compared to the rising enrollments of students. As each report came out, local and state governments requested more aid from the federal government, signaling a dramatic shift in the control over American schools. Attempts to attach strings to education dollars, most often to promote federal funding of parochial schools or integration, caused legislation designed to address the problem to fail. For example, in 1956 Representative Adam Clayton Powell attached an

FEDERAL HOUSING

"U.S. Education is undoubtedly worse than it was 25 years ago. All we can say of American education is that it's a colossal housing project designed to keep young people out of worse places until they are able to go to work."
— Dr. Robert M. Hutchins, 1951.

Due to school-building shortages during the Korean War, these students make do in an airplane that has been converted into a classroom.

amendment to a construction bill (HR 7535) that called for the allocation of aid only to states that complied with the *Brown* v. *Board of Education, Topeka, Kansas* decision in the integration of schools. That amendment caused the defeat of a measure that would have allocated $1.6 billion over four years for construction.

Continued Overcrowding. As of 1953 the nation had allocated over $350 million for the construction of schools. In each subsequent year at least $150 million more was earmarked for construction; between 1950 and 1960 the value of construction for educational buildings (in 1957–1959 dollars) rose from $1.133 billion to $2.818 billion. Even so, by the end of the decade many children still attended overcrowded, deteriorating schools. Some school districts were forced to split the school day into two sessions in order to find the space to instruct the growing classes. In 1956 it was estimated that $16 billion would be needed by 1959 to meet the growing enrollments. In 1957 a $1.5 billion education construction bill failed in Congress. Federal legislators openly expressed the hope that funding school construction would become a responsibility born by state and local governments. Federal spending bills began calling for "matching funds" from state and local governments, an ironic twist considering education had been solely in the domain of state and local governments until the 1930s. The federal grants to state and local governments peaked in 1955 with 9.6 percent of all grants going to education compared to 3.7 percent in 1950 and 6 percent in 1959.

War Needs. Not only did restrictions on funding affect building construction, but steel shortages due to strikes throughout the decade hindered the process. Allocations for school construction could not meet the demand for new buildings. The NEA and other agencies worked to increase the steel allocations, but, especially during the Korean War, steel had destinations other than the classrooms.

One-Room Schoolhouses. Existing school structures posed still other problems. In 1951 Commissioner McGrath reported "one out of every five schoolhouses now in use throughout the United States should be abandoned or extensively remodeled because they are fire hazards, obsolete, or health risks." Twenty-five percent of elementary school students attended schools with no indoor toilet facilities. As class sizes soared, up to fifty students jammed into single rooms with poor ventilation. There were still 39,061 one-room, one-teacher schools operating in 1955.

Source:
Earl James McGrath, *Education the Wellspring of Democracy* (Tuscaloosa: University of Alabama Press, 1951).

TEACHERS

College Training. Concerns about the quality of the nation's teachers grew as the number of students in the school system increased. In 1950 the American Association of Colleges for Teacher Education stated that 90 percent of college professors were poor teachers. The National Education Association's Commission on Teacher Education and Professional Standards, in February 1951, reported that less than 50 percent of the twelve hundred colleges and universities offering training in education met "reasonable standards." It labeled training as "chaotic," and the associations urged a national organization to improve training for teachers and the professors who taught them. That, coupled with the massive dismissals due to the "Red Scares," left the educational system lacking an adequate teacher base.

Teacher Accreditation. In 1952 the National Committee on Accreditation urged reform of accreditation for several fields of higher education, especially schools of education and teacher-education departments. Instead of more than three hundred independent college-accrediting agencies, the higher educational system should fall

M.A. IN TEACHING

In 1951 the Ford Foundation established the Fund for the Advancement of Education to support experimental programs for improved teacher education. The development of a master of arts in teaching became one of the group's earliest accomplishments. The degree grew out of the "fifth year" programs started at Harvard in 1936. These programs gave traditional liberal arts graduates an opportunity to learn teaching methods during a "fifth year." The Fund for the Advancement of Education piloted programs to turn that fifth year into a master's program which continued to grow in future decades.

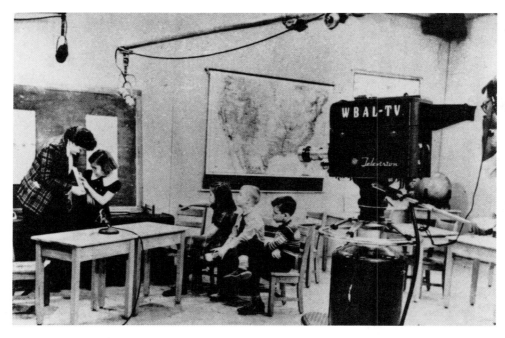

After a city-employee strike in 1953 closed schools in Baltimore, Maryland, city television stations aired educational programs as substitutes for the classroom.

into six regional associations, the committee recommended. This would make steps to standardize requirements for teacher licensing easier. By 1959, forty states required at least a bachelor's degree for teacher certification (compared to six in 1937), and efforts were made to intensify the requirements even beyond that.

Filling Vacancies. In 1950, 914,000 teachers were in classrooms with over twenty-nine million elementary and secondary students (a 1 to 33 ratio). It was estimated by the NEA in 1952 that the nation had only one qualified teacher for every five vacancies. States issued thousands of temporary or emergency certificates in an attempt to alleviate some shortages. But a vast number of schools were forced to split the day into two sessions to serve more students. The new suburban schools as well as the ever-crowded urban centers needed teachers. Colleges and universities, already pressured to meet higher standards, struggled to produce large numbers of graduates. States, in response, implemented scholarship programs to encourage college students to work in education. The numbers of new teachers, however, still trailed the number of students entering school.

Recruitment. In 1956, as shortages continued, the Labor Department announced that it would recruit retired officers and other armed forces personnel for high-school–teaching positions. That won the support of the NEA, which projected the end of shortages by 1962 as a result of increases in college graduates majoring in education. Other groups called upon to teach included mathematicians, physicists, chemists, and engineers — all employed in private industry. Indeed, some observers charged that industry had "raided" college graduates and

wooed them away from education with more lucrative salaries. Plans were made by the federal government to form a national educational reserve to meet teacher shortages. The result of all these efforts was that in 1960 there were only 1,464,000 teachers in public elementary and secondary schools to serve a student population of over 34 million students. The student-teacher ratio was 32.2 to one in elementary school and 15.4 to one in secondary schools.

Teacher Salaries. Many graduates avoided teaching as a profession due to low average pay. The U.S. Office of Education put the average pay for U.S. public elementary and secondary teachers in 1950 at just over $3,000 a year. (College-level teachers fared a bit better with an average annual salary of $4,354). But in the rural South salaries were less than half of the national average. Recruiting teachers to that region proved increasingly difficult. Worse, the turnover rate for teachers increased over the decade. By 1953 the rate was highest since the end of World War II.

National Disgrace. The NEA's 1953 annual convention declared teachers' salaries to be a "national disgrace" and called for efforts to increase the minimum scale to help recruit new people to the field of education. More teachers left the field than entered it because of low pay and classroom overcrowding (one-third of children were in classes of 36 or more, one-eleventh in classes of 41 or more in 1953). By 1959 the average teacher salary had climbed to $5,100 ($6,711 for college teachers).

Teacher Strikes. Several teacher unions waged strikes against local school districts over pay increases during the 1950s. A twenty-two day strike in Minneapolis closed the public school system in 1951 as teachers, janitors, and clerks demanded more money. As strikes in Connecticut increased, the state supreme court finally ruled that teachers had no right to strike or bargain collectively. Parents and administrators expressed outrage at the teaching days lost. Increasingly the public viewed strikes by teachers as a threat to public safety. Garfield, New Jersey, teachers went out on strike in 1953 after funds earmarked for a pay raise had been used elsewhere. Teachers strikes in Baltimore the same year resulted in the use of television programs to educate those students affected by closed schools.

More Money! The NEA called for the federal government to help states pay teachers' salaries in 1954. It contended that quality teachers for quality education demanded increased compensation. Those efforts proved fruitless as federal funding focused on research and development and construction while day-to-day expenses, such as salaries, remained in the hands of the state and local budgets.

University of Southern California professor Frank C. Baxter
teaching Shakespeare on television

TELEVISION'S EFFECT ON EDUCATION

The Tube Invasion. Many Americans found a new source of entertainment in the 1950s — television. Before long, critics worried that the "boob tube" would have harmful effects on education. In 1950, 3.875 million American households, or 9 percent, owned a television. By 1960 that number had increased to 45.75 million, or 87.1 percent. This dramatic jump led experts in several fields to examine the effect of television on the nation's children.

An Educational Opportunity. Television without doubt increased the amount of information available to children and their parents. Up-to-the-minute *visual* news about the country and the world became readily available. Universities that could afford the high start-up costs could potentially establish production facilities and become the cultural and intellectual beacons. Many predicted great educational opportunities arising from television. McGrath stated, "Through the use of television, educational institutions will be able to bring the greatest teachers, the finest artists, scientists, and philosophers into schools and homes."

Closed Circuits. Television and other audiovisual media became highly valued teaching tools during the 1950s. The movie industry spent millions of dollars tapping into the educational market. Sciences, life skills, and social studies all lent themselves to television instruction. Closed-circuit televisions were used in high schools and universities on the principle that they could reach more students with greater amounts of information. By 1955 programs were directed at nursery-school–aged children.

Cheap Tutors. The Federal Communication Commission set aside 82 VHF and 127 UHF channels for the sole purpose of educational television in March 1951. In October 1951 "The Living Blackboard" began broadcasting educational television programs to hospitalized and homebound students in New York. Western Reserve University (Cleveland, Ohio) became the first university to offer full-credit courses by television, with courses in literature and psychology. By 1955 thirty-five colleges and universities had such courses in a wide variety of subjects. During a 1953 strike by Baltimore city employees, which closed 107 of the 174 schools, commercial television stations broadcast lessons for the eighty thousand children affected. Television lessons also provided a cheaper alternative for shut-in students than costly private tutors.

The Drawbacks. But some investigations showed startling problems with the home use of televisions. Comparisons between school time and television time were studied at Burdick Junior High School in Stamford, Connecticut, during the spring of 1950. The results revealed that children watched noneducational television twenty-seven hours a week, almost as much time as they spent in school. In 1952 Xavier University found that "poor television habits, lower IQ's, lower parental control, and poorer school achievement tended to be related." Teenage students revealed a preference for television over reading. A particularly disturbing problem was the potential effect of commercials that bombarded children of all ages with pleas to buy a variety of products, shaping tastes and forging attitudes.

A Force to Contend With. The overall effect of television remained unclear at the close of the decade. Positive influences in the school setting could easily be un-

The opening session of the 1955 White House Conference on Education

done by poor viewing habits at home. Yet the "tube" was clearly not going away, and educators would have to decide to use it or oppose it.

Sources:

Caleb Gattegno, *Towards a Visual Culture: Educating through Television* (New York: Outerbridge & Dienstfrey, 1969);

Charles Arthur Siepmann, *TV and Our School Crisis* (New York: Dodd, Mead, 1958).

U.S. VS. SOVIET SCHOOLS

Red Education. A two-year study by the Office of Education released in November 1957 revealed a basic difference between the U.S. and Soviet school systems. Soviet education was authoritarian and aimed at the fulfillment of the state's needs. Soviet students had a rigid program of study, small class sizes, and well-educated teachers. That contrasted with the U.S. system, wherein "the goal of education is the development of each individual . . . with freedom and with opportunity to choose his life's work in his best interests" and in which curricula, class sizes, and teacher shortages were pervasive problems. The study also noted that the clear emphasis placed upon science and technology in Soviet schools was lacking in the U.S. system. To many Americans the flight of *Sputnik* a month earlier underscored the need for change.

Cultural Exchange. In 1958 a Soviet-U.S. cultural exchange agreement brought twenty Soviet students and youth leaders to the United States in July. They complained that U.S. education was expensive and militarized — an ironic comment coming from an education system built solely to support the country's war machine. In addition, they felt U.S. students knew little of the Soviet Union.

Desire. On the other hand, U.S. education commissioner Lawrence Derthick, after leading a one-month survey of the Soviet education system, stated that the Soviet Union was pledged to "reach and over reach America." He contended that the Russians had "a burning desire to surpass the United States in education, in production, in standard of living, in world trade — and in athletics."

Source:

National Education Association of the United States, Division of Travel Service, A Firsthand Report on Soviet Schools: *Based on a Trip through the Soviet Union of Soviet Socialist Republics by a Group of Sixty-four American Educators* (Washington, D.C.: National Education Association of the United States, 1960).

WHITE HOUSE CONFERENCE ON EDUCATION

Agenda. The White Conference on Education, held 28 November–1 December 1955, was the first of its kind. It involved citizens and educators in a study of current educational problems. Money had been allocated earlier in the year for each state to hold its own conference, culminating with the national event. The agenda comprised six topics: (1) What should the schools accomplish? (2) In what ways can the schools be operated more efficiently and economically? (3) What are the school building needs? (4) How can enough good teachers be secured and kept on the job? (5) How can the schools be financed, built, and operated? and (6) How can a continuing public interest in education be obtained?

Plan. The conference produced a plan for Congress to fund. HEW Secretary Folsom planned to design a proposals around three principles: (1) state and local efforts should not be reduced by federal aid for school buildings; (2) need should be the basis for assistance; and (3) local school-system freedom should be maintained. The third point resulted from fears about the federal government's intrusion into education and the loss of local control.

Report. A report on the conference appeared in April 1956. It contended that "The schools have fallen far behind both the aspirations of the American people and their capabilities . . . There is growing resolve throughout the nation to close the gap between educational ideals and educational realities." Overall, the conference set the tone for education-funding requests for the coming years and further pushed the federal government into the domain of state control over education.

WHY JOHNNY CAN'T READ

Phonics Is the Answer. In 1955 Rudolf Flesch published his influential work, *Why Johnny Can't Read and What You Can Do About It.* He discussed the reading problems of the nation's children and how television had a negative effect on reading ability. Television programs brought about memorization through word associations and promoted learning through pictures — not true reading ability. The answer, according to Flesch, was phonics. Phonetic practice enabled students to sound out words unfamiliar to them, and although comprehension came

---

SEUSS ON THE LOOSE

As educators debated the root of poor reading, Theodore S. Geisel, known to millions of children as Dr. Seuss, set out to change the nature of children's books. Starting with *The Cat in the Hat* and *The Grinch Who Stole Christmas* in 1957, he made reading and learning through whimsical rhyme fun and enjoyable. Over the next three decades over eighty-eight books in the Dr. Seuss series would be included in The Cat in the Hat library, and millions of children would learn how to read from Dr. Seuss.

---

later through experience, phonics would make good readers.

Sight Reading. The debate between proponents of phonics and sight reading, or recognizing words by sight, did not begin with Flesch. In 1954 *Collier's* ran a six-part study of education entitled "The Struggle for Our Children's Minds," which included a look at phonics. Parents complained that sight reading led to the misunderstanding of words. For example, children would see a scene with a word underneath it and assume it only meant one thing: *meadow* would be read as *pasture*. On the other hand, sight reading was fun and effective, adherents argued. The debate over how to teach reading would continue throughout the decade without resolution.

Source:
Rudolf Flesch, *Why Johnny Can't Read and What You Can Do About It* (New York: Harper, 1955).

HEADLINE MAKERS

JAMES B. CONANT
1893 – 1978

PRESIDENT OF HARVARD UNIVERSITY (1933-1953)

Calling for Education Reform. In 1953 James B. Conant vacated his position as president of Harvard University to become the U.S. high commissioner for Germany. He did not abandon his role as an innovator in education, however. Throughout the decade he continued to draw publicity as he pressed for reforms in America's school system. His call for higher standards in American education culminated in the 1959 publication of *The American High School Today,* which sold over half a million copies.

Revamping the Public High Schools. While at Harvard, Conant gained a reputation for championing the concept of liberal education, with its emphasis on a broad curriculum of study for college freshmen and sophomores. After leaving Harvard, he began to focus his attention on American high schools. Proclaiming the "typical" American high school to be a myth, Conant argued that schools differed widely from one education district to the next, given America's cultural and geographic diversity. He called for comprehensive high schools that would offer a wide range of academic and vocational classes so that all students of varying intellectual abilities would be best served. In such schools courses of study would be tailored to meet an individual student's abilities and aspirations.

Education and Democracy. Inherent in his recommendations was a criticism of private schools. Private education, Conant believed, ran counter to his notion of the comprehensive school that would bring together students of not only various intellectual abilities, but of differing cultural backgrounds as well. He asserted that his comprehensive school would capture the spirit of American democracy and promote upward social mobility. He continued his push for public-school reform during the 1960s.

Sources:
James B. Conant, *The American High School Today* (New York: McGraw-Hill, 1959);

Conant, "A Hard Look at Our High Schools," *Look,* 23 (February 1959): 27–32;

Conant, *My Several Lives: Memoirs of a Social Inventor* (New York: Harper & Row, 1970).

ORVAL E. FAUBUS
1910 –

GOVERNOR OF ARKANSAS (1954-1967)

Reputation as a Segregationist. Known as a strong segregationist, Gov. Orval Faubus brought about the single most controversial reaction to *Brown* v. *Board of Education, Topeka, Kansas* in 1957. Earlier in the year Faubus signed four bills that created an anti-integration investigation committee; authorized parents to refuse to send their children to integrated schools; required organizations such as the National Association for the Advancement of Colored People to publish membership roles and financial data; and authorized the use of school-district funds to hire lawyers and pay for other legal costs to fight integration. He was determined to keep Arkansas segregated despite federal rulings to the contrary.

Little Rock Crisis. The events in Little Rock shook the country, and the American public viewed Faubus several times on television defending his segregationist beliefs. He saw the black students as the "cause" of the problems and encouraged violence to maintain the status quo. As federal troops took control of the situation, Faubus charged that the president had overstepped his authority by interfering with state and local rights to control education. Over the next two years Faubus emphasized the theme of federal abuse of power, charging that Supreme Court decisions were illegal and continuing the debate over the proper actions for Little Rock schools to take.

His Popular Appeal. Faubus's political career boomed after Little Rock. In 1958 Faubus won an almost unprecedented third term as governor in a Democratic primary (he would go on to a fifth term). Generally viewed as a rejection of President Dwight D. Eisenhower's use of federal troops in Little Rock, the vote was cited by Faubus as evidence that his stand against integration had the support of the people of Arkansas. The governor would not give up despite signs that the federal government would support integration. At the close of the decade Faubus pledged to continue the fight and stated "mass integration would not be accepted."

Sources:
Elizabeth Huckaby, *Crisis at Central High School* (Baton Rouge: Louisiana State University Press, 1980);

Robert Sherrill, *Gothic Politics in the Deep South: Stars of the New Confederacy* (New York: Grossman Publishers, 1968).

THURGOOD MARSHALL
1908 - 1993

DIRECTOR OF LEGAL DEFENSE AND EDUCATIONAL FUND OF NAACP (1939–1961); ASSOCIATE JUSTICE OF THE SUPREME COURT (1967–1991)

Championing Civil Rights. Marshall's years at the NAACP were spent representing people who had been denied their legal rights because of their race. He won twenty-nine of the thirty-two civil rights cases he brought before the Supreme Court including the 1950 *Sweatt* v. *Painter* which set the ground for *Brown*.

In the National Spotlight. Marshall's most notable case, *Brown* v. *Board of Education of Topeka, Kansas,* put segregation squarely before the nation in 1954. He argued, along with George Hayes and James Nabrit, Jr., that the separated schools for black and white children were not equal and black students were being denied the equal protection under the law guaranteed by the Fourteenth Amendment.

Supreme Court Justice. His appointment to the Supreme Court by President Lyndon B. Johnson in 1967 made him the first black to sit on the court. He was a respected justice throughout his term on the court, which ended with his retirement in 1992.

Source:
Carl Thomas Rowan, *Dream Makers, Dream Breakers: The World of Justice Thurgood Marshall* (Boston: Little, Brown: 1993).

PEOPLE IN THE NEWS

Horace Mann Bond was influential in the integration of Lincoln (Pennsylvania) University. He was the first black to become president of the school (1945–1957) and became dean of the School of Education at Atlanta University in 1957.

The 1954 class-action suit named after eleven-year-old **Linda Brown,** *Brown* v. *Board of Education of Topeka, Kansas,* ended racial segregation in the public schools.

Autherine Lucy was admitted to the University of Alabama by court order in 1957. After riots broke out, university officials removed her from campus. She made several allegations against the university regarding her poor treatment which resulted in her permanent expulsion from the school. This action made her a symbol of the struggle of desegregation.

Sol Markoff, associate general director of the National Child Labor Committee, in 1952 criticized Congress for spending $6.5 million yearly to study migratory birds and refusing to fund $181,000 for better education for migrant workers' children.

In 1955 the University of Iowa's **Dora Lee Martin**, seventeen, became the school's first black campus sweetheart after integration in 1952.

Sen. Joseph R. McCarthy, in 1952 and 1953, stated it was his personal crusade to rid the universities and colleges of subversives. His death in 1957 marked the anticlimax of the "Red Scare" earlier in the decade.

Adm. Hyman Rickover, a critic of U.S. education and the "father of the nuclear navy," thought the country was losing the battle with the Soviets due to its poor education system. In 1959 he proposed a program to educate the nation's children through a selective school system similar to the European track education systems. That system would seek out and better educate the gifted.

Walter Ridley in 1953 became the first black to receive a Ph.D. from a southern institution.

Eleanor Roosevelt spoke against the use of federal funds for parochial schools in 1952. She stated that she had never asked anyone to pay for her children's private education and therefore taxpayers should not pay for such education now.

Mrs. Mary Schoenheit, a former schoolteacher, won a court decision in 1957 that found her personal tutoring of her seven-year-old daughter was "substantially equivalent" to public education and legally adequate. She had contended that public schools produced "trained seals" and was once prosecuted and jailed for refusing to send her child to a public school.

In 1957 **Barbara Smith**, a nineteen-year-old black, was removed from the leading role in a school play by University of Texas officials. The officials contended that the role "calls for a white person."

Gov. Adlai Stevenson, speaking at the 1952 Democratic Convention, reflected upon the educational system: "The softness which has crept into our educational system is a reflection of something much broader, of a national complacency, of a confusion of priorities. . . . We have lacked, I fear, the deep inner conviction that education in its broadest sense unlocks the door of our future, and that it gives us the tools without which 'the pursuit of happiness' become a hollow chasing after triviality, a mindless boredom relieved only by the stimulus of sensationalism or quenched with a tranquilzer pill."

Mrs. Charles E. White became the first black elected to public office in Houston, Texas, where in 1958 she defeated two white males to become a city public school system trustee.

In 1953 **Mrs. Thomas J. White**, a member of the Indiana Textbook Committee, demanded the removal of *Robin Hood* from schools. She referred to the theme of robbing the rich and giving to the poor as part of the Communist code.

AWARDS

TEACHER OF THE YEAR

1952: Geraldone Wheldon Jones — First Grade Hope
Public School, Santa Barbara, California

1953: Dorthy Hamilton — Social Studies
Milford High School, Milford, Connecticut

1954: Willard Wideberg — Seventh Grade
Dekalb Junior High School, Dekalb, Illinois

1955: Margaret Perry — Fourth Grade
Monmouth Elementary, Monmouth, Oregon

1956: Richard Nelson — Science
Flathead Country High School, Kalispell, Montana

1957: Eugene G. Bizzell — Speech, English and Debate
A. N. McCallum High School, Austin, Texas,
and Mary F. Schwartz — Third Grade
Bristol Elementary, Kansas City, Missouri

1958: Jean Listebarger Humphrey — Second Grade
Edwards Elementary, Ames, Iowa

1959: Edna Donley — Mathematics and Speech
Alva High School, Alva, Oklahoma

DEATHS

Harold Allen, member of the National Education Association staff for twenty-six years, instrumental in rural and agricultural education, 3 November 1958.

Mary Ritter Beard, 82, U.S. historian who worked to include women in the predominantly male-centered history works, 14 August 1958.

Dr. Mary Kendrick Benedict, 81, first president of Sweet Briar College (Virginia), 10 February 1956.

Mildred C. Berleman, former editor of *American Teacher*, (1942–54), 8 November 1955.

Katherine Devereux Blake, 92, pioneer in education for women, organized first evening high school for women, 2 February 1950.

Ward C. Bowen, 64, chief of Audio and Visual Aids bureau and director of visual education for New York State Education Department, advisory consultant with CBS educational television, 1956.

Isaiah Brown, president emeritus of Johns Hopkins University and one of the world's leading geographers, 6 January 1950.

Samuel P. Capen, 78, first director of the American Council of Education, 22 June 1956.

Philander Priestley Claxton, 94, U.S. commissioner of education, 1911–1921, 12 January 1951.

Dr. Edmund E. Day, 67, president emeritus of Cornell University, one of the leaders responsible for Education Policies Commission of the NEA, March 23, 1951.

John Dewey, 92, distinguished philosopher and educator, known as the Father of Progressive Education in the United States, 1 June 1952.

Frederic Ernst, New York City deputy superintendent, responsible for radio and TV instruction for shut-in students, 30 May 1953.

Clyde A. Erwin, North Carolina state superintendent, involved with planning the 1952 Democratic platform, 19 July 1952.

William B. Featherstone, served as chief of educational division for the U.S. armed forces in Austria and supervised rehabilitation of Austrian schools during World War II, 12 April 1951.

Dr. Grace M. Fernald, 70, widely known for her work on problems of retarded school children, 17 January 1950.

Dr. Frank Pierpont Graves, 87, a member of the New York State Education Committee and holder of forty-three academic degrees, 13 September 1956.

Michi Kawia, 75, Christian educator who worked in Japan, 11 February 1952.

Clara Savage Littledale, 64, editor of *Parents' Magazine* since its founding in 1926, 9 January 1956.

E. E. Oberholtzer, 74, president emeritus and one founder of University of Houston, 1954.

Wesley E. Peik, dean of College of Education, University of Minnesota, instrumental in NEA's National Commission on Teacher Education and Professional standards, spearheaded development of national accrediting program, 6 December 1951.

Cyrus Perry, 54, legal counsel for National Commission for the Defense of Democracy thru Education, 27 December 1955.

Charles Allen Prosser, 81, nationally known leader in vocational education, 26 November 1952.

Margaretta Baldwin Reeve, 83, honorary president of National Congress of Parents and Teachers; helped establish several journals for the PTA, 1955.

Bertha E. Roberts, held highest administrative position, deputy superintendent of elementary schools, ever occupied by a woman in San Francisco school system, 15 December 1955.

Joseph Rosier, 81, former president of the NEA, worked for increased funding for education during the Depression, 7 October 1951.

William Russell, 65, president emeritus of Teachers College, Columbia University; director of National Citizenship Education Program for Department of Justice; president of World Organization of the Teaching Profession, 27 March 1956.

John Amherst Sexton, pioneered the 6-4-4 program in Pasadena, California, wherein a two-year junior college was incorporated into the senior high school, 14 April 1952.

Frank Palmer Speare, 85, founder and president emeritus of Northeastern University (Boston), 1954.

Thomas C. Trueblood, organized and taught first college credit course in public speaking (University of Michigan), 4 June 1951.

Carter Godwin Woodson, 74, founder and director of Association for Study of Negro Life and History, 3 April 1950.

George F. Zook, 66, retired president of American Council on Education and former U.S. commissioner of education, 17 August 1951.

PUBLICATIONS

Philippe Aries, *Centuries of Childhood* (New York: Knopf, 1962);

Association for Childhood Education International, *Continuous Learning* (Washington, D.C., 1951);

Association for Supervision and Curriculum Development, *Growing Up in an Anxious Age* (Washington, D.C., 1952);

Alfred Bestor, *The Restoration of Learning* (New York: Knopf, 1955);

William F. Buckley, *God and Man at Yale* (Chicago: Regnery, 1951);

Leslie Lee Chisholm, *The Work of the Modern High School* (New York: Macmillan, 1953);

Columbia University Teachers College, *Are Liberal Arts Colleges Becoming Professional Schools?* (New York: Columbia University Teachers College, 1958);

James B. Conant, *Citadel of Learning* (New Haven: Yale University Press, 1956);

Conant, *The Revolutionary Transformation of the American High School* (Cambridge, Mass.: Harvard University Press, 1959);

Lester Donald Crow, *High School Education* (New York: Odyssey Press, 1951);

Monroe E. Deutsch, *The College from Within* (Berkeley: University of California Press, 1952);

William Clyde De Vane, *The American University in the Twentieth Century* (Baton Rouge: Louisiana State University Press, 1957);

James Henry Dougherty, *Elementary School Organization and Management* (New York: Macmillan, 1950);

Benjamin Fine and Lillian Fine, *How to Get the Best Education For Your Child* (New York: Putnam, 1959);

Fine, *1,000,000 Delinquents* (Cleveland: World, 1955);

Rudolf Flesch, *Why Johnny Can't Read and What You Can Do About It* (New York: Harper, 1955);

C. G. F. Franzen, *Foundations of Secondary Education* (New York: Harper, 1955);

George Willard Frasier, *An Introduction to the Study of Education* (New York: Harper, 1951);

John M. Gran, *How to Understand and Teach Teen-agers* (Minneapolis, Minn.: T. S. Denison, 1958);

Albert Donavon Graves, *American Secondary Education* (Boston: Heath, 1951);

Hilde T. Himmelweit, A. N. Oppenheim, and Pamela Vince, *Television and the Child: An Empirical Study of the Effect of Television on the Young* (London: Oxford University Press, 1958);

Himmelweit, Oppenheim, and Vince, *Television and the Teaching of English* (New York: Appleton-Century-Crofts, 1961);

Robert M. Hutchins, *Conflict in Education in a Democratic Society* (New York: Harper, 1953);

Hutchins, *Some Observations on American Education* (Cambridge, U.K.: Cambridge University Press, 1956);

Christine Porter Ingram, *Education of the Slow-Learning Child*, second edition (New York: Ronald Press, 1953);

Philip E. Jacob, *Changing Values in College* (New York: Harper, 1957);

Gilbert Clarence Kettelkamp, *Teaching Adolescents* (Boston: Heath, 1954);

Russell Kirk, *Academic Freedom* (Chicago: Regnery, 1955);

John Francis Latimer, *What's Happened to Our High Schools* (Washington, D.C.: Public Affairs Press, 1958);

Gordon C. Lee, *An Introduction to Education in America* (New York: Holt, 1957);

Jonathan Murray Lee, *The Child and His Curriculum* (New York: Appleton-Century-Crofts, 1950);

Albert Lynd, *Quackery in the Public Schools* (Boston: Grossett & Dunlap, 1953);

Charles Marshall MacConnell, *New Schools for a New Culture* (New York: Harper, 1953);

Frederick Mayer, *Philosophy of Education for Our Time* (New York: Odyssey, 1958);

Bernard E. Meland, *Higher Education and the Spirit* (Chicago: University of Chicago Press, 1953);

Ernest O. Melby and Morton Puner, eds., *Freedom and Public Education* (New York: Praeger, 1953);

Cecil Vernon Millard, *School and Child: A Case History* (East Lansing: Michigan State College Press, 1954);

Philip W. Perdew, *The American Secondary School in Action* (Boston: Allyn & Bacon, 1959);

Hyman G. Rickover, *Education and Freedom* (New York: Dutton, 1959);

Wilbur Schramm, *The Impact of Educational Television* (Urbana: University of Illinois Press, 1960);

Schramm, J. Lyle, and I. deSola Pool, *The People Look at Educational Television* (Stanford, Cal.: Stanford University Press, 1963);

Emma Dickson Sheehy, *The Fives and Sixes Go to School* (New York: Holt, 1954);

Harold Spears, *The High School for Today* (New York: American Book, 1950);

Lindley Joseph Stiles, *Democratic Teaching in Secondary Schools* (Philadelphia: Lippincott, 1950);

Agatha Townshend, *College Freshmen Speak Out* (New York: Harper, 1956);

Rosalind Marie Zapf, *Democratic Processes in the Secondary Classroom* (Englewood Cliffs, N. J.: Prentice-Hall, 1959).

Elementary school children watching a music lesson broadcast on television, 1952

CHAPTER FIVE
FASHION

by JAN COLLINS STUCKER

CONTENTS

Sidebars and tables are listed in italics

1950

- William J. Levitt expands his mass-production techniques of building identical boxlike houses in Levittown, New York, assembled by crews using precut materials, thus accelerating the rush to suburbia.

- The White House is gutted and remodeled during the first year of a three-year project. Only the outside walls remain unchanged during the rebuilding.

- New York's United Nations Secretariat building, featuring all-glass east and west facades, is completed to provide offices for the UN's thirty-four hundred employees on land overlooking the East River.

- The "Sun House" at Dover, Massachusetts, heated solely by stored-up rays of the sun and erected by the Massachusetts Institute of Technology, is occupied in comfort by a New England family throughout the winter, opening up the possibilities of solar heat for house warming.

- Miss Clairol hair coloring is introduced; it takes only half the application time needed by other hair colorings.

- Sales of at-home leisure wear grow with the increased number of television sets purchased for entertainment.

- Orlon is introduced by E. I. du Pont de Nemours, which had begun developing the wool-like fiber in 1941.

- Cotton's share of the U.S. textile market falls to 65 percent, down from 80 percent in 1940, and man-made fibers — mostly rayons and acetates — increase their share to more than 20 percent.

1951

- The first all-glass-and-steel apartment building, designed by Ludwig Mies van der Rohe, is completed on Lake Shore Drive in Chicago.

- The American Association of Textile Chemists and Colorists proclaims that a "full-fledged textile revolution" — production and demand for man-made fibers — is in progress.

- The popularity of tubular metal furniture grows.

- The Chemise Lacoste is exported to the United States for the first time by the French Izod Company. The long-tailed all-cotton "alligator" tennis shirt is soon to become a U.S. status symbol.

- Victor Gruen Associates is founded by Austrian-American architect Victor Gruen. Gruen's architecture, engineering, urban-planning firm will have a major impact on U.S. building design and city planning.

- A second Levittown is started by Levitt and Sons for seventeen thousand families in Bucks County, Pennsylvania, with schools and churches to be built on land donated by the developers. The inexpensive three- to four-bedroom houses (the price includes major appliances) encourage thousands of Americans to leave the city and move into suburban developments as scores of builders adopt the methods pioneered by Levitt.

1952

- The McDonald's Golden Arches, modeled on the flamboyant "coffee house" architecture of California, is designed.

- The inventor Buckminster Fuller displays at the Museum of Modern Art in New York his strong but lightweight geodesic dome, which eventually revolutionized construction.

- New York City's Lever House opens 29 April on Park Avenue. The heat-resistant glass windows in the twenty-four-story glass-walled building are sealed, and the centrally air-conditioned building uses an enormous amount of energy. It becomes an example for energy-wasting architecture.

- Revolutionary new materials such as melamine, a lightweight plastic, are introduced for use in furniture and dinnerware.

- Strongly modern furniture designs account for 60 percent of all new furniture patterns.

- Entirely new synthetic yarns are introduced; viscose rayon, acetate, and nylon production reach new highs.

- Femininity triumphs in women's wear as cinched waistlines, molded bodices, and yards of wide skirts worn over stiff petticoats are "in."

- Four-inch stiletto heels are introduced, much to the dismay of floor manufacturers.

- "Never wear a white shirt before sundown," says ads for Hathaway shirts. Four out of five shirts sold to men in America are white, but the ratio will fall to two out of five in the next fifteen years, and all-cotton shirts will give way to blends of cotton and synthetic fibers.

1953

- Architects of America designs new "super" shopping centers that spread throughout suburbia.

- Plastic women's shoes become popular after Marilyn Monroe wears them in the film *How to Marry a Millionaire*.

- Bermuda shorts for men appear in offices and are even worn by some executives.

1954

- A major technological conference on plastic as a building material is held.

- Seamless nylon stockings are introduced.

- French designer Christian Dior ignites another fashion firecracker in America with his popular "H" look.

- Americans move into single-family homes — most in the suburbs — at an astounding rate; the numbers are up 33 percent over those of 1953.

- The world's largest shopping center, with one hundred stores opens in March at Detroit's Northland.

- Geodesics, Inc., and Synergetics, Inc., are established to produce seven-room circular aluminum Dymaxion houses and geodesic domes designed by Buckminster Fuller.

1955

- No-iron Dacron is put on the market by DuPont.
- A patent for Velcro is granted to engineer George deMestral.
- Minnie and Mickey Mouse and other Disney motifs are stamped on millions of T-shirts, bags.

1956

- Elvis Presley's blue suede shoes, black leather jackets, doubled-high collars, sideburns, and long, greased hair are copied by masses of American teenage boys.
- "Does she or doesn't she?" ask advertisements for Miss Clairol hair coloring. The ads picture children with mothers to show that nice women can color their hair, too.
- Eero Saarinen's TWA Terminal at Kennedy Airport in New York opens. Saarinen also completes his seven-year project of designing the General Motors Technical Center in Michigan.
- Plastic invades the furniture industry.
- The National Automobile Show is reestablished after a lapse of sixteen years, giving U.S. car designers a showplace for new models.

1957

- In May The American Institute of Architects celebrates its one hundredth birthday.
- Japanese architectural influence begins to be seen in America as some U.S. builders import top Japanese architects.
- Los Angeles adopts a revised building code that permits construction of high-rise buildings. The code reflects earthquake-stress engineering technology.
- Christian Dior introduces the popular chemise dress (also known as "the sack") — his concession to comfort.
- Blue jeans surge in popularity as a symbol of teen revolt in the wake of Jack Kerouac's *On The Road*.
- "Beatnik" clothing, featuring khaki pants, sweaters, sandal.

1958

- Buckminster Fuller's geodesic dome at Baton Rouge is unveiled.
- Full-skirted "rock 'n' roll" dresses layered with petticoats become fashionable for teenage girls.
- The new "trapeze" dresses designed by Frenchman Yves St. Laurent, the successor to Christian Dior, are a hit.
- The U.S. textile industry consolidates and moves south. Some 90 percent of all cotton fabrics are produced in the South by early 1958, as well as 73 percent of man-made fabrics. Within two years man-made fabrics increase their share of the market to 28 percent, with polyesters taking 11 percent of the market.

1959

- The first Barbie Doll, with an extensive wardrobe of fabric (not paper) clothes.

OVERVIEW

Fond Memories. Nostalgia for the 1950s began while memories of the decade were still fresh. Tail-finned cars, hula hoops, poodle skirts, Elvis Presley, mothers in aprons, and "Leave It To Beaver" conjure up images of a genial time that seems better, softer, simpler. Indeed, the years from 1950 to 1959 were a time of optimism, domesticity, security through compliance with the system, and apparent simplicity.

Simplicity. In the realm of fashion (clothing, architecture, furniture, interior design, and autos), simplicity was certainly the key in all areas except, conspicuously, the chrome-laden cars with their huge tail fins that looked as if they were suited to a vehicle about to blast off into the stratosphere.

"New Look." In terms of clothing, women's "New Look" fashions, which had been introduced in 1947, were *not* simple as far as construction went. Hips were padded, skirts were full, and tailoring was complicated. But clothing for women *was* simple as far as the motivation went: women were supposed to be women again after years of wartime deprivations, and that meant sensuous designs. These sexy outfits were especially popular in evening wear, with sequined gowns and narrow, clinging sheaths.

"American Look." Men's clothing was self-consciously conformist and somber: it was the man in the gray flannel suit. Fashion could not get much more simple than that. But women's fashions were adventuresome. The 1950s was the decade when a group of young American designers offered the simple and comfortable sportswear that became known as the American Look and took the fashion world by storm.

Imaginative Structures. Architecture in the 1950s was generally stark, with unadorned glass-and-steel skyscrapers mushrooming across corporate America. Frank Lloyd Wright, considered the greatest architect of the twentieth century, fought against this trend with his imaginative structures that hugged the earth and reflected the natural surroundings. But he was in the minority.

Levitt. The mass-produced houses that sprang up in suburbia were also simple in the extreme — and conformist as well. Built on concrete slabs with no basements, these so-called Levittown houses were nearly identical in floor plan. Lots were of uniform size, with trees planted every twenty-eight feet. Many of these boxlike houses survived forty years of constant use, serving as ample bases for remodeling and structural additions prompted by changing lifestyles.

Furniture. Furniture in the 1950s was likewise the epitome of simplicity. It was called American Modern; it was austere, functional, mass-produced, and often made of synthetic materials such as molded plastic and plywood laminate. This style was perfect for the smaller rooms of low-ceiling homes of suburban homes, where couples moved in droves.

Space. As for interior design, what could be more simple than lots of space? "Open" plans of the era called for flowing space in both homes and offices. There were fewer walls, making for less demarcated rooms, so the function of the room could change according to the occasion.

The Guise of Simplicity. But the irony of all this is that the decade of the 1950s was not really a simple time after all. The "simplicity" and naive optimism of the 1950s, in fact, were failed attempts to insulate people from postwar and cold-war fears. The so-called simplicity was actually a refuge from the cauldron of complex issues simmering during 1950s America.

Blind Optimism. The upheavals of the 1960s and 1970s — characterized by the antiwar movement, the civil rights movement, the women's movement, the environmental movement, and the rebirth of social individualism — sprang with a vengeance from the bourgeois cocoon of the 1950s. By refusing to focus on these problems and spending time instead on conspicuous consumption, people magnified the consequences. Americans' blind optimism in the 1950s guaranteed that the decades to follow would be anything but simple.

TOPICS IN THE NEWS

WOMEN'S FASHION: FEMININITY IS THE KEY

Back Home. By 1950 women were long gone from the factory jobs of World War II and were back home (usually in the kitchen and wearing aprons, to judge from advertisements of that era). Domesticity and femininity were the watchwords, and women wore wasp waists, voluminous skirts, and pearls by day and clingy, sequined gowns by night.

The "New Look." Christian Dior's "New Look" took the fashion world by storm in 1947. Emphasizing the natural curves of the female figure, the shape of Dior's fashions resembled an hourglass. The bosom was emphasized by skintight tailoring; hips were padded; the skirt was midcalf in length, full, and "extravagant in its use of fabric"; the waist was slender, or "wasp." By 1950 the sensuous Dior designs and the hourglass figure reigned supreme in the postwar United States, where, as sociologists have noted, sexuality and maternity were the way to restore the population.

Women by Day. Career women in the 1950s (and there were not many of them) wore wool suits with slim sheath skirts and straight, short jackets over silk blouses. The ideal silhouette was long-legged and shapely. Dresses hung at midcalf. Gloves were a must: a woman

HAIR IMITATES ART

Claiming to have been inspired by the work of artist Alexander Calder, leading New York hairstylist Victor Vito began cutting women's hair so that it would "move and dance like a mobile" with the toss of a head. Models sporting the short hairdos appeared in a 1954 issue of McCall's shaking their heads to prove Vito's point. Although none of his models especially evoked Calder's work, Vito insisted that the spirit of the mobile was captured in the "young and carefree" haircut that needed "little upkeep."

Source: *McCall's* (21 June 1954): 14.

Representative of the "New Look" in fashion, a dress designed by Christian Dior

dressed in a suit always wore them. Hats, too, were essential, although less so than they had been in the 1940s. According to a 1959 survey the average American woman owned four chapeaus. Some were large, although most were small pillboxes or berets. Handbags in brightly colored lizard skin were favored. Shoes, usually with impossibly high stiletto heels, matched the outfit. All of this would be encased in a clutch coat, often of mohair or textured cloth, that had no buttons — hence the name *clutch.*

Work Clothes. Less formal workingwomen donned "separates" (originally designed by American designer Claire McCardell), consisting of skirts and tops that could be interchanged at will, giving women a variety of outfits at a lower cost. Pop-it necklaces, which could be lengthened from choker to waist-length by snapping on extra beads, were a favorite with this group (and with teenagers, too).

The Sack and Other Fashion Ideas. The chemise, also known as the "sack" dress, made the biggest fashion splash in women's day wear in the 1950s. This type of dress, which looked like a bag, was not popular for long, since the hips and bust were completely hidden. After a

The gray flannel suit

year, says author Richard Horn, "the sack was sacked." The hooded dress made of a single tube-shaped length of hip-clinging knit also caught on in the 1950s. Housewives in the 1950s wore shirtwaist dresses (often with pearls), housedresses, slacks, and dungarees. The theme was comfort.

Women by Night. Women wore essentially simple clothing in the daytime; nights were different. Evening dresses in the 1950s were either full-skirted, ethereal, and romantic — in exotic hues and materials such as silk and taffeta — or they were narrow, clinging sheaths, often slathered with the shimmering sequins popularized by Marilyn Monroe and Jane Russell.

Colors. Colors varied, with black and white particularly favored for fall and winter. Synthetics, which are viewed as somewhat tacky today, were not thought so then. Rayon and rayon blends were particularly popular in evening frocks.

Accentuating Curves. All evening styles emphasized women's bodies (the "ideal" woman in the 1950s was curvier and considerably less angular than today's ultra-thin, waiflike models). Most dresses were tightly fitted, sleeveless, and strapless. They also sported plunging necklines and back lines yet concealed elaborate foundations that enhanced a woman's figure.

DIOR AND THE FULL-FIGURED GAL — BOSOM BUDDIES NO MORE?

Christian Dior, father of the New Look, nearly instigated a fashion riot during a 1954 Paris exhibition showcasing his latest style, the "H" look. Dior's boyish models looked like flappers of the 1920s as they strutted among the buyers and fashion critics in straight, flat dresses that de-emphasized the breasts and lowered the waistline to the hips. The word was soon out that Dior had "abolished bosoms," and outraged U.S. fashion editors accustomed to shapliness in Dior design cried foul. Hollywood slaves to fashion also seemed on the verge of revolt: "I am not built for any kind of boy's fashions," curvy Marilyn Monroe flatly claimed, "so why should I wear them?" Television's busty Dagmar added, "Frankly, honey, the instrument hasn't been made that can flatten me out." When asked to comment on Dior's lowering of the waistline, tough guy Marlon Brando insensitively shot from the hip, "Emphasizing women's hips is like putting falsies on a cow." By the fall, 1955 Dior had yielded to American critics and introduced the "Y" look—dresses, shaped like upside-down Coke bottles, that flattered the bosom.

Sources: *Time* (9 August 1954): 29;

Time (5 September 1955): 68-69.

Claire McCardell, center, oversees the making of her new line of American leisure wear in 1955.

Accessories and Cosmetics. Fur stoles and capes were popular. Handbags and satin pumps matched the dress. Gloves were always worn. Hair was short and swept back off one's face, and really adventurous women colored their hair so that it matched their evening clothes. Arched eyebrows and dark lips completed the look.

Don't Forget the Makeup. Makeup was an essential part of a woman's appearance in the 1950s. There was an excessive emphasis on painted lips and eyes, and those lips were usually colored fire-engine red. Charles Revson, president of Revlon, said in the 1950s that "most women lead lives of quiet desperation. Cosmetics are a wonderful escape from it — if you play it right."

Source:
Richard Horn, *Fifties Style, Then and Now* (New York: Beech Tree, 1985), pp. 142–145, 150–153.

MEN'S FASHIONS: GRAY FLANNEL SUITS

Conform — Or Else. In the 1950s conformity was the password of men's fashions. And as long as "conformity was the order of the day, there was a uniform to go with it," according to author Richard Horn: "a three-button, single-breasted, charcoal gray flannel suit, with narrow shoulders, narrow, small-notched lapels, flaps on the pockets, and pleatless, tapering trousers. A white or pale blue cotton broadcloth shirt with a button-down collar and button cuffs, trim ties with regimental stripes and small knots, and trim black leather shoes that rose at the ankle and the toe. . . . A drip-dry beige raincoat, a Ches-terfield with black velvet collar, or a single-breasted, straight-lined tweed overcoat with raglan sleeves was donned upon stepping out of corporate headquaters and

A CALL TO BARE ARMS

Despite Manhattan's unbearably hot and steamy summertime weather, city fashion czars, claimed the *New York Daily News* in July 1951, continued to insist that men endure the dog days with their shirtsleeves covered. Hot as hell and not wanting to take it anymore, a *Daily News* columnist urged "outright rebellion against any and all social edicts which say a guy has to pull a hot jacket over a carcass which already, probably, is steaming like a 1908 Maxwell. Down with any heartless females and etiquette fanatics who'd still like to see us looking like boiled lobsters and feeling like steamed clams." According to a July Gallup poll, however, jacketless men already had the sympathies of seven out of ten women surveyed. Yet *Time* magazine reported that the *Daily News* crusade was having little impact in revising lunchtime couture for the hot and hungry businessman. Snooty maître d's in Manhattan's posh restaurants continued to accost their shirtsleeved male patrons, demanding they put on a jacket and tie.

Source: *Time* (23 July 1951): 13.

A bathing suit designed by Claire McCardell typifies the American Look.

onto the street. Any hat would have been narrow-brimmed and worn brim up or brim down, sometimes with a pinched crown. Hair was worn in a crew — or semi—crew — cut. Jewelry was minimal — no more than a wristwatch and, if the man was married, a wedding band."

Alternatives. Not every man wore gray flannel suits, of course. Corporate types sometimes wore dark blue suits. And blue-collar laborers did not wear suits. By the mid 1950s, suits made of "miracle" synthetic fabrics such as Dacron blends that were lightweight and spot- and wrinkle-resistant were gaining popularity in colors such as beige, blue, and brown. Nonetheless, men's formal fashions in the 1950s were generally somber.

Sports Clothes. Men's clothes for leisure time, on the other hand, were more fun than work outfits. Bermuda shorts made a big splash in the 1950s, with some men even wearing them to parties and the country club with sports jackets and knee-length socks. Though tweed jackets with gray flannel slacks were standard among conservative dressers, sports jackets came in a variety of cas-

ually festive styles for more adventuresome men. They boasted colorful madras plaids, large bright checks, or smaller houndstooth checks. Continental jackets had lightly padded shoulders and hung straight in the back. Slim-cut slacks were sometimes worn cuffless and with a trim belt often in a bright color. Long- or short-sleeved sport shirts came in lightweight, washable synthetics such as Dacron; as a bonus they were wrinkle-free. Gaudy Hawaiian "aloha" shirts were popular during the 1950s, too, particularly at the ubiquitous backyard barbecues.

Outerwear. Heavy duffel coats held together by wooden toggles and hemp loops rather than zippers or buttons came into fashion in the 1950s. So did the thigh-length car coat. But the best-known outerwear of this era was the Eisenhower jacket, named after President Dwight D. Eisenhower: it was "jaunty, blousy, and waist-length."

Who Cares? Perhaps because their range of fashion choices was so limited, men in the 1950s did not care as much about clothes as women did. As an article in *Newsweek* in 1957 put it, "men prefer to spend the extra money they're earning on things other than clothes," that is, on their homes and growing families. Probably because of the relative disinterest from men, styles did not change measurably from year to year in the 1950s as they did for women.

Source:
Richard Horn, *Fifties Style, Then and Now* (New York: Beech Tree, 1985), pp. 146 –149.

AMERICAN DESIGNERS TAKE THE REINS

Postwar Style. Before World War II American fashion had little sense of national identity or style. Since the nineteenth century, in fact, Paris couturiers had set fashion trends for women in both Europe and America. Before the 1950s America's only distinctive contribution to international fashion was via Hollywood movies. This situation changed in the 1950s with the emergence of more than two dozen energetic and imaginative young men and women on the American fashion scene.

The "American Look." "The 'American Look' is a young look because it comes from young minds," said a 1955 *Look* magazine article. "It's an American look because these designers are independent and free-wheeling, wary of imitating, anxious to create. They share a pox-on-Paris spirit." These young American designers ranged in age from twenty-four to thirty-five in 1955, and they included such names as Anne Klein, Claire McCardell, Kasper, Rudi Gernreich, and James Galanos. They had a common purpose: to give American women comfortable yet chic sportswear that fit their active lifestyles and complimented the wearer, not necessarily the designer.

Simple and Comfortable. American women in the 1950s were busy wives and mothers. Backyard barbecues, weekend car trips, get-togethers in front of the television, chauffeuring children to school, sports, and parties —

Long, flowing sleeves and ankle-length, billowy skirts might be a matter of habit for most nuns, but not for the nine sisters of the Roman Catholic Society of Christ Our King. Located in Danville, Virginia, the small order worked a farm, and traditional nun garb was presenting practical difficulties—such as how to handle a Dodge truck without an unholy mess of cloth getting in the way. In 1951 the sisters confessed their fashion problem to renowned Manhattan designer Hattie Carnegie, who had modernized the WAC uniform. In answering the sisters' prayers, Carnegie's solution called for a plain, yet shapely, two-piece dress in gray wool with close-fitting sleeves, Peter Pan collar, and gored skirt. The design combined the simplicity of pilgrim wear with the chic lines sported by even the most trendy of secular women. Carnegie's work was free of charge.

Source: *Time* (17 September 1951): 93.

this active life required relaxed, comfortable, yet sophisticated clothing. As a young New York mother told *Time* magazine (2 May 1955), "When I get dressed up, I have little time to make up to the dress; I want the dress to make up to me."

Leisure Wear. American Look clothes were intended not so much for work as for leisure, but a leisure, as a cover story on McCardell said, "of action." They were mass-produced, simply made, of clean lines, durable (especially those made of synthetics), and easy to wear.

No Need to Break the Bank. American women loved the fact that this comfortable, functional clothing was inexpensive. Almost everyone could afford McCardell's creations, for example, which ranged from bathing suits and play clothes ($10 to $50) to dresses ($20 to $100) to suits and coats ($89 to $150). "The best-dressed women in the world are to be found on almost any street in America," said *Life* magazine in 1956. "Without the small fortune it takes to outfit a fashionable woman abroad, women across the U.S. can out-dress all others because of a unique $8 billion ready-to-wear industry which puts no price barriers on style."

What Was Popular. Jersey jumpers, tailored slacks, play shorts, Bermuda shorts, housedresses, and short-sleeved golf dresses were popular. So were mix-and-match separates — a madras skirt "topped, perhaps, with a simple tailored blouse boasting a Peter Pan collar, or a dirndl skirt worn with a peasant blouse," according to Richard Horn. Dungarees were worn only around the house. Ponchos and shawls were worn in cool weather,

along with a short-sleeved sweater with a matching cardigan, in cashmere or angora.

International Influence. The American designers of the American Look were considered trend-setting revolutionaries. The look was influential abroad, particularly in Italy, where it influenced the designers of sportswear. Paris also tried the style, with no less a master than Dior declaring that *la mode sport* in America is "beyond doubt excellent."

Source:
Richard Horn, *Fifties Style, Then and Now* (New York: Beech Tree, 1985), p. 155.

YOUTH-CENTERED FASHION

Consumerism at an Early Age. With the prosperity of the 1950s in full swing, American clothing manufacturers discovered — or perhaps created — new markets eager to buy their goods: children and teenagers. Television and printed advertisements instilled in 1950s kids at an early age a rampant consumerism that their parents had never had. The oldsters, after all, had grown up during the Depresssion, when thriftiness was next to godliness.

Born to Spend. But children and teens of the 1950s identified with a fifteen-year-old Los Angeles girl quoted in a 1957 *Newsweek* article: "We just find it neat to spend money." In 1957 teens' disposable income was estimated at $9 billion. Intensive research into this "hitherto untapped teen market" began after World War II, and by the mid 1950s fashion manufacturers were masters at manipulating teens' tastes.

Swept up in the Elvis Presley rage, seventeen-year-old Susan Hull of Grand Rapids, Michigan, stunned her boyfriend and made the pages of *Life* magazine when she cut off her foot-long ponytail, dyed black what hair remained, and slicked it back in homage to the King of Rock 'n' Roll. In reacting to his girlfriend's new coiffure, Lew Potter voiced the bitterness of many Michigan boyfriends and husbands whose Presley-obsessed women were flocking to the barber chair: "I could hang you for that." If Michigan men were truly looking for someone to hang, however, they could have turned on Grand Rapids beautician Glenwood Dodgson, who created the new look for women—complete with stray locks dangling over the forehead and sideburns. Charging $1.50 a cut, Dodgson in March 1957 reported that he had made Presleys of a thousand women—ranging in age from three to sixty—in a six-week period.

Source: *Life*, 42, (25 March 1957): 55.

Not like Their Parents. On the other hand, young people in the 1950s did their own manipulating by deciding to reject their parents' styles and make their own mark. *Vogue* commented on the trend in November 1952, when it described a "blueprint teenager" complete with bobby socks, ponytail, and the boyfriend's sweater. Young fashions became a regular feature in that magazine in 1953. *Harper's Bazaar* started a regular section called "The Young Outlook" in 1958. England's Mary Quant began making youth-centered fashions in 1955 and had a successful trip to America in 1959. Announcing that "snobbery has gone out of fashion," Quant offered kicky outfits specifically for women under twenty-five, rather than popular fashions that had been designed for film stars and wealthy princesses. For young people, suddenly, dictates from Paris were irrelevant.

The "Preppy" Look. Quant's more radical designs became widely popular in America in the 1960s. But in the mid to late 1950s both boys and girls had their own versions of the "preppy" look. Preppy boys wore baggy pants, V−necked sweaters, and Top Siders or dirty white bucks. They sported crew cuts or else, in Horn's words, "the long-but-not-too-long carefully combed and parted, wholesome-looking rocker hairstyles favored by such teen trendsetters as Ricky Nelson of 'Ozzie and Harriet' fame." For dressy occasions they donned a sports jacket and slacks, with loafers or white bucks.

Preppy on the Dance Floor. Preppy girls wore sweaters, poodle skirts, bobby socks, and saddle shoes. The dirndl dress (sleeveless, or with puffed sleeves, and plenty of petticoats underneath) became the first popular fashion designed strictly for youth. Billowing circle skirts and cinch belts were perfect for rock 'n' roll dancing or the Bunny Hop. Baggy pants were also favored by girls, as were long, pleated, plaid skirts. At night teens glittered with paste-on rhinestones. Hair was cut into short, curly "poodle" cuts or shaggy Italian styles, or it was swept back into a ponytail or teased and sprayed into an elaborate bouffant.

The "Greaser" Look. "Greasers," by contrast, were the all-American rebels. Inspired in part by movie star Marlon Brando in "The Wild One," the idea, Horn says, "was to look poor, tough, and hard — cold as ice, angry as hell, macho, arrogant, and dressed to kill." Tight black jeans, black boots, shiny shirts, black leather jackets, and T-shirts with rolled-up cuffs (for storing cigarettes) constituted the greaser look, as portrayed years later by Fonzie in television's "Happy Days." Boys' hair was worn long and greased with Vaseline, molded into a duck tail (or "D.A." for "duck's ass") like Elvis Presley's. (A Massachusetts school banned the D.A. in 1957, fearful that it was fostering rebellious attitudes.)

Tough Girls. Their girlfriends were a tough group, too, wearing heavy makeup, tight sweaters, short skirts, and stockings. Some girls wore their hair greased into duck tails, and some smoked cigarettes, too. The dress of both male and female greasers screamed rebellion, and society heartily disapproved.

Accessorizing. Couples, of both styles, also made fashion statements. Preppies exchanged class rings, which girls wore on necklaces, and had matching ID tags. When in college, this group's fraternities sponsored elaborate pinning ceremonies. Greasers, by contrast, rarely bothered with class rings; they sported tattoos and heavy ID bracelets, instead, and girls wore their boyfriends' leather jackets. But whether you were a preppy or a greaser, by mid decade the youth culture and its fashions reigned supreme.

Source:
Richard Horn, *Fifties Style, Then and Now* (New York: Beech Tree, 1985), pp. 159–160.

1950s ARCHITECTURE

American Dominance. In the 1950s America exerted an enormous influence on world architectural design, not only because of the volume of work being done but also because the most exciting new forms were being conceived and executed in the United States. Wealthy clients and the large number of emigrants from throughout the world made the United States the undisputed center of architectural innovation.

Great Architects. With a few exceptions (Le Corbusier in France, Yoshimura in Japan, and Oscar Niemeyer in Brazil), architects everywhere found themselves copying American trends rather than originating their own. Great architects such as Frank Lloyd Wright, Walter Gropius, Ludwig Mies van der Rohe, Eero Saarinen, Philip Johnson, and Edward Durrell Stone were all at work in 1950s America — and the quality and amount of their output were staggering. The trend was unabashedly modern, although by the late 1950s more ornamentation and exuberance were creeping in — the first stirrings of the postmodern era of architecture.

Frank Lloyd Wright. Experts believe the greatest lasting influence on architecture in the 1950s and 1960s was that of Wright and Mies van der Rohe. Already an old man in 1950 (he died at age eighty-nine in 1959), Wright continued to design astonishing buildings throughout the decade. His Price Tower (1953–1956) in Bartlesville, Oklahoma, was an imaginative variation on the high-rise housing structure. His Solomon R. Guggenheim Museum (1956–1959) in New York was a free-form structure in an urban context, and it was extremely controversial. Wright also designed several fascinating religious buildings near the end of his life, including the Unitarian Church (completed after his death in 1965) in Madison, Wisconsin, and the Orthodox Church (1961) near Milwaukee. Wright's stunning originality made him suspect to modern purists, who wanted everything simple, stark, and similar. But Wright's legacy endures. The fact that American architecture was so influential in the 1950s —

and throughout the twentieth century — is due in large measure to the contributions of Wright.

Mies van der Rohe. Mies van der Rohe's influence came through his architectural designs and also through his teaching position at the Illinois Institute of Technology in Chicago, where he influenced countless aspiring architects. Among his buildings is the entire campus complex of the Illinois Institute of Technology, done between 1938 and 1955. Disciples of Mies van der Rohe were everywhere in 1950s America. They designed unadorned glass-and-steel buildings (with concrete slabs creating the ceilings and floors) for large corporations across the country — though not usually with the flair of their master. The architects of the firm of Skidmore, Owings & Merrill were some of the better-known disciples of Mies van der Rohe. In designing buildings that were impersonal in appearance, they worked in anti-individualistic committees — or "teams" — that had little to no direct contact with a client. The company's 1952 Lever House in New York was a good example of this impersonal, anonymous architecture.

1950s High Spirits. By the mid to late 1950s some other American architects besides Wright were using flamboyant forms and decorations in their buildings. Morris Lapidus's flashy Fontainebleau Hotel in Miami Beach had a sweeping, arc-shaped facade that was "blatantly hedonistic," according to author Horn. Some of John Lautner's 1950s houses look like flying saucers — objects of much interest at the time. Stone's United States Pavilion at the 1958 Brussels World's Fair also was flying saucer shaped. Lautner's Amphitheater House in Los Angeles had exterior walls that could be swung open like doors "so that its inhabitants could take fullest advantage of the view." By the end of the 1950s the stark modern designs were being phased out, and postmodern ornamentation was "in."

Sources:
Richard Horn, *Fifties Style, Then and Now* (New York: Beech Tree, 1985);

The H. C. Price Company Tower, designed by Frank Lloyd Wright, in Bartlesville, Oklahoma

Udo Kultermann, *Architecture in the 20th Century* (New York: Reinhold, 1993);

Tom Wolfe, *From Bauhaus to Our House* (New York: Farrar, Straus & Giroux, 1981).

THE "GOOGIE SCHOOL OF ARCHITECTURE"

Euphoria Personified. The optimism and euphoria that swept the country after World War II infused the outlook of 1950s architects. These men and women, already influenced by the brilliant Frank Lloyd Wright, had access to amazing new construction materials and building techniques generated by war technologies. Now it was time to design the postwar nation: the future was theirs.

Cars. Simultaneously, the car culture exploded. Huge, flashy American cars laden with shiny chrome and fitted with futuristic tail fins traveled the roads between the cities and the burgeoning suburbs in ever-increasing numbers.

Question: How is it possible to lure the people in those cars off the highways and into the coffee shops and

The Lever House, designed by Skidmore, Owings & Merrill, in New York City typifies the architectural style inspired by Mies van der Rohe.

gic symbols of the era. Ironically, many of the more controversial design elements in the Googie buildings have now become commonplace in both commercial and residential architecture.

California Crazy. The Googie style of architecture was born in California, particularly in 1950s Los Angeles, in part because the city's mild weather was perfect for drive-in coffee shops and restaurants. Bright flashy colors, exposed neon tubing, glistening metallic reflections, and lustrous interior lighting personified Coffee Shop Modern. These artistic elements also spread to the design of supermarkets, car washes, bowling alleys, motels, highrises, homes, and even a few churches. By the mid to late 1950s Googie architecture had moved east and permeated the entire country.

Favorite Symbols and Shapes. The boomerang was a favorite symbol that showed up in much Googie architecture. It was so ubiquitous, in fact, that writer Tom Wolfe suggested that the entire style be called "Boomerang Modern." The dingbat, the starburst, the sputnik, the spiky ball (a variation on the atomic symbol), and the frozen sparkler were also widely used in signs and ornaments. Americans in the 1950s were obviously fascinated by space imagery. Other favorite shapes used in Googie architecture included parabolas, pylons, trapezoids, arrows of all kinds, slanting darts, and soaring prows.

Rules of Googie.

Be abstract.

Ignore gravity; whenever possible, the building must seem to hang from the sky.

Mix together two or three structural systems.

McDonald's. The 3-D, twenty-five-foot, gleaming metal parabola reaching into the sky was the original

drive-in restaurants that sprang up across America? Answer: Use outrageous buildings as advertisements. There would be wild shapes, brilliant colors, and bright, spotless interiors combined with controversial metal-framed, angular designs, lavish use of glass and stone, stylized lettering, and integrated landscaping. Detractors titled these structures "Coffee Shop Modern" and the "Googie School of Architecture" after a particularly fanciful coffee shop in Los Angeles. "It starts off on the level like any other building," wrote an architectural critic about the original Googie's coffee shop in 1952. "But suddenly it breaks for the sky. The bright red roof of cellular steel decking suddenly tilts upward as if swung on a hinge, and the whole building goes up with it like a rocket ramp. But there is another building next door. So the flight stops as suddenly as it began." At night the interiors of these places were visible through clear plate-glass windows. It was modern, flamboyant architecture at its most outlandish.

Gone Googie. Today much of the Googie architecture of the 1950s is gone, razed and replaced with more staid designs. But a few Googie designs remain as nostal-

The McDonald's golden arch in the 1950s is an example of the "Googie" style.

Construction workers in 1950 mass-produce houses in Levittown, New York.

symbol of McDonald's in the 1950s. The golden arches exemplify Googie architecture. In the late 1960s public taste changed, and the McDonald's Corporation introduced a new prototype: a low-profile mansard roof and staid brick-and-shingle textures. But the golden arches were retained as the corporation's logo.

Sources:

Alan Hess, *Googie: Fifties Coffee Shop Architecture* (San Francisco: Chronicle Books, 1986);

Richard Horn, *Fifties Style, Then and Now* (New York: Beech Tree, 1985).

SUBURBIA

Coming Home. As World War II ended, more than ten million soldiers were discharged from the U.S. armed forces. Where were they going to live? The answer, it turned out, was suburbia — 1950s style.

House Builder Levitt. There were suburbs in America before the 1950s, but these were nothing like Levittown and its imitators. On 3 July 1950 developer William J. Levitt appeared on the cover of *Time* magazine, standing in front of a row of identical boxlike houses on newly bulldozed land. The caption read: "HOUSE BUILDER LEVITT: For Sale: a new way of life." First on Long Island, then near Philadelphia, and finally in New Jersey, Levitt built his dream houses and in the process created the suburbia of the 1950s.

The Levitt Design. Levitt and his sons, who had built houses for the navy during World War II, brought mass-production techniques to house building. The Levittown houses, built on concrete slabs with no basements, were nearly identical in floor plan, although there were some slight variations in exteriors and color. The original designs had two bedrooms and one bathroom, and a family could expand the house by converting the attic or adding on. Lots were of uniform size (sixty by one hundred feet) with a tree planted every twenty-eight feet (two-and-a-half trees per home). In the beginning the Levitts included free televisions sets and a Bendix washing machine as incentives.

An Orderly Neighborhood. The early deeds to the Levitts' houses specified that no fences were to be built, lawns were to be mowed at least once a week in season, and laundry could be hung only on rotary racks, not on clotheslines, and never on weekends.

Record Growth. A 1949 housing act helped finance suburban projects, and the low Levittown prices helped even more. World War II veterans — anxious for clean, less expensive, safe places for their children — streamed out of the cities and queued up to buy the new tract housing. Soon scores of builders adopted the methods pioneered by Levitt.

Housing Boom. In 1950, 1.4 million new housing units were built, mostly in the suburbs. This rate continued throughout the 1950s, as an average of three thousand acres of farmland *per day* was bulldozed into tract housing. By 1952 Levittown's population (in Long Island) had jumped to ten thousand, and a second Levittown in Pennsylvania was built for seventeen thousand families.

No Architectural Distinction. In terms of style, the suburban tract housing followed none of the principles of Wright or Mies van der Rohe or any other of the famous architects of the 1950s, except for the occasional inclusion of multipurpose rooms. Indeed, the Federal Housing Authority "refused to finance developers whose designs they deemed too Modern-looking, assuming that it was a fad that sooner or later would pass."

Patterned Lives. Block after block of identical houses dotted suburbia. Children quickly memorized the exact route to their homes, lest they get hopelessly lost among the similar structures. Only the strange color combinations inside some of these homes gave them any individuality. Early American furniture was popular in suburbia, as were antiques. The houses had few interior walls, ostensibly to cut down building costs. But this also promoted the family "togetherness" that seemed so important in the 1950s.

The Community. Soon shopping centers were built, followed by schools, libraries, movie theaters, restaurants, and churches — all in the same boxlike version of modern architecture that developers liked and, apparently, so did consumers.

The Same People, Too. The 1950s suburban communities tended to attract similar people: young, white, middle-class, and newly married. Blacks, Jews, and Hispanics were not welcome; neither were singles, gays, the elderly, or unmarried people living together. Only the nuclear family was acceptable, with the young married couples usually between the ages of twenty-five and thirty-five. Most had at least one child. Incomes averaged between six thousand and seven thousand dollars.

Suburban Psychosis. Suburban life was orderly and convenient, but also unreal and sterile. It produced harried husbands, bored wives, and alienated children. Not surprisingly, the middle-class children who grew up in 1950s suburbia began the counterculture of the 1960s.

Sources:
Richard Horn, *Fifties Style, Then and Now* (New York: Beech Tree, 1985), pp. 132–133.
Douglas T. Miller and Marion Nowak, *The Fifties: The Way We Really Were* (Garden City, N.Y.: Doubleday, 1977), pp. 133–134, 137.

ARCHITECTURE: SPACE AND COLOR

Central Feature. Space — lots of it — was the key feature of interior design in the 1950s. Influenced by the severe designs of Mies van der Rohe and other Bauhaus architects who sought an integration of visual arts into society, both American homes and public buildings were built with lots of spare, open space. *House Beautiful* magazine was lyrical about "our wonderful 20th century concept of space . . . the free and easy movement from the house to the garden and back to the house . . . vistas for the eye to roam or relax in — indoors and out and upwards." Said designer George Nelson in *Living Spaces:* "It is not efficiency that we are looking for, but freedom from dimensional barriers."

Breaking Down Barriers. At the same time, walls and rooms became scarce. Wright's concept of "open" architectural plans meshed with the idea of flowing space, and great rooms — actually, no demarcated rooms at all — were the result. There was a bonus: the function of the room could change according to the occasion.

Furniture. Furniture was also spare and was grouped according to function. There was probably no wall between the living room and dining room; the furniture identified the room. Recessed lighting fixtures replaced space-consuming lamps, and flooring materials "were continuous throughout a space, to enhance the sense of openness." There was minimal clutter in 1950s homes — few ornamentations or gewgaws. They would, after all, take up space.

GUGGENHEIM MUSEUM "NEITHER COMMUNIST NOR SOCIALIST"

During the 1950s many American artists became targets of the House Committee on Un-American Activities, which sought to purge the country of Communist influence. Writers, painters, movie directors, and actors were accused of subverting democracy by producing "Red Art." Architects as well felt the heat in the emotionally charged political atmosphere—and often felt compelled to use cold-war rhetoric in explaining and defending their designs. In 1953 Frank Lloyd Wright rushed to a hearing in Manhattan held to decide the fate of his Guggenheim Museum design. Many New Yorkers felt that the museum would be too radical in appearance and inappropriate as an art gallery. Furthermore, city officials charged that the blueprints did not conform to Manhattan building codes. Wright agreed to make several cosmetic changes in the blueprints to meet the building codes but vowed to fight his critics on other aesthetic issues. With a characteristic flair for the dramatic, he boldly proclaimed his museum to be a "democratic" symbol, unlike the "fascist" design of most city skyscrapers. He then took a swipe at those who would criticize his building as un-American: "This building is neither Communist nor Socialist, but characteristic of the new aristocracy born of freedom to maintain it. The reactionary . . . will not really like it."

Source: *Time* (10 August 1953): 70.

A 1950s living room representative of "open"
architectural design

Offices, Too. Open plans were the preferred look in offices, too. CEOs were sold on the idea that open space encouraged communication and greater intimacy among workers, thereby helping the company run more smoothly. The spare, lean office furniture designed in the 1950s by Charles Eames, Eero Saarinen, George Nelson, Florence Knoll, and others fit right in. A pamphlet published in 1957 by the Connecticut General Life Insurance Company talked about the advantages of open space: "An unexpected dividend is the greater intimacy in which we spend our working day. In vertical buildings, where quick elevators take one from a small work level to the street level, there are few spontaneous meetings, few casual interchanges of work experiences. Here in the . . . lounges and on the daily routes of travel through the buildings, we are getting to know each other better."

Privacy? What Privacy? With few walls (except glass ones) in houses and offices of the 1950s, privacy was hard to come by, but 1950s designers came up with solutions: screens, freestanding storage units, and curtains. All were used to divide one large space into smaller spaces and give some privacy as well. The screens of the 1950s were imaginative: some were fiberglass, some were bamboo, some were strips of plastic beads. Plastic accordion walls were popular, too. In offices bookcases and storage units were used to divide vast spaces into smaller, more-private nooks.

Colorful Colors. Americans in the 1950s liked bright, bold colors as much as they liked space. Splashes of color warmed up the severe architecture and simple furniture of the era. Colors were displayed exuberantly, sometimes as accents, sometimes covering entire rooms. One designer, Donald Deskey, even came up with a line of "splotchily colored furniture . . . made of cast aluminum and polychrome Micarta. In tones ranging from blue-into-violet to red-into-sienna, they provided some of the color accents thought to be so appropriate for the more sophisti-

cated space of the fifties." Even some bomb shelters were colorful. Writer William Manchester described one in Los Angeles with "brightly painted concrete walls [and] shamrock green plastic carpeting."

Source:
Richard Horn, *Fifties Style, Then and Now* (New York: Beech Tree, 1985), pp. 106–118.

THOSE FABULOUS CARS

Cruisin'. If any invention typified the wildly optimistic mood of America in the 1950s, it was the decade's large, long, sleek automobiles. Unlike architects, furniture designers, and fashion designers of the era, who produced simple, unornamented products in subdued colors, designers of the fabulous 1950s cars produced gleaming, exuberant creations of chrome and power — and in delicious ice cream colors, too.

Impractical but Stylish. By 1954 there were forty-seven million passenger cars in the United States, and by 1960, 80 percent of American families owned cars. The cars were totally impractical. Their gas mileage was abysmal. They were designed for style, not safety. They were so long that they were hard to park, especially in cities. Their fancy grilles and acres of chrome were difficult to keep clean. But their shiny exteriors and spacious interior design screamed power and status. Moreover, they had those fabulous fins.

Fabulous Fins. The fins had their genesis in 1941, when Harley Earl, chief stylist for General Motors

THE MAKING OF A LEMON

The first Edsel rolled off the Ford assembly line in 1958; it was discontinued two years later, having become the joke of the automobile industry. In a remarkably short time the Edsel became synonymous with botched market research, as Ford executives had spent much energy and money in determining wrongly that the box-shaped car would be snatched up by a growing market—those families earning more than $5,000 a year. Advertising campaigns portrayed the Edsel as the perfect car for the up-and-coming man and wife who had outgrown their hot rods yet still did not want anything to do with the large, boat-shaped Pontiacs, Dodges, and Buicks that screamed middle age. By the time the first Edsel appeared, however, demand among young middle-class families had shifted to sleekly designed compacts. The Edsel's design was hardly sleek; its grille with the large oval center—the Edsel's most comic feature—has been described as resembling "an Oldsmobile sucking a lemon."

Source: *Time* (30 November 1959).

A 1959 Cadillac Eldorado Biarritz convertible

(GM), saw the U.S. Air Force's twin-tailed P-38 "lightning" fighter plane. Why not similar tail fins for cars, Earl wondered? He directed GM artists to design tail fins of all types to be adapted for use on automobiles. In 1948 Cadillac introduced the first (fairly modest) aircraft-style tail fins. Within ten years the fins would grow to an incredible size, resembling everything from propeller airplanes to rockets. Even better, the fins supposedly had a functional purpose: they were said to aid aerodynamic stability.

"Finomania." By the mid 1950s, according to *Motor Trend* magazine, "finomania exploded." Chrysler, which had lagged behind the rest of the industry in design innovation, took advantage of the public's fascination for big fins. The company's 1957 models sported highly stylized fins that stretched from the middle to the tail end of the car. In 1959 Cadillac introduced the fins to outdo all fins in its Eldorado Biarritz convertible.

Fins Peak. Fins peaked in 1959, becoming progressively smaller accessories until they disappeared in the 1960s, unfortunately for Chrysler, who had planned a big, single, off-center fin for a future model, starting in a ridge on the hood and then running along the roof, rising in a single rib at the tail. With the end of "finomania," however, the new model never made it to the showroom floor.

Detroit's Complacency. In the postwar years Detroit complacently built the cars it thought America wanted. The cars grew bigger, faster, gaudier, heavier, and more self-indulgent. They also had eight-cylinder engines and a seemingly limitless choice of body styles, engines, transmissions, and options. Motors were hawked in terms of raw power — "Rocket 88," then "98." Style was the American auto industry's god. Safe cars, said William Mitchell, GM's styling director, only appeal to "squares," and, he added, "there ain't no squares anymore."

Fabulous Fantasies. Americans in the 1950s were accused of worshiping their cars, and, in a way, they did. Eric Larrabee wrote that "the car is an instrument against the very *idea* of chores and inconveniences, regardless of the reality. To be splendid and irrational is of its nature." The 1960s realities of assassination, war, and antiwar demonstrations had not yet arrived. During the 1950s, says Richard Horn, "Americans could afford to avoid reality, forget about space races and financial woes, and go through life as if it were one big, open road leading toward a wonderful future . . . . no vehicle could have been more appropriate for the journey than the now-classic 1950s automobile."

Sources:

Richard Horn, *Fifties Style, Then and Now* (New York: Beech Tree, 1985), pp. 12–15;

Douglas T. Miller and Marion Nowak, *The Fifties: The Way We Really Were* (Garden City, N.Y.: Doubleday, 1977), pp. 139–141;

Marco Ruiz and others, *100 Years of the Automobile, 1886–1986*, translated by Arnoldo Mondadori (New York: Gallery Books, 1985), pp. 92–101.

1950s KITSCH

Decorating Whimsically. Most American furniture in the 1950s was lean and spare, with virtually no curlicues or ornamentation of any kind. Indeed, American modern furniture designers prided themselves on simple, almost stark designs. How did interior designers and consumers spell relief in the 1950s? It was spelled "kitsch" — a German colloquialism for trash or rubbish. Kitsch has been called — only partly tongue-in-cheek — the only art form developed by the middle class.

1950s Pop. The zany, playful, extreme accessories and decorations of the 1950s are called kitsch or "1950s pop." To call them whimsical is an understatement. The 1950s accessories were simply marvelous to the extreme.

A marshmallow sofa designed by George Nelson, 1956

Wild Lamps. There are some first-class examples of 1950s kitsch in lamps of the decade. There were lamps whose bases were ladies' legs; "bubble" lamps that hung in clusters; a weird chandelier called "Sputnik" after the Soviet satellite; and lamps patterned after Gumby, a popular 1950s doll; lamps whose bases were ceramic hula dancers, ballerinas, Spanish dancers, or African princesses.

Ball Clock. Clocks from the 1950s are easily recognizable, from their pastel plastic cases to their odd shapes — often boomerangs, balls, or molecules. One of the most famous, and a big seller during the 1950s, was a Ball Clock designed in 1949 by George Nelson and Company of New York. Starkly simple in appearance, the clock featured twelve small balls stuck on the ends of twelve sticks, with each ball representing one of the hours. The clock's hands were fastened to another larger circle set in the middle of the twelve balls — all extremely 1950s.

"Golliwogs." Odd planters called "golliwogs" were also the rage and can still be found today in shops that specialize in 1950s designs. The golliwogs were made of hand-painted aluminum set on a cast-iron base, and they had people's stylized faces and bodies. Some were almost life-size.

Odd Knickknacks. Candleholders were imaginative and strange, and ashtrays (pastel-colored, boomerang-shaped ones were popular, as were those that resembled amoebas) outdid themselves. Large, free-form ashtrays were a sort of sculpture for those who could not afford artwork. Wall masks — often painted wood and pseudo-African — also graced the walls of many 1950s tract houses and apartments.

Marshmallow Sofa. Sofas and chairs were also available in pop styles. One of the most famous was the "marshmallow" sofa, designed by George Nelson and Company. The couch consisted of eighteen round, soft pillows that looked like marshmallows, attached to the seat and the back of a curved iron frame.

Patterns and Wall Covers. Like accessories, playful fabrics and wall coverings were also used to soften the stark modern interior of the 1950s. The boomerang shape — everywhere in the 1950s — was on a Formica pattern for kitchen counters. Wallpaper patterns inspired by primitive art were also popular, as were labyrinthine designs. Wild geometric designs were considered highbrow. A few avant-garde homes suspended neon shapes in boomerang motifs from the ceiling of rooms used for entertaining, but mostly this motif was used in kicky cafés.

Sources:
Bevis Hillier, *Austerity Binge: The Decorative Arts of the Forties and Fifties* (London: Studio Vista, 1975), p. 161;

Richard Horn, *Fifties Style, Then and Now* (New York: Beech Tree, 1985), pp. 94–101.

AMERICAN MODERN TAKES A BOW

American Modern. Prewar furnishings did not work in postwar homes. Young people married earlier, had more babies, and moved to suburbia, where the homes were different from town houses or city apartments. Increased building costs shrank room sizes, lowered ceilings, and reduced the number of rooms and closets. Double-duty living areas, more open and spacious rooms, and fewer walls were also the style of the day.

Modern Furniture for the Modern House. Lower, more simple furniture was needed, and talented architects and designers were more than willing to oblige. Indeed, many of the most influential designers of furniture and home furnishings in the 1950s were architects, for they designed the modern houses that could not be furnished with what was on the market. Today, one refers to 1950s furniture as "American modern" — austere, functional, mass-produced, often of synthetic materials like molded plastic and plywood laminate. But American modern is actually an amalgam of the German Bauhaus principles and Scandinavian influence.

Bauhaus Heads West. The Bauhaus, a German architectural school begun by Walter Gropius, was founded on the principles of industrial technology and prices affordable to the masses. When the Bauhaus was closed by the Nazis in the 1930s, several of its leading proponents came to American universities, where they taught modern design. At about the same time Scandinavian design — the so-called Danish modern look — became influential in America.

New Design Meets America's Tastes. In the late 1940s and the 1950s American designers such as Charles Eames, Eero Saarinen, Hans and Florence Knoll, George Nelson, and Harry Bertoia created furniture that combined Bauhaus and twentieth-century Scandinavian design aesthetics. The result was a completely new style that

The simple curves and unadorned style of the Eames chair are characteristic of 1950s American modern interior design.

appealed to a victorious America: American modern. It was characterized by straight lines or simple curves, broad and unusually flat surfaces, and the absence of carving or other ornamentation. It was, as writer Tom Wolfe called it, bare and spare. And it was often made of revolutionary new materials.

MOMA. The American modern look was given wholehearted support and nudges by the Museum of Modern Art (MOMA) in New York City. Its directors liked the Bauhaus outlook and wanted the American public to like it, too. Throughout the late 1930s and into the 1940s MOMA sponsored several exhibits to introduce Americans to functional, mass-produced, trim furniture and housewares. Eames and Saarinen won best of show at one of these early exhibits. Many of the winning designs eventually went into mass production and were sold throughout the country.

New Materials and Technology. Without the revolutionary synthetic materials invented in the 1940s, and without the technological advances made during World War II, it is unlikely that American modern furniture would have evolved as it did. These technological advances made during the war — especially in the aircraft industry — were later applied to furniture design. The synthetic materials developed before and during the war included melamine (a crystalline compound used in making molded plastic products) and plywood laminates. All were put to good use in the new furniture.

The Classics. As postwar Americans got richer, classic American modern furniture was introduced primarily by the Herman Miller Company and Knoll Associates. The furniture was intentionally impersonal, and it was made of "honest design" — that is, plastic looked like plastic, and joints were not hidden. It was supposed to be part of American modern's charm. There were the Eames molded plywood chairs (1946) and plastic shell chairs (1949), Eames storage units (1950), wire chairs (1951), lounge chairs and ottomans (1956), and the aluminum group (1958). Eames's plywood chairs were practically indestructible and became standard in offices worldwide. Most of his designs remain classics.

"Womb" Chair. Nelson designed several innovative storage systems still being used today. Saarinen's famous "Womb" chair came out in 1948, and his "Pedestal" tables and chairs in 1955 and 1957. The sculptor Bertoia introduced his chairs of welded steel latticework in 1952. The famous Hardoy chair (also known as the "Butterfly") came out in the mid 1950s. It remains popular — and inexpensive — today.

Office, Not Home. Much of the American modern furniture of the 1950s was ultimately used in offices rather than private homes. Indeed, much of this furniture was designed with corporate settings in mind. Knoll Associates, which distributed many of the American modern designs, in fact targeted architects and designers, not the general public, as their most likely customers.

1952 BEST-DRESSED MEN SELECTED BY THE CUSTOM TAILORS GUILD

1. Bernard Baruch (investor)

Runners-up:

Hank Greenberg (Cleveland Indians general manager)

Conrad Hilton (hotel magnate)

Guy Lombardo (bandleader)

Alfred Gwynne Vanderbilt (socialite)

Arthur Murray (dance teacher)

Yul Brynner (actor)

Robert Montgomery (actor)

Gene Kelly (dancer and entertainer)

Harry E. Gould (industrialist)

Source: *Time* (6 October 1952): 47.

Sources:

Cherie Fehrman and Kenneth Fehrman, *Postwar Interior Design: 1945–1960* (New York: Reinhold, 1987);

Olga Gueft, "Decade of Modern: How It Grew," *New York Times Magazine*, 9 March 1958, pp. 54–55;

Richard Horn, *Fifties Style, Then and Now* (New York: Beech Tree, 1985), pp. 80–89;

Lesley Jackson, *The New Look: Design in the Fifties* (London: Thames & Hudson, 1991), pp. 38–41.

1952 BEST DRESSED WOMEN SELECTED BY THE NEW YORK DRESS INSTITUTE

1. Duchess of Windsor (tops best-dressed list for tenth consecutive year)

Runners-up:

Mrs. William Paley (New York)

Duchess of Kent

Mrs. Byron Foy (New York)

Mme. Louis Arppels (Paris)

Marlene Dietrich (actress)

Mrs. William Randolph Hearst, Jr.

Mrs. Winston Guest (Boston)

Countess Rodolfo Crespi (Rome)

Mme. Henri Bonnet (wife of French ambassador to America)

Mrs. Dwight D. Eisenhower (wife of U.S. president-elect)

Oveta Culp Hobby (federal security administrator-designate)

[Note: In the 5 January 1952 issue of the *New Yorker*, E.J. Kahn, Jr.—who had received a best-dressed ballot from the New York Dress Institute—questioned the Institute's confusing forms of address for the year's more than one hundred most fashionable candidates: Why should only the famous (with the notable exception of Mamie Eisenhower) and employed be referred to by their names alone? In the case of "Oveta Culp Hobby" Kahn asserts that "perhaps she was disallowed her rightful use of "Mrs." because she was once a WAC and the Dress Institute has some reservations about lady soldiers." Kahn also noted glaring omissions in the list of candidates. Queen Elizabeth did not make the cut, but her mother-in-law did. In a self-proclaimed act of chivalry and diplomacy, he cast a write-in vote for Her Royal Highness. For the sake of his marriage, he also wrote in his wife.]

Source: *New York Times*, 17 December 1952: 38;
New Yorker (5 January 1952): 49–52.

HEADLINE MAKERS

GABRIELLE "COCO" CHANEL
1883-1971

FRENCH COUTURIERE;
POPULARIZED SIMPLE, WEARABLE CLOTHING

No More Tight Corsets. In 1919 French designer Gabrielle "Coco" Chanel released women from the tight corsets of the era and introduced them to comfortable jersey clothing. In 1954, after fifteen years of retirement and just six months before her seventy-first birthday, she made a comeback and freed women once again from highly structured, constricting designs — this time the clothing of the "New Look." Critics were lukewarm, but women, particularly American women, loved her casual, softly shaped clothes and snapped them up. These designs ushered in a new relaxation in fashion that continues today.

Early Years. Little is known of Chanel's early years except that she was orphaned as a young child. She started in fashion in 1910, making hats in Paris. Chanel opened her first dress shop in Paris in 1914 and closed it in 1939 at the onset of World War II. But in the period between the world wars she revolutionized women's fashion with her straight, simple, uncorseted, and, above all, comfortable "Chanel Look." She also popularized short hair for women in the 1920s and introduced shorter skirts. She created her famous Chanel No. 5 perfume in 1922.

Later Years. In 1954 Chanel said her competitive spirit was aroused because Parisian high fashion had been taken over by men. "There are too many men in this business," she told a magazine interviewer in May 1954, "and they don't know how to make clothes for women. All this fantastic pinching and puffing. How can a woman wear a dress that's cut so she can't lift up her arm to pick up a telephone?" She had a knack for knowing what women wanted, and women responded enthusiastically. In the 1950s her famous Chanel suit — a collarless, braid-trimmed cardigan jacket and slim, graceful skirt — was an enormous hit. She also popularized pea jackets and bell-bottom trousers plus magnificent jewelry worn with sportswear.

Broadway. In 1969 Coco Chanel's life was the basis for *Coco*, a Broadway musical starring Katharine Hepburn. Chanel died in 1971, working to the end on a new collection.

CHRISTIAN DIOR
1905-1957

FRENCH FASHION DESIGNER AND CREATOR OF
THE "NEW LOOK"

COFFIN

Diplomatic Training. Christian Dior, son of a wealthy Norman manufacturer of chemicals and fertilizer, wanted to be an architect, but his family insisted he enter the diplomatic service. He prepared for a diplomatic career at the Ecole des Sciences Politiques but abandoned diplomacy in 1928 and became an art dealer. Illness forced him to give up that business in 1934, and when he returned to Paris a year later, it was as a fashion illustrator — first of hats, later of dresses.

"The New Look." In 1946, when World War II cloth rationing was lifted, Dior opened his own salon. In the spring of 1947 the success of his first collection, called the "New Look," propelled him to the top of the French fashion industry. His idealized, ultrafeminine silhouette featured tiny waists; long, full skirts; padded busts; and rounded shoulders. Everything was made exquisitely of the best materials available. The New Look changed the shape of women's clothing and lifted the French fashion industry out of the doldrums. For this feat a grateful French government awarded him the Legion of Honor.

Subsequent Designs. His successive collections (including the "H-Line" in 1954 and the "A-Line" in 1955) continued to be popular, and throughout the 1950s the fashion world looked to Paris and Dior for inspiration and style. He expanded his company into eight firms and sixteen associate firms in twenty-four countries, reportedly grossing some $20 million a year. His Dior label went on jewelry, scarves, men's ties, furs, stockings, gloves, and ready-to-wear clothing.

House of Dior. After his death the House of Dior continued under other designers, including his protégé Yves St. Laurent until 1960, then Marc Bohan. Thirty years later the House of Dior continues to set the pace for high fashion throughout the world.

CHARLES EAMES

1907-1978

ARCHITECT AND DESIGNER OF FAMOUS FORM-FITTING CHAIRS

"Extraordinarily Comfortable." Although he worked with a variety of fabrics, machinery, and buildings, Charles Eames was best known for the series of chairs that still bear his name. In the 1950s his extraordinarily comfortable chairs, built low and responsive to the body, were snapped up by consumers wanting the new American Modern furniture but wanting comfort, too.

Flunked Architecture. Born in Saint Louis to a Civil War veteran, Eames won a scholarship to study architecture at Washington University but flunked out, partly because he spent too much time working in one of the city's large architectural firms and partly because the traditional teachers at his university disapproved of Frank Lloyd Wright, one of Eames's idols. In 1929 Eames went to Europe, where he learned about the work of the great German Bauhaus architects. He opened an architectural office back in Saint Louis in 1930.

Cranbrook Academy of Art. In the late 1930s Eames was offered a fellowship to study at the Cranbrook Academy of Art of Bloomfield Hills, Michigan. Working with the director's son, Eero Saarinen, he entered a molded-plywood chair in the Organic Design Competition conducted in 1940–1941 by the Museum of Modern Art in New York City. The chair, which for the first time used bare plywood shaped to fit the contours of the human body, won first prize in the international competition and established the two designers as leading innovators. Later Eames's chairs were fashioned of tubular steel, wire mesh, and molded plastic. His simple and functional chairs and tables were considered revolutionary because they were made almost wholly by machines. The chairs were unusually comfortable primarily due to rubber shock mounts that joined backs and seats to the chair frame — an innovation Eames had learned from engine design.

Other Talents. Later in life Eames became a documentary filmmaker, winning awards from the Edinburgh International Film Festival (1954 and 1957), the San Francisco International Film Festival (1958), and the American Film Festival (1959). But his name is still synonymous with his chairs. Three of those chairs appear on a list called "The 100 Best Designed Products," compiled in 1959 by the world's leading designers and released by the Institute of Design of the Illinois Institute of Technology.

R(ICHARD) BUCKMINSTER FULLER (JR.)

1895-1983

ENGINEER, AUTHOR, AND INVENTOR OF THE GEODESIC DOME

Man of Many Talents. "Bucky" Fuller was an inventor, engineer, architect, mathematician, cartographer, philosopher, scientist, environmentalist, poet, author, and educator who, because of his wide range of interests and abilities, has been compared with Leonardo da Vinci. He is most famous for his creation of geodesic domes — structures of honeycombed triangles encompassing maximum space and strength with minimal materials. Since their invention in 1947 geodesic domes have been used in thousands of structures throughout the world.

Early Handicaps. Fuller had impaired vision as a child, and he was fitted for his first eyeglasses at the age of four. "I was filled with wonder at the beauty of the world and I have never lost my delight in it," Fuller told one of his biographers. In kindergarten he built his first tetrahedronal octet truss (three squares combined into eight triangles) out of toothpicks and dried peas. Many years later this construct became a key element of his geodesic domes.

Post-Harvard. Fuller was expelled twice from Harvard — once for "irresponsible conduct" after a spree in New York City, a second time for "lack of sustained interest in the process within the university." The second expulsion ended his formal education. He worked at a variety of jobs for more than a dozen years before he began patenting the first of his two thousand inventions. Believing that all human needs could be met through technology and planning, Fuller worked for several years on the mathematics of the science of geodesics. He constructed his first sizable geodesic dome in 1948 with the help of students at Black Mountain College in North Carolina. In 1953 Fuller designed a ninety-three-foot cover for the Dearborn plant rotunda of the Ford Motor Company. Thereafter his geodesic domes began to gain general acceptance. He created the famous American domed pavilion for the Montreal World's Fair in 1967. He designed plastic and fiberglass geodesic enclosures used for military radar installations and a two-hundred-foot golden dome in Moscow that became the site of Soviet premier Nikita S. Khrushchev's much publicized "kitchen debate" with American vice-president Richard Nixon. Khrushchev later remarked: "I would like to have Mr. J. Buckingham [sic] Fuller come to Russia and teach our engineers."

Uniquely American Contribution. By the early 1960s Fuller's geodesic dome was generally recognized as a uniquely American contribution to architecture. During the late 1960s Fuller became a hero of the counterculture with his books and his World Game — a computerized interplay of world resources and world strategies. But he will always be known for the geodesic dome. According to *Time* magazine in 1964: [the dome is] "a kind of benchmark of the universe, what seventeenth-century mystic Jakob Boehme might call 'a signature of God.'"

CLAIRE MCCARDELL
1905-1958

CREATOR OF THE "AMERICAN LOOK" IN FASHION

Paper Dolls. The daughter of a banker and state senator, Claire McCardell as a small child cut out and dressed paper dolls from her mother's fashion magazines. After high school she attended the Parsons School of Design in New York, later studying at the school's Paris division for a year.

For Ordinary Women. Unlike other designers of the time who copied the stilted Parisian fashions, McCardell decided to modify them to fit the ordinary woman's pocketbook and demand for comfort as well as fashion. McCardell is credited with originating the so-called American Look of the 1950s, the forerunner of today's comfortable, easy fashions. Clothes should be comfortable as well as handsome, she said, and should be appropriate to the occasion. They should fit well and be attractive.

American Fabrics. McCardell used such American fabrics as calico, seersucker, ticking, gingham, denim, and wool jersey to make simple, relaxed, wearable clothes. She picked up many details from men's clothing, such as large pockets, shirtsleeve shoulders, blue-jeans topstitching, trouser pleats, rivets, and gripper fastenings. Among her innovations were ballet slippers as dress accessories, the monastic dress, harem pajamas, the "Pop-over" wraparound housedress, and the diaper bathing

suit. She also pioneered the idea of interchangeable separates. In addition, McCardell designed sunglasses, infants' and children's wear, children's shoes, and jewelry.

Many Awards. McCardell received many honors, including the American Fashion Critics Award and the Neiman-Marcus Award. In 1950 President Harry S Truman presented her with the Women's National Press Club Award. Her designs were consciously contemporary, and most look contemporary forty years later .

NORMAN NORELL
1900-1972

POPULARIZED THE CULOTTE; AMERICAN PACESETTER IN THE WORLD OF HIGH FASHION

Clothes-Conscious Mother. Born Norman Levinson in Noblesville, Indiana, Norell learned about high fashion at an early age from his mother, who subscribed to French fashion magazines and dressed in avant-garde styles. He studied at the Parsons School of Design in New York City and later became a costume designer for Paramount. In 1928 Norell went to work for the legendary Hattie Carnegie, with whom he stayed until 1940, when he went out on his own.

High Fashion. Norell was one of the few American dress designers considered to be an equal by many Parisian couturiers in the 1940s and 1950s, when Paris still ruled the fashion world. Considered the father of American high fashion (Hattie Carnegie was the mother), Norell created designs that were sophisticated, dramatic, and of the highest workmanship. He was the first to show long evening skirts topped with sweaters. His long, glittering, sequined dresses, popularized by Marilyn Monroe and Jane Russell, never went out of style. The smoking robe, the chemise, the jumper, and the pantsuit were part of his collection. His culotte, a divided skirt that looks like a conventional skirt but allows for easy movement, was heavily copied by competitors.

The Artificial "Norell Look." Dramatic by nature, Norell was well known for the artificial "Norell Look" he created for his models: whitened faces, burnt-corked eyelids, and shingled haircuts.

Council of Fashion Designers. Norell was the founder and first president of the Council of Fashion Designers of America. He was also elected the first Hall of Fame designer by the American press in 1956 after receiving three Coty American Fashion Critics awards. In 1962 he was the first designer to receive an honorary degree of doctor of fine arts, conferred on him by the Pratt Institute in Brooklyn.

MARY QUANT

1934-

BAILEY

Early Life. Mary Quant studied at Goldsmith's College of Art in London, where she met Alexander Plunket-Greene. The two opened a small boutique called Bazaar in London's Chelsea district in 1955. Two years later they were married.

Making Her Own Designs. In the beginning Bazaar sold clothing from outside designers, but Quant soon became frustrated at the dearth of appropriate styles for young people. Clothes for youth should reflect that youthfulness, Quant believed; they should be spirited and unconventional, not stuffy and boring. Quant enrolled in night classes, bought material from Harrod's department store in London, and made up her own styles — aimed at independent, affluent working girls in their late teens or early twenties. The styles were a sensation, with a permanent line of young people waiting to get into the store.

Mod and Mini. Quant is given credit for starting the Chelsea or Mod look of the mid 1950s and creating the miniskirts of the 1960s. She used denim, colored flannel, and vinyl in clothes specifically for the young. And she showed her fashions with colored tights, not staid hosiery. Within seven years Quant's business was worth more than $2 million and was supplying 150 shops in Britain and 320 stores in the United States. Quant's Bazaar became a well-known meeting place for young people, and Chelsea became celebrated in movies, books, and songs.

Pivotal Figure. Quant made London the fashion capital of the world from the mid 1950s through the late 1960s. She was a major figure in the fashion earthquake of the time that reflected important social changes taking place around the world.

EERO SAARINEN

1910-1961

Early Life. Son of well-known Finnish architect and educator Eliel Saarinen, Eero Saarinen moved to the United States with his family in 1923. It was at the Cranbrook Academy of Art in Bloomfield Hills, Michigan, headed by the elder Saarinen, that Eero blossomed.

Organic Design. After winning first prize with Charles Eames in the 1940–1941 Museum of Modern Art's Organic Design in Home Furnishings competition, Saarinen began working on an "organic" chair design. He believed that a chair was incomplete without a person sitting in it, and he was determined to design a truly organic chair in which all parts blended in a unity of design. The result was the Womb chair, so called because its comfortable construction encouraged the sitter to assume a fetal position. The construction was of a molded plastic shell and fabric-covered latex foam upholstery on a steel frame with nylon swivel guides. There was also an accompanying ottoman. The chair is considered by many to be one of the most comfortable contemporary chairs ever made, and it was wildly popular in the 1950s. It still sells well.

Pedestal Group. In the 1950s Saarinen became dedicated to designing a chair in which body and base were a unified structure. This design led to his successful Pedestal group in 1957 consisting of an armchair, two stools, a side chair, and several tables.

Architect, Too. As an architect Saarinen had many outstanding achievements, including the winning design for the Smithsonian Art Gallery in Washington, D.C. His designs also included the master plan for the University of Michigan's Ann Arbor campus; the TWA Terminal at Kennedy Airport in New York; the Ingalls Ice Hockey Rink at Yale University; the Columbia Broadcasting System headquarters building in New York; Dulles International Airport outside Washington, D.C.; the General Motors Technical Center in Warren, Michigan; the United States Embassy in London; and the chapel at the Massachusetts Institute of Technology. He always described his work as rooted in the "organic approach," that is, one that "grows together with and out of the total concept of a building."

Untimely Death. Saarinen died at the age of fifty-one after surgery for a brain tumor. But he made an unforgettable mark in the fields of architecture and interior design.

YVES ST. LAURENT

1936-

EDDY VAN DER VEEN

Born in Algeria. Born and raised in Oran, Algeria, Yves St. Laurent went to Paris at age seventeen to try his luck in theatrical and fashion design. After winning first prize for a cocktail dress he designed for the International Wool Secretariat competition, he was taken to meet Christian Dior, the famous designer. After a fifteen-minute interview Dior hired the nineteen-year-old St. Laurent. Dior became St. Laurent's mentor and said of him, "St. Laurent is my right arm. I need him."

House of Dior. Dior died unexpectedly in October 1957, and twenty-one-year-old St. Laurent was named to succeed the master as head designer of the House of Dior. His first showing, in 1958, was a smash hit as his Trapeze, or "little-girl look," took the fashion world by storm. After the showing Parisians demonstrated in the street and chanted, "St. Laurent has saved France." The Trapeze was as popular in America as elsewhere in the late 1950s. His last fashion collection for the House of Dior was in 1960, when he introduced the "chic beatnik" look, featuring knit turtleneck collars, heavy-knit sleeves, and black leather jackets edged in fur.

His Own House. In 1962 St. Laurent opened his own house of haute couture. He began his Rive Gauche ready-to-wear label in 1966, and in 1974 he established his menswear. Since then his name and initials have been licensed for everything from sweaters and dresses to bed and bath linens, from eyeglasses to children's clothes. He has also created several perfumes, including the popular *Paris.*

Influence Continues. St. Laurent's label retained its popularity in America and around the world among high-fashion buyers. His day clothes are of the best fabric, simple, and of a slightly boyish quality. His evening clothes are soft and luxurious. In 1983 the Costume Institute of the Metropolitan Museum of Art mounted a retrospective of twenty-five years of his work, the first time a living designer had been so honored.

LUDWIG MIES VAN DER ROHE

1886-1969

FOREMOST ARCHITECT OF CORPORATE AMERICA

ROBERT DAMORA

Bauhaus-Trained. Considered one of the founders of modern architecture, Ludwig Mies van der Rohe's directed his concepts toward industrialization and harmonious proportions. Mies practiced architecture in Berlin, Germany, from 1911 to 1937, serving as the last director of the famous Bauhaus school from 1930 to 1933. He became internationally famous after World War I with his design of two steel skyscrapers entirely sheathed in glass. These were fore-runners of his creations in the United States, where he settled in 1938 after fleeing from Nazi Germany.

Glass and Steel. In the 1950s Mies's glass-and-steel skyscrapers ("glass-and-steel boxes," his detractors called them) were adopted by much of corporate America. Chief executive officers liked the well-ordered look of Mies's sleek, geometric buildings; his creations became a symbol of corporate power and spawned imitations all over America. Mies's famous buildings included the Seagram Corporation headquarters in New York City, which set a precedent for that city's commercial architecture, and the Lake Shore Drive Apartments in Chicago, a pair of rectangular, twenty-five-story towers called the world's first all-glass-and-steel apartment building. He also designed houses for individuals. One of those commissions resulted in the famous Farnsworth House in Fox River, Illinois, whose owner ended up suing Mies because the house was too impractical and too costly to live in. (The house was a pair of horizontal slabs floating from eight welded beams. The owner lost the suit.) Mies also designed the one-hundred-acre campus of the Illinois Institute of Technology, the first modern American campus ever built as a single, conforming architectural unit.

Beyond U.S. Borders. Mies also designed many famous buildings outside the United States — in Mexico, Germany (the National Gallery in Berlin, 1963–1968), and Canada. His influence was felt worldwide, and the early work of such well-known architects as Minoru Yamasaki, Philip Johnson, Ieoh M. Pei, and C. Fing Murphy was clearly influenced by Mies's concepts.

Form Follows Function. Mies followed his famous maxim, "form follows function," to the letter, and so did many of his imitators. Numerous architects copied his designs while cutting costs, often using cheaper, prefabricated materials. The buildings looked rational and neat, perfect for the optimistic, booming economy of the 1950s. Throughout the decade Mies's glass-and-steel creations and others like them popped up all over America.

FRANK LLOYD WRIGHT

1869-1959

GREATEST ARCHITECT OF THE TWENTIETH CENTURY

Trailblazer. A trailblazer in modern American architecture, Frank Lloyd Wright left a legacy of more than seven hundred buildings that spanned more than half a century, from the Robie House in Chicago (1904) to the Guggenheim Museum in New York City (1959). Already elderly when the 1950s began, Wright continued to be active, designing provocative, exuberant masterpieces until his death.

Always an Architect. From the beginning Anna Wright, a Wisconsin schoolteacher, wanted her son to become an architect. Since the University of Wisconsin offered no courses in architecture, he enrolled as a civil engineer in 1884 but left the university without graduating and went to Chicago in 1887, when many of his early designs were completed. He called himself a farm boy, and in 1900 Wright designed the first of his famous "prairie houses" (a low, ground-hugging type of bungalow ideally suited to the Midwest), for which there was no precedent.

Organic Approach. Wright believed a building's form was derived from nature and should harmonize with it. Although he had no single architectural style, his work was characterized by broad lines, stark surfaces, curves, and natural materials. He was famous for the organic growth of his houses from interior to exterior, for blending the houses with their natural surroundings, and for using various building materials according to their inherent characteristics. His focus on curves intensified during the 1950s, culminating in the Guggenheim Museum in New York City in 1959. This concrete structure has the form of a spiral ramp to provide continuous gallery space. Wright originated many design concepts that are reflected in modern houses, including the "open" plan, built-in furniture, radiant floor heating, and "indoor-out-door integration" accomplished by glass walls and corners.

Other Undertakings. Wright's architectural style was wholly American, but his most famous international work is probably the Imperial Hotel in Tokyo (1915–1922). His training as an engineer helped enormously because the vast structure had to be made to withstand earthquakes. The problem was solved through a unique use of concrete-supported cantilevered floors and a foundation floating on a cushion of soft mud. The hotel survived the major earthquake of 1923 without damage. Wright was also famous for his many "Usonian" homes — Wright's name for an ideal, democratic America. These houses were medium-sized and medium-priced. One of his most beautiful houses is Falling Water in Bear Run, Pennsylvania, cantilevered over a waterfall.

Gold Medal. Wright received countless awards over his long lifetime, but perhaps the most significant was the Gold Medal Award of the National Institute of Arts and Letters, which he received in 1953. His vision of freedom and spaciousness in homes and buildings truly liberated twentieth-century architecture.

PEOPLE IN THE NEWS

In 1953 twenty-nine-year-old **Pierre Cardin** showed his first couture collection in Paris. He was an instant sensation in Europe and America.

American designer **Bonnie Cashin** in 1953 opened her own studio in New York. Her distinctively avantgarde sportswear and layered coordinates, often made of leather, were prophetic of future decades.

In 1951 American designer **James Galanos** began his own business in Los Angeles with two hundred dollars and two assistants. His ready-to-wear clothes became a symbol of luxury.

French designer **Hubert de Givenchy** in 1952 launched his first fashion collection in his Paris boutique. The collection consisted of mix-and-match blouses, skirts, and trousers — mostly in casual, inexpensive cotton. The look quickly spread across the Atlantic.

Architect **Douglas Honnold** in 1950 designed a prototype built in several California cities for Biff's Drive-in with neon tubing and metallic reflections. This look spread throughout the country.

In 1955 architect **Philip Johnson**'s New Harmony Shrine in New Harmony, Indiana, a bell-shaped structure with shingle roof that was inspired by Hindu temples, was so complicated that an IBM computer took two weeks to calculate its compound curves.

Anne Klein, an important designer in the 1960s and early 1970s, started her climb in the 1950s. She pioneered a movement to transform junior-size clothes from little-girl style to adult sophistication.

In 1955, for the first time ever, three young American designers won the "Winnie," also known as the Coty American Fashion Critics' Award. They were **Anne Klein, Jeanne Campbell**, and **Herbert Kasper**.

Interior and furniture designers **Hans and Florence Knoll** in 1955 marketed the Hardoy chair (also known as the "Butterfly").

Erwine and Estelle Laverne, furniture designers, in 1957 designed their famous "Champagne" chair, a variation on Eero Saarinen's "Tulip" chair but made from transparent Plexiglass.

In 1952 architect **Stanley Clark Meston** of Fontana, California, designed the now-famous McDonald's golden arches.

Architect/designer **George Nelson** introduced the Comprehensive Storage System (CSS) in 1955 to Americans. The CSS consisted of shelving and storage units slung between adjustable aluminum poles, designed to expand both vertically and horizontally. It spawned hundreds of imitations.

Actor **Fess Parker**, star of the Disney television show "Davy Crockett," started a new fashion trend in late 1954: coonskin caps. During the next year the price of of coonskins soared to eight dollars a pound.

Throughout the 1950s red-haired **Suzy Parker** epitomized women's fashion. Because of her chameleonlike quality of looking just right in any clothes in any setting, her portrait graced more than sixty magazine covers during the decade.

In 1952 **Pope Pius XII** granted permission for the modification of Catholic nuns' habits. In America designer Hattie Carnegie came up with a simple black dress that also became a ready-to-wear success. Christian Dior followed suit and designed a habit for French nuns in 1960.

Virginia Pope, who pioneered fashion reporting, in 1952 began the "Fashions of the Times" supplement in the *New York Times*.

Jean Schlumberger was the winner in 1958 of the first Coty American Fashion Critics' Special Award given for jewelry.

John Van Kort in 1954 presented his popular "Profile" collection from Drexel furniture makers — blending features reminiscent of contemporary Scandinavian design with a solid look people associated with traditional furniture. It became a major moneymaker.

DEATHS

Anthony L. Aste, 88, former bootblack who founded Griffin Shoe Polish Company, 8 December 1954.

James Baird, 79, American civil engineer, 16 May 1953.

Alexander Samuel Beck, 93, founder of A. S. Beck shoe stores, 11 April 1955.

Arthur Besse, 64, president of the National Association of Wool Manufacturers since 1933, 24 November 1951.

Walter W. Birge, 74, pioneer in the development of rayon, 13 June 1952.

Arthur W. Bush, 78, a founder of the Nunn-Bush Shoe Co., 13 November 1950.

Hattie Carnegie (Henrietta Kanengeiser), 69, first American custom designer with ready-to-wear labels; she set the pace of fashion design for a generation, 22 February 1956.

John J. Cavanaugh, 93, men's hat designer, founder of Dobbs Stores, 24 January 1957.

Edna Woolman Chase, 80, editor of *Vogue* from 1914–1952; she initiated women's fashion shows in the United States, 20 March 1957.

John H. Cheatham, 67, president of Dundee Mills, former president of American Cotton Manufacturers Association, 17 February 1950.

E. Harold Cluett, 79, former chairman of Cluett, Peabody shirtmakers, 4 February 1954.

Harvey Corbett, 81, American architect, designer of Rockefeller Center, 21 April 1954.

Charles W. Ervin, 87, public-relations adviser of CIO Amalgamated Clothing Workers Union since 1924, 5 February 1953.

Jacques Fath, 42, one of the first French designers to venture in the ready-wear market, 11 November 1954.

Norman Bel Geddes, 65, designer noted for the 1939 New York World Fair's Futurama, 8 May 1958.

Mrs. Charles Dana Gibson, 83, the original Gibson girl model, 20 April 1956.

Edwin Goodman, 76, founder and chairman of Bergdorf Goodman on Fifth Avenue in New York, 19 August 1953.

Talbot Faulkner Hamlin, 67, architect, 7 October 1956.

Shortridge Hardesty, 72, designer of New York World's Fair Trylon and Perisphere, 16 October 1956.

George Simmons Harris, 69, chairman of Dan River Mills, founder and former chairman of Cotton Textile Institute, 16 February 1950.

Emil Alvan Hartman, 57, founder and director of the Fashion Academy, 10 December 1951.

Daniel Paul Higgins, 67, architect, designer of the Jefferson Memorial and National Gallery of Art, 26 December 1953.

Myron Hunt, 84, architect, designer of the Hollywood and Rose bowls, 26 May 1952.

Francis Y. Joannes, 76, architect and designer, 21 June 1952.

Omar (Alexander) Kiam, 60, New York and Hollywood dress designer, 29 March 1954.

Lucien Lelong, 68, French fashion designer and leader of international haute couture, 10 May 1958.

Joseph J. Lerner, 67, chairman of Lerner Stores, 18 July 1954.

Thomas I. Levitt, 63, president of National Retail Furniture Association, 31 January 1953.

Austin T. Levy, 70, who built a $10 million textile business and turned most of it over to his employees, 24 November 1951.

Chapin Marcus, 66, jewelry designer, former president of Marcus & Co. of New York, 20 April 1950.

Frank E. Masland, 84, chairman of C. S. Masland & Sons, one of the nation's leading carpet makers, 1 December 1951.

Michael Maximillian, 58, leading fur designer, 17 September 1953.

Max Meyer, 76, mediator of labor disputes in the New York garment industry, 31 January 1953.

George Miller, 61, president and board chairman of I. Miller & Sons, a women's shoe manufacturer, 4 October 1950.

Charles Nessler, 78, inventor of permanent waving and false eyelashes, 22 January 1951.

Eliel Saarinen, 76, architect and city planner, 1 July 1950.

Dorothy Shaver, 66, president of Lord & Taylor's from 1945 to 1959, who encouraged American designers to challenge Parisian fashion supremacy, 28 June 1959.

Sylvan I. Stroock, 65, leading textile manufacturer and producer of unusual fabrics, 17 May 1952.

Dr. Gideon Sundback, 74, the man who perfected the zipper, 21 June 1954.

Frederick F. Umhey, 60, executive secretary since 1934 of the International Ladies Garment Workers Union, 26 January 1955.

William Van Alen, 71, designer of the Chrysler Building in New York and pioneer in the use of steel in construction, 24 May 1954.

Ralph Hewitt Widdicombe, 86, furniture designer, 15 November 1959.

Frank Lloyd Wright, 89, considered the greatest architect of the twentieth century, 9 April 1959.

AWARDS

COTY AMERICAN FASHION CRITICS' AWARD

(The "Winnie" — to an individual selected as the leading designer of American women's fashions)

1950 — Charles James

Bonnie Cashin

1951 — Jane Derby

1952 — Ben Zuckerman

Ben Sommers

1953 — Thomas F. Brigance

1954 — James Galanos

1955 — Anne Klein

Jeanne Campbell

Herbert Kasper

1956 — Luis Estevez

Sally Victor

1957 — Leslie Morris

Sydney Wragge

1958 — Arnold Scaasi
1959 — No Award

RETURN AWARD

(Award to a designer whose work merits a top award for a second time)

1951 — Norman Norell
1952 — No Award
1953 — No Award
1954 — No Award
1955 — No Award
1956 — James Galanos
1957 — No Award
1958 — Ben Zuckerman
1959 — No Award

HALL OF FAME

("Winnie" designer chosen three separate times as best of the year — begun in 1956)

1956 — Norman Norell
1957 — No Award
1958 — Claire McCardell
1959 — Pauline Trigere
    James Galanos

SPECIAL AWARDS

(Honoring noteworthy contributions to fashion)

1950 — Mabel and Charles Julianelli
    Nancy Melcher
1951 — Vera Maxwell
    Anne Fogarty
    Sylvia Pedlar
1952 — Harvey Berin
    Karen Stark
    Sydney Wragge
1953 — Helen Lee
    Mattie Talmack
    John Moore

1954 — Charles James
1955 — Adolfo
1956 — Gertrude and Robert Goldworm
1957 — Emeric Partos
1958 — Donald Brooks
    Jean Schlumberger
1959 — No Award

NEIMAN-MARCUS AWARD FOR DISTINGUISHED SERVICE IN THE FIELD OF FASHION

1950 — Bonnie Cashin
Pauline Trigere
Gloria Swanson
Fleur Meyer
1951 — Michelle Murphy
Ernestine Cannon
Jane Derby
Ben Zuckerman
Jacques Lesur
1952 — Anne Fogarty
Roger Fare
Vincent Monte Santo
Dolores Del Rio
1953 — Charles James
Marchesa Olga di Gresy
Ben Sommers
Gilbert and Helen Orcel
1954 — James Galanos
Emilio Pucci
Mr. and Mrs. Herbert Levine
1955 — Pierre Balmain
Florence Eiseman
Vera Maxwell
Sally Kirkland
Henry Dreyfuss
The Princess of Monaco
1956 — Giuliana Camerino
Cecil Beaton
Marie-Louise Bousquet
1957 — Gabrielle "Coco" Chanel
1958 — Yves St. Laurent

Jens Quisgaard

Helen Lee

1959 — Anne Klein

Arnold Scaasi

Rosalind Russell

Piero Fornasetti

Emme

THOMAS B. CLARKE PRIZE (GIVEN BY THE NATIONAL ACADEMY OF DESIGN FOR INTERIOR DESIGN)

1950 — Hazel J. Teyral

1951 — Lee Jackson

1952 — Doris Rosenthal

1953 — Sigmund Menkes

1954 — Fletcher Martin

1955 — Thomas Yerxa

1956 — Adolf Konrad

1957 — Morton Roberts

1958 — Robert Sivard

1959 — Hughie Lee-Smith

AMERICAN INSTITUTE OF ARCHITECTS (AIA)

AIA Gold Medal (Awarded annually to an individual for distinguished service to the architectural profession or to the institute. It is the institute's highest honor.)

1950 — Sir Patrick Abercrombie, London

1951 — Bernard Ralph Maybeck, San Francisco

1952 — Auguste Perret, Paris

1953 — Williams Adams Delano, New York

1954 — No Award

1955 — William Marinus Dudok, Netherlands

1956 — Clarence S. Stein, New York

1957 — Ralph Walker, New York

  Luis Skidmore, New York

1958 — John Wellborn Root, Chicago

1959 — Walter Gropius, Cambridge, Massachusetts

AIA Craftsmanship Medal

1950 — Joseph Gardinar Reynolds, Jr., Stained Glass

1951 — No Award

1952 — George Nakashima, Furniture

1953 — Emil Frei, Stained Glass

1954 — Maria Montoya Martinez, Pottery

1955 — John Howard Benson, Calligraphy

1956 — Harry Bertoia, Metal Design

1957 — Charles Eames, Furniture

1958 — Francois Lorin, Stained Glass

1959 — No Award

AIA Edward C. Kemper Award (To AIA members for "significant contributions to the profession of architecture and to the Institute.")

1950 — William Perkins

1951 — Marshall Shaffer

1952 — William Stanley Parker

1953 — Gerrit J. DeGelleke

1954 — Henry H. Saylor

1955 — Turpin C. Bannister

1956 — Theodore Irving Coe

1957 — David C. Baer

1958 — Edmund R. Purves

1959 — Bradley P. Kidder

AIA Honor Awards (Initiated to encourage appreciation of excellence in architecture in the United States and by American architects working abroad.)

1950 — A. Quincy Jones, Jr.

Harold M. Jeatley

Ketchum, Gina and Sharpe Associates

1951 — Thorshov and Cerney

Stone and Pitts

1952 — Skidmore, Owings & Merrill

William S. Beckett

1953 — Saarinen, Saarinen & Associates

Smith, Hinchman and Grylls

1954 — Richard P. Neutra and Dion Neutra

Vincent G. King

John P. Wiltshire and J. Herschel Fisher

Curtis and Davis

Perkins and Will

Caudill, Rowlett, Scott Associates

Marsh Smith and Powell

1955 — Ralph Rapson and John van der Meulen

Eero Saarinen and Associates

Smith, Hinchman & Grylls

Ernest J. Kump

Charles B. Genther of Pace Associates

1956 — Hellmuth, Yamasaki & Leinweber

Skidmore, Owings & Merrill

Philip C. Johnson

John Lyon Reid & Partners

Wurster, Bernardi & Emmons

1957 — Anderson, Beckwith and Haible

Warren H. Ashley

Eliot Noyes

Caudill, Rowlett, Scott & Associates

Antonin Raymond and L. L. Rado

Anshen and Allen

1958 — Skidmore, Owings & Merrill

Edward D. Stone

Mario J. Ciampi

Pereira and Luckman

1959 — Colbert, Lowrey & Associates

Kenneth W. Brooks and Bruce W. Walker

Minoru Yamasaki & Associates

Eero Saarinen & Associates

I. M. Pei & Associates

PUBLICATIONS

Richard Horn, *Fifties Style, Then and Now* (New York: Beech Tree, 1985);

Peter Lewis, *The Fifties* (New York: Lippincott, 1958).

Architecture & Design

Joseph Alsop, "I'm Guilty! I Built a Modern House," *Saturday Evening Post*, 222 (20 May 1950): 31;

"Architectural Oscars," *Time*, 67 (16 April 1956): 86;

J. A. Barry, "Frank Lloyd Wright: The Man Who Liberated Architecture," *House Beautiful*, 97 (November 1955): 240–245;

J. Burchard and A. Bush-Brown, "100 Years of American Architecture," *New York Times Magazine*, 12 May 1957, pp. 26–27;

Cherie Fehrman and Kenneth Fehrman, *Postwar Interior Design: 1945–1960* (New York: Reinhold, 1987);

O. Gueft, "Furniture — Decade of Modern: How It Grew," *New York Times Magazine*, part 2, 9 May 1958, pp. 54–55;

John A. Gunnell, ed., *Standard Catalog of American Cars, 1946–1975* (Iola, Wis.: Krause Publications, 1982);

Alan Hess, *Googie: Fifties Coffee Shop Architecture* (San Francisco: Chronicle Books, 1986);

Bevis Hillier, *Austerity Binge: The Decorative Arts of the Forties and Fifties* (London: Cassell & Collier Macmillan, 1975);

"Houses Women Would Like, and The Houses They Get," *U.S. News*, 40 (4 May 1956): 54+;

C. Kellogg, "American Design at the Fair," *New York Times Magazine*, 6 April 1958, pp. 52–53;

J. McAndrew, "Our Architecture Is Our Portrait," *New York Times Magazine*, 18 January 1953, pp. 12–14;

"Modern Furniture in the American Tradition," *New York Times Magazine*, 21 May 1950, pp. 54–55;

"New Architecture," *Time*, 73 (27 April 1959): 67–68;

"Pope on Fashions," *America*, 97 (27 July 1957): 435;

"This Is American Architecture," *Design*, 59 (January 1958): 112;

Architectural Digest, periodical;

Architectural Record, periodical;

Better Homes and Gardens, periodical;

Designer, periodical founded in 1957;

Historic Preservation, periodical;

House and Garden, periodical;

Interior Design, periodical;

Landscape Architecture, periodical.

Fashion

"American Look," *Time,* 65 (2 May 1955): 85–86;

"America's Young Designers," *Look,* 19 (4 October 1955): 52–55;

Bettina Ballard, *In My Fashion* (New York: D. McKay, 1960);

Garrett Davis Byrnes, *Fashion in Newspapers* (New York: Columbia University Press, 1951);

Jane Dorner, *Fashion in the Forties and Fifties* (London: Ian Allen, 1975);

Beryl William Epstein, *Young Faces in Fashion* (Philadelphia: Lippincott, 1956);

"Fashion: Sense or Nonsense," *Scholastic,* 65 (5 January 1955): 7–8;

Lesley Jackson, *The New Look: Design in the Fifties* (London: Thames & Hudson, 1991);

"25 Years of Fun with Fashion," *Mademoiselle,* 50 (February 1960): 76–81;

Randle Bond Truett, *The First Ladies in Fashion* (New York: Hastings House, 1954);

Brides, periodical;

Fashion Calendar, periodical;

Gentlemen's Quarterly, periodical founded in 1957;

Glamour, periodical;

Harper's Bazaar, periodical;

Mademoiselle, periodical;

McCall's, periodical;

Modern Bride, periodical;

Vogue, periodical.

CHAPTER SIX

GOVERNMENT AND POLITICS

by LARRY SCHWEIKART and DENNIS LYNCH

CONTENTS

1950

- Soviet-spy scandals rock the United States and Britain.

- Attempts to reach an agreement with the Soviet Union on control of the atomic bomb fails.

25 Jan. Alger Hiss, the State Department official under investigation for his Communist ties, receives a five-year prison sentence for perjury.

9 Feb. Sen. Joseph McCarthy (R-Wis.) charges that there are 205 Communists working in the State Department.

1 Mar. The House votes to establish the National Science Foundation.

26 Mar. Sen. Estes Kefauver (D-Tennessee) opens a nationwide crime inquiry through the Senate Crime Investigating Committee.

27 June In response to the North Korean invasion of South Korea, President Harry S Truman orders U.S. air and naval forces under Gen. Douglas MacArthur to Korea.

1 Nov. Puerto Rican Nationalists attempt to assassinate President Truman in Washington, D.C.

1951

- Communist Chinese troops enter the Korean conflict; combatants fight to a stalemate by year's end, then agree to a negotiated truce.

7 Mar. • Gen. Douglas MacArthur warns Truman that a stalemate will develop in Korea unless United Nations troops are permitted to move against China.

5 Apr. • Julius and Ethel Rosenberg receive death sentences for transmitting U.S. atomic-bomb information to the Soviet Union.

5 Apr. • General MacArthur advocates using Chiang Kai-shek's Nationalist Chinese (based in Taiwan) to open a front against the mainland Red Chinese in the Korean War.

11 Apr. • President Truman dismisses General MacArthur from command of UN, Allied, and U.S. forces in the Far East.

9 Aug. • Senator McCarthy names twenty-six members of the State Department who are suspected of disloyalty.

1952

29 Mar. President Truman announces at a Jefferson-Jackson Day dinner that he will not be a candidate for reelection.

June–7 July Gen. Dwight D. Eisenhower builds support for his presidential nomination for the Republican party in the 1952 election, winning the nomination on 7 July. Richard Nixon is nominated as the vice-presidential candidate.

21–24 July The Democratic convention nominates Illinois governor Adlai E. Stevenson for president.

1953

23 Sept.	Nixon, responding to media reports that he had pocketed a political-expense fund, makes a powerful televised appeal to the public in which he states, "I'm not a quitter," and in which he observes that the only gift his family received from his life in politics was a cocker spaniel named Checkers.
1 Oct.	Reports circulate that the United States has exploded a hydrogen bomb.
24 Oct.	Republican presidential nominee Eisenhower promises to go to Korea to seek "an early & honorable end" to the war.
4 Nov.	Eisenhower wins election by a popular vote of 32.9 million to 26.5 million and carries thirty-nine states to Stevenson's nine.

1954

15 Mar.	Sen. Robert A. Taft calls for an investigation of the Voice of America radio-broadcasting station.
27 Mar.	The Senate confirms Charles E. Bohlen as ambassador to the U.S.S.R. despite stiff opposition by Senator McCarthy.
27 July	Armistice concluded in Korea that left country divided. United States guaranteed economic aid and military security.

- Army-McCarthy hearings reach a climax; McCarthy is discredited.
- The Senate considers statehood bills for Alaska and Hawaii.
- An Eisenhower-supported tax cut passes.

18 Feb.	Senator McCarthy assails Brig. Gen. Ralph W. Zwicker for harboring Communists in the army.
20 Feb.	Army Secretary Robert T. Stevens orders Brig. Gen. Zwicker not to answer McCarthy's summonses to appear before his investigating committee.
1 Mar.	Puerto Rican Nationalists shoot five members of Congress in the House of Representatives.
12 Apr.	Atomic scientist J. Robert Oppenheimer is declared a security risk for his associations with Communists.
17 May	The U.S. Supreme Court rules segregation is illegal in public schools.
17 June	The Senate ends its eight-week probe into the dispute between Senator McCarthy and the U.S. Army.
27 Sept.	The U.S. Senate Select Committee recommends the censure of Senator McCarthy for contempt of the Senate Privileges and Elections Subcommittee.
2 Dec.	The U.S. Senate votes to condemn but not censure McCarthy.

1955

- The eighty-fourth Congress has a record eighteen women (sixteen in the House, one in the Senate, and one nonvoting delegate from Hawaii).

- The U.S. opposes the entry of additional Communist nations, especially "Red" China, into the United Nations.

24 Sept. President Eisenhower suffers a heart attack.

5 Dec. A boycott of the Montgomery, Alabama, city bus lines begins after Rosa Parks, a black woman, is fined for refusing to give up her seat to a white passenger.

1956

- President Eisenhower runs for reelection against Adlai Stevenson.

- The Eisenhower administration faces a crisis in Egypt as Israeli-Anglo-French forces invade the Sinai Peninsula and capture the Gaza Strip in a dispute over the Suez Canal as the U.S. refuses to intervene.

- Soviet tanks crush an uprising in Hungary, while the United States stays out.

- *Congressional Quarterly* reports that ten registered lobbies account for more than one-third of all lobbying funds.

4 Feb. A House banking subcommittee charges that the slum-clearance and urban-redevelopment programs are bogged down by the Eisenhower administration's bungling, roadblocks, and strangling red tape.

25 Feb. Sen. Harry F. Byrd (D-Virginia) calls on southern states to organize massive resistance to enforced school desegregation.

16 Aug. Stevenson and Estes Kefauver win the nomination of the Democratic party for president and vice-president, respectively, in the fall elections.

Oct. Stevenson's proposal to end hydrogen-bomb testing becomes a major campaign issue; Eisenhower stresses a sound economy.

6 Nov. President Eisenhower and Vice-president Nixon are reelected in a landslide victory over Stevenson and Kefauver (457 electoral votes to 74; 33.2 million popular votes to 24.1 million).

1957

- Democrats control both houses of Congress (233 to 200 in House; 49 to 46 in the Senate).

- The Eisenhower administration runs a second consecutive budget surplus.

May 8–19: South Vietnam president Ngo Dinh Diem is welcomed at the White House as Eisenhower pledges further aid to the nation within U.S. constitutional processes.

19 Sept. Secretary of Defense Charles E. Wilson orders reduction of U.S. armed forces by one hundred thousand to bring the total strength to 2.6 million under arms.

24 Sept. President Eisenhower orders U.S. Army paratroopers to prevent interference with racial integration at Central High School in Little Rock, Arkansas.

5 Oct. The U.S.S.R. launches *Sputnik,* the first artificial earth satellite, into space, opening the possibility of atomic attack on the continental United States by Soviet missiles.

5 Nov.   Secretary of State John Foster Dulles admits that the Soviets have outdistanced the United States in certain aspects of missile development; the *New York Herald Tribune* reports that the U.S. government has asked U.S. companies for plans for rockets capable of reaching the moon.

1958

- The U.S. launch of the *Explorer* satellite puts the United States in the space race.

- The Senate Select Committee on Improper Labor-Management Activities investigates the Teamsters Union.

26 Mar.   President Eisenhower indicates he will accept a "reliable agreement halting nuclear testing."

30 Apr.   The U.S. Senate votes for aid in the form of guaranteed loans to the nation's financially pressed railroads.

8 May   President Eisenhower orders federalized Arkansas National Guardsmen removed from Central High School in Little Rock, Arkansas.

26 Aug.   The residents of Alaska approve statehood.

1959

5 Feb.   President Eisenhower asks Congress in a special session to enact a seven-point civil rights program.

23 Apr.   Soviet premier Nikita S. Khrushchev rejects President Eisenhower's proposals to end nuclear bomb tests.

16 June   The Federal Communications Commission upholds the "equal time" rule for political candidates.

21 Aug.   Hawaii becomes the fiftieth state.

16 Nov.   The Justice Department initiates a law suit in U.S. District Court to end "white primaries" in Tennessee, where blacks had been prohibited from voting.

OVERVIEW

1950s Politics Sentimentalized. Current baby-boomer nostalgia has, for the most part, washed over — and sanitized — the political history of the 1950s. When compared to the turbulent decades that would follow and the world war that had preceded in the 1940s, the 1950s would appear from the present, popular perspective to represent a peaceful interlude in twentieth-century power politics — a kind of return to innocence from which the American people would emerge the "children of Eisenhower." Indeed, two-term president Dwight D. Eisenhower, the decade's dominant political presence, was a paternal figure. Running on the 1952 Republican platform at the age of sixty-two, he was an international hero who had organized the Allied victory over the Nazis and briefly served as president of Columbia University. He had a kind face and a smile that beamed confidence and optimism. A high handicapper, he spent a good deal of time at the golf course — more time there, contended some political wags, than in the Oval Office. But if he had a weakness for play, it was something the American people were more than willing to forgive in him as a fatherly indulgence; for, as a young Jack Kerouac and an equally drunk fellow Beat poet once sarcastically phrased it in an obscene letter meant for the White House, Eisenhower *was* the "Great White Father."

Politics of Fear. But Eisenhower was much more than a golf-playing figurehead: he was a shrewd and savvy politician, as his more current biographers and many historians convincingly argue. A state of relative peace and prosperity likewise camouflaged a highly charged, rough-and-tumble political landscape. Politics in the 1950s were driven by immediate fears that the American way of life was being threatened by a philosophy that ran counter to, and called for the destruction of, democracy. American's fear of communism during the 1950s is often looked back on as having been fueled by naive generalization and paranoia. When understood in the context of the times, however, American fears were hardly naive. After World War II the Soviets had acted quickly to annex most of Eastern Europe. In 1949 China had fallen to the Communists. In June 1950 the United Nations intervened in the Korean border conflict, and the United States once again sent troops to war — this time to contain Communist aggression.

Korean War. American military presence in Korea provided one of the most dramatic examples of emerging U.S. cold-war policy. At the end of World War II the Allied leaders had reached an agreement in which the Japanese occupying North Korea would surrender to the Soviets, the Japanese in the south to the Americans. Both the Soviet Union and the United States came to regard the Korean peninsula with increasing importance: each of the two superpowers sought a firm foothold in Asia from which it could wield influence over the region or at the very least contain the influence of its rival. At first Americans praised President Harry S Truman for committing U.S. troops to Korea to halt Communist aggression. But when UN forces led by Gen. Douglas MacArthur approached the Chinese border in pursuit of North Korean forces, the Chinese intervened. MacArthur's aggressive strategy of bringing the war to China was in direct conflict with Truman's policy of containment. Truman fired his general, touching off one of the fiercest debates on American international conduct the country had ever experienced. From then on the question of Communist intentions regarding American interests — and how America ought to respond — dominated an increasingly frightening political discourse.

McCarthyism. In 1950 an obscure senator from Wisconsin, Joseph R. McCarthy, used a women's Republican club meeting in Wheeling, West Virginia, to make public the stunning claim that 205 Communist-party members worked in the State Department. His charges could not easily be dismissed by an American public already made suspicious by claims that the State Department had not done enough to support anticommunist forces in China. Charges of fellow traveling — "Red-baiting" — became a potent part of campaign strategy in elections taking place at all levels of American government. Richard Nixon, a junior Republican senator from California who had used such campaign tactics to gain political office, saw his political clout skyrocket at the beginning of the decade due to his key role in exposing Alger Hiss, a midlevel government official with ties to the State Department, as a Communist spy. McCarthy's allegations would lead further Senate hearings and more accusations, capturing the public's attention and further increasing the Wisconsin senator's power. Indeed, two presidential administrations were powerless to put a halt to McCarthyism, despite both Truman's and Eisenhower's deep dislike for the senator's bullying tactics.

A New Era in Government. Tired of New Deal bureaucracy and war and scared of the Communist presence that had engulfed Eastern Europe and China — and that had supposedly infiltrated their government — Americans entered the 1950s a beleaguered people yet politicized as they had never been before in the twentieth century. They voted in record numbers in the 1952 elections, and, in proclaiming an electoral majority for Eisenhower over Democratic opponent Adlai Stevenson, they ushered in a watershed moment in American politics. Out were twenty years of Democratic control of the White House. Out was Truman — the last American president without a college degree — whom the Republicans had portrayed as the last vestige of New Deal, partisan policy making and final reminder of Franklin D. Roosevelt's alleged appeasement of the Soviets at the 1945 Yalta Conference. It was an era of governing that was to appeal to Middle America's political sensibilities. Eisenhower Republicans pledged to cut defense spending while simultaneously engaging Communist aggression both abroad and at home; limit the federal government's role in the business and private sectors; and invigorate a maturing sense of America's role as a superpower.

The Politics of Image. Policy makers at even the highest levels of government, however, were placed under ever-increasing public scrutiny as more Americans were buying television sets for their living rooms and dens. The 1950s, to be sure, ushered in the era of political image making — an art that in its infancy was used by McCarthy both effectively, to bring popularity to him and his anticommunist crusade at the beginning of the decade, and ineptly, in the televised Army-McCarthy hearings of 1954 in which he appeared as a mean-spirited political buffoon. The widely watched television appearances of Richard Nixon were key to his political successes and failures during the period: Nixon's effectively maudlin Checkers speech, in which he defended himself against charges that he had misused campaign funds, went out to approximately fifty-eight million Americans, whose sympathies saved his vice-presidential spot on the 1952 Republican ticket; an even larger television audience watched as a pale and heavily perspiring Nixon debated his opponent in the 1960 presidential election — a young, handsome, and tanned John F. Kennedy. By the end of the decade the *images* of politics had become enmeshed in American popular culture and had arguably become a more important political tool than the ability to articulate the issues themselves.

TOPICS IN THE NEWS

COLD WAR: THE BOMB

Its Public and Political Acceptance. After U.S. bombers shocked the world in August 1945 by dropping horrendously destructive atomic bombs on Hiroshima and Nagasaki to end World War II, the administration of President Harry S Truman pledged never again to introduce atomic weapons into a conflict. By November 1950, however, the president was reconsidering. Responding to reports by military advisers that A-bombs could shorten the Korean War by efficiently destroying Soviet military bases in Asia and forcing the Soviet and Chinese Communists to think twice before intervening, Truman made veiled references to the option of atomic force to end the conflict.

Public Support for the Bomb. If Truman had decided to employ atomic weapons in Korea, he would have had little trouble selling the idea to the American people. In 1949 a Gallup poll determined that 70 percent of Americans were against their government's pledge of no first use. By the winter of 1951, 51 percent supported using the bomb against "military targets" in Asia. As the American fear of Communist aggression grew, so too did infatuation with the bomb as a symbol of U.S. military and technological superiority. Sen. Margaret Chase Smith (R-Maine) appealed to the feeling of moral superiority of many Americans in the summer of 1951 when she suggested that the United States "drop the atomic bomb on these barbarians" if the Korean peace talks failed. Clearly both President Truman and his successor in 1953, President Eisenhower, had a mandate to stockpile weapons of mass destruction and declare the nation's resolve in using them if faced with a Communist threat.

The Bomb and Political Realities. As is often the case, however, public perception and political reality did not go hand in hand. The complexities of the emerging new world order meant that the Truman and Eisenhower administrations — despite their saber rattling — often had to give ground to the Soviets on political fronts. In 1949 the Soviet Union had successfully tested its first atomic bomb, and at the beginning of 1950 it seemed to be keeping pace with the Americans in developing the next generation of nuclear weapons — hydrogen bombs.

A Foreign-Policy Tool. With both sides having deployed hundreds of H-bombs by the mid 1950s — and each well on its way toward developing the kind of rocketry needed to deliver them — it became clear to foreign-policy experts that the arms race had become necessary if

A 43,600-pound bomb dwarfs color guards at a 1951 military ceremony attended by President
Harry S Truman, right.

BOMB SHELTERS: "LIFE SAFES" OR "DEATH TRAPS?"

Throughout the decade construction firms cashed in on public fear of atomic annihilation and were offering a wide array of bomb shelters, or "life safes," ranging from a $13.50 backyard foxhole to a spacious $5,500 underground suite complete with all the household amenities—and a Geiger counter to boot. Public fear of the Soviets' ability to deliver the bomb over long distances became more acute and widespread in 1957, when Russian scientists were able to launch a satellite into orbit. Civil Defense Administrator Val Peterson, who had dismissed bomb shelters as "death traps," suddenly was being urged by citizen groups to consider a nationwide shelter program. With the Eisenhower administration being characterized as uncaring in its approach to civil defense, Peterson displayed a new attitude in March 1957 and told reporters that he "believes in bomb shelters" but insisted that the construction cost for a national shelter program would run as high as $32 billion — numbers that infuriated Eisenhower critics who charged Peterson with callously placing a cost on human lives.

Sources: *Nation* (23 March 1957): 246;
Time (5 February 1951): 12.

---

wars between the East and the West were to be avoided. Each side needed to maintain enough weapons to be able to strike back forcefully if attacked, deterring a potential aggressor by the possibility of massive retaliation; the result was a balance of destructive power. So long as the balance was maintained, the cold war would remain a battle of words and threats.

The Bomb and Government Policy. In April 1950 Paul H. Nitze, director of policy planning in the State Department under Truman, completed a key defense-policy document, National Security Council memorandum–68 (NSC-68). Nitze recommended massive increases in defense spending to respond to the Communist menace. The money was mostly to be spent on conventional forces, but Nitze's plan also underscored America's need to develop the hydrogen bomb. The Democratic president agreed, despite strong Republican opposition.

New Look Policy. Among the top goals of the Republican Eisenhower administration in 1953 were to tighten the country's purse strings and lower defense spending. As a result Eisenhower adopted a new cold war strategy called the New Look policy. It supported nuclear armament over troop deployments to avoid the costs of full-scale conventional warfare. Eisenhower's secretary of state, John Foster Dulles, immediately began a program

of attacking the political "taboo" that had surrounded the use of the bomb since Hiroshima and Nagasaki. "No use in having stuff, and never being able to use it," he insisted. Truman's pledge of no first use was soon replaced with a policy that would allow for atomic strikes in response to even a conventional armed attack. In 1953 Eisenhower strongly hinted that "it might be cheaper, dollar-wise," to rely on A-bombs instead of ground troops to end the Korean War. Unlike Truman, however, Eisenhower had the weight of accepted policy to back up his threats.

"Atoms for Peace." Eisenhower had a broader vision of atomic power than the New Look policy suggested, however. In a speech delivered to the United Nations on 8 October 1953, Eisenhower proposed "atoms for peace." His hopes were sincere, for he understood that an arms race could drive the superpowers into bankruptcy. Nonetheless, the Soviet Union looked upon Eisenhower's proposal with cynicism, partly because Eisenhower's own administration did not pursue his ideas of peaceful uses of atomic energy with any vigor. The speech did lead to the establishment of the International Atomic Energy Agency to monitor atomic research and testing globally, but the lack of cooperation between the superpowers often crippled its effectiveness.

Bombs and Rockets. After the Soviets successfully launched *Sputnik* on 4 October 1957, American confidence and feelings of military superiority gave way to fear. It seemed that the Soviet Union had gained an edge in rocket technology, and Americans felt that Eisenhower had not been vigilant enough. It no longer seemed to matter how many bombs the government stored if the Soviets could launch an attack from Soviet soil or, worse, rain bombs on the United States from outer space. By the end of the decade missile development had become a dominant political issue. Despite the fact that by 1960 the United States had regained a technological advantage over the Soviet Union, the Democrats were successful in playing off American fears that the Soviets had better — and more — delivery systems. The new Democratic president, John F. Kennedy, entered the White House in January 1961 with a mandate to build more bombs and more missiles.

Sources:
Stephen E. Ambrose, *Eisenhower: The President* (New York: Simon & Schuster, 1984);
James Gilbert, *Another Chance: Postwar America, 1945–1968* (Philadelphia, Pa.: Temple University Press, 1981).

COLD WAR: THE KOREAN CONFLICT

A Return to War. Following U.S. involvement in two world wars within a twenty-five-year period, many Americans thought they had fought their last war when Japan surrendered in 1945. They were wrong. On 25 June 1950 North Korean Communist troops crossed the 38th parallel into South Korea. Two days later President Truman said that the United States would oppose Commu-

President-elect Dwight Eisenhower eats with American troops during his November 1952 visit to Korea.

nist "armed invasion and war," and he ordered U.S. air and naval forces, under the command of Gen. Douglas MacArthur, to aid in the defense of South Korea.

Rival Blocs. The United States, however, did not want to become the "world's policeman": that was the job of the United Nations (UN). Formed in 1945, the global organization was founded with the purpose of regulating international conflict and, if need be, of bringing the forces of all the nations of the world against any aggressor. Since the end of World War II, however, two rival blocs had arisen: the West, led by the United States, the democratic and free nations of Western Europe, and Japan; and the East, composed mainly of nations with Communist governments and led by the Soviet Union. Furthermore China, a new and unpredictable player on the international scene, entered into the cold war when the Communists took over in 1949 and drove the pro-West government to the island of Formosa (Taiwan).

The Cold War Heats Up. Cold war politics were further exacerbated prior to the Korean War when the Soviet Union exploded its own atomic bomb in 1949, ending the American monopoly on atomic weapons. The outbreak of hostilities in Korea thus presented to the Truman administration a host of tricky questions: How could the West contain Communist aggression in Korea without bringing in neighboring Communist China? Could the United Nations function as a world policeman,

or would the United States have to "go it alone" in Korea? And did an East-West confrontation have to escalate into "total war" — involving the use of atomic bombs — between the two competing blocs?

UN Involvement. One of the questions was answered quickly. Hours after the invasion, the UN Security Council, which had the authority to deploy troops, passed a resolution calling for all UN nations to "render every assistance to the UN" in supporting the U.S. decision to defend South Korea. The Soviet Union, due to its protest of another issue, was absent from the Security Council meeting. By July ground forces in Korea flew the UN banner instead of the American flag.

Communists Capture Seoul. Between 25 June and 28 June the North Koreans overwhelmed the South's forces and captured Seoul, the South Korean capital. On 4 July U.S. ground forces arrived. At first, however, MacArthur's men fared little better than the South Koreans: U.S. troops no sooner arrived than they began retreating, while the North's troops had overrun most of the South. Gen. Omar Bradley, chairman of the Joint Chiefs of Staff, said things were not "desperate but they are very serious." Congressman Lloyd Bentsen, Jr. (D-Texas), drew cheers in the House of Representatives when he proposed that Truman demand that the North Koreans withdraw or the United States would use atomic bombs on their cities.

Chinese Involvement. On 15 September MacArthur led a daring landing at Inchon, a port 150 miles behind the North Korean lines, taking the North by surprise. As a consequence North Korean forces rapidly retreated back toward the 38th parallel. In October South Korean forces crossed the 38th parallel. At that point the Communist Chinese had not intervened, but American leaders were concerned that penetration too far into the North would draw the Chinese into the conflict. U.S. forces also began crossing the 38th parallel, and the UN army was quickly approaching the Yalu River, the border between North Korea and China. Communist Chinese forces swarmed across the Yalu River on 26 November, and overnight the enemy armies increased by 275,000, also opening the possibility that millions more Chinese might reinforce those troops. Eventually numbering 2.1 million, the Chinese troops drove the UN forces back to the 38th parallel, where the war was stalemated.

Negotiating a Peace. The United States stood on a threshold. It could have moved into a "total war" mode, deploying millions of soldiers and rationing materials. But it was doubtful that the American public would have supported another total-war effort so soon after World War II. Another alternative for the United States was to use atomic bombs to pound China and North Korea into submission; however, such a move might have provoked a military response from the Soviet Union in support of the Communists. Or the United States could negotiate a

Troops at Fort Monmouth, New Jersey, guard an antenna used to track *Sputnik*.

peace. Truman and the United Nations chose the latter alternative.

P'anmunjom Talks. While attacks and counterattacks along the 38th parallel produced no long-term strategic change in the war, negotiators in 1951 started to meet at P'anmunjom. By fall both sides had started to talk, and by February 1952 the P'anmunjom talks had yielded an agreement on how to proceed after an armistice. Among other points the exchange of prisoners remained a problem, as many North Korean prisoners did not want to return to the Communists. Dwight D. Eisenhower in his presidential campaign promised to "go to Korea" and broker a peace. Meanwhile aerial combat between Chinese MiG fighters and U.S. jets continued. An armistice was signed on 27 July 1953, with neither side able to claim victory.

Source:
Bruce Cummings, *The Origins of the Korean War: Liberation and the Emergence of Separate Regimes, 1945–1947* (Princeton, N.J.: Princeton University Press, 1981).

COLD WAR: SPUTNIK

Public Fear and Outrage. Many Americans reacted with disbelief and fear when the Soviet Union launched the world's first man-made satellite into orbit on 4 October 1957: the Soviets — supposedly well behind the United States technologically, militarily, and economi-

cally — had managed to beat the Americans into space. Eisenhower, often portrayed as having been caught off guard by *Sputnik,* noted that it came as a "distinct surprise," but what really shocked him was "the intensity of public concern." Democrats pounced on *Sputnik* as an issue of national defense. Democratic senator Henry Jackson of Washington described the launch as a "devastating blow to the prestige of the United States as the leader of the scientific and technical world." Some U.S. scientists who had worked for the air force or on the army's missile projects thought the feat unimpressive; still others, including celebrated rocket scientist Wernher von Braun, claimed that Truman had ignored space and as a consequence was responsible for the slow start of the American rocket program. America had focused much of its energy on air-breathing propulsion, especially jet fighters and bombers, not on heavy rockets.

Ike Plays Down *Sputnik*. When Eisenhower called an advisory meeting on 8 October 1957 to discuss the event and determine what the administration should do, he learned that military rockets could have accomplished the task years earlier, but that the Defense Department had decided that it was more within the peaceful character of the satellite program to allow the development of an earth satellite to come from outside the military. Secretary of Defense Charles Wilson dismissed *Sputnik* as a "neat scientific trick." At a press conference Eisenhower said that *Sputnik* "does not raise my apprehensions, not

Soviet premier Nikita S. Khrushchev and American vice-president Richard Nixon debate the merits of modern kitchen appliances at the 1959 American Exhibition held in Moscow.

one iota. I see nothing at this moment, at this stage of development, that is significant in that development as far as security is concerned." Nevertheless, many scientists and politicians were shocked and wanted to know how the United States could "catch up" with the Soviets. The national-security threat posed by a potentially armed satellite flying high over American airspace, combined with the public's belief that only federal spending could diminish the perceived Soviet lead in space, forced Congress and the president into action.

Sputnik **Shoots Federal Spending into Orbit.** After meeting with a group of top scientists on 15 October, Eisenhower appointed Dr. James Killian, president of the Massachusetts Institute of Technology, as the first presidential science adviser and created the President's Science Advisory Committee. Congress passed the National Defense Education Act (NDEA) to encourage a new generation of Americans to study science in college. Under increasing pressure spending on aerospace soared. The cost of military R&D stood at $822 million in 1950, but a decade later it topped $2.196 billion. Total federal R&D in aerospace rose from $934 million in 1950 to $2.4 billion in 1960.

The Space Race. In December 1957 an attempt to put a satellite into orbit with the navy's Vangard rocket failed when the rocket exploded. On 31 January 1958, the United States finally launched a satellite, *Explorer I,* on a modified Jupiter-C rocket. The launch, however, turned out to be something of an embarrassment when compared with the Soviet achievement: weighing thirty-one

UNCLE SAM, SCIENCE'S SUGAR DADDY

Money Spent on Science. Even before the Soviet launching of Sputnik on 4 October 1957 officially ushered in the space race, Uncle Sam had started to fund scientific research and development (R&D) at an increasing pace. In 1953, for example, more than 53 percent of all R&D funding came from the federal government. By 1960 more than 64 percent came out of Uncle Sam's pocket. Indeed in 1959, when space-race funding really kicked in, the federal government's share of R&D exceeded 65 percent of the $19.6 billion total. From 1953 to 1960 the total amount spent by the federal government on R&D tripled in constant dollars.

Funding from the Private Sector. Compared to government spending on basic research, contributions made by other sectors seemed stingy: industry, the second largest contributor to R&D in 1953, only invested $153 million, while colleges and universities put in a paltry $10 million; other nonprofit institutions added $27 million. By 1960 the share contributed by colleges and universities had grown sixfold, but most of that money went to educate a new generation of scientists to counter the Soviet missile threat.

pounds, *Explorer I* was dwarfed by the three-thousand-pound satellite the Russians launched in May. Other American launches followed, and Eisenhower found himself under increasing pressure from virtually everyone — Democrats, most Republicans, scientists, the media — to step up the space race. Critics demanded Eisenhower bring integration and order to the space program and create a separate department of space. Despite his reservations and fear that a separate department would emphasize satellites over missiles, on 2 April 1958 Eisenhower asked Congress to establish the National Aeronautics and Space Administration (NASA), superseding the old National Advisory Committee on Aeronautics (NACA). On 12 January 1959 NASA selected the McDonnell Aircraft Corporation to design, develop, and construct the *Mercury* space capsule to put an American in space.

Source:
James Gilbert, *Another Chance: Postwar America, 1945–1968* (Philadelphia, Pa.: Temple University Press, 1981).

GOVERNMENT AND BUSINESS

Consumerism and the American Dream. America emerged from World War II as the dominant world power player — not only militarily but economically as well. Ravaged by war, European industry was at a standstill, and the Continent was open to receive American-made products. At home pent-up consumer demand — caused by government-sponsored rationing during the world war and the Korean War — exploded, and American plants ran at full capacity to provide their customers with automobiles, television sets, household appliances — all the amenities of an American way of life that was becoming increasingly defined by the tastes of a burgeoning middle class with more money to spend. America was evolving into a consumer-oriented society during the 1950s, and the pursuit of modern goods and appliances that made everyday life easier became identified with the American Dream. In 1959, while viewing an American kitchen display at the trade fair in Moscow, Richard Nixon defended this relationship between consumerism and American democratic principles during a spirited, impromptu debate with Nikita Khrushchev. The Soviet leader suggested that the large variety of U.S. products aimed at modernizing domestic life — and Americans' insatiable appetite for these products — had turned the American people lazy, a charge to which Nixon replied: "To us, diversity, the right to choose, the fact that we have a thousand different builders, that's the spice of life."

Big Business Becomes Bigger. The "kitchen debate" scored big political points for Nixon back home. Yet, despite Nixon's ringing defense of capitalism, both the American government and people had grown increasingly wary of big business, which was growing bigger. Between 1949 and 1955 the number of mergers rose by 300 percent. More and more the decision-making power regard-

Secretary of Defense Charles E. Wilson, former head of General Motors, surrounded by models of
military hardware

PHOTO BY HANK WALKER

ing the setting of prices and the developing of product lines was being controlled by a single megacorporation — the result of large mergers — within a given industry. Small businesses felt that their ability to compete was being undercut by merging big business. Many feared that the power and influence of the big corporations had become too great and widespread.

Uncle Sam Investigates Big Business. Government responded to the calls for control of big business by launching a record number of antitrust suits. Armed with the Celler-Kefauver Act of 1950, which allowed government investigators to use a company's market share as an indicator of monopoly, the feds waged an aggressive legal campaign against industry-dominating corporations. In 1952, for instance, the Federal Trade Commission filed suit against five U.S. oil companies for taking part in an international oil cartel that controlled 65 percent of the world's oil reserves. Senate investigations targeted the National Broadcasting Company and the Columbia Broadcasting System, two companies which accounted for 46 percent of the income earned by the television industry. The pricing policies of companies such as Eastman-Kodak were examined by congressional committees, and picture studios were forced to relinquish control of their theater chains. The individuals and families behind big business also did not escape scrutiny. The du Pont family was forced to divest their controlling interest in General Motors, U.S. Rubber, and E. I. du Pont de Nemours and Company.

The Democrats and Big Business. Prior to 1953 the Democrats had been in power for nearly twenty years, during which time, claimed many industry heads (who were for the most part Republicans), American business had been forced by government to bow to the whims of federal regulators and union officials, who held the presidency in their back pocket. The Democrats, on the other hand, charged that big business operated according to its own agenda, with little concern for the working man or national interests beyond what it could make in profits. Although relations between business and government during the World War II years had been characterized by a rare spirit of cooperation for the sake of the war effort, industry leaders had grown tired of continued government regulations in the immediate postwar years. But, with American entry into the Korean War in 1950, a Democratic president was once again asking business to cooperate with government to serve higher national interests. In April 1952 President Harry S Truman used his executive powers to seize the steel industry. In justifying an action that amounted to the nationalization of an industry that served as a backbone of the American economy, Truman cited the inability of steel executives to bargain with labor, the unwillingness of the industry to accept the prices recommended by the War Labor Board, and the importance of maintaining high levels of steel production to serve the war effort. What followed was a public-relations battle between the executive office and big business from which Truman never fully recovered. Steel executives purchased airtime on radio and television to lambaste the president, publicly comparing Truman to Benito Mussolini and Adolf Hitler. To add to Truman's humiliation, the Supreme Court ruled in June 1952 that his actions had been unconstitutional.

Ike's Big-Business Administration. Business leaders welcomed Dwight D. Eisenhower's presidency with open arms. The Republicans' return to power meant the possibility that government might once again be probusiness in setting its policies on industry, labor relations, and trade. Furthermore, in forming his cabinet Eisenhower was reaching into America's corporate boardrooms and plucking out those men who shared his vision of no-nonsense government and fiscal responsibility. The selection of such men as Charles E. Wilson, president of General Motors, and George M. Humphrey, president of M. A. Hanna Company, to key government posts made many Americans uneasy, however, despite the otherwise high marks of approval they were giving Eisenhower in his first days in office. A January 1953 Gallup poll showed Ike's approval rating at 78 percent, but when those polled were asked, "Has Dwight Eisenhower done anything so far that you disapprove of ?," one of the few criticisms offered was that Ike's cabinet appointments had created a big-business administration.

Labor Representation in Cabinet. Yet it soon became clear that Ike had no intention of catering to the interests of big business. Indeed, one of his cabinet appointments — the American Federation of Labor's plumber's union head Martin Durkin as secretary of labor — bewildered Republican officials and businessmen, who were fearing imminent drastic changes in the Taft-Hartley Act, which to the anger of labor leaders had outlawed the closed shop. The appointment of a union man to oversee delicate labor relations angered Robert Taft and prompted the *New Republic* to comment wryly, "Ike had picked a cabinet of eight millionaires and one plumber."

Fighting the Monopolies. Under Eisenhower government regulators continued to target those businesses that were thought to be monopolistic. The way of doing business in entire industries was altered: the Bank Holding Company Act of 1956, for instance, called for multibank holding companies to divest their holdings in nonbanking businesses. In reaction to what they deemed to be heavy-handed governmental interference, business leaders fought back through what became two powerful lobbying groups, the National Chamber of Commerce and the National Association of Manufacturers.

Ike's Internationalist Trade Policies. Moreover, many American industrialists were less than pleased to learn that Eisenhower was an internationalist when it came to issues of trade. Most leaders of basic industry, such as steel executives, were fiercely protectionist in their desire to seal off domestic markets from foreign competition. Eisenhower did not want to alienate himself politically from industrialists over issues of trade, yet he felt that a more lax foreign-trade policy was a necessary part of U.S. cold-war strategy: the United States needed to open economic channels to those European and Asian countries which were in danger of falling under Communist influence. Through various commissions and the Council on Foreign Economic Policy, Ike worked to reverse the protectionist policies of Truman and the anti-free-trade sentiments that existed among industry executives and union leaders who feared that foreign competition would lead to price hikes and a suspension of wage increases.

The Military-Industrial Complex. During his farewell speech broadcast on radio and television on 17 January 1961, Eisenhower uttered his most memorable lines delivered during his presidency. He warned that the government and the American people "must guard against the acquisition of unwarranted influence, whether sought or unsought, by the military-industrial complex. The potential for the disastrous rise of misplaced power exists and will persist." At a postspeech news conference Ike was characteristically vague when asked to elaborate on what he meant by "military-industrial complex" and whether or not the corporate world posed an immediate threat to the inner workings of democracy. Yet the speech managed to create a sensation among the press and the public, for its message was an ominous departure from what Americans had come to expect from their president: expressions of confidence and optimism that through much of the 1950s held sway over public opinion.

The Business of Making Bombs and Rockets. Eisenhower's vivid warning that corporate boardrooms had the potential to control the political apparatus heightened public fears that big business had grown too big. Yet it was precisely public fear that had contributed to the growth of the military-industrial complex — missile-making companies such as Grumman, McDonnell, Martin, and Northrop which by 1958 were completely devoted to filling military orders and which filled their top executive positions with retired military generals. The Sputnik scare in 1957 had created the perception that the United States lagged behind the Soviet Union in missile development. In fact, Eisenhower had intelligence information at his fingertips which proved that just the opposite was true — that the Americans continued to outpace the Soviets in developing military technology. But to divulge the information would have been tantamount to admitting that the Americans had been spying on the Soviets. Meanwhile an outraged American public demanded massive federal spending in research and development to counter the Soviet menace — exactly the kind of spending increase that Eisenhower had fought to avoid. In sizing up the economic boon *Sputnik* would have on the American technology industry, a spokesman for an aircraft and missile company was quoted in *Nation* as saying, "The boys are going to be jumping all over themselves to see who'll get in the first bill to increase funds for missiles and manned aircraft after Congress reconvenes."

Source:

Altofler, "Who Will Make the Missiles?," *Nation,* 185 (7 December 1957): 428–431;

Stephen E. Ambrose, *Eisenhower: The President* (N.p., Simon & Schuster, 1984);

Paul A. C. Koistinen, *The Military Industrial Complex: A Historical Perspective* (New York: Praeger, 1980).

GOVERNMENT AND EDUCATION

Government Takes a More Active Role. Public education once had been the sole domain of the state and local governments. Local school boards selected texts, hired teachers, and even determined where children of different colors could attend school. The 1950s, however, brought Uncle Sam into education as never before, dramatically shifting the balance of power between states and the national government and making equal access to education a civil right.

Midcentury White House Conference. An early indicator that the government planned to take a more active role in education came in December 1950, when the Midcentury White House Conference on Children and

Youth convened. Some six thousand delegates and observers attended meetings held to discuss how the American educational system might be improved. The conference recommended increased federal aid to states for education, government support for college tuition, abolition of racial segregation in schools, reserving of educational-television channels by the Federal Communications Commission (FCC), and government efforts to provide school lunches for poor children.

Department of Health, Education, and Welfare. In 1953 President Dwight D. Eisenhower created the Department of Health, Education, and Welfare (HEW) — which absorbed the Office of Education, created in 1867 by Andrew Johnson — and named Oveta Culp Hobby the department's first secretary. Although the department spent most of its time and energy on the problem of polio, it coordinated various federal activities regarding the state of education, especially after desegregation in the schools emerged as a pressing issue.

Integration. On 17 May 1954, the Supreme Court decided *Brown* v. *the Board of Education of Topeka, Kansas,* ruling that "the doctrine of 'separate but equal' has no place" in public education and ordering that those U.S. public schools that were segregated — 40 percent of the public schools — should be desegregated in a prompt and reasonable manner. Although after his retirement Eisenhower claimed that he had agreed in principal with the Court's decision on desegregation, as president he refused to make public his support of the ruling. He counted many wealthy southerners among his friends and shared their belief that institutionalized racial segregation in the South could not be changed overnight. At a White House party held prior to the *Brown* decision, Eisenhower took Chief Justice Earl Warren aside and voiced his sympathy with the southerners and their fight

President Dwight D. Eisenhower discusses the Little Rock Central High School crisis with Arkansas Democratic congressmen Brook Hays, center, and Arkansas governor Orval Faubus at the president's vacation headquarters in Newport, Rhode Island, 14 September 1951.

to maintain segregation in the schools: "These are not bad people. All they are concerned about is to see that their sweet little girls are not required to sit alongside some big overgrown Negroes." Furthermore, Ike feared that if the Court ordered integration in the schools then the executive office could do little to either distance itself from the ruling or enforce it — resulting in a political nightmare for an administration that wanted to stay out of state and local politics.

The Little Rock Crisis. In March 1956, 101 southern members of the House and Senate struck back at the Court and signed a pledge to overturn the *Brown* deci-sion. The situation came to a head at Central High School in Little Rock, Arkansas, in 1957. Integration was scheduled to proceed at the school, but, according to Arkansas governor Orval Faubus, the threat of violence and bloodshed was so great as to require a stay on the integration order. A chancery court agreed, but a federal court overruled the lower court, restoring the integration order. Faubus, under the auspices of keeping the peace, called out the Arkansas National Guard to prevent any black students from enrolling. On 3 September nine black students attempted to enroll, and the guard turned them away.

Showdown between a Governor and a President. In a meeting with Eisenhower on 14 September, Faubus seemed willing to end the test of wills between him and the federal government and redirect the guard to escort the black students into the school. The guard's orders remained the same, however, after Faubus returned to Little Rock, and on 23 September the students made another attempt to enter the school, only to face an angry mob. An outraged Eisenhower, who thought he had a deal with the Arkansas governor and in no mood for vigilante tactics, nationalized the Arkansas Guard, sup-plementing them with 101st Airborne troops, and had the soldiers escort the students into Central High on 25 September. Federalized state militia continued as a pres-ence in the school for the remainder of the year, when eight of the nine completed the term and one graduated. Faubus continued a rearguard action against desegrega-tion by closing Central High in 1958, but the Supreme Court moved to end such "evasive schemes" used to per-petuate segregation. When Eisenhower was asked if his action in Little Rock meant executive support for the *Brown* decision, he continued to shy away from an en-dorsement of civil rights and instead spoke of his com-mitment to upholding the law.

White House Conference on Education. The White House sponsored the 1955 Conference on Education, which addressed the goals of schools, the construction and financing of schools, the operation of schools, and the productivity of education. The conference report, is-sued in April 1956, urged greater federal funding for education. Later that year, partly as a result of the confer-ence report, Eisenhower created a thirty-three-member committee to study the problems of higher education. In 1956 the committee proposed that the federal govern-ment needed to develop a policy on aid to education beyond the high-school level, and the states needed to undertake surveys of future enrollments, facilities, and staff needs. The final report, in 1957, called for an em-phasis on teacher recruitment, income-tax deductions for college expenses, and long-range planning for college fa-cilities.

Source:
Henry R. Nau, *The Myth of America's Decline: Leading the World Econ-omy into the 1990s* (New York: Oxford University Press, 1990).

AN ATTEMPT ON TRUMAN'S LIFE

On 1 November 1950, days after a small group of Nationalists had taken to the streets of Puerto Rico, violently protesting U.S. rule, two men— later identified as Puerto Rican Nationalists Oscar Collazo and Griselio Torresola—took to the streets of Washington, D.C., with the intention of assassinating President Harry S Truman. Collazo and Torresola came surprisingly close to killing Truman, considering that they had no real plan of action and could not even be sure that the presi-dent was at home in the Blair House—Truman's residence while the White House was being reno-vated. A Secret Service agent's nightmare, the four-story Blair House sits fully exposed to Penn-sylvania Avenue traffic and passers-by, who if so compelled could peak through the windows to catch a glimpse of presidential life. The two men easily made their way to the Blair House front door before pulling a pistol on a presidential guard. Having heard shots, Truman woke from a nap and stood in his underwear, watching the gun battle from a window. Torresola and one of the guards were killed in the exchange. Many political pundits commented on the irony of the assassina-tion attempt, for Truman had been perceived as a strong advocate of Puerto Rican self-rule. Truman, however, seemed unphased by the attempt on his life, and the next morning he took his customary brisk stroll through the capital city. When asked to comment on the gunplay, the president re-sponded in typically terse fashion: "A president has to expect those things." The surviving would-be assassin, Collazo, was handed a death sentence, which Truman commuted to life imprisonment in 1951. President Jimmy Carter freed Collazo in 1979.

Sources: *Time*, 56 (13 November 1950): 20;

New Republic, 123 (13 November 1950): 6.

Helicopters and Baby Kissing. By 1950 Madison Avenue copywriters and their pithy slogans were figuring prominently in the campaigns of vote-hungry politicians. But the 1950 elections in Connecticut soon captured the nation's attention: two ad men had teamed up to sell themselves as candidates. Democratic gov. Chester Bowles, up for re-election, and his choice for the vacant Senate seat, William Benton — the two being former partners in the New York advertising firm of Benton and Bowles — toured the state in a helicopter sporting a large placard that read Here's Bill Benton! A sound truck blaring campaign slogans would arrive ahead of the helicopter to attract a crowd, and Benton and Bowles would descend from the skies to pass out campaign buttons and kiss the babies of the dazzled citizenry.

Whiffenpoofers Get Out the Vote. Not to be out-done, Benton's Republican opponent Prescott S. Bush — Yale class of 1917 and father of future president George Bush — took to the television waves with his former college quartet, the Whiffenpoofers, to serenade the traditionally conservative Connecticut voter with a rendition of "Shine On, Harvest Moon." Also taking on the Madison Avenue high-flying political machine was Congressman John Davis Lodge in his race

against Bowles for the governor's seat. Lodge realized that if his campaign were to be successful it had better fall into step with the times, and he began spicing up his political rallies with high-kicking dances performed by his wife, Francesca Bragiotti, a former actress. At the very least, rationalized the Lodge campaign tacticians, the highly visible appearance of Italian-American Bragiotti would corner the much-sought-after Italian vote for their Waspish candidate. Lodge, however, eventually fired his wife from her role in the campaign, deciding that her leggy performances were a bit too distasteful, even in an election year.

Just the Issues. It seemed that the only Connecticut candidate in the off-year election attempting to stay entirely clear of hucksterism was in the other Senate race: the staid Democratic senator Brien McMahon would make television appearances from behind his desk to discuss his record and his current work on the Atomic Energy Committee. Some political wags cynically predicted that McMahon's issue-centered campaign style would mean certain defeat for the candidate, but they were wrong. McMahon won. Lodge won the governor's race, and Bush lost to Benton.

NATIONAL POLITICS: ELECTION 1950

A Wartime Campaign. The hot issues during the congressional campaigns of 1950 were inflation and the Korean War, which had erupted in June. In launching their attack on Truman's domestic policies, the Republicans adopted the theme "Liberty against Socialism"; GOP leaders announced that their campaign would oppose Truman's Fair Deal as a program "modeled on the Socialist governments of Europe." Gen. Dwight D. Eisenhower, likely to be a front-runner for the Republican presidential nomination in 1952, also joined in the fray by claiming that America suffered from "creeping paralysis" brought on by the increased size of the federal government. The Republicans stepped up their attack in April, alleging that Truman had "lost" China to the Communists. Democrats countered that the Republicans' baseless accusations and their criticisms of the president had compromised national security and made America appear weak in the eyes of the world. The campaign climate turned uglier as Democrats lambasted the GOP for turning its back on schoolchildren and farmers by not

having supported federal aid packages for education and agriculture.

Record Voter Turnout. The intensity of the campaign and the immediacy of the issues made for a record voter turnout in an off-year election. Forty-one million ballots were cast, leaving the Democrats in control of both houses of Congress. There were, however, clear signs that the Democratic stranglehold on congressional politics

House	81st Congress	82nd Congress	Net Gain/Loss
Democrats	263	235	-27
Republicans	171	199	27

Senate	Holdovers	Reelected	Net Gain/Loss
Democrats	31	12	-5
Republicans	29	10	5

was loosening. In the House the Democrats' majority margin slipped from eighty-eight seats to thirty-six. The elections left the Democrats with only a two-seat advantage in the Senate.

Sources:

"Opening Shots Fired in the 1950 Election Campaign," *Congressional Digest*, 29 (March 1950): 65–66;

"Who Has Done More for You Lately?" *Business Week* (22 April 1950): 21.

NATIONAL POLITICS: REPUBLICAN PRIMARIES AND CONVENTION 1952

1952 Republican Primaries. Although Eisenhower still had not officially declared his intention to seek the Republican nomination, officials within the Dewey-controlled East Coast Republican-party machine placed General Eisenhower's name on the ballot in New Hampshire, the first — and arguably most important — of the primaries. Eisenhower — or Ike, as he was known politically, to suggest a more congenial image for voters — scored a victory of 46,661 to 35,838 votes over Robert Taft in New Hampshire, despite that Eisenhower had not campaigned and that he had not publicly expressed his positions on the issues. Frustrated Taft supporters spoke of Ike as the "phantom candidate."

Eisenhower's Candidacy. On 11 April Eisenhower announced his retirement as head of NATO, and the highly popular general began to campaign actively. Taft finished the primaries with nearly a hundred more delegates than Eisenhower — and only seventy-four more needed to secure the nomination. Yet, opinion polls were showing that Eisenhower enjoyed stronger voter appeal than Taft. "Ikemen" had the political momentum on the eve of the convention and had begun to work on the Republicans in the Harold Stassen and Earl Warren camps, hoping to convince them that a ticket headed by Taft would be unelectable in November.

The California Voting Bloc. California had been a winner-take-all primary, giving all seventy delegates to favorite-son candidate Warren. In holding firm control over such a significant voting bloc, the California governor went to Chicago hoping for a Taft-Eisenhower deadlock — in which case Warren might emerge as the convention's compromise choice. But little support from the all-important Midwest and East Coast political machines had been thrown to Warren's dark-horse candidacy and Warren delegates soon became the target of political piracy at the hands of Ikemen and Taftmen hoping to deliver votes to their candidate. California junior senator Richard Nixon proved to be one of the key political raiders.

Nixon Delivers Votes to Ike. Although as a California delegate he was pledged to Warren, Nixon sensed an Eisenhower victory and, like many young party lions, began to hitch his political fortunes to the Ike bandwagon. In July he boarded the California delegation's Chicago-bound train and moved among the delegates, bemoaning Warren's and Taft's latest standing in the public-opinion polls and suggesting the need for California to back a winner. Enraged by Nixon's show of disloyalty to Warren, delegates asked that Nixon be thrown from the train. At the convention, however, he would be successful in persuading California to vote in favor of a resolution that would allow pro-Ike southern delegates — whose credentials the Taftmen opposed — to be seated on the convention floor. In successfully crossing Warren before and during the convention, Nixon added significantly to his political clout and strengthened his claim to a vice-presidential spot on an Eisenhower ticket.

POLITICAL HIJACKING?: A STORY OF PARTY POLITICS LOUISIANA STYLE

The battle between pro-Ike and pro-Taft delegations in the South produced lurid tales of political chicanery — tales told by aggrieved delegates and outraged politicians, and spiced with a language more befitting of a gangster movie. Ikemen went to Chicago looking to avenge the "The Texas Steal," in which the Texas Taft boys used strong-arm tactics to take over county and state conventions and pull off a political heist. Taftmen vowed to run the "double-crossers" and the "Republicans for a day" out of the Grand Old Party and on the state convention floors were often seen spitting on the Ike delegates. But some of the most sensational stories came out of Louisiana, where tales of corruption and political slight of hand were a traditional part of the party machine. In the spring of 1952, the *New Orleans Item* ran a series of articles on alleged political hijacking at the state and local levels. The reports focused on Taft-supporter Robert Butler, who called a convention of West Baton Rouge Parish Republicans to be held in his mother's house. Four men showed up, each a supporter of Eisenhower. Butler quickly nominated and elected himself the convention chairman, proclaimed himself the parish delegate, banged the gavel to adjourn the meeting, and escorted the men — who were howling in protest — out the door. The Eisenhower Four held a rump meeting and sent their own delegate to the state convention. But the members of the credentials committee, named by the Taft machine, threw him out. The story gained national attention and further fueled criticisms that the Republican rank and file in the South had little say-so in local and state party politics — that, indeed, the party of Lincoln had become "all rank and damned little file."

Delegates hold a demonstration in celebration of the nomination of Dwight D. Eisenhower at the 1952 Republican Convention.

Preconvention Power Politics. The preconvention political battles had been particularly intense in the South, with the Taft and Eisenhower camps accusing each other of stealing delegates. Although rooted primarily in the Midwest, the Taft political machine enjoyed widespread influence over southern Republicans, who tended to share the Ohio senator's isolationist views on foreign policy and trade — and, more important, perceived Taft's antagonism toward unions and New Deal social programs as being sympathetic to southern interests. By and large, it was the Taftmen who ran the Republican party in the South; those who had managed to gain local office in a region dominated by Democrats owed their political fortunes to Taft-wing support. As such, when southern local conventions were called, the Taft Republicans were appalled at the large numbers of Eisenhower supporters in attendance. Bitterly referred to by the Taftmen as "Republicans for a day," Ike supporters were accused of being party outsiders who sought to pack the conventions. Ikemen, however, claimed that they were being shut out of the state conventions and "steamrolled" in local party meetings. In many cases they broke from the party machine and held rump meetings, which resulted in contesting pro-Ike and pro-Taft delegations being sent to the state conventions. Moderate Republican cried foul, charging that Taft-controlled party executive committees

in Texas, Louisiana, and Georgia simply overlooked the contesting Ike delegates and sent a disproportionate number of Taftmen packing for Chicago. With the South controlling nearly 100 votes at the Republican convention, the rules surrounding delegate credentials was the hottest issue leading up to July — and threatened to destroy the Republican party in the South.

The War over Credentials. The Republican brass met in Chicago the week before the convention to decide the delegate issue. Hoping to play on the widely held belief that Taft had dabbled in dirty politics in the southern primaries, Ikemen wanted the emotional deliberations to be broadcast on television and radio: "Let the people see and hear the evidence," declared Dewey. National Committee Chairman Guy Gabrielson, a Taft supporter, attempted to head off a potential public-relations debacle and, behind closed doors, offered a compromise split of the contested delegates. Ike's negotiators refused the deal, knowing that continued heated debate on the issue during the convention might begin to erode Taft's power base and attract delegates to the Eisenhower camp.

Republican Convention. The first to be televised, the Republican convention drew an estimated audience of 75 million. There had been many journalists prior to the convention who had suggested that the American people's first glimpse into the party process of anointing a

Standing with their wives, Pat Nixon, left, and Mamie Eisenhower, California sen. Richard M. Nixon and Gen. Dwight Eisenhower raise their hands as victors at the 1952 Republican Convention.

candidate might be their last. The Republican conventions had a reputation for being staid, predictable, often boring affairs — especially when compared to the raucous party the Democrats threw every four years. From 7 to 11 July in Chicago, however, the Republicans produced one of the most extraordinary political dramas in the history of the Grand Old Party. Republicans looked more like Democrats as they exchanged heated accusations, fought blood wars over parliamentary procedure, and scrambled to solidify power bases in a struggle for control of a divided party.

A Two-man Race. The Republican primaries had created a two-man race for the nomination. Taft and Eisenhower came to Chicago with a clear advantage in number of delegates over Stassen, MacArthur, and Warren. Taft had further cause for optimism; he had nearly 100 more delegates than Eisenhower — and only 75 more needed to secure the nomination. Furthermore, the convention would be Taft-controlled. National Committee Chairman Gabrielson and fellow Taftmen dominated the convention committees. Even the convention's list of speakers was loaded with Taft partisans. MacArthur, who if not drafted for the nomination was ready to throw his delegates and support behind Taft, was named by Gabrielson to deliver the keynote address. Virtually all of the senators on the list represented the pro-Taft right wing of the party: James Kem of Missouri and Harry Cain of Washington delivered proisolationist speeches,

and Joe McCarthy accused the Democrats of being soft on communism in his characteristic slash-and-burn style.

The Fair Play Rule. Ike's floor strategists had to act quickly the first day of the convention to ignite a fight over the contested delegates and credentials procedures. Dewey and Eisenhower's campaign coordinator, Henry Cabot Lodge, proposed a new rule that would forbid many of the contested delegates from voting on the credentials of others. To underscore their charges of delegation tampering, Dewey and Lodge named their proposal the "fair play" amendment — further infuriating Taft supporters. The Taftmen found themselves in the awkward position of having to reject a proposal entitled fair play in order to protect their delegates' votes on the floor. In convincing fashion Ikemen won the rules fight in a floor vote, and Taft's strategists were suddenly on the defensive. They retreated from the fight over the contested Texas and Georgia delegates. Meanwhile, as television cameras watched, Lodge rallied the delegates who had previously been refused credentials and declared, "We're going right ahead on the floor!"

An Attack on Dewey. Having bungled the parliamentary debate, the brass in the Taft camp regrouped and decided to launch an offensive from behind the speaker's podium. Their target would be Thomas E. Dewey — Northeast liberal party boss, loser in the last two presidential elections, and highly visible supporter of Eisen-

Conventions Enter America's Living Rooms. With television cameras running, Taft made his first entrance into the convention hall. But it was an experience he would have rather missed. Frenzied, banner-waving supporters rushed Taft in an attempt to get close to the candidate — and, guessed Taft, in an attempt to get on national television. His suit and sense of decorum having been ruffled by the spectacle, Taft snarled, "That is a good example of why we don't have TV at national committee meetings." But despite the annoyance he and many other politicians felt at having the wheeling-dealing aspect of party politics exposed in American living rooms, television arrived on the American political scene as a major force. The three major networks spent ten million on covering the two conventions — both having an estimated viewing audience of 75 million.

Television's Political Influence. Indeed, the presence of television cameras shaped the conduct and atmosphere of the conventions in ways party bosses never dreamed possible. Chicago's International Amphitheater was chosen in favor of the more convenient Chicago Stadium by both parties as the convention site because it had additional room for television coverage. Wary of the political damage that could be caused by the camera's eye, campaign leaders warned their delegates not to look tired on the convention floor or, worse, fall asleep during their candidate's speech. Convention television coverage also meant that the political speechwriters had to go back to work writing new material for the candidates; having previously relied on stump speeches often delivered hundreds of times by the first day of the convention, politicians could not risk having a speech heard twice by the average American, who already had come to doubt that politicians had any new ideas.

Walkie-Lookies, or Peepie-Creepies. The difficulties of covering a convention on television called for innovations by the networks. On the convention floor the "periscope camera" was used to shoot above the heads of the delegates. Portable cameras — called walkie-lookies, or peepie-creepies — were also used to take extreme close-up shots of the conventioneers. Despite the possibility of brief fame promised by the roving cameras, unsuspecting delegates soon became disenchanted with the walkie-lookie, which often snuck up on them at inopportune moments. At one point during the Republican convention, Guy Gabrielson from behind the podium spotted one of the portable cameras and cried, "There's a talkie-walkie. No talkie-walkie allowed on the floor — no sir!"

hower. Speakers excoriated Dewey as "the most cold-blooded, ruthless, selfish political boss in the United States today," insinuating that any product of the Dewey machine — namely Eisenhower — must be tainted. Sen. Everett Dirksen, a rabid Taft supporter, reminded the conventioneers that Dewey was the Grand Old Party's two-time loser — that he "had a habit of winning conventions and losing elections." Triggering the convention's most memorable demonstration, Dirksen pointed a finger at Dewey, who stood with his New York delegation, and bellowed, "You have taken us down the path to defeat . . . don't take us down that road again." Television audiences watched stunned as Taftmen paraded on the convention floor, jeering at the New York delegation. Dewey, however, sat smiling through the demonstration. Many of the undecided delegates had already bought Dewey's "Taft Can't Win" argument, and the convention was slipping away from the Ohio senator.

A First-ballot Victory. The debate on parliamentary rulings had signaled disaster for Taft. Eisenhower's roll-call victories in the fight for Georgia, Texas, and Louisiana delegates had added 68 Ike votes to the convention floor. 604 votes were need for the nomination, however, and the Taft camp predicted that Eisenhower could manage only 560 votes on the first ballot. If stopped at 560, reasoned Taft, delegates convinced that Ike lacked the strength to take the nomination would come back into the Taft fold in a second roll call. The first roll call was held on 10 July, and Eisenhower took 595 votes. The total was devastating to Taft. With only nine votes needed for a first-ballot Eisenhower nomination, states eager to secure presidential patronage began jumping on the Eisenhower bandwagon. Minnesota's political boss, Walter Judd, was the first to reach the Republican chairman and announce a switch of Minnesota votes to Eisenhower. Having watched the drama unfold on television from his hotel suite, Ike immediately called Taft's headquarters across the street then paid a visit. A pale and badly shaken Taft offered the nominee an unenthusiastic handshake and the promise of his support.

Sources:

Richard C. Bain, *Convention Decision and Voting Records* (Washington, D.C.: Brookings Institution, 1960);

"Bitter Beginning," *Life*, 33 (14 July 1952);

Paul T. David, Ralph M. Godman, and Richard C. Bain, *The Politics of National Conventions* (Washington, D.C.: Brookings Institution, 1960);

Harry S Truman stands with Adlai Stevenson at the 1952 Democratic Convention.

"National Affairs," *Time* 60 (14 July 1952): 17–24; (21 July 1952): 11–21.

NATIONAL POLITICS: DEMOCRATIC PRIMARIES AND CONVENTION 1952

Democratic Primaries. Estes Kefauver's campaign performance dominated the Democratic primaries. His surprise victory over Harry S Truman in New Hampshire embarrassed the president and quickened his decision not to seek another term. Yet, despite Kefauver's impressive showing in the northern primaries, several of his victories came in states such as Illinois, New Jersey, and Massachusetts, where the delegates were required by law to remain unpledged. Furthermore, fellow southerners regarded the famous senator from Tennessee to be a traitor to the white South on issues of segregation — and were eager to hand him a string of defeats in the Dixie primaries. Sen. Richard Russell — a Georgia conservative and an anti–Fair Deal candidate who had campaigned little in the early northern primaries — easily defeated Kefauver in Florida, signaling the South's solidarity in their opposition to the Tennessee senator.

Democrats Search for a Candidate. The party brass in the northeastern and midwestern urban centers also were prepared to withhold delegates from Kefauver. As chairman of the Senate Crime Investigating Committee, popularly referred to as the Kefauver committee, the Tennessee senator had helped expose the link between organized crime and the big city Democratic bosses. Truman also was less than enamored of Kefauver, who had openly attacked the administration for having failed to address corruption in government. Party leaders clamored for an alternative candidate to Kefauver. Truman thought he had found his man in Illinois governor Adlai Stevenson. Although he had built a reputation as a reformer of Illinois politics, Stevenson had the strong support of the state Democratic political machine. Stevenson had also worked in the Roosevelt administration as a New Dealer and was perceived to be an ally of organized labor and of the Truman administration.

An Attempt to Draft Stevenson. As titular head of the Democratic party, Truman promised Stevenson the nomination if he were to run. But Stevenson demurred, claiming that he wanted to remain a governor and had little desire to seek the presidency. Stevenson's coyness outraged Truman, who began to swing his support to his seventy-four-year-old vice-president, Alben Barkley, just prior to the opening of the convention. The hope among administration insiders what that Barkley's great popularity (he was the first vice-president to be affectionately dubbed the "Veep") and his Kentucky roots might produce a groundswell of support from both northerners and southerners on the convention floor. But organized labor was opposed to a Barkley candidacy — ostensibly because of his age. By the first day of the convention, none of the declared candidates had emerged as a front-runner for the nomination. The hopes of the party leaders and the attention of the press and the nation remained fixed on Stevenson, who nevertheless continued to insist that he was not a candidate.

1952 Democratic Convention. The Democratic Convention opened under the glow of television camera lights in Chicago's International Amphitheater on 20 July — days after the Republican drama had climaxed in the same setting. The Democrats, however, came to Chicago knowing that they could not afford the kind of political fireworks that had characterized the Republican's divisive convention. The current Democratic administration was unpopular, and still lingering were memories of the 1948 Democratic convention, when southern delegations walked out in protest over a civil rights plank that had been authored by northern party leaders. With millions of Americans watching, the party was determined to put on a show of unity and assure the masses that Democrats were still capable of governing. Yet the ability of the party to run a smooth convention and nominate an electable candidate was in doubt. The two key questions being asked by politicians and pundit alike on the opening day were Will Stevenson run? and Will the southern conservatives bolt?

Stevenson's Reluctance. On the first day of the convention, newsmen eavesdropped on a closed-door session of the Illinois delegation. Pressed by Illinois delegates to announce his candidacy, Stevenson was overheard to say that he was not "temperamentally, physically, or mentally" equipped for the presidency. When asked by Chicago political boss Jack Arvey if he would accept a draft, Stevenson refused to give a firm answer. Later that day he delivered a characteristically eloquent welcoming speech to the delegates, who interrupted Stevenson countless times to march through the aisles and roar their approval. Although his speech made no mention of a Stevenson candidacy, the Illinois governor — whether intentionally or unintentionally — clearly had placed himself in a position to walk away with the nomination. By having refused Truman's preconvention overtures, he had distanced himself from the unpopular Truman-wing of the party. The rest of the candidates had little choice but to hop on the Stevenson bandwagon. Kefauver had the most committed delegates (251 1/2) but no other support. Oklahoma senator Robert Kerr was perceived to be a big-business candidate and a slave to oil interests — and therefore was unacceptable to labor. A Russell candidacy would falter outside the South, and the liberal campaign of wealthy presidential adviser W. Averell Harriman had no momentum beyond the borders of New York, his native state.

North–South Negotiations. In dealing with the southern conservatives, northern party leaders and administration strategists hoped to avoid the ugly North-South fight that had occurred in 1948. The northerners were prepared to further water down the already vague civil rights plank of the 1948 convention in return for a "loyalty pledge": Dixiecrats would promise to place the convention's nominees on the ballots in their states. Most of the South agreed to take the pledge as along as it applied to "this convention only." Virginia, South Carolina, and Louisiana refused to sign, reserving the right to break away and hold a rump convention. It soon was evident, however, than even the most ardent Dixiecrats had no intention of bolting from the convention. They had become too powerful a force to be easily reckoned with, and Georgia favorite-son Russell held 268 delegates. In response to the possibility of a walkout, Virginia governor Harry Byrd wryly declared, "We'll just sit here and maybe they'll have to throw us out."

The First Nominating Ballot. In deciding on whether to seat those delegations that had not signed the loyalty pledge, those on the convention floor understood that a proseating vote would mean a vote for Stevenson; for the liberal Harriman-Kefauver forces strenuously opposed seating the Virginia delegation. But a pro-Virginia motion was passed, and soon a strong anti-Kefauver voting bloc composed of the southern renegade states was in position on the convention floor. After the first nominating ballot, Kefauver retained his lead but was well short of the numbers of delegates needed to secure the nomination. Stevenson's momentum became evident on the second ballot, picking up more than two new votes to every new one cast for Kefauver. Sensing a lost cause, Kefauver delegates began to defect to the Stevenson camp. In one last desperate attempt to stop Stevenson, Kefauver tried to interrupt the third ballot but was turned back from the podium by the powerful convention chairman and Speaker of the House Sam Rayburn. "Never in the history of a Democratic Convention has a roll call been interrupted for any purpose," growled Rayburn.

A Third-Ballot Victory. Stevenson's victory on the third ballot had been anticlimactic; the "candidate who would not campaign" had emerged as the odds-on favorite for the nomination well before the doors of the convention had opened. His reluctance to be drafted as a candidate for an office he "did not seek" appealed to a party that sought to slough off its image as a corrupt political machine which produced power-hungry and cynical politicians. Stevenson deliberately cast his acceptance speech in biblical language, suggesting that a sacred covenant had been reached between a united Democratic party bent on taking the high road and a reluctant nominee chosen to conduct a crusade: "I have asked the merciful Father of us all to let this cup pass from me. But from such dread responsibility one does not shrink in fear, in self-interest, or in false humility. So, if this cup may not pass from me, except I drink it, Thy will be done." Some political editorialists later criticized the "Stevenson in the Garden" speech as tactless, but the New Testament rhetoric worked magic on delegates and party brass.

Selecting a Running Mate. Having given his acceptance, Stevenson and party leaders retreated into the smoke-filled back room, located directly behind the speaker's podium, to conduct the less-than-spiritual quest for a running mate. Further appeasement of the volatile southern delegations was at the heart of the selection process, and the leaders settled on Sen. John Sparkman of Alabama. Sparkman was a southern moderate who had not bolted along with the Dixiecrats in 1948 but had nevertheless distanced himself from the Truman wing of the party.

Sources:

Richard C. Bain, *Convention Decision and Voting Records* (Washington, D.C.: Brookings Institution, 1960);

Paul T. David, Ralph M. Godman, and Richard C. Bain, *The Politics of National Conventions* (Washington, D.C.: Brookings Institution, 1960);

"National Affairs" *Time* 60 (14 July 1952): 17–24; (21 July 1952): 11–21.

NATIONAL POLITICS: ELECTION 1952

Truman's Unpopularity. Truman did not run for re-election in 1952, his approval ratings in the Gallup poll having dropped to a dismal 30 percent. To test his voter appeal, Truman had placed his name on the New Hampshire ballot during the Democratic primaries, but he was defeated by Sen. Estes Kefauver of Tennessee. The defeat was a particularly humiliating one for an incumbent president. Americans were tired of the Korean War, continued inflation, and the kind of pork-barrel government spending that many associated with twenty years of Democratic leadership. Truman's political clout had been further undermined by Sen. Joseph McCarthy and his cronies, whose sensational charges that the Defense Department was harboring Communists were grabbing headlines and politicizing a fearful population.

Rough Politicking and Brave Campaigns. The Republicans successfully drafted Eisenhower to head up their presidential ticket. Ike's promises to clean up gov-

INTERNATIONAL NEWS

Dwight D. Eisenhower and wife Mamie pose with a November 1952 headline announcing his victory in the presidential elections.

Many thought the thirty-minute speech to be maudlin, mawkish, and third-rate theater. Gen. Lucius Clay proclaimed it the "corniest thing I ever heard," but he marveled at its effectiveness when he came across a teary elevator man obviously touched by the contents of the speech — mostly a list of Richard M. Nixon's financial assets and liabilities that painted a portrait of Nixon as an Everyman and a victim of vicious slander. The message behind the detailed list of debts owed was excruciatingly clear: his political career was in jeopardy, and his television audience of fifty-eight million — at that time a record number — would decide if he was guilty of using an eighteen-thousand-dollar campaign fund for personal use. Whether disgusted by Nixon's shameless play for Middle America's sympathy or moved to tears by the vice-presidential nominee's mortgage, few could deny that Nixon, with the help of television and family dog Checkers, pulled off a political escape act of history-making proportions. His daughter loved the dog, Nixon told his television audience in mock seriousness, and even though Checkers was a present given to the Nixon family by a Republican supporter, Nixon was going to keep him. Many viewers winced at Nixon's attempt at humor, but he had nevertheless succeeded in using the hot new medium of television to appear to be a man battered and backed into a corner by his political enemies yet still capable of at least trying to deliver a funny line. At the end of the speech he asked viewers to contact the Republican National Committee with their verdict. His allotted time ran out in the middle of his appeal to "wire and write," and he felt certain that the speech had been a flop. The Republican National Committee, however, soon reported the receipt of three hundred thousand letters and telegrams, virtually all in support of Nixon.

ernment, balance the budget, and put an end to the Korean War had massive appeal. His running mate, Richard M. Nixon — the young Republican senator from California who had exposed Alger Hiss as a Communist spy — took up the banner of anticommunism and acted as the ticket's political pit bull. He pressed ahead with allegations of fellow traveling in the Democratic-controlled government — charges that Gov. Adlai Stevenson of Illinois, Democratic presidential hopeful, often had to counter with eloquent speeches that denounced witch-hunt politics and championed civil liberties. Many of these speeches were delivered to hostile audiences who equated civil liberties with "Commies' rights." For this reason Stevenson's 1952 campaign has been considered one of the bravest in American political history.

Political Images. Dubbed an egghead by columnist Stewart Alsop, Stevenson infused his rhetoric with a philosophical tone that defied conventional campaign wisdom and made him the darling of intellectuals. Republican campaign strategists, however, had their candidate decrease his reliance on the stump speech. They had come to realize that most Americans living in an increasingly fast-paced society would favor a political message that was quickly and charismatically delivered. Eisenhower took to the television airwaves — a medium Stevenson despised — to deliver fifteen-second sound bites. What the political ads lacked in substance they made up for in powerful images of a robust and confident Ike who spoke directly to the average American.

Nixon and Television. Television proved to be a dominant force in the 1952 campaign. In September the new medium came to the Republicans' rescue after the *New York Post* had run the story that Nixon had received a slush fund of eighteen thousand dollars from wealthy supporters. An estimated television audience of fifty-eight million watched as Nixon successfully defended his conduct — and his place on the ticket. Two months later Eisenhower and Nixon scored an easy victory in an election that saw a record voter turnout.

Republican Sweep. In the congressional elections eleven women were elected to the House and one was reelected to the Senate. For the first time a mother-son team (Ohio Republicans Francis and Oliver Bolton) were voted into Congress. The Republican election sweep split

Senate	Holdovers	Reelected	New	Net Gain/Loss
Democrats	35	8	4	-6
Republicans	26	17	6	6

House	82nd Congress	83rd Congress	Net Gain/Loss
Democrats	232	213	-19
Republicans	202	22	19
Independents	1	1	-

many of the once-solid Democratic delegations and forged inroads in southern politics, a traditional Democratic stronghold.

Sources:

Porter McKeever, *Adlai Stevenson: His Life and* Legacy (N.Y.: Morrow, 1989);

Time, 60 (6 October 1952): 20–23.

NATIONAL POLITICS: ELECTION 1954

Republicans Gain Ground in Congress. In the Senate the Republicans took a four-seat majority and struck a balance with the Democrats in the House (with Vice-president Nixon counting as the tie-breaking vote). The new Republican National Committee chairman, Leonard Hall, had begun to effect a long-term strategy of solidifying Republican gains by singing the praises of the Eisenhower administration; candidates running on the GOP platform pounded home the message that life was once again good. The Korean War had ended, the dollar was

President Dwight D. Eisenhower and Republican National chairman Leonard Hall keep close tabs on the 1954 congressional election returns.

sound, and the administration had made significant strides toward balancing the budget. Republicans also reminded voters of the Democrats' soft record on communism.

Democrats on Defensive. For the first time in many years, the Democratic political machine appeared to be in disarray as it tried to get out from under the financial and political debts chalked up by Stevenson's unsuccessful 1952 presidential campaign. The Democrats attempted to reunify under National Party chairman Stephen A. Mitchell. Faced with the overwhelming popularity of Eisenhower (whose approval ratings in the Gallup poll had been hovering around 75 percent) and the certainty that relatively large numbers of Republican candidates would hitch a ride into Congress on the president's long coattails, the Democrats strove to distance themselves from Truman's economic and foreign-policy record. For the most part, Democratic candidates stuck to local issues. Those in the southern and plains states focused on the economic hardships of farmers, while northeastern and midwestern urban Democrats rallied around their labor constituency in denouncing the Taft-Hartley Act. Democrats also played on public fear that big business had too much say in the Eisenhower administration and that efforts to balance the budget would mean cuts in defense dollars and a compromised national security.

Sources:

Richard C. Bain, *Convention Decisions and Voting Records* (Washington, D.C.: The Brookings Institute, 1960);

Time, 60 (6 October 1952): 20–23.

Governors	1952	1954	Net Gain/ Loss
Democrats	18	27	+9
Republicans	30	21	-9

NATIONAL POLITICS: DEMOCRATIC PRIMARIES AND CONVENTION 1956

1956 Democratic Primaries. Preconvention campaigning pitted Adlai Stevenson against Estes Kefauver, who surprised many in his own party by announcing that he would contest key primaries. No longer the shy, reluctant candidate, Stevenson had announced his candidacy in November 1955 with assurances from the Democratic kingmakers that the nomination was his for the taking. Kefauver, however, continued to stress his independence from the party machinery and officially sounded his challenge one month later. He stunned Stevenson in the New Hampshire primary and scored an even more shocking victory in Minnesota, where Stevenson had campaigned heavily with the support of Minnesota favorite-son Hubert Humphrey. Contributing to Kefauver's success was a chatty, grassroots campaign style. Buttonhol-

ing a passerby, the Tennessean would offer a firm handshake and drawl, "My name is Estes Kefauver. I'm running for President of the United States. I'd sure appreciate it if you'll help me." These homey solicitations of potential voters were often followed up by a letter of thanks.

Baby Kissing and Barnstorming. Kefauver's campaign of personality galled Stevenson. After the New Hampshire and Minnesota losses, he felt that Kefauver had played down the issues and instead had turned the political race into a baby-kissing contest — a contest that the often aloof and patrician Stevenson was sure to lose. Since 1952 Kefauver's power base had remained narrow, and there existed little chance for the Tennessean to win at the convention; yet further Kefauver primary victories could deny Stevenson the nomination. Despite their boss's misgivings, Stevenson strategists rushed into Florida, California, and Oregon — the other primaries contested by Kefauver — determined to match their opposition's door-to-door tactics. In these states the revamped Stevenson campaign proved a success, and on 1 August Kefauver announced his withdrawal from the race in favor of Stevenson. But Kefauver's barnstorming efforts had managed to draw blood. He had landed 156 delegates, and other Democratic hopefuls were gathering in the wings, sensing that the primary losses had proven Stevenson vulnerable. New York governor Averell Harriman headed to Chicago thinking that he would be the man to seize the nomination if the Stevenson machine were to stall on the convention floor. Senators Lyndon Johnson of Texas and Stuart Symington of Missouri held favorite-son backing in their respective states and went to Chicago hoping they might parlay their delegates and influence into an upset convention victory.

Democratic Convention. Having secured at least a tenuous cease-fire between northern and southern delegations in 1952, Democratic party leaders hoped that the '56 convention in Chicago would be muted and tranquil. There were stirrings of opposition in some wings of the party, yet Stevenson remained not only confident that the nomination would be his, but his on the first ballot. By 13 August, the opening day of the convention, Stevenson had begun drafting his acceptance speech.

Furious Southerners. Signs began to appear prior to the first day of the convention, however, that Stevenson might be in for more of a struggle than he had imagined. He nearly managed to incite a southern revolt after having made to a reporter an offhand comment in support of school desegregation: the party platform, blurted Stevenson, "should express unequivocal approval of the Court's decision . . . although it seems odd that you have to express your approval of the Constitution and its institutions." Furious southern delegates who had been working with their northern counterparts on a compromise civil-rights plank threatened to shift the South's support to Lyndon Johnson, who was the plank's key architect.

Truman's Arrival. Stevenson was able to soothe tempers by announcing that he had no intention of influencing the construction of the party platform. But trouble for Stevenson again appeared, this time in the form of Harry Truman. The former president arrived in Chicago playing the role of elder statesman and kingmaker. Treating the convention as his last hoorah, he grabbed newspaper headlines — and attention away from Stevenson — by hinting to reporters that he might not support the candidate from Illinois ("I'm not a bandwagon fellow. Don't get that in your head.") but coyly refused to say whom he would endorse. Asked by a reporter if he was just trying to baffle conventioneers, Truman grinned and replied, "That is exactly right."

Truman's Endorsement. Truman had political scores to settle with Stevenson. Still bristling over having been spurned by Stevenson in 1952, Truman was determined to throw the convention wide open. On 11 August the former president held a much anticipated televised press conference to announce his endorsement. His statement included one more barely concealed jab at Stevenson ("this convention must name a man who has the experience and the ability to act as president immediately upon assuming that office without risking a period of costly trial and error"), and then the bombshell was dropped: "In the light of my knowledge of the office of president, I believe that the man best qualified . . . is Governor Harriman."

Counting Frenzy. The Truman announcement created a frenzy among delegate counters in the first hours of the convention. Stevenson had suspected that most of the uncommitted delegates and favorite-son supporters — such as the fifty-six Texas delegates who stood behind Lyndon Johnson — would be delivered to the Stevenson camp without fuss. The possibility of a Stevenson-Harriman deadlock, however, raised hopes for Johnson's nomination. Similarly, Stuart Symington of Missouri was sitting on his delegates in an attempt to create a bandwagon of his own. Stevenson's convention-floor strategists rushed from one caucus to the next in an effort to convince delegations not to defect. Pennsylvania delegates considering a jump to Harriman, for instance, were given a lecture on the political "facts of life": the current Pennsylvania governor was a Stevenson man, and if a delegate wished to remain on good terms with leaders in the state capital, then he had better vote for Stevenson.

A Stevenson Victory. By nominating day Stevenson's men had managed to put out most of the brush fires that had been ignited by Truman's grandstanding. The Stevenson totals determined by a roll call dwarfed those of the other candidates, and a motion was passed that Stevenson's nomination be made unanimous. Truman had continued to hit hard at Stevenson in interviews given to reporters, but the former president had to suffer the indignation of being, in effect, reprimanded by party boss Sam Rayburn, who *sent* for Truman and then chided him for his "Give'm hell" tactics. Clearly no longer a potent power in a party run by a new generation, Truman was forced to congratulate Stevenson publicly on his decisive roll-call victory and recognize the Illinois candidate's tenaciousness as a fighter, because "he's given some of us here a pretty good licking."

An Open Nomination for a Running Mate. In a surprise move that created a second convention of sorts, Stevenson turned the matter of choosing a running mate over to the delegates. Democratic strategists hoped that a wide-open nomination would place more heat on Richard Nixon from within the embattled vice-president's own Republican ranks. Nixon's place on the Republican ticket was in doubt, and in preparing for their upcoming convention some Republicans were calling for an open nomination to decide his political fate.

Estes Kefauver won the vice-presidential spot on the ticket, but not until after a rising young star in Democratic politics, Sen. John Kennedy of Massachusetts, came within 38.5 votes of winning the nomination on the second ballot.

Sources:
Richard C. Bain, *Convention Decision and Voting Records* (Washington, D.C.: The Brookings Institution, 1960);

Paul T. David, Ralph M. Godman, and Richard C. Bain, *The Politics of National Conventions* (Washington, D.C.: The Brookings Institution, 1960);

"The Platform Democrats Will Stand On," *U.S. News and World Report,* 41 (24 August 1956): 102–115.

President Dwight D. Eisenhower recovers from a heart attack suffered in September 1955.

NATIONAL POLITICS: REPUBLICAN CONVENTION 1956

Republican Convention. From 20 to 23 August, Republican delegates convened in San Francisco's Cow Palace to rally around Ike, whose immense popularity most believed would ensure victory in the November polls. Those who tuned in to watch the convention witnessed none of the acrimony that had transformed the '52 convention into nail-biting political drama. Even the "Dump Nixon" movement that had been spearheaded by administration official Harold Stassen failed to raise any serious doubt about the vice-president's claim to a renomination. Party leaders had moved quickly to portray Stassen as a lone renegade and his attempt to oust Nixon as inept. Indeed, on nomination day Stassen found himself in the awkward position of having to bow to the demands of Republican brass and deliver a seconding speech for Nixon's nomination.

Republican Harmony. "Spontaneous" demonstrations — prearranged months in advance and commandeered on the convention floor by the Young Republicans — created an atmosphere more often associated with a campaign stop than a party convention. Even the convention politics surrounding the formation of a party platform signaled unanimity among the delegates: easily approved, the platform sang Ike's praises and listed his good works in office.

Sources:

Richard C. Bain, *Convention Decision and Voting Records* (Washington, D.C.: The Brookings Institution, 1960);

Paul T. David, Ralph M. Godman, and Richard C. Bain, *The Politics of National Conventions* (Washington, D.C.: The Brookings Institution, 1960);

"What the Two Parties Stand for in 1956," *U.S. News and World Report*, 41 (17 August 1956): 37–38.

NATIONAL POLITICS: ELECTION 1956

Ike-Nixon Again. Eisenhower and Nixon ran for reelection against a Democratic ticket that was once again headed by Stevenson. Senator Kefauver was the Democrats' vice-presidential nominee. Stevenson had outdueled Kefauver during the Democratic primaries and went on to win the nomination over Gov. Averell Harriman of New York at a raucous party convention. Southern Democrats had split with northern liberals over a civil rights platform, but a compromise was finally reached. Kefauver emerged from the convention on the offensive, attacking Republicans for fostering racial segregation and challenging Eisenhower to put a unilateral end to H-bomb testing. The Democrats also continued to champion the causes of labor in 1956 and pressed for a four-day workweek. But, in fact, they had little ammunition with which they could attack the Republicans on the domestic economic front. Under Ike the rate of inflation had been reduced to 1 percent, and the middle class continued to grow and prosper. A congressional battle over farm price supports in early 1956, however, gave a Democratic ticket an issue which had strong appeal with the Middle American voter: Democrats wanted support payments to be doled out under a fixed rate; Ike wanted that rate to be flexible. In April, Eisenhower vetoed a farm bill that had been heavily amended by the Democrats, who found themselves cast as the party sympathetic to the plight of the American farmer.

Ike's Health an Issue. Eisenhower entered the election year as popular as ever, if not more so. A March Gallup poll showed that 76 percent approved of the way Ike was handling his job. Yet he had expressed to friends and advisers his desire to retire from politics. In September 1955 Eisenhower had suffered a heart attack that, although described by his physicians as "moderate," left both him and the American public with serious doubts about his ability to survive another term in office. These doubts became a major campaign issue when Eisenhower announced in February of 1956 his intention to run for reelection after getting the go-ahead from his doctors. In order to convince Americans that he remained a fit and vigorous world leader, Ike was forced to hit the campaign trail more aggressively than he thought was becoming of an incumbent with a glowing record in office. In June Eisenhower suffered an ileitis attack and had to undergo intestinal-bypass surgery. Following the operation *Chicago Daily News* reporter William McGaffin suggested to Ike that the American people so loved the sixty-five-year-old president that they might vote *against* him, fearing that the demands of the presidency might kill him.

Nixon a Heart Beat Away? The issue of Ike's health raised hard questions about the political fate of Vice-president Nixon. He had received high marks from the public and the press for his leadership after Eisenhower's heart attack, yet there were clearly many voters who were pro-Ike and anti-Nixon, especially with Nixon only an erratic heartbeat away from the presidency. Of those polled by Gallup in April, 19 percent believed Nixon would help the Republican ticket; 32 percent believed he was a political liability. Republican National Committee chairman Leonard Hall tried to quash any Democratic attempt to play on the connection between a Nixon vice-presidency and Ike's health by repeatedly proclaiming that "the American people simply won't stand for tactics of that kind." But the issue continued to be raised by Eisenhower himself, who in press conferences would praise the vice-president's intellect, loyalty, and record of service but refuse to name Nixon as his running mate for 1956, claiming that an endorsement of Nixon should be determined at an open Republican convention. The press was left to assume that even the administration was buying into a morbid logic: if Ike is unwilling publicly to proclaim Nixon fit to remain as his vice-president and potential successor, then Ike must have serious doubts about his chances to survive four more years in the job, despite his claims to the contrary.

Harold Stassen, head of the movement to dump Richard Nixon from the Republican ticket in favor of Massachusetts governor Christian A. Herter, speaks to reporters at the opening of the Eisenhower-Herter campaign headquarters in Washington, D.C.

Ike's Doubts about Nixon. The press was correct. Privately Eisenhower believed Nixon was still too politically immature and inexperienced to play the president's successor and tried to persuade Nixon to remove himself from the ticket and take a seat in the cabinet. During one of these conversations Eisenhower broached the topic of his health and Nixon's presidential aspirations with disarming frankness, telling Nixon that he would be better off serving in the cabinet unless "you calculate that I won't last five years." An informal list of acceptable Eisenhower running mates — including Earl Warren and Gov. Frank Lausche of Ohio, a Democrat — began to float among White House advisers.

"Dump Nixon" Campaign. To make matters worse for the already besieged vice-president, a "Dump Nixon" campaign went public on 23 July, when Harold Stassen, the president's special assistant on disarmament, called a press conference and dropped the bombshell announcement that he was planning on supporting Gov. Christian A. Herter of Massachusetts for vice-president. He claimed that a privately funded poll showed that an "Eisenhower-Herter ticket will run at least 6 percent stronger than an Eisenhower-Nixon ticket." Furthermore, he stated that Eisenhower had prior knowledge of his announcement, which many political pundits interpreted as Ike's blessing. The Stassen press conference undermined the fragile peace between the Eisenhower moderates and the conservative Old Guard Republicans,

who supported Nixon as their link to the White House. Political infighting erupted. In an attempt at damage control, Hall announced that Stassen would nominate Nixon at the convention, but rumors of a Nixon replacement persisted, much to the joy of Democrats. Republicans polled at the end of July, however, were expressing a clear preference for Nixon on the ticket, and by August those administration officials most likely behind the at-

Senate	Holdovers	Reelected	New	Net Gain/Loss
Democrats	34	17	7	2
Republicans	33	8	6	-2

House	83rd Congress	84th Congress	Net Gain/Loss
Democrats	215	232	17
Republicans	219	203	-16

Governors	1954	1956	Net Gain/Loss
Democrats	27	29	+2
Republicans	21	19	-2

tempted palace coup were adamantly denying the existence of a "Dump Nixon" campaign.

A Landslide. The Stassen debacle proved to have little effect at the polling booth. Also, by the end of the year the increasingly volatile political climate in Eastern Europe had underscored the need for a strong military. Stevenson's response to defense issues — particularly his calls for a halt to nuclear testing and the draft — had made him extremely vulnerable to Republican criticism. By midnight of November 6, election day, it had become clear that Ike would win by a landslide, and the president began to turn surly while waiting for a Stevenson concession speech. Aides overheard their boss mutter, "What in the name of God is the monkey waiting for? Polishing his prose?" Eisenhower won by ten million votes, doubling the margin of his 1952 victory.

Sources:

"The Battle Stassen Started: A Blow-by-Blow Account," *U.S. News and World Report"* (3 August 1956): 36–46;

"What the Two Parties Stand for in 1956," *U.S. News and World Report*, 41 (17 August 1956): 37–38.

Senate	Holdovers	Reelected	New	Net Gain/Loss
Democrats	36	13	15	15
Republicans	26	8	-	-13

House	84th Congress	85th Congress	Net Gain/Loss
Democrats	235	283	48
Republicans	200	153	-48

Governors	1956	1958	Net Gain/Loss
Democrats	29	35	6
Republicans	19	14	-6

NATIONAL POLITICS: ELECTION 1958

Democrats Rebound. In the off-year elections of 1958 the voters handed the Republican party its worst political defeat in over twenty-five years. The congressional polls sent Democrats to Washington in droves, creating a new Congress in which Democrats would outnumber Republicans in both houses by nearly two to one. Results in the gubernatorial campaigns added to the Republicans' humiliation: the Democrats picked up six governor seats; the Republicans lost five.

Ike Criticized. Sensing voter discontent over unemployment and fear that America was losing the cold war, a revitalized Democratic party had launched a highly aggressive campaign that was not afraid to take on the White House. The issue of a "missile gap" — the belief, created by the 1957 launching of *Sputnik*, that the Soviets had better rockets and more of them — had damaged Eisenhower's approval ratings, which dropped below 60 percent. Ike was vulnerable to widespread criticism for the first time in his presidency, and Old Guard and Eisenhower Republicans alike found themselves on the defensive in an election year.

Attacking Republicans on the Domestic Front. The charge that Eisenhower had not been vigilant enough in protecting U.S. interests in the global arena allowed Democrats to accuse Ike of being out of touch with the domestic issues as well. Southern Democrats blamed the Republican administration for forced integration in the South. They cited Eisenhower's commitment of federal troops to Central High School in Little Rock — which had defied the court order to desegregate — as an example of Republican heavy-handedness. Democrats in industrial regions outside of the South rallied around labor, which had become increasingly politicized due to increasing rates of unemployment and the antiunion measures of the Taft-Hartley Act.

Republican Old Guard Purged. Despite the devastating election results for the Republican party, Eisenhower emerged from 1958 with a much stronger power base. The election had purged the GOP of many of the Old Guard who had strongly opposed much of the president's foreign policy. Furthermore, Ike had much in common with conservative southern Democrats, who now wielded considerable power in Congress. Both wanted a balanced budget, decreased defense spending, and no new social programs. The Republican arguably the most apprehensive about the GOP's political future was Nixon. The old guard had been his power base, and now that they had been swept away there were few friendly faces among moderate Republicans to which he could turn. He had hoped that succeeding Eisenhower would be easy business in 1960, but the conservative Republican political machine was in shambles.

Sources:

Richard C. Bain, *Convention Decision and Voting Records* (Washington, D.C.: Brookings Institution, 1960);

Paul T. David, Ralph M. Godman, and Richard C. Bain, *The Politics of National Conventions* (Washington, D.C.: Brookings Institution, 1960).

THE PRESS AND THE PRESIDENCY

White House–Press Relations. The relationship between the executive office and the White House press corps has always been more or less adversarial, as newshounds spar with administration officials who seek to control the flow of information from the White House. Prior to the 1950s, however, the White House held a clear advantage in its information battle with reporters. Presidents effectively managed the news by dictating to

President Harry S Truman at a 15 January 1951 press conference

reporters the kind of questions that could be asked — and how they could be asked. Furthermore, meetings between the press and the president often were called at the last minute and held in the Oval Office with newsmen gathered around the president's desk. The setting and the format highlighted the fact that any White House information gathering would be conducted on the president's turf in accordance with his ground rules. Much of this changed radically in the 1950s, and the way was paved for the modern era of White House press coverage.

Truman and the Press. In April 1950 Truman moved the press conferences from the Oval Office to the old State Department Indian Treaty Room. Reporters were seated ahead of time, would stand when Truman entered, then would once again take their seats. The president conducted a question-and-answer format by calling on reporters, who would identify themselves before asking their questions. These sessions were often much shorter than those held by Truman's predecessor, Franklin D. Roosevelt — often lasting less than fifteen minutes. Furthermore, whereas Roosevelt averaged two conferences a week, Truman only averaged one. During his second term, he gave the public limited access to the often feisty press conferences by allowing prerecorded excerpts of the meetings to be broadcast on radio.

Truman's Cool Relations with Reporters. Unlike Roosevelt, Truman did not attempt to woo the newspapers, and many of the changes he introduced to the press conference — such as dispensing with the chitchat, reducing the number of conferences held, and creating a more formal atmosphere — reflected the cool relations between him and the press corps. Answers to reporters' questions were often brusque and spiced with obscenities. He would shoot from the cuff in his exchanges with

newsmen, and his unrehearsed answers frequently landed him in trouble. When asked if the issue of Communist infiltration in government was a red herring used to distract public attention from more-pressing issues, Truman readily agreed; Republicans and columnists hostile to the administration responded by accusing Truman of being soft on communism. After having ordered the steel mills seized to avoid labor strife, Truman was asked if he could use the same presidential powers to nationalize the media. His reply, which suggested that he could and would if it were in the best interest of the country, touched off a firestorm of protest among reporters.

Truman Honesty. Despite Truman's abrupt and sometimes dismissive style with reporters (he did not hesitate to answer a question with "it's none of your business"), many newsmen later would recall the Truman-era press conferences with fondness. Truman rarely equivocated in his responses to the press, and the information that did flow out of the White House tended to be trustworthy. Although, unlike most past presidents, Truman did not cultivate friendships with reporters, he did allow exclusive interviews. *New York Times* correspondent Arthur Krock — who landed the first-ever presidential exclusive with Roosevelt — was the first to receive an exclusive interview with Truman. The interview got front-page attention in February 1950 and landed Krock a Pulitzer Prize. The *Times* had been highly critical of Truman, and in commenting on Krock's coup, columnist Doris Fleeson asserted that anyone "who can kick the President's teeth down his throat 364 days a year, then pull an exclusive interview from his bleeding mouth on the 365th, deserves a cheer." Truman dismissed any notion that the Krock interview signaled a thawing of relations between him and the press, but his willingness to talk to Krock did demonstrate the president's refusal to shy away from even the most hostile members of the press corps.

Eisenhower and the Press. Eisenhower and his press secretary James Haggerty instituted further changes in dealing with newsmen. Beginning in December 1954 reporters were allowed to quote the president directly. Furthermore, tapes of *all* news conferences were released for delayed radio broadcast — with Haggerty reserving the right to edit. In January 1955 Haggerty allowed television cameras into the press conferences. Although the meetings between Ike and the newsmen were not broadcast live — and Haggerty retained his editing privileges — for the first time the American people could hear and *see* the news-gathering process at work in the White House.

A Friend of Reporters. Unlike Truman, Eisenhower had friends in newspaper publishing, and in answering reporters' questions, he avoided the kind of heated exchanges that had characterized the Truman press conferences. Ike also did not share Truman's blunt style of reply. A typical Eisenhower answer at a press conference was often rambling and incoherent — the message often lost in the president's tortured syntax. His bumbling left many with the impression that their president was not particularly sharp and that he was ill informed on the issues. This, however, was far from the case. Ike was a veteran when it came to dealing with the press. As commander of the Allied forces during World War II, he understood the importance of communicating a sense that the war was going well without offering any tactical information. As president, he gave the same kind of evasive yet good-natured responses to tough questions. Prior to addressing reporters at a news conference held after the Soviets had launched *Sputnik,* Haggerty cautioned Ike not to take any questions regarding the "missile gap," the widely held perception that the Soviet Union was building more intercontinental ballistic missiles than the United States. Ike beamed at Haggerty and told his press secretary that if the question arose he would not duck; he would just confuse them. The question was asked, and Ike launched into a response that was somehow as reassuring to the American people as it was confusing and devoid of any meaning.

Source:
Carolyn Smith, *Presidential Press Conferences: A Critical Approach* (New York: Praeger, 1990).

SPENDING AND THE FEDERAL GOVERNMENT

The Growing Budget. Uncle Sam has never had trouble spending the taxpayers' money. By 1960 it had more money to spend than ever: the federal budget grew from $42.6 billion in 1950 to $92.1 billion in 1959. After World War II the government had sharply reduced its expenditures on defense from a wartime high of $83

WHAT DID GOVERNMENT WORKERS MAKE?

The article title "I Road Uncle Sam's Gravy Train" appeared in the 9 January 1954 issue of the *Saturday Evening Post* and shocked many average Americans: Thomas Drake Durrance confessed that as a government worker he lived the high life off the taxpayer's dollar. Prior to taking a government job, Durrance worked as an editor in Washington, D.C.; but, typical of young American urban couples of the 1950s, he could not afford a family car or a full-time maid. After he took a job with the U.S. Economic Co-operation Administration as a class-three foreign-service staff officer (an FSS-3) with the title of assistant economic commissioner, "luxury followed luxury in . . . dizzy succession." Foreign-service officers, Durrance discovered, "were participants in an unconscionable exploitation of the fellow taxpayers we left behind." His position paid $7,380 a year, plus extra tax-free allowances of $3,370, for a total income of $10,750. He had a nursemaid for his daughter, a cook, and a butler. He traveled first-class and stayed in the best hotels. Cars awaited whenever he or his family needed transportation. As Durrance observed, "never had so many taxpayers donated so much to maintain so few in a style to which they were so completely unaccustomed." Given such opulence, one wonders why students were not attracted to the federal government: a 1952 study published in the August 1954 issue of *Scientific Monthly* showed that of six hundred college seniors only 5.2 percent had selected the federal government as an employer. Science majors — at 4 percent — were the least likely to move into government service.

Sources: *Saturday Evening Post* (9 January 1954): 17+;
Scientific Monthly (August 1958).

---

billion in 1945 to $42.7 billion in 1946. By 1950 national defense spending — at $13.7 billion — only consumed approximately 35 percent of federal government outlays. Although defense spending soared again during the Korean conflict by more than 75 percent, it fell again by 1960 to less than 60 percent. Payments to individuals, which in later decades often meant welfare or social security, remained at roughly 30 percent of the government's outlays during the 1950s. The budget category "All Other" — which included spending on education, highways, and, toward the end of the decade, nonmilitary space projects — started at more than 10 percent and shrank to approximately 7 percent, with net interest making up the difference.

Although some foreign-service officials may have lived luxuriously, the big money was still being made in the private sector during the 1950s. Average 1955 salaries for government and corporate positions are compared below.

Cabinet Member $22,500	Company President $120,000
Bureau Head $14,800	Executive Vice-president $80,000
Budget Director $17,500	Comptroller $35,000
Division Head $12,030	Plant Manager $25,000
Engineer $9,360	Engineer $19,600
Junior Engineer $4,035	Junior Engineer $4,300
Lawyer $7,960	Lawyer $8,700
Payroll Clerk $3,700	Payroll Clerk $3,200
Typist $3,175	Typist $2,912
Duplicating-Machine Operator $2,800	Duplicating Machine Operator $2,600

"How Good is a Government Job?," *U.S. News & World Report* (8 July 1955): 50–51.

Capitol Hill Spending. As a percentage of the gross national product (GNP), defense fell from 14 percent in 1952 to 10 percent a decade later; payments to individuals grew from 3 to 5 percent; and all other gradually expanded to about 3 percent. When comparing U.S. expenditures in "transfers and subsidies" to those of other developed nations between 1955 and 1957, the United States lagged behind, ahead only of Japan. But U.S. spending as "consumption" — such as purchases of goods and services, including military hardware — led the world. Defense expenditures went from $13.2 billion in 1949 to $49 billion in 1959, while government funds used for "investment" hovered near the bottom. Clearly the United States paid a price for the military requirement to defend the free world during the cold war. Interest rates reached 5 percent in 1959, and prices during the 1950s soared to 124 percent of their 1949 high.

Government Workers. The rising federal budget in part reflected the cost of a growing federal payroll. During the 1950s workers in federal, state, and local government comprised nearly 38 percent of all service-oriented workers.

Source:
Henry R. Nau, *The Myth of America's Decline: Leading the World Economy into the 1990s* (New York: Oxford University Press, 1990).

SPENDING AT THE STATE AND LOCAL LEVELS

State Bureaucracy. Throughout his two terms as president, Eisenhower worked to curb the size of government. But an entirely separate layer of government bureaucracy had grown at the state and local levels. In 1950 only three states — New York, Pennsylvania, and California — had general revenues and borrowing over $1 billion; state governments' total revenue and borrowing exceeded $13 billion, with tax revenues topping $11.8 billion. By 1959 seven states exceeded $1 billion in revenues and borrowing, and California hit a whopping $3 billion in revenues. Even states traditionally considered "poor," such as Mississippi, took in more than $320 million. By 1960 general revenues and borrowing by the states exceeded $27 billion, of which taxes accounted for only $18 billion.

Local and State Spending. States dramatically increased their spending on highways over the decade, going from $567 million in 1950 to more than $7.3 billion in 1960. Expenditures on education soared; local funding of public secondary education in 1950 constituted 66 percent of all funding, while state and federal spending comprised 33 percent. A decade later local funding of public secondary education fell by 5 percent, and state and federal spending rose by 5 percent. In 1950 state spending on education and transfers for education totaled $2.8 billion; by 1959 it had risen to $8.1 billion.

State Borrowing Increases. State governments' debts grew as they increasingly borrowed to finance their activities. Borrowing accounted for approximately 10 percent of state funds in 1950, costing a total of $87 million in interest. By decade's end, borrowing had risen to nearly 30 percent, racking up interest payments of more than $2.5 billion. Some states, such as Montana, barely financed half their activities out of taxes. Others, such as Michigan, borrowed for only about 25 percent of their needs.

Source:

Henry R. Nau, *The Myth of America's Decline: Leading the World Economy into the 1990s* (New York: Oxford University Press, 1990).

HEADLINE MAKERS

DEAN ACHESON
1893-1971

U.S. SECRETARY OF STATE, 1949-1953

Controversial Secretary of State. Although considered one of the most successful architects of American foreign policy, Dean Acheson won many enemies by ignoring public opinion. Some blamed Acheson and his policy of Communist containment for American entry into the Korean War. Others such as Sen. Joseph McCarthy accused Acheson of being soft on communism for not having been vigilant enough in protecting U.S. interests in China. Acheson was often pressured by members of both political parties to resign. His Old World demeanor and English attire made him an easy target for those who thought him to be effete and out of touch.

Background. A protege of Felix Frankfurter at Harvard Law School, Acheson first worked in Washington as a law clerk for Supreme Court Justice Louis D. Brandeis. He subsequently became a partner and a leading figure in the powerful Washington lawfirm Covington and Burling. He entered government service during World War II, when he became assistant secretary of state with the responsibility to help manage the land-lease program, which provided $39 billion in aid to American allies. Under Harry S Truman, Acheson was promoted undersecretary of state in 1945 and then to secretary of state in 1949 suceeding George Marshall. He contributed heavily to both the Truman Doctrine and the Marshall Plan, which defined American foreign policy during the early years of the cold war.

Making Foreign Policy. Acheson saw the creation of economic blocs as the remedy for Soviet expansionism and worked to reindustrialize West Germany. Acheson devised the plans to integrate a rearmed Germany into the North Atlantic Treaty Organization. In Asia he sided with the French in Indochina and saw the split between the Russian and Chinese Communists as early as 1949. Acheson supported the removal of Gen. Douglas MacArthur as supreme commander in Korea, mainly because he wanted the resources going to the Far East to be diverted back to Europe. He continued to be a strong voice for a conservative, anti-Soviet foreign policy throughout the 1950s.

Hawkish Adviser. As an adviser to President John F. Kennedy, Acheson increasingly came to be viewed as a "hawk," advocating dealing with the Soviets through superior military and strategic strength. Overruled in his recommendation for a direct strike against the Soviet missiles placed in Cuba in October 1962, Acheson nevertheless argued forcefully for continued U.S. presence in Vietnam.

Source:
Douglas Brinkley, *Dean Acheson and the Making of U.S. Foreign Policy* (New York: St. Martin's Press, 1992).

DWIGHT D. EISENHOWER
1890-1969

PRESIDENT OF THE UNITED STATES, 1953-1961

Ike's Presidency Reconsidered. Dwight D. ("Ike") Eisenhower was once portrayed as a dull, somewhat lazy president; in a 1962 poll of historians he was ranked twenty-second of thirty-one presidents. In the minds of more-recent historians, however, Ike is considered to have been a shrewd, moderate, sensible, deeply patriotic man — and today is ranked often among the top ten of U.S. presidents. Eisenhower could campaign with Richard Nixon but distance himself from Nixon's partisan and often inflammatory rhetoric. Eisenhower, above all others, could warn of the threats posed by the "Military-Industrial Complex" at a time when the American public was responding favorably to calls for increased defense spending.

Role as President. His reputation as a do-nothing president in part was due to his belief in governmental noninterference in state and local politics. He did not believe that as president his role was to initiate social change. Instead, he believed his job was to represent the voice of reason in warning against federal spending sprees and peacefully ushering the United States through dangerous times. Faced with challenges from the Democrats to increase military spending after the Soviets launched *Sputnik*, Ike resisted. Criticized for not doing enough on civil rights, Eisenhower nevertheless remained determined to let the social movement follow its own natural course. (In one case, however, he did bring presidential dictum to bear on state matters by sending federal troops into Little Rock, Arkansas. He maintained that he did so to restore social order rather than to enforce a federal mandate.) Having inherited high price levels from Truman, Ike demanded and received budgets nearly in balance, and twice the administration even ran surpluses.

Government Continues to Grow. Yet despite his proclamation in 1950 that further growth of government was "a creeping paralysis" and a greater danger to freedom than the atomic bomb, government contined to grow during his years in office. Vast new bureaucracies such as the National Aeronautics and Space Administration were created. Ike signed legislation ensuring the expansion of federal power, such as the National Highway Act. Eisenhower presided over the creation of a new cabinet-level department, Health, Education, and Welfare. Although he publicly denounced the "Military-Industrial Complex" at the end of his second term, his foreign policies had entangled the United States in Vietnam (then called Indochina) and had permitted the Communist takeover of Cuba. He kept the United States out of Egypt during the Suez Crisis and out of Hungary in 1956, yet his perceived complacency about the new Soviet missile threat — which terrified most Americans — left him open to charges that he had allowed a "missile gap" to develop. Ironically, when Ike scored successes — by limiting government's role in shaping the economy, for example — they were credited to factors outside the White House.

Post-Eisenhower Era. After Ike's presidency, the federal bureaucracy, already primed to grow dramatically, exploded with the dual stimuli of the war on poverty and the war in Vietnam. Eisenhower died in 1969, at the peak of the Vietnam War, a conflict whose embers he had at least fanned a little.

Source:
Stephen E. Ambrose, *Eisenhower: The President* (New York: Simon & Schuster, 1984).

WILLIAM AVERELL HARRIMAN

1891-1986

NEW YORK GOVERNOR, 1954-1958

Truman Adviser. A longtime government administrator and ambassador to the Soviet Union from 1943 to 1946, Averell Harriman, along with Dean Acheson, supported the "peace-through-strength" approach to dealing with the Soviet Union as President Harry S Truman's special adviser in 1951 and 1952.

Background. Averell Harriman was born into one of the wealthiest families in America. His father had amassed a $100 million fortune in the railroad and shipping businesses and had founded one of the leading Wall Street investment houses. Educated at Groton and Yale, Harriman was an international businessman before he entered government in 1941 as President Franklin D. Roosevelt's special representative to oversee land-lease assistance to Great Britain. In 1943 he became the first U.S. ambassador to the Soviet Union. He was subsequently ambassador to Great Britain, secretary of commerce, and President Truman's special representative to oversee distribution of funds under the Marshall Plan. Harriman brought a wealth of international experience to the political arena.

Presidential Candidate and New York Governor. Harriman unsuccessfully challenged Adlai Stevenson for the 1952 Democratic presidential nomination. In 1954, however, he was elected governor of New York as a New Dealer. As governor, Harriman supported an antidiscrimination commission, a war on poverty, and consumer interests. In 1958 he lost a reelection bid to Republican Nelson Rockefeller. Although he never harbored any conviction that the United States could agree on all matters with the Soviets, Harriman did advocate negotiations to reduce armaments and nuclear weapons. He traveled to the Soviet Union in 1959 to meet with Nikita Khrushchev and other Soviet leaders. He returned to the United States advocating "competitive coexistence with the Soviets," believing the two countries could continue in their power struggle without much threat of war.

Source:
Rudy Abramson, *Spanning the Century: The Life of W. Averell Harriman, 1891–1986* (New York: Morrow, 1992).

ALGER HISS

1904–

ALLEGED SPY FOR THE SOVIET UNION

A Career in Government. To many, Alger Hiss is a symbol of cold-war tensions and anticommunism run amok in the late 1940s and 1950s. As a highly placed State Department official, who also had access to secret documents pertaining to American national security, Hiss had represented the United States in some of the most crucial meetings of the post–World War II era. He had accompanied President Franklin D. Roosevelt to the Yalta Conference in 1945; helped create the United Nations, serving as temporary secretary-general at the San Francisco Conference later that year; and served as principal adviser to the U.S. delegation to the United Nations.

Accused and Tried. On 3 August 1948 Whittaker Chambers, an editor at *Time* magazine and former Communist, appeared before the House Un-American Activities Committee (HUAC) and testified that in the 1930s he had been a part of a Communist cell that included several government officials — Hiss among them. Hiss denied the allegations and, after Chambers repeated his claims, sued Chambers for libel. During a pretrial hearing, the Hiss-Chambers affair took on more significant meaning when Chambers contradicted his HUAC testimony in claiming that the Communist cell had engaged in spying and that Hiss had stolen government documents. To substantiate his claims, Chambers handed five rolls of microfilm over to Rep. Richard Nixon, who headed the HUAC subcommittee in charge of the Chambers affair. The film came to be known as the "pumpkin papers" because Chambers had hidden it in a pumpkin on his farm; the microfilm, Chambers claimed, had been given to him by Hiss in 1938. Hiss was indicted for perjury — the statute of limitations having run out on treason — and in 1949 was tried twice, the first trial ending in a hung jury, the second in a conviction. Hiss entered prison on 22 March 1951 and served three years and eight months of a five-year sentence.

Aftermath of the Hiss-Chambers Affair. As a result of the affair, Chambers became a best-selling author (*Witness*, 1952) and respected conservative thinker. Nixon had proved a force for cleaning out Communists and had gained national attention as a hard-nosed congressional investigator and spear-carrier of the conservative movement. Hiss continued to protest his innocence into the 1990s, when Russian historians produced new evidence from the Soviet archives to show Hiss was not involved. But other historians immediately criticized the evidence as unreliable, and the controversy has raged on.

Source:
John Chabot Smith, *Alger Hiss, the True Story* (New York: Holt, Rinehart & Winston, 1976).

ESTES KEFAUVER

1903–1963

DEMOCRATIC VICE-PRESIDENTIAL CANDIDATE, 1956

Reputation as a Grassroots Campaigner and Antimob Crusader. As a candidate for the 1952 and 1956 Democratic presidential nominations, Estes Kefauver employed a grassroots style of campaigning that won the hearts of many who had grown tired of party-machine politics. The senator from Tennessee had won a national reputation as a political crusader in 1950–1951, when he headed up a Senate investigative committee on organized crime. In 1939 Kefauver easily won a House seat.

An Independent Thinker. Despite having been sent to Washington with the help of Tennessee's Democratic party machine, Kefauver soon established his independence as a political thinker. His voting pattern on issues of civil rights often ran counter to that of his southern colleagues. In 1942 he voted for anti–poll tax legislation (the poll tax being one method used by racist whites to keep poor blacks away from the voting booth), and in so doing he provoked the ire of Mississippi's fiery prosegregationist legislator, John Rankin, who pointed a finger at the Tennessean and shouted, "Shame on you, Estes Kefauver." Rankin's famous line would be used many times again on the House and Senate floors and in party conventions to denounce the man who was quickly gaining a reputation as a liberal southern Democrat.

The "Coonskin Crusade." Kefauver ran for the Senate in 1948 in what would prove to be one of the most exciting campaigns in Tennessee history. His candidacy was bitterly opposed by state party bosses, who used red-baiting tactics throughout the campaign to assail his voting record and label him "pink." Kefauver sought to emphasize his political independence, and he began traveling the state with a live raccoon to symbolize his connection with pre-party-machine frontier politics. The live raccoon was later replaced by a coonskin cap. The campaign gimmick was a stunning success and created something of a fad. He would address thousands of coonskin-cap-wearing supporters. Kefauver won a close election, and in so doing he dealt a crushing blow to the state party bosses.

The Kefauver Committee. Kefauver had become interested in the growth of organized crime when he served as the chairman of a House subcommittee charged with investigating a corrupt federal judge; and in January 1950 he introduced a resolution on the Senate floor calling for an investigation of organized crime. A Senate committee, with Kefauver as its chairman, was soon formed. Popularly known as the

Kefauver committee, the special body was given three responsibilities: (1) determine whether organized crime used interstate-commerce facilities to circumvent federal law; (2) investigate the "manner and extent" of such criminal operations; and (3) determine whether these corrupting influences were spreading. The committee's hearings were held in fourteen major U.S. cities and held the American public spellbound. The hearings in New York were televised, and many Americans sat glued to their television sets as the committee members grilled known hoodlums such as Frank Costello. Costello's testimony provided fascinating television imagery; to protect his identity, the gangster asked that his face not be shown, and instead the camera focused on his hands, which he increasingly wrung as the questions got tougher. The crime hearings also implicated many urban Democratic political bosses — an exposure of the dirtier side of politics that the bosses never forgot and for which Kefauver would later pay at the Democratic conventions.

Convention Losses. Kefauver went to both the 1952 and 1956 Democratic conventions with large numbers of delegates from states mostly outside of the South. His maverick style as a campaigner and a legislator, however, alienated him from too many in the party. Fellow southerners were by and large opposed to his candidacy due to his liberal-to-moderate stance on issues such as civil rights. Northern urban political bosses — who controlled the labor vote — had their score to settle with the Tennessean and worked hard to block his candidacy. In 1952 he was beaten out by Adlai Stevenson for the presidential nomination. In 1956 Stevenson's organizational strength forced Kefauver to relinquish his campaign during the primaries. At the convention, however, Kefauver managed to win a vice-presidential spot on the Stevenson ticket. Kefauver proved to be a tireless campaigner as Stevenson's running mate. Yet the incumbent team of Dwight D. Eisenhower and Richard M. Nixon was too strong and too popular for the Democrats. Kefauver returned to the Senate, where he continued to attract national attention for his refusal to join the Dixiecrats' anti-civil-rights voting bloc.

JOSEPH RAYMOND MCCARTHY

1909-1957

U.S. SENATOR, 1947-1957

Hunting Communists. Beginning with a speech in Wheeling, West Virginia, on 9 February 1950 in which he claimed to have a list containing the names of 205 known Communists in the U.S. State Department, Republican senator Joseph McCarthy of Wisconsin became synonymous with investigations of Communists. He took the Senate floor later that month to elaborate on his accusations. During his series of speeches to the Senate, McCarthy's numbers varied, ranging from 205 to 57 Communists. When challenged by majority leader Democratic senator Scott Lucas to "name them all," McCarthy responded that "it would be improper to make the names public until the appropriate Senate committee can meet in executive session and get them. . . . If we should label one man a Communist when he is not a Communist, I think it would be too bad." Critics labeled those comments window dressing: McCarthy, they argued, never had any evidence. Nevertheless, in making his claims McCarthy soon emerged as one of the most powerful — and most feared — men on Capitol Hill. He had touched a nerve in an American people already fearful of Communist aggression, and few politicians were willing to denounce McCarthy.

The Tydings and McCarran Committees. McCarthy's revelations, offered with the assistance of pugnacious Chief Counsel Roy Cohn, first resulted in a specially formed subcommittee headed by Democratic senator Millard Tydings of Maryland, wherein McCarthy accused Owen Lattimore, a consultant to the State Department and a Johns Hopkins University professor, of subversive ties and claimed that the Truman administration held evidence against Lattimore and others in its files. The Tydings committee report charged McCarthy with "fraud and hoax," claiming he had not produced the name of one Communist in the State Department. But the public apparently did not agree. Polls showed that more than 40 percent of the public believed McCarthy's allegations. A second committee, headed by Sen. Pat McCarran of Nevada, from 1951 to 1952 examined McCarthy's allegations. The committee claimed to find credibility in McCarthy's accusations and labeled Lattimore "a conscious, articulate instrument of the Soviet conspiracy." A stunned nation paid close attention as others such as Annie Lee Moss, an elderly black woman who handled coded messages in the Pentagon, were hauled in front of the committee to answer charges that they were card-carrying Reds.

The Permanent Investigations Subcommittee. An obscure senator prior to 1950, his political future in doubt, McCarthy had found a potent political weapon in anticommunism and won reelection in 1952; he became chairman of the Committee on Government Operations, a body in charge of investigating petty violations within the federal government. McCarthy, however, soon appointed himself head of the committee's Permanent Investigations Subcommittee, which held the power to subpoena, and opened inquiries into the Army Signal Corps at Fort Monmouth, New Jersey, after allegations of spying and sabotage there. A full-scale investigation ensued in 1954 in which the U.S. Army counsel Joseph Welch clashed with the senator on national television. The army maintained that McCarthy had sought preferential treatment for a staff member of his, G. David Schine, and McCarthy responded that the army used Schine to get him to call off his investigation. McCarthy's antics on national television turned the tide of public opinion against him, and a Senate committee condemned McCarthy for defiling the integrity of the Senate. McCarthy lost influence after 1954 and lost his committee chairmanship in 1956. He even charged that Dwight D. Eisenhower was guilty of continuing the "20 years of treason" started by the Roosevelt and Truman administrations — a charge that the popular Eisenhower quickly shook, but one that tainted McCarthy himself as lacking patriotism.

The End of the McCarthy Era. On 2 May 1957 McCarthy died of complications associated with alcoholism. Prior to his death McCarthy attempted to regain the national spotlight by proclaiming himself a champion of civil liberties. Few listened, however. He had gained a reputation for anticommunist excesses and witch-hunting, and for besmirching the character of hundreds of individuals. Subsequent committees did find that some individuals he had named as Communist indeed were, and that when examined, McCarthy's evidence stood up more than critics cared to admit. One historian of the Eisenhower era noted that McCarthy's "appeal was very much in the American mainstream" and "not a phenomenon at all." Above all, he left a legacy of controversy, and the term *McCarthyism* became synonymous with inquisitorial tactics.

Source:
William Bragg Ewald, Jr., *Who Killed Joe McCarthy?* (New York: Simon & Schuster, 1984).

RICHARD M. NIXON

1913-

VICE-PRESIDENT OF THE UNITED STATES, 1953–1961

Reputation as an Anticommunist Crusader. Nixon entered the national political spotlight in the late 1940s as the man most responsible for exposing Alger Hiss, a former State Department official and alleged Communist spy. Although Nixon was mostly moderate and internationalist in his political sentiments, the Hiss case made the young California congressman the darling of the Republican party's right wing. During the 1950s he capitalized on his reputation as a crusader against communism in his rise to the Senate and to the vice-presidency.

Role in the Hiss-Chambers Affair. In 1946 Nixon challenged Democratic representative Jerry Voorhis for his House seat. Nixon scored an upset victory over the five-term incumbent after having conducted a hard-hitting campaign in which he subjected Voorhis to red-baiting. As a Republican representative, Nixon served as chairman of the House Un-American Activities Committee, responsible for investigating charges made by Whittaker Chambers, a senior editor at *Time* magazine and a former Communist. In his testimony Chambers named former government official Alger Hiss as a member of the Communist party; Hiss maintained his innocence. But further Nixon-led investigations into Hiss's alleged involvement in the Communist party revealed that Hiss may have stolen government documents from the State Department. Hiss was convicted of perjury in 1950, and for his dogged pursuit of the alleged spy Nixon became a political star.

"Tricky Dick." In that year he returned to California and used his newfound political clout to launch a successful campaign against Democratic representative Helen Gahagan Douglas for a vacated Senate seat. Yet, despite Nixon's trouncing of Douglas at the polls, many were horrified by the mean-spiritedness and red-baiting that had characterized the Nixon campaign. The *Independent Review,* a California newspaper, dubbed him "Tricky Dick" — a nickname he never was able to shake during his political career.

A Respected Partisan. As a Republican senator, Nixon proved to be a tireless partisan in his attacks on the Truman administration and its policies. By the 1952 Republican convention he had become successful in creating for himself a solid power base among conservative Republicans and enjoyed the gratitude of the party brass for having campaigned and raised money for the Republican cause. He proved instrumental in helping deliver the nomination to Gen. Dwight D. Eisenhower and was at the top of Ike's list of potential running mates.

Vice-presidential Candidate. As the Republicans' vice-presidential candidate, Nixon mercilessly slashed at Democratic presidential candidate Adlai Stevenson. Nixon increasingly accepted the burden of having to perform the "dirty business" of making accusations and in so doing allowed Ike to take the political high road during the campaign. At one point Nixon's place on the Republican ticket was in doubt after newspapers revealed the existence of an eighteen-thousand-dollar fund allegedly set up for his personal use. Nixon acquitted himself in dramatic fashion by hitting the television airwaves to explain the fund and deliver an emotional defense of his actions.

A Valuable Vice-president. As vice-president, Nixon was kept well informed by Eisenhower and the president's men; Ike wanted to ensure a smooth transition if ever he had to hand over the reins of government to the number-two man. Furthermore, Eisenhower and his advisers understood that Nixon's experience and savvy as a legislator would serve as significant assets to a cabinet composed mainly of businessmen with little to no government experience. Nixon often was consulted by administration officials who wondered how to secure votes on the House and Senate floors, and the vice-president labored behind the scenes to whip up support for White House legislation. He also continued to take on tasks and issues that Ike would not touch: as a champion of civil rights, Nixon was recognized by black leaders as the White House official most sympathetic with their cause — and most instrumental in pushing through civil-rights legislation.

Relationship with Eisenhower. Nixon often did not see eye to eye with Eisenhower, especially concerning issues of foreign policy and defense. The vice-president nevertheless kept his objections to himself and publicly endeavored to play the role of team player. When Ike suffered a heart attack in 1955, Nixon scored high marks for conveying to the public a sense of leadership and the reassurance that the executive office would conduct business as usual in a time of crisis. Eisenhower often commented warmly on his vice-president's loyalty, yet he held misgivings about Nixon's ability to serve as a successful president. Ike feared that his young vice-president was too strident in his partisan attacks on the Democrats and too immature to preside over a superpower in dangerous times.

A Political Survivor. Prior to the 1956 presidential elections many pundits questioned Nixon's political future, and the vice-president had to survive a "Dump Nixon" campaign organized by some White House officials. By the end of the decade, however, Nixon had Ike's public support and endorsement for the 1960 presidential elections. The Republicans had taken a severe pounding in the 1958 congressional elections, however, and Nixon was forced to campaign as the nominee of a weakened and politically vulnerable party. After his bid for the presidency was defeated by John F. Kennedy, Nixon returned to California and worked to shore up his power base for another political campaign.

Source:
Stephen E. Ambrose, *Nixon: The Education of a Politician, 1913–1962* (New York: Simon & Schuster, 1987).

ADLAI EWING STEVENSON
1900-1965

DEMOCRATIC PRESIDENTIAL CANDIDATE, 1952, 1956

Democratic Presidential Hopeful. In the 1950s Adlai Stevenson came into the national limelight as a successful Illinois governor who battled the excesses of McCarthyism and as the Democratic heir apparent to President Harry S Truman.

Reluctant Candidate. The Democratic presidential candidate in 1952 and 1956, Stevenson ran campaigns that became famous for his eloquent stump speeches and for the candidate's emphasis on issue-oriented substance rather than on style and image. In early 1952 Truman asked Stevenson to run for the nomination, but Stevenson refused. Instead, he wanted to return to the governor's mansion in Illinois and finish the programs he had started. Despite his many statements that he did not want the presidential nomination, even with Truman's support, Stevenson was drafted on the third ballot.

Intellectual Campaigner. Often hailed as one of the most intellectual men ever to run for the presidency, Stevenson, according to one biographer, conducted a campaign that raised "American political thinking to a high plane." The majority of voters, however, seemed to find highbrow traits irrelevant in a candidate. Indeed, the more educated the voter, the less likely he was to have voted for Stevenson. High-school-educated voters favored Dwight D. Eisenhower 55 to 45 percent, while college-educated voters more overwhelmingly approved of the Republican candidate 66 to 34 percent. Part of Eisenhower's appeal may have been his war-hero reputation and folksy demeanor. The vote also indicated a partial rejection of Truman's foreign and domestic policies; Truman, in the eyes of the public, had gotten the United States into another war and did not appear to give the generals the authority to win it. When combined with a shaky domestic economic program, Stevenson's intellectual capabilities hardly mattered to the Middle American voter.

Working Toward Another Campaign. Undaunted, Stevenson concluded that he would get his turn in the White House in four more years, after Eisenhower discredited himself. Stevenson already had impressive foreign experience, having worked on the founding of the United Nations with the U.S. delegation under Edward Stettinius and having served as a troubleshooter for President Franklin D. Roosevelt and Gen. George C. Marshall from 1941 to 1947. Further enhancing his image as the world sophisticate, he embarked on a six-month trip to Asia and the Middle East in 1953 to bolster his foreign policy experience and to see firsthand the newly emerging nations. While on that trip, he recounted his experiences in articles written for *Look* magazine and in a book published in 1954, *Call to Greatness*. He then returned to America to build the party machinery that he thought would carry him to victory in 1956. During the 1954 congressional campaigns, he launched an attack on the Eisenhower administration, calling Vice-president Richard Nixon a "white-collar McCarthy." By 1955 Stevenson had announced his candidacy, and he won the 1956 Democratic nomination from Estes Kefauver. Stevenson called upon the convention to name the vice-presidential nominee. It gave him Kefauver.

The Rematch. In the rematch with Eisenhower, Stevenson tried to emphasize the importance of establishing nuclear-test bans — at times calling for a unilateral ban — and decreasing U.S.-Soviet tensions. He also campaigned for increased federal spending on poverty, education, and the elderly. After his defeat, he blamed the media for failing to cover the issues: but it had covered the issues that the public thought relevant, including a stronger defense against worldwide Soviet aggression and a tighter rein on federal government spending. Americans did not favor massive poverty relief programs; nor did most Americans see nuclear tests as a greater threat than Soviet expansionism.

Democratic Elder Statesman. Stevenson remained the voice of Democratic liberalism through most of the 1950s and, after the 1956 election, traveled and rejuvenated his legal work. Under the Kennedy administration, Stevenson served as ambassador to the United Nations. He would later advise President Lyndon B. Johnson.

Source:
Porter McKeever, *Adlai Stevenson: His Life and Legacy* (New York: Morrow, 1989).

ROBERT ALPHONSO TAFT
1889-1953

U.S. SENATOR

Emerging as Leader of Republican Conservatives. The son of twenty-seventh U.S. president William Howard Taft, Robert A. Taft entered the political arena as assistant general counsel to food administrator Herbert Hoover during World War I. In 1938 he was elected to the Senate from Ohio, running on an anti–New Deal platform. After the end of World War II Taft emerged as a leader of a Republican conservative wing that opposed prounion legislation and spearheaded efforts to lower top tax rates. Yet despite his immense power on Capitol Hill, he failed in his 1952 bid against Dwight D. Eisenhower for the Republican presidential nomination.

Championing Isolationism. "Mr. Republican," as he was called, was often at loggerheads with the Truman administration over the proper response to the Soviet threat. He opposed, for example, overseas military commitments, arguing that the United States was better off relying on nuclear power to deter the Soviets and that U.S. defense policy should first concern itself with the defense of home soil. During the Korean War Taft continued to criticize interventionist foreign policy. He later lead the opposition against strategies of containment that Eisenhower largely inherited from Truman; Taft consistently questioned the wisdom and cost of deploying American troops in Europe.

Seeking the Republican Nomination. In 1940 and in 1944 Taft's name emerged as a potential Republican nominee. In 1948 Taft fell short of gaining his party's support when liberal eastern Republican Thomas Dewey of New York won the nomination on the third ballot. In 1950 Taft began gearing up for the 1952 nomination and joined Sen. Joseph McCarthy in claiming that Truman "lost" China and in charging that Communists had infiltrated the U.S. State Department. Yet again Taft's bid for the Republican nomination was foiled as Dewey and Henry Cabot Lodge, Jr., threw their support behind Gen. Dwight D. ("Ike") Eisenhower, the internationalist-minded war hero with broad voter appeal.

Taft's Failings as a Candidate. Taft the candidate was the victim of his own drab personality. He lacked the polished oratorical skills of many of the younger Republican party lions such as Richard Nixon, and he failed to generate much real passion among the voters; nor was it possible for him to capture the nomination from inside the Republican political machine without the support of the eastern establishment. At the convention, when it was clear he would lose to General Eisenhower, Taft retreated in silence.

Taft Becomes a White House Ally. Weeks later Eisenhower's forces found that they desperately needed Taft's political clout and resources in the election, and Ike met with him at Morningside Heights in New York City. The two men struck a deal: in return for the Ohio senator's support both in the election and in training the White House staff afterward, Eisenhower would cut spending and stand firm against government expansion, issues that Ike was inclined to support anyway. Despite continued foreign-policy debate, Taft and the new president got along well, and the senator even attempted to temper the outbreaks of McCarthy. In July 1953 Robert Taft died of a brain hemorrhage resulting from cancer. Eisenhower lost a valuable ally on Capitol Hill, and the American conservative movement lost one of its primary voices.

Source:
James T. Patterson, *Mr. Republican: A Biography of Robert A. Taft* (Boston: Houghton Mifflin, 1972).

PEOPLE IN THE NEWS

On 21 January 1950 **Whittaker Chambers**, former editor of *Time* magazine, told reporters, "my work is now finished. . . . I have told the FBI all I know," after a federal jury in New York found Alger Hiss, a former State Department official whom Chambers had accused of spying for the Communist underground, guilty of perjury.

On 27 April 1955 Gen. **J. Lawton Collins**, special envoi to Vietnam, said the United States faced a "strange" and "almost an inexplicable situation" in trying to fight communism in Asia.

On 24 September 1957 Texas governor **Price Daniel** criticized the use of federal troops to integrate Little Rock Central High School, calling the action "reminiscent of the tactics of Reconstruction days."

On 16 February 1955 U.S. Secretary of State **John Foster Dulles** assured the exiled Nationalist Chinese government in Formosa that it would "not be forcibly taken over by the Communists" of mainland China.

In a 13 February 1950 speech Gen. **Dwight D. Eisenhower** said that the increasing size and power of the federal government was a "creeping paralysis" and a greater danger to freedom than the atomic bomb.

On 17 June 1953 President **Dwight D. Eisenhower** called the Tennessee Valley Authority an example of "creeping socialism."

On 24 September 1957, as he dispatched federal troops to Little Rock, Arkansas, to prevent interference with court-ordered integration efforts there, President **Dwight D. Eisenhower** said that "under the leadership of demagogic extremists, disorderly mobs had deliberately prevented the carrying-out of proper orders from a federal court."

On 18 March 1959 President **Dwight D. Eisenhower** pledged a reduction in taxes as part of a plan to boost an economic recovery.

On 16 February 1959 Democratic senator and presidential candidate **John F. Kennedy** of Massachusetts, in order to quell fears that the Vatican might influence White House decision making if he were elected the country's first Roman Catholic president, announced

his opposition to church-state ties, an American ambassador to the Vatican, and federal funding of parochial schools.

On 12 February 1959 Democratic senator **Michael J. Mansfield** of Montana proposed that East and West Germany use United Nations secretary-general Dag Hammarskjöld as a mediator to help settle their differences.

On 6 January 1950 Democratic senator **Pat McCarran** of Nevada criticized the Truman administration for lacking a policy that would help Europeans displaced by World War II and protect them from becoming "ready recruits in subversive organizations in Europe."

On 24 September 1957 Vice-president **Richard Nixon**, referring to Arkansas governor Orval Faubus's decision to call out the state militia to prohibit black students from entering Central High School in Little Rock, noted that Faubus "actually tended to invite violence [and the governor] should have used the Guard not to keep Negro children from going to school but to see that they were able to go."

On 1 August 1959 Vice-president **Richard Nixon** went on Moscow radio and television to warn the Soviet people that in promoting the spread of communism throughout the world they would extend the "era of fear, suspicion, and tension."

In 1951 McCarthy critic and political columnist **Drew Pearson** sued Sen. Joseph McCarthy for bodily injury following a fight between the two men at a Washington dinner party. McCarthy had slapped Pearson and kneed him in the groin.

On 18 August 1958 Rear Adm. **Hyman G. Rickover** received a gold medal from Congress for his part in successfully "directing the development and reconstruction of the world's first nuclear powered ships."

On 1 June 1950 seven liberal Republican senators, led by **Margaret Chase Smith** of Maine, the Senate's only woman, issued a "Declaration of Conscience," denouncing McCarthy's tactics.

On 1 November 1958 former Democratic presidential nominee **Adlai Stevenson** claimed that under the Eisenhower administration the world had become "more dangerous."

On 5 June 1950 Georgia governor **Herman Talmadge** pledged, "as long as I am Governor, Negroes will not be admitted to white schools."

On 27 December 1952 President **Harry S Truman** told reporters that Gen. Douglas MacArthur "wanted to involve [the United States] in an all-out war in the Far East."

On 19 February 1958 former president **Harry S Truman** accused the Eisenhower administration of ruining the national economy and leading the country to the brink of another depression.

On 6 February 1950 Democratic senator **Millard Tydings** of Maryland, chairman of the Armed Services Committee, appealed to President Harry S Truman to "end the world's nightmare of fear" by calling a world conference to outlaw all weapons "stronger than a rifle."

In a 7 September 1952 article appearing in *This Week*, former vice-president **Henry A. Wallace** conceded that he had been soft on communism prior to 1949, when he had become convinced that the Soviets "wanted the Cold War continued indefinitely, even at the peril of accidently provoking a hot war."

On 13 May 1958 **Roy Wilkins**, executive secretary of the National Association for the Advancement of Colored People (NAACP), suggested that President Eisenhower had failed to give "leadership and heart" to civil rights forces when the president suggested that blacks have "patience and forebearance" in their campaign for equal rights.

DEATHS

Ralph Henry Ackerman, 64, U.S. ambassador to the Dominican Republic (1948–1952), 12 January 1957.

Warren R. Austin, 78, U.S. Ambasador to the United Nations (1946–1954) October 1956.

William Augustus Ayres, 84, congressman (D.) from Kansas (1915–1921, 1923–1935), and member of Federal Trade Commission (1934–1951), 17 February 1952.

Robert M. Barnett, 57, U.S. government personnel expert and liaison officer with the International Labor Organization, 1 January 1953.

Roy Hood Beeler, 72, Tennessee attorney general since 1932, 23 September 1954.

Charles Wayland Brooks, 59, U.S. senator from Illinois (R) from 1939 –1948, 14 January 1957.

Joseph R. Bryson, 60, congressman (D) from South Carolina, 10 March 1953.

William Thomas Byrne, 75, congressman (D.) from New York (1935–1951), 27 January 1952.

David D. Caldwell, 83, special assistant to the U.S. attorney general, specialist in government procedure, 4 March 1953.

Ralph Henry Cameron, 89, U.S. senator (R) from Arizona (1921–1927) and leader in Arizona's drive for statehood while a territorial delegate, 12 February 1953.

Raymond J. Cannon, 60, congressman (D.) from Wisconsin (1932–1938), 25 November 1951.

Virgil M. Chapman, 55, senator (D.) from Kentucky (1948–1951), 8 March 1951.

Dr. Philander P. Claxton, 94, U.S. commissioner of education (1911–1921), founder of the University of Tennessee department of education, 12 January 1957.

Edward Eugene Cox, 72, congressman (D.) from Georgia (1925–1951), 24 December 1952.

John William Davis, 81, Democratic presidential nominee in 1924 and ambassador to Britain (1918–1921), 24 March 1955.

Gen. Charles Gates Dawes, vice-president under Calvin Coolidge, and winner of 1925 Nobel Peace Prize, 23 April 1951.

John J. Dempsey, 78, representative (D) from New Mexico and former under secretary of the Interior (1941–1942), 11 March 1958.

Martin Patrick Durkin, 61, secretary of labor (1953) and president of the United Assodiation of Plumbers and Steamfitters, AFL, 13 November 1955.

Charles A. Eaton, 84, representative (R) from New Jersey (1925–1953), 23 January 1953.

Robert B. Ennis, 71, Maryland State Central Committee chairman (D), 18 February 1953.

Frank Fellows, 61, congressman (R.) from Maine (1941–1951), 27 August 1951.

Judge Jerome N. Frank, 67, judge of U.S. Second Circuit Court of Appeals (1941–1957); Securities and Exchange Commission chairman (1939–1941), 13 January 1957.

Sen. Perer Goelet Gerry, 78, congressman (D) for twenty-six years from Rhode Island and grandson of Elbridge Gerry, 31 October 1957.

Dwight H. Green, 61, governor (R) of Illinois (1940–1948) and federal prosecutor who sent Al Capone to jail in 1931, 20 February 1958.

Alexander J. Groesbeck, 79, governor of Michigan (R) from 1921–1927, 10 March 1953.

Chalmers Hamill, 70, former head of the Justice Department's Small Business Unit, 4 November 1954.

Leland Harrison, 68, minister to Switzerland (1937–1947), and assistant secretary of State (1922–1927), 7 June 1951.

Charles Belknap Henderson, 81, member of the Reconstruction Finance Corporation and chairman (1941–1947); U.S. senator from Nevada (D), 1918–1921, 8 November 1954.

Samuel Francis Hobbs, 64, congressman (D.) from Alabama (1935–1951), 31 May 1952.

Rush Drew Holt, 49, Senator (D) from West Virginia (1935–1940), 8 February 1955.

Lansing W. Hoyt, 69, Republican party leader who backed Gen. Douglas MacArthur for president in 1944, 1948, and 1952, 12 January 1954.

Edward Eyre Hunt, 67, chief of U.S. State Department Protective Services Division since 1947, 5 March 1953.

Harold LeClaire Ickes, 77, secretary of the interior (1933–1946), 3 February 1952.

Pete Jarman, 62, ambassador to Australia (1949–1953) and congressman (D) from Alabama (1937–1949), 17 February 1955.

Adm. C. Turner Joy, 61, chief negotiator for the United Nations in Korea, 6 June 1956.

John Kee, 77 congressman (D.) from West Virginia (1933–1951), 8 May 1951.

Frank B. Keefe, 64, congressman (R). from Wisconsin (1938–1950), 5 February 1952.

Harley M. Kilgore, 63, chairman of the senate judiciary committee and three-term congressman (D) from West Virginia, 28 February 1954.

Isabella Greenway King, 67, congressman (D) from Arizona (1933–1936), 18 December 1953.

Richard Miflin Kleeberg, Sr., 67, congressman (R) from Alabama (1937–1949), 17 February 1955.

George S. Long, 74, representative (D) from Louisiana and brother of Huey P. Long, 22 March 1958.

Francis Patrick Matthews, 65, secretary of the navy (1949–1951), and ambassador to Ireland, 18 October 1952.

Joseph Raymond McCarthy, 48, senator (R) from Wisconsin, 2 May 1957.

John McDowell, 55, representative (R) from Pennsylvania who instigated House Un-American Activities Committee investigation of Alger Hill, 11 December 1957.

Joseph V. McGee, 66, acting mayor of New York in 1932 while James J. Walker was being investigated, 28 January 1956.

Kenneth McKellar, 88, forty-one-year representative (D) of Tennessee in Congress, 25 October 1957.

John F. Montgomery, 76, U.S. minister to Hungary (1933–1941), 7 November 1954.

Harold B. Murchie, 64, Chief Justice of the Maine Supreme Court, 7 March 1953.

William Henry "Alfalfa Bill" Murray, 86, 1932 presidential contender, 15 October 1956.

Mathew M. Neely, 83, Senator (D) from West Virginia who charged that President Eisenhower began going to church only after his election, 18 January 1958.

David K. Niles, 62, special administrative assistant to presidents Franklin D. Roosevelt and Harry S. Truman, 28 September 1952.

Gilbert Mason Oweltt, 64, state senator and powerful force in Pennsylvania politics, 24 January 1957.

Paul L. Patterson, governor (R) of Oregon, 31 January 1956.

Thomas Wharton Phillips, Jr., 81, representative (R) from Pennsylvania (1923–1927), 2 January 1956.

Chauncey W. Reed, congressman from Illinois for thirty-two years and ranking Republican on the House Judiciary Committee, 20 February 1956.

David Aiken Reed, 72, U.S. senator (R) from Pennsylvania (1922–1935), former chairman of the Senate Military Affairs Committee, 10 February 1953.

Adolph Joachim Sabath, 86, congressman (D) from Illinois (1907–1952), 6 November 1952.

Bertrand Snell, 87, representative (R) from New York (1931–1938) and former minority leader of the house, 2 February 1958.

Paulina Longworth Sturm, 31, granddaughter of President Theodore Roosevelt known as the "St. Valentine

Baby" of Alice Roosevelt and Ohio congressman Nicholas Longworth, 27 January 1957.

Robert A. Taft, 63, senator (R) from Ohio (1939–1953) and Republican presidential nominee in 1948 and 1952, 31 July 1953.

Elbert D. Thomas, 69, U.S. high commissioner for ninety-six groups of United Nations trust territory islands in the Pacific, and U.S. senator (D) from Utah (1932–1950), 11 February 1953.

William D. Upshaw, 86, congressman (D) from Georgia (1919–1927 and Prohibition Party presidential candidate in 1932, 21 November 1952.

Arthur T. Vanderbilt, 68, New Jersey political activist (R) before he was appointed to United States Supreme Court in 1948, 24 June 1957.

George Wadsworth, 64, advisor to Presidents Roosevelt, Truman, and Eisenhower on the Middle East, 5 March 1958.

Kenneth S. Wherry, 59, senator (R.), from Nebraska (1943–), 29 November 1951.

Roy O. Woodruff, 76, congressman (R) from Michigan (1913–1915, 1921–1952), 12 February 1953.

PUBLICATIONS

Max Beloff, *The American Federal Government* (New York: Oxford University Press, 1959);

Ralph Barton Berry, *The Citizen Decides: A Guide to Responsible Thinking in Time of Crisis* (Bloomington: Indiana University Press, 1951);

Daniel J. Boorstin, *The Genius of American Politics* Chicago: University of Chicago Press, 1953);

Chester Bowles, *American Politics in a Revolutionary World* (Cambridge, Mass.: Harvard University Press, 1956);

Franklin L. Burdette, *Readings for Republicans (New York: Oceana, 1960);*

Noel fairchild Busch, *Adlai E. Stevenson of Illinois: A Portrait* (New York: Farrar, Straus & Young, 1952);

Marquis William Childs, *Eisenhower for President? or, Who Will Get Us Out of the Mess We Are In? (New York: Exposition Press, 1951);*

Horace Coon, *Triumph of the Eggheads* (New York: Random House, 1955);

Elmer Holmes Davis, *But We Were Born Free* (Indianapolis: Bobbs-Merrill, 1954);

Robert J. Donovan, *Eisenhower: The Inside Story* (New York: Harper, 1956);

John Foster Dulles, *War or Peace* (New York: Macmillan, 1950);

Arthur Alphonse Ekich, *The Decline of American Liberalism* (New York: Longmans, Green, 1955);

Milton Friedman and Rose Friedman, *Capitalism and Freedom* (Chicago: University of Chicago Press, 1962);

Lawrence H. Fuchs, *The Political Behaviour of American Jews* (Glencoe, Ill.: Free Press, 1956);

John Gunther, *Eisenhower, the Man and the Symbol* (New York: Harper, 1952);

Louis Harris, *Is There a Republican Majority? Political Trends, 1952–1956* (New York: Harper, 1954);

Gordon A. Harrison, *The Road to the Right: The Tradition and Hope of American Conservatism* (New York: William Morrow, 1954);

Louis Hartz, *The Liberal Tradition in America* (New York: Harcourt, Brace & World, 1955);

Quincy Home and Arthur Schlesinger, *Guide to Politics, 1954* (New York: Dial Press, 1954);

Marinn Doris Irish, *The Politics of American Democracy* (Englewood Cliffs, N.J.: Prentice-Hall, 1959);

Walter Johnson, *How We Drafted Stevenson* (New York: Knopf, 1955);

James Keogh, *This Is Nixon* (New York: Putnam's, 1956);

Russell Kirk, *The Conservative Mind* (Chicago: H. Regnery, 1953);

Arthur Larson, *A Republican Looks at His Party* (New York: Harper, 1956);

David Low, *The Fearful Fifties: A History of the Decade* (New York: Simon & Schuster, 1960);

Samuel Lubell, *Revolt of the Moderates* (New York: Harper, 1956);

Clarence Manion, *The Key to Peace: A Formula for the Perpetuation of Real Americanism* (Chicago: Heritage Foundation, 1950);

John Bartlow Martin, *Adlai Stevenson* (New York: Harper, 1952);

Martin Merson, *Private Diary of a Public Servant* (New York: Macmillan, 1955);

Raymond Moley, *How to Keep Our Liberty: A Program for Political Action* (New York: Knopf, 1952);

Judah Nadich, *Eisenhower and the Jews* (New York, 1953);

Merlo John Pusey, *Eisenhower the President* (New York: Macmillan, 1956);

Benjamin F. Reading, *Democracy Can Succeed — How?* (New York: Parthenon Press, 1956);

Edward Reed, ed. *Readings for Democrats* (New York: Oceana, 1960);

Clinton Lawrence Rossiter, *Conservatism in America* (New York: Knopf, 1955);

Marty Snyder, *My Friend Ike* (New York: F. Fell, 1956);

Adlai E. Stevenson, *The New America* (New York: Harper, 1957);

Stevenson, *What I Think* (New York: Harper, 1956);

Ralph de Toledano, *Nixon* (New York: Holt, 1956);

Arthur Bernon Tourtellot, *An Anatomy of American Politics: Innovation versus Conservatism* (Indianapolis: Bobbs-Merrill, 1950);

Francis Graham Wilson, *The Case for Conservatism* (Seattle: University of Wahington Press, 1951).

Commentary, periodical;

Congressional Quarterly Service weekly report, periodical;

Foreign Affairs, periodical;

Nation, periodical;

National Review, periodical founded in 1955;

New Republic, periodical.

CHAPTER SEVEN

LAW AND JUSTICE

by ROBERT DEEB
and
CHARLES D. BROWER

CONTENTS

Sidebars and tables are listed in italics.

1950

- The Court also rules that once a state university admits a black student, the school cannot deny that student access to any of its facilities.

- The Federal Bureau of Investigation releases its first Ten Most Wanted list.

20 Feb. The Supreme Court upholds the legality of warrantless searches of a lawfully arrested person and the immediate premises where the arrest occurred.

10 Apr. The Supreme Court upholds the convictions of Hollywood Ten screenwriters John Howard Lawson and Dalton Trumbo for contempt of Congress.

24 Apr. The Supreme Court reverses a criminal conviction based on an indictment by a grand jury that excluded blacks.

8 May The Supreme Court upholds provisions of the Taft-Hartley Labor Act which deny unions access to the National Labor Relations Board if their officers refuse to swear they are not affiliated with the Communist party.

26 May The first meeting of the U.S. Senate Special Committee to Investigate Organized Crime in Interstate Commerce (the Kefauver committee) is held in Miami, Florida.

5 June The Supreme Court unanimously holds that a state may not bar a black admission to its law school despite a "black" law school being available.

23 Sept. Congress overrides President Harry S Truman's veto of the Internal Security Act of 1950.

1951

- President Truman issues Executive Order 10241, which provides that an employee may be dismissed if an employer doubts his or her loyalty to the government.

15 Jan. The Supreme Court finds a New York City ordinance barring worship services on public streets without a permit unconstitutional.

26 Feb. The Twenty-second Amendment to the Constitution is adopted, limiting presidential tenure to two terms.

8 Mar. Martha Beck and Raymond Fernandez, the Lonely Hearts Killers, are executed for three murders; they likely committed seventeen more.

29 Mar. Julius and Ethel Rosenberg are convicted of violating the Espionage Act of 1917 by passing atomic secrets to the Soviet Union.

4 June The Supreme Court finds that restraints on speeches advocating the forceful overthrow of the government do not abridge First Amendment rights. It also finds that a law demanding that public employees take a loyalty oath is not unconstitutional.

1952

- The police force of Milwaukee, Wisconsin, becomes the first to recruit and train officers using the cadet system.

2 Jan. The Supreme Court finds that police officers' use of a stomach pump on an unconsenting suspect to extract evidence of drugs violates Fourth Amendment protection against unreasonable search and seizure.

28 Feb.   The Kefauver committee releases a report on its findings on organized crime.

26 May   The Supreme Court overturns a lower court's ban of the film The Miracle, thus establishing that movies are a constitutionally protected form of expression.

2 June   The Supreme Court affirms a district court injunction preventing President Truman from seizing the nation's steel mills.

12 Nov.   An all-white jury in North Carolina convicts a black man of assault for leering at a white woman seventy-five feet away.

1953

4 May   The Supreme Court finds that Texas's Jaybird party primary excluded African-Americans, violating the Fifteenth Amendment's guarantee of voting rights to all citizens regardless of race.

19 June   The Rosenbergs are executed after the Supreme Court lifts a stay of execution.

25 Aug.   The American Bar Association adopts a resolution to oust Communists from the legal profession.

8 Sept.   Chief Justice of the United States Fred Vinson dies of a heart attack.

30 Sept.   Earl Warren is appointed chief justice of the United States.

1954

3 May   The Supreme Court rules that the systematic exclusion of Mexican Americans from jury duty in Texas violates the Fourteenth Amendment.

17 May   The Supreme Court rules that separate public schools for white and black students violate the equal protection clause of the Fourteenth Amendment, expressly overruling the "separate but equal" doctrine as applied to public schools. The Court rules that the congressionally segregated public school system of the District of Columbia violates the Fifth Amendment's due process guarantee of personal liberty.

14 June   President Dwight D. Eisenhower signs a bill amending the pledge of allegiance to include the words "under God" after "one nation."

24 Aug.   President Eisenhower signs the Communist Control Act, effectively outlawing the Communist party.

1955

28 Mar.   John Marshall Harlan is sworn in as an associate justice to the Supreme Court.

31 May   The Supreme Court relegates school desegregation to the supervision of the federal district courts, stipulating that local school officials must proceed toward desegregation "with all deliberate speed."

3 June   Convicted murderer Barbara Graham is executed; in 1958 her story is made into the movie I Want to Live! starring Susan Hayward.

1956

23 June	The U.S. Court of Appeals upholds the natural right of all citizens to travel abroad, ruling that the State Department could not refuse a citizen a passport without due process.
23 Sept.	In Mississippi Roy Bryant and J. W. Milam are acquitted by an all-male, all-white jury of murdering fourteen-year-old Emmett Till, an African-American who allegedly propositioned Bryant's wife; the two later confess to the murder.
1 Nov.	John Gilbert Graham, in an attempt to collect on his mother's life-insurance policy, places a bomb in the airplane she is boarding; the resulting explosion kills her and forty-three others.
7 Nov.	The Supreme Court rules that a civilian cannot be tried by court martial for crimes he committed while in the service.

1957

12 Jan.	The FBI announces that it has arrested six men in the Brinks robbery.
5 Apr.	New York labor columnist Victor Riesel is blinded when acid is thrown in his face by thugs allegedly acting on the wishes of Teamsters Union vice-president Jimmy Hoffa.
26 Apr.	The Supreme Court rules that a defendant should not be denied the right to a transcript of his trial because he could not afford to pay for it, affirming that laws and rights should apply equally to rich and poor.
11 June	The Supreme Court rules that only federal employees in sensitive jobs could be dismissed as security risks.
7 Sept.	Supreme Court Justice Sherman Minton announces his retirement due to poor health.
29 Sept.	President Eisenhower names William J. Brennan, Jr., as Minton's replacement on the Supreme Court.
13 Nov.	The Supreme Court rules that an Alabama law and a Montgomery, Alabama, ordinance requiring racial segregation on interstate buses are unconstitutional.

22 Jan.	Police in Waterbury, Connecticut, arrest George Metesky, the "Mad Bomber" who had left more than thirty bombs around New York City over sixteen years.
26 Feb.	A Senate committee investigating labor racketeering hears testimony linking the Teamsters Union to racketeers in Portland, Oregon.
2 Mar.	Judge Charles E. Whittaker of Missouri is nominated to the Supreme Court by President Eisenhower to replace retiring justice Stanley Reed.
17 June	"Red Monday." The Supreme Court holds that prosecutions of persons under the Smith Act for advocating the violent overthrow of the government must be based on more than accusations. The Court overturns the conviction of a union official for contempt of Congress after the official refused to answer questions about acquaintances' associations with the Communist party.
24 June	The Supreme Court finds that obscene material is not protected by the First Amendment guarantees of freedom of speech and the press.

29 Aug.	Congress passes the Civil Rights Act of 1957, which provides penalties for the violation of voting rights and creates the Civil Rights Commission.
November	Mass murderer Ed Gein, whose exploits inspired the movies *Psycho* and *The Texas Chainsaw Massacre*, is arrested in Plainfield, Wisconsin.

1958

Mar.	Nathan Leopold is paroled thirty-four years after he and Richard Loeb kidnapped and murdered fourteen-year-old Bobby Franks.
31 Mar.	The Supreme Court declares a statute unconstitutional which deprives a native-born American of his citizenship for deserting the armed forces. The Court upholds the right of federal courts to punish criminal contempt without a jury trial.
4 Apr.	Cheryl Crane, the fourteen-year-old daughter of actress Lana Turner, stabs Turner's husband, gangster Johnny Stompanato, after she overhears Stompanato threaten her mother; the killing is ruled "justifiable homicide."
30 June	The Supreme Court rules that a state order requiring the NAACP to produce its membership lists is a violation of the First Amendment rights to freedom of speech and assembly.
25 Aug.	Chief Justice Warren calls a special session of the Supreme Court to rule on the integration of Central High School in Little Rock, Arkansas.
4 Sept.	The Department of Justice invokes the powers of the 1957 Civil Rights Act for the first time to stop alleged violations of African-Americans' voting rights in Terrell County, Georgia.
12 Sept.	The Supreme Court denounces Arkansas officials for delaying desegregation mandates.
29 Sept.	Gov. James Folsom of Alabama commutes to life imprisonment the death sentence against an African-American man convicted of robbing a woman of less than two dollars.
7 Oct.	President Eisenhower appoints Judge Potter Stewart to replace retiring Supreme Court Justice Harold Burton.

1959

•	The Supreme Court rules that state and federal governments can each prosecute a criminal for the same crime.
2 Jan.	The Teamsters Union announces that it is abandoning plans to organize the New York City police force.
25 June	Nineteen-year-old Charles Starkweather is electrocuted for the eleven murders he and Caril Ann Fugate committed during a week-long murder spree.
20 July	Federal judge Frederick van Pelt Bryan overrules the postmaster general's ban on D. H. Lawrence's *Lady Chatterley's Lover*.
18 Sept.	Teamsters president Jimmy Hoffa is ordered by the Department of Labor to remove all union officials with criminal records.
8 Nov.	Undercover detectives disguised as beatniks arrest more than one hundred people in narcotics raids in New York City.

OVERVIEW

"A Wave of Crime." Crime was on the minds of Americans during the 1950s. They watched it on television nightly; it was fictionalized on *The Untouchables*, for example, which told weekly stories of the battles between government agents and gangsters; and real accounts were broadcast of the hearings during the U.S. Senate's Kefauver committee investigating organized crime, which was almost as exciting as an episode of *The Untouchables*. Americans read daily in their newspapers of escalating crime which was witnessed on the streets.

Statistics. A six-part series titled "Crime in the United States" in *Life* magazine began, "The nation in the fall of 1957 appears to be threatened by a catastrophic wave of crime." The statistics seemed to tell the story: in 1957 the Federal Bureau of Investigation reported an all-time high level of major crimes for the previous year, up more than 13 percent from 1956 and 40 percent from ten years before. In 1960 a *U.S. News & World Report* article offered even more-alarming numbers: between 1940 and 1960 the rate of serious crime had more than doubled, up 128 percent.

Challenging the Statistics. But not all of the experts were convinced. Possible explanations were offered as to why the increase seemed so extreme. Reports from local police forces, for example, on which the FBI numbers were based, were of questionable accuracy. As the police became more efficient, they kept better records and reported more arrests. Some statistics did not take into consideration changes in population, which could account for surprising drops or jumps in the crime rates. Laws themselves were changed so that what was a crime in 1960 might not have been one in 1940, and vice versa. Further, as some sociologists speculated, the rise in crime might have been temporary, a growing pain of the postwar building boom.

The Juvenile Delinquent. Still, it seemed undeniable that crime in the 1950s was increasing at a faster pace than the population. Americans were concerned not only about the number of crimes but the nature of them. They were disturbed by the trend toward more-wantonly brutal crimes and especially by the sharp increase in juvenile crime. Again the statistics may have been inflated by various factors. Even so, arrests of persons under age eighteen doubled between 1948 and 1959, while the population in that age group increased by less than one-half. The public seized upon a new threat to society: the juvenile delinquent.

The Mobster. Another criminal specter that haunted the 1950s was the gangster. The public fascination with organized crime was both reflected in and fueled by the popularity of fictional television crime fighters, the Kefauver committee hearings, books such as Jack Lait and Lee Mortimer's *Chicago Confidential* (1950) and Virgil W. Peterson's *Barbarians in Our Midst* (1952), and the real-life exploits of Frank Costello and Mickey Cohen. While the police, the government, and the press were never able actually to prove their claims of the existence of an overlord who controlled all mob activity, such a figure loomed large in America's imagination.

Who's Watching the Watchmen? Law-abiding Americans looked to the criminal justice system—the police, the courts, and the prisons — to protect them and to maintain order. Sometimes they wondered if their faith was misplaced. Stories of police corruption or incompetence appeared regularly during the decade. Law enforcement as a whole, however, improved. The attention paid to the system's "bad apples" by lawmakers, the courts, and the media helped keep all police forces more honest and fair. New technologies and better communication between police around the nation made them more efficient. Further, as the links between social forces and criminal behavior were better understood, police were expected to take a more positive role in maintaining a healthy community.

Congress Joins the Fight. Crime fighting during the 1950s, however, was not solely the jurisdiction of the nation's police. The country's elected officials got in on the act as well. Much publicity surrounded the investigations by the Senate's Special Committee to Investigate Organized Crime in Interstate Commerce, headed by Sen. Estes Kefauver, and the Select Committee on Improper Activities in the Labor or Management Field, chaired by Sen. John L. McClellan. Critics charged that political ambitions as much as a desire for justice motivated the senators' crusades. But the hearings, much of which Americans watched avidly on television, revealed

HOW MUCH DID LAWYERS MAKE?

In 1954, according to a study by the Department of Commerce, the average income of lawyers in the United States was $10,220, more than twice as much as the average family income of the time. Slightly more than a quarter of these lawyers made less than $5,000 a year, and 18 percent earned $15,000 a year or more. The majority, almost two-thirds, earned between $5,000 and $10,000 yearly. A lawyer's earnings could also vary widely depending on where he practiced, the study found. Those who practiced in a city with a population of one million or more earned more than twice as much as those in small towns of a thousand people or less. Average income also varied from state to state, with California offering the nation's high ($12,180) and Florida the nation's low ($7,830).

The study also reported that fewer lawyers were practicing on their own as opposed to forming partnerships or working for firms. In 1947 almost three-quarters of the country's lawyers had an individual practice; by 1954 that number had fallen to 65 percent, and with good reason, as far as earning power was concerned: lawyers in firms of between five and eight members earned more than three times as much as lawyers in solo practices, and lawyers in firms of nine or more earned nearly five times as much.

Source: *Personnel & Guidance Journal* (March 1957): 413.

---

to many for the first time the inner workings of organized crime and the corruption and violence that dominated the country's largest labor unions.

Blind Justice? According to a basic principle of American government, anyone accused of a crime will have his day in court and may expect the administration of "blind" justice. But justice during the 1950s could not really be considered blind. It was often apparent that the judiciary treated the rich differently from the poor, whites differently from minorities, and those who held unpopular views differently from "loyal" Americans. Sentencing and court procedures varied considerably from state to state, and judges too often based their rulings on the quality of the opposing legal counsels or the popular opinions of the day. Some of these problems are natural products of the American legal system. But others — such as inequalities based on race or class — the federal courts, especially the

U.S. Supreme Court, devoted much time and effort to resolving.

A Good Lawyer is Hard to Find. Even if he had the means to pay for counsel, a defendant in the courts of the 1950s might have had a hard time finding a good lawyer. The "Crime in the U.S." series in *Life* reported that many lawyers were avoiding trial work altogether for other, more lucrative options. Lloyd Wright, president of the American Bar Association, told his colleagues in 1957: "Material rewards must no longer be an excuse for so many of our topflight members of the profession to contribute to the uplifting and establishment of a thoroughly responsible bar for the practice of criminal law."

Equal Protection. For the defendant without means, getting good legal representation was unlikely. Legal-aid societies in large cities provided some help. Only eight states in 1957 had public defenders — full-time public employees whose job is to defend the poor in criminal courts — and those states did not provide them in all courts. A Supreme Court decision of 1956, *Griffin* v. *Illinois*, was the first of several Warren court decisions that stressed equal protection for the haves and have-nots under the law.

Judicial Activism. "Equal protection of the laws" is an American right set forth in the Fourteenth Amendment to the Constitution. Under Chief Justice Earl Warren, appointed in 1953, the Supreme Court applied that notion to social, as well as criminal, justice. The decisions of the Warren court ushered in the new age of judicial activism; the Court used its power to overturn unjust laws in order to guarantee the rights of Americans. In 1954 the decision in *Brown* v. *Board of Education, Topeka, Kansas* — one of a handful of the most important Supreme Court rulings in American history — destroyed the legal basis for separating school students on the basis of race.

An Unpopular Decision. The uproar following *Brown* and subsequent decisions was intense. State politicians and school officials, who no longer had the law on their side, struggled to find new ways to keep the racist system alive. Some schools even closed rather than admit African-American students. After some initial hesitation President Dwight D. Eisenhower demonstrated his support for federal court decisions by sending armed troops, when necessary, to force compliance. Clearly, segregation, or even much foot-dragging in the process of integration, would no longer be tolerated. In the battle the federal courts provoked between the national government and various local governments, the smaller bodies were destined to lose.

Sources:
"Upsurge in Crime — and Why," *U.S. News & World Report* (26 September 1960): 58–64;

Robert Wallace, "Crime in the U.S.," *Life* (9 September 1957): 47–69.

TOPICS IN THE NEWS

THE BRINK'S ROBBERY

"Crime of the Century." Probably no single crime attracted more publicity during the 1950s than the robbery on 17 January 1950 of the Brink's armored-car company in Boston. On that night seven masked gunmen broke into the company's offices, tied up the guards, and walked out with almost $2.8 million in cash, checks, and money orders — the largest amount stolen in a single robbery to that date. The robbers planned the heist carefully and nearly got away with it. The Federal Bureau of Investigation, who referred to the robbery as "the crime of the century," solved the case eleven days before the statute of limitations (the date after which the robbers could no longer be prosecuted) ran out.

A Dishonest Living. The robbery was the brainchild of Tony (the Pig) Pino, a professional safecracker who by his thirtieth birthday had been arrested some twenty-five times. Released from prison in 1944, Pino soon returned to his chosen career, making a modest living for himself by shoplifting and minor robberies. He was an ambitious criminal, though, and as early as 1945 he had started planning the job that would be his masterpiece. He was inspired one night as he happened to pass Brink's North Terminal Garage while employees loaded bag after bag of money into armored cars.

The Five-year Plan. For the next five years Pino worked out the details for the "Brink's job." In various disguises he entered the Brink's offices and memorized details of the office's layout. He followed the daily operations of the business to determine on what days the most money would be in the building. And he began to recruit the accomplices he would need: acquaintances from prison, small-time criminals like himself.

Golden Opportunities. Soon Pino and his group began testing the armored-car company's security in earnest. They followed the Brink's armored cars and learned all their routes. When the opportunity presented itself, they would sneak up on an unguarded car, open it with a

Eight members of the gang that committed the Brink's robbery. Tony Pino, who planned and organized the heist, is fifth from left.

In 1956 *Harper's* magazine profiled the cream of America's lawyers, the partners of large firms (fifteen or more partners) who oversee the legal affairs of corporations, financial institutions, and wealthy individuals. Most large cities had at least one of these firms, but more than half of them were located on or near Wall Street, New York City's financial district. These lawyers were the most highly paid in the country, and they wielded considerable influence for such a small segment of society. As *Harper's* reported, "Graduates of Wall Street firms are presently Secretary of State, Ambassador to Great Britain, Chairmen of U.S. Steel and Chase-Manhattan Bank. Among the present crop of partners in Wall Street law firms are men who were recently Secretaries of the Army and the Air Force, our Special Negotiator in Korea, head of our delegation to the United Nations General Assembly, the director of the OSS. No other profession — not even the military — matches the quantity of national leadership that has been drawn from this one, small segment of the Bar."

Source: Martin Meyer, "The Wall Street Lawyers," *Harper's*, (January 1956): 31–37; (February 1956): 50–56.

key they had stolen from the company garage, and make off with a sack of money. They also robbed the safes of Brink's customers, using the security company's delivery schedule to determine when its customers would have the most money on the premises. In this way, reported Noel Behn in his *Big Stick-Up at Brink's!* (1977), the thieves stole almost four hundred thousand dollars from Brink's and its customers between 1946 and 1950.

No Security. In the last two years before the robbery, members of Pino's group broke into the Brink's offices repeatedly, researching their crime. Every detail of the company's operations was available to them. They discovered that the company's security system was amazingly primitive. Only the alarm system on the company vault gave them pause. So Pino made his last strategy decision: they would have to rob Brink's when the vault was open — armed robbery instead of burglary.

Clueless. The highly publicized Brink's job was the culmination of years of crimes. As they had rehearsed, the group left no usable evidence behind. Reporters and an army of police trampled the crime scene. Despite an unpromising lack of leads the FBI — which had claimed that the robbery should be considered a federal crime — took up the search. Unfortunately the agents had few regular dealings with street criminals of the sort that had robbed Brink's. When their investigation seemed to turn

up nothing, the public began to regard the case with amusement: Ed Sullivan and Fred Allen joked about the case on national television.

Under Their Noses. Although the investigators did not know it, they were almost immediately on the right track. Ten of the group's eleven members were part of the long list of suspects the FBI compiled. But checking every lead took time, and money — the investigation eventually cost an estimated $29 million. Eventually the heavy police pressure, including surveillance and arrest on other charges, took its toll on the suspects. One of the robbers, "Specs" O'Keefe (whom the other members of the gang had tried to kill), confessed just eleven days before the sixth anniversary of the crime. O'Keefe got a comparatively short sentence because of his cooperation; the other eight surviving Brink's robbers each received multiple life sentences, of which they served an average of fourteen years.

Source:
Noel Behn, *Big Stick-Up at Brink's!* (New York: Putnam, 1977).

BROWN V. BOARD OF EDUCATION TOPEKA, KANSAS

Topeka, Kansas, Two Sets of Rights. The Fourteenth Amendment to the U.S. Constitution, adopted in 1866, guarantees that no state may "abridge the privileges or immunities of citizens of the United States" nor "deny to any person within its jurisdiction the equal protection of the laws." These words give all Americans, regardless of race, equal rights and equal protection under state and federal laws. Yet at the beginning of the 1950s society was still separated into black and white. Hotels, trains, parks, restaurants, apartment houses, and even state voting precincts were segregated by race through state statutes, called "Jim Crow" laws. African-Americans were criminally prosecuted and jailed for attempting to ride the same trains or eat in the same restaurants as whites.

National Guardsmen denying student Elizabeth Eckford entrance to Central High School in Little Rock, Arkansas, 4 September 1957

THURGOOD MARSHALL

While deciding the landmark *Brown* v. *Board of Education* case the Supreme Court heard arguments from a lawyer who would one day be a justice himself: Thurgood Marshall. In 1954 Marshall was no stranger to the men of the high court. As a lawyer for the National Association for the Advancement of Colored People, he had argued cases before the Court for ten years, starting with the appeal of W. D. Lyons, a young man unfairly convicted of murder, in 1944. The *Lyons* case was one of the few that Marshall lost: he eventually won twenty-nine out of the thirty-two cases he represented.

The *Brown* decision was one of his most significant victories. As Marshall biographer Carl Rowan wrote, "There may never have been any days of oral argument before the Supreme Court to equal the depth of passion, the agony of the justices, that erupted in this *Brown* case." Certainly there had been few cases before the Court with such enormous social implications. With characteristic frankness Marshall urged the justices to make a decent decision.

"I got the feeling on hearing the discussion yesterday that when you put a white child in a school with a whole lot of colored children, the child would fall apart or something," Marshall asserted. "Everybody knows that is not true. Those same kids in Virginia and South Carolina — and I have seen them do it — they play in the streets together, they play on the farms together, they separate to go to school, they come out of school and play ball together. They have to be separated in school. . . . Why, of all the multitudinous groups of people in the country, [do] you have to single out the Negroes and give them this separate treatment? . . .

"The only thing it can be is an inherent determination that the people who were formerly in slavery, regardless of anything else, shall be kept as near that stage as possible. And now is the time, we submit, that this Court should make clear that this is not what our Constitution stands for."

Source: Carl Rowan, *Dream Makers, Dream Breakers: The World of Justice Thurgood Marshall* (Boston: Little, Brown, 1993).

Separate but Equal. The constitutionality of these state laws was first considered by the Supreme Court in *Plessy* v. *Ferguson* (1896). Homer Plessy was an African-American who attempted to ride in a whites-only railroad car in Louisiana. Plessy was charged with violating Louisiana's Jim Crow law, and he argued all the way to the Supreme Court that the law was unconstitutional. In a seven-to-one vote, the 1896 Court declared that the amendment did not prohibit state laws from treating people differently according to the color of their skins as long as that treatment was "equal." The "separate but equal" doctrine created by the *Plessy* decision lasted for nearly sixty years, until the 1954 decision of *Brown* v. *Board of Education*.

The Long Journey Begins. The *Brown* case began in Topeka, Kansas, at the beginning of the 1950 school year, when Oliver Brown was told that his eight-year-old daughter Linda could not attend the neighborhood elementary school four blocks from their home. The principal of the school explained to Brown that Kansas law required African-Americans to attend segregated schools. Brown joined with other African-American families to protest the law and engaged the National Association for the Advancement of Colored People to argue their cause. They started a lawsuit against the board of education of Topeka, claiming that segregation violated their children's constitutional rights under the Fourteenth Amendment. For four years they lost their case, appealing it to progressively higher courts. In 1954 *Brown* v. *Board of Education* reached the U.S. Supreme Court along with three other similar cases.

Separate Is Not Equal. The plaintiffs' attorney, Thurgood Marshall, later a Supreme Court justice, argued that racially segregated public schools were not "equal" and could not be made "equal"; therefore the laws were in violation of the Fourteenth Amendment. He claimed that the only way for the Court to uphold segregation in 1954 was "to find that for some reason Negroes are inferior to all other human beings." The Supreme Court agreed and unanimously rejected the "separate but equal" doctrine of *Plessy* v. *Ferguson*. Chief Justice Earl Warren, writing the opinion of the Court, highlighted the fundamental importance of education to American children. He then stated unequivocally that segregation of public schools based solely on race deprives minority children of the values of education. In conclusion the opinion read, "in the field of public education the doctrine of 'separate but equal' has no place."

"All Deliberate Speed." The *Brown* decision hit the country like a bombshell. Reversing segregation was not going to come easily, and the Court realized the tremendous resistance local politicians and school boards would have to its decision. Therefore the *Brown* decision called for a reargument on the issue of how to bring about the constitutional mandate of desegregation. The following year, in *Brown II*, the Warren Court charged local federal district courts with the task of assessing local obstacles to integration and deciding whether local school boards were implementing good-faith attempts at desegregation. The nation's public schools were ordered to desegregate "with all deliberate speed."

Stiff Resistance. The judicial branch of the government, however, can only pronounce the law. It is up to the executive branch, led by the president, to enforce it. Federal district courts did their best to make local school boards conform to the "all deliberate speed" mandate, but their orders and injunctions had little effect. Desegregation was extremely unpopular, and many states threatened to close their public schools rather than allow them to become integrated. Attempts by African-American students to follow court-ordered integration resulted in riots in cities such as Milford, Delaware; Mansfield, Texas; Clinton, Tennessee; and New Orleans, Louisiana. President Dwight D. Eisenhower, who believed that the Court had attempted to force the nation to integrate too quickly, offered no help. For several years after the *Brown* decision, very little was done on local levels to proceed toward desegregation. Nevertheless, African-Americans continued to push for their rights.

Amid Three Armies. The situation came to a head in Little Rock, Arkansas. In a halfhearted attempt to follow the federal court order, in 1957 the Little Rock school board initiated a plan to integrate the public schools one grade at a time, starting with the twelfth grade in 1959. African-American families and the NAACP saw this move as much too slow. They took their case back to federal court and won an order allowing nine African-American students to enter Little Rock's Central High School for the fall semester. Under the direction of Arkansas governor Orval Faubus, however, armed troops from the Arkansas National Guard blocked the entrance of the school from the nine students. This situation continued for three weeks until newspapers across the country showed a picture of fifteen-year-old Elizabeth Eckford turned away from the school, with guardsmen and white students screaming insults at her. President Eisenhower could not delay enforcing citizen's rights any longer. He sent one thousand air force paratroopers to Little Rock, where they surrounded the school. Amid three small armies — federal, state, and the news media — nine African-American students began their first day of high school at Little Rock Central.

***Cooper* v. *Aaron*.** Lawyers for the school board argued that after the Little Rock incident public hostility was so extreme and severe that it was impossible to run a sound educational program. The board's case, *Cooper* v. *Aaron*, quickly reached the Supreme Court. On 12 September 1958 the Court denounced Arkansas's position in a unanimous and resounding decision. Writing for the Court, Justice William Brennan dismissed an anti-integration amendment Arkansas had added to its constitution, stating that "the federal judiciary is supreme in the exposition of the law of the Constitution and that principle [is] a permanent and indispensable feature of our constitutional system." He reaffirmed the Court's reversal of the "separate but equal" doctrine of 1896. The principles of the *Brown* case, Brennan wrote, "are indispensable for the protection of the freedoms guaranteed by the fundamen-

tal charter for all of us. Our constitutional idea of equal justice under law is thus made a living truth." After the *Cooper* decision no state could again argue that segregation was constitutional.

Sources:

Elizabeth Huckaby, *Crisis at Central High: Little Rock, 1957–58* (Baton Rouge & London: Louisiana State University Press, 1980);

Arnold S. Rice, *The Warren Court, 1953–1969* (Millwood, N.Y.: Associated Faculty Press, 1987).

THE EMMETT TILL CASE

Chilling Circumstances. The circumstances surrounding the death of Emmett Till provide chilling insight into the racism that dominated the South in the 1950s. Till was a fourteen-year-old Chicago native visiting relatives in Mississippi. While out with his cousins and friends on the night of 24 August 1955, he allegedly accosted a white woman in the grocery store owned by her husband. Accounts vary as to what Till actually said or did. According to the woman Till grabbed her and made lewd remarks. Some witnesses claimed that he only whistled at her. Still others asserted that he made no advances at all, that he whistled habitually to control a speech defect.

A Brutal Murder. Roy Bryant considered his wife's honor tainted by the incident. Several nights after the episode, Bryant, his half brother J. W. Milam, and possibly other accomplices kidnapped Till from his relatives' home in the middle of the night. The two men beat him severely and, apparently enraged that he had a picture of a white woman in his wallet, shot Till and threw him in a nearby river. Several days later the body was found, and Bryant and Milam were charged with murder.

BATHED IN THE SPIRIT

The following account of a murderer's spiritual redemption is from *Life* magazine, 3 April 1950:

"In Charleston, West Virginia, one night last July two men who had been drinking heavily all day suddenly knocked down a perfect stranger and, holding back the crowd with a knife, took turns senselessly stomping him to death. Last month one of the men, 26-year-old Harry Burdette, a professional pool-hall gambler, whose electrocution is scheduled for April 14, asked a minister to baptize him. Guarded by the sheriff and 10 deputies armed with shotguns, he was escorted to a nearby creek. While a crowd of 1,500 lined the bank to watch, two ministers of the Free Salvation Baptist church lowered him into the icy water. 'I am now prepared to die,' said Burdette, who had meanwhile converted seven fellow prisoners."

Emmett Till

A Surprise Verdict. Mississippi politicians and newspapers unanimously condemned the murderers and promised swift justice. However, Mississippians became more defensive as for weeks the press bombarded them with harsh condemnations of racial violence in the South. The highly publicized trial of the two men was charged with racial tension. African-American politicians and reporters from the North were treated contemptuously and were segregated in the courtroom. The prosecution was poorly prepared, and the substance of the defense was the astounding claim that Till was not actually dead. The badly decomposed body was identified only by Till's ring on its finger. The sheriff of Tallahatchee County, who investigated the case, speculated on the witness stand that an unnamed group of "rabble-rousers" had planted the evidence. The all-male, all-white jury was apparently convinced: they acquitted Bryant and Milam after deliberating slightly longer than an hour.

The World Reacts. News of the verdict was received around the country and the world with astonishment. A survey of European reactions conducted by the American Jewish Committee reported that American prestige had been "seriously damaged" by the outcome of the trial. The press in Mississippi, on the other hand, closed ranks and praised the fairness of the trial.

The Killers Tell the Truth. The truth of what happened that night became public knowledge several months after the trial. William Bradford Huie, an Ala-

bama journalist in Mississippi to report on the aftermath of the case, offered Bryant and Milam money to tell their story. Since the two could no longer be prosecuted for a crime of which they had already been acquitted, they gladly told for a fee of how they had beaten and killed young Till. Huie reported what the killers told him in the 24 January 1956 issue of *Look* magazine. Now publicly exposed as murderers, Bryant and Milam were ostracized by the community, and both moved elsewhere within a year. Emmett Till in death became a martyr for the civil rights movement, a symbol of the racial hatred African-Americans had yet to overcome.

Source:
Stephen J. Whitfield, *A Death in the Delta: The Story of Emmett Till* (New York: Free Press, 1988).

THE FIRST AMENDMENT IN THE 1950S

A Lasting Controversy. The First Amendment to the Constitution forbids Congress from making any law "abridging the freedom of speech, or of the press." The courts have traditionally ruled, however, that the framers of the Constitution never intended to protect *all* forms of expression. Some works, in fact, are considered so offensive to society's standards of decency that they are banned from any public display. How to tell the difference between a work that is unpopular but tolerable and one that is completely unacceptable has been an ongoing concern of the American court system. During the 1950s the Supreme Court made several significant decisions regarding the controversy.

Is Sacrilege Illegal? In 1952, in the case of *Burstyn* v. *Wilson*, the Court struck down the state of New York's ban on the film *The Miracle*. The Italian film told the story of a young peasant girl who is impregnated by a hobo she mistakes for Saint Joseph; she goes mad and claims she is the Virgin Mary about to give birth to Jesus. The New York State Board of Regents ruled that the exhibitor who had shown the film had committed sacrilege. The appeal reached the Supreme Court, which ruled that "under the First and Fourteenth Amendments a state may not ban a film on the basis of a censor's conclusion that it is 'sacrilegious.' " This decision marked the first instance of a film had being extended the full protection of the First Amendment.

Two Cases of Indecency. On 24 June 1957 the Court handed down decisions in two cases related to the free-expression issue. In one, *Alberts* v. *California*, salesman David Alberts had been convicted under a California law prohibiting "lewdly keeping for sale" and advertising indecent books; he claimed that his Fourteenth Amendment guarantee of due process of law had been ignored. In the other, more important case, *Roth* v. *United States*, Samuel Roth, a pornographic-book seller, argued that not only had his right to due process been denied, but that the laws against obscene material violated the First Amendment and its guarantee of free expression.

No Protection. The First Amendment issue was the most important feature of either case. Justice William Brennan, in the majority opinion, wrote that "All ideas having even the slightest redeeming social importance . . . have the full protection of the guarantees [of the First Amendment] . . . But implicit in the history of the First Amendment is the rejection of obscenity as utterly without redeeming social importance." Having thus affirmed government's ability to restrict obscenity, the justice turned to the thornier issue of definitions.

A New Standard. Brennan suggested the following test of obscenity: "Whether to the average person, applying contemporary community standards, the dominant theme of the material taken as a whole appeals to prurient interests [arouses lust]." The standard, however, raised as many questions as it answered. Who was the average person? What was his community, exactly? What specific standards was he to apply? The dissenting opinion, written by Justice William Douglas, warned that the standard could lead to "community censorship in one of its worst forms." Douglas wrote, "I have the same confidence in the ability of our people to reject noxious literature as I have in their capacity to sort out the true from the false in theology, economics, politics or any other field" — in other words, not much. Still, the *Roth* standard set the patterns for the future definitions of obscenity.

Ideas Cannot Be Banned. The Court had the opportunity to test the *Roth* standard in 1959, in the case of *Kingsley International Pictures Corp.* v. *Regents*. The previous year the New York Board of Regents had ruled that a film version of D. H. Lawrence's *Lady Chatterley's Lover* was immoral because it portrayed adultery as a "desirable, acceptable, and proper pattern of behavior." The Supreme Court unanimously overturned the state's ban. For the Court the presence of serious ideas, even those contrary to the public morality, was enough to lift a work above those that merely arouse lust.

No Solution in Sight. With respect to the free-expression guarantees of the First Amendment, the Court ended the decade roughly as it began. There were still limits on free expression and still no successful definition of those limits. The tension, possibly unresolvable, between the public danger posed by immoral works and the public danger posed by banning them remained a controversial issue for American courts.

Sources:

Morris Leopold Ernst, *Censorship: The Search for the Obscene* (New York: Macmillan, 1964);

"On Sex and Obscenity," *Time* (8 July 1957): 10–11.

J. EDGAR HOOVER AND THE FBI

A Better Bureau. During the 1950s, as for several decades before and several decades after, J. Edgar Hoover *was* the Federal Bureau of Investigation. When he was named director of the national police agency in 1924, he was faced with the task of changing it from a corrupt and

J. Edgar Hoover

inefficient organization to an effective one. He had demonstrated his qualifications for the job by overseeing the infamous Palmer raids against American radicals in 1919–1920. In short order the new director purged the bureau of its dishonest and incompetent agents and replaced them with qualified, loyal men.

Birth of the G-Man. Through the 1930s and 1940s Hoover and his reformed FBI became more and more popular with the American public. During the Depression the "G-men," as federal agents were called, consistently made headlines by capturing or killing gangsters such as John Dillinger, George "Machine Gun" Kelly, and Charles "Pretty Boy" Floyd. Hoover shifted the bureau's focus to espionage and subversive elements in the tense years of World War II. As the cold war developed in the late years of the 1940s, Hoover considered Communists and Communist sympathizers to be risks to the nation's security and, therefore, to be the FBI's highest priority.

The Battle against Disloyalty. By 1950, then, Hoover had positioned himself and his bureau as the country's main protectors against subversion. In Hoover's mind the importance of this mission ultimately put the FBI's activities beyond the scope of the president, Congress, or the country's courts. The basis of the FBI's power was the files it maintained on tens of thousands of Americans

During the 1950s several incidents pointed to a lack of proper security precautions in the nation's airline industry. In 1950 thirty-one-year-old John Henry Grant took his wife and two children to Los Angeles Municipal Airport to load them onto a passenger plane for San Diego. He also included in their baggage a homemade time bomb, set to explode while the plane was in flight. At the airport Grant bought twenty-five thousand dollars worth of insurance on his family. Grant was foiled, however, when the rigged suitcase burst into flames while being loaded. He confessed that he was seeing another woman on the side and paying child support to a third. Blowing up his family seemed like the best way to uncomplicate his life.

The passengers on a DC-6B plane leaving Stapleton Airport in Denver on 1 November 1955 were not as fortunate. On that date John Graham loaded twenty-five sticks of dynamite on to the plane with his mother, who was traveling to Alaska. Ten minutes into the flight the plane crashed in flames, killing all forty-four persons aboard. Graham drew attention to himself by nervously buying insurance at the airport; after an investigation the FBI found material to make a bomb in Graham's home. He was executed for the mass murder on 11 January 1957.

In the 1960s, spurred by these and similar events and a rash of "skyjackings," airlines and airports began to pay more attention to security. Passengers and their carry-on items had to pass through metal detectors, and any bags were X-rayed before they were loaded into the luggage compartment.

Source: *Time*, 1 May 1950, p. 20; Carl Sifakis, *The Encyclopedia of American Crime* (New York: Facts on File, 1982).

---

who by the FBI's standards were not sufficiently loyal citizens. Often the information in the files had been gained by unwarranted and even illegal invasions of privacy. Hoover jealously guarded the secrecy of these files but would leak information in them to allies in the war against subversion, such as his personal friend Sen. Joseph McCarthy or the House Un-American Activities Committee (HUAC). In this way Hoover kept the bureau above the political squabbling that characterized congressional smear campaigns, but at the same time he helped discredit American Communists.

The FBI Picks Congress. As a subdivision of the Department of Justice, the FBI is overseen by the attorney general and, ultimately, the president. Hoover, however, did not always feel bound to honor this official chain of command. In the early 1950s, for example, his relationship with President Truman was strained, largely because Hoover felt that Truman was soft on the issue of disloyal Americans. Consequently, in the bitter feud with Congress that marked Truman's last years in office, Hoover sided with HUAC and the Senate Internal Security Subcommittee (SISS) against the president.

Changing Sides. When Eisenhower took office in 1953, on the other hand, Hoover felt that he and the new president were much more in agreement on the loyalty issue. At the same time the congressional Communist hunters had several times revealed the source of their information, to the embarrassment of the FBI. When Senator McCarthy overreached and took on the army in 1954, his former ally Hoover helped to discredit him.

Under Eisenhower, Hoover was relatively free to pursue his investigations.

Defenders of Freedom. Throughout this period Hoover and the FBI were enormously popular with the American people. Books such as Don Whitehead's *The FBI Story* (1956), which was made into a film starring Jimmy Stewart in 1959, portray FBI agents as heroic, but average, defenders of American freedom. *Masters of Deceit* (1958), ironically credited to Hoover but written by FBI employees, chronicles the bureau's running battle against subversion. More-critical works on the bureau, such as Max Lowenthal's *The FBI* (1950), were squelched by Hoover and the critics themselves denounced as disloyal.

A Threat to the Establishment. In the late 1950s Hoover's chief concern was no longer the rest of the country's. A variety of factors — including a temporary easing of tensions in U.S.-Soviet relations and the civil rights movement — pushed the issue of domestic communism into the background. Hoover hated civil rights activists for the threat they represented to established authority, and he tried to smear them as Communist dupes. He also withheld FBI resources in the investigation of racially charged crimes in the South.

The FBI versus the Court. Hoover saw the national strife over racial justice to be largely the fault of the Supreme Court, whose 1954 *Brown* decision destroyed the legal basis for segregation. He maintained throughout the rest of the decade that the Warren court's liberalism was eroding the government's authority. After the "Red Monday" decisions of 1957 reversed many of the worst excesses of McCarthyism, Hoover recorded in a memo that the "Party as a whole is jubilant over these decisions." When the Court ruled in *Jencks* v. *United States* (1959) that accused Communists were entitled to see the FBI file on them to help in preparing their defenses, Hoover contended that it struck at the heart of the bureau's effectiveness. "The courts themselves must eventually . . . join all forces for good in protecting society," he cautioned.

Out of Step. As the decade closed Hoover could perhaps feel the nation leaving him behind. The election of President John F. Kennedy in 1960 underscored the country's new, progressive mood. Compared to the Kennedys (the president and his brother Robert, the new attorney general), Hoover seemed stodgy and old. The 1960s would find Hoover and his bureau increasingly out of touch with American society, a far cry from the celebrity and influence he had commanded in the 1950s and before.

Sources:

Fred J. Cook, "The FBI," *Nation*, 187 (18 October 1958): 221–280;

Richard Gid Powers, *Secrecy and Power: The Life of J. Edgar Hoover* (New York: Free Press / Macmillan, 1987);

Athan Theoharis, *Spying on Americans: Political Surveillance from Hoover to the Huston Plan* (Philadelphia: Temple University Press, 1978).

JUVENILE DELINQUENCY

A Disturbing Trend. Juvenile delinquency was considered a major social problem in the 1950s. Americans under the age of eighteen were committing serious crimes in growing numbers; their elders were horrified at the severity of the crimes and at the young criminals' disregard for authority. Most of all, though, people were concerned about what the rate of juvenile crime said about how the nation was raising its children. Of course, there had always been youth crime in America, even vicious youth crime. But in the 1950s, because of the growth of cities across the United States, it became a national cause for concern.

Junior Crime Wave. As early as 1953 the statistics suggested a youth crime wave. FBI director J. Edgar Hoover reported: "persons under the age of 18 committed 53.6 percent of all car thefts; 49.3 percent of all burglaries; 18 percent of all robberies, and 16.2 percent of all rapes. These are the statistics reported to the FBI by 1,174 cities." Moreover, with the post–World War II baby boom creating more potential juvenile delinquents, experts expected the trend toward lawlessness to continue indefinitely. A 1959 study cited in *Personnel and Guidance Journal* claimed that about one-third — almost six-hundred thousand — of crimes being committed by teenagers went undetected by the police.

Many Causes, Many Answers. Judges, law-enforcement officials, psychologists, and other experts suggested a variety of causes of juvenile crime, from lack of a good home life to too much comic-book reading. In order to stem the junior crime wave, parents, teachers, and policemen were all expected to be stricter but at the same time more understanding. On a social level Americans were all asked to bear the burden of funding better institutions and more trained counselors to address the needs of the youthful offender.

Rebels without a Cause. The older generation might have thought that young criminals represented a threat to American society and its values, but to their children the juvenile delinquent was a "rebel without a cause," as the title of the 1955 film goes. The popular-music and movie industries were quick to recognize a new market. Rock 'n' roll music was just different and dangerous enough to horrify parents and delight teenagers. Movies such as *The Cool and the Crazy* and *Riot in Juvenile Prison* usually ended on the side of traditional values, but they also provided plenty of the wild parties, rock music, drag races, and gang fights their young audiences paid to see.

Sources:

Max F. Baer, "The National Juvenile Delinquency Picture," *Personnel & Guidance Journal*, 38 (December 1959): 278–279;

Mark Thomas McGee, *The J.D. Films: Juvenile Delinquency in the Movies* (Jefferson, N.C.: McFarland, 1982);

"Why Law Fails to Stop Teenage Crime," *U.S. News & World Report* (14 January 1955): 64–75.

THE KEFAUVER COMMITTEE AND ORGANIZED CRIME

Crime Buster from Tennessee. The Kefauver committee, which has been called "probably the most important probe of organized crime" in U.S. history, revealed to Americans the activities of criminal operations earning millions of dollars yearly and of the corrupt public officials who allowed such operations to flourish. It was formed as the Senate Special Committee to Investigate Organized Crime in Interstate Commerce, but it came to be called the Kefauver committee after Sen. Estes Kefauver. The energetic Tennessee Democrat, looking to make a name for himself in his first term in the Senate, sponsored the resolution which created the committee and was its chairman. In order for the resolution to pass, Kefauver had to overcome stiff opposition from elder senators who distrusted their junior colleague's ambitions.

Murder in Kansas City. The murder of two gangsters on 6 April 1950 in a Democratic clubhouse in Kansas City, Missouri, brought the issue of organized crime back into the headlines. For the Republicans the incident provided an opportunity to make an embarrassing connection between the Democrats and corruption in President Harry S Truman's home state; and Democrats, rather than appear afraid of an investigation of big-city political machines, agreed that federal action against the "National Crime Syndicate" was necessary. After some squabbling between the two parties, the membership of the committee — Kefauver, two fellow Democrats, and

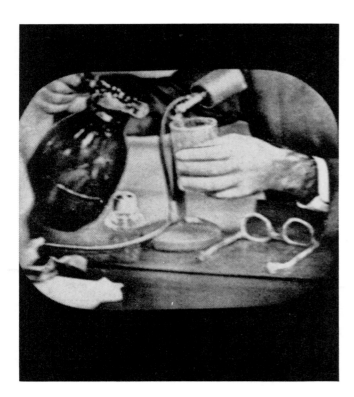

Scene from television coverage of Frank Costello's testimony before Estes Kefauver's U.S. Senate Committee to Investigate Organized Crime

two Republicans — was settled. Public hearings began in Miami, Florida, on 26 May 1950.

"Taking the Fifth." Over the next ten months the committee traveled the country from Miami to Saint Louis, New York, Cleveland, Chicago, and Los Angeles, among other cities. They listened to hundreds of hours of testimony from police experts, corrupt public officials, and underworld notables. So many of the crime figures questioned tried to invoke their constitutional right against self-incrimination guaranteed in the Fifth Amendment that "taking the Fifth" became part of the national vocabulary. Others tried to avoid appearing before the committee altogether: "Kefauveritis" was the name given to the variety of mysterious ailments that suddenly afflicted gangsters on the day they were scheduled to testify.

Star Witnesses. Probably the most dramatic hearings in the Kefauver investigation were those held in New York City. Frank Costello, considered the head of the New York–Miami syndicate, testified only on the condition that his face not be shown on television, so the cameras focused on his hands for the duration of his appearance. As an attempt to protect his identity the ploy was unsuccessful: by the time the committee was through with him, Costello was a ruined man. His testimony had made him an unwelcome presence among both his legitimate and underworld associates. The other star of the New York hearings was Virginia Hill, whom the press had labeled the "Queen of the Mob" although she never

actually wielded any authority in the underworld. Rather, she was infamous for her series of gangland husbands and lovers. After her testimony, perhaps upset by her unchivalrous treatment in the newspapers, Hill lashed out at a crowd of reporters, slapping one and screaming, "I hope an atom bomb falls on all of you!"

The Syndicates Revealed. On the basis of information they received, the committee developed a picture of organized crime in 1950s America. It was dominated by two syndicates, one operating in New York and the other based in Chicago; both also had operations in Florida. The committee claimed — but was never completely able to substantiate — that both of these syndicates were coordinated and controlled by the Mafia, presided over by Charles "Lucky" Luciano. (Most of the gangsters who testified, perhaps fearing reprisals, denied ever having even heard the word *Mafia* before.) The syndicates made most of their money from gambling, and they operated relatively free from legal harassment by bribing or intimidating elected officials and law-enforcement personnel.

Making Sense. As the committee's hearings drew to a close early in 1951, critics and supporters alike tried to make sense of the issues that had been raised. Many of the mobsters questioned had been unsure of their rights: the hearings were not criminal trials, yet those testifying were often accused of criminal activities. They were allowed not to incriminate themselves, but they had no opportunity to cross-examine other hearing witnesses who incriminated them. These issues were compounded by the presence of the television cameras, which convicted many of the witnesses in the eyes of the public, even though none of them had been formally indicted.

A Confused Atmosphere. Witnesses claimed that they had difficulty testifying under the hot, bright television lights. The committee, however, seemed reluctant to limit use of the cameras, leading critics to charge that media coverage was more important to committee members than justice. Kefauver inadvertently encouraged such a view by seemingly rushing his book, *Crime in America* (1951), and a series of articles he wrote for the *Saturday Evening Post* into print before the final report of the hearings had appeared.

A Service to the Nation. Kefauver asserted, though, that the committee had on balance done the nation a service. Many of the methods and faces of organized crime had been exposed to the public for the first time. Privately funded crime committees were formed around the country to address criminal activity at the local level. The Justice Department and Internal Revenue Service stepped up efforts to prosecute mobsters on racketeering and tax evasion charges. And voters rejected candidates with links to the underworld. Still, for all the public interest generated by the hearings, concrete results are harder to measure; as William Howard Moore wrote in *The Kefauver Committee and the Politics of Crime* (1974), "So inadequate are crime statistics and definitions . . . no one can document whether organized crime and corruption declined or increased during the 1950s."

Sources:

Estes Kefauver, *Crime in America*, edited by Sidney Shalett (Garden City, N.Y.: Doubleday, 1951);

William Howard Moore, *The Kefauver Committee and the Politics of Crime, 1950–1952* (Columbia: University of Missouri Press, 1974).

THE MCCLELLAN COMMITTEE AND LABOR RACKETEERING

Congress Considers the Unions. The two most significant congressional probes of criminal activity during the 1950s were the Kefauver committee and the Senate Select Committee on Improper Activities in the Labor-Management Field, or the McClellan committee, after Arkansas senator John L. McClellan, the committee's chairman. The goal of the committee was to investigate allegations of corruption and abuse of power in the country's labor unions, especially the International Brotherhood of Teamsters, the largest and strongest union in America. The investigation resulted in the prosecution and disgrace of more than a few top labor leaders. A round of housecleaning among the nation's unions followed, but the reputation of organized labor in America was seriously — and perhaps permanently — damaged.

The Racketeers. A labor union operates on the principle that its members, by acting together, can secure for themselves equitable pay, working conditions, and benefits. But by the 1950s many unions had strayed from that original purpose. Corrupt union officials made themselves rich through a variety of rackets, or crooked schemes. The most common was simple theft of union funds: in larger unions, with thousands of dues-paying members, considerable sums of money were there for the taking. Other rackets included negotiating sweetheart deals with business owners, selling out the interests of union members in return for bribes from management; and extorting money from businessmen with threats of pickets or other labor unrest. Racketeers stayed in authority through rigged elections and intimidation tactics.

A Question of Jurisdiction. Such practices had been an ugly part of American business for decades, and in the 1950s the government was moved to act. The Senate Permanent Subcommittee on Investigations, with McClellan as its chair and young lawyer Robert Kennedy as its chief counsel, began in January 1957 to investigate the possibility that union corruption had inflated prices on government purchases. The union men called to testify stonewalled, however, claiming that the subcommittee had no proper jurisdiction. In response the Senate created a committee specifically charged with investigating labor corruption. McClellan was appointed its chairman, and Kennedy again served as chief counsel. Kennedy's brother Massachusetts senator John F. Kennedy also served on the committee.

Talented Lawyers. McClellan was considered an odd choice for the committee's chair: the southern Democrat was one of the more conservative senators of either party and was thought to be antilabor, which he denied. He was a talented lawyer, however, able to grasp the complexities of labor-management relations. Much of the success of the committee could be attributed to Robert Kennedy, who along with his staff traveled the country from coast to coast, chasing down evidence. The exhausting effort paid off: more than one racketeer was tripped up by the wealth of research the committee had at its disposal.

A Big Fish. The biggest fish netted by the committee was Dave Beck, president of the Teamsters Union at the time. As the head of a union with 1.4 million members, Beck was an extremely powerful, well-connected, and — as the committee demonstrated — greedy man. Although he claimed (with some justification) that he had done much for his Teamsters, he also pilfered IBT funds wantonly. His thefts from the union ranged from the astounding — $200,000 that he used to build a palatial home in Seattle, Washington—to the ridiculous — $3.50 for a bow tie, all at a time when the average Teamster's salary was around $5,000. On the basis of the committee's investigation, Beck was indicted and convicted on tax evasion and grand larceny charges.

MISTAKEN IDENTITY

The police of New Rochelle, a suburb of New York City in Westchester County, nearly created an embarrassing international incident in June 1950, when they accidentally arrested the wives of several of Pakistan's delegates to the United Nations. When the women, dressed in native outfits of their country, entered a Bloomingdale's department store in New Rochelle, they were mistaken by an alert patrolman for "gypsies." As one of New Rochelle's finest explained: "You know gypsies — always out to commit some larceny by theft."

Soon two detectives were on the scene, and the women were taken into custody. At the station they were identified, and the police apologized for their error. Pakistan, however, demanded an official apology for the indignity. The police of New Rochelle, however, claimed that they were simply doing their job. "I tried to explain," said Lt. Lawrence Ruehl, "that when gypsies turn up in the city, our men are on the alert for mischief."

Source: *Time* (25 June 1951): 27.

Hoffa Gets Away. Poised to take control of the IBT after Beck's downfall was Jimmy Hoffa, the union's vice-president, himself a target of the committee's probe. In fact Hoffa narrowly escaped conviction on the charge that he had bribed a lawyer in order to have an insider on the committee's staff. Using his acquittal as proof that he was "clean," Hoffa won the Teamsters Union presidency in October 1957 at the union's annual meeting. Hoffa was confident that the McClellan committee could not touch him: when Kennedy confronted him with evidence that he had stolen union money, consorted with gangsters, and fraudulently exaggerated union membership, Hoffa nonchalantly claimed that poor memory kept him from answering the charges. Not until the 1960s, after persistent effort from Kennedy (U.S. attorney general during his brother John F. Kennedy's presidency), was Hoffa finally brought to justice.

Labor Cleans House. The rest of American labor, meanwhile, scrambled to distance itself from its bad apples. The AFL-CIO, the large federation of unions formed in 1955, supported the committee's investigation and promised one of its own. Its executive board expelled the Brotherhood of Teamsters, the Laundry Workers Union, and the Bakers Union, all implicated during the McClellan probe. Because of its size and its importance to industry, the IBT was probably less hurt by the expulsion than was the AFL-CIO. Member unions of the AFL-CIO and businesses around the country still had to deal with the Teamsters, since the Teamsters controlled virtually all American trucking and shipping.

New Rules for Unions. The AFL-CIO had hoped that by taking a tough stand on corruption it could avoid heavy government regulation. Clearly, though, some sort of federal action was required. During the 1958 legislative year an antiracketeering bill that was fairly sympathetic to labor failed to pass the full Congress. The next year, a coalition of Republicans and conservative southern Democrats ensured passage of the Labor-Management Reporting and Disclosure Act. The act provided a worker's bill of rights, guaranteeing a union member's right to have a say in the running of his union and protecting him from intimidation. The bill also required each union to provide regular, detailed accounts of its finances and membership. The decade closed with American labor on the defensive. Honest and dishonest unions alike found that they had to pay a price for labor racketeering.

Sources:
"Can the Labor Racketeer Be Stopped?," *U.S. News & World Report* (10 October 1958): 52–65;

"Here's What the Labor Probe Means," *Nation's Business*, 45 (April 1957): 32–35, 102–107;

"Labor on Trial," "Dave & the Green Stuff," *Time*, 69 (8 April 1957): 15–20;

John L. McClellan, *Crime Without Punishment* (New York: Duell, Sloan & Pearce, 1962);

"When Senators Asked Questions, This Is What a Big Union Did," *U.S. News & World Report*, 42 (1 February 1957): 89–93;

"Why Union Men Are Complaining," *U.S. News & World Report*, 42 (29 March 1957): 29–33.

PRISON LIFE IN THE 1950S

A World Behind Bars. Americans of the 1950s did not like to dwell on one aspect of the growing crime problem: the nation's increasingly crowded prisons. By the end of the decade, the U.S. prison population — 22,492 men and women in federal penitentiaries, 185,021 in state facilities — equaled the population of a city the size of Tulsa, Oklahoma. They made sure, often in violent ways, that the outside world could not ignore them. Between 1950 and 1953 people were shocked by a succession of riots in federal and state penitentiaries around the country, twenty in 1952 alone. With a few shameful exceptions, prisons in America were more humane than they had ever been. Yet convicts from New Jersey to Louisiana to California were demonstrating that something was fundamentally wrong with the penitentiary system.

An Abiding Question. Were prisons intended to reform convicts, to punish them, or simply to separate them from society? This was a basic question that experts, from law-enforcement officials to social scientists, had been asking since the earliest modern prisons of the 1820s. In the 1950s it still went unanswered. Clearly convicts were not being reformed. A *Nation's Business* magazine article from December 1954 reported that 62 percent of the convicts released from prison would be back. "There is not the slightest reason to believe that the remaining 38 [percent] have abandoned crime," the article continued. "Many of them learn enough in jail not to repeat previous mistakes in technique."

Influential Company. Penologists (experts on prisons) would have preferred to see convicts learning a trade. But not many facilities of the time taught job skills. Businesses in the outside world worried about competition from prisons acting as low-cost factories. Consequently, the convicts were left with either meaningless toil or languishing in their cells. The company of their fellow criminals had a much more significant influence on them than poorly planned work programs. A warden from a prison in Jefferson City, Missouri, the site of a bloody riot in 1954, was quoted in *Life* magazine as saying, "If we rehabilitate anybody here, it's by accident."

An Inexact Science. Nor were prisons effectively protecting society from its dangerous members. As previously mentioned, more than 60 percent of convicts were leaving to commit crimes again. The policy of indeterminate sentencing, in which the possibility of parole was offered as an incentive to good behavior, was an inexact science. The press seized on examples of dangerous criminals who had served abbreviated sentences; meanwhile, nonviolent offenders stayed behind bars. Penologists, according to *Life*, believed that "one quarter to one half of all the men in prison today could safely be

By the 1950s the more vicious cruelties of prison life—beatings, torture, starvation, filthiness—had been almost completely eliminated from American facilities. There were, however, a few unfortunate exceptions, especially in poor southern states. One such prison was Louisiana's Angola state penitentiary, where, as *Newsweek* reported on 12 March 1951, thirty-seven prisoners crippled themselves, some permanently, by slicing the tendons in their heels with razor blades. Warden Rudolph Easterly tried to downplay the incident, but such a graphic protest was difficult to ignore. Governor Earl Long appointed a committee to investigate conditions at Angola.

At the prison the committee found the miserable results of several decades of neglect by the Louisiana state government, beginning during the reign of Governor Long's brother, Huey, in 1928. Prisoners lived crowded together by the hundreds into wooden, tumbledown barracks. Four toilets without seats and four showers were shared among 250 men. Beatings were common. Prisoners were loaned as manual laborers to outside businesses. They were offered little medical treatment and no rehabilitation.

Long had not expected the committee to make a serious investigation, but the scandal over the disgraceful conditions at Angola contributed to the governor's downfall. Prison reform became a major issue of Louisiana's gubernatorial election of 1952, when Robert F. Kennon defeated Long's handpicked successor. Acknowledging that "Angola was one of the big reasons I was elected," Kennon immediately set about authorizing the necessary funds and enlightened leadership "to change Angola from one of the worst prisons in the country to one of the best."

Source: Edward W. Stagg with John Lear, "America's Worst Prison," *Collier's*, 130 (22 November 1952): 13–16.

among inmates became more common as the growing number of inmates overwhelmed prison authorities. The American Prison Association believed that no prison could be effectively run with more than twelve hundred inmates; yet, in the 1950s, facilities around the country housed two to three times as many. Life behind bars was a dehumanizing experience, certainly a punishment; but no humane person could claim that this was a productive goal in itself.

Heroic Contributions. It was not impossible, however, for convicts to make positive contributions to the society that had locked them away. Some made heroic sacrifices in order to further medical research, often without any promise of reward. In February 1953 at Sing Sing prison in New York, sixty-two volunteers were injected with syphilis. During the Korean War, when the country had a vital interest in maintaining a supply of uncontaminated blood, convicts became guinea pigs in the fight against serum hepatitis. During the studies three prisoners lost their lives to the disease.

Sources:
Ernest Havemann, "The Paradox of the Prisons," *Life* (30 September 1957): 85–115;

Bill Slocum, "U.S. Prisons: A $215,000,000 Blunder," *Nation's Business* (December 1954): 86–90;

Don Wharton, "Prisoners Who Volunteer, Blood, Flesh — And Their Lives," *American Mercury* (December 1954): 51–55.

RED MONDAY

Talking Communism. One evening in 1950, a year after the Communist revolution in China, a Houston couple sat down in a local Chinese restaurant. The woman, a radio writer, asked the Asian owner some questions regarding a program she was producing on recent developments in China. A man seated at a nearby table overheard the conversation, rushed to the nearest phone, and informed the police that people were "talking Communism." The police then arrested the couple and incarcerated them for fourteen hours before concluding that there was no case.

A History of Paranoia. This was not an isolated incident. Several decades worth of anticommunist paranoia reached a fever pitch during the 1950s. By 1957 nearly six million persons had been investigated by administrative agencies and legislative committees because of their alleged disloyalty to the United States, with only a handful of dubious convictions resulting. Congress had long been investigating with deep concern the presence of Communists in the United States, starting with the formation of the House Un-American Activities Committee (HUAC) in 1938. In 1940, ostensibly as a measure against enemy agitators in the tense days just before World War II, Congress passed the Alien Registration Act, or Smith Act. The Smith Act, which provided the legal basis for many of the prosecutions of leftists during the 1950s, made it illegal to advocate or organize any group with the

released on parole and that their chances of going straight would in fact be improved by releasing them at the psychologically correct moment rather than keeping them confined." But there simply were not enough qualified experts to make such delicate judgments for each convict.

No Room. Whether it was intentionally the case or not, the only thing prisons seemed to do effectively was punish. Lack of privacy, one of the harsh realities of prison life, became a serious problem due to overcrowding. Cells designed to house two prisoners sometimes held three or four. Discipline suffered and violence

purpose of overthrowing the United States government by force or violence.

"McCarthyism." Later, after World War II and the emergence of a powerful, expanding Communist Soviet Union, the U.S. government increased its distrust of the American Communist party. In 1947 the Harry S Truman administration issued a loyalty order, which required Federal Bureau of Investigation checks on all federal employees. Sen. Joseph McCarthy accused the government of violating that order at a woman's club meeting in Wheeling, West Virginia, 9 February 1950, when he alleged that the State Department knowingly employed Communists. With this statement the senator introduced the public to his strategy of attacking fellow Americans through innuendo and distortion of the truth. "McCarthyism" is the popular name for the anticommunist hysteria that gripped the country during the decade. A national survey showed more than half of Americans believed that Communists should be jailed, and seventy-eight percent thought it a good idea to report to the FBI neighbors and acquaintances whom they suspected of being Communists.

Nipping Revolutions in the Bud. Conservative Supreme Court decisions regarding First Amendment freedoms of speech and assembly reflected the country's anxious mood. The 1950 ruling in *American Communications Association* v. *Douds* restricted freedom of speech, allowing the government to demand that union officers swear that they are not Communists before appearing before the National Labor Relations Board. In *Dennis* v. *United States*, after a sensational New York trial, a federal jury found eleven members of the American Communist party guilty of violating the Smith Act. The Supreme Court upheld the convictions in 1951 despite the defendants' contentions that they were merely meeting to discuss ideas, not taking actual steps to overthrow the government. The country must be free to nip revolutions in the bud, the Court ruled, rather than wait until actual revolution is under way.

"Red Monday." By the mid 1950s McCarthyism had peaked. McCarthy self-destructed in 1954 when he pushed the Senate Investigations Subcommittee, of which he was the chairman, into a politically disastrous confrontation with the U.S. Army. Soon after he was formally condemned by his fellow senators for "conduct unbecoming a member of the United States Senate." And on 17 June 1957, the Warren court gave Americans back some of the rights McCarthyism had taken away. The date was dubbed "Red Monday" by the press, who claimed that the four decisions the Court handed down that day marked a victory for communism.

Service v. *Dulles*. The first and least controversial of the four decisions was *Service* v. *Dulles*. Service was a career foreign-service officer dismissed from his position even though the State Department Loyalty Board concluded that he was neither disloyal nor a security risk.

The Court ruled that the dismissal was arbitrary and contrary to the State Department's own regulations.

More Than an Idea. The second, and more important decision of Red Monday curtailed the effectiveness of *Dennis* v. *United States*. *Yates* v. *United States*, like *Dennis*, involved Communist party members convicted of conspiring and teaching the overthrow of the government under the Smith Act. In this case, however, the Court differentiated between discussion of political ideas — which is protected by the First Amendment — and active participation in the overthrow of the government. The Court held that to restrict one's freedom of speech, the government must show that the speech advocated revolution as more than an idea. In other words, the government may criminalize active plans to overthrow it, but not political discussions of whether or not it should be overthrown.

No Power to Expose. The last two decisions, *Watkins* v. *United States* and *Sweezy* v. *New Hampshire*, involved legislative investigatory power. *Watkins* involved a union organizer who admitted he was a member of the American Communist party. He had been convicted of contempt of Congress for refusing to identify other members of the party before the House Un-American Activities Committee. In *Sweezy*, a university professor had been convicted of contempt for refusing to identify members of the Progressive party before the New Hampshire legislature. The Supreme Court overturned both the *Watkins* and *Sweezy* convictions. The Court could see no justification in narrowing the First Amendment simply for the sake of obtaining names, especially when it had never been shown that any of the targeted people or organizations actively advocated the overthrow of the government. As Chief Justice Warren put it, "There is no congressional power to expose for the sake of exposure."

Congressional Outrage. These decisions outraged a number of congressmen, particularly those whose platforms rested on exposing alleged revolutionaries and perpetuating McCarthyism. One legislator, Senator Jenner of Indiana, went so far as to propose a bill that would have deprived the Supreme Court of jurisdiction to review cases involving congressional investigations. However, a majority of legislators and the public had become weary and disillusioned with the witch-hunt atmosphere of McCarthyism, and the bill never became law. "Red Monday" still remains a victory for individual rights, supporting the freedoms of speech and association in the face of impulsive, aimless, and unwarranted governmental persecution.

THE SUPREME COURT OF THE 1950s

A Change in Philosophy. Looking at the ideological change in the United States Supreme Court during the 1950s, one would think that it underwent a drastic change in personnel. However, changes in three seats on the Court, between 1953 and 1956, made the difference:

with this turnover in justices came a turnover in the way the Court saw its role in government.

One Vote in Nine. The most visible and significant change in the Court occurred when Earl Warren became chief justice in 1953, replacing Fred M. Vinson, who had led the conservative Court since 1946. Warren has been celebrated as the force behind the Court's active drive toward establishing human and civil rights. (Certainly the John Birch Society thought so: they waged a campaign to impeach him.) Nevertheless, a chief justice has just one of nine votes, and no chief justice can command the beliefs and decisions of his associates.

The Liberal Voice. The seeds of change were planted when President Franklin D. Roosevelt appointed Alabama native Hugo Lafayette Black to the Court in 1937. Black was recognized as the leader of the Court's liberal wing, and in many ways it was his philosophy of judicial activism that the Warren court adopted. He envisioned the Court's role as that of a protector of civil liberties, especially those written into the Bill of Rights. If Congress or the president had not specifically written those rights into law, Black felt it was up to the courts to affirm them. He also considered the Bill of Rights binding on state governments through the Due Process Clause of the Fourteenth Amendment. This conviction increasingly influenced the Warren court's decisions during the 1950s and 1960s.

A Strong Ally. Black had a close ally in another Roosevelt appointee, Justice William O. Douglas. Douglas was a brilliant man: a Columbia law school graduate, an eminent law professor, and chairman of the Securities and Exchange Commission before his appointment to the Supreme Court at the age of forty. His tenure on the Court spanned thirty-six years, from 1939 to 1975.

BIRDS OF A FEATHER

One crime story of the 1950s suggested that the underworld was a small world after all. It began in 1950, when armed robbers held up the Manufacturer's Trust Company in the Queens section of New York City. Two of the robbers were identified as Willie ("the Actor") Sutton and Thomas Kling, both career criminals. Subsequently, each was added to the FBI's "Most Wanted" list, Sutton in March and Kling in July 1950.

Both remained free for almost two years. Sutton was recognized in New York by a subway passenger named Arnold Schuster, who reported the fugitive to the police. Kling, coincidentally, was captured by authorities two days later. Kling and Sutton were tried together for the robbery in Queens, and both received stiff prison sentences.

Unfortunately for Arnold Schuster, he became something of a celebrity for his role in capturing Willie Sutton. When Mafia chieftain Albert Anastasia saw Schuster on television, he flew into a rage and ordered that the "squealer" be killed. The task fell to Frederick J. Tenuto, a mob hit man who was also a "Top Tenner." Less than a month after Sutton's capture, Schuster was murdered near his Brooklyn home. Realizing that the hit on Schuster had probably been unwise, Anastasia covered his tracks by having Tenuto assassinated as well.

Source: Michael and Judy Ann Newton, *The FBI Most Wanted: An Encyclopedia* (New York & London: Garland, 1989).

Douglas was well known as a maverick: as one law clerk wrote, the justice "was just as happy signing a one-man dissent as picking up four more votes." As did Black, Douglas believed that it was the Court's duty to enforce actively the provisions of the Bill of Rights, especially in the face of state and federal legislative attempts to curb the freedoms it guaranteed.

Judicial Restraint. Opposed to the liberal viewpoints of Black and Douglas were the conservative justices Felix Frankfurter and Robert H. Jackson. Both of the latter were exceptional justices. Frankfurter had arrived in America from his native Austria when he was twelve years old. By the time of his appointment as associate justice to the Court by Franklin D. Roosevelt in January 1939, he had distinguished himself as a public servant and legal scholar. Through the 1920s and 1930s he was a strong supporter of liberal social causes, but as a justice he was the Court's spokesman for the conservative approach of judicial restraint. Justice Frankfurter viewed the Court, essentially, as an undemocratic leg of government, one

Willie "The Actor" Sutton, third from left, with attorneys before his 1953 trial for an April 1950 bank robbery

The Warren court: standing, from left, Tom C. Clark, Robert H. Jackson, Harold H. Burton, Sherman Minton; seated, Felix Frankfurter, Hugo L. Black, Chief Justice Earl Warren, Stanley F. Reed, William O. Douglas

that should interpret the words of the Constitution strictly and defer to the decisions of the other two representative branches on most occasions.

Bitter Feuds. Justice Black regarded this approach as a rejection of the judiciary's role under the Constitution. Justice Frankfurter, never a reticent figure, saw Black's and Douglas's activist approach as "self-righteous, self-deluded, part fanatic, part demagogue." Justice Jackson, another Roosevelt appointee, had originally taken up the activist cause with Black and Douglas. By 1946, however, after a two-year absence from the Court to serve as the chief prosecutor in the Nuremberg war-crime trials of Nazis, his sympathies had shifted, and he became Frankfurter's close ally. Books have been written of the intense internal feuds that took place within the Court: at times the rift between the two liberals and the two conservatives became so emotional that the groups hardly spoke with one another.

Middle Ground. Between the two factions was a moderate gray area comprising Justices Stanley Reed, Sherman Minton, Harold Burton, and Tom Clark. All were fairly conservative, especially in relation to Black and Douglas, but all could be swayed in their opinions. Indeed, Clark slowly came under the influence of the activist Warren court and, by the 1960s, became a crucial Warren supporter. Reed and Burton departed from the Court in the late 1950s, solidifying the shift in the Court's philosophy under Warren. But when Warren took the role of chief justice, the Court consisted of four justices evenly split into two opposing groups and four

moderate justices who could be swayed either way by the forceful personalities of the others.

A Dynamic Choice. Warren was not known for his legal scholarship abilities, yet his dynamic personality and prominence in the Republican party made President Eisenhower sure he would make a fine, conservative chief justice. In the beginning Warren did follow Frankfurter's philosophy of judicial restraint. Of course, many in the nation doubted this when, during his first term on the Court, Warren rounded all the justices together to join in the celebrated decision of *Brown* v. *Board of Education*. (See the section in this chapter on the *Brown* case.)

A Conservative Choice. Justice Jackson died in 1954. Annoyed at the rift in the nation over the *Brown* decision and determined to keep the Court conservative, President Eisenhower appointed court of appeals justice John Marshall Harlan to fill Jackson's vacancy. Educated at Princeton University, Harlan had been a Rhodes scholar and a successful Wall Street attorney before being appointed to federal court. Harlan was a learned and conscientious justice who believed in judicial restraint. Frankfurter took an immediate liking to him, as did the public.

Reviving the Constitution. However, Harlan's appointment failed to keep the Court conservative. By the middle of the decade Warren's adherence to Frankfurter's stance began to waver. This was near the height of McCarthyism: the Court regularly heard cases in which accused Communists claimed that their Fifth Amendment protection against self-incrimination and their Sixth Amendment right to confront an accusing witness had been violated. People were losing their careers and reputations in front of congressional "red-hunting" committees, which argued that these rights did not apply to their investigations. Warren was interested in what was just and felt, as did many people at the time, that the anticommunists were trampling the Constitution in their hunt for subversives. By the "Red Monday" decisions Warren had steered himself and the Court down the road of protecting and enlarging the constitutional definitions of human and civil rights.

Triumph of Activism. In 1956 Justice Minton resigned, and President Eisenhower appointed William J. Brennan, Jr., to the Court. Justice Brennan was a well-respected New Jersey Supreme Court judge. The chief justice immediately took a liking to Brennan's affable style, which was much like his own. To Eisenhower's dismay, Warren's influence on the new justice had him siding with the Black-Douglas philosophy from the beginning. With four strong activists on the Court and three moderates, Frankfurter's position lost ground. By the close of the decade, positions of moderates Burton and Reed were filled by Charles Whittaker and Potter Stewart, the latter also liberal minded. The activist ideology that began with Roosevelt's appointments of Justices Black and Douglas in the 1930s had firm hold of the Court under Earl Warren and was to continue until the 1970s.

Sources:
Robert Mayer, *The Court and the American Crises, 1930–1952* (Millwood, N.Y.: Associated Faculty Press, 1987);

Arnold S. Rice, *The Warren Court, 1953–1969* (Millwood, N.Y.: Associated Faculty Press, 1987).

ANCIENT JUSTICE

As late as the 1950s some American judges were still using unusual methods to arrive at a suspect's guilt or innocence. In March 1951 in Charleston, South Carolina, Magistrate Gene Herron balanced a Bible on the forefingers of a woman accused of stealing money from a restaurant. "By Saint Peter, by Saint Paul / By the grace of God who made us all, / If this woman took the money, / Let the Bible fall," intoned the judge. The Bible fell.

Afterward, the woman confessed and led the police to the missing money, which she had hidden in her house.

Source: *Time*, (5 March 1951): 24.

THE TEN MOST WANTED

Valuable Publicity. The Federal Bureau of Investigation's "Most Wanted" program began in March 1950, after a news story distributed by the International News Service on the "toughest" criminals currently at large appeared in 1949. The success of that story convinced the bureau that publicity might be a valuable tool in the capture of wanted fugitives. The more known a fugitive's face was through news reports and widely circulated wanted posters, the greater the chance he would be recognized and apprehended.

The "Top Tenners." Most of the "top tenners" were career criminals who had committed the federal offense of crossing state lines to flee prosecution or imprisonment. Some critics of the list contended that these

WORDSMITHS BEHIND BARS

One convict, Morris Lipsius of New York City's lower East Side, found an unusual way to go straight after his release from prison. He became a writer. Lipsius, a product of a broken home who had been on his own since the age of thirteen, seemed to be well on his way to the life of a career criminal. But while serving a sentence for armed robbery at New York's Great Meadow prison, Lipsius began working for Rabbi Hyman Goldin, the prison's Jewish chaplain. At Goldin's suggestion, Lipsius and a fellow inmate, Frank O'Leary, began gathering material for a dictionary compiling the slang used by criminals. In the course of their "field research" the two convicts became experts on the subject. With Rabbi Goldin they became coeditors of *The Dictionary of American Underworld Lingo*, which was published in 1950. Their new-found literary careers gave O'Leary and Lipsius (released in 1948 and 1949, respectively) an honest basis on which to build their lives outside.

The dictionary revealed the rich, colorful "slanguage" of the criminal subculture. For example, *boodle, buck, buttons, cabbage, cush, geedus, gelt, kale, silk,* and *spinach* are all listed as synonyms for money. One's face can be called a *kisse*r, *moosh, mugg,* or *squash*. A graveyard is a *bone-orchard*. To escape was to *beat the pups* or *take it on the Dan O'Leary* (no relation).

Source: "The Lexicographers in Stir," *New Yorker,* 27 (1 December 1951): 101+.

"small-time" criminals were less worthy of the FBI's attention than racketeers or drug traffickers. In the cases of criminals whose cases had already been highly publicized, the bureau argued, the suspects' whereabouts are usually known, and so there was no reason to include them on the list.

Early Success. When the list was begun on 14 March 1950, Thomas Holden was the first fugitive named. He was a bank robber from the 1920s who at that time was being sought for the murder of his wife and brothers-in-law. The bureau's third addition to the list, William Nesbit, a jewel thief and vicious killer who had escaped from prison in 1946, became the program's first success. A pair of teenagers recognized Nesbit from his picture in the newspaper on 18 March 1950, just two days after he was named to the list. Of the original ten "Most Wanted" fugitives, nine were captured, most of them identified by alert citizens within a year after they were named to the list.

Successful Results. The listing program continued to enjoy a high level of success throughout the 1950s. Of the 122 fugitives named to the list during the decade (one, Nick Montos, had the dubious distinction of being named twice), only six were never captured. Two were found dead. The remaining 114 were almost all captured as a direct result of the unwelcome publicity resulting from being a "top tenner." Most of them surrendered to authorities without resistance. After making the list, they suspected their capture was only a matter of time.

Source:

Micahel and Judy Ann Newton, *The FBI Most Wanted: An Encyclopedia* (New York & London: Garland, 1989).

YOUNGSTOWN SHEET & TUBE COMPANY V. SAWYER

Memories of Rationing. At the outset of the Korean War in 1950, Americans remembered well the rationing and the scarcity of consumer goods during World War II. Fearing a recurrence of these hardships, they began hoarding goods, which caused prices to increase. In an effort to halt inflation, President Harry S Truman established administrative agencies to control wages and prices. The program worked for awhile until the newly established Office of Price Stabilization recommended increases in wages for steelworkers but not in steel prices. In the administration's opinion, steel companies already enjoyed more-than-adequate profits due to the increased demand and production of steel induced by the Korean War. The steel companies did not agree and refused to give the workers raises.

Taking Over the Mills. On 5 April 1952, at the height of the war, the steelworkers union threatened a nationwide strike. President Truman feared the catastrophic results that a national steel-mill shutdown might have on the war effort, and he ordered Secretary of Commerce Charles Sawyer to take possession of the mills, essentially nationalizing them. Under the Taft-Hartley Act of 1947, Truman could have ordered the union not to strike in the face of a national emergency. However, he chose instead to direct the Commerce Department to operate the mills.

Inherent Power to Act. The steel industry sought an injunction against Truman's action, arguing that neither Congress nor the Constitution gave the president authority to seize their property. The Truman administration, on the other hand, argued that the Constitution gives the president "inherent power" to act in the national interest, despite the lack of specific authority from Congress. The case of *Youngstown Sheet & Tube Company* v. *Sawyer* involved not only one of the nation's most powerful industries, but also a conflict between the legislative and executive branches of government, all set against the pressures of the Korean War.

"Supreme Law of the Land." The Supreme Court outlined the constitutional limitations of the president in its opinion and found that Truman had overstepped his powers. Article VI of the Constitution designated federal statutes as the "supreme law of the land" which means that when Congress writes laws for the executive branch to carry out, the president may not choose to ignore them. In strong words the Court pointed to the antistrike provisions Congress wrote into the Taft-Hartley Act as the only legal means the president had to stop the mills from closing. Wrote the Court: "Congress has not left seizure of private property an open field but has covered it by three statutory policies inconsistent with this seizure."

"At Its Lowest Ebb." Three justices dissented, most strongly on the grounds that this type of seizure had not been expressly forbidden by Congress. The power to stop the threatened strike was simply an alternative and did not preclude the president's seizure remedy. However, the majority's words that the president's power is "at its lowest ebb" when he reacts contrary to "the expressed or implied will of Congress" remain the rule today. The *Youngstown* decision stands as a reminder that under the Constitution the president must obey the laws as Congress writes them.

HEADLINE MAKERS

CARYL CHESSMAN
19??–1960
CONVICTED RAPIST AND KIDNAPPER

A Question of Fairness. The story of Caryl Chessman, who was arrested and eventually executed as California's "Red Light Bandit," captured national attention during the 1950s. The question of Chessman's guilt or innocence became less important than the question of whether or not he had received a fair trial. Chessman, in his efforts to avoid the gas chamber, became an author, a self-educated legal scholar, and a celebrity.

The "Red Light Bandit." The "Red Light Bandit" was responsible for a series of crimes in southern California in the 1940s. He accosted couples parked in secluded areas, robbed them at gunpoint, and on occasion took the women back to his car and sexually assaulted them. He got his name from the red searchlight mounted on his car, the sort that police vehicles used. On 23 January 1948 Chessman, a small-time hood then on parole, was arrested in a car matching the description of the bandit's, and inside the glove compartment were a gun and small flashlight of the type the bandit had used. While in custody Chessman confessed to the crimes; he later claimed that the confession had been tortured out of him.

A Vague Law. Chessman was prosecuted under California's "Little Lindbergh Law," which specified that any kidnapping in which robbery was the motive and in which the victim was physically harmed could be punished by death. By this law Chessman's crimes could be considered capital offenses, although the law—as the popular name of it implies — was written with kidnapping for ransom in mind. (The California legislature, in fact, changed the law shortly after Chessman's conviction

to eliminate the confusion.) Chessman was positively identified as the bandit by several of the victims, (but never in a lineup) — and once when he was taken to a victim's house in handcuffs. Several other victims said that Chessman was not their attacker, but he was never given their names so that he could call them for his defense.

Chessman's Defense. Unable to afford adequate legal representation, Chessman decided to represent himself in court. His jailers hampered his efforts to prepare his defense, however, and the judge in the trial behaved in a prejudicial manner toward him. Chessman was convicted, and the jury recommended the death penalty on 21 May 1948.

A Basis for Appeal. Every death-sentence case, according to California law, is given an automatic appeal. This process requires a verbatim transcript of the trial, prepared and verified by the court reporter who took the original notes. However, the reporter in the Chessman trial died before he could prepare the transcript. The prosecutor suggested another reporter, Stanley Fraser, who could interpret the late reporter's shorthand and prepare the record. Subsequently it was learned that Fraser was a chronic alcoholic, extremely unreliable, and the prosecutor's uncle. Most of Chessman's appeals started from the premise that these circumstances invalidated the testimony.

Appeal Denied. Chessman appealed his conviction repeatedly, avoiding eight scheduled executions in the process, some by only a few hours. When his case reached the U.S. Supreme Court, the Court ruled that he had not received fair treatment and ordered a hearing to determine the validity of the transcript. Despite expert testimony that the transcript was hopelessly muddled, and admissions by Fraser that he had left out whole sections and changed statements that did not make sense to him, the transcript was allowed to stand. Chessman was denied a new trial.

From Criminal to Celebrity. Over the years Chessman's case had become a national, even world-wide sensation. Much of its notoriety stemmed from the books Chessman himself wrote. The first, *Cell 2455, Death Row* (1954), was a best-seller, was translated into a dozen languages and even made into a film in 1955. Millions around the world signed petitions encouraging California to spare his life, and notables such as Eleanor Roosevelt, Billy Graham, and Robert Frost, among many others, pleaded on his behalf but to no avail: his options exhausted, Chessman died in the gas chamber on 2 May 1960, twelve years after his original conviction.

Sources:

Caryl Chessman, *Cell 2455, Death Row* (Westport, Conn.: Greenwood Press, 1954);

Gene Marine, "Seventh Execution of Caryl Chessman," *Nation* (October 17, 1959): 226–233.

HERBERT A. PHILBRICK

1915–

FBI COUNTERSPY

NEW YORK DAILY MIRROR

A Patriot and Hero. The title of Herbert Philbrick's best-selling autobiography, *I Led Three Lives*, describes how its author spent the 1940s: first, as an advertising executive; second, as a member of the Communist party; and third, as an agent for the Federal Bureau of Investigation, informing on communist activities. In the 1950s, when fear of and fascination with communist conspiracies reached a peak, Philbrick was considered a patriot and a hero for his work as a double agent.

A Communist Front. Philbrick first became affiliated with the Communist party in 1940 in Boston, his hometown. He had studied engineering in college, but worked as a salesman for an advertising agency. In that capacity he entered the offices of the Massachusetts Youth Council one day. The council, Philbrick was told, coordinated the activities of "progressive youth groups" and served as an advocate of young people. Philbrick was given the opportunity to organize a neighborhood youth group in the nearby suburb of Cambridge. His enthusiasm for the project, however, was soon dispelled when he realized that the council he helped establish was a "front," a supposedly legitimate organization disguising communist activities.

A Dangerous Decision. Philbrick, angered that people's good intentions were being exploited for communist purposes, reported his concerns to the FBI. On a federal agent's advice he stayed with the group, waiting for his cohorts in the council to lift the facade and actually reveal themselves as Communists. On the same day

that Philbrick was invited to join the Communist Youth League, a sort of training organization for the actual party, he also officially became an informant for the FBI. Philbrick's decision even to pose as a Communist was potentially dangerous to his livelihood and reputation. If he were exposed as a member of the party, he could not use his status as an FBI informer as an excuse: the government, his contact in the bureau informed him, would disavow any connection to him.

Stressful Years. Philbrick's duties as an undercover agent were to supply the FBI with as many details as he could as to the members, objectives, and practices of the Communist party. He filed regular reports and passed along to the bureau party textbooks and pamphlets. He was not paid for his work, but he was reimbursed for his expenses. As a Communist he was expected to put his advertising skills to work for the party, writing pamphlets and coordinating propaganda campaigns. What he later wrote of his experiences confirmed Americans' fears that many left-wing civil rights or pacifist groups were influenced, or sometimes controlled outright, by Communists. Philbrick's years as a Communist were stressful for him: he had to hide his party membership from all but his fellow members, and, of course, he kept his other secret from them.

A Household Name. On 20 July 1948 twelve leading Communists were arrested on charges of violating the Smith Act, conspiring to encourage the forceful overthrow of the U.S. government. Over Philbrick's objections, the government decided that he should abandon his undercover activities and testify at the trial of "the Twelve." He revealed his activities publicly in court in April 1949. After almost ten years of secrecy, Philbrick soon became a household name. His 1952 book describing his experiences was widely read and inspired a television series of the same name with Richard Carlson as Philbrick. The series, which had Philbrick foiling Communist attempts at subversion on a weekly basis, bore little resemblance to any of his actual three lives, although Philbrick was a technical adviser for the show.

Source:

Herbert A. Philbrick, *I Led 3 Lives: Citizen, "Communist," Counterspy* (New York: McGraw-Hill, 1952).

ETHEL & JULIUS ROSENBERG

1915–1953 – 1918–1953

EXECUTED "ATOMIC" SPIES

INTERNATIONAL NEWS PHOTO

Convicted by Circumstance. Ethel and Julius Rosenberg were convicted of conspiracy to commit espionage for their alleged roles in passing atomic secrets to the Soviet Union. No hard evidence against them was offered at their trial, although they had been implicated by several of their coconspirators, including Ethel's brother David Greenglass and Max Elitcher, a college classmate of Julius's. The Rosenbergs maintained their innocence throughout their trial. The fact that they were convicted on circumstantial evidence and the severity of their sentence indicate how seriously Americans took two of the greatest fears of the 1950s: communism and the atomic bomb.

A Communist Couple. Julius Rosenberg met his future wife, Ethel Greenglass, at a 1936 New Year's Eve benefit for the International Seamen's Union. Ethel was a strong union sympathizer, and she found that she and Julius held many political views in common. Julius, a student in electrical engineering at City College of New York, had joined the Young Communist League in 1934. After he graduated college in 1939, the couple married and moved into a small Brooklyn apartment. Soon Julius found work as an engineer inspector for the U.S. Army Signal Corps. For a while the Rosenbergs were active participants in the Communist party. They brought Ethel's younger brother David into the party and, later, David's wife Ruth. But after Ethel had a child in 1943, the Rosenbergs dropped out of the party and appeared to fall into a simple, domestic life.

A Spy Ring Discovered. David Greenglass was stationed as a machinist at Los Alamos, New Mexico, the site of the first atomic bomb test, during the Manhattan Project. On 15 June 1950 Greenglass confessed to the Federal Bureau of Investigation that he had passed information about the project to Harry Gold, a Swiss immigrant. Gold had already confessed to conspiring with Dr. Karl Fuchs, a high-level atomic scientist on the Manhattan Project, to pass atomic secrets to the Soviets. Greenglass also claimed that he had handed over documents to his twenty-six-year-old sister, Ethel, and her husband Julius Rosenberg. The next day FBI agents showed up at the Rosenbergs' apartment.

The Noose Tightens. Julius Rosenberg told the agents that his brother-in-law was a liar. His refusal to cooperate convinced the FBI that he was hiding something and that they were about to uncover a spy ring of unprecedented importance. Intensifying and broadening its investigation, the bureau found Max Elitcher, who told agents that Rosenberg had approached him various times during the mid 1940s attempting to obtain classified information to which Elitcher had access through his work with air force and navy contracts. The FBI felt it now had its case.

Questionable Procedures. On 17 August 1950 a federal grand jury indicted the Rosenbergs for conspiracy to commit espionage. Lack of direct evidence kept them from being charged with the more serious crime, treason. Their trial began on 6 March 1951 with Morton Sobell, who had been implicated by Elitcher as Rosenberg's accomplice, as the third defendant. The hysterical publicity and questionable procedures of prosecutor Irving Saypol

compromised the fairness of the trial. Saypol told the jury that "the evidence of the treasonable acts of these three defendants you will find overwhelming," even though the defendants were not accused of treason. During the trial the prosecutor announced in a national news conference that he had secured sworn affidavits from an old friend of the Rosenbergs's, William Perl, which conclusively proved the conspiracy. Saypol decided against putting Perl on the stand, however, when Perl admitted to lying in his affidavits.

Incriminating Flights. One by one, Greenglass, his wife, Gold, and Elitcher took the stand and testified that the Rosenbergs were involved in a spy ring, although Elitcher admitted that he never actually passed any documents to Julius Rosenberg. Sobell never took the stand. The Rosenbergs denied any wrongdoing on their part. When Saypol questioned them about their past affiliations with the Communist party, they pleaded the Fifth Amendment and refused to answer. A large part of Saypol's case rested on Sobell's flight to Mexico and Julius Rosenberg's attempt to obtain a passport after Fuch's confession. The defendants' attempted flight damned them in the eyes of the jury. After a day of deliberating, the jury found all three defendants guilty of conspiracy.

"Worse Than Murder." Now Judge Irving Kaufman had the responsibility of imposing the punishment. Although the defendants had not been convicted of treason, the judge appeared to pass sentence on unproven acts and an uncharged crime. Announcing that their crime was "worse than murder," he explained that "putting into the hands of the Russians the A-bomb has already caused, in my opinion, the Communist aggression in Korea, with the resultant casualties exceeding 50,000 and who knows but what that millions more innocent people may pay the price of your treason." On 5 April 1951 Kaufman sentenced the Rosenbergs to die in the electric chair and Sobell to thirty years in prison.

International Protests. The Rosenbergs unsuccessfully appealed their convictions for two years, eventually taking their case to the Supreme Court. Meanwhile, the public interest in their case reached international proportions. There were many demonstrations urging the commutation of their death sentences. Some chivalrous supporters were against the idea of executing a woman, but most protested the hysteria of the trial and the extreme severity of the punishment. On 18 June 1953 there were demonstrations in support of the couple in Paris and New York. The following evening, shortly before 8:00 P.M., the Rosenbergs were electrocuted in Sing Sing prison in New York.

Sources:

Alvin H. Goldstein, *The Unquiet Death of Ethel and Julius Rosenberg* (New York: Hill, 1975);

Joseph F. Sharlitt, *Fatal Error: The Miscarriage of Justice That Sealed the Rosenbergs' Fate* (New York: Scribners, 1989).

CHARLES STARKWEATHER
1940-1959

Executed "Thrill Killer"

LIFE

Teenage Killers. Eighteen-year-old Charles Starkweather and his fourteen-year-old girlfriend Caril Ann Fugate shocked the nation in 1958 with a murder spree that crossed two states and took eleven lives, including those of Fugate's mother, stepfather, and two-year-old sister. Starkweather, who idolized the late teen-rebel movie star James Dean, killed his first victim, Robert Colvert, during a gas-station holdup on 1 December 1957. Over a month later, during a visit to Fugate's home, he argued with Fugate's parents and killed both of them and their youngest daughter. For the next several days Starkweather and Fugate stayed at the house, Caril Ann turning away any visitors that appeared. Then they left in Starkweather's car.

An End to the Terror. In the days that followed Starkweather murdered seven more people in Nebraska and Wyoming. He and Fugate would rob their victims of any valuables or guns and then speed off in the victim's car. The couple was apprehended shortly after Starkweather's last murder, when a passerby struggled with him over a gun. When a deputy sheriff arrived on the scene, Fugate ran to him for protection, apparently terrified that Starkweather was going to kill her. Starkweather leapt into his stolen car and led police on a high-speed chase before he was finally captured.

Expert Testimony. Starkweather's trial was highly publicized. His court-appointed lawyers offered an insanity defense on his behalf, arguing that Starkweather could not tell right from wrong and therefore could not be held responsible for his crimes. Experts speculated that a blow to the head Starkweather suffered several years before might explain his murderous behavior. The jury, however, was not convinced. Starkweather was convicted, and he went to the electric chair on 25 June 1959.

The Most Trigger-Happy Person. What crimes, if any, Caril Ann Fugate committed was never determined. Initially Starkweather claimed that she was a hostage and took no part in the killings. Later, however, he changed his story: Caril Ann had killed several of their victims, he said, and was "the most trigger happy person I ever saw." Fugate insisted that she was always too afraid to try to escape, although Starkweather had frequently given her guns to hold and left her alone for hours at a time. She was tried and convicted for one of the murders Starkweather had consistently admitted to committing. Fugate was sentenced to life in prison and released on parole in 1977. Her and Starkweather's exploits inspired a film, *Badlands* (1973), which starred Martin Sheen and Sissy Spacek as the murderous couple.

Source:

Ninette Beaver, B. K. Ripley, and Patrick Trese, *Caril* (Philadelphia & New York: Lippincott, 1974).

EARL WARREN
1891-1974

Chief Justice of the U.S. Supreme Court

GALE PORTRAIT GALLERY

A Revolution Made by Judges. President Dwight D. Eisenhower once called his appointment of Earl Warren to the Chief Justice of the United States "the biggest damnfool mistake I ever made." Eisenhower regretted his choice because he had appointed Warren for his "integrity, honesty, and middle-of-the-road philosophy" — and while Warren's tenure on the Supreme Court certainly embodied those first two qualities, it just as certainly rejected the third. In fact, under Warren the Court practiced what is called "judicial activism," rejecting the tendency of more-conservative Courts to make decisions based on precedent, following the reasoning and authority of earlier, similar decisions. The Warren court frequently overruled earlier decisions, greatly expanding Americans' civil and individual rights even when there was no precedent for such rulings. The changes in the constitutional rights of Americans during the Warren-court era have been described as "a revolution made by judges."

Early Career. Earl Warren was born in Los Angeles on 19 March 1891. His father, a Norwegian immigrant, worked as a railroad car repairman. The young Warren worked his way through college and law school at the University of California, Berkeley; he was employed at odd jobs, including railroad callboy, mechanic's helper, and iceman. After being admitted to the California bar in 1914, Warren practiced law in San Francisco until World War I. After the war, Warren became a $150-a-month assistant prosecutor for Alameda County, California. He was elected district attorney of Alameda County in 1925. Warren next ran for and won the office of state attorney general in 1939. In 1942 he was elected governor of California. Californians were so fond of the governor that he was endorsed by both the Democratic and Republican parties before he won the 1946 governor's race.

A Controversial Appointment. Warren had been regarded throughout the early part of his career as a staunch, law-and-order Republican. His successful tenure as California's governor, as well as his position as Thomas Dewey's running mate on the 1948 GOP presidential ticket, had made him one of that party's most prominent members. When the Republicans regained the presidency in 1952, therefore, Warren expected to have a role in the Eisenhower administration. That role, after the unexpected death of Chief Justice Fred Vinson in September 1953, turned out to be as presiding judge in the highest court in America. It was a somewhat controversial appointment, the first — but by no stretch the greatest — controversy that marked Warren's association with the Supreme Court.

"Super Chief." For Warren, who was used to having the resources of a large state government under his control, being chief justice was considerably different from being governor of California. The chief has no direct power to command his fellow justices, but he does preside over the open court and the conferences in which the justices discuss decisions. Perhaps most important, the chief assigns the writing of opinions — essays explaining the reasons for the Court's decision and specifying how the decision should be applied. This job is vital to determining the evolution of the law, but also to maintaining harmony on the Court. Chief Justice Warren found that he had to tread carefully in order to keep the peace between the Court's great rivals: Justices Felix Frankfurter and Robert H. Jackson on the conservative side, and their opponents, the liberal justices Hugo L. Black and William O. Douglas. The justices of the Warren court, who all had more judicial experience than their chief, agreed that Warren assigned opinions and presided over discussions and oral arguments fairly and diplomatically.

Stepping Down. After Robert Kennedy's assassination, Warren feared that nothing could stop Richard M. Nixon from winning the 1968 presidential race. The two men had been bitter enemies since their days as California politicians nearly twenty years before. At age seventy-seven, the chief justice knew that he could not outlast a four-year conservative administration. To prevent Nixon from appointing his successor, Warren submitted his resignation to President Lyndon Johnson on 11 June 1968.

A Campaign Issue. Nixon's campaign had made the Warren court a major issue. He accused the court of "seriously weakening the peace forces and strengthening the criminal forces in our society," and he promised to appoint only justices who would "interpret, not try to make laws." Warren turned to President Johnson to appoint "someone who felt as he did" to the position of chief justice. The plan never worked, however. Johnson's planned replacement, Justice Abe Fortas, failed to pass the Senate confirmation, and Warren was unable to retire until after Nixon's election. President Nixon appointed Warren E. Burger as Warren's successor, and the Senate confirmed Burger overwhelmingly. Warren continued to be active in government, giving speeches and attending conferences and ceremonies. He died following a heart attack on 9 July 1974.

Sources:
Bernard Schwartz, *Super Chief: Earl Warren and His Supreme Court* (New York: New York University Press, 1983);

John Downing Weaver, *Warren: The Man, the Court, and the Era* (Boston & Toronto: Little, Brown, 1967).

PEOPLE IN THE NEWS

In 1956 **John Ogden Bigelow,** attorney and jurist, was nearly denied a position on the board of governors of Rutgers University because as a lawyer he had defended accused Communist schoolteacher **Richard Lowenstein;** after bitter debate and personal appeals from New Jersey's governor, the state senate finally agreed to confirm Bigelow.

In 1953 **Herbert Brownell, Jr.,** became U.S. attorney general under President Dwight Eisenhower. He served in the post until his resignation in October 1957. During his first year as attorney general, in November 1953, Brownell made headlines by accusing the Harry S Truman administration of promoting known-Communist **Harry Dexter White** to a high-level position in the State Department.

In 1954 **Roy Cohn,** chief counsel for the Senate Permanent Investigations Subcommittee, resigned from the position after facing considerable criticism during that year's army-McCarthy hearings.

Beginning in 1952 **Reed Cozart,** a pioneer in prison reform, led the effort to transform Louisiana's Angola prison from "America's worst prison" to a modern, humane facility.

In 1953 six-year-old **Bobby Greenlease,** son of a wealthy Missouri auto dealer, was kidnapped; the kidnappers received $600,000 in ransom from the boy's parents. Bobby was never returned, however: the kidnappers, **Carl Austin Hall** and **Bonnie Brown Heady,** had murdered him almost as soon as they had kidnapped him. The couple was apprehended, and a little less than half of the ransom money was recovered, although they had only spent a few thousand. The FBI suspected that a member or members of the Saint Louis police force had stolen the rest.

In April 1959 **Judge Learned Hand** celebrated his fiftieth year as a federal judge. He was credited by his peers as having established in his written opinions many of the principles on which American jurisprudence was based.

In 1958 **Nathan Leopold,** who with **Richard Loeb** committed one of the most sensational murders of the twentieth century, was released on parole after thirty-three years of imprisonment. Loeb had been killed in prison in 1936.

In 1957 a Florida judge awarded custody of six-year-old **Hildy McCoy** to the couple who had raised her since shortly after her birth. Custody was contested by Hildy's biological mother, a Roman Catholic who wanted to ensure that the girl was adopted by a Catholic family.

In 1957 **George Metesky,** a quiet resident of Waterbury, Connecticut, was arrested as the "Mad Bomber" who had terrorized New York City by planting thirty-two bombs over sixteen years, causing explosions that injured fifteen persons.

In 1951 **William O'Dwyer,** U.S. ambassador to Mexico, was accused by the Kefauver committee of allowing crime to flourish during his tenures as district attorney of Brooklyn and mayor of New York.

In 1955 the Supreme Court ruled that **Dr. John Bennett Peters,** a professor of medicine at Yale University, had been wrongfully dismissed by the U.S. Loyalty Review Board from a consultant's position with the Public Health Service. The Court ruled that the board had exceeded its authority, pointedly refusing to rule on the constitutionality of that authority.

In 1951 the case of **William W. Remington,** an economist for the Department of Commerce, gained public attention. Remington was found guilty of perjury by a federal jury in New York for denying that he was a member of the Communist party. His conviction was reversed on appeal, but in October 1951 he was reindicted and reconvicted. In November 1954 he was killed in a brutal beating in prison.

In 1956 **Victor Riesel,** a newspaper columnist and outspoken critic of labor racketeering, was blinded by an unknown assailant who threw sulfuric acid in his face,

apparently to discourage him from testifying before a congressional committee.

In September 1957 **Terrence Roberts, Elizabeth Eckford, Melba Pattillo, Gloria Ray, Thelma Mothershed, Carlotta Walls, Minnijean Brown, Ernest Green,** and **Jefferson Thomas** were are denied admittance to Central High School in Little Rock, Arkansas. In the national press they were known as the "Little Rock Nine," on whose behalf the federal government interceded to enforce the Supreme Court's integration mandates.

In November 1957 **William P. Rogers** replaced **Herbert Brownell, Jr.,** as President Eisenhower's attorney general. Rogers clarified and effectively administered the federal government's school-desegregation policy. He served as attorney general for the rest of Eisenhower's presidency.

In 1951 **Stanley R. Schrotel** became chief of police for Cincinnati, Ohio, and over the decade changed the Cincinnati police force from a scandal-ridden one to a model of efficiency and honesty with a worldwide reputation.

In 1954 **Dr. Sam Sheppard** was convicted of his wife's murder after a highly publicized trial. Twelve years later, a second trial was held with young lawyer **F. Lee Bailey** representing Sheppard. In this second trial Sheppard was acquitted.

In January 1959 **Marie Torre,** a syndicated columnist who wrote about celebrity news, went to prison for ten days rather than reveal the source of a rumor that **Judy Garland** was suffering from an "inferiority complex" and obesity. Garland, in response, had sued the CBS network, where the rumor had supposedly originated.

In November 1959 **Charles Van Doren,** who had become a national celebrity on the basis of his appearances on the NBC game show *Twenty-One,* admitted before a congressional subcommittee that he had been coached in questions, answers, and even mannerisms during his reign as champion on the show.

In 1956 **Peter Howard Weinberger,** month-old infant son of Mr. and Mrs. Morris Weinberger of Westbury, Long Island, New York, was kidnapped and held for ransom; after two months of searching and several false arrests, Nassau County police arrested New York cabdriver **Angelo LaMarca.** LaMarca confessed that he had abandoned the child in a wooded area, where police found the body.

In 1954 **Joseph Nye Welch,** a Boston lawyer, was thrust into national prominence as the skillful counsel for the army in the televised army-McCarthy hearings.

DEATHS

Alberto Anastasia, 55, "Lord High Executioner" of organized crime's Murder, Inc., 25 October 1957.

Wendell Berge, 52, head of the Department of Justice's Anti-Trust Division (1943–1947), 24 September 1955.

Emanuel H. Bloch, 52, attorney who defended Ethel and Julius Rosenberg, 30 January 1954.

Charles Culp Burlingham, 100, attorney and advocate of civil reform in New York City, 6 June 1959.

Francis Gordon Caffey, 82, federal judge who presided at the twenty-seven-month trial of the antitrust case against the Aluminum Company of America (ALCOA), 20 September 1951.

William L. Clark, 66, chief justice of the U.S. Court of Appeals in West Germany (1948–1953), 9 October 1957.

Bartley C. Crum, 59, noted divorce attorney, obtained a million-dollar settlement for actress Rita Hayworth from Prince Aly Khan, 9 December 1959.

Homer Cummings, 86, U.S. attorney general (1933–1939), proposed to President Franklin Roosevelt the idea of "packing" the Supreme Court with justices sympathetic to Roosevelt's policies, 10 September 1956.

William J. Foley, 65, district attorney of Boston (1926–1952), 1 December 1952.

William L. Frierson, 83, U.S. solicitor general (1920–1921), 25 May 1953.

Henry William Goddard, 79, judge of the Federal District Court, Southern District of New York (1923–1954), 26 August 1955.

T. Alan Goldsborough, 73, federal district judge (1939–1951), 16 June 1951.

Rudolph Halley, 43, counsel for the Senate Crime Investigating Committee (1950), 19 November 1956.

Augustus Noble Hand, 85, judge of the U.S. Circuit Court of Appeals, Second District (1927–1953), 28 October 1954.

Arthur Garfield Hays, 73, attorney and civil rights activist who served as counsel without fee to Thomas Scopes, Nicola Sacco and Bartolomeo Vanzetti, and the Scottsboro defendants, 14 December 1954.

Dr. Edward Oscar Heinrich, 72, American criminologist and innovator in methods of crime detection, 29 September 1953.

Ligon Johnson, 78, noted copyright lawyer and counsel to much of the film industry, 29 March 1951.

Frederick Katzmann, 78, district attorney who prosecuted the case against Sacco and Vanzetti, 15 October 1953.

Joseph B. Keenan, 66, attorney who served as prosecutor in the 1945 Japanese war-crimes trials, 8 December 1954.

Edward J. McGoldrick, 80, New York Supreme Court justice (1929–1951), 8 January 1951.

Terence J. McManus, 79, noted New York lawyer, 19 May 1950.

Joseph Morelli, 70, allegedly the actual perpetrator of the crimes for which Sacco and Vanzetti were executed, 26 August 1950.

Seth Whitley Richardson, 73, chief counsel for the 1946 congressional investigation of Pearl Harbor and former chairman of the Subversive Activities Control Board, 17 March 1953.

Owen Josephus Roberts, 80, associate justice of the U.S. Supreme Court (1930–1945), 17 May 1955.

Charles J. Scully, 68, FBI agent who exposed stock swindling in the 1920s, 4 August 1952.

Charles B. Sears, 80, a presiding justice at the Nuremberg war-crimes trials, 17 December 1950.

Charles Warren, 86, Pulitzer Prize–winning author of *The Supreme Court in United States History* (1923), 16 August 1954.

Jesse E. Wilkins, 54, attorney, the first African-American to hold a subcabinet post (assistant secretary of labor, 1954–1958), 19 January 1959.

PUBLICATIONS

David Abrahamson, *Who Are the Guilty? A Study of Education and Crime* (New York: Rinehart, 1952);

Charles Abrams, *Forbidden Neighbors* (New York: Harper, 1955);

Jack Anderson, *The Kefauver Story* (New York: Dial, 1956);

Louis E. Burnham, *Behind the Lynching of Emmett Louis Till* (New York: Freedom Associates, 1955);

Paul A. Carter, *Another Part of the Fifties* (New York: Columbia University Press, 1983);

Donald Clemmer, *The Prison Community* (New York: Rinehart, 1958);

Benjamin Fine, *1,000,000 Delinquents* (Cleveland: World, 1955);

John Joseph Floherty, *Our F.B.I.* (Philadelphia: Lippincott, 1951);

Karen Sue Foley, *The Political Blacklist in the Broadcast Industry: The Decade of the 1950's* (New York: Arno, 1979);

Foley, *Television and the Red Menace* (New York: Praeger, 1985);

J. Edgar Hoover, *Masters of Deceit* (New York: Holt, 1958);

John Kenneth Jones, *The FBI in Action* (New York: New American Library, 1957);

Estes Kefauver, *Crime in AMerica* (Garden City, N.Y.: Doubleday, 1951);

The Kefauver Committee Report on Organized Crime (New York: Didier, 1951);

Richard Kluger, *Simple Justice: The History of Brown vs. Board of Education and Black America's Struggle for Equality* (Mew York: Knopf, 1975);

Max Lowenthal, *The Federal Bureau of Investigation* (Westport, Conn.: Greenwood Press, 1950);

John L. McClellan, *Crime Without Punishment* (New York: Duell, Sloan & Pearce, 1962);

St. Clair McKelmay, *True Tales from the Annals of Crime and Rascality* (New York: Random House, 1951);

William Charles Ousler, *Narcotics: America's Peril* (Garden City, N.Y.: Doubleday, 1952);

Austin Larimore Porterfield, *Mid-Century Crime in Our Culture* (FortWorth, 1954);

Red Channels: The Report of Communist Influence in Radio and Television (N.p., 1950);

Quentin James Reynolds, *Courtroom: The Story of Samuel S. Liebowitz* (New Yorl: Farrar, Straus, 1950);

Malcolm Pitman Sharp, *Was Justice Done?* (New York: Monthly Review Press, 1956);

Andrew Tully, *Treasury Agent: The Inside Story* (New York: Simon & Schuster, 1958);

John Wexley, *The Judgment of Julius and Ethel Rosenberg* (New York: Cameron & Kahn, 1955);

Don Whitehead, *The FBI Story* (New York: Random House, 1956);

ABA Journal, periodical;

Business Lawyer, periodical;

Master Detective, periodical;

Official Detective Stories, periodical;

Police Chief, periodical;

True Detective, periodical founded in 1950.

CHAPTER EIGHT
LIFESTYLES AND SOCIAL TRENDS

by CHARLES D. BROWER

CONTENTS

Sidebars and tables are listed in italics.

1950

- Levittown, near Hicksville, Long Island, adds a new suburban home every fifteen minutes.

- The Henry J, a domestically produced compact car, is introduced by the automaker Henry J. Kaiser.

- *Prevention* magazine, which champions folk remedies over established medical practices, debuts, helping to launch a folk-remedies craze.

- *Look Younger, Live Longer* by Gayelord Hauser is published; the book becomes a best-seller and boosts demand for "wonder foods" such as yogurt and blackstrap molasses.

- Smokey the Bear, an orphaned bear cub, becomes the symbol of the U.S. Forestry Service, beginning a twenty-five-year career.

- *Betty Crocker's Picture Cookbook*, based on General Mills's fictitious spokeswoman, is published.

17 July   A survey by the University of Michigan library shows that almost half of the U.S. population does not read books.

1951

- A Denver grocery-store chain revives the use of trading stamps by offering S&H stamps to store customers.

- Gerber Products Company starts using the flavor additive MSG (monosodium glutamate) to make its baby foods taste better to mothers.

- The French clothes manufacturer Izod introduces the Lacoste shirt to the United States; the tennis shirts, which sport the alligator symbol associated with French tennis star René Lacoste, become status symbols.

12 Feb.   The U.S. Office of Naval Research reports that purported flying saucers can almost always be attributed to high-altitude weather balloons used for cosmic-ray research.

1 July   The largest unsegregated audience in Atlanta since Reconstruction meets at the convention of the National Association for the Advancement of Colored People.

5 Nov.   The New Jersey Turnpike opens.

1952

- More than fifty-two million automobiles ride American highways, up from twenty-five million in 1945.

- *Amy Vanderbilt's Complete Book of Etiquette* is published.

- The first Holiday Inn motel opens in Memphis, Tennessee.

- A contraceptive pill for women is developed by G. D. Searle laboratories in Chicago.

17 July   The U.S. Air Force reports a wave of UFO sightings, sixty in the previous two weeks.

26 Nov.   *Bwana Devil,* the first full-length 3-D movie requiring the use of polarized eyeglasses, premieres.

30 Dec.   The Tuskegee Institute reports that 1952 was the first in seventy-one years in which no lynchings were reported.

1953

- Alfred Kinsey's *Sexual Behavior in the Human Female* is published.
- Chevrolet introduces the two-seat Corvette sports car.
- The Kellogg Company introduces Sugar Smacks breakfast cereal, which is 56 percent sugar.
- Cigarette makers respond to reports of a link between smoking and cancer by introducing "safer" filter-tipped cigarettes.
- Sara Lee Kitchens begins to mass-market frozen cakes and pies successfully.

14 Apr.   The air force publication *Air Training* reports that one thousand flying saucer sightings were reported to the government's Air Intelligence Center during 1952.

26 Oct.   The Songwriter's Protective Association reports that coin-operated jukeboxes gross nearly $1 billion annually in the United States.

1954

- C. A. Swanson and Sons introduces frozen TV dinners.
- The cha-cha, based on the Cuban Chanzon, becomes a popular dance in U.S. dance halls.

31 Aug.   Hurricane Carol batters the mid Atlantic and northeastern United States, killing fifty-three.

15–16 Oct.   Hurricane Hazel causes 249 deaths in the U.S., carving a path of destruction from the Carolinas to New York.

27 Oct.   Twenty-six American publishers announce the formation of the Comics Code, regulating the contents of comic books.

15 Dec.   The United States observes the first Safe Driving Day, sponsored by the Presidential Traffic Safety Commission.

1955

- Ford introduces the two-seat Thunderbird sports car.
- The Coca-Cola Company officially uses the name Coke for the first time.
- The popularity of "Davy Crockett" inspires Americans to buy $100 million in merchandise related to the show.

19 Feb.   The Senate committee investigating juvenile delinquency denounces comic books as offering "short courses in crime."

July	WED Enterprises, owned by Walt Disney, opens Disneyland in Anaheim, California, and introduces "The Mickey Mouse Club" on afternoon television.
25 Oct.	Basing his statement on a 316-page summary of the U.S. Air Force's investigation into flying saucer sightings, secretary of the U.S. Air Force Donald Quarles claims he is convinced that no saucers have flown over the United States.

1956

29 June	The Federal Aid Highway Act is passed by Congress, authorizing $33.5 billion to build 42,500 miles of interstate highways.
11 Nov.	The U.S. Census Bureau reports that women outnumber men in the United States by 1.381 million.

1957

•	Wham-O Manufacturing introduces the Frisbee and the hula hoop.
Jan.	"American Bandstand," hosted by Philadelphia disc jockey Dick Clark, debuts on the ABC network.
2 Jan.	The Immigration and Naturalization Service announces that 350,000 immigrants, the most since quotas were established in 1924, entered the country in 1956.
10 Oct.	Secretary of State John Foster Dulles and Attorney General Herbert Brownell announce that fingerprinting will no longer be required of foreigners entering the United States for a year or less.
23 Dec.	The U.S. Census Bureau announces that the United States, with its three million square miles of land, had an average of fifty-seven persons per square mile.

1958

•	Pizza Hut, eventually the largest chain of pizzerias in the United States, opens its first restaurant in Kansas City, Missouri.
18 Jan.	New York City police break up a white-supremacist youth gang, with members ranging from sixteen to twenty-one years of age.
25 Feb.– 5 Mar.	Wood alcohol poisoning kills twenty-seven people in New York City who drank a homemade liquor called King Kong.
19 Mar.	Kentucky governor Albert B. Chandler signs into law a bill abolishing daylight savings time in the state and making it a crime to display publicly the incorrect time.
24 Mar.	Elvis Presley is inducted into the U.S. Army.

1959

•	The Ford Falcon, the first attempt on the part of the Big Three automakers to compete in the compact-car market, is introduced.
•	Supermarkets comprise 11 percent of U.S. grocery stores but are responsible for 69 percent of the country's food sales.
3 Apr.	University of Florida president S. Wayne Reitz reveals that fourteen employees were dismissed for homosexual activities.

5 May   Judge Jennie Loitman Barron of the Massachusetts Superior Court was named Mother of the Year by the American Mothers Committee.

19 May   The U.S. Public Roads Bureau reports that there are a record 68,299,408 registered vehicles on the road, approximately 1 for every 2.5 Americans.

15 Nov.   The Clutter family of Holcomb, Kansas, are found murdered in their home; the circumstances of their deaths inspire Truman Capote's *In Cold Blood* (1965).

OVERVIEW

Baby Boom. The 1950s was a decade of unprecedented economic and population growth for the United States. The baby boom that had begun in the years immediately following World War II continued well into the decade. From 1948 to 1953 more children were born than in the previous thirty years, and in 1954 the country experienced the largest one-year population gain in history. Some experts worried about society's ability to handle the added burden of so many new Americans. But each new American was also a new consumer, and most people thought optimistically that the high birthrate would help to support the expanding economy.

Immigration. Adding to the burgeoning population was a steady flow of immigrants, including war refugees from World War II and war brides from Korea. In the fifteen years after the Korean War, seventeen thousand Koreans immigrated to the country, many the wives and children of American soldiers. Many immigrants came from Europe, fleeing the Communist domination that had settled over Eastern Europe in the early days of the cold war. Allowed into the country under the 1948 Displaced Persons Act, these émigrés frequently established themselves in academic posts and industrial research. Another source of immigration to the United States was its neighbor to the south, Mexico. More than 275,000 Mexicans became U.S. citizens during the decade. Most settled in California, New Mexico, Arizona, and Texas and provided the majority of farm labor for the southwestern agricultural sector.

Youth. The high birthrate lowered the average age: by 1958 one-third of the population was younger than fifteen years old. As the country got younger, Americans began to pay more attention to the tastes and concerns of its children and teenagers. Another factor of the baby boom was that the average marrying age dropped; consequently teens began dating at a younger age too. The elaborate courtship rituals of teenagers became the subject of much discussion. Most offensive to many parents was the music that accompanied teen dating, a mix of black and country and western music and rock 'n' roll. The music celebrated teenagers' new-found sense of their importance and their emotional highs and lows. It contributed to the generation gap that became a canyon in the next decade, as did confused, charismatic young rebels such as the beatniks and film actors James Dean and Marlon Brando.

Fads. But rock 'n' roll was about fun too, which was all most kids wanted. A succession of toys and fads added to the fun of the 1950s; most it was designed for kids, but their elders often played along. Miniature ten-gallon hats and toy guns and holsters were popular among children, probably because of the number of western series that filled the airwaves in the early days of television. Slinkies, Silly Putty, and Frisbees all first appeared during the decade. But the toy most associated with the decade is the hula hoop, first marketed by Wham-O Manufacturing in 1958. The extreme popularity of the simple toy caused observers abroad and at home to wonder about the stability of American culture, but that did not stop young and old alike from swinging their hips.

Transportation. If America of the 1950s was a growing society, it was also a society on the move. Life was getting faster. There were more-powerful cars to drive and more and better roads on which to drive them. During the decade the American affair with the automobile became a full-blown romance. Drive-in businesses made it possible for customers to bank, watch a movie, or eat a meal without leaving their cars. When parking in inner cities became difficult, shopping malls sprang up at an incredible rate to serve the car-driving public.

New Roads. Greater mobility also provided Americans of the decade the freedom to travel. The National Highway Act of 1956 provided $26 billion to construct forty-one-thousand miles of interstate roads. The project took years to complete, but before the end of the decade new, efficient routes between major cities took Americans from one end of the country to the other. National parks, often a brief drive in the family car away, became popular vacation sites. New businesses such as the Holiday Inn motel chain catered exclusively to the needs of the traveler.

Dissenters from "Progress." Many Americans had new cars and new homes, furnished with new televisions and appliances. Yet something seemed wrong. Social critics noted that as America became more powerful and prosperous, individuals seemed to become more alienated. The observations of John Kenneth Galbraith, C. Wright Mills, and David Riesman reminded Americans of the dark side of affluence. From their books a picture of a different American emerged: one pressured to conform, hemmed in by an entrenched power elite, beset with choices, and yoked to an unfulfilling job.

Civil Rights. In his work on the country's conformity and alienation Riesman calls Americans the "lonely crowd." Yet there was another crowd that was even lonelier. Blacks were denied much of the prosperity that marked the decade. While nearly half of working white Americans of the decade could call themselves middle class, less than one-fifth of their black counterparts could do so. Landmark legal decisions regarding black educational opportunities were resisted until well into the next decade, denying most black students the opportunity to prepare for a career in mainstream society. Yet important groundwork for the more dramatic civil-rights advancements of the 1960s was laid.

Women's Rights. Women were also largely denied access to public power. The feminine ideal of the decade was the perfect wife and mother, and women who reached age thirty without marrying were viewed with suspicion. Domestic training for American girls started in childhood; few women were encouraged to pursue self-fulfillment through a career. Rather, a woman's success should be supporting a successful husband. Mrs. Dale Carnegie spoke for the generation in 1955 when she wrote in *Better Homes and Gardens:* "there is simply no room for split-level thinking — or doing — when Mr. and Mrs. set their sights on a happy home, a host of friends, and a bright future through success in HIS job."

Sex. Attitudes about the relationship between men and women outside of marriage underwent some revisions during the decade. Dr. Alfred Kinsey, in his *Sexual Behavior in the Human Female* (1953), reported that 25 percent of six thousand women surveyed admitted having extramarital affairs. Movie stars such as Marilyn Monroe and Brigitte Bardot exhibited a greater freedom with their sexuality, and an enterprising midwestern entrepreneur, Hugh Hefner, began *Playboy* magazine in 1953, which proudly represented a new, pleasure-seeking lifestyle.

Questions About the Future. While the 1950s was America's first decade as a world superpower, Americans at home sought to understand how their lives were changing. Mass culture had brought a greater degree of material wealth to a greater number of Americans, but at what cost? The concerns of poorer citizens without access to power in Washington were often ignored. The Protestant work ethic, announced many observers, was dead. Society was progressing, but many Americans did not share in the that progress. Others questioned whether or not that progress was positive. It was an age of anxiety.

TOPICS IN THE NEWS

THE BABY BOOM

Victory and Prosperity. During the Great Depression the marriage rate fell as uncertainty over economic conditions caused people to postpone decisions that would significantly affect their lives. Birthrates also dropped: pessimism shrouded Americans' expectations of a promising future for themselves and their children. After World War II ended, however, prospects seemed considerably brighter. Young Americans returned home from war in 1945 ready to reap the benefits of victory and a prospering economy. Accordingly, there were almost 2.3 million marriages in 1946, an increase of more than six hundred thousand over the previous year. Many of these newlyweds had children within a year: a record 3.8 million babies were born in 1947. This was the first year of the baby boom, which lasted for most of the 1950s. Between 1948 and 1953 more babies were born than had been over the previous thirty years. In 1954 a record birthrate, a low death rate, and an influx of 144,000 immigrants created the largest one-year population gain in U.S. history.

Booming Population. Experts correctly predicted that the boom would subside slightly toward the end of the decade, as the smaller generations of the 1930s and war years reached child-bearing age. But overall the U.S. population increased dramatically in the decade, from 150 million in 1950 to 179 million according to the 1960 census. This was by far the largest ten-year increase in population to that date. And by the middle of the next decade, when the baby boomers themselves started to have children, birthrates gathered steam again.

Effects of the Boom. Experts were divided as to the potential effects of the baby boom. During the 1950s economists frequently pointed to the growing population as a safeguard against economic stagnation. Each new birth represented new demands for food, clothing, and toys. In 1958, by which time children fifteen years old and younger made up nearly a third of the U.S. population, *Life* reported on the economic consequences of the boom. Babies were the potential market for eight hundred dollars in products in their first year. Toy sales that year reached $1.25 billion, and diaper services were a $50-million business. The American Seating Company

---

THE MAN OF THE HOUSE

In the March 1956 issue of *Reader's Digest* British author Philip Wylie laid the blame for the problem of rebellious youth squarely on Dad: "American men are lousy fathers," the article's title claimed. While the American father is busy overachieving, Wylie suggested, his family is without a male role model at home. "There are 168 hours in a week. The average man spends about 40 of them at work. Allow another 15 hours for commuting time, lunch, overtime, etc. Then set aside 56 hours, eight each night, for sleep. That adds up to 111 hours — leaving Dad 57 hours for eating, relaxing, or whatever he wants to do." And, Wylie asked, should Dad not want to spend at least some of that time with the kids?

Source: "American Dads are Lousy Fathers," *Reader's Digest* (March 1956): 99–100.

---

of Grand Rapids, Michigan, a major supplier of school furniture, tripled its business in the thirteen years following the end of World War II. Clearly, each little bundle of joy was also a blessing to American businessmen.

Effects on Education. Some people, however, worried about the burden the swelling population placed on society. Educators warned of coming teacher and classroom shortages — crowded schools plagued the educational system throughout the decade. Greater amounts of public money were needed for education, health care, and other social services. Agricultural experts doubted that the American farmer could keep up with growing demands. Social commentators could only wonder about the effect of the falling average age — which pointed to an increasing number of younger Americans compared to the decreasing number of older Americans. By the mid 1960s, when the first baby boomers entered college, the concerns of youth were having a profound impact on society. The baby boom provided new opportunities for Ameri-

One of the stranger results of the Cold War was the American mania in the 1950s to build their own backyard bomb shelters. The importance for shelter from nuclear war was stressed by the government in the Gaither report made for the National Security Council in the 1950s. Popular magazines followed suit by publishing stories about how to design fallout shelters and how these shelters might be stocked with necessary foods and sanitary items. *Popular Mechanics*, *Time*, and *Life* all ran detailed articles on shelter design during the 1950s.

The fear of nuclear holocaust led both citizens and governments to invest in building the shelters. Individuals could construct shelters large enough for their families and stock the shelters with enough supplies to last the fourteen days experts predicted that fallout would be at its highest. Walter Kidde Nuclear Laboratories was urged by civil defense authorities during the mid 1950s to design shelters for purchase by individuals. The luxury model, which sold for three thousand dollars, was fourteen feet long and eight feet in diameter. The self-contained unit came with an electronic generator, an air filtration system, canned water, five bunks with air mattresses, blankets, storage shelves, and safety suits to be used when entering the post-nuclear-war world. A smaller unit sold for twenty-five hundred dollars.

Governments could adapt basements to fallout shelters or construct separate facilities. An extensive plan for building a nationwide system of underground shelters was outlined by the research engineer Willard Bascom in the 18 March 1957 issue of *Life*. Also recommended by physicist Edward Teller, the father of the hydrogen bomb, the system of shelters would have been prohibitively expensive, estimated at three hundred dollars per person actually saved. The shelters proposed would be built in five-hundred-foot sections, each containing sleeping, recreation, commissary, and medical facilities for one thousand people.

All the public discussion about nuclear war and the need for bomb shelters added to the change in public attitudes during the 1950s. The idea of atomic war was a fearful prospect, as the images of Hiroshima and Nagasaki were still fresh in the public mind. The fallout shelter had a curious effect on that fear. Government and media images of fallout shelters tried to sell the public on the idea that atomic warfare would be an inconvenience that would interrupt, but not end, the accustomed pattern of life. This feeling was expressed in an article in the 10 August 1959 issue of *Life*. The article featured a story about a Miami, Florida, couple who spent their fourteen-day honeymoon in an underground shelter at the behest of a shelter-building company.

The fallout shelter was an enduring symbol of the cold war and the fear of atomic war. Many citizens only had to walk into their backyards to be confronted with the reality of preparation for war.

Sources: "Atomic Hideouts," *Popular Mechanics* (November 1958): 146–148;

"Back-yard Bomb Shelter," *Popular Mechanics* (October 1951): 112–113;

"Scientific Blueprint for Nuclear Survival," *Life*, 42 (18 March 1957): 146–148, 150, 153–154, 156, 159–160, 162;

"Their Sheltered Honeymoon," *Life*, 47 (10 August 1959): 51–52.

can retailers, but it offered new challenges to teachers, parents, and policy makers.

Sources:

Landon V. Jones, *Great Expectations: America and the Baby Boom Generation* (New York: Coward, McCann & Geoghegan, 1980);

Elaine Tyler May, *Homeward Bound: American Families in the Cold War Era* (New York: Basic Books, 1988).

BLACK AMERICANS AND SOCIETY

From Jim Crow to *Brown*. America in the 1950s was not nearly the "land of opportunity" for blacks that it was for their white fellow citizens. Throughout the decade "Jim Crow" laws around the country — but especially in the South — forbade almost all interaction between black and white Americans. Beginning with the *Brown v. the Board of Education of Topeka, Kansas* Supreme Court decision in 1954, the country took a series of important early steps toward racial equality during the decade. But change was slow in coming.

Poor Education. Although the *Brown* decision guaranteed black students the legal right to the same education in the same schools as white students, many schools resisted integration until well into the 1960s. Consequently few black students received a quality education. Their schools were poorly funded and understaffed compared to those attended by white students. These deficiencies probably contributed to the fact that fewer black students during the decade graduated from high school than white students. The scholastic achievements of black students suffered in comparison to whites in other ways as well. The 1960 U.S. census revealed that between 20 and 30 percent of black students (depending on the region of the country) were behind their proper grades by age fifteen — a much higher percentage than white students of the same age.

College and Careers. With a comparatively poor public-school education, blacks were less likely to pursue college careers than whites. By decade's end the proportion of blacks with four or more years of college was at 3 percent (the proportion of whites, 8 percent, was small as well but considerably higher). The cost of a college education kept all but a few students from pursuing a degree, and even those blacks with professional training had few doors open to them. Almost three-fifths of black professionals during the decade were teachers and clergymen; significantly fewer were doctors or lawyers; and, as *Newsweek* reported in 1955, there were only forty black certified public accountants in the country. Nearly all of these professionals had received their training at black colleges and were therefore generally considered unacceptable by white employers. Black professionals, whatever their training, dealt almost exclusively with a clientele of the same race.

Out of the Middle Class. Thus the rapidly growing middle class, to which so much attention was devoted during the decade, hardly included the country's fifteen million or so blacks. The proportion of blacks who could include themselves in the middle class according to the 1960 census was a paltry 13.4 percent, compared to nearly half of the white population. Although the average annual income of black workers had risen 300 percent since 1940, it was only thirteen hundred dollars — less than one-half the average salary of a white worker in 1955. Black workers were further hampered by underrepresentation in the nation's unions. Railroad brotherhoods, craft unions, and machinist unions all discouraged black membership. In 1955 Lester Granger of the National Urban League summed up job opportunities for blacks in each region of the United States: "Fair to good in the Middle Atlantic States, Northeast, and Midwest; poor to fair in the Border States, Northwest, Southwest; poor in the Deep South."

Black Middle Class. Since blacks were almost completely shut out of the newly prosperous middle class, a parallel black middle class, which had its roots several decades earlier, continued to develop. Social clubs, whose doings were covered in the society columns of black newspapers, provided opportunities for members of the black bourgeoisie to achieve the social respectability they felt they deserved. They also desired the same material luxuries that members of the white middle class enjoyed during the decade, although they were less able to afford them. E. Franklin Frazier, a sociologist who wrote several pioneering works on blacks, observed that middle-class blacks often spent beyond their means because they saw themselves as members of a social elite compared to other blacks in their community. As he wrote in *The Negro in the United States* (1954), "A teacher or a physician [in the black community] is not simply a professional worker but generally regards himself as a member of an aristocracy which requires certain standards of consumption" — standards they could rarely afford to meet.

Power of Money. Blacks were able to make inroads into mainstream American society because of the $15 billion they spent annually; their spending played an important part in the mushrooming American economy. White-owned companies realized more frequently the value of hiring blacks to meet labor demands but also to create more consumers. RCA, International Harvester, and Westinghouse were a few of the large companies willing to open their doors to black employees during the decade. As RCA president Frank M. Folsom remarked, "Equal job opportunities for Negroes and other minority groups will increase the income of this part of our population and hence widen the market for many products, including our own."

Sources:

Bart Landry, *The New Black Middle Class* (Berkeley: University of California Press, 1987);

Clem Morgello, "The Rise of Negroes in Industry: Problems . . . and Progress," *Newsweek* (12 September 1955): 86–88;

Daniel O. Price, *Changing Characteristics of the Negro Population* (Washington, D.C.: U.S. Government Printing Office, 1969).

THE CAR CULTURE

Return to Prosperity. Americans had suffered through fifteen years of economic hardship and material shortages from the beginning of the Great Depression through the end of World War II. Small wonder, then, that as soldiers returned home and economic prospects seemed much brighter, people were in a mood to buy. During the war automobile production had dropped drastically as automakers were enlisted in the war effort. The number of registered cars on the road plummeted by four million: as they became inoperable, their owners were unable to repair or replace them. Out of the 25.8 million registered cars in 1945, *Fortune* magazine reported that half of them were at least ten years old. Millions of these cars were ready for the scrap heap.

Production Surge. American automakers were glad to satisfy the pent-up demand for cars, of course, but they could do so only gradually. The process of converting back to civilian production went more slowly than Detroit hoped: only seventy thousand new cars came off the assembly line in 1945, far short of the predicted five hundred thousand. By 1950, however, production surged to a record eight million automobiles. Even at that high level of production the autos were bought as quickly as they reached the showroom. In 1955 there were fifty-two million cars on the nation's roads, double the amount ten years before. The country was in the grip of an "automania" that meant substantial changes in the American way of life.

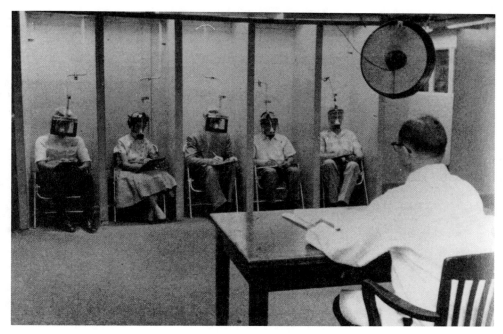

A smog irritation test being conducted on volunteers at the Stanford Research Institute's Atmospheric Chemistry Laboratory

Commuting. All those cars gave Americans a greater mobility than they had previously had. People were free to live outside of cities, for example, and commute to work or to shop. A 1957 study of urban problems titled *The Exploding Metropolis* reported that in America's twenty-five largest cities, an average of 60 percent of the people who entered downtown did so by car. New York City, because of its efficient mass-transit system, comprised the low end of this average (17 percent), while in San Antonio a high 78 percent of commuters provided their own transportation. As more cars swarmed into the cities, parking became a serious problem. In the middle of the decade the city of Boston determined that while an average of 150,000 cars entered the city daily, it only had parking space for 110,000 cars. The city's solution was to build parking garages underground; but as more parking became available, more people drove downtown. So the problem remained unsolved.

Pollution. The great increases in traffic also led to serious atmospheric pollution problems over the nation's cities. Smog, the combination of smoke and fog, became a familiar condition to Americans during the decade. Automobile exhaust was by far the largest contributor to these ever-present blankets of haze. In Los Angeles the enormous number of motor vehicles and the city's location — between a mountain range and the Pacific Ocean, in a basin of stagnant air — combined to make the problem especially acute. The city's Atmospheric Pollution Control Board declared frequent smog alerts, during which all nonessential traffic was supposed to stop and people with respiratory illnesses were instructed to stay indoors. But the problem was by no means limited to Los

Angeles. In the early 1960s Congress took steps to control the pollution problem by mandating that automakers develop smog-control devices for their cars.

Shopping Malls. As traffic and pollution problems plagued the cities, businesses relocated to the urban fringe. Shopping malls, clusters of stores under one roof, popped up in suburbs across the nation; they offered "plenty of free parking" as a major draw. Some suburban

FAMILIES ON WHEELS

Harper's magazine reported a growing phenomenon of the decade in its June 1958 issue. Alvin L. Schorr reported that more American families were living in trailer parks, in mobile homes they could relocate on short notice. These new mobile families challenged American notions of a stable home life, although, as Schorr pointed out, these families were rarely the source of any strife in the community. Most of them were headed by temporary workers who before long moved on to new job opportunities. When one of these transient Americans was asked by a social worker about his home state, he replied, "Do you mean where I was born, where I live, where my folks live, or where I last voted?"

Source: Alvin L. Schorr, "Families on Wheels," *Harper's,* 216 (June 1958): 71–75.

For years Walt Disney dreamed of constructing a theme park populated by the characters and settings his movie studio had created. By 1952 he had established WED Enterprises, and within that company a staff immediately set to work designing the park and deciding upon its location. Within two years construction of Disneyland began in Anaheim, California, thirty minutes from Los Angeles by freeway.

Many observers thought that Disney's theme park was doomed to failure. Disney had no intention of creating a conventional park with roller coasters, Ferris wheels, and hot dogs and beer. He envisioned a place that catered equally to children and adults. Investors were initially skeptical: during the 1950s it seemed as if amusement parks had permanently lost their popularity. Disney was obliged to find much of the funding himself. A fortunate agreement with the ABC television network, for whom Disney's studio produced the popular series "Disneyland," gave Disney not only the money to begin building but also an outlet for promoting his grand scheme.

When Disneyland opened on 18 July 1955, the park had barely been completed. Crews worked around the clock for two weeks prior to the opening. For Disney the day was enormously satisfying. As Richard Schickel wrote, "Disneyland, to him, was a living monument to himself and to his ideas of what constituted the good, true and beautiful in this world." For inspiration Disney and his designers drew from American history (Mark Twain's Riverboat Ride and Frontierland) and from memorable Disney movie creations (Dumbo's Flying Elephant Ride or the Nautilus Ride based on *20,000 Leagues Under the Sea*). Disney himself had a hand in every detail of his dream world, from constructing the rides to replacing plants that had been trampled by guests. He believed that the key to success was to create a friendly atmosphere for patrons of the park. Park employees, who were trained at "Disneyland University," were drilled on the park's philosophy, that "*every* guest receives VIP treatment." "Disneyland is a first-name place," they were reminded. "The only 'Mr.' here is 'Mr. Toad.'"

Not all of the early response to Disneyland was positive. Julian Halevy complained in the *Nation* in 1958 that "As in the Disney movies, the whole world, the universe, and all man's striving for dominion over self and nature, have been reduced to a sickening blend of cheap formulas packaged to sell." But such criticisms were drowned out by the park's tremendous early success. Slightly more than a million people visited the park in its first six months of operation, and in its first full year, 1956, it earned $10 million. In its first ten years of business Disneyland magically earned almost $200 million dollars.

Source: Richard Schickel, *The Disney Version* (New York: Simon & Schuster, 1968).

---

businesses encouraged Americans never to leave their cars at all. By the end of the decade thousands of drive-in theaters and tens of thousands of drive-in restaurants were serving motorists around the country. Other businesses, laundries and even banks, began accepting drive-in customers as well.

Highway System. People also used their cars for more-ambitious journeys than to the store or office. Vacationing by auto was a phenomenon of the decade, encouraged by the National Highway Act of 1956, which provided for the building of forty-one thousand miles of safe modern highways crisscrossing the country. For the comfort of motorists the highways also featured picnic and rest areas. Private businessmen also benefited from the new American wanderlust: travelers could find gas stations, motels, restaurants, and campgrounds at any stop along the way. Several entrepreneurs began earning their fortunes during the decade by catering specifically to the American away from home. Holiday Inns, for example, started by Tennessee architect Charles Kemmons Wilson in 1954, thrived by offering uniform service and lodging to the weary vacationer.

New Problems. With all the services it provided, the car had become an accepted — almost necessary — member of the American family. Still, disenchantment with automobiles had begun to set in. Many objected to the sales tactics of auto dealers, who, as Sen. A. S. Mike Monroney put it, displayed the attitude toward customers one would expect to find at "an Oriental Bazaar." Dealers relied on a variety of tricks of the trade, including the "switch," where buyers are lured in with an advertised special and then pressured to buy a more expensive model. Dealers argued that such tactics were necessary to sell the large numbers of cars and accessories the automakers forced on them.

A display of comic books discontinued through the efforts of the Comic Code Authority

Planned Obsolescence. Faced with a saturated market in the later years of the decade, the "Big Three" automakers — Ford, General Motors, and Chrysler — had to resort to tricks of their own in order to move their products. "Planned obsolescence," the idea that cars should be built to last only a few years, was one strategy to guarantee regular auto purchases. Another was to make yearly innovations and to advertise them heavily. These innovations had to do with a car's look far more than its safety or efficiency. Ford in 1956 offered a series of "Lifeguard Design" features, and its sales dropped by two hundred thousand cars. The drop could have been due to many factors, but it seemed to confirm the opinion of industry experts: "Ford is selling safety, but Chevy is selling cars."

Styling. During the decade Detroit concentrated on style. The tail fin, that legendary appendage of 1950s autos, made its first appearance on the 1948 Cadillac. General Motors chief stylist, Harley Earl, had borrowed the look from the P-38 fighter plane. On an airplane the tail fins helped stabilize the craft, but on a car they were purely for show. (When touring the United States in 1959, Soviet premier Nikita Khrushchev pointed at a Cadillac tail fin and asked, "What does that thing do?" The answer, as Khrushchev well knew, was that it did nothing.) Tail fins grew to absurd heights and slanted from the car at odd angles. Decked out with fins and with similarly useless bumper bullets, fake vents, and massive grills and trimmed with a generous amount of chrome, the American auto of the 1950s could be a strange sight. Americans of the decade thought the strangest-looking of the lot was Ford's 1958 Edsel, a notorious model that lost the company a quarter-billion dollars and whose name became synonymous with failure.

Small Cars. After the Edsel, automakers retreated somewhat from big cars with unusual styling; it seemed as if the public had lost its taste for such extravagance. Throughout the decade automakers believed that Americans valued size in a car, despite problems parking such behemoths and keeping them filled with gas. And that was confirmed with high profits. Sales of small foreign cars such as Volkswagens and Renaults climbed steadily during the decade, however; and when U.S. sales reached 10 percent of the market, the Big Three acted. In 1959 Ford introduced the compact Falcon, Chevrolet debuted the Corvair, and Chrysler introduced the Valiant. Consumers responded favorably: Falcon sales topped five hundred thousand that year. Detroit's taste for the exaggerated car designs of the 1950s had passed.

Sources:

James J. Flink, *The Car Culture* (Cambridge, Mass.: MIT Press, 1975);

John Keats, *The Insolent Chariots* (Philadelphia: Lippincott, 1958);

Stephen W. Sears, *The American Heritage History of the Automobile in America* (New York: American Heritage Publishing/Simon & Schuster, 1977).

COMIC BOOKS AND JUVENILE DELINQUENCY

Increasing Youth Crime. During the decade the problem of juvenile delinquency reached alarming proportions. As director of the Federal Bureau of Investigations J. Edgar Hoover reported in 1953, that "persons under the age of 18 committed 53.6 percent of all car thefts; 49.3 percent of all burglaries; 18 percent of all robberies, and 16.2 percent of all rapes."

Sadistic Acts. Americans were concerned not only by the number of youth crimes but by their ferocity. Reports abounded of sadistic acts committed by young criminals who often expressed no remorse. Dr. Frederic Wertham reported of a teenager who tortured a four-year-old boy because he "just felt like doing it." Dr. Wertham was one of the many self-proclaimed experts who offered an explanation for the alleged juvenile crime wave. A leader of the New York psychiatric community, he published the book *Seduction of the Innocent* in 1954, based on seven years of research. The book laid the lion's share of the blame for juvenile delinquency on comic books, which had previously been considered harmless entertainment for children. According to Dr. Wertham, comics were a "locust plague" that had settled on the children of America. Crime comics, which featured graphic depictions of torture, murder, and mutilation, were singled out as the most harmful. But even such icons as Batman and Superman came under fire: Superman was condemned as a symbol of "violent race superiority," and the Dynamic Duo of Batman and Robin was "like a wish dream of two homosexuals living together." Under the influence of such reading matter, Dr. Wertham asserted, children would inevitably suffer psychological harm.

Senate Hearings. Wertham's thesis was accepted by many people looking for a scapegoat for the juvenile-delinquency problem. He was asked to speak to community groups around the country and in 1954 was one of the star witnesses before the Senate subcommittee, headed by Senator Estes Kefauver, investigating the causes of juvenile crime. Testifying for comic books was William Gaines, the editor of EC Comics, publisher of some of the industry's grisliest horror titles. Gaines, and the industry in general, mistakenly underestimated the seriousness of Wertham's charges: they counterattacked with portrayals of meddlesome quack psychiatrists in their titles.

Self-Regulation. It soon became clear, however, that some form of regulation of the industry was inevitable. Rather than wait for regulations to be imposed by the government, comics publishers created the Comics Code Authority in 1954 to establish a set of guidelines as to what was and was not acceptable in comic books. Under the code, crime could be depicted only as "a sordid and unpleasant activity," no comic could use "Horror" or "Terror" as part of its title, and "Scenes dealing . . . with walking dead, torture, vampirism, ghouls, cannibalism and werewolfism are prohibited," among other restrictions. To the comic book fans of later decades, many of whom remembered fondly the comics of the 1950s, the establishment of the Comics Code marked the end of the medium's creative golden age.

Sources:

William W. Savage, *Comic Books and America, 1945–1954* (Norman: University of Oklahoma Press, 1990);

Frederic Wertham, *Seduction of the Innocent* (New York: Rinehart, 1954).

Girl placing sorority medallion around the neck of her boyfriend

COURTSHIP IN THE 1950S

Younger Marriages. During the 1950s Americans were marrying at a younger age than they had in generations. As Brett Harvey reported in *The Fifties: A Woman's Oral History,* "the median marriage age dropped from 24.3 to 22.6 for men [during the decade], and from 21.5 to 20.4 for women." Women were more likely to marry in their teens than were men: by 1959, 47 percent of all brides were younger than nineteen. This trend was a continuation of the marriage boom of the late 1940s, which was originally thought to be a temporary response by young Americans to the end of the war. By the 1950s, however, the trend seemed to be longer-lived, and it had the endorsement of many of the nation's experts. As Dr. David R. Mace, professor of human relations at Drew University, wrote in *Woman's Home Companion* in 1949, " When two people are ready for sexual intercourse at the fully human level they are ready for marriage — and they *should* marry. Not to do so is moral cowardice. And society has no right to stand in their way." The trend toward earlier marriage tended to reinforce itself: young people who waited longer than everyone else to marry might miss their chance.

Early Courtship. As Americans married at an earlier age, it was necessary for them to get an earlier start on dating. By 1956, as Phyllis McGinley wrote in *Good Housekeeping,* younger dating had gotten a little ridiculous: "pushed and prodded and egged on by their mothers or the PTA or scoutmasters, sixth-grade children are now making dates on the telephone and ineptly jitterbugging together every weekend evening." Earlier, in 1949, anthropologist Margaret Mead suggested that parents supported preteen dating so that they could influence their child's choice of a mate. In any event, as Beth L. Bailey noted in *From Front Porch to Back Seat*, "Thirteen-year-olds who did not yet date were called 'late bloomers.' "

Going Steady. As teenagers reached high-school age they tended to pair off into "steady" dating partners. This contradicted the dating practices their parents followed when they were young. The popular young people of the preceding few generations "played the field" more, having many dates with a variety of their peers. "Going steady" symbolized an intention to marry. But by the 1950s, as a poll in 1959 indicated, nearly three-quarters of all high-school students supported the idea of dating only one person at a time, and most of them probably had no serious intention of marrying their current sweethearts.

Dating Rules. Most communities of teenagers had precise rules of conduct for "steadies" to follow. Boys were expected to call and see their girlfriends a certain number of times a week. Neither boy nor girl could date anyone else, and each had to inform the other of any plans. In most places steadies were expected to make some sort of outward show of their commitment to each other, as with a ring in marriage. Rings for steadies were popular too; other popular tokens were ID bracelets and matching "steady jackets."

Generation Gap. Going steady contributed to the generation gap that widened increasingly during the decade. Parents feared, probably correctly, that steady dating led to a greater degree of sexual familiarity between partners. In direct contrast to their children's attitudes, two-thirds of adults in 1955 felt that high-school students should not limit themselves to dating one person. Written agreements — compacts — between groups of parents and groups of teens in communities around the country were popular ways to calm parents' concerns about unchaperoned socializing. Teens would agree to rules of proper and improper behavior for parties or dating, and parents would agree to be supportive with allowances, transportation, and respectful attitudes.

Sources:

Beth L. Bailey, *From Front Porch to Back Seat* (Baltimore & London: Johns Hopkins University Press, 1988);

Phyllis McGinley, "The Fearful Aspect of Too-Early Dating," *Good Housekeeping* (April 1956): 60–61, 287–288;

Ellen K. Rothman, *Hands and Hearts* (New York: Basic Books, 1984).

FADS OF THE 1950S

Davy Crockett. As in any other decade, a series of brief fashions in dress and pastimes captured the public's imagination during the 1950s. Many of these fads were inspired by what Americans saw on television, which

Children displaying examples of the Davy Crockett fad

most of them encountered for the first time during the decade. In 1955 children and adults alike were swept up in the merchandising blitz surrounding Walt Disney's television series "Davy Crockett." Four million recordings of "The Ballad of Davy Crockett," the show's theme song, and fourteen million Davy Crockett books were sold to eager fans. Little pioneers wore replicas of the coonskin cap their hero wore, so that the price of raccoon tails shot from twenty-five cents to eight dollars a pound. Some three thousand items of merchandise were licensed to cash in on the popularity of the Tennessee woodsman, including lunch boxes, bath towels, ukuleles, and women's underwear. Minor sports such as professional wrestling and roller derby were also extremely popular during the decade primarily because of exposure on television. The new medium itself, in fact, was something of a fad during the 1950s because of its novelty, and early stars and shows fascinated the public as few have since.

Dance. Dance crazes of the 1950s were also influenced by television. Young people watched Dick Clark's "American Bandstand," which debuted in 1957, to learn the latest steps. The stroll, a line dance with hand clapping, was especially popular. For their parents, "The Arthur Murray Party" was broadcast weekly throughout the decade; dance instructor Murray popularized several ballroom dances, including the cha-cha and the merengue.

College Fads. College students, always on the lookout for new fads, latched on to quite a few. Panty raids were popular during the 1950s and were, as Peter L. Skolnik puts it, "generally greeted with equal enthusiasm by the raiders and the raided." Only occasionally did the raids get out of hand and turn into full-scale riots. Mostly they

A hula-hoop contest

Sources:

B. Ray, "The Nifty Fifties," *Life*, 72 (16 June 1972): 38–46;

Peter L. Skolnik, *Fads: America's Crazes, Fevers & Fancies* (New York: Crowell, 1978).

SEX

Changes in Attitudes. Sexual attitudes during the 1950s were in a state of transition. On one hand, as Albert Ellis writes in *The American Sexual Tragedy* (1954), a woman was obliged "to make herself infinitely sexually desirable — but finally approachable only in legal marriage." But men were encouraged to adopt the swinging bachelor's lifestyle represented by *Playboy* magazine, which debuted in 1953. The magazine's notorious pictorials of naked women, *Playboy* publisher Hugh Hefner explained, were symbols "of disobedience, a triumph of sexuality, an end of Puritanism." Hefner's announcement of the death of puritanism might have been a bit premature — the sexual revolution was still a decade away — but sexual values were clearly changing. And perhaps, as such scientific studies as the one conducted by Alfred Kinsey and associates seem to suggest, Americans were never particularly puritanical.

Kinsey Reports. The two Kinsey reports on human sexuality are the results of interviews with more than sixteen thousand men and women conducted during the 1940s by the staff of the Institute for Sex Research, Indiana University, under the direction of the head of the institute, zoologist Kinsey. The sex researchers crisscrossed the country, hampered at first by a meager budget and wartime shortages; but with generous grants from the Rockefeller Foundation the institute was eventually able to accumulate a wealth of data. The first report of the institute's findings, a huge, scholarly tome called *Sexual Behavior in the Human Male*, was published in 1948. To the surprise of everyone — including Kinsey — the book was an instant best-seller. Soon Kinsey was nationally known as the "sex doctor." The institute's findings, which

were harmless fun. Collegians also stuffed themselves into cars (a variation of the telephone-booth stuffing of old). In 1959 "hunkering" was a popular campus fad: students squatted on their haunches to study or just hang around.

Advances in Toys. Many new toys, some made possible by technological advances from World War II, competed for the attention of the country's youngest consumers. The success of western movies and television shows led to heavy sales of toy guns, holsters, and spurs, to the tune of $283 million. Thirty million children wore propeller beanies in 1952. Slinkies, wire coils that walked down stairs "alone or in pairs," were popular toys during the decade, as was Silly Putty, a moldable glob of silicone, thirty-two million of which were sold between 1949 and 1954.

Hula Hoop. The most popular toy of the decade, however, among children and adults was the hula hoop. Arthur Melin and Richard Knerr, owners of Wham-O Manufacturing, introduced the hoop in 1957, inspired by an Australian variety of calisthenics. Soon people everywhere were swinging the plastic hoops around their hips. Some one hundred million of the hoops were sold around the world in 1958, not all by Wham-O, which had difficulty patenting such a simple toy. The Soviet Union condemned the hoop as exemplifying the "emptiness of American culture," and Japan outlawed it, but everywhere else, and in America especially, few missed out on the fun. More-skillful hoopers learned to spin them on their arms and legs or around their necks, or to spin more than one hoop at a time.

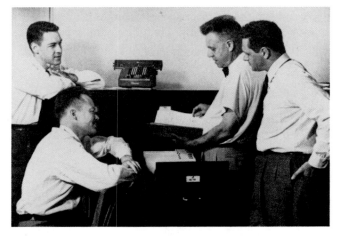

The Kinsey research team: Clyde E. Martin, Paul H. Gebhard, Alfred C. Kinsey, and Wardell B. Pomeroy

THE KINSEY REPORT

In 1953 *Sexual Behavior in the Human Female* by Alfred Kinsey, the first major study of American women's sexual practices, was published. Although the Kinsey report, as it was known, was a serious scientific study, it created a sensation uncommon to the scientific community.

The scientific method involved interviews with 5,940 female volunteers. Kinsey found that half of the women were no longer virgins when they married. Among married women, about one fourth had committed adultery by age forty. About half the adulterous wives had only one partner outside the marriage, and a third had committed adultery only once or a few times. Women were generally found to have a much lower sex drive than men. While an earlier report found that men were frequently preoccupied with sexual thoughts, women were found to daydream seldom about sex.

Shattering to males were the findings related to sexual maturity. Males tended to reach a peak of sexual ability in the late teens and decline precipitously from then on. Females, however, did not reach a sexual peak until their late twenties. The decline with age after this point was much more gradual in females than in males.

Some of Kinsey's theories based on his findings were as shocking to the public as the findings themselves. Kinsey suggested that teaching girls to remain virgins until marriage might be counterproductive. Since half failed to achieve this status, the result was often prolonged guilt. Perhaps it would be better to teach young women to have a limited sexual experience before a marital commitment, Kinsey suggested. Such ideas were not accepted in America in the 1950s.

Kinsey's major conclusions from the report were lost in the controversy over the topic and some of the lesser recommendations. Kinsey pointed out a potential problem in communication. Basically, males and females see the world differently. If they are to communicate in harmony, each gender must understand how the other thinks. Without a willingness to do this, the result is conflict in male-female relationships.

showed that premarital and extra-marital sex and homosexuality were much more common than people wanted to believe, outraged church leaders and other establishment figures. To them the results of the sex research struck at the heart of the nation's morality.

Criticism of Kinsey. Undeterred by the critics, who Kinsey felt were arguing from emotion rather than science, the institute continued to evaluate its data. Kinsey knew that a second book on female sexuality would almost certainly cause more furor than its predecessor: now the researchers were indicting the sanctity of American womanhood. As expected, *Sexual Behavior in the Human Female* (1953) was met with heavy sales and vehement criticism. Evangelist Billy Graham claimed that it was "impossible to estimate the damage this book will do" to American morals. Again critics attacked Kinsey for the institute's unwillingness to make a moral judgment on its findings. This time the Rockefeller Foundation seemed to agree and withdrew funding for further research. Kinsey, already a chronic workaholic, did not handle the added stress well. Hospitalized several times over the next three years, he died in August 1956.

Sexual Preoccupation. As if to prove the worst fears of Kinsey's critics, society did seem to be more preoccupied with sex. Novels that offered explicit (for the time) depictions of sexual themes were no longer hidden away but instead made the best-seller lists. One of the most popular authors of the decade, Mickey Spillane, laced his Mike Hammer novels with heavy doses of sex and violence; critics sneered, but millions of readers responded enthusiastically. Only slightly more genteel was Grace Metalious's *Peyton Place* (1956), one of the decade's runaway best-sellers, which depicts the sexual intrigue (including such taboos as incest and abortion) behind a small-town facade. Sex became the chief selling device for paperbacks (such as Spillane's novels) whose cover illustrations promised seamy sex — frequently more than the novel actually delivered.

Sex in Hollywood. Motion pictures were also beginning to take a greater degree of sexual license. For the movie industry it was a matter of necessity. The enormous success of television had cut drastically into Hollywood's earnings: attendance at movie houses had dropped in some cities by as much as 40 percent. One response was to put things in movies that television could not show. Since the 1920s the contents of movies had been regulated by a production code the industry itself had created. In 1956 the Motion Picture Association of America announced revisions to the code, allowing for screen treatments of such adult subjects as prostitution, abortion, and miscegenation.

Rock 'n' Roll. A further assault on American modesty came from the younger generation, who was listening to and creating a new type of music — rock 'n' roll. Even if parents did not recognize the subject of songs such as "Shake, Rattle and Roll," "Brown-Eyed Handsome Man," and "Tutti Frutti," they worried that wild dancing and "jungle rhythms" would cause their children to give in to their baser instincts. Something always seemed

The credit card was not only a business and economic breakthrough, it was also a technical revolution. The original cards did not include holograms and were made of paper. However, they were instrumental in moving credit flow from the business sector to the private consumer sector. The technological breakthrough was not in developing a new material or manufacturing technique. Rather, it was the application of a simple concept on a wide scale. How a little piece of paper became a technological and social milestone involves an interesting story of embarrassment.

Long before automated teller machines, cash was obtained at the bank during banking hours. Credit accounts were established on faith. One business sent material to another business, and the receiver sent a check after receiving the goods. This is credit, based on the faith that the receiver will pay for the goods and not sneak off with them in the middle of the night. The concept is rather old. Until 1950, though, it had only minor applications to the average consumer. A bank would lend someone money to buy a home, a car, or a washing machine. It had faith that the person would repay the loan. That faith, however, was improved by the knowledge that the bank could come and repossess the home, car, or washer if the consumer did not repay the money owed.

Then Frank X. McNamara had a bad day in 1950. This attorney was dining in a Manhattan restaurant when he suddenly realized he was short of cash. His embarrassment led to his revolutionary idea. He formed the Diner's Club. At twenty-seven fancy New York restaurants, the Diner's Club members could show their club cards instead of paying cash. In essence, the Diner's Club paid the bill by lending the money to the club member. Thus the restaurant got paid even if the bank was closed, and the Diner's Club would guarantee payment. In effect, the Diner's Club was giving its members unsecured loans simply for the asking. Obviously people had to meet strict income and credit criteria to join. Still, it opened a world of credit to the consumer which had not been available before and was convenient as well.

The idea caught on quickly. The club was billing $1 million the year after it was founded. When American Express started issuing credit cards in 1958, they signed up over 250,000 members in a three-month period. Banks began issuing credit cards, but they were only used on a limited, local basis. Capitalizing on McNamara's idea, Bank of America issued BankAmericards. These could be used nationally, and later internationally, at a wide variety of places. BankAmericard later became Visa, and other banks in Chicago and California developed cards that became today's MasterCard. So now that automated tellers give access to cash twenty-four hours every day, many can use credit cards to avoid carrying cash and all because of Frank McNamara's being embarrassed in 1950.

---

raunchy about rock 'n' roll, even when no one was saying anything dirty. When Elvis Presley gave his hip-swinging performances on "The Ed Sullivan Show" in 1956, it was clear that sexual energy was what propelled the music along. Rock 'n' roll, with its celebration of teen hormones, probably contributed more than any other factor to widening the generation gap and launching the sexual revolution.

Sources:

Albert Ellis, *The American Sexual Tragedy* (New York: Twayne, 1954);

Institute for Sex Research, *Sexual Behavior in the Human Female* (Philadelphia: Saunders, 1953).

SOCIAL THEORY OF THE 1950S

Anxious Society. While it might not have been apparent to many people at the time, American society in the 1950s was less stable than it seemed. The Depression, World War II, and the unprecedented growth and prosperity of the postwar period had wrought fundamental changes in American life. Economists, psychologists, and sociologists wrote best-selling books during the decade charging that these changes were not altogether for the better. The titles of these books — *The Affluent Society* (1958), *The Lonely Crowd* (1950), *The Organization Man* (1956) — became catchphrases which described the pressures and anxieties of contemporary life. A running theme throughout these works was that America was growing and changing more quickly than its citizens could comprehend.

Inner or Other. The first of these books to appear during the decade was *The Lonely Crowd* (1950) by David Riesman, a sociologist from the University of Chicago, and a colleague, Nathan Glazer. The authors' thesis was that Americans had become "other-directed" — pressed to conform to social values dictated by institutions and mass media — rather than "inner-directed" — holding to a personal set of ambitions and beliefs. The highest goal of such conformists was to be a valued member of the community. To a certain degree "other-directedness" is responsible for cooperation and tolerance in society, but it can also lead to alienation when a group is held together not by personal convictions but by its members' desire to belong. Other-directed Americans were at once in a crowd and lonely.

End of Individualism? William Whyte's *The Organization Man* made a point similar to Riesman's. Whyte claimed that big business, bureaucracy, and suburban living had smothered the puritan ethic, which championed hard work and self-motivation. The work ethic of the organization man dictated only that he contribute to the success of the organization. The phenomenon was most closely associated with the business world; but academia, government, religion — all increasingly structured — likewise subtly discouraged individual initiative. Again, as with Riesman and Glazer's idea of "other-directedness," there was a tension: cooperation among its members is necessary to the success of an organization, but creativity and innovation are as well.

Dynamics of Power. Also published in 1956 was *The Power Elite* by the maverick scholar C. Wright Mills. Mills was a brilliant professor of sociology at Columbia University who rode a motorcycle and dressed in flannel shirts and combat boots. He first came to national attention with the publication of his *White Collar* (1951), a stinging depiction of a class of workers with middle-class pretensions who are likely paid less than their blue-collar counterparts. In *The Power Elite* Mills turned from the pretenders to those actually in control. He described the developing close relationship among heads of industry and heads of state and the military, what President Dwight D. Eisenhower called the "military-industrial complex" in 1961. Some critics charged (as they had with *White Collar*) that Mills's analysis of social dynamics was too simplistic; but others believed that he rescued 1950s liberals from stagnation by making adversaries of the rich and powerful.

Conventional Wisdom. *The Affluent Society* was the work that made economist John Kenneth Galbraith a household name. Galbraith, a Canadian, was active in American politics, campaigning for Adlai Stevenson during his 1952 presidential bid and for John F. Kennedy in 1960. He was also chairman of the Democratic Advisory Committee during the Eisenhower presidency. Although an avowed liberal, Galbraith took both liberals and conservatives to task for relying too much on what he called "conventional wisdom": outdated beliefs that obscure social issues rather than explain them. Specifically, in *The Affluent Society* he attacked the conventional wisdom that prosperity was based on the increased production of consumer goods. Consumerism, Galbraith argued, led to "social imbalance," in which citizens were rich in material goods but real social progress — better schools, highways, and medical care — was considered an unwanted burden.

C. Wright Mills on his motorcycle

THE AFFLUENT SOCIETY

One passage of *The Affluent Society* that John Kenneth Galbraith nearly deleted from his final draft of the book turned out to be the most quoted from it:

> The family which takes its mauve and cerise, air-conditioned, power-steered, and power-braked automobile out for a tour passes through cities that are badly paved, made hideous by litter, blighted buildings, billboards, and posts for wires that should have long since been put underground. They pass on into a countryside that has been rendered largely invisible by commercial art.... They picnic on exquisitely packaged food from a portable icebox by a polluted stream and go on to spend the night at a park which is a menace to public health and morals. Just before dozing off on an air mattress, beneath a nylon tent, amid the stench of decaying refuse, they may reflect on the curious unevenness of their blessings. Is this, indeed, the American genius?

Source: John Kenneth Galbraith, *The Affluent Society* (Boston: Houghton Mifflin, 1958).

Social Position. Several other key works of social criticism influenced people's thinking during the time. Vance Packard's *The Status Seekers* (1959) made the case that Americans obsessively strove for higher social position through the purchase of status symbols such as expensive cars, houses, clothing, and appliances. This social climbing was, of course, encouraged by producers and advertisers of such items. With its broad generalizations, *The Status Seekers* was not really considered a work of serious scholarship, but it was widely read and discussed. *Growing Up Absurd* by Paul Goodman was published in 1960 but developed from magazine articles the author had written in the latter half of the 1950s. Goodman placed the blame for the growing youth rebellion squarely on the society that provided them with no clear system of values. Another book of the 1960s that had its genesis in the previous decade was by Betty Friedan, who found that no magazine wanted to print an article she had written on the stifled aspirations of American women. Taking a cue from Packard, she expanded her article to book length and saw it published as the early bible of American feminism, *The Feminine Mystique*, in 1963.

Sources:

John Kenneth Galbraith, *A Life in Our Times* (Boston: Houghton Mifflin, 1981);

David Halberstam, *The Fifties* (New York: Villard, 1993);

Rick Tilman, *C. Wright Mills: A Native Radical and His American Intellectual Roots* (University Park & London: Pennsylvania State University Press, 1984).

SUBURBIA

History of American Suburbs. The American suburbs, the residential ideal of the 1950s, have a long tradition in the country's history. The U.S. Bureau of the Census first used the term *suburb* to designate an area that had economic ties to a nearby city (because the population worked and spent money there) but was outside the city limits. Suburbs had actually been around since much earlier, in the nineteenth century, for as long as families had wanted to escape the cramped conditions of inner-city life. In the 1920s planned residential communities sprang up, as land developers divided vacant areas within the city into lots to sell to hopeful home builders. But the Great Depression ended most private construction in the country, and many lots remained undeveloped or with partially built houses that would never be completed.

New Suburbs. With the boom in marriage and birthrates following World War II, growth of the suburbs began again. Real-estate organizations now sold lots with houses already built on them in a small variety of conservative styles: ranch or split-level, Colonial, Tudor, or Spanish. Developers were financed by the Federal Housing Administration (FHA), which was created by President Franklin D. Roosevelt during the Depression. The FHA encouraged home buying by offering low-payment, low-interest loans for purchases. Additionally, veterans returning from the war were offered even better lending rates and longer-term mortgages through the Veterans Administration (VA). Because of FHA and VA loans, houses were more affordable than ever before.

Levittown. Perhaps the most famous of these early mass-produced neighborhoods was Levittown, a suburb thirty miles east of New York City. Initially the construc-

A family standing in front of their Levittown house

Teenagers frequently use slang to talk to each other in order to create a sense of community and to keep their elders from knowing what they are saying. Movies such as *American Graffiti* and *Grease* and the television series "Happy Days" made a fad in the 1970s and 1980s out of 1950s teen slang but did not hint at the diversity of that decade's youth lingo, which varied widely from region to region.

In Saint Louis teens called a movie a "hecklthon," and if it was a really good one it was "real George." In Atlanta a "pink" was a snob; "Joe Roe" and "Joe Doe" were names for blind dates; and if someone tried to be a big wheel but did not make it he was a "hub cap." In New Orleans something exciting was a "large charge." Friends greeted each other with "What's your tale, nightingale?" and said goodbye with "Black time's here, termite." In Salt Lake City "she" meant yes and "schnay" meant no. In Boston, serious students were "book gooks," and if a girl wanted to know how much something cost, she would ask, "What's the geetafrate?"

Source: *Newsweek*, 38 (8 October 1951): 28–29.

---

tion firm owned by the seventy-year-old Abraham Levitt and his two sons planned to build a community of two thousand sixty-dollars-per-month rental units for veterans. By 1948 Levitt and Sons had obtained the necessary land to build six thousand houses. By this time federal regulations had made it cheaper to sell the houses than to rent them. Even so, the Levitt company found no shortage of young couples prepared to make the commitment. With each expansion of Levittown, crowds camped out for the opportunity to buy the new units. When the suburb was completed in November 1951, it comprised 17,447 homes, as well as schools, stores, parks, and a community center.

Identical Floorplans. The houses in which Levittowners lived were very much alike. Their facades and color schemes varied slightly, but their floor plans were exactly the same. The first floor of each house consisted of two bedrooms, a kitchen, a living room, a bath, and a stairway leading to an unfinished attic. The house resided on a lot approximately sixty-by-one-hundred feet. Each house was furnished with a refrigerator, an electric stove, a washing machine, and, for the 1950 model, a television set built into the living room wall. After 1949 the Levitt company also offered a ranch-style home which was slightly larger than the original "Cape Cod" model but laid out along essentially the same plan. The Cape Cods sold for $6,990–$7,990, and the

"Ranches" for between $8,000 and $9,500. These houses, especially if their owners improved upon them, could be resold for as much as $18,000, although a couple that could afford to pay that much for a home probably did not live in Levittown, which had a reputation as a low-income community.

Housing the Young. Levittown and the other suburbs like it were populated mainly by young families. The average age of a Levittown adult in 1957 was thirty-five. The average number of children in each home was 2.13, meaning that more children than adults lived in the community. A majority — nearly three-quarters — of suburban businessmen commuted to a nearby city for their jobs; but as businesses also began to move from the city, this figure dropped slightly, to 60 percent. Wives stayed in the suburbs almost exclusively, occupying their days tending to home and family or shopping at one of the growing number of nearby shopping malls. Because of the various demands of house, family, lawn, and community, the suburban couple often developed a division of labor in which each took on some of the other's traditional roles. Harold Wattel describes the situation in *The Suburban Community* (1958): "Father will do the family's weekly food shopping while mother may help paint the house; the male will help maintain the . . . tile floors while the female will represent the family at a civic meeting; the husband will participate actively in the local Parent-Teachers Association, while the wife keeps the family's monthly accounts."

A Sense of Community. The young suburban families naturally socialized with their neighbors, informally or as part of church and citizens' groups, the PTA, or Little League sports. A self-survey conducted among the residents of Levittown in 1956 showed that 76 percent of the respondents considered themselves primarily residents of Levittown, and 70 percent were willing to work to improve the neighborhood. Clearly a sense of community prevailed. At the same time, social critics warned that the positive aspects of community living were balanced by a pressure to conform, to keep as neat a lawn and own as many appliances as one's neighbors. In his novel *The Man in the Gray Flannel Suit* (1955), Sloan Wilson gives fictional life to the drive to "keep up with the Joneses"; by the end of the novel Tom and Betsy Rath decide to reject the hollow values of corporate and suburban America. The Raths might have inspired those couples already tiring of the pressures of suburban living, but most families remained sold on life on the urban fringe. According to the Levittown self-survey, 94 percent of the community's residents would recommend it to others.

Sources:

Kenneth T. Jackson, *Crabgrass Frontier: The Suburbanization of America* (New York: Oxford University Press, 1985);

Gwendolyn Wright, *Building the Dream: A Social History of Housing in America* (New York: Pantheon, 1981).

DIVORCE

As important as home and family were during the 1950s, failed marriages were becoming more prominent. The annual number of marriages actually declined over the course of the decade, as the wave of marriages following World War II began to subside. There were 1.66 million marriages in 1950 and 1.52 million in 1960. At the same time the divorce rate rose slightly, from 385,000 in 1950 to 393,000 in 1960. In 1950, 1 in every 4.3 marriages failed, and by the end of the decade that ratio had changed to 1 in every 3.8. In other words, despite the emphasis on domestic life that characterized the decade, the institution of marriage actually lost ground. One reason for the higher divorce rate was the successful economy, which made it possible for more women to consider leaving their husbands.

WOMEN'S ROLES IN THE 1950S

Standard Roles, But Changing. Housekeeping and raising a family were considered ideal female roles during the 1950s, although that standard was less rigid than in previous decades. With marriage and birthrates booming, women were becoming wives and mothers at unprecedented levels. But more women were entering the workplace as well. During World War II women by the millions took factory jobs to make up for the domestic manpower shortage. After the war the number of working women dropped, but by 1950 it was climbing again, at the rate of a million a year. By 1956, 35 percent of all adult women were members of the labor force, and nearly a quarter of all married women were working. As A. W. Zelomek, president of the International Statistical Bureau, reported in *A Changing America* (1959), two out of five women with husbands and school-age children worked outside the home. However, working women had yet to attain many positions of influence: in 1957 the overwhelming majority, more than 70 percent, held clerical, assembly-line, or service jobs. Only 12 percent practiced a profession, and 6 percent held management positions.

Rising Opportunities. Many women were torn between traditional expectations and the opportunities available to them. The percentage of women among college students dropped during the decade, to a low of 35 percent in 1958; during the war the majority of collegians had been women, but in the postwar years colleges preferred to accept veterans studying through the GI Bill. A 1959 study determined that 37 percent of female college students were leaving school before they graduated, most for marriage. Even those who stayed in school were not thought to be preparing for a career, the way their male counterparts were. Lynn White, Jr., president of Mills College, proposed in his *Educating Our Daughters* (1950) that the curriculum for female students should prepare women to "foster the intellectual and emotional life of her family and community." Female students taking liberal-arts and professional courses were also encouraged to take classes in interior decoration and family finance. Throughout the decade the male president of all-female Radcliffe College told his incoming freshmen students that their education would make them "splendid wives and mothers, and their reward might be to marry Harvard men."

THE TV DINNER

World War II caused TV dinners to be created. With so many men off fighting the war, women entered the workforce in large numbers for the first time to support the war effort. After the war many women kept their jobs. Thus, there was a need for quick, easy meals (which even workingwomen were usually responsible for preparing) for two-worker families at the end of the day.

Clarke and Gilbert Swanson of Omaha saw the need and began selling frozen potpies in 1951 on a national scale. Meanwhile, a lawyer named Cecil Johnson had trademarked the name "TV Dinner." The Swansons acquired Johnson's trademark and began preparing complete dinners in sectional aluminum trays in 1953. The first included one section of turkey with dressing and gravy, another section of flavored sweet potatoes, and a third section of buttered peas. The original packages were designed to show the dinners on a television screen.

In 1953 five thousand dinners were sent to supermarket shelves in the first order. When Campbell Soup bought Swanson in 1955, twenty-five million dinners a year were being sold. These included fish, beef, and chicken varieties. The TV dinner trademark expired in 1973.

Two innovations were necessary to make mass-produced TV dinners a success story. One was the development of the supermarket chain store, which facilitated distribution. The other was the fast freezing techniques developed earlier by Clarence Birdseye that allowed frozen foods to retain their flavor.

Source: Kenneth Morris, Marc Robinson, and Richard Kroll, eds., *American Dreams: One-Hundred Years of Business Ideas and Innovation from the* Wall Street Journal (New York: Light Bulb Press, 1990).

Media Perceptions. The belief in a woman's destined social role was reinforced by the popular media of the day. Since women bought 65 to 80 percent of all goods sold in the United States, advertisements and product designs were frequently aimed at feminine concerns, at least as male advertising executives saw them. The magazines of the time were filled with images of dedicated housewives whose only pleasures were that their families were satisfied and their chores made easier. Ironically, as their household responsibilities consumed less of their time, women had more freedom to explore interests other than home and family. While advertisers continued to depict women as domestic servants, real women were finding fulfillment in jobs, volunteer work, and social organizations as well as homemaking.

Danger to Family. Women who spent too much time outside the home, social commentators were quick to warn, were endangering their families, neglecting their husbands and especially their children. *Life* magazine, in a special issue devoted to the American woman, deplored the "changing roles" of married couples and placed most of the blame on the increasingly aggressive wife: "They should use [their minds] in every conceivable way . . . so long as their primary focus of interest and activity is the home." The article continued: "If they are truly feminine women, with truly feminine attitudes, they will . . . accept their wifely functions with good humor and pleasure."

Changing Duties. Deplorable or not, the pressures of job, home, and family forced both husbands and wives to accept changing domestic duties. With a wife making most of the family's purchases, it made sense that she also controlled the family finances. But if a husband used the car to commute to work, he might buy groceries himself. Frequently, since the wife was at home more than her husband, she would perform much of the manual labor around the house and lawn, traditionally considered "man's work." Fathers might chauffeur the children or represent the couple at school meetings. Children were often obliged to help their busy parents. Experts on family life were not necessarily willing to say that these changes were positive, but American women were grateful for the new opportunities.

Public Power. In the realm of public policy women made few significant gains during the decade. Women had secured suffrage only recently, when the Nineteenth Amendment to the Constitution was ratified in 1920. By the 1950s only a few women held national office: out of the 531 members of Congress in 1956, 16 were women. And in the upper house, the Senate, Margaret Chase Smith, a Republican from Maine, was the only female member. Women had made some inroads, however, in diplomatic and cabinet-level positions. Eugenie Anderson, the first woman U.S. ambassador, served as chief diplomat to Denmark from 1949 to 1953. Anna Rosenberg was assistant secretary of defense during the Harry S Truman administration, and President Eisenhower appointed Oveta Culp Hobby, the World War II director

BARBIE

To the uninitiated, the development of the Barbie doll may not seem like a major technological breakthrough. During her first eight years Barbie brought in $500 million. This little moneymaker was the product of simple observation by a mother named Ruth Handler.

Ruth Handler and her husband were already accomplished toy designers. Her husband, Elliot, made his fortune in furniture making. Ruth suggested making furniture for dollhouses. This led to Mattel Creations (from the names of the company's two partners, Harold MATson and ELliot Handler, Ruth's husband). After several successful toy inventions, Mattel was growing rapidly. Ruth Handler's observational powers led to the 1959 invention of the Barbie doll and the astounding rise of Mattel in the corporate world.

Ruth Handler was watching her daughter, named Barbara (Barbie), playing with dolls. Barbara had lots of baby dolls to play with. Instead of playing with the baby dolls, though, Barbara would prefer paper dolls of teenagers. These had paper clothing and other articles to accompany them. Ruth Handler had the idea of making a real doll that looked like a teenager. The doll would also have clothes, jewelry, purses, and so forth — "Each sold separately," of course. Furniture for the new doll's house was also available. Ruth Handler had Mattel technicians build the doll to her specifications. Naming it was easy, also. Barbie was named after the Handler's daughter, Barbara. Mattel named the male doll after the Handler's son Ken.

As is often true, ingenuity went unrecognized. The Handlers gave the Barbie doll a debut at a toy show in New York in 1959. The reaction from the others who attended the show was immediate. They told the Handlers that the doll would never sell. Eight years later Ruth Handler had made $500 million from the sale of Barbie.

It is interesting that Ruth Handler later made another observation that turned tragedy into good fortune. During the 1970s she retired from Mattel after removal of her left breast for cancer. Trying to look and feel like a normal woman, she sought a breast prosthesis. None was adequate. Handler began working with designers and technicians to fill the needs of cancer victims. The result was the Nearly Me products produced by Ruthton, Inc.

of the Women's Army Corps, as his first secretary of health, education, and welfare.

Sources:

Betty Friedan, *The Feminine Mystique* (New York: Norton, 1963);

Brett Harvey, *The Fifties: A Women's Oral History* (New York: HarperCollins, 1993).

YOUTH

Rise of Youth Power. During the 1950s young Americans gained both in number and economic clout and so had a considerable influence over popular culture. Movies, music, magazines, and clothes — all reflected teenage interests and concerns that were distinct from those of their parents. Teens were eager consumers, with $7 billion to spend annually by mid decade. In 1956 according to *Scholastic* magazine, the average teenager had a weekly income of $10.55; just prior to the start of World War II that was the average weekly disposable income for an entire family. With more money inevitably came a certain degree of independence — less parental support was needed for socializing and purchasing. Parents might have worried that their children had too much freedom; but teens, like almost everyone else, benefited from the prosperity of postwar America.

Rock 'n' Roll. The cornerstone of youth culture during the decade was rock 'n' roll, which transformed antisocial behavior into a multimillion-dollar industry. "Rock and Roll is Here to Stay," recorded by Danny and the Juniors in 1957, was an accurate, even understated, prophecy. At first it was portrayed as the music of hoodlums in *The Blackboard Jungle* (1955), and parents feared that it was a primary cause of juvenile delinquency. But rock 'n' roll was, in fact, a fairly harmless form of rebellion. Soon movies such as *Rock Around the Clock* and *Don't Knock the Rock* (both 1956) showed that the music's reputation for causing trouble was undeserved and that kids were only out to have fun. Teenagers' fascination with the new sound resulted in booming sales of 45-rpm singles, portable radios, and portable record players (which teens could buy for a dollar down and a dollar a week). For the radio industry, reeling from the tremendous success of television, rock 'n' roll provided a whole new target audience. Rock music also made an impact on television, as performers sang on prime-time shows with great success. Locally produced dance shows — televised "hops" — became popular. One such show, "American Bandstand," begun by Philadelphia disc jockey Dick Clark in 1952, had enduring national success.

"American Bandstand" host Dick Clark, right, during a Record Review Panel segment

Courtship Rituals. Because one of the main topics of rock 'n' roll was love — teen love in all its aspects, from eternal and passionate to deceptive and frustrating — it provided the perfect musical accompaniment to a favorite hobby of young Americans, dating. Courtship rituals among high-school students became more elaborate, and who was dating whom received weekly attention in school newspapers. "Dos and don'ts" were the frequent subject of articles in teen magazines, and whether a boy and girl should go steady was a hotly debated issue.

College. Many young men and women attended college after high school, but for different reasons. While men were there to train for careers, women quite often attended college to find a husband. In 1956 one-fourth of female students were marrying while still in school, and by the end of the decade two out of three coeds were dropping out before receiving their degrees. For many young women there was simply no practical reason to complete their education. There was no social pressure on them to have careers, but there was considerable pressure on them to become wives and mothers.

Sources:

Brett Harvey, *The Fifties: A Women's Oral History* (New York: HarperCollins, 1993);

Elaine Tyler May, *Homeward Bound: American Families in the Cold War Era* (New York: Basic Books, 1988);

Hermann Remmers, *The American Teenager* (Indianapolis: Bobbs-Merrill, 1957);

Ernest Allyn Smith, *American Youth Culture: Group Life in Teenage Society* (New York: Free Press, 1962).

HEADLINE MAKERS

MAMIE DOUD EISENHOWER

1896-1979

Early Life. Mamie Eisenhower was the first lady of the United States at a time when home and family were considered to be of paramount importance. As first ladies often are, she was expected to serve as a role model for the American wife. Mamie Doud and Dwight D. "Ike" Eisenhower met in 1915 in San Antonio, Texas, where Eisenhower was a young army officer and high-school football coach and Mamie was wintering with her parents. They were married the next year. For Mamie, life as a military wife was initially harsh: the Douds were a close and socially prominent family, and life with Ike was relatively lean and lonely. Over the next several decades she dutifully followed her husband when she could, and raised the family herself when she could not. Her husband, meanwhile, became increasingly prominent as a military leader.

New Pressures. At the end of World War II Eisenhower was a national hero, and for his wife this meant a measure of celebrity to which she was unaccustomed as well as the opportunity to meet important world leaders. The general became president of Columbia University in 1948; throughout Ike's tenure at Columbia Mrs. Eisenhower was a gracious hostess to scores of famous visitors. When her husband decided to enter the presidential campaign in 1952, Mamie — a self-professed homebody — found that she would have to shed her aversion to public life: "there would be nothing he would ask during the campaign that I would not do," she recalled. As a campaign wife she subjected herself to daily appearances and interviews and answered thousands of letters.

Life in the White House. After Eisenhower won the presidency, Mrs. Eisenhower was able to return to a degree of domestic stability in the White House. By this time she was used to overseeing a staff, and she saw that the executive mansion was run efficiently. She also lent her services to charitable causes, and she made the White House more historic by leading a drive to recover authentic presidential antiques. She and her husband observed a division of labor ("Ike took care of the office — I ran the house") although the president valued his wife's insights into political personalities of the time.

Public Ideal. For the eight years of the Eisenhower presidency Mamie Eisenhower represented the public ideal of the American wife: exuding quiet strength, finding satisfaction in domestic duties, supporting her husband unhesitatingly. Eisenhower observed of her: "I personally think that Mamie's biggest contribution was to make the White House livable, comfortable, and meaningful for the people who came in. She was always helpful and ready to do anything. She exuded hospitality. She saw that as one of her functions and performed it, no matter how tired she was." When Eisenhower left office in 1961, he and Mrs. Eisenhower were at last allowed something like a peaceful retirement, although Eisenhower kept busy in the role of elder statesman until his death in 1969. Mamie Eisenhower lived quietly after her husband's death until her own death in 1979.

Sources:

Dorothy Brandon, *Mamie Doud Eisenhower* (New York: Scribners, 1954);

Steve Neal, *The Eisenhowers: Reluctant Dynasty* (Garden City, N.Y.: Doubleday, 1978).

JOHN KENNETH GALBRAITH

1908-

ECONOMIST AND TEACHER

Criticizing Materialism. John Kenneth Galbraith made his name in 1958 with the publication of *The Affluent Society*, a critical look at the "conventional wisdom" that dominated American economic and social life at the time. The book was a rarity, a scholarly work on economics that received mainstream attention and became a best-seller. Its popularity was even more surprising, perhaps, considering its stinging indictment of modern materialist society, which, Galbraith claimed, champions private wealth and productivity over public needs.

Early Life. Galbraith was born to Scottish-Canadians on the shore of Lake Erie near the United States–Canada border. He graduated from an agricultural branch of the University of Toronto and then pursued advanced degrees in economics from the University of California. In 1934 he accepted an offer to teach at Harvard University. For the next ten years he worked at a variety of scholarly positions; he also became involved in government service. In 1941 he was in Washington, D.C., as deputy administrator of the Office of Price Administration, a position which, as John S. Gambs reports, "made him virtually the economic czar of the United States until he left in 1943."

Political Roles. In 1952 Galbraith played an important role in the presidential election as a speechwriter for Democratic candidate Adlai Stevenson, along with literary critic Bernard De Voto and playwright Archibald MacLeish. After Stevenson lost the election to Dwight D. Eisenhower, Galbraith found a role in the Republican administration as the chairman of the Democratic Advisory Council. In the late years of the decade he campaigned actively for John F. Kennedy, and in 1960, after Kennedy's successful presidential bid, he was named U.S. ambassador to India.

Inspired by India. Galbraith had first visited India in 1956, and his fascination with the country partly inspired his most famous work, *The Affluent Society*. In a desperately poor society such as India's, almost all of the products consumed are urgently needed — food, clothing, and shelter. As a society becomes more prosperous, many unnecessary goods are produced as well, and they must be purchased in order to maintain the country's high level of production and employment. In affluent societies, Galbraith claimed, demand followed production, and people bought products because they were persuaded to do so by advertisers.

Social Imbalance. This commitment to private affluence, Galbraith argued, led to social imbalance: social programs and environmental concerns were ignored, and production of more cars and televisions was viewed as social progress. Only by adopting a new standard of productivity, one that led to real social progress, could balance be achieved. Critics of *The Affluent Society* argued that Galbraith was attempting to deny a basic American social freedom: free Americans were first and foremost free to buy things. But many of Galbraith's ideas had an impact on the policies of Presidents Kennedy and Lyndon B. Johnson. Urban renewal and conservationism, concepts that were to become part of Johnson's Great Society, were all advocated in *The Affluent Society*.

Later Work. After the Kennedy years Galbraith returned to scholarly activity. He has traveled and written extensively over the last several decades, using Harvard as his home base. His varied literary output includes several memoirs of his eventful life. Although conventional wisdom has remained firmly entrenched, Galbraith has continued to kick at some of the props supporting it.

Sources:

John Kenneth Galbraith, *A Life in Our Times* (Boston: Houghton Mifflin, 1981);

John S. Gambs, *John Kenneth Galbraith* (Boston: Twayne, 1975).

GAYELORD HAUSER
1895-1984

NUTRITION EXPERT

AP

Changing Eating Habits. Gayelord Hauser was the author of several influential books on health in the 1950s, most notably *Look Younger, Live Longer* (1950) and *Be Happier, Be Healthier* (1952). Other nutrition experts questioned the value of Hauser's advice, and he was investigated by the federal government several times. His ideas on diet, however, undoubtedly affected the eating habits of many Americans during the decade.

Early Life. Hauser immigrated to the United States from Germany when he was sixteen years old. He contracted tuberculosis of the hip, and doctors predicted he would be crippled for life. At a doctor's recommendation he turned to "food science" as a source of therapy, and after a few weeks of salads, soups, and fruit juices he was cured permanently. From then on Hauser was devoted to studying the healing properties of food. He traveled to Europe and studied under a variety of nutritionists. Returning to the United States in 1923, he began to lecture in the Midwest and became a partner in a health-food company.

Health Manuals. Hauser moved to Hollywood in 1927 and became known for a series of health manuals he wrote in the 1930s, including *Harmonized Food Selection, With the Famous Hauser Body-Building System* (1930) and *Keener Vision Without Glasses* (1932). He became the diet adviser to celebrities, such as Marlene Dietrich, Paulette Goddard, and Greta Garbo and even to members of royalty, including Queen Alexandra of Yugoslavia and the duchess of Windsor.

Wonder Foods. Hauser did not achieve national fame, however, until the publication of *Look Younger, Live Longer* in 1950. The book stressed the value of five "wonder foods": brewer's yeast, powdered skim milk, yogurt, wheat germ, and blackstrap molasses. The book sold sensationally, staying on the best-seller lists for months. By 1953 it had sold five hundred thousand copies and had been translated into twelve languages. Hauser wrote daily syndicated newspaper columns and made frequent television appearances. Sales of the five wonder foods, most of them considered throwaway products, suddenly skyrocketed.

FDA Controversy. Hauser's theories on a healthy lifestyle were not universally admired. In March 1951 the Food and Drug Administration seized copies of Hauser's book and jars of blackstrap molasses, claiming that Hauser made grossly exaggerated claims in the book as to the syrup's health value. Officials reminded the public that Hauser, who used the title doctor, actually had no formal medical training, degree, or license. Hauser was careful, however, to make no claims that could be clearly called fraudulent. After another best-seller, *Be Happier, Be Healthier,* in which Hauser also suggested the importance of sunbaths and lying on "slant boards," his popularity seemed to subside. He still preached his message of a healthy diet to a smaller group of loyal followers. By the time of his death at age eighty-nine in 1984, he was largely forgotten.

Sources:

Noel F. Busch, "You Can Live to be a Hundred, He Says," *Saturday Evening Post,* 224 (11 August 1951): 30, 107–110;

"Live Longer, Lasses," *Newsweek,* 37 (26 March 1951): 58–59.

HUGH HEFNER
1926-
MAGAZINE PUBLISHER

BETTMANN ARCHIVES

New Openness. When *Playboy* first hit the newsstands in 1953, it represented a new openness about sexuality that was beginning to influence American life. The magazine, which was the brainchild of a would-be cartoonist from Chicago named Hugh Hefner, was originally to be called "Stag Party," but Hefner, who wanted to suggest sophistication as well as high living and wild parties, eventually settled on *Playboy.* Hefner hoped to make his magazine the equal of others that featured female nudity as well as articles, such as *Esquire,* for which Hefner had also worked and which had recently stopped featuring suggestive photography.

Marilyn Monroe. *Playboy* was an instant sensation, mainly because Hefner had shrewdly purchased a nude photograph of actress Marilyn Monroe; it had been taken before her success in Hollywood, and Hefner used it as the centerfold of his first issue. Monroe was a star by the time the magazine was published, and the first issue sold out quickly. That issue included an editorial by Hefner that espoused the *Playboy* philosophy that was to become familiar over the years:

> We like our apartment. We enjoy mixing up cocktails and an *hors d'oeuvre* or two, putting a little mood music on the phonograph and inviting in a female acquaintance for a quiet discussion on Picasso, Nietzsche, jazz, sex. . . . If we are able to give the American male a few extra laughs and a little diversion from the anxieties of the Atomic Age, we'll feel we've justified our existence.

Trappings of Success. The immediate success of the magazine prompted Hefner to establish a proper office and staff for the magazine, and as of the fourth issue the *Playboy* empire was officially under way. Hefner's devotion to the magazine in its early years precipitated the breakup of his marriage: Hefner and his wife Millie were separated in 1957 and divorced in 1959. As he and his wife became increasingly estranged, Hefner and his associates began to embody the lifestyle about which they wrote, having almost weekly parties at the *Playboy* editorial offices. When the success of the magazine came to the attention of the mainstream public, Hefner was happy to portray himself as the playboy his magazine described. In 1959 he even hosted the television series "Playboy's Penthouse," a weekly talk show set in a bachelor pad, featuring plenty of the magazine's "playmates" and celebrities such as comedian Lenny Bruce and singers Ella Fitzgerald and Nat King Cole.

Pursuit of Pleasure. For Hefner, his magazine and image were responses to the new mood of the country. He felt that the puritan ethic was eroding and that the pursuit of pleasure and material gain was the way of life for many Americans. As Hefner has been quoted, "If you had to sum up the idea of *Playboy,* it is antipuritanism. Not just in regard to sex, but the whole range of play and pleasure." For many the *Playboy* philosophy proved to be a welcome antidote from the repressive atmosphere of the 1950s. Over the years it has continued to have its followers, and Hefner's small magazine for men has become an empire extending well beyond magazine publishing.

Source:

Frank Brady, *Hefner* (New York: Macmillan, 1974).

GRACE KELLY
1925-1982
ACTRESS AND PRINCESS

PARAMOUNT PICTURES

Fairy Tale. During the 1950s Grace Kelly was a socialite, a movie star, and, finally, a princess. To many Americans her life represented the closest thing to a fairy tale the country had ever produced. She was one of the Kellys of Germantown, Pennsylvania, a family that numbered noted playwrights, athletes, and entrepreneurs among them. Grace's father, John Kelly, made his wealth with Kelly for Bricks, an inherited business that he developed into a major industry of Philadelphia. Grace was a young woman with an independent spirit and a desire to act on stage. While attending the American Academy of Dramatic Arts in New York in 1947, she supported herself by modeling. After graduating from the academy she found only a few small roles on stage and in films over the next several years.

Big Break. Kelly's career took a giant step forward when she was selected as the "fresh face" to appear opposite Gary Cooper in the western *High Noon* (1952). The beautiful young starlet was an immediate success. Over the next few years she starred in several memorable films, including *Mogambo* (1953), costarring with Clark Gable, and three films for director Alfred Hitchcock, *Dial M for Murder* (1954), *Rear Window* (1954), and *To Catch a Thief* (1955). In 1955 she also won the Academy Award for Best Actress for her role in *The Country Girl*. It seemed that she had a promising career as a screen actress ahead of her. Yet within two years after winning the Oscar she had given up a chance to become movie royalty for the real thing.

Royal Romance. In 1955 Kelly met Prince Ranier, the regent of the small Mediterranean country of Monaco, while she was on the French Riviera at the Cannes Film Festival. Neither thought much of the meeting at first, but on their second meeting, at the home of a friend of the Kelly family in the United States, they discovered a powerful mutual attraction. Within four days the couple was engaged. Playwright Anita Loos, when she heard of the engagement, remarked, "And now, to top everything, she's going to become a princess and live in fairyland!"

Wedding and After. The fairy-tale marriage occurred in Monaco on 19 April 1956. For more than twenty-five years Princess Grace attended to the social and charitable responsibilities her position entailed; she was well loved by the people of Monaco. The royal couple had three children, two daughters and a son. In 1982, while driving along the Moyenne Corniche, a mountain highway in her adopted country, Princess Grace suffered a stroke, and her car plummeted off a cliff. Her daughter, seventeen-year-old Princess Stephanie, was in the car with her and was not hurt, but Grace died of the injuries she sustained. Both Monaco and America mourned her passing.

Sources:
Howell Conant, "Hollywood's Queen Becomes a Princess," *Collier's* (2 March 1956): 22–27;

Gant Gaither, *Princess of Monaco: The Story of Grace Kelly* (New York: Holt, 1957).

C. WRIGHT MILLS

1916-1962

SOCIAL THINKER AND THEORIST

Dissenter. C. Wright Mills has been referred to as America's "foremost dissenter"; he rose to prominence during the 1950s as a dynamic liberal social thinker. David Halberstam observed that he provided an intellectual bridge between old Left — the Communists of the Great Depression and their sympathizers — and the New Left of the 1960s.

Early Life. Mills spent an alienated and lonely childhood in West Texas and then Dallas. In college he studied sociology and philosophy, first at the University of Texas at Austin and then at the University of Wisconsin. Throughout his academic career he impressed his professors with his brilliance, his appetite for knowledge, and his brashness. One professor said of him, "The prevailing legend about him is to the effect that he takes people up and pursues them furiously until they get so tired of it they rebuff him (or until he has milked them dry and drops them). Mills received his doctorate in 1942, the same year he was rejected for service in World War II because of high blood pressure.

Outsider. Mills imagined himself as the perpetual outsider, and from that position he developed his theories of American life. His first book, *The New Men of Power*, was published in 1948. In 1951 he published *White Collar*, an important look at the new middle class of the postwar era. His most famous book was published in 1956 — *The Power Elite*. In it he discussed the forces that dominated American life: he believed that all decisions on national issues were made by an interwoven body of the executive branch of the government with its army of bureaucrats, military policy makers, and corporate leaders. Since they controlled all access to power, those outside the power elite are denied any influence. While the country seemed to be growing stronger, then, most Americans felt that they were less in control of their own lives. Mills did not propose that there was a conspiracy among the power elite; since they all had the same interests at heart, it was only natural that they cooperated.

Radical Social Critic. *The Power Elite* was widely discussed and brought Mills to national prominence as a radical social critic of the status quo. He relished the notoriety and cultivated an image of himself as different from other intellectuals. Throughout his writing career he was also a maverick professor at Columbia University: he rode a motorcycle to campus and stomped into the classroom in big leather boots and a lumberjack's shirt. He was a capable carpenter who built his own home. He believed in hard living, and his heavy drinking and smoking aggravated the vascular condition that had kept him out of military service. Mills had his first heart attack in 1958; he died of heart failure in 1962.

Early Death. Because of his untimely death, Mills was unable to see the impact his thinking had on the radicalism of the 1960s. For that generation the enemy to society was the entrenched "military-industrial complex," to which President Dwight D. Eisenhower gave its name, but Mills had already anticipated in *The Power Elite*.

Sources:
David Halberstam, *The Fifties* (New York: Villard, 1993);

Irving Louis Horowitz, *C. Wright Mills: An American Utopian* (New York: Free Press, 1983);

Rick Tilman, *C. Wright Mills: A Native Radical and His American Intellectual Roots* (University Park & London: Pennsylvania State University Press, 1984).

PEOPLE IN THE NEWS

On 12 April 1956 **Mrs .Joseph Wright Alsop,** widowed mother of columnists Joseph and Stewart Alsop, married **Francis W. Cole,** retired chairman of the board of Travelers Insurance Company, on 12 April 1956.

Josephine Baker filed charges of sexual discrimination against Sherman Billingsley's Stork Club in New York City on 21 December 1951.

Malcolm Bingay, editorial director of the *Detroit Free Press,* was critically injured on 17 January 1950 at a gourmet dinner sponsored by the AFL Cooks' Union when a container of hot coffee and brandy exploded.

Actress **Ingrid Bergman** on 25 January 1950 filed suit for divorce from **Dr. Peter Lindstrom** so she could marry Italian film director **Roberto Rossellini.**

Radcliffe College senior **Audrey Bruce,** the heiress to the fortune of Andrew Mellon, revealed on 22 April 1956 that she had married Boston art-gallery consultant **Stephen Currier** on 15 November 1955.

Dr. James Lee Dickey, a black physician in Taylor, Texas, was named "Man of the Year" in Taylor on 28 January 1953.

C. L. Grimes, a moonshiner, walked fourteen miles to Savannah, Georgia, with severe stomach cramps to surrender to authorities. He pleaded with them to confiscate his entire supply. "If it did this to me, it would probably kill anybody else."

Bill Hendrix, member of the Imperial Council of the Ku Klux Klan, announced that the organization will accept Catholics as members, since its fight is against "integration, communism, and federal controls."

Skater and actress **Sonja Henie** was sworn in as a U.S. citizen on 3 January 1950.

Socialite **Barbara Hutton** was married to her sixth husband, former tennis star **Baron Gottfried von Cramm,** on 8 November 1953.

Helen Keller received the first award of President Dwight D. Eisenhower's Committee on Employment of the Physically Handicapped, 14 November 1955.

Richard Knerr and **Arthur Melin,** the owners of Wham-O Manufacturing, introduced to the public two of the most popular toys of the decade, the frisbee and the hula hoop.

Erma Leach, 25, set the world flagpole-sitting record on 1 January 1951, when she ended a 152-day stay on top of a sixty-foot pole.

John Maragon, who rose from bootblack to Truman White House confidante, was indicted on four counts of perjury on 3 January 1950.

Rosemary Meyer, a former secretary for Perry Como, married singer **Julius La Rosa** on 7 April 1956.

On 14 February 1950 **Nancy Sinatra** announced she was seeking a divorce from singer **Frank Sinatra.**

In January 1953 **Hugh Alexander Morris Gene Saul Ralph Giles Gilbert Motoer Marquis Miles Marion Mayo John Charles James Gordon Bennett Adams Christopher Columbus Elijah Green Eversole Bradley Kincaid Robert Jefferson Breckenridge Stallard** was inducted into the U.S. Navy. On the navy roster his name read **Bennett (NMI) Stallard.** The NMI stood for No Middle Initial.

In August 1958 **Trigger, Roy Rogers's** costar for twenty years in numerous movies retired to "a life of ease at Rogers' California ranch."

Pamela Wilde became engaged to "Today" host **Dave Garroway** on 23 March 1956.

DEATHS

Jimmy (James Crawford) Angel, 57, soldier of fortune and gold prospector who discovered Angel Falls (world's highest waterfall) in Venezuela in 1929, 8 December 1956.

Lolita Sheldon Armour, 83, widow of meat packer J. Ogden Armour, Chicago society leader, 6 February 1953.

Judge George A. Batlett, 82, Reno judge who granted more than twenty thousand divorces, 1 June 1951.

Raymond Benjamin, 79, confidant of former president Herbert Hoover, grand exalted ruler of the Elks (1914–1915), 18 June 1952.

Oscar H. Bentson, 76, founder of Agriculture Department 4-H Clubs for farm youth, former director of Boy Scouts' Rural Scouting Service, 15 August 1951.

Dr. James Bernstein, 84, New York doctor who headed the Hebrew Sheltering and Immigrant Aid Society, 1932–1942, which helped refugees from Germany resettle in the United States, 28 June 1959.

Edna Blue, 49, a founder and international chairman of the Foster Parents' Plan for War Children, 24 March 1951.

William Bodine, 71, Philadelphia civic leader, 8 September 1959.

John Boettiger, 50, former son-in-law of Franklin D. Roosevelt, 31 October 1950.

Owen E. Brennan, 45, New Orleans restaurant owner and founder of *Brennan's,* 4 November 1955.

Israel A. Broadsword, 105, one of the last four GAR (Union) veterans of the Civil War, 25 July 1952.

Roger Lee Brodie, 16 months, weaker brother of surviving Rodney Brodie, Siamese twins joined at the tip of their skulls, 20 January 1953.

Edgar G. Brown, 56, National Negro Council founder-director, 9 April 1954.

Peaches Browning (Mrs. Francis Heenan Wilson), 46, whose brief marriage at age fifteen to Edward W. ("Daddy") Browning in 1926 caused widespread publicity, 23 August 1956.

Frank Buck, 66, big-game hunter who captured, not killed, his prey, 25 March 1950.

Clara Bradley Burdette, 98, founder of several national women's organizations allied with the General Federation of Women's Clubs, 6 January 1954.

Mathilda Burling, 78, founder (1925) of Gold Star Mothers (mothers of U.S. servicemen killed in World War I), 21 July 1958.

Allen Tibbals Burns, 77, social worker who aided U.S. immigrants and World War I famine victims, executive director of Community Chests and Councils of America, 9 March 1953.

William Jordon Bush, 107, one of the last seven veterans of the Confederate army, 11 November 1952.

Albert C. Chire, 62, Federal Housing Administration chief engineer (1934 –1942) who set many of the technical standards for low-cost housing, 9 September 1958.

Rear Adm. Wat Tyler Cluverius, 77, survivor of the sinking of the *Maine* (1898), veteran of both world wars, 28 October 1952.

Edith Rubridge Cohoe, 75, who learned to fly a plane at age sixty-one, gaining the title of the "flying grandmother," 1956.

Dr. James A. Colescott, 53, former imperial wizard of the Ku Klux Klan, which he disbanded in 1944, 11 January 1950.

Francis Dana Coman, 56, polar explorer, 28 January 1952.

Elizabeth Sprague Coolidge, 89, wealthy patron of chamber music ensembles and projects, 4 November 1953.

Grace Anna Goodhue Coolidge, 78, widow of former president Calvin Coolidge, 8 July 1957.

Ernest K. Coulter, 80, founder of the Big Brother movement to guide and protect boys, 1 May 1952.

Jacob Sechler Coxey, 97, "general" who led "Coxey's Army" of unemployed in a march on Washington from Massillon, Ohio, in 1894, 18 May 1951.

Louise E. du Pont Crowinshield, philanthropist active in restoring historic colonial buildings, 11 July 1958.

Grace Cummins, 71, social worker and Presbyterian leader, originator of released-time plan for giving children religious instruction outside public schools, 20 March 1953.

Neva R. Deardorff, 71, social-welfare statistical expert, former president of the Child Welfare League of America, 21 August 1958.

William I. Dotson, 62, attorney who was the first man recruited into Alcoholics Anonymous, 17 September 1954.

Jean McGinley Draper, 69, a leader in the national movement for the repeal of Prohibition, 26 September 1954.

Marjories Gould Drexel, granddaughter of Jay Gould, widow of Anthony J. Drexel, New York banker, 29 November 1955.

William J. ("Big Bill") Duffy, 69, Prohibition-era speak-easy operator who managed the Italian heavyweight Primo Carnera to the world title in the 1930s, 25 May 1952.

Lincoln Ellsworth, 71, explorer, first man to fly across both polar regions, 26 May 1951.

Fala, 11, late president Franklin D. Roosevelt's black Scottish terrier who sat in on many history-making conferences, 5 April 1952.

John Andrews Fitch, 78, labor and social relations professor at Columbia University's School for Social Work, 1917–1946, 15 June 1959.

Brig. Gen. Frederick S. Foltz, 94, oldest West Point alumnus who fought the northwestern Indians in the 1880s, 28 August 1952.

Katherine Ford, 53, Detroit society leader and wife of industrialist–music patron John B. Ford, Jr., 31 May 1953.

Capt. Ragnar T. Freng, 52, pilot of the first U.S. commercial passenger flight (1922), 9 July 1952.

Ruth Bernard Fromenson, 73, cofounder of Hadassah (Women's Zionist Organization of America), 26 January 1953.

Irene Lanhorne (Mrs. Charles Dana) Gibson, 83, the "Gibson Girl" made famous in the early 1900s as a model through illustrations by her husband-artist, 20 April 1956.

John Mark Glen, 91, social worker, general director of the Russell Sage Foundation (1907–1931), 20 April 1950.

Josephine Goldmark, 73, leader in movement for social legislation, 15 December 1950.

Waxley Gordon (Irving Wexler), 63, Prohibition-era bootlegger and underworld figure, 24 June 1952.

Hunter B. Grant, 67, founder of first Boy Scouts of America troop, 23 June 1954.

M. Louise Gross, 67, founder-president of Women's Moderation Union, foe of Prohibition, 26 November 1951.

Samuel W. Gumpertz, 84, circus showman, manager of Houdini and Ringling Circus, 22 June 1952.

Fleet Adm. William F. Halsey, 76, U.S. Navy leader in World War II whose flagship *Missouri* was the scene of Japan's formal surrender, 16 August 1959.

Ralph Warner Harbison, 83, national president of the Young Men's Christian Association, 12 December 1959.

James A. Hard, 111, oldest U.S. Civil War veteran, next-to-last survivor of the Union army, 11 March 1953.

Ira Hayes, 32, American Indian immortalized in the famous photograph of the flag-raising on Mountain Suribachi during the battle for Iwo Jima in World War II, 24 January 1955.

Capt. Hugh Herndon, Jr., 48, American Airlines official, the first pilot to fly the North Pacific nonstop (1931), 5 April 1952.

Duncan Hines, 78, gourmet and author of *Adventures in Good Eating*, 26 March 1959.

Burton Holmes, 88, lecturer, photographer, and originator of the travelogue, 22 July 1958.

Hunting Horse, 107, American Indian of the Kiowa tribe, last surviving Indian scout for Gen. George Armstrong Custer, 1 July 1953.

James R. Howard, 80, farmer and first president of the American Farm Bureau Federation, 27 January 1954.

Eddie Jacobson, 64, former partner of President Harry S Truman in a Kansas City haberdashery (1922), 25 October 1955.

Joseph Smith Jessop, 83, patriarch of the Short Creek, Arizona, colony of polygamists raided and broken up in July 1953, 1 September 1953.

Marguerite C. Johnson, 57, public safety director (fire, police, and communications departments), Dearborn, Michigan, and the only woman police commissioner in the United States, 3 March 1959.

Osa Johnson, 58, big-game hunter, author, and filmmaker who worked as a team with her late husband Martin Johnson, 7 January 1953.

Rosalie M. Jonas, 91, promoter of welfare projects of black children in Harlem, 4 January 1953.

Eugene Kinkle Jones, 69, executive secretary of the National Urban League, 11 January 1954.

Thomas Jesse Jones, 76, Welsh-born pioneer in black education and U.S. race relations, director emeritus of the Phelps-Stokes Fund, founder of the Commission on Interracial Cooperation, 5 January 1950.

Peggy Hopkins (Mrs. Andrew C. Meyers, née Marguerite Upton) Joyce, 62, former Ziegfeld Follies girl noted for six marriages, 12 June 1957.

Thomas A. Keen, inventor of the mechanical rabbit used in dog races, former associate of Al Capone, 5 February 1952.

Paul Underwood Kellogg, 79, pioneer social worker whose study of the Pittsburgh steel industry led to the end of the seven-day workweek, 1 November 1958.

Alvin Anthony (Shipwreck) Kelly, 67, stuntman famous for flagpole sitting in the 1920s, 11 October 1952.

Iven C. Kincheloe, 30, U.S. Air Force captain, holder of the American altitude record (126,000 feet), and one of a small group picked for pioneer space travel, 26 July 1958.

Alfred Kinsey, 62, author of *Sexual Behavior in the Human Male* and *Sexual Behavior in the Human Female*, 25 August 1956.

Mabel Kittredge, 87, school-lunch crusader, a member of President Herbert Hoover's food committee in World War I, 8 May 1955.

Eduard Christian Lindeman, 67, president of the National Conference of Social Work, 13 April 1953.

Samuel McCune Lindsay, 90, former Columbia University social legislation professor, housing and labor expert, 11 November 1959.

Katherine Ludington, 83, woman's suffrage leader, National League of Women Voters cofounder, 7 March 1953.

William A. Lundy, 109, one of the last three surviving Confederate veterans, 1 September 1957.

William Allen Magee, 106, one of the last three GAR survivors, bugler for Gen. William Tecumseh Sherman's Civil War army, 23 January 1953.

Benjamin C. Marsh, 74, a campaigner for public welfare causes and the first Washington lobbyist registered under a law passed in 1946, 30 December 1952.

Vivian C. McCollum, 57, Young Men's Christian Association president since 1956, 26 August 1959.

Vida Milholland, woman's suffrage leader during World War I, 29 November 1952.

Capt. Joseph McConnell, Jr., 32, world's leading jet ace, 25 August 1954.

Daisy Orr Miller, 78, president of the Animal Protective Union, known as the "dog detective" for locating lost animals, 2 December 1955.

Col. Zack T. Miller, 74, owner of the 101 Ranch (once the largest in Oklahoma), 3 January 1952.

Helen Moore, 92, retired social worker, editor of research publications for the Russell Sage Foundation, 2 August 1954.

James ("Dinty") Moore, 83, New York restaurateur known as the "Corned Beef and Cabbage King," 25 December 1952.

Joseph Morelli, 70, criminal, thought to have been responsible for the crime for which Nicola Sacco and Bartolomeo Vanzetti were convicted, 26 August 1950.

Anne Morgan, 78, daughter of banker John Pierpont Morgan, one of the world's richest women, and noted for her philanthropies in France, 29 January 1952.

Brig. Gen. Thomas Bentley Mott, 87, soldier who represented Gen. John Pershing on the staff of Marshall Ferdinand Foch in World War I, 17 January 1952.

Clem (Uncle Pike) Noble, 123, former slave, believed to have been the second oldest person in the world, 18 March 1954.

Howard Washington Odum, 70, New York City University sociologist who worked for better race relations, 8 November 1954.

Esther Gracie Ogden, 89, suffragette and former secretary of the Foreign Policy Association, 13 January 1956.

Joanne Connelly Ortez-Patino, 27, socialite, 2 July 1957.

Mary White Ovington, 86, one of the founders of the National Association for the Advancement of Colored People, 15 July 1951.

Isabel Townsend Pell, 51, American "Frederika" or girl with the blond hair who led Marquis resistance groups on the French Riviera during World War II, 5 June 1952.

Edwin McNeill Poteat, 60, Baptist minister, anti-segregationist, chairman of Protestants and Other Americans United for Separation of Church and State, 17 December 1955.

Gladys (Mrs. Vernon) Presley, 42, mother of Elvis Presley, 14 August 1958.

Roger Preston, 54, Boston financier and civic leader, 28 November 1954.

Laura B. Prisk, 75, the "Mother of Flag Day," who crusaded to have 14 June declared a legal holiday, 30 May 1950.

Harold Purcell, 72, Roman Catholic editor-priest who promoted the $5-million City of St. Jude in Montgomery, Alabama, for the needy of all races, 22 October 1952.

Lawson Purdy, 95, New York City civil leader in housing reform, former president of Russell Sage Foundation, National Municipal League, and Department of Taxes and Assessments (1906–1917), 30 August 1959.

Mabel Gilmore Reinecke, 65, U.S. collector of internal revenue during Presidents Warren G. Harding and Calvin Coolidge administrations, the first woman to receive a Presidential commission to a federal executive position, 8 March 1958.

Lady Ribblesdale (Mrs. Ava Willing Ribblesdale), 89, socialite, first wife of Col. John Jacob Astor and widow of Queen Victoria's lord-in-waiting whose title she renounced in 1940, 9 June 1958.

Thomas Evans Riddle, 107, one of five surviving U.S. Civil War veterans, 2 April 1954.

Edith Conway Ringling, 84, cofounder with husband Charles Ringling of the Ringling–Barnum and Bailey Circus, 23 September 1953.

Robert Edward Ringling, 52, chairman of Ringling Brothers and Barnum and Bailey Circus, 2 January 1950.

Edgar M. Robinson, 84, an organizer of the Boy Scouts of America and Young Men's Christian Association boys' leader, 9 April 1951.

John B. Salling, 112, one of two surviving Civil War Confederate veterans, 16 March 1959.

Mabel Young Sanborn, 87, last surviving of Brigham Young's fifty-six children, 20 September 1950.

Aaron L. Sapiro, 75, attorney who sued Henry Ford for $1 million in 1927 for maligning Jews, 23 November 1959.

Clarence Saunders, 72, founder of first self-service grocery chain (Piggly Wiggly in Memphis, Tennessee) who made and lost two fortunes, 14 October 1953.

Alan Magee Scaife, 58, Pittsburgh industrialist and philanthropist (Scaife Foundation), 24 July 1958.

Arnold Schuster, 24, whose tip led to the arrest of bank robber Willie Sutton, 8 March 1952.

Walter E. ("Death Valley Scottie") Scott, 81, gold prospector whose spectacular spending sprees were financed secretly by a Chicago millionaire, 6 January 1954.

Grace Gallatin Thompson Seton, 83, author, lecturer, explorer, cofounder of the Camp Fire Girls in 1910, 19 March 1959.

Samuel James Seymour, 96, last known witness to the assassination of President Abraham Lincoln, 13 April 1956.

Dora Monness Shapiro, 72, philanthropist, Jewish welfare worker, 13 November 1952.

Mary Kingsbury Simkhovitch, 84, New York social worker, founder of Greenwich House, 15 December 1951.

Ida B. Wise Smith, 81, president of the Women's Christian Temperance Union (1933–1944), 16 February 1952.

Robert Holbrook Smith, 71, a founder of Alcoholics Anonymous, 16 November 1950.

Fred Snite, Jr., 44, polio victim who spent eighteen years in an iron lung, 12 November 1954.

Dr. Abraham Stone, 68, pioneer in birth control and marriage counseling, director of the Margaret Sanger Research Bureau, 3 July 1959.

Birdsall Sweet, 32, polio sufferer who spent nineteen years in an iron lung, 17 April 1950.

Adm. Robert A. Theobold, 73, commander of the Pearl Harbor destroyer flotilla at the time of the Japanese attack in 1941, 13 May 1957.

Chief Thunderwater (Oghema Niagara), 85, head of the Supreme Council of Indian Tribes in the United States and Canada, 10 June 1950.

Roger ("Terrible") Touhey, 61, gangster of the Prohibition era, 16 December 1959.

William D. Townsend, 106, one of the last five Confederate army survivors, 22 February 1953.

Florence Adele Vanderbilt Twombly, 98, only surviving grandchild of Commodore Cornelius Vanderbilt, 10 April 1952.

Grace Wilson Vanderbilt, 82, widow of Brig. Gen. Cornelius Vanderbilt, society leader in New York City and Newport, 7 January 1953.

Harriet E. Vittum, 81, pioneer Chicago social worker and suffragette, 16 December 1953.

Florence Dahl Walrathe, 81, founder of the Cradle Society (1923) which worked to place infants for adoption, 7 November 1958.

Frieda Schiff Warburg, 82, widow of Felix Warburg, philanthropist who donated her New York City home as a Jewish museum, 1 September 1958.

Harry P. Wareham, 68, organizer of the first Community Chest drive, 11 June 1951.

Simon Taylor Webb, 83, Casey Jones fireman who leaped from the Illinois Central's Cannon Ball Express just before it crashed in 1900, killing its now-immortal engineer, Casey, 13 July 1957.

George S. Welch, 36, first U.S. Army pilot to shoot down a Japanese plane during the Pearl Harbor attack, 12 October 1954.

Bouck White, 76, who preached social revolution in his Church of the Social Revolution during World War I in New York, 7 January 1951.

William Fitzhugh Whitehouse, 76, Newport civic and society leader, 27 May 1955.

Brig. Gen. Wilbur Elliott Wilder, 95, oldest living holder of the Congressional Medal of Honor, which he won fighting the Apaches, 30 January 1952.

Charles Finn Williams, 79, Cincinnati philanthropist, art collector, Catholic lay leader, 11 September 1952.

Harison Williams, 80, utilities financier, husband of "best dressed" society leader Mona Strader Williams, 10 November 1953.

Walter Williams, 117, reputed to be the last survivor of the Civil War whose contention that he served in the Confederate army under Gen. John B. Hood was the subject of a newspaper controversy in 1959, 19 December 1959.

J. Finley Wilson, 70, grand exalted ruler of the Negro Elks (1922–1950), 19 February 1952.

Elma H. Wischmeier, 52, the millionth automobile traffic victim recorded since 1899, 21 December 1951.

Albert Woolson, 109, last surviving veteran of the Union army, 2 August 1956.

PUBLICATIONS

Gary M. Abshire, "Robbie," in *Science Fiction Thinking Machines,* edited by Groff Conklin (New York: Vanguard, 1954);

Leland Dewitt Bladwin, *The Meaning of America* (Pittsburgh: University of Pittsburgh Press, 1955);

Wini Breines, *Young, White, and Miserable: Growing Up Female in the Fifties* (Boston: Beacon, 1992);

Paul G. Brewster, *American Nonsinging Games* (Norman: University of Oklahoma Press, 1953);

Brewster, *Children's Games and Rhymes* (Chapel Hill: University of North Carolina Press, 1952);

Bob Brown and Eleanor Parker, *Culinary Americana: 1860–1960* (New York: Roving Eye Press, 1961);

Groff Conklin, ed., *Science Fiction Thinking Machines* (New York: Vanguard, 1954);

Margaret Cussler and Mary Louise de Give, *Twixt the Cup and the Lip: Psychological and Socio-cultural Factors Affecting Food Habits* (New York: Twayne, 1952);

Peter F. Drucker, *The New Society* (New York: Harper, 1950);

H. Warren Dunham, ed., *The City in Mid-Century* (Detroit: Wayne State University Press, 1957);

William Y. Elliott, *Television's Impact on American Culture* (East Lansing: Michigan State University Press, 1956);

Erik Erikson, *Childhood and Society* (New York: Norton, 1950);

Fortune Editors, *The Exploding Metropolis* (Garden City, N.Y.: Doubleday, 1958);

John K. Galbraith, *The Affluent Society* (Boston: Houghton Mifflin, 1958);

Galbraith, *American Capitalism: The Concept of Countervailing Power* (Boston: Houghton Mifflin, 1956);

Sidonie M. Gruenberg and Hilda Sidney Krech, *The Many Lives of Modern Woman: A Guide to Happiness in Her Complex Role* (Garden City, N.Y.: Doubleday, 1952);

Harry Harrison, ed., *War with the Robots* (New York: Pyramid Books, 1962);

Hilda T. Himmelweit, A. N. Oppenheim, and Pamela Vince, *Television and the Child: An Empirical Study of the Effect of Television on the Young* (London: Oxford University Press, 1958);

Eric Hoffer, *The True Believer: Thoughts on the Nature of Mass Movements* (New York: NAL, 1951);

Johan Huizinga, *Homo Ludens: A Study of the Play Element in Culture* (Boston: Beacon, 1960);

Robert Jungk, *Tomorrow is Already Here* (New York: Simon & Schuster, 1954);

Orrin E. Klapp, *Heroes, Villains, and Fools: The Changing American Character* (Englewood Cliffs, N. J.: Prentice-Hall, 1961);

John A. Kouwenhoven, *The Beer Can by the Highway* (Garden City, N.Y.: Doubleday, 1961);

Louis Kronenberger, *Company Manners: A Cultural Inquiry into American Life* (Indianapolis: Bobbs-Merrill, 1954);

Robert Lindner, *Must You Conform?* (New York: Rinehart, 1956);

Lawrence Lipton, *The Holy Barbarians* (New York: Messner, 1959);

Marjorie Longley, Louis Silverstein, and Samuel A. Tower, *America's Taste: 1851–1959* (New York: Simon & Schuster, 1960);

David Low, *The Fearful Fifties: A History of the Decade* (New York: Simon & Schuster, 1960);

Leo Lowenthal, *Literature, Popular Culture, and Society* (Englewood Cliffs, N. J.: Prentice-Hall, 1961);

Herbert Lewis Marx, Jr., ed., *Television and Radio in American Life,* The Reference Shelf, vol. 25, no. 2 (New York: H. W. Wilson, 1953);

Kenneth McArdle, ed., *A Cavalcade of "Collier's"* (New York: Barnes, 1959);

Inez McClintock and Marshall McClintock, *Toys in America* (Washington, D.C.: Public Affairs Press, 1961);

Douglas T. Miller, *The Fifties: The Way We Really Were* (Garden City, N.Y.: Doubleday, 1960);

C. Wright Mills, *The Power Elite* (New York: Oxford University Press, 1956);

Mills, *White Collar: The American Middle Classes* (New York: Oxford University Press, 1951);

Vance Packard, *The Status Seekers* (New York: McKay, 1959);

David Potter, *People of Plenty: Economic Abundance and American Character* (Chicago: University of Chicago Press, 1954);

David Riesman and Nathan Glazer, *The Lonely Crowd: A Study of the Changing American Character* (New Haven: Yale University Press, 1950);

Bernard Rosenberg and David Manning White, eds., *Mass Culture: Popular Arts in America* (Glencoe, Ill.: Free Press, 1957);

A. C. Spectorsky, *The Exurbanites* (Philadelphia: Lippincott, 1955);

E. N. Todhunter, "The History of Food Patterns in the U.S.A.," in *Proceedings of the Third International Congress on Dietetics* (New York: Nutrition Foundation, 1961);

Alan Valentine, *The Age of Conformity* (Chicago: Regnery, 1954);

Better Homes and Gardens, periodical;

Collier's, periodical;

Coronet, periodical;

Good Housekeeping, periodical;

Ladies' Home Journal, periodical;

Life, periodical;

Look, periodical;

McCalls, periodical;

Reader's Digest, periodical;

Saturday Evening Post, periodical;

Seventeen, periodical;

Woman's Home Companion, periodical.

The Davy Crockett craze reached its peak in 1955, when sales of Davy Crockett merchandise reached $100 million. Department stores reported enrolling as many as fifteen thousand members in a two-week period.

MEDIA

by JAMES W. HIPP

CONTENTS

Sidebars and tables are listed in italics.

1950

- 101 television stations are operating.

- 4,835,000 television sets are installed.

21 Feb. The Justice Department files a civil antitrust suit charging Lee and Jacob Shubert with monopolizing U.S. theater ownership.

13 Apr. The Federal Communications Commission (FCC) warns radio stations that present editorial opinions on controversial issues that they have a "duty to seek out, aid and encourage the broadcast of opposing views."

11 Oct. The FCC votes to allow CBS to begin color television broadcasts starting 20 November.

12 Dec. CBS asks twenty-four hundred employees to sign loyalty oaths.

1951

- A coast-to-coast cable link is completed, allowing simultaneous bicoastal broadcasting.

- Marquette University televises the first course over television.

25 June CBS begins broadcasting color commercial television programs; conventional black-and-white sets are unable to receive them.

5 Aug. The Ford Foundation allots $1.2 million for cultural and public-service television broadcasts.

9 Sept. The soap operas "Search for Tomorrow" and "Love of Life" premiere on CBS.

15 Oct. "I Love Lucy" premieres on CBS.

18 Nov. The CBS television show "See It Now," starring Edward R. Murrow, premieres.

1952

- The FCC lifts the freeze on television broadcast licenses which had been imposed in 1948. The action reinvigorates the television business.

- The transistor radio is introduced in the United States by Sony Corporation.

16 Jan. "The Today Show" premieres on NBC.

Aug. *Mad* comic books, forerunners of *Mad* magazine, are introduced.

20 Aug. *American Mercury* magazine is sold.

1953

- RCA demonstrates videotape recording.

- 55 percent of American families owns a television.

- 311 television stations are in operation.

8 Nov. Photoengravers go on strike in New York City for eleven days, leaving the city without a daily newspaper for the first time since 1778.

27 Nov. The FCC rules that no person or firm may have a financial interest in more than five television stations.

1954

- Newspaper vending machines first appear.

4 Apr. Walt Disney signs an agreement with the ABC television network to produce twenty-six television films per year.

11 Sept. The Miss America pageant is first televised; Lee Ann Meriweather, Miss California, is the winner.

25 Oct. President Dwight D. Eisenhower holds the first televised cabinet meeting.

27 Oct. Twenty-six comic-book publishers announce the adoption of a code restricting violent or vulgar scenes.

1955

19 Jan. President Dwight D. Eisenhower holds the first televised presidential news conference.

22 Feb. The owners of the *Kansas City Star* are convicted in federal court of attempting to monopolize news coverage and advertising in the Kansas City area.

6 Apr. Zenith Radio Corporation denounces CBS for "unwarranted censorship" and withdraws as sponsor of "Omnibus" when CBS refuses to let Zenith air a commercial for Phonevision, a subscription television service opposed by the networks.

18 July Howard Hughes sells RKO Radio Pictures and its pre-1948 movie titles to General Tire for $25 million.

1956

- CBS moves production of several of its shows, including "Playhouse 90," to Television City in California.

14 Jan. Detroit newspaper deliverers end a six-week strike by accepting a two-year contract containing increased pay and benefits.

20 June Loew's Inc. releases M-G-M's pre-1949 film library, except *Gone With the Wind,* for television broadcast.

Aug. *American* magazine, first published in 1876 as *Frank Leslie's Popular Monthly,* is discontinued by the Crowell-Collier company.

30 Nov. The first commercial use by television of videotape for "Douglas Edwards with the News" occurrs on CBS.

1957

4 Jan. Alliance of Television Film Producers agrees to adopt the ethical-production code of the National Association of Radio and Television Broadcasters.

7 Mar. The publisher and the distributor of *Confidential* magazine are indicted on charges of mailing obscene or crime-inciting material.

25 May Comedian Sid Caesar quits NBC after the mutual cancellation of the remaining seven years of his $100,000 per year contract.

1958

3 Mar.   Richard Mack resigns as FCC member after admitting to the Special House Subcommittee on Legislative Oversight that he received loans and gifts of stock from a friend who is interested in the FCC award of a valuable Miami television channel.

24 May   United Press Association and International News Service merge to form United Press International (UPI).

18 Sept.   FCC announces that it would consider applications from television stations to test subscription television telecasts experimentally over a three-year period.

11 Oct.   In a new guideline interpreting the equal time clause, the FCC says television and radio stations must give equal time to all legally qualified political candidates.

16 Oct.   Sponsors drops the NBC quiz show "21," under grand jury investigation for pre-arrangement of quiz contest results.

1959

28 July   The Senate passes and sends to the House a bill exempting radio and television news shows from an FCC requirement that all competing political candidates be given equal time if any one of them appeared on a broadcast.

6 Oct.   The Special House Subcommittee on Legislative Oversight begins a probe into television quiz programs.

16 Oct.   CBS President Frank Stanton bans quiz shows from the network.

3 Nov.   Bandleader Xavier Cugat testifies that he received questions and answers on CBS's "$64,000 Question."

OVERVIEW

The Decade of Television. The stereotype that labels the 1950s as a sleepy, conformist decade is at no time less true than when discussing the media. The 1950s were revolutionary years in the media. During the decade the technology and content of radio, television, newspapers, magazines, and the movies entered a period of rapid change. In the aftermath of the Great Depression and World War II, the pent-up demand for goods and services and the unexploited supply of new technologies combined to bring a nearly unprecedented wave of radical change to many areas of American life. The rise of television as an entertainment center for the American public was the dominant media trend of the 1950s. Television supplanted radio as the primary source of entertainment, dramatic, comedic, and variety programs; radio by the end of the decade was primarily given only to popular music, news, and sports programming.

Competing with Television. Changes in the other media, while driven by many of the same social and economic forces affecting television, came to be seen by many as driven by television itself. Radio, newspapers, magazines, and movies all began to compete with television. The success of these outlets was measured by how well they withstood the challenge television presented in terms of audience size and advertising dollars.

Growth of the Market. The potential size of the television audience was estimated at 9.8 million households in December 1951. By October 1959 this figure had grown to 45 million households. The number of radio-equipped households reached 50 million in 1959. But radio had the most to lose from the emerging television medium. The three major radio networks, the National Broadcasting Company (NBC), the Columbia Broadcasting System (CBS), and the American Broadcasting Company (ABC), all implemented plans to move into television broadcasting. Of these the most important was NBC. In June 1946 an internal company memo had proposed that radio network profits be plowed into the development of television technology and programming. This meant that network radio would subsidize the medium that would supplant it as the entertainment choice of millions of Americans.

Milking Radio. With little money available, radio producers were unable to invest in new programming, and by the mid 1950s many of the top radio shows — and their stars — had transferred to television. With their traditional formats gutted, local and network radio programmers turned to recorded music. They also began the exploitation of market niches, such as "Negro" radio. The development was assisted by the 1947 invention of the transistor, technology which allowed the miniaturization of electronics. The development of portable radios greatly aided programmers in their search for new and prosperous markets. By 1956 over 3.1 million transistor radios were being sold annually.

Magazine Starts and Closings. The print media — newspapers and magazines — were not immune to the postwar changes. Television networks and the new radio stations, which were carrying increasingly more local advertising rather than national spots, competed for advertising dollars. Advertising revenues for magazines and newspapers increased, as did circulation, but profits weakened as production and distribution costs increased. In 1954 magazine net profits slumped to 2.8 percent from 8.3 percent in 1948. By the end of the decade many famous magazine titles, *Collier's, Woman's Home Companion,* the *American,* and *Town Journal* among them, had folded. But there were major magazine start-ups. Henry Luce started *Sports Illustrated* as an addition to his stable, already containing, among others, *Life* and *Time. Sports Illustrated* first appeared on 12 August 1954, reaching a first-year circulation of six hundred thousand readers. A new conservative political magazine, *National Review,* debuted in 1955.

Tightening Newspaper Market. Newspapers remained the primary source of local, national, and international news for most Americans. But, like radio stations, newspapers were faced with the dilemma of revenues that did not keep up with quickly rising expenses. The years of economic hardship and wartime deprivation were replaced by years of relative economic prosperity. The resulting escalation of wages, newsprint prices, and costs of investing in new technology weighed heavily on profit margins. Closures and mergers became more common. Fourteen papers were either closed or merged in 1950.

The two Atlanta newspapers, the *Journal* and the *Constitution,* merged, and the *New York Sun* and the *Oakland Post-Enquirer* ceased publication in 1950. At the end of 1959 there were 1,745 daily newspapers, a decline of 2 percent from the 1949 number. By 1955, 94 percent of all communities with daily newspapers were served by newspapers owned by a single company.

The Movie Industry. Movie producers felt particularly threatened by television, as executives and critics predicted that people would remain at home and watch television rather than travel to a theater to see a movie. These threats were exaggerated, but the 1950s brought great change to movies and the industry which produced and distributed them. The antitrust investigation and lawsuit launched by the U.S. government in the late 1940s were finally settled in the early 1950s, and the ramifications were widespread. Movie studios were forced to sell the theater chains that they owned and controlled. Movies became more expensive to produce, fewer were made, and profits became tighter at the movie studios. Also, the voluntary censorship program that producers had operated since the late 1920s fell apart because of the studios' inability to control distribution. Movie theaters, sold by the production companies because of the antitrust ruling, fought for the reduced number of movies. As a result of the competition, many theaters closed, and profits shrank at the remaining outlets.

Decade of Radical Change. The changes in the media brought about during the 1950s left industries in 1959 radically changed from their condition in 1949. The implications of these changes were still to be worked out in the succeeding decades. What was clear was that the media had staked their claim to being the most influential industries in American society.

TOPICS IN THE NEWS

AUDIENCE RATINGS

Need for Ratings. "How many people were watching?" That question captivated (and still captivates) television executives and advertisers. To find the answer, television networks and individual stations began in the late 1940s to hire firms to do the surveys that determined program popularity and audience. With such information the networks and stations could determine what they might charge companies to advertise on particular shows.

History of Ratings. The idea of audience testing was not new. The radio networks and individual stations had begun in 1930 to test the level of audiences by the use of telephone interviews. New techniques were then developed to improve the validity of survey results. The most important of these were the printed roster, in which listeners marked down on a preprinted list the programs they watched; the mechanical recorder; and the interview. While the radio-ratings service field was very competitive — dominated by such firms as Cooperative Analysis of Broadcasting, C. E. Hooper, A. C. Nielsen — the television end of the industry was the kingdom of Nielsen in the 1950s.

NBC's Gambit. How Nielsen became king is a story of wrong guesses and missed opportunities. Late in the 1940s, as television was not yet widely available, no company offered a television rating service. NBC was especially interested in the performance of its shows and offered C. E. Hooper a list of the twenty thousand television-set owners in New York as an inducement to start a New York City service. The list of owners, frequently updated by the Manhattan RCA television distributor, would provide the raw material needed to initiate a telephone survey. Hooper was a radio fan and did not think television would survive. He was persuaded in 1948 to begin the ratings service when RCA showed him his first televised New York Yankees baseball game. RCA also threatened to provide the owner list to another firm.

Hooper's Misjudgment. Hooper's television service took off and within two years was established in all major cities. In 1950 Hooper was interested in selling his national radio ratings service in order to concentrate on the local ratings business. A. C. Nielsen bargained with Hooper for the national service, but he was really interested in television. Nielsen shrewdly offered to take the national television ratings system off Hooper's hands along with the national radio service. With Hooper's belief in the ultimate failure of television undiminished, he sold the national television ratings system to Nielsen.

Nielsen Television Index. The basis of the Nielsen rating service was the Nielsen Television Index, a meter

A. C. Nielsen with one of his audience-measuring devices

system that recorded what station a viewer had tuned in and for how long. During the early and mid 1950s, when many cities had only one or two stations, networks and affiliates were less concerned with the popularity of individual shows. What was important was the network lineup on particular nights, which, if popular, could dominate viewing. This thinking became commonplace among the networks; it was still common in the 1980s and early 1990s to hear advertisements touting a particular network's "Thursday night" or "Saturday night" comedies, for instance. By the end of the 1950s the television market was varied enough that the ratings for individual shows became important.

The Endurance of Ratings. Ratings themselves lent at least the perception of objectivity to the buying and selling of television advertising, a business worth $1 billion in 1955. As television grew during the 1950s and after to become the primary medium for national product advertising, the ratings companies were compelled to develop more-precise statistical measures to produce numbers to convince companies to buy advertising on particular shows. Ratings were the business end of the creative process. Poor ratings could kill a critically acclaimed show, and high ratings could save a show denounced as the worst drivel. Critics pointed to ratings as causing a tilt from art to commerce in determining television lineups.

Sources:
Hugh Malcolm Bevill, Jr., *Audience Ratings: Radio, Television, Cable* (Hillsdale, N.J.: Lawrence Erlbaum Associates, 1988);

Karen S. Buzzard, *Chains of Gold: Marketing the Ratings and Rating the Markets* (Metuchen, N.J.: Scarecrow Press, 1990).

COLLIER'S CLOSES

Magazine Economics. The closing of *Collier's* magazine in 1956 shockingly illustrated the postwar changes in magazine economics and the entertainment and editorial tastes of the American reading public. A venerable name in magazine history, *Collier's* had reached its peak of circulation of above four million at the time of its demise. But rising costs and competition from television and more nimble and aggressive magazines had cut drastically into advertising revenues.

Early History. The magazine began publishing as *Once a Week* in 1888 and as *Collier's* in 1895. It finally became consistently profitable in 1929 as circulation broke through the two million mark. During the Great Depression *Collier's* prospered. This was the result of the magazine editors' decision in 1925 to reverse their stand and editorialize against Prohibition; after the Eighteenth Amendment to the Constitution was repealed in 1933 and liquor again flowed legally, *Collier's* became a favorite of liquor advertisers.

Editorial High Point. The 1930s were its editorial high point. Editorial precision, however, was never the hallmark of what was a competent, popular, general-interest magazine. The lack of a precise market to which

THE LORAIN (OHIO) JOURNAL CASE

On 11 December 1951, the United States Supreme Court ruled that the *Lorain* (Ohio) *Journal* could not legally refuse advertising in order to coerce clients not to advertise on radio. The Elyria, Ohio, radio station WEOL initiated the lawsuit in 1948 when the *Journal* refused to accept advertising from businesses that used WEOL. The radio station asserted that the *Journal* had engaged in illegal restraint of trade prohibited by the Sherman Anti-Trust Act. As part of the judgment, the *Journal* was forced to print the details of the court's decision once a week for twenty-five weeks. Civil libertarians decried the decision, saying that it made the *Journal* the first U.S. newspaper to be told by a court what to print.

the editors could attract advertisers was a serious problem in the postwar magazine world.

Postwar Decline. Beginning in 1947 *Collier's* advertising revenue dropped every year except 1953, when the weekly switched to biweekly publication. Revenues dropped after World War II partly because of the new outlets for advertisers. Magazines not only had to compete with newspapers and each other but also with radio and the new medium of television. Even rising circulation could not offset stagnant advertising rates. Falling revenues combined with increasing operating costs — salaries, postage, paper — to squeeze the bottom line.

Management Problems. But it was not purely economic factors that drove *Collier's* into oblivion. The management of the Crowell-Collier Corporation, the owner of *Collier's*, also contributed to the demise of the magazine through their ill-judged business decisions. In 1932 Crowell-Collier began declaring large dividends to shareholders, paying an average $2 million yearly until 1953, when the firm began to lose large amounts of money. The big dividends removed the funds needed for new editorial investment in the magazine.

Competition with Television. Editorially, the magazine found itself competing in a new media world. *Collier's*, which looked at the venerable *Saturday Evening Post* as its main competition, was, according to *Printer's Ink*, "almost in direct competition with TV in the fiction-entertainment area." Oblivious to its new competition, *Collier's* was fighting blind.

Specialization. Too late, the editors and management realized that the magazine world had also changed. Specialization hit the industry, and new magazines with narrow foci were launched even as the older general-interest magazines were folding. *Playboy*, founded in 1953 by Hugh Hefner, targeted men with its pictorials of nude and provocatively dressed women. *Sports Illustrated*, first published in 1954 by Henry Luce's *Time* empire, targeted sports fans, mostly men. Specialization aided in attracting advertisers, who could choose what type of reader would see their ads.

Decline of General-Interest Magazines. Such trends worked against magazines such as *Collier's*. The number of general-interest magazines dwindled in the 1950s and 1960s. Important names in magazine history disappeared — *Collier's*, the *American, Woman's Home Companion, Liberty* — but the number of new magazines increased to fill the void.

Sources:

Hollis Alpert, "What Killed Collier's," *Saturday Review*, 40 (11 May 1957): 9–11, 42–44;

James Playsted Wood, *Magazines in the United States*, third edition (New York: Ronald Press, 1971).

DRIVE-INS

Drive-In Boom. Though they first appeared after World War I and in significant numbers in the first years after World War II, drive-in theaters boomed in popularity during the 1950s. In 1948 there were only 820 drive-ins operating in the United States. In 1952 this number had ballooned to over 3,000. The prosperity of postwar America was the source of this increase, as workers and farmers, newly flush with cash and driving new automobiles, sought recreation. The drive-ins catered to a new audience of moviegoers who did not frequent the traditional movie theater. In 1950 the *Saturday Evening Post* described the appeal of drive-ins to people with special needs:

> Leading the list are moderate-income families who bring the kids to save on babysitters. Furthermore they don't have to dress up, find a parking place, walk a few blocks to a ticket booth and then stand in line. The drive-ins make it easy for them and for workers and farmers, who can come in their working clothes straight from the evening's chores, and for the aged and the physically handicapped.

The Quality of Drive-In Movies. The quality of the drive-in movies seemed to matter little. Most drive-ins showed second- and third-run features, long since gone from traditional theaters. Some showed newer, low-budget, poor-quality fare. The fare did not seem to affect revenues, a large percentage of which (forty cents of every dollar) came from concessions. One drive-in operator was quoted as saying that "the worse the pictures are, the more stuff we sell."

Surprise Success. In the early 1950s the average drive-in had a capacity of five hundred to six hundred cars and could operate twenty-six weeks a year — longer in warm climates. Later in the decade one chain of drive-ins had an average capacity of nearly two thousand vehicles. In 1950 drive-ins sold upward of seven million tickets weekly. Because the drive-ins attracted a different audience than did traditional theaters, the success of these outdoor movie emporiums was entirely unexpected by the theater industry. In 1952 a traditional film exhibitor derided the drive-in entrepreneur's prospects as being no better than those of running a novelty shop:

> It's like midget golf. Lotta poor fellas are going to lose their shirts on it. It's got so every farmer has a piece of land near a highway thinks all he needs is a bulldozer to grade it, and a bank to put up some money for a screen and a sound system and he's in business.

Peak of Popularity. The 1950s were the peak of popularity for the drive-ins, which in the 1960s and 1970s regained the unsavory reputation they held in the prewar years. But they remain a symbol of America's postwar prosperity and burgeoning car culture.

Sources:

"The Colossal Drive-In," *Newsweek*, 50 (22 July 1957): 85–87;

"Drive-In Business Burns Up the Prairies," *Life*, 31 (24 September 1951): 104;

"Drive-Ins/Theaters," *Architectural Record*, 108 (August 1950): 140–145;

John Durant, "The Movies Take to the Pasture," *Saturday Evening Post*, 223 (14 October 1950): 24–25, 85, 89–90;

Al Hine, "The Drive-Ins," *Holiday*, 12 (July 1952): 6, 8, 9, 11.

THE HOLLYWOOD TEN

Dalton Trumbo. In 1957, when Robert Rich was announced as the winner of the Academy Award for Best Screenplay, few realized that the name was a pseudonym. Robert Rich was the pen name of screenwriter Dalton Trumbo, a member of the so-called Hollywood Ten, who had been cited in 1947 for contempt of Congress and sentenced to varying terms in prison. He had also been a victim of the Hollywood blacklist that prohibited real or suspected Communist party members from working openly in the movie industry.

HUAC and Hollywood. The Hollywood Ten case began in postwar America during the first rustlings of the cold war. The House Un-American Activities Committee (HUAC), which had been permanently established in 1938, decided in 1947 to conduct hearings on communist influence in Hollywood. In November HUAC subpoenaed forty-one people involved in making Hollywood movies. Nineteen of those subpoenaed protested loudly that they would under no circumstances cooperate with HUAC.

Hearings. During the hearings, which ran from 28 October to 30 October 1947, ten witnesses refused to answer the committee's famous question: "Are you now or have you ever been a member of the Communist party?" All ten were cited for contempt of Congress and were sentenced to between six months and one year in federal prison and fines of one thousand dollars. In addition to Trumbo the ten included Alvah Bessie, Herbert Biberman, Lester Cole, Edward Dmytryk, Ring Lardner,

The Hollywood Ten stand outside district court in Washington, D.C., on 9 January 1950 before their arraignment on contempt of Congress charges.

Jr., John Howard Lawson, Albert Maltz, Samuel Ornitz, and Adrian Scott.

Blacklist. After the hearings, in November, Hollywood executives met at the Waldorf-Astoria Hotel in New York to devise some way to avoid looking like harborers of communists. The blacklist was the result. All members of the Hollywood Ten and other real or perceived communist sympathizers would be fired and refused further work in the movie industry. The ten re-

BLACKLIST ANNOUNCEMENT

Text of the blacklist announcement by Eric Johnston, Motion Picture Association of America, 26 November 1947:

"We will forthwith discharge or suspend without compensation those in our employ and will not re-employ any of the ten until such time as he is acquitted or has purged himself of contempt and declares under oath that he is not a Communist.

On the broader issue of alleged subversive and disloyal elements in Hollywood, our members are likewise prepared to take positive action.

We will not knowingly employ a Communist or a member of any party or group which advocates the overthrow of the Government of the United States by force, or by any illegal or unconstitutional methods."

mained free from prison while appeals progressed. On 10 April 1950 the Supreme Court refused to review their case.

Underground Work. The Hollywood Ten found during their prison terms and after their releases that the blacklist was not airtight. But it remained humiliating and personally costly. The victims of the public blacklist still wrote movie screenplays, and the screenplays were still bought. But during the time of the blacklist, the blacklisted writers had to resort to subterfuge, selling their scripts under false names for reduced prices. They also had to bear with absurdly short deadlines and slow payments. For example, during the time of the blacklist Trumbo completed eighteen screenplays for an average fee of $1,750 each.

Breaking the Blacklist. Trumbo's 1957 Academy Award was the beginning of the breakdown of the blacklist. In 1958 the award for best adapted screenplay went to Pierre Boulle for the script from his novel *Bridge on the River Kwai.* In fact, the screenplay was written by Carl Foreman and Michael Wilson, two writers on the blacklist. In 1960 the blacklist was formally breached when producer Otto Preminger publicly announced that Trumbo was the screenwriter for his upcoming film of Leon Uris's novel *Exodus.* The economic and social suffering of the Hollywood Ten and the other victims of the blacklist ultimately served no purpose except to show the futility of censorship and blacklisting.

Sources:
Bruce Cook, *Dalton Trumbo* (New York: Scribners, 1977);

"Dalton Trumbo, Film Writer, Dies; Oscar Winner Had Been Blacklisted," *New York Times*, 11 September 1976, p. 22;

Bernard F. Dick, *Radical Innocence: A Critical Study of the Hollywood Ten* (Lexington: University of Kentucky Press, 1989);

Stefan Kanfer, *A Journal of the Plague Years* (New York: Atheneum, 1973);

Dalton Trumbo, *Additional Dialogue: Letters of Dalton Trumbo, 1942–1962*, edited by Helen Manfull (New York: M. Evans, 1970).

"I LOVE LUCY"

Significance. "I Love Lucy" was one of the most successful television shows in the history of American broadcasting. First broadcast on Monday night, 15 October 1951, on the CBS television network, the show captured the loyalty of millions of viewers with its comic depiction of marital life. The story of its development and its long prime-time run illustrates many of the forces and trends that shaped television in the 1950s.

Ball's Career. In the mid 1940s actress and comedienne Lucille Ball was the star of a CBS radio program called "My Favorite Husband." When television began to search for programming, CBS executives approached Ball about switching from radio to television. Ball and her husband, Cuban bandleader Desi Arnaz, responded to the approach in 1950 by buying the RKO film studio properties and ambitiously forming their own production company, Desilu, to develop and produce television shows. William S. Paley, CBS president, rejected Ball's ideas for an adaptation of "My Favorite Husband"; in response Ball and Arnaz developed an entirely new project. Desilu planned a filmed program rather than a live show.

Pilot Show. Desilu produced the pilot program for "I Love Lucy" for five thousand dollars; CBS had no financial interest in the show as yet. Desilu's advertising agency arranged sponsorship for the show before it had acquired a network time slot on which to be shown. Faced with the prospect of losing one of its stars to a rival network, CBS bargained hard to keep Ball on the network.

The Cast. "I Love Lucy" starred Ball as Lucy Ricardo, a New York housewife, and Arnaz as her husband, Ricky, a Cuban bandleader. Paley, other CBS executives, and the show's sponsor, the Philip Morris Company, were vehemently opposed to Arnaz being cast as Lucy's husband. Ball was adamant that he remain. When confronted with the network's belief that her television marriage to a Cuban bandleader would be unbelievable, Ball replied, "What do you mean nobody'll believe it? We *are* married."

Also featured were the Ricardos' landlords and best friends, Fred and Ethel Mertz (played by William Frawley and Vivian Vance). The premise of the series, which had Lucy and Ethel continually frustrating their husbands with crazy schemes, was a familiar one to domestic situation comedies; but the comic talents of the four stars, particularly Ball, lifted the series above the average.

The Public's Reaction. The reaction of the public to the show was overwhelmingly positive. Within four

A scene from "I Love Lucy"; Lucille Ball, left, Desi Arnaz, center, and William Frawley

months the show was number one in the ratings in New York. The Chicago department store Marshall Field began to close on Monday nights so as not to compete with "I Love Lucy." By early 1952 over 10 million households were regularly watching the show. In October 1952 it was the highest-rated show in television. The 19 January 1953 episode, on which Lucy gave birth to the Ricardos' child, was watched by an estimated 44 million people, twice the number of viewers of the Dwight D. Eisenhower inauguration.

The End of Production. In September 1956, while the series was still one of the highest rated on the air, the two stars ended regular production. Until 1961 the CBS network continued to show reruns of earlier episodes in prime time with occasional new hour-long episodes.

Film vs. Live. The success of "I Love Lucy" reinforced trends already evident in the trade. One trend was the growing prevalence of taped programs. Network executives, such as Paley and David Sarnoff of NBC, preferred live television to film. The executives feared that producers of filmed programs, in many cases Hollywood movie companies, would sell their programs directly to the affiliates, the local television stations that broadcast the programs. The affiliates could then sell advertising time themselves and bypass the networks entirely. This fear proved overblown; affiliates remained under tight control by the networks and continued to rely on their advertising contracts.

Critical Dislike of Film. Critics opposed filmed programs. Jack Gould, television critic of the *New York Times*, wrote against the use of film, especially Hollywood-produced film, in television:

> On every count — technically and qualitatively — the films cannot compare with "live" shows and they are hurting video. . . . There is simply no substitute for the intangible excitement and sense of anticipation that is inherent in the performance that takes place at the moment one is watching.

A Classic Form. Regardless of the views of the critics, audiences appeared to prefer filmed shows. Film lent itself to series in which characters, settings, and basic plot forms — set up in the initial episode — did not vary from week to week. "I Love Lucy" was a classic in this sense, and its success hastened the demise of live television.

Sources:

Bart Andrews, *Lucy & Ricky & Fred & Ethel: The Story of "I Love Lucy"* (New York: Dutton, 1976);

William Boddy, *Fifties Television: The Industry and Its Critics* (Urbana & Chicago: University of Illinois Press, 1990);

David Halberstam, *The Fifties* (New York: Villard, 1993);

Sally Bedell Smith, *In All His Glory: The Life of William S. Paley* (New York: Simon & Schuster, 1990).

THE TOP-TEN SHOWS IN THE 1951 TELEVISION SEASON

1. Texaco Star Theater — NBC

2. Fireside Theatre — NBC

3. Philco TV Playhouse — NBC

4. Your Show of Shows — NBC

5. The Colgate Comedy Hour — NBC

6. Gillette Cavalcade of Sports — NBC

7. The Lone Ranger — ABC

8. Arthur Godfrey's Talent Scouts — CBS

9. Hopalong Cassidy — NBC

10. Mama — CBS

THE TOP-TEN SHOWS IN THE 1959 TELEVISION SEASON

1. Gunsmoke — CBS

2. Wagon Train — NBC

3. Have Gun Will Travel — CBS

4. The Danny Thomas Show — CBS

5. The Red Skelton Show — CBS

6. Father Knows Best — CBS

7. 77 Sunset Strip — ABC

8. The Price Is Right — NBC

9. Wanted: Dead or Alive — CBS

10. Perry Mason — CBS

THE MOVIE INDUSTRY

Antitrust. In 1948 the Supreme Court ordered the major Hollywood studios to sell their theater holdings, ruling that the system of film distribution was anticompetitive, and the way Hollywood movies had been produced and delivered to audiences since their beginnings abruptly changed. The Supreme Court decision had many unintended and surprising effects, not the least of which was to restructure the business radically.

Selling the Theater Chains. Early in 1951 the major movie studios — Universal, Columbia, Paramount, Warner Bros., M-G-M, 20th Century–Fox, and RKO Radio — agreed with the Justice Department on the details of selling the theater holdings. The theater chains were sold, freeing a market that for decades had been run as separate monopolies, each studio distributing its own films to its own theaters. The sales had the effect of reducing the number of films produced by the studios, since there was no theater that was obliged to show them without question. In 1954 the seven largest movie studios planned to make fewer than 100 movies as opposed to the 320–400 per year that was common in the late 1940s. With the reduction in the number of movies, the theater owners were hard-pressed to keep the screens busy.

Declining Business. The emergence of television as an entertainment medium also affected film production. The studio heads were terrified of the threat that in-home visual entertainment, including in-home movies, presented to the movie business. In 1951 20th Century–Fox lowered the salaries of its top 130 executives — some as much as 50 percent — because of slumping profits. Fox president Spyros P. Skouras blamed "this great new medium, television." The moviegoing audience declined from 63 million in 1950 to 58 million in 1952. That same year approximately 640 theaters went out of business.

Moving into Television. RKO Radio, one of the major studios, went out of the movie production business altogether in 1957, its pieces sold by owner Howard Hughes. Though not a direct result of competition from television, the sale was influenced by reduced profits in the movie business. Ironically, the RKO Radio studios were bought by Desilu Productions, a television produc-

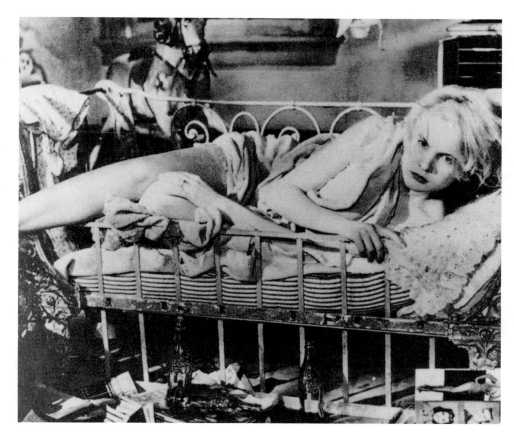

Carroll Baker in *Baby Doll*

tion company owned by Lucille Ball and Desi Arnaz. The RKO Radio film library was sold to General Tire to be shown on television. 20th Century–Fox drilled wells to search for oil on its property formerly used to shoot films. Many of the studios — Warner Bros., Republic, 20th Century–Fox, Columbia — set up subsidiaries to produce movies and television shows for broadcast on network television.

End of the Production Code. In addition to restructuring the movie business and reducing the number of films made, the Supreme Court decision and the subsequent Justice Department settlement indirectly affected the content of the films that were made. Since 1922 the movie industry had undertaken the task of regulating the moral content of movies through the Motion Picture Producers and Distributors of America (MPPADA) to counteract a public protest about film industry morals. This regulation was possible because of the control the studios held over both production and exhibition. The guidelines controlled the way the movies handled such things as cursing, kissing, criminal acts, cruelty to animals, and a myriad of other human behaviors. The MPPADA studios controlled the production of the movies and could deny distribution of those movies that violated the guidelines.

Independent Producers. The freeing of the exhibition market opened the opportunity for independent producers — who were not part of the MPPADA — to gain theater access for their movies whether or not they adhered to the code. Even studio movies, under the influence of the more adventurous independent producers and under the pressure of falling profits and smaller movie audiences, began to experiment with language, sex, violence, and other aspects of behavior that until then had been heavily regulated. Movies that in the early 1950s pushed the previously observed limits of morality include *A Streetcar Named Desire* (1951), *The Moon Is Blue* (1953), *The French Line* (1954), and *Baby Doll* (1956).

Increased Financial Risk. But the more adventurous movies did little to reverse the trend toward lower attendance and profits. In 1955 the audience was estimated at 50 million, a figure that was an improvement over 1953 numbers. As the audiences dwindled, producers began to spend more on the fewer movies being made, filling them with bigger stars and higher production values. The spectaculars did seem to attract larger crowds, but they had to bring in more money just to pay for themselves. In 1948 the highest grossing film was *Road to Rio* with $4.5 million. In 1952 there were four films that grossed more than $6 million, with the largest take being $12 million by *The Greatest Show on Earth*. The biggest change in the movies was the financial risk: the hits made more money, but the flops lost more.

Sources:
Business Week (6 June 1953): 141;

"General Tire Goes Hollywood," *Business Week* (23 July 1955): 32;

A newsstand during the 1954 newspaper strike in New York City

Will H. Hays, *The Memoirs of Will H. Hays* (Garden City, N.Y.: Doubleday, 1955);

Gertrude Jobes, *Motion Picture Empire* (Hamden, Conn.: Archon Books, 1966);

Raymond Moley, *The Hays Office* (Indianapolis: Bobbs-Merrill, 1945);

Ethan Mordden, *The Hollywood Studios* (New York: Knopf, 1988).

NEWSPAPERS IN THE 1950S

A Turbulent Decade. The 1950s was a turbulent decade for the newspaper industry. In the aftermath of World War II, the economic realities of a radically changed world hit newspapers especially hard. Between 1950 and 1958, 180 daily newspapers either suspended publication, merged, or converted to weekly papers. Many papers also suffered crushing strikes, as labor attempted to raise wages and keep employment levels high.

Return to Normal. After World War II the economy returned to normal for the first time since the beginning of the Great Depression in 1929. As a result, long-stagnant prices and wages began to rise. Newsprint, the paper on which the newspapers were printed and the basic commodity of the industry, rose from a price of $44 a ton in 1938 to $88 a ton in 1947 and $134 a ton in 1958. Labor unions demanded increased wages, keeping personnel costs high. Revenues, on the other hand, grew slowly if at all.

New Competition. In the 1950s newspapers competed with a new information, entertainment, and adver-

tising medium: television. Not only did television have the advantage of novelty, but it also made fewer demands on the intelligence and literacy of the audience. Television's share of the advertising market grew from 1 percent in 1949 to 30 percent in 1957, while the newspaper share slumped during the same period from 36 percent to 33 percent.

Strikes. Newspaper strikes became more common, with a huge strike in New York City over wages in 1953. Strikes also stopped presses in Maine and Connecticut that year. Detroit and Cleveland newspapers were shut down in late 1955 and early 1956. There were strike-related shutdowns at papers in Saint Louis, Kansas City, Boston, San Jose, and Reno in 1959.

One Paper's Story. A prime example of the effect of these trends is found in the story of the *New York Herald Tribune*. In 1946 the *Herald Tribune* made a record profit of over $1 million. But while the paper sold for 5¢ a copy, it cost 9¢ a copy to produce; the difference had to come from advertising revenues. By 1950 profits had decreased to the break-even point. The editorial staff struggled to increase the circulation of the paper by adopting the techniques and subject matter of the populist tabloid newspapers. Celebrity news, less international news, gossip columns, cash prize puzzles, a television magazine, and a Sunday magazine became the selling points of what previously had been known simply as a newspaper of high quality with good writing and reporting. Profits returned, but the competitive pressures did not lessen. The competition in the New York market — the city still had six major daily papers in 1957, in addition to strong suburban papers and many ethnic and niche publications — held the price of the newspaper to a nickel. By 1958 the paper was losing massive amounts of money, and it was sold to new ownership.

Effects of Change. In New York City the newspaper industry deferred the drastic effects of the competition of the 1950s until the 1960s; by 1967 only three daily papers remained. But the effects of rising costs and stagnant revenues were felt all over the country. The *Oakland (California) Post-Enquirer* closed in 1950, as did the *San Diego (California) Journal*. The two Atlanta newspapers merged in 1950 to form the *Atlanta Journal-Constitution*; the same year the two Birmingham, Alabama, newspapers merged into the *Birmingham Post-Herald*. Twenty daily papers shut down in 1954, the largest number since 1941. Among them were the *Washington Times-Herald*, sold to the *Washington Post*, and the *Brooklyn Eagle*, closed after 114 years of publishing.

Fewer Newspapers. Newspapers underwent radical change during the 1950s. While competition increased among the different media, many cities saw less competition among newspapers alone. Newspapers, in the face of the television juggernaut, became less reporters of news and more sources of entertainment and information.

Sources:

Richard Kluger, *The Paper: The Life and Times of the New York Herald Tribune* (New York: Knopf, 1986);

Joseph Kraft, "*The New York Herald Tribune*: What goes on here," *Harper's*, 219 (August 1959): 39–45;

Newsweek, 35 (26 June 1950): 69–70;

Newsweek, 36 (17 July 1953): 55–56;

Newsweek, 42 (14 December 1953): 29–32;

U.S. News and World Report, 35 (25 December 1953): 70–72.

PEANUTS

Childhood Seriousness. The comic strip *Peanuts*, written and drawn by Charles Schulz, was immensely popular in the 1950s. First syndicated in eight newspapers in 1950, the comic strip *Peanuts* was the most successful strip of the decade. By the end of the 1950s the strip appeared in more than four hundred newspapers in the United States and in thirty-five foreign papers. The strip was notable in that its characters, all children, acted and talked through their childhood activities with all the seriousness and insecurities of adults. As the *Saturday Evening Post* commented in 1957, readers of the comic strip imagined Schulz as a "superintellectual."

Mistaken Intellectual. In 1956 a staffer for Adlai Stevenson telephoned Schulz to ask him to support her candidate. During their conversation she called Schulz, on the basis of his comic strip *Peanuts,* "the youngest existentialist." Schulz politely declined to endorse Stevenson but did have one question: "What is an existentialist?"

Charles M. Schulz, creator of *Peanuts*

Early Years. Schulz began his career as a cartoonist in Saint Paul, Minnesota, in 1949 drawing cartoons that were published once a week in a Saint Paul newspaper. He began selling cartoons to the *Saturday Evening Post* in 1950. Later that year he sent eight of the cartoons published in the *Post* and a selection of his Saint Paul publications to the United Features Syndicate. In October *Peanuts* premiered in eight newspapers. The strip steadily grew in popularity. A Sunday strip was added, and Schulz began to publish book collections of his strips.

Wide Success. In 1958 Schulz was making ninety thousand dollars per year from his cartoons and books, and newspaper circulation of *Peanuts* was continuing to rise. Charlie Brown, Lucy, Snoopy, Linus, Schroeder, Peppermint Patty, Sally, and the rest of the *Peanuts* cast became a stock part of American popular culture. The Coasters' 1959 song "Charlie Brown" exemplifies the cultural role the comic strip had come to play, as the reference to it was indirect but unmistakable. *Peanuts* continued to grow in readership as one of the most popular of postwar comic strips.

Sources:

"Child's Garden of Reverses," *Time*, 71 (3 November 1958): 58;

"A Handful of Peanuts," *Look*, 22 (22 July 1958): 66–68;

Hugh Morrow, "The Success of an Utter Failure," *Saturday Evening Post* (12 January 1957): 34–35, 70–72;

Gerald Weales, "Good Grief, More Peanuts!," *Reporter*, 20 (30 April 1959): 45–46.

POLITICAL MAGAZINES

New War of Ideas. The 1950s ushered in the modern era of American political thought. World War II had thrust the nation into the position of leader of the Western democracies in a world increasingly divided along ideological lines defined by the cold war. The Communist governments of the Soviet Union and mainland China were poised to challenge U.S. influences, and fearful Americans began to peer beyond their country's borders and consider the potentially devastating impact of foreign affairs on their lives. The cold war was thus not only characterized by spy intrigue and threats exchanged by Eastern and Western officials, it was also fought on the domestic front. The war of ideas between the American Right and Left was the struggle to forge a political philosophy that would usher the American people through dangerous times. The struggle was fought increasingly between the covers of magazines.

The Left. The *Nation* and the *New Republic* were the most influential political magazines of the American Left. Founded in 1865, the *Nation* had a long tradition of criticizing the conservative influences in American government and society. In 1955 Carey McWilliams became editor of the *Nation* and devoted the magazine to espousing civil rights, arms control, and social programs that would move beyond the limits set by Franklin D. Roosevelt's New Deal and Harry S Truman's Fair Deal. During the early 1950s the magazine also ran columns that were favorable toward the Soviet Union and often sought to explain Communist expansion in terms related to Russian historical interests. Many critics accused the *Nation* of being too ready to accept Soviet policy.

The Moderates. The *New Republic* tended toward a more moderately liberal stance than did the *Nation*. Founded in 1914, the *New Republic* attracted more than forty-one thousand subscribers after World War II, when Michael Straight became the magazine's owner and named Henry Wallace the editor. By the 1950s the number of subscribers had peaked at ninety-six thousand, and the magazine became an important voice for Stevenson Democrats who sought social and economic reforms. The magazine typified American liberalism in denouncing communism — yet saving its most hard-hitting criticism for Sen. Joseph McCarthy and his witch-hunting tactics. It remained essentially a voice of the status quo of American liberalism.

The New Left. On the academic front a new generation of leftist historians and political scientists was emerging during the decade. Called the New Left and composed of scholars such as William Appleman Williams, Gabriel Kolko, and Walter Lafeber, the group took a dim view of America's militaristic campaign against communism in Asia. Toward the end of the decade it was criticizing U.S. foreign policy as being rooted in expansionist and imperialist motives. There was no major magazine allied solely with this movement.

The Right. Many right-wing intellectuals soon realized that the American conservative movement lacked definition and was too closely associated with the ex-

TRUMAN BATTLES A CRITIC

On 5 December 1950 Margaret Truman, the twenty-five-year-old daughter of President Harry S Truman, gave a concert of vocal music at Constitution Hall in Washington, D.C. Appropriate to a budding vocalist of still-immature talent who was also the President's daughter, Margaret's performance was duly noted in the Washington papers. In an especially scathing review Paul Hume in the *Washington Post* passed harsh judgment on Margaret's singing and her prospects for a career, saying, in part,

> . . . Miss Truman cannot sing very well. She is flat a good deal of the time — more last night than at any time we have heard her in past years . . . Miss Truman has not improved in the years we have heard her . . . she still cannot sing with anything approaching professional finish.

When the president read the review the next morning, he impetuously, and unknown to his staff, sent an emotional letter to Hume. The editors at the *Post* did not print the letter but a copy made its way to the *Washington News*, a tabloid that jumped at printing the letter on page 1:

> Mr. Hume: I've just read your lousy review of Margaret's concert. I've come to the conclusion that you are an "eight ulcer man on four ulcer pay."
>
> It seems to me that you are a frustrated old man who wishes he could have been successful. When you write such poppy-cock as was in the back section of the paper you work for it shows conclusively that you're off the beam and at least four of your ulcers are at work.
>
> Some day I hope to meet you. When that happens you'll need a new nose, a lot of beefsteak for black eyes, and perhaps a supporter below!
>
> [Westbrook] Pegler, a gutter snipe, is a gentleman alongside you. I hope you'll accept that statement as a worse insult than a reflection on your ancestry.

The earthy language and physical threats of the letter did very little to endear Truman to the public. Letters and calls to the White House ran two to one against him. Most agreed with a letter that said "you showed the whole world that you are nothing but a selfish little pipsqueak." The episode showed the power of the press and, in politics, the need for careful press management.

Source: David McCullough, *Truman* (New York: Simon & Schuster, 1992).

Edward R. Murrow, left, and producer Fred Friendly

cesses of McCarthyism. The isolationist views of conservative Republican Robert Taft no longer had currency in the increasingly international atmosphere of American politics. In his attempt to consolidate the Right, William F. Buckley, Jr., founded the *National Review* in 1955. His magazine attacked communism as economically flawed, socially destructive, and intellectually and morally corrupt. In so doing, Buckley sought to move the conservatives' attack against the Left to a higher philosophical ground. Although by the end of the decade the magazine's circulation had reached only about thirty thousand, Buckley had largely succeeded in creating a conservative coalition of the religious Right, economic libertarians, and anti-Communists. He also worked to eliminate the more racist and antireligious elements from the *National Review* conservative coalition and established a more internationalist wing of conservatism. By doing so he made his brand of right-wing ideology fashionable for many of the intellectual elite and also for cold war strategists.

Sources:

John P. Diggins, *The American Left in the Twentieth Century* (New York: Harcourt Brace Jovanovich, 1973);

George H. Nash, *The Conservative Intellectual Movement in America Since 1945* (New York: Basic Books, 1979);

Theodore Peterson, *Magazines in the Twentieth Century* (Urbana: University of Illinois Press, 1979).

"SEE IT NOW" CANCELED

Significance of Cancellation. The 1958 cancellation of Edward R. Murrow's repected news and documentary television show "See It Now" by CBS showed many the growing importance of profit over public interest in broadcasting.

Financial Costs. "See It Now" first aired on 18 November 1951. Though the first two shows were without a sponsor, by the third episode ALCOA (Aluminum Company of America) had signed up to pay CBS thirty-four thousand dollars a week to air its commercials during the show and an additional twenty-three thousand dollars to subsidize production costs; anything above that figure was paid by the network. As "See It Now" garnered positive reviews and respectable ratings, network chief William S. Paley resigned himself to the fact that the show made the network no money.

Controversial Subjects. But "See It Now" was also controversial. On many occasions Paley had to endure angry phone calls from irate congressmen and business leaders, upset that Murrow had questioned their behavior. Still Paley persevered with the show, partly out of reluctance to end a show of such importance and partly out of his friendship and respect for Murrow.

A Glimpse of the Future. In 1955 "The $64,000 Question" premiered on CBS. Watching the show, Murrow turned to his coproducer Fred Friendly and asked how long he thought "See It Now" could keep its prime-time slot in the face of such popular and low-cost competition. In the 1955 season "See It Now" was reduced from a weekly schedule to six to eight shows a year.

Responsibilities of Success. The nature of CBS had changed. It was no longer a small, unprofitable television network but a thriving media and manufacturing conglomerate. Paley had more at stake than the network's reputation or a friend's respect. He ran a company that had made profits of $16 million in 1955 and was subject to the expectations of shareholders. But Paley was still willing to swallow the forgone profits of scheduling "See

Rehearsal shot from "The Goldbergs," a radio serial that successfully made the jump to television

It Now" in a prime-time slot. He was not so willing in 1958.

Final Conflict. In an argument arising over an episode advocating statehood for Hawaii and Alaska, Paley demanding that equal time be provided to an opponent of statehood and Murrow resisting, "See It Now" was canceled. The headaches of dealing with Murrow and outraged viewers demanding equal time were no longer worth the prestige of good critical press. The last show was broadcast on 7 July 1958. Critics were outraged. John Crosby wrote powerfully of its demise in the *New York Herald Tribune:*

> There have some dull "See It Now" shows, and some have been better than others, but it is by every criterion television's most brilliant, most decorated, most imaginative, most courageous and most important program. The fact that CBS cannot afford it but can afford "Beat the Clock" is shocking.

Source:
"A Fond Farewell," *Newsweek* (23 May 1955): 100;

Joseph F. Persico, *Edward R. Murrow* (New York: McGraw-Hill, 1988);

Sally Bedell Smith, *In All His Glory: The Life of William S. Paley* (New York: Simon & Schuster, 1990).

SOAP OPERAS FROM RADIO TO TELEVISION

The Rise of the Soap Opera. Gilbert Seldes writes that "the daytime serial was the great invention of radio." Three "women's serial dramas" — daily radio programs intended for an audience of women, featuring a stable cast and a melodramatic, domestic story which advanced slowly — premiered in 1931. The three were "Clara, Lu and Em"; "The Goldbergs"; and "Myrt and Marge." The shows, in the beginning only fifteen minutes long, soon became a staple on radio. By 1939 the number of shows had grown to sixty-one. In 1950 the four television networks — NBC, CBS, ABC, and Du Mont — devoted seventy-five hours per week to daytime serials.

Importance of the Sponsor. From the early years of the serials, most were sponsored by soap manufacturers who were interested in advertising their products to women. The daytime serials became so associated with the sponsors that in 1939 some wag coined the term *soap opera* to describe them. Humorist James Thurber memorably described the fifteen-minute radio serial formula:

> Between thick slices of advertising, spread twelve minutes of dialogue, add predicament, villainy, and female suffering in equal measure, throw in a dash of nobility, sprinkle with tears, season with organ music, cover with a rich announcer sauce, and serve five times a week.

Unsure of Success. With the advent of commercial television in the 1950s, network executives doubted the possibilities for the television success of soap operas. Many did not believe that women would sit and watch the same melodrama they previously listened to while performing housework. Once again had the networks had misgauged the response of the audience.

Soapmakers Bonanza. The sponsors, however, realized the potential of television. They knew that exclusive sponsorship of the daytime programs enhanced their ability to sell products. They thought that television would

The 2 June 1953 coronation of British queen Elizabeth II drove the already furious competition among the television networks to a new height. While all four networks — NBC, CBS, ABC, and Du Mont — planned coverage, NBC and CBS engaged in a frenzied race to provide the first taped coverage of the royal events. With combined costs running in excess of five hundred thousand dollars, the two largest networks spent months planning strategies to film independently the coronation and surrounding hoopla. The networks made elaborate, and some would say ridiculous, plans to speed the pictures back to the United States. NBC wanted to bounce a television signal off the moon; CBS wanted to use a guided missile. More-practical ideas triumphed, however, and both networks planned to use high-speed airplanes to fly the tape back to broadcast studios in the United States. The CBS plane arrived in Boston well ahead of NBC's. But the Canadian Broadcasting Corporation (CBC), with the aid of the Royal Canadian Air Force, was the first broadcaster to receive film of the coronation and quickly began showing the event out of their Montreal studios. Much to the chagrin of CBS, both ABC and NBC cut into the CBC signal and beat CBS onto the air. As for the competition, the winner was ABC, who showed the coronation without spending an excessive amount of money.

Sources: "Long Live the Queen!," *Time*, 61 (25 May 1953): 67–68; "Who's on First?," *Newsweek*, 41 (15 June 1953): 92.

---

be a bonanza. Procter and Gamble and Colgate-Palmolive were the two most important sponsors of soap operas. Procter and Gamble quickly exploited what it saw as the great advertising potential of television. In 1951 the company formed its own television production company to produce soap operas. Procter and Gamble's large stake in soap-opera production contributed much to its rise by 1954 to be the largest television advertiser. From $7.2 million in 1951 Procter and Gamble's television advertising budget rose to $23.7 million in 1954.

On Television. The soap opera made the switch from radio to television in the 1950s with ease. In 1950, the year that CBS introduced the first television serial, "The First Hundred Years," there were twenty-seven such serials on the radio. In February 1954 there were seven soaps on television. The television soaps quickly matched and even exceeded the audience of their radio counterparts. The television version of "Guiding Light" was watched in 3.75 million homes in 1954 and ranked fourth among

daytime programs. The radio version of the same soap was also ranked fourth among daytime radio programs, yet was listened to in only 2.7 million homes. The shows were televised live daily and were initially fifteen minutes long; late in the decade most soaps expanded to thirty minutes. The time slots for the shows were from 12 noon to 2 P.M. and from 4 P.M. to 5 P.M.

Stubborn Radio Success. Despite the increasing emphasis on television soap operas, radio serials continued to be popular through the middle of the decade. In 1952 the five top-rated radio soap operas were on CBS. The list included "The Romance of Helen Trent," "Our Gal Sunday," "Ma Perkins," "The Guiding Light," and "Big Sister." The audience for the shows in 1952 reached as high as 4 million viewers. But both networks and advertisers quickly realized that the radio soaps were a dying breed. From a high of thirty-five programs on the air in 1952, the number fell to twenty-six in 1955. After 1955 the number of programs on radio dwindled, until by the 1959–1960 season there were only eight on the air: one on NBC and seven on CBS. At the end of that season NBC canceled its remaining soap, and CBS canceled one. CBS closed its radio soap shop in November 1960.

Enduring Soap Opera. Soap operas became the longest running shows on television and also the most profitable. "The Guiding Light" premiered on CBS in 1952 and remains on the air in 1993. "Search for Tomorrow," which premiered on CBS in 1951, continued on the network until 1982 and then on NBC until 1986. The relatively low costs of producing the shows and their high ratings ensured their popularity with the sponsors. The melodramatic stories of interpersonal relationships have led to an enduring popularity of the soap opera, regardless of the medium.

Sources:
Murial G. Cantor and Suzanne Pingree, *The Soap Opera* (Beverly Hills, Cal.: Sage, 1983);

J. Fred MacDonald, *Radio Programming in American Life from 1920 to 1960* (Chicago: Nelson-Hall, 1978);

Mary Mannes, "Channels: Soft Soap," *Reporter* (23 September 1954): 48–49;

Gilbert Seldes, "Darkness Before Noon," *Saturday Review* (5 December 1953): 53–54;

"Soap in Your Eyes," *Newsweek* (1 February 1954): 74–75;

Christopher H. Sterling and John M. Kitross, *Stay Tuned: A Concise History of American Broadcasting* (Belmont, Cal.: Wadsworth, 1978).

"THE TODAY SHOW"

A Risky Morning Show. On 14 January 1952, at 7:00 A.M., NBC premiered "The Today Show." A risky offering in the until-then-barren early-morning television hours, "Today" faced problems that other television programs did not face. First, "Today" faced an audience that was more concerned with preparing for work or school than watching a television show. NBC executive Pat

"Today" host Dave Garroway watches as J. Fred Muggs frolics in cake.

Weaver, who proposed the show to the network, outlined in a planning memo what the show hoped to accomplish:

> We are not trying to get people to rise earlier to see the show, nor to stay at home and be late. . . . We therefore must repeat key information . . . all important hunks or points should be made in each of the two hours . . . We are not trying to get a 10 rating for two hours, but we are trying to get sixty per cent of all sets to turn on the show, with time from the viewers varying between a fast two-minute look at the time and the headline from a bachelor who eats out and has a big apartment . . . to a longish hour from a large family . . . where the father hits the road at 7:50 and the kids leave for school at 8:40.

Affiliate Doubts. Second, the show's producers had to negotiate with the network affiliates, the local broadcast stations, to convince them to carry the show. Affiliates, the majority of which did not carry any shows before 10:00 A.M., were reluctant to add the show since it would leave them with an empty hour between the end of "The Today Show" at 9:00 A.M. and the beginning of their broadcast day. Weaver finally persuaded thirty-one affiliates by agreeing to give each station five minutes of every half hour for their own local newscasts, a concession which gave them a larger stake in the success of the show.

The Show's Cast. "Today" was hosted by Dave Garroway, an affable eccentric. The news was delivered by Jim Fleming, a former foreign correspondent. Garroway's assistant on the telecast was Jack Lescoulie. Garroway's on-air persona was so laid-back early in the show's run as to be laughable. An early Garroway interview on "Today" shows the tenor of his laconic style:

Garroway: "Hello, Ed Lasker in Frankfurt. Tell me the news in your part of the world."

Lasker: "The big news is the weather. We had our first big storm of the year. We're really chilly."

Garroway: "You're not alone. Good-bye, Ed."

Need for Spice. Garroway was charming but also slightly boring. In January 1953 the ratings for the show were respectable but not large. The number of affiliates had grown to forty. The "Today" producers decided that the show needed someone, or something, to add spice to the mix.

Chimp to the Rescue. Early in 1953 the show introduced a new cast member, a chimpanzee named J. Fred Muggs. Introduced as comic relief, the chimp had the double effect of attracting children and, through them, their parents to the show and of making Dave Garroway seem more serious by comparison. Whatever the effects, the ratings of "Today" skyrocketed.

Success and the Monkey's Departure. Muggs remained on the show until mid 1957, when the chimp's erratic behavior — he made a habit of biting Garroway and terrorizing "Today" guests — became too much of a burden. By this time the show was a ratings and financial success, and the network had few qualms about dismissing the chimp. Still, NBC felt it necessary to provide a replacement chimp, Mr. Kokomo, who did not remain for long and was the last animal star of "Today."

Enduring Popularity. From a risky venture in the beginning, "Today" became during the 1950s a fixture of the emerging television culture of the United States. It

On 19 October 1953 the young singer Julius La Rosa was fired by Arthur Godfrey from Godfrey's daily television show. What was notable in this mundane business decision was that Godfrey carried out the firing without warning live on television. After La Rosa finished singing a song near the end of the Monday morning show, Godfrey faced the camera and issued a thirty-eight-word statement:

> That was Julie's swan song with us. He goes now out on his own, as his own star, soon to be seen on his own program, and I know you wish him Godspeed as I do. Bye, Bye.

The singer was shocked, as were the estimated 7 million viewers. Godfrey justified the firing on the grounds that La Rosa had "lost his humility." He claimed that the singer had written him a note, saying that "in the future, when you wish to talk to me, please see my agent."

La Rosa disputed Godfrey's account, denying that he had approached Godfrey with anything resembling the haughtiness reported. The real problem, La Rosa explained, was that he had signed a contract with an outside agent, General Artists Corporation. Whatever the reason, the incident boosted La Rosa's career. On the day following his dismissal, La Rosa was hired to appear on Ed Sullivan's "Toast of the Town" show at three times his Godfrey salary of nine hundred dollars per week.

During the two years following his firing by Godfrey, La Rosa grossed over $1 million and had over thirty hit records. La Rosa — whose conversation was reported by *Look* to be filled with lines such as, "Cyrano de Bergerac said, 'I carry my adornments on my soul' . . . Man, that gasses me." — thanked the firing for an intellectual rebirth as well as a financial windfall.

Explaining why he had read Winston Churchill's World War II histories, works by Voltaire, and biographies of Michelangelo and Saint Francis of Assisi during the two years on his own, La Rosa said,

> I started to read when I got off the Godfrey show, partly because of shock. I wanted to find out the reason behind things that happen to you. Also, I began being exposed to people who'd drop names like Schopenhauer or Kant. Then I'd say, "Who's he? Playing first base for the Giants?" I wanted to see for myself what they were talking about, and I also wanted to find out if these talkers were phonies or if they really knew.

The firing of La Rosa had the opposite effect of that Godfrey intended, establishing a career rather than ending it. As *New York Times* critic Jack Gould commented,

> [Godfrey's] error actually was in forgetting his own humility while complaining that others had. After all, he was doing what he thought best for his own career, yet at the same time he was objecting to Mr. La Rosa following his example.

Sources: "Godfery Confirms Dismissing La Rosa," *New York Times*, 22 October 1953, p. 42;

Jack Gould, "More About Dispute With La Rosa and Public Reaction," *New York Times*, 26 October 1953, p. 32;

Eleanor Harris, "Julius La Rosa's Life Since Godfrey," *Look*, 20 (15 May 1956): 67–81.

also showed the networks that television viewing was not limited to the time slots that had proved popular with radio. Still broadcast in the 1990s, "Today" has become the longest-running television show in history.

Source:
Robert Metz, *The Today Show* (Chicago: Playboy, 1977).

TV GUIDE

Annenberg's Idea. In 1952 Walter Annenberg, the president of Triangle Publications, the publisher of the *Philadelphia Inquirer* and *Daily Racing Form*, had a brainstorm. Astounded by the success of the *TV Digest*, a Philadelphia area publication featuring television listings — circulation exceeded 180,000 — Annenberg's idea was to launch a national publication that promised local television listings while offering national editorial and advertising scope.

Local Magazines. Inquiring whether other such magazines existed across the country, he was told that *TV Guide* in New York had circulation exceeding 400,000 and that *TV Forecast* in Chicago reached 100,000 readers. So Annenberg bought them at a cost of several million dollars. *TV Digest*, *TV Guide*, and *TV Forecast* became the first three local bureaus of *TV Guide*. More bureaus were signed up by franchising the national section of *TV Guide* to local magazines in Boston; Davenport, Iowa; Minneapolis; and Wilkes-Barre, Pennsylvania. Teams were sent to Los Angeles and Cincinnati to start local operations from scratch.

The First Issue. By the end of March 1953, four months after Annenberg's initial idea, ten cities were

"Dragnet" star Jack Webb reading the 1954 fall preview issue of *TV Guide*

Sources:

TV Guide: The First 25 Years, edited and compiled by Jay S. Harris (New York: Simon & Schuster, 1978);

"TV Guide," *New York Times*, 17 January 1953, p. 27.

TELEVISION CRITICS

News Coverage. The development of television as a new entertainment medium was news in the 1950s: coverage of television in newspapers increased by 500 percent from 1953 to 1955. Along with this increased coverage came the rise of the television critic. Writing in both newspapers and magazines, these men — there were few female critics in the 1950s (Janet Kern of the *Chicago Tribune* was the most prominent) — debated and commented on not only the content of television shows but the nature of the medium itself.

The Elite. The two most respected television critics of the 1950s were Jack Gould of the *New York Times* and John Crosby of the *New York Herald Tribune*. Their careers have paralleled each other. In the manner of newspapermen of the time, neither Gould nor Crosby graduated from college, though Crosby did attend Yale University for two years. Both men trained on the *Herald Tribune* by covering Broadway theater. In 1945, the beginning of the end of the radio era, Gould was hired by the *Times* as radio editor. A year later Crosby became radio columnist for the *Herald Tribune*. With the relative decline of the importance of radio and the meteoric rise of television, the direction of both men turned toward television.

equipped for *TV Guide*. The magazine was first published on 3 April 1953. The cover of the first issue, which cost fifteen cents, featured a photograph of Desi Arnaz, Jr., Lucille Ball's recently born baby, whose birth was fictionalized as that of Little Ricky on the 19 January 1953 episode of "I Love Lucy."

Early Pullback and Growth. The inaugural issue sold 1.56 million copies in ten cities. During summer 1953 five new city editions were added in Rochester, New York; Pittsburgh; Detroit; Cleveland; and San Francisco. Sales, however, slumped after the initial rush. By mid August circulation was nearly 200,000 less than in April, and, by the beginning of the fall 1953 season, magazine officials were hoping that the slump in sales was due only to the reduced amount of summer television watching. September brought smiles to *TV Guide* sales representatives. The 4 September 1953 issue sold more than 1.6 million copies. The sales of the September 11 fall preview issue reached almost 1.75 million.

Significance. *TV Guide* continued to grow throughout the decade; by 1959 there were fifty-three regional editions that pushed circulation to more than 6 million every week. Its success established the extent of television's dominance over the entertainment business and its growing influence on other media.

John Crosby of the *New York Herald Tribune*

Gould's Viewing. Being a television critic involved watching a lot of television. Gould and Crosby developed different strategies of viewing. Gould watched twenty-five to thirty hours of television per week from his home in Old Greenwich, Connecticut. His viewing room contained two television sets, one color and one black and white. A third set was available when needed. Most of his work was reviews of television shows phoned into New York in time for the early editions of the *Times*.

Crosby's Viewing. Crosby, on the other hand, did not concern himself with timely reviews for the early editions. His viewing in preparation for writing his syndicated column — his pieces were carried in 103 newspapers in 1956 — took place at his New York apartment on a single television set. Crosby did not attempt to be an objective reporter, as did Gould, but instead used a highly personal style to reflect his own opinions and tastes.

Jack Gould of the *New York Times*

CRITIC JOHN CROSBY'S APPEARANCE ON TELEVISION

John Crosby, the television critic of the *New York Herald Tribune*, made what many called a foolhardy decision in 1957: to host the CBS program "The Seven Lively Arts," an anthology series featuring dramatizations of literary works and historical events.

In addition to creating questions of conflict of interest — would Crosby be more kind to CBS shows now that he was employed by the networks? — Crosby subjected himself to the same criticisms he himself mercilessly applied in his syndicated column. Except for his self-selected stand-in at the *Herald Tribune*, George Axelrod, the critics were unrestrained in their negative notices of the 3 November premiere. Typical of the reviews was that of Jack O'Brian of the *New York Journal-American*:

> He seemed to smile as if in constant pain. Close-ups did him few favors, for they presented his face with a seemingly endless mouth . . . which when speaking seemed to be pulled vertically apart as if with unseen strings.

Despite the criticism Crosby remained on the program through the end of its run on 16 February 1958. His reputation as a fair and impartial critic was unsullied, and he continued to attack bad programming, regardless of the network on which it appeared.

Sources: "Dual Role," *Time*, 69 (10 June 1957): 46, 48;

"Turning the Tables," *Newsweek*, 49 (18 November 1957): 78.

The Role of the Critic. As with all genres of criticism, debate raged about the importance or effectiveness of the critics. Both men saw their role as instructing the producers rather than the consumers of television. In Gould's words, "the critic's function is to bring to top management the ideas that an underling is not able to bring up from below." While unsure about the importance of the work performed by television critics, Crosby thought that "television is damn lucky that it has two guys like Jack Gould and myself."

Sources:

"Big Men on the Papers," *Newsweek*, 49 (15 April 1957): 104, 107;

"Out of the Blue," *Time*, 68 (20 August 1956): 71-72;

Christopher H. Sterling and John M. Kitross, *Stay Tuned: A Concise History of American Broadcasting* (Belmont, Cal.: Wadsworth, 1978).

TELEVISION NEWS

Television vs. Radio. In addition to becoming the primary source of home entertainment in the 1950s, television also became a major source of news and information. Many commentators regarded television as inherently lowbrow and not disposed to serious news gathering and reporting. H. V. Kaltenborn, a distinguished radio news analyst, stated in 1956 that "there are no advantages to TV newscasting. . . . Pictures are a distraction. Remembering camera angles is a bother. TV news should pay more attention to intelligent discourse."

Chet Huntley, NBC news anchor, broadcast these nostrums over ABC Radio on 3 January 1955.

Resolved: To take a walk each morning around a given issue or problem or controversy and report on all the aspects seen or heard — all 360 aspects, if there be that many.

To show some improvement this year in learning how to depreciate my own opinions.

To stop and think at least thirty minutes before offering one of my own opinions in a broadcast.

That if my own opinion must be used, to label it as just opinion with the biggest verbal sign or billboard I know how to make.

To remember, at least once a week, for the next fifty-two weeks, that Providence, unfortunately, did not endow me with complete wisdom or infallibility.

To practice faithfully throughout the coming year to learn how to utter those noble and refreshing words "I was wrong," just in case that uncomfortable situation should arise.

To narrow down almost to infinity, or at least keep to a minimum, the number of your fellow citizens to whom you would deny the privilege of being heard, if you had the power. Rather, to remember that they don't deserve silencing — just answering.

To remember that "success" in the profession of journalism is, to be sure, measured by your actual and potential rendering of service; but it's also restrained by the fact that the bigger you are, the bigger and more serious your mistakes.

To remember that only a William Jennings Bryan and a few others seemed to produce their best effort in the first draft, and Bryan never got to be President. In other words, give strength to cut and edit and rewrite.

To face the East each morning and thank Mr. Sulzberger for the New York *Times*.

To be more decent to my sponsor . . . To do some more serious thinking and wondering whether television is a medium for the reporting of day-to-day news or whether it's more exclusively suited for the documentary.

To waste no more time in search for the "gimmick" or "gadget" for the so-cute and so-contrived television show.

To become a better and more persistent gadfly on the hides of my bosses throughout the coming year in a campaign which is mottoed "There's no such thing as too much news."

To live with the annoying proposition that a little insecurity may be good for a journalist.

And finally — when all the rules, the prohibitions, the restrictions, and points of policy have been violated — to ask only this: a fairly respectable rating on those good questions, "Is he fair, is he decent, and does he have a shred of integrity?" A set of resolutions and entreaties of this nature by all engaged in the business of buying and selling or giving away ideas might cause even journalists to make some contribution this year to our chances of enduring the uncertainties and confusions with more natural composure and inner strength, unwasted by the exertions of emotional brawls.

Source: *Reporter*, 12 (27 January, 1955): 4.

Distraction of Entertainment. Television news from the beginning was believed to value pictures, personality, and technology over good writing, competence, and content. The technology was seen as an obstacle to good news reporting. *New York Times* correspondent A. M. Rosenthal said in 1953 that television "is not interested primarily in news but in entertainment." The technology required by television broadcasting, he said, forced newsmen to work in a "hectic, noisy, movie-set atmosphere."

Third-Generation News. There was confusion in the 1950s over the place of news in television. One source of this confusion was that television news was seen as the third generation of professional news. The first generation, and the most respected, was print journalism. When radio was developed as an entertainment and information source, its role in news reporting and broadcasting was roundly denigrated by the print media. The same process occurred with television news.

Dominance by CBS. Building on its reputation as a radio news broadcaster, CBS developed the most renowned television news team of the 1950s. With newscasters and reporters such as Edward R. Murrow, Charles

Chet Huntley, left, and David Brinkley, newscasters for NBC

Collingwood, Walter Cronkite, and Eric Sevareid, CBS began to erode the distrust with which many in the public regarded television news. The first regular television news show was "Douglas Edwards With the News," first broadcast in 1948 on CBS. NBC followed the next year with "The Camel News Caravan," which starred John Cameron Swayze. CBS continued to lead the ratings race through the decade, but the competition in the fifteen-minute evening news slot became more fierce from 1956 on.

Huntley and Brinkley. For the 1956 political conventions, NBC brought together Chet Huntley and David Brinkley to form a news team. The network was attempting to find a recipe to counteract the widespread public perception that their news programs were, in the words of *Coronet*, "bland and unprovocative." The convention went so well that the two were set up on the evening news show, renamed "The Huntley-Brinkley Report." The pair quickly became popular with viewers, who seemed to respond to their air of competence; restrained, ironic moralism; and gentle humor. Their popularity was reflected in the ratings; Huntley and Brinkley finally overtook their CBS counterparts in 1960. In addition to being popular in the audience ratings, Huntley and Brinkley were respected by news makers. In an August 1959 poll of members of Congress, 32.8 percent regarded the "Huntley-Brinkley Report" as their favorite newscast. The second-place finisher was John Daly's newscast on ABC with 16.1 percent.

Slow Progess. Yet television news was still regarded as a less-than-serious news source in the 1950s. It was not until the early 1960s, with the Richard M. Nixon–John F. Kennedy presidential debates in 1960 and the Kennedy assassination in 1963, that television showed its importance as a news source. During events such as these, television proved that it could shape as well as report the news, a realization that would have a revolutionary effect on journalism.

Sources:
Hollis Alpert, "TV's Unique Tandem: Huntley-Brinkley," *Coronet*, 49 (February 1961): 162–169;

"The Evening Duet," *Time* (19 October 1959): 92;

"Good News and Bad News," *Newsweek* (7 January 1957): 64–65;

William Pfaff, "News on the Networks," *Commonweal*, 60 (9 April 1954): 11–14;

Robert Louis Shayon, "Mileage in Morality," *Saturday Review*, 40 (28 December 1957): 24;

"Television and Newsmen," *Time* (2 November 1953): 49;

"Television in Controversy: The Debate and the Defense," *Newsweek*, 43 (29 March 1954): 50–52.

HEADLINE MAKERS

JOSEPH AND STEWART ALSOP
1910-1989; 1914-1974
COLUMNISTS

NEWSWEEK-GEORGE TAMES

Inside Information. Syndicated in up to two hundred newspapers by the *New York Herald Tribune* from 1946 to 1958, Joseph Alsop and his brother Stewart were two of the most influential newspaper columnists of the 1950s. Earning sixty thousand dollars for their column and espousing a hard line against the Soviet Union and communism, the Alsops used their contacts within official Washington, D.C., to report inside information on world affairs. The Alsops' column, "Matter of Fact," which appeared four times a week, provided, as Edgar Kemler in the *Nation* commented in 1954, the "only remaining pipelines into the National Security Council."

Impending Doom. Their column first appeared on 1 January 1946, the first in a long litany that predicted impending doom for the United States and the world. The Alsopian habit of making dire predictions garnered them many nicknames, including "the Brothers Cassandra," "disaster experts," "Old Testament prophets," and the "All-slops," the last given them by Sen. Joseph McCarthy.

Background. The Alsops came from an upper-class background, their mother being a niece of Theodore Roosevelt, a first cousin of Eleanor Roosevelt, and a sixth cousin of Franklin Roosevelt. The Alsop brothers possessed markedly different personalities. Joseph described himself as "ornate," and his manner was criticized by other commentators as arrogant. He kept his vow, made early in life, to insult at least one person a day. Stewart, on the other hand, was more pleasant and easygoing.

Predictions. Yet they shared a profound pessimism about world prospects which led to their dark predictions. Although they did not pretend infallibility, the Alsops

did have a respectable track record at interpreting trends in national and international politics. Their most notable predictions included the 1948 Communist coup in Czechoslovakia and their 1948 warning about an impending war in Korea. But some prognostications went awry. They predicted in 1948, along with many other commentators, that Thomas Dewey would defeat President Harry S Truman. They forecast that the United States would go to war with the Soviet Union in 1952.

Close to the White House. Despite the hit-and-miss nature of their column, the Alsops cultivated a close relationship with the White House, regardless of the occupant. Readers knew that by reading "Matter of Fact" they were reading the inside Washington scoop, filtered through the urbane, acerbic, and doom-struck writing of the Alsop brothers.

Sources:

Joseph Alsop and Adam Platt, *I've Seen the Best of It: Memoirs* (New York: Norton, 1992);

"Alsop's Fables," *Time,* 67 (18 June 1956): 66;

"Brothers in Arms," *Newsweek,* 50 (11 November 1957): 81–82;

Patrick Donovan, "Alsop's Fables for Our Terrible Time," *New Republic,* 139 (29 December 1958): 17–18;

Edgar Kemler, "Celestial Pipe Line," *Nation,* 178 (2 January 1954): 5–10;

Walter T. Ridder, "The Brothers Cassandra, Joseph and Stewart," *Reporter,* 11 (21 October 1954): 34–38.

HARRY ASHMORE
1916-
NEWSPAPER EDITOR

GREG VILLET, LIFE

New Breed. The winner of the 1958 Pulitzer Prize for editorial writing, Harry Ashmore, the editor of the *Arkansas Gazette* in Little Rock, was part of the new breed of southern newspaper editors in the 1950s that eschewed the narrow racial conservatism of previous eras in favor of religious and racial tolerance. Ashmore, Jonathan

Daniels of the *Raleigh* (N.C.) *News and Observer*, George Bingham of the *Louisville Courier-Journal* and *Louisville Times*, and Gene Patterson and Ralph McGill of the *Atlanta Journal* and *Constitution* were at the forefront of editors who took controversial stands as spokesmen for an enlightened South.

Background. Born in Greenville, South Carolina, and a 1937 graduate of Clemson College, Ashmore began his journalistic career that same year with the *Greenville Piedmont*. Following his service in the U.S. Army from 1942 to 1946, Ashmore was named associate editor of the *Charlotte* (N.C.) *News*. He succeeded to editor in 1947 and began writing editorials in favor of two-party politics, voting rights for blacks, increased funding for education, and racial harmony. Ashmore's editorials garnered national attention and gained for him an appointment in 1947 as the editorial-page editor of the *Gazette*. He was named executive editor in 1948.

Little Rock. Ashmore's tenure at the *Gazette*, which lasted until 1959, coincided with the most volatile period in the history of Arkansas race relations. In the wake of the 17 May 1954 *Brown* v. *Board of Education* Supreme Court decision outlawing segregated schools, Little Rock Central High School was ordered to be desegregated. On 2 September 1957 Arkansas governor Orval Faubus sent National Guard troops to prevent nine blacks from attending the school. President Dwight D. Eisenhower sent federal troops in response. Ashmore's editorial on 4 September showed his basic philosophy in opposing resistance to integration:

> Somehow, sometime, every Arkansan is going to have to be counted. . . . We are going to have to decide what kind of people we are — whether we obey the law only when we approve of it, or whether we obey it no matter how distasteful we find it.

Public Outcry. Governor Faubus labeled Ashmore "an ardent integrationist." The Capital Citizen's Council named him "Public Enemy Number 1." Despite falling circulation, from one hundred thousand to ninety thousand, Ashmore and the *Gazette* stood ground. By mid 1958 circulation had firmed, and Ashmore and the paper gained national recognition for their editorial position and reporting excellence. The Pulitzer committee credited Ashmore for "the forcefulness, dispassionate analysis and clarity" of his editorials. In also awarding the *Gazette* a Pulitzer for its reporting, the committee praised the paper under Ashmore's leadership for "demonstrating the highest qualities of civic leadership, journalistic responsibility, and moral courage in the face of mounting public tension."

Moral Courage. Ashmore was one of the southern editors who exemplified the moral courage that the civil rights movement demanded of those who took difficult positions in dangerous times.

Sources:
New York Times, 6 May 1958, p. 38;

"Southerner by Inclination," *Time* (21 April 1947): 52;
Time (21 April 1947).

MILTON BERLE

1908-
COMEDIAN AND ACTOR

The First Star. Milton Berle was television's first star and helped establish home television as an entertainment medium. Starring in the NBC comedy-variety series "Texaco Star Theatre" from 1948 to 1956, Berle became known as "Mr. Television." The popularity of his show, which aired every Tuesday evening at eight o'clock, helped secure an audience for the fledgling medium during its early years.

Vaudeville. Born in 1908 to show-business parents, Berle began performing professionally in vaudeville at the age of five, honing the skills as a comedian that prepared him for his radio and television career. Vaudeville was adapted to television as the variety show, and Berle was one of the first in television to take advantage of the public's familiarity with the form.

Show Format. The show was a live musical-comedy act with Berle acting as master of ceremonies and participant. Filled with sight gags, songs, dancing, comedy routines, jokes about current topics and New York City, and Berle's signature routine, dressing as a woman, the show was a manic sixty minutes written, scored, rehearsed, and broadcast for thirty-nine weeks a year. It was live television at its best and an example of why live television was so difficult to sustain. The show was popular from the beginning with both critics and audiences. Jay Gould of the *New York Times* called it television's "first smash hit"; the audience figures were startling.

New York Effect. In 1948 there were only half a million television sets in the United States, most of them in New York City. In the fall of that year "Texaco Star Theatre" achieved the amazing rating of 94.7, which meant that 94.7 percent of those half million sets were tuned into the show.

Ratings Decline. The audience in the late 1940s and early 1950s was disproportionately Jewish and urban, groups that identified closely with Berle, his style, and his comedic references. As the number of televisions grew and the audience expanded to include more rural areas, Berle's ratings declined from the unsustainable levels of 1948. Still, Berle commanded an immense audience, and he commanded a salary to match. In 1951 NBC was concerned that he might jump to another network and signed Berle to a thirty-year contract worth $200,000 annually. But the show's rating continued to decline, and in 1956 it was canceled. Berle's contract was reduced to $120,000 per year.

Mr. Television. After "Texaco Star Theatre" was canceled, Berle returned in 1958 with a new show on NBC. "The Kraft Music Hall" featured Berle until 1959, but the show lacked the freshness and energy of the earlier Berle vehicle. Though he never again reached the same level of success, Berle continued to be known as "Mr. Television" and to be revered for his early work in establishing television's dominant role in the popular culture of the 1950s.

Sources:

Goodman Ace, "Berle's Still Berling," *Look,* 17 (7 April 1953): 52–54;

Alfred Bester, "The Good Old Days of Mr. Television," *Holiday,* 23 (February 1958): 97, 99–100, 102–103, 105;

Joel Edwards, "Behind the Scenes with Milton Berle," *Coronet,* 29 (April 1951): 83–87;

David Halberstam, *The Fifties* (New York: Villard, 1993).

WILLIAM M. GAINES

1922-1992

MAGAZINE PUBLISHER

Growth in Circulation. The publisher of the most unlikely magazine success story of the 1950s, William M. Gaines made *Mad* magazine a household name and an icon for American youth. The magazine, a compendium of satire and humor aimed at the high-school and college market, grew from a circulation of 195,000 in 1953 to a level of 1.3 million in 1958. In 1959 *Mad* was chosen as the favorite magazine by 58 percent of college students and 43 percent of high-school students. The editorial rationale is that "anything, even death and destruction, can have a humorous side."

Background. Gaines began his publishing career when he inherited a comic-book publishing firm, Educational Comics, from his father in 1947. EC, as the firm was called, published a weak line of children's comics and by 1948 was one hundred thousand dollars in debt. In 1950 Gaines developed a new line of horror comics, the first two titled *The Crypt of Terror* and *The Vault of Horror.* The horror series, which expanded to seven titles, was tremendously successful and helped wipe out the EC debt by the end of 1952.

***Mad* Comics.** In summer 1952 Gaines oversaw the development of the first EC humor comic, tentatively called *Mad Dog* but shortened by the time of the first issue to *Mad.* It was immediately successful and prosperous. The prosperity did not last, however. In 1953 comic books became the focus of a Senate investigation, led by Sen. Estes Kefauver, into juvenile delinquency. Horror comics were blamed for all sorts of juvenile crime, and the public responded by demanding comic-book regulation.

Comic-book wholesale distributors reacted by refusing to carry horror comics.

Censorship. Gaines saw that his livelihood was severely threatened. The comic-book producers formed the Comics Magazine Association (CMA) in 1954 to regulate the industry themselves rather than leave it to the government. The CMA decided to ban horror comics, a decision that greatly reduced the profits of EC Comics. In order to circumvent the comic-book censors, Gaines decided to change *Mad* from a comic-book format to a magazine format. In addition to using higher-quality paper, Gaines raised the price from ten cents to twenty-five cents. With the new format removing the threat of censorship, *Mad* reached new levels of popularity. By 1958 the magazine made a profit of $43,000 per issue.

Unexploited Market. With *Mad* Gaines stumbled on an unexploited market of late adolescent and college age youth. Gaines and *Mad* were influential in identifying the youth market so expertly exploited by others in the 1960s and beyond. In his biography of Gaines, Frank Jacobs summarizes both the appeal and the controversy surrounding *Mad:*

> Because it contains so many pictures, many people call it a comic. Because it appeals to so many youngsters, many people think it is not fit reading for adults. Because it assails both political fringes, it is damned by both of them. Because it attacks sacred institutions, it is called un-American. Because it refuses to print pornography, it is called square. Because it hits everything, it is accused of lacking a point a view.

Sources:

"Crazy Like a Fox," *Newsweek* (31 August 1959): 57;

Richard Gehman, "It's Just Plain Mad," *Coronet,* 48 (May 1960): 96–103;

Frank Jacobs, *The Mad World of William M. Gaines* (Secaucus, N.J.: Lyle Stuart, 1972);

"Maddiction," *Time* (7 July 1958): 63.

JACKIE GLEASON

1916-1987

COMEDIAN AND ACTOR

Meteoric Rise. Jackie Gleason enjoyed a meteoric rise in television during the early 1950s. From humble beginnings in Brooklyn, New York, Gleason worked his way to success through all kinds of show business jobs — at different times Gleason was a bouncer, carnival barker, radio disc jockey, and cabaret performer — before signing a one-year contract with Warner Bros. Pictures in 1941. After appearing in three movies for Warner Bros. and one for 20th Century–Fox in 1941 and 1942, Gleason returned to New York to work on Broadway and in comedy clubs. He continued to work in clubs and at resorts for seven years, until he was signed in 1949 by the Du Mont television network to star in the adaption to television of the "Life of Riley" radio series.

"Cavalcade of Stars." After twenty-six weeks as Chester A. Riley, Gleason was named host of the Du Mont television show "Cavalcade of Stars." It was this show that Gleason used to hone the characters that made him a television institution. Ralph Kramden, the Poor Soul, Joe the Bartender, and Reginald Van Gleason III all made their television debuts on "Cavalcade of Stars." Gleason's presence raised the show's ratings from nine to thirty-eight in two years, garnering the attention of the other networks. The executives at CBS were especially interested in the fact that Gleason could draw such ratings on DuMont, a network without a nationwide audience.

Move to CBS. His contract with DuMont due to expire in 1952, Gleason approached CBS about signing with them. The contract was a blockbuster. CBS promised to cover the production costs for "The Jackie Gleason Show" — three hundred thousand dollars annually — and Gleason was promised a ten-thousand-dollars-per-week salary. Premiering 20 September 1952, "The Jackie Gleason Show" was in the top ten and had reached second place by 1954. The show's popularity in its Saturday night 8:00 time slot gained Gleason the nickname "Mr. Saturday Night."

New Contract. In 1954 Gleason canceled "The Jackie Gleason Show" in favor of a weekly half-hour broadcast of "The Honeymooners," a Gleason's skit that featured Brooklyn bus driver Ralph Kramden. The contract that produced the switch in shows was the biggest in television's short history. CBS agreed to pay Gleason a total of eleven million dollars for two years of shows, with an option for a third year. In 1956 Gleason began a thirty-minute "Jackie Gleason Show." He starred in shows that ran on the network in various forms until 1971.

Classic Comedian. During his television career Gleason was a bigger-than-life character. Not always consistent or reliable, Gleason was the classic television comedian. Jim Bishop, in his 1956 biography of Gleason, attempts to summarize the contradictions:

> Gleason, I am convinced, has a king-sized soul. And a loud conscience. These, coupled with a body which was intended to enjoy all of the sensual pleasures, making for a disparate, sometimes desperate, character. He has a gargantuan appetite for food, women, music and charity. They do not all pull in the same direction.

Sources:
Jim Bishop, *The Golden Ham: A Candid Biography of Jackie Gleason* (New York: Simon & Schuster, 1956);

"Jack for Jackie," *Time* (3 January 1955): 52;

Eric Pace, "Jackie Gleason Dies of Cancer; Comedian and Actor Was 71," *New York Times*, 25 June 1987, pp. A1, B16;

Sally Bedell Smith, *In All His Glory: The Life of William S. Paley* (New York: Simon & Schuster, 1990).

MARGUERITE HIGGINS
1920-1966
NEWSPAPER CORRESPONDENT

© 1950, TIME INC.

War Correspondent. Marguerite Higgins was the most publicized newspaperwoman of the 1950s. Although a seasoned reporter from her experience during World War II — she was with Allied troops as they liberated the Dachau and Buchenwald concentration camps in 1945 — Higgins first gained widespread public notice as a war correspondent during the Korean War.

Korean War. Higgins joined the staff of the *New York Herald Tribune* in 1942 and remained with the paper throughout her career. From 1946 to 1950 she served as Berlin bureau chief for the *Herald Tribune*. In 1950 she was transferred to Tokyo as chief of the Far East bureau just before the invasion of South Korea by North Korea. She arrived in Korea two days after the initial Communist invasion and remained near the front for much of the war, to the dismay of both Homer Bigart, the official *Herald Tribune* war correspondent, and the U.S. Army.

Feud with Bigart. For much of the war Higgins shared the front page with Bigart, both of them filing competing stories. The *Herald Tribune* often printed both dispatches. The relationship between the two reporters was competitive and tinged with bitterness. A colleague captured the flavor of the situation: "As soon as Homer kills off Maggie or Maggie kills off Homer the competition will wane and so will the coverage of the Korean War."

Discrimination. A more serious disagreement arose with the army. In July 1950 Lt. Gen. Walton H. Walker ordered Higgins back to Japan, saying that war was no place for a woman. In Japan Higgins immediately appealed the decision to Gen. Douglas MacArthur in language that foreshadowed the woman's movement of later decades: "I'm not working in Korea as a woman. I am there as a war correspondent." MacArthur returned her to Korea, this time as a worldwide sensation. For her exploits in Korea — and no doubt because of the publicity surrounding them — Higgins shared the Pulitzer Prize for international reporting given in 1951 with five other reporters, all of them men: Keyes Beech and Fred Sparks of the *Chicago Daily News*, Relmin Marin and Don Whitehead of the Associated Press, and Homer Bigart. She was also named 1951 "Woman of the Year" by the Associated Press.

Sources:

Marguerite Higgins, *War in Korea: The Report of a Woman War Correspondent* (Garden City, N.Y.: Doubleday, 1951);

"Last Word," *Time*, 56 (31 July 1950): 53;

Antoinette May, *Witness To War: A Biography of Marguerite Higgins* (New York: Beaufort Books, 1983);

Carl Mydans, "Girl War Correspondent: The New York Herald Tribune's Maggie Higgins Is Winning Battle of the Sexes on the Korean Front," *Life*, 29 (2 October 1950): 51–52, 54, 56, 59–60;

"Pride of the Regiment," *Time*, 56 (25 September 1950): 63–64.

HENRY R. LUCE

1898-1967
EDITOR AND MAGAZINE PUBLISHER

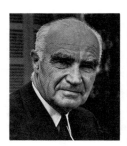

Magazine Empire. As the most powerful American media figure during most of the twentieth century, Henry R. Luce through his publishing empire dominated the magazine industry during the 1950s and wielded strong political influence. The cofounder (with friend and partner Briton Hadden) of *Time*, the first modern news magazine, Luce affected the way in which many Americans received their news. His other magazine ventures, including *Fortune*, *Life*, and *Sports Illustrated*, helped secure a media empire that in 1959 grossed more than $271 million.

Background. Luce's parents were Presbyterian missionaries, and he was born in China, where he lived until the age of fourteen. He arrived in the United States at age fifteen, enrolling at the prestigious Hotchkiss School in Connecticut. He met Hadden at Hotchkiss, working with him at the school newspaper and creating a journalistic vision they would continue to develop while at Yale University and afterward.

Launching *Time*. Luce and Hadden graduated from Yale in 1920. Luce first went to Oxford, then to work for Ben Hecht at the *Chicago Daily News*. In 1922 he rejoined Hadden, then a reporter at the *Baltimore News*. A year later the two resigned from the *News* to launch *Time*. Selling stock in the new enterprise, Luce and Hadden began the magazine in 1923 with an investment of eighty-six thousand dollars.

Hadden's Death. The first issue was dated 3 March 1923 and sold twelve thousand copies. Luce handled the business aspects of the operation, while Hadden was the editor. In 1929 Luce and Hadden planned the start of a business magazine, to be called *Fortune*. Before the first issue, however, Hadden died. Luce was shaken, but he persevered in putting out the first monthly issue, which appeared in February 1930. Its expensive one-dollar-per-copy price was unheard of. Despite the stock-market crash of the previous October and the incipient Depression, the magazine was a success.

Political Power. Luce continued to build his empire, expanding it into book publishing, radio- and television-station ownership, and television programming. But the media power of the Luce empire expanded inevitably toward political power. Luce was an ardent Republican and a staunch cold warrior. He used his editorial power at *Time* and *Fortune* to circulate his views on capitalism, labor, communism, and, especially, Communist China. His support of Chiang Kai-shek, the Chinese Nationalist leader, after World War II in the Chinese revolution influenced U.S. foreign policy for almost thirty years. He was regarded as controversial due to the stands he and his magazines took, but he never claimed to be totally objective. "Show me a man who claims he is objective," he once told an interviewer, "and I'll show you a man with illusions."

Launch of *Sports Illustrated*. The decade of the 1950s was the pinnacle of Luce's political influence. It was also the decade that saw Luce's last big magazine launch, that of *Sports Illustrated*. Although not a sportsman himself, Luce perceived a market for a recreation magazine in a postwar society that promised more leisure time. To prepare himself to publish such a magazine, Luce took courses in baseball, boxing, and horse racing. *Sports Illustrated* was an immediate success, with sales of 550,000 copies for its first issue, which was dated 16 August 1954.

International Influence. The raw numbers associated with the phenomenal success of Luce's media empire tend to understate his cultural import. The German magazine *Der Spiegel* summarized in 1961 Luce's influence in the United States and the world:

> No man has, over the last two decades, more incisively shaped the image of America as seen by the rest of the world, and the American's image of the world, than *Time* and *Life* editor Henry Robinson Luce.

> Every third U.S. family buys every week a Luce product; 94 percent of all Americans over 12 know *Time*. Luceferic printed products are the intellectual supplement of Coca-Cola, Marilyn Monroe and dollar diplomacy.

> No American without a political office — with the possible exception of Henry Ford — has had greater influence on American society. Luce was the first — between the wars — to use the term American Century. Recently, at a party on board [Aristotle] Onassis' yacht *Christina*, Winston Churchill counted him among the seven most powerful men in the United States, and President Eisenhower, while still in office, called him "a great American."

Last of an Era. In a society entering a period of revolutionary change brought about by the new medium of television, Luce was the last U.S. print-media figure who commanded worldwide power.

Sources:

John J. Abele, "Publisher Stepped Down in '64 as Editor in Chief," *New York Times*, 1 March 1967, p. 33;

Noel F. Busch, *Briton Hadden: A Biography of the Co-Founder of Time* (New York: Farrar, Straus, 1949);

W. A. Swanberg, *Luce and His Empire* (New York: Scribners, 1972);

Alden Whitman, "Created the News Magazine," *New York Times*, 1 March 1967, pp. 1, 33.

EDWARD R. MURROW

1908-1965

TELEVISION NEWS REPORTER

GALE PICTURE GALLERY

Early Career in Radio. Edward R. Murrow virtually invented modern radio and television news. Renowned for his thoroughness, fairness, and curiously charismatic seriousness, Murrow began his career at CBS News in 1935 not as a broadcaster but as the CBS "director of talks," or educational programs. He served as CBS representative in Europe beginning in 1937; he began his radio broadcasting career by covering the forced merger of Austria with Germany in 1938, beaming reports of the entrance of German troops into Vienna. He gained notoriety for his dramatic radio coverage of the Battle of Britain. But his television documentary news programs, "See It Now" and "CBS Reports," made him a fixture of 1950s television. In the public eye Murrow became the very ideal of a television newsman and a prime source of the great reputation of CBS News.

Broadcaster. Not trained as a journalist or a broadcaster, it was those two fields which soon gathered his attention. In 1938 Murrow found himself in Vienna as Adolf Hitler sent troops to force a merger of Austria with Germany. Given a short deadline and with no experienced radio journalist available, Morrow made his first broadcast on 13 March 1938. The thrill of being in the midst of historic events and reporting their significance to the world captured Murrow's imagination.

The Battle of Britain. Murrow became a public figure through his broadcasts from London during the Battle of Britain, when the Nazi air force attempted to bomb England into surrender. During these radio reports he would sign on saying "This is London." The simple phrase, understated yet dramatic, became synonymous with Murrow. After the war Murrow was named vicepresident of CBS for public affairs. He served in that post until 1947, when he returned to the air. "Hear It Now," which first was broadcast in 1950, was Murrow's most respected show on radio.

Suspicious of Television. Murrow was suspicious of television and thought it unsuited to serious journalism, but in 1951 he tried television when he was given the opportunity to adapt the radio program to the new medium. With Fred Friendly, his coproducer and collaborator, Murrow intended "See It Now" to make headlines, not merely to report them. For the first six months, the show was broadcast at 3:30 on Sunday afternoon; its success in both the ratings and with the critics convinced the network to move the show to 6:30 P.M. As coproducer, narrator, and occasional interviewer, Murrow brought integrity and respectability to television news. The first show featured a report on the Korean War that followed the activities of Fox Company, Second Platoon, Nineteenth Infantry Regiment. The report was realistic in a way that World War II newsreels had not been. Murrow reported early in the segment that half the men seen were missing in action or had been killed or wounded since the filming ended. At the end of the segment, the platoon members turned to the camera and stated their names and hometowns. The association of names and faces with the violence of battle brought the war closer to home than the headlines of a newspaper.

Provocative Issues. With Murrow's approach the show was inherently topical and controversial. Examples of subjects covered included the tragedy of racial prejudice in the South, the turmoil surrounding nuclear physicist Robert Oppenheimer, and the controversy and fear concerning nuclear weapons. Television critic Gilbert Seldes called "See It Now" "the most important show on the air."

Joseph McCarthy. At no time was it more important than in March 1954, when it broadcast a show on Sen. Joseph R. McCarthy, then at the peak of his influence and popularity. Murrow used careful editing and his own personal outrage to highlight the cruelty and irrationality of the McCarthy Senate-sanctioned hunt for communists in the government. "See It Now" made a powerful and risky statement against McCarthy which helped bring that suspicious and paranoid era to an end.

Documentaries. In addition to "See It Now," Murrow worked on "Person to Person," a lighter television show of interviews with celebrities in their homes. He initiated "CBS Reports," a highly acclaimed series of hour-long documentaries. The most renowned of these was "Harvest of Shame," an exposé of the harsh conditions under which migrant laborers were exploited in American agriculture. He also hosted "Small World," a show which linked three people around the country by remote hookups and discussed general topics. One such show featured James Thurber, Siobhan McKenna, and Noel Coward on the nature of comedy.

Decline. But the pace of working nonstop for so many years and growing suspicion about the ultimately profit-oriented heart of television began to take its toll on Murrow. As the decade ended and after "See It Now" was canceled, he was a bitter man. While serving as director of the U.S. Information Agency in the John F. Kennedy administration, he was diagnosed with lung cancer. In 1965 he underwent an operation for a brain tumor and died on 27 April 1965. His career remains a model and a source of inspiration for serious television journalists.

Sources:

William Boddy, *Fifties Television: The Industry and Its Critics* (Urbana & Chicago: University of Illinois Press, 1990);

Joseph E. Persico, *Edward R. Murrow: An American Original* (New York: McGraw-Hill, 1988);

Charles Wertenbaker, "The World on His Back," *New Yorker*, 29 (26 December 1953): 28-45.

WILLIAM S. PALEY

1901-1990

TELEVISION NETWORK EXECUTIVE

Tycoon. William S. Paley was the most dynamic tycoon in the television industry of the 1950s. As president and chairman of the Columbia Broadcasting System (CBS), Paley built a struggling radio network into a radio and television empire. No person had greater influence on the development of television, its broadcasting content, and its cultural power.

Early Career. Born in Chicago in 1901, Paley began his career in the Congress Cigar Company, which the Paley family owned. As vice-president of Congress, Paley contracted in the mid 1920s to advertise on the Columbia Phonograph Broadcasting System, a small struggling radio network headquartered in Philadelphia and owned by United Independent Broadcastings. His interest in broadcasting piqued, Paley bought United in 1928 for five hundred thousand dollars and renamed it Columbia Broadcasting System. By 1929 he had increased the size of the network from sixteen stations to forty-nine.

Programming Strategies. Paley continued to expand at CBS during the onset of the Depression and initiated broadcasting strategies that he would later carry to television. He scoured the hinterlands for little-known quality vocalists and musicians — Fats Waller, the Mills Brothers, the Boswell Sisters, and Kate Smith, among them — and brought them to radio. In 1931 he signed Bing Crosby to a fifteen-hundred-dollar-per-week contract to perform six times a week at 11 P.M. for fifteen minutes. He also signed to CBS many famous radio comedians, including George Burns and Gracie Allen, Jack Benny, and Fred Allen. When these did not put CBS at the top of the ratings, he bought stars from competitor NBC: Al Jolson, Nelson Eddy, and Maj. Edward Bowes were three that Paley lured to his network. Paley spared no expense in attracting the best and most popular performers to CBS.

Introduction to Television. Paley's introduction to television came during its experimental stage in the 1930s; CBS opened its first experimental station, WXAB in New York, on 21 July 1931. During the rest of the decade and through the mid 1940s CBS did little to develop its television franchise. CBS executive Frank Stanton later commented, "Before the war we did the minimum to keep our television license. NBC was way ahead of us. [David] Sarnoff [NBC and RCA executive and founding father of broadcast television] was the visionary. He had the guts."

Buying Talent. After World War II Paley decided that the same strategy he had used in radio — buying talent — would also be successful in television. In the late 1940s CBS took out a $5 million bank loan and used the proceeds to sign up many of NBC's television stars. Paley was able to offer on CBS television such established stars as Benny, Red Skelton, Edgar Bergen and Charlie McCarthy, Frank Sinatra, and Amos 'n Andy. The result was that CBS began to dominate the ratings, a domination that continued into the 1970s.

News. Under Paley's leadership CBS also gained a great reputation for its news division. The roots of this reputation were in the 1930s, when Paley oversaw the building of a radio-news division that proved its worth during World War II. The television news division later included such renowned newsmen as Edward R. Murrow, Eric Sevareid, William Shirer, Howard K. Smith, and Walter Cronkite. Paley took great pride in CBS News and believed it to be an important part of the overall success of the network. He did not flinch at the costs of maintaining a top-flight news gathering and reporting organization. In 1956 these costs were more than $7 million.

Influence. Paley's brashness and boldness helped define the direction that television broadcasting took in the late 1940s and 1950s. His notions of quality became the standard for many viewers of television. Along with Sarnoff, Paley must be ranked as one of the two most influential figures in television history.

Sources:

"Good News and Bad News," *Newsweek* (7 January 1957): 64–65;

William S. Paley, *As It Happened: A Memoir* (Garden City, N.Y.: Doubleday, 1979);

Sally Bedell Smith, *In All His Glory: The Life of William S. Paley* (New York: Simon & Schuster, 1990).

DAVID SARNOFF

1891-1971

TELEVISION NETWORK EXECUTIVE

Background. Born in Minsk, Russia, David Sarnoff immigrated to America in 1900 to reside with his family in a tenement on New York City's Lower East Side. To support his family, nine-year-old David, the eldest son, almost immediately found work selling newspapers. Soon he had his first real job, as a five-dollars-a-week messenger boy. In 1906 he took a position with American Marconi, the American office of the first wireless-telegraph company, Marconi Wireless. As a telegrapher for Marconi, Sarnoff stayed at his post for three straight days after the sinking of the SS *Titanic* on 14 April 1912, receiving wireless transmissions of the names of the dead and survivors. The *Titanic* tragedy had the effect of boosting the infant wireless industry, which could communicate with vessels at sea.

Forming RCA. Sarnoff's fortunes rose with American Marconi's, and when the company merged with several others to form the Radio Corporation of American (RCA) in 1919, he was one of the conglomerate's junior executives. As an officer of RCA, Sarnoff was responsible for the company's change of emphasis from transoceanic communication to commercial radio broadcasting. To that end RCA established the National Broadcasting Company (NBC) in 1926, which offered entertainment and news to owners of "receiver sets" in New York City. Soon NBC was broadcasting nationwide over chains of transmitters that relayed radio signals far from their starting point.

President of RCA. Sarnoff became president of RCA in 1930. Over the next two decades the company entered the movie and phonograph industries, and NBC dominated radio entertainment. By the early 1940s Sarnoff was ready to lead his company into television, with which RCA had been experimenting for years. Sarnoff had seen enormous potential in the broadcasting of images as well as sound since the 1920s. World War II interfered with RCA's plans, however, and the company was not allowed to begin mass production of television receivers until 1946.

Color Television. In the 1950s Sarnoff strongly backed NBC's attempts to manufacture color television sets and to broadcast in color. He was successful in getting television sets approved by the Federal Communications Commission (FCC) that were "color compatible," meaning that they could pick up either black-and-white or color broadcasts. However, Sarnoff's corporate rival, William S. Paley of CBS, quickly overcame RCA's lead in manufacturing color sets and overtook NBC in television broadcasting. Sarnoff retired from RCA in 1970 and died a year later.

ED SULLIVAN
1902-1974
TELEVISION HOST

King of Variety Shows. Ed Sullivan was the king of variety shows in the 1950s. With his CBS shows the "Toast of the Town" and "The Ed Sullivan Show," Sullivan parlayed his expressionless manner and untelegenic face into a television institution.

Early Career. Sullivan first gained prominence in 1932 as the author of the "Little Old New York" column, which was published in the *New York Daily News* and syndicated to newspapers across the United States. The same year he began a radio variety show that was notable for broadcasting Jack Benny, Irving Berlin, and George M. Cohan, among others. In 1942 he began a network radio show on CBS called "Ed Sullivan Entertains."

Television Premiere. His premiere on television occurred without his knowledge. Sullivan was the master of ceremonies of the annual Harvest Moon Ball, a dance competition sponsored by the *Daily News* and held in Madison Square Garden. In 1947 CBS televised the competition without Sullivan's knowing about it. On the basis of his performance, Sullivan was engaged by CBS to become the host of "Toast of the Town." The hour-long variety show premiered on 20 June 1948 with Dean Martin and Jerry Lewis and Richard Rodgers and Oscar Hammerstein II among the guest stars.

Network Moneymaker. For the first five seasons the show was popular, though not a consistent finisher in the twenty top-rated programs. By the 1954 season "Toast of the Town" was a common resident of the top twenty. Regardless of its place in the ratings, Sullivan's show was a prestigious moneymaker for CBS. In 1951 Lincoln Mercury, the sponsor of "Toast of the Town," paid CBS over $2.2 million to advertise on the show for one year. Sullivan was also well paid, receiving $125,000 a year in 1951. Sullivan was amazed at the money figures associated with him and his show, musing in *Time* in 1951 that Rodgers and Hammerstein had appeared on the premiere of "Toast of the Town" for $270.

Critic's Disbelief. If Sullivan was amazed at the monetary success of the show, critics were incredulous that Sullivan's wooden personality could gain the following of such a large audience. John Crosby in the *New York Herald Tribune* described him as "totally innocent of any of the tricks of stage presence." Sullivan himself said, in one of his better-known lines, "when I walk on the stage I apparently look as if I'd just been embalmed." His hunched shoulders, his greeting, and his promise to the audience every week that he had "a really big shew" became the stuff of comedy routines across the country.

Importance of Talent. But the secret of Sullivan's success on "Talk of the Town" and "The Ed Sullivan Show," as it was known from 1955, was his ability to choose and attract performers to appear. He introduced many performers to television in the 1950s, including Bob Hope, Lena Horne, Jack Benny, and, most famously, Elvis Presley. On Elvis's second appearance on the show, Sullivan demanded that the camera show Elvis only from the waist up, so the singer's gyrating hips would not offend Middle America.

Continued Success. The "Ed Sullivan Show" continued in its Sunday 8:00 P.M. time slot until 1971, when Sullivan retired. By that time it had become the most popular television variety show in history. Its host was one of the most recognizable and popular figures in television.

Sources:

Richard B. Gehman, "Ed Sullivan: TV's Miracle Man," *Coronet*, 31 (8 March 1952): 53–58;

Philip Hamburger, "Variety," *New Yorker*, 30 (18 December 1954): 89–91;

"The Toast of the Town," *Time* (25 June 1951): 49–50;

"Why Ed Rates High," *Newsweek*, 36 (21 December 1953): 82–83.

PEOPLE IN THE NEWS

Samuel Blackman was named general news editor of the Associated Press in December 1958.

Dick Clark hosted the national premiere of his "American Bandstand" music show on ABC on 7 October 1957.

In 1957 **Nat King Cole** became the first black performer to have his own television show. Because southern stations threatened a boycott, no national advertiser could be found, and the show was canceled in 1958.

After eight years on the show, **Dorothy Collins** and her husband, **Raymond Scott,** were dropped from "Hit Parade" in February 1957.

John Denson was named editor of *Newsweek* on 22 July 1956.

In 1954 **Roscoe Drummond** was hired from the *Christian Science Monitor* to be the Washington bureau chief for the *New York Herald Tribune.*

Pauline Frederick was hired in 1953 as an NBC news correspondent. Her hiring opened many career doors for women.

Radio disc jockey **Alan Freed** hosted the first prime-time television special featuring rock 'n' roll music on 4 May 1957.

Radio and television personality **Arthur Godfrey** underwent surgery for lung cancer on 30 April 1959.

In 1951 graphic designer **William Golden** conceived the CBS Eye as the network symbol.

Sen. Robert Hendrickson (R–New Jersey), chairman of a Senate subcommitte investigating the impact of television on juvenile violence, urged the government to regulate television content.

Rosel Hyde, a member of the FCC, testified on 20 October 1954 that censorship of television by the government would be "dangerous and undemocratic" and called for an industry-appointed "czar" to police televised violence.

The *New York Times* published on 14 February 1950 an exclusive interview by **Arthur Krock** with President Harry S Truman. Other news reporters were furious at the exclusivity, but Krock won a Pulitzer Prize for the interview.

Louis R. Lautier of the *Atlantic Daily World* became the first black member of the National Press Club in February 1955.

Walter Lippman, Joseph and **Stewart Alsop, Howard K. Smith,** and **Edward R. Murrow** were presented Overseas Press Club awards on 29 March 1954.

Boston University president **Daniel Marsh** told graduating seniors on 4 June 1950 that "if the television craze continues with the present level of programs, we are destined to have a nation of morons."

In July 1950 **Daniel D. Mich** was named editorial director of *McCall's* magazine.

William N. Otis, an Associated Press correspondent, was sentenced in March 1951 to ten years' imprisonment for espionage by Czechoslovakian officials.

Syndicated newspaper columnist **Drew Pearson** was punched up by Sen. **Joseph McCarthy** at a Washington cocktail party on 13 December 1950.

Newspaper columnist **Westbrook Pegler** and two Hearst firms are ordered by a federal jury to pay $175,000 to writer Quentin Reynolds in settlement of libel charges.

Gerald Pill, editor of *Scientific American,* revealed in March 1950 that thirty thousand copies of the magazine were burned at the behest of the Atomic Energy Commission because it contained technical data on the H-bomb that Pill said already had been published elsewhere.

In May 1955 **Ogden Rogers Reid** succeeded his brother **Whitelaw Reid** as editor of the *New York Herald Tribune.*

On 13 March 1950 NBC barred singer and leftist **Paul Robeson** from appearing on a television special starring **Eleanor Roosevelt.**

RCA chairman **David Sarnoff** filed a statement on 6 June 1955 with the FCC opposing subscription television service.

CBS news commentator **Eric Sevareid** was awarded an Alfred I. duPont award for public service in radio and television broadcasting on 24 March 1955.

In July 1950 **Prof. Walter A. Steigleman,** after five years of research, reported that the stress of newspaper editorial work reduced life expectancy by one to three years.

CBS president **Frank Stanton** barred quiz-show programs from his network on 16 October 1959 in reaction to the scandal concerning quiz shows.

Margaret Truman debuted as a radio actress on 26 April 1951 in a NBC radio adaption of the film *Jackpot.*

Pat Weaver, creator of "The Today Show," became the president of NBC in December 1953. He served in that post until December 1955.

In 1958 **John Hay Whitney** bought the *New York Herald Tribune.*

AWARDS

Emmy Awards

1950

Best Sports Program: "Rams Football" (KNBH)

Best Variety Show: "The Alan Young Show" (KTTV, CBS)

Best Dramatic Show: "Pulitzer Prize Playhouse" (KECA-TV)

Best News Program: "KTLA Newsreel"

Most Outstanding Personality: Groucho Marx (KNBH, NBC)

1951

Best Dramatic Show: "Studio One" (CBS)

Best Comedy Show: "Red Skelton Show" (NBC)

Best Variety Show: "Your Show of Shows" (NBC)

Special Achievement Award: U.S. senator Estes Kefauver, for outstanding public service on television

1952

Best Dramatic Program: "Robert Montgomery Presents" (NBC)

Best Variety Program: "Your Show of Shows" (NBC)

Best Public Affairs Program: "See It Now" (CBS)

Best Mystery, Action, or Adventure Program: "Dragnet" (NBC)

Best Situation Comedy: "I Love Lucy" (CBS)

Most Outstanding Personality: Bishop Fulton J. Sheen (Dumont)

1953

Best Dramatic Program: "U.S. Steel Hour" (ABC)

Best Situation Comedy: "I Love Lucy" (CBS)

Best Variety Program: "Omnibus" (CBS)

Best Program of News or Sports: "See It Now" (CBS)

Best Public Affairs Program: "Victory at Sea" (NBC)

Best Mystery, Action or Adventure Program: "Dragnet" (NBC)

Most Outstanding Personality: Edward R. Murrow (CBS)

1954

Best Cultural, Religious or Educational Program: "Omnibus" (CBS)

Best Sports Program: "Gillette Cavalcade of Sports" (NBC)

Best Daytime Program: "Art Linkletter's House Party" (CBS)

Best News Reporter or Commentator: John Daly (ABC)

Best Mystery or Intrigue Series: "Dragnet" (NBC)

Best Variety Series Including Musical Varieties: "Disneyland" (ABC)

Best Situation Comedy Series: "Make Room For Daddy" (ABC)

Best Dramatic Series: "U.S. Steel Hour" (ABC)

Most Outstanding New Personality: George Gobel (NBC)

1955

Best Contribution to Daytime Programming: "Matinee Theatre" (NBC)

Best Special Events or News Program: "A-Bomb Test Coverage" (CBS)

Best Documentary Program (Religious, Informational, Educational or Interview): "Omnibus" (CBS)

Best Action or Adventure Series: "Disneyland" (ABC)

Best Comedy Series: Phil Silvers's "You'll Never Get Rich" (CBS)

Best Variety Series: "Ed Sullivan Show" (CBS)

Best Music Series: "Your Hit Parade" (NBC)

Best Dramatic Series: "Producers' Showcase" (NBC)

Best News Commentator or Reporter: Edward R. Murrow (CBS)

Governor's Award (The First Presidential-size Emmy to be awarded): President Dwight D. Eisenhower, for his use and encouragement of television

1956

Best New Program Series: "Playhouse 90" (CBS)

Best Series (Half hour or less): "Phil Silvers Show" (CBS)

Best Series (One hour or more): "Caesar's Hour" (NBC)

Best Public Service Series: "See It Now" (CBS)

Best Coverage of a Newsworthy Event: "Years of Crisis," year-end report with Edward R. Murrow and other correspondents (CBS)

Best News Commentator: Edward R. Murrow (CBS)

1957

Best New Program Series of the Year: "Seven Lively Arts" (CBS)

Best Dramatic Anthology Series: "Playhouse 90" (CBS)

Best Dramatic Series With Continuing Characters: "Gunsmoke" (CBS)

Best Comedy Series: "Phil Silvers Show" (CBS)

Best Public Service Program or Series: "Omnibus" (ABC and NBC)

Trustees' Award: Jack Benny, for his significant contributions to the television industry as a showman. For the high standard, for all to emulate, set by his personal skill and excellence as a performer. For the consistency, quality, and good taste of his programs through many years and many media.

1958–1959

Best Dramatic Series (One hour or longer): "Playhouse 90" (CBS)

Best Dramatic Series (Less than one hour): "Alcoa-Goodyear Theatre" (NBC)

Best Comedy Series: "Jack Benny Show" (CBS)

Best Musical or Variety Series: "Dinah Shore Chevy Show" (NBC)

Best Public Service Program or Series: "Omnibus" (NBC)

Best News Reporting Series: "Huntley-Brinkley Report" (NBC)

Best News Commentator or Analyst: Edward R. Murrow (CBS)

Trustees' Award: Bob Hope. Presented with appreciation and admiration for bringing the great gift of laughter to all peoples of all nations; for selflessly entertaining American troops throughout the world over many years; and for making television finer by these deeds and by the consistently high quality of his television programs through the years.

1959–1960

Outstanding Program Achievement in the Field of Humor: "Art Carney Special" (NBC)

Outstanding Program Achievement in the Field of Drama: "Playhouse 90" (CBS)

Outstanding Program Achievement in the Field of Variety: "Fabulous Fifties" (CBS)

Outstanding Program Achievement in the Field of News: "Huntley-Brinkley Report" (NBC)

Outstanding Program Achievement in the Field of Public Affairs and Education: "Twentieth Century" (CBS)

Trustees' Award: Dr. Frank Stanton, president, The Columbia Broadcasting System, Inc., by forthright and courageous action, has advanced immeasurably the freedom of television as an arm of the free press and in so doing has strengthened the total freedom of television. In honoring Dr. Stanton, the Trustees seek to express their deep concern for television's freedom to carry out its vital responsibilities as a medium of information and discussion.

Trustees' Citation: The Ampex Corporation, The Radio Corporation of America, Michael R. Gargiulo, Richard Gillaspy. In recognition of the corporate effort of all phases of television production. For capturing on video tape the Nixon-Khrushchev debate of July 25, 1959, in Moscow at the American Color Television Exhibit, and for making the extraordinary public event available to the American people through its television network.

PULITZER PRIZES IN JOURNALISM

MERITORIOUS PUBLIC SERVICE

1950 *Chicago Daily News* and *St. Louis Post-Dispatch*

1951 *Miami Herald* and *Brooklyn Eagle*

1952 *St. Louis Post-Dispatch*

1953 *Whiteville* (N.C.) *News Reporter* and *Tabor City* (N.C.) *Tribune*

1954 *Newsday*

1955 *Columbus* (Ga.) *Ledger* and *Sunday Ledger-Enquirer*

1956 *Watsonville* (Cal.) *Register-Pajaronian*

1957 *Chicago Daily News*

1958 *Arkansas Gazette*

1959 *Utica* (N.Y.) *Observer-Dispatch* and *Utica Daily Press*

REPORTING

1950 Meyer Berger, *New York Times*

1951 Edward S. Montgomery, *San Francisco Examiner*

1952 George de Carvalho, *San Francisco Chronicle*

LOCAL GENERAL REPORTING

1953 *Providence* (R.I.) *Journal-Bulletin*

1954 *Vicksburg* (Miss.) *Sunday Post-Herald*

1955 Mrs. Caro Brown, *Alice* (Tex.) *Daily Echo*

1956 Lee Hills, *Detroit Free Press*

1957 *Salt Lake Tribune*

1958 *Fargo* (N.D.) *Forum*

1959 Mary Lou Werner, *Washington* (D.C.) *Star*

LOCAL SPECIALIZED AND INVESTIGATIVE REPORTING

1953 Edward J. Mowery, *New York World-Telegram*

1954 Alvin Scott McCoy, *Kansas City Star*

1955 Roland Kenneth Towery, *Cuero* (Tex.) *Record*

1956 Arthur Daley, *New York Times*

1957 Wallace Turner and William Lambert, *Portland Oregonian*

1958 George Beveridge, *Washington* (D.C.) *Evening Star*

1959 John Harold Brislin, *Scranton* (Pa.) *Tribune*

NATIONAL REPORTING

1950 Edwin O. Guthman, *Seattle Times*

1951 No award

1952 Anthony Leviero, *New York Times*

1953 Don Whitehead, Associated Press

1954 Richard Wilson, Cowles Newspapers

1955 Anthony Lewis, *Washington Daily News*

1956 Charles L. Bartlett, *Chattanooga Times*

1957 James Reston, *New York Times*

1958 Relman Morin, Associated Press, and Clark Mollenhoff, *Des Moines Register & Tribune*

1959 Howard Van Smith, *Miami News*

INTERNATIONAL REPORTING

1950 Edmund Stevens, *Christian Science Monitor*

1951 Keyes Beech and Fred Sparks, *Chicago Daily News;* Marguerite Higgins and Homer William Bigart, *New York Herald Tribune;* Relman Morin and Don Whitehead, Associated Press

1952 John M. Hightower, Associated Press

1953 Austin Wehrwein, *Milwaukee Journal*

1954 Jim G. Lucas, Scripps Howard Newspapers

1955 Harrison E. Salisbury, *New York Times*

1956 William Randolph Hearst, Jr., Kingsbury Smith, and Frank Conniff, International News Service

1957 Russell Jones, United Press

1958 *New York Times*

1959 Joseph Martin and Philip Santora, *New York Daily News*

EDITORIALS

1950 Carl M. Saunders, *Jackson* (Mich.) *Citizen Patriot*

1951 William H. Fitzpatrick, *New Orleans States*

1952 Louis LaCoss, *St. Louis Globe Democrat*

1953 Vermont Royster, *Wall Street Journal*

1954 Don Murray, *Boston Herald*

1955 Royce Howes, *Detroit Free Press*

1956 Lauren K. Soth, *Des Moines Register & Tribune*

1957 Buford Boone, *Tuscaloosa* (Ala.) *News*

1958 Harry S. Ashmore, *Arkansas Gazette*

1959 Ralph McGill, *Atlanta Constitution*

EDITORIAL CARTOONS

1950 James T. Berryman, *Washington* (D.C.) *Evening Star*

1951 Reginald W. Manning, *Arizona Republic*

1952 Fred L. Packer, *New York Mirror*

1953 Edward D. Kuekes, *Cleveland Plain Dealer*

1954 Herbert L. Block (Herblock), *Washington Post & Times-Herald*

1955 D. R. Fitzpatrick, *St. Louis Post-Dispatch*

1956 Robert York, *Louisville* (Ky.) *Times*

1957 Tom Little, *Nashville Tennessean*

1958 Bruce M. Shanks, *Buffalo* (N.Y.) *Evening News*

1959 William H. (Bill) Mauldin, *St. Louis Post-Dispatch*

PHOTOGRAPHY

1950 Bill Crouch, *Oakland* (Cal.) *Tribune*

1951 Max Desfor, Associated Press

1952 John Robinson and Don Ultang, *Des Moines Register & Tribune*

1953 William M. Gallagher, *Flint* (Mich.) *Journal*

1954 Mrs. Walter M. Schau, San Anselmo, Cal.

1955 John L. Gaunt, Jr., *Los Angeles Times*

1956 *New York Daily News*

1957 Harry A. Trask, *Boston Traveler*

1958 William C. Beall, *Washington* (D.C.) *Daily News*

1959 William Seaman, *Minneapolis Star*

SPECIAL CITATIONS — JOURNALISM

1951 C. L. Sulzberger, *New York Times*, and Arthur Krock, *New York Times*

1952 Max Kase, *New York Journal-American*

1952 *Kansas City Star*

1953 *New York Times*, Review of the Week

1958 Walter Lippmann, *New York Herald Tribune*

DEATHS

Julius Ochs Adler, 62, general manager of the *New York Times*, publisher of the *Chattanooga Times*, 3 October 1955.

Frederick Lewis Allen, 63, editor in chief, *Harper's* magazine (1941–1953), 13 February 1954.

Bert Andrews, 52, chief Washington correspondent of the *New York Herald Tribune*, Pulitzer Prize winner (1947), 21 August 1953.

Edwin Howard Armstrong, inventor of FM radio, 1 February 1954.

John Balaban, 62, motion picture executive and president of Balaban & Katz Corporation since 1949, 4 April 1957.

Suzan Ball, 22, television actress, 5 August 1955.

Marshal Ballard, 74, editor of the *New Orleans Item* (1906–1947), 24 March 1953.

Meyer Berger, 60, newspaperman, *New York Times* correspondent (1928–1959), 1950 Pulitzer Prize winner, 8 February 1959.

Stephen Bonsal, 86, foreign correspondent, diplomat, author, 1944 Pulitzer Prize winner for *Unfinished Business,* 8 June 1951.

Edna Woolman Chase, 80, editor of *Vogue* magazine (1914–1952), initiated women's fashion shows in the United States, 20 March 1957.

Lou Costello, 52, comedian in motion pictures and television, part of Abbott and Costello comedy team, 3 March 1959.

Russell Wheeler Davenport, 54, former managing editor, *Fortune* magazine, 19 April 1954.

Elmer Davis, 68, news broadcaster and analyst, noted for his opposition to Sen. Joseph McCarthy, 18 May 1958.

Cecil B. De Mille, 77, motion picture pioneer, producer of multimillion-dollar spectacles, including *Greatest Show on Earth, The Ten Commandments, Sampson and Delilah,* 21 January 1959.

George Gard "Buddy" De Sylva, 54, former production head at Paramount Pictures, 11 July 1950.

Olin (Edwin) Downes, 69, music critic for the *New York Times* since 1924, 22 August 1955.

Stephen T. Early, 61, newsman, President Franklin D. Roosevelt's press secretary (1933–1945), 11 August 1951.

John H. Fahey, 77, newspaper publisher (*New York Evening Post, Boston Traveler,* others), 19 November 1950.

Douglas Southall Freeman, 67, historian, newspaper editor, Pulitzer Prize–winning biographer, 13 June 1953.

Frank Ernest Gannett, 81, publisher, founder of several rural newspapers and radio and television stations, 1940 candidate for Republican presidential nomination, 3 December 1957.

Robert Garland, 60, drama critic for the *New York Journal-American* (1943–1951), 27 December 1955.

Edgar A. Guest, 77, English-born writer of inspirational verse syndicated in nearly three hundred American newspapers, 5 August 1959.

Arthur A. Hargrave, 101, reputedly the oldest American newspaper publisher (the *Rockville* (Ind.) *Republican,* since 1888), 13 September 1957.

William Randolph Hearst, 88, newspaper publisher, 14 August 1951.

Don Hollenbeck, 49, radio and television commentator, 22 June 1954.

Louis Isaac Jaffe, editor of the *Norfolk Virginia-Pilot,* 1929 Pulitzer Prize winner for editorial writing, 12 March 1950.

Edwin Leland James, 61, *New York Times* managing editor since 1932, 3 December 1951.

Alva Johnston, 1923 Pulitzer Prize winner for reporting, 23 November 1950.

John Oliver La Gorce, 80, geographer, author and publicist, edited *National Geographic* (1954–1957), served as a member of National Geographic Society for fifty-four years, 23 December 1959.

Jacquin Leonard (Jack) Lait, 71, editor of the *New York Mirror* since 1936, 1 April 1954.

Clark Lee, 49, Associated Press and International News Service correspondent in World War II, 15 February 1953.

Louis B. Mayer, 72, Russian-born movie producer, "starmaker," former vice-president of M-G-M, 29 October 1957.

Anne O'Hare McCormick, 72, *New York Times* staff writer, winner of the 1937 foreign correspondence Pulitzer Prize, 29 May 1954.

Robert Rutherford McCormick, 74, editor and publisher of the *Chicago Tribune* since 1910, 1 April 1955.

John Augustin McNulty, veteran sketchwriter for the *New Yorker,* 29 July 1956.

Eugene Meyer, 83, publicist and financier, former editor of the *Washington Post* (1940–1946) and first president of the International Bank for Reconstruction and Development, 17 July 1959.

Harry Moore, 70, best known for his role as Kingfish on the "Amos 'n Andy" television show, 13 December 1958.

Harry Mountfort, 79, editor of *Vanity Fair,* 4 June 1950.

Fred Little Packer, 1951 Pulitzer Prize–winning cartoonist for the *New York Mirror,* 8 December 1956.

Geoffrey Parsons, former chief editorial writer for the *New York Herald Tribune,* 8 December 1956.

Joseph Pulitzer, 70, editor and publisher of the *St. Louis Post-Dispatch* since 1912, 30 March 1955.

E. Lansing Ray, 71, editor and publisher of the *St. Louis Globe-Democrat,* 30 August 1955.

Harold Wallace Ross, 59, founder/editor of the *New Yorker* magazine, 6 December 1951.

Sid Silverman, 52, publisher of *Variety,* 10 March 1950.

Preston Sturges, 60, motion-picture director and producer, won a 1940 Oscar for writing and directing *The Great McGinty,* 6 August 1959.

Herbert Bayard Swope, 76, reporter and executive director of *The World* (1920–1929), adviser to prominent officials, 20 June 1958.

William O. Taylor, 84, editor and publisher of the *Boston Globe* since 1921, 15 July 1955.

Michael Todd (Avrom Hirsch Goldbogen), 50, theatrical and motion-picture producer *(Around the World in 80 Days),* 22 March 1958.

Arch Ward, 58, *Chicago Tribune* sports editor, 8 July 1955.

Harry M. Warner, 76, Polish-born motion-picture pioneer and cofounder with his two brothers of Warner Bros. film studios, 25 July 1958.

Col. Stanley Washburn, 72, noted war correspondent and soldier, 14 December 1950.

PUBLICATIONS

Robert Lee Bailey, *An Examination of Prime Time Netword Television Special Programs, 1948–1966* (New York: Arno, 1979);

Erik Barnouw, *The Image Empire: A History of Broadcasting in the United States from 1953* (New York: Oxford University Press, 1970);

Bliss, Edward, Jr. *In Search of Light: The Broadcasts of Edward R. Murrow, 1938–1961.* New York: Alfred A. Knopf, 1967.

William Boddy, *Fifties Television: The Industry and Its Critics* (Urbana & Chicago: University of Illinois Press, 1990);

William Y. Elliott, *Television's Impact on American Culture.* (East Lansing: Michigan State University Press, 1956)

Karen Sue Foley, *The Political Blacklist in the Broadcast Industry: The Decade of the 1950's.* (New York: Arno, 1979);

Larry James Gianokos, *Television Drama Series Programming: A Comprehensive Chronicle, 1947–1959* (Metuchen, N.J.: Scarecrow Press, 1980);

Thomas F. Gordon and Mary Ellen Verna, *Mass Communication Effects and Processes: A Comprehensive Bibliography, 1950–1975* (Beverly Hills, Calif.: Sage, 1978);

Ben Gross, *I Looked and I Listened: Informal Recollections of Radio and Television* (New York: Random House, 1954);

Wilson Hicks, *Words and Pictures* (New York: Harper, 1952);

Hilde T. Himmelweit, A. N. Oppenheim, and Pamela Vince, *Television and the Child: An Empirical Study of the Effect of Television on the Young* (London: Oxford University Press, 1958);

Donald H. Kirkley, *A Deceptive Study of the Network Television During the Seasons 1955–56–1962–63* (New York: Arno, 1979);.

Penelope Houston, *The Contemporary Cinema, 1945–1963* (Baltimore: Penguin, 1963);

Houston, *Introduction to the Art of the Movies* (New York: Noonday Press, 1960);

Siegfried Kracauer, *Theory of Film* (New York: Oxford University Press, 1960);

Helen Otis Lamont, ed., *A Diamond of Years: The Best of the "Woman's Home Companion."* (Garden City, N.Y.: Doubleday, 1961);

Robert Larka, *Television's Private Eye: An Examination of Twenty Years of Programming of a Particular Genre, 1949–1969* (New York: Arno, 1979);

Ernest Lindgren, *The Art of the Film* (New York: Macmillan, 1963);

J. Fred MacDonald, *Blacks and White TV: Afro-Americans in Television Since 1948* (Chicago: Nelson Hall, 1979);

Herbert L. Marx, ed. *Television and Radio in American Life* (New York: H. W. Wilson, 1953);

Kenneth McArdle, ed., *A Cavalcade of "Collier's"* (New York: Barnes, 1959);

Frank Luther Mott, *American Journalism: A History, 1690–1960* third edition (New York: Macmillan, 1962);

Everrett C. Parker, David W. Barry, and Dallas W. Smythe. *The Television-Radio Audience and Religion* (New York: Harper Brothers, 1955);

Jeb Perry, *Television and the Teaching of English* (New York: Appleton-Century-Crofts, 1961);

Theodore Peterson, *Magazines in the Twentieth Century* (Urbana: University of Illinois Press, 1964);

Red Channels: The Report of Communist Influence in Radio and Television (N.p., 1950);

Wilbur Schramm, *The Impact of Educational Television* (Urbana: University of Illinois Press, 1960);

Gilbert Seldes, *The Great Audience* (New York: Viking, 1950);

Seldes, *The New Mass Media: Challenge to a Free Society* (Washimgton, D.C.: American Association of University Women, 1962);

Seldes, *The Public Arts* (Mew York: Simon & Schuster, 1956);

Harrison B. Summers, *A Thirty Year History of Programs Carried on National Radio Networks in the United States 1926–1956* (Columbus; Ohio State University Press, 1958);

Richard Thruelson and John Kobler, eds., *Adventures of the Mind* (New York: Knopf, 1959);

C. Robertson Trowbridge, *Magazines in the United States,* third edition (New York: Ronald Press, 1956);

Jack Webb, *The Badge* (Englewood Cliffs, N.J.: Prentice-Hall, 1958);

Helen Woodward, *The Lady Persuaders* (New York: Obolensky, 1960).

Broadcasting, periodical

Editor and Publisher, periodical

Television Age, periodical

TV Guide, periodical

TV News Nagazine, periodical

RCA Television assembly line, 1950

MEDICINE
AND
HEALTH

by RICHARD LAYMAN

CONTENTS

Sidebars and tables are listed in italics.

1950

- A human aorta transplant is performed, the hepititis A virus is isolated and photographed, and penicillin is synthesized.

26 Jan. A new antibiotic, Terramycin, is developed.

7 Mar. Blood tests for tuberculosis are introduced.

14 Apr. Stomach cancers are detected using swallowed radioactive pills.

18 Apr. A patient pronounced dead during surgery is revived through heart massage.

1951

- The nausea-inducing drug antabus is marketed as a cure for alcoholism. Antibiotics are used to stimulate growth in farm animals.

25 July The full-body X-ray machine is developed.

3-7 Sept. A report suggests that some cancers may be caused by viruses.

9 Oct. Leg veins are transplanted to repair faulty arteries.

1952

- A heart-lung machine is developed. The polio rate is at an all-time high: fifty-five thousand people are stricken.

30 Jan. A cardiac-arrest patient is revived by electric shock.

10 Feb. The 190-million-volt deuteron ray combats cancer without breaking the skin.

8 Mar. A mechanical heart keeps a patient alive for eighty minutes.

21 Apr. Holes in a heart wall are repaired surgically.

19 Sept. An artificial heart valve is installed in a human.

13 Nov. An artificial pacemaker is used to regulate heart rhythm.

1953

- A heart-lung machine is perfected. A method for long-term preservation of blood using glycerin is developed. Psychologists suggest that a sleeping person may learn from a tape recording played within earshot.

11 Apr. The Department of Health, Education, and Welfare is created.

5-9 Oct. A human aorta is repaired using animal tissue.

4 Nov. A two-million-volt anticancer X-ray machine is developed.

11 Nov. The polio virus is photographed.

8 Dec. Skin cancer is produced in mice by painting their skins with cigarette tar.

1954

- Full-scale open-heart surgery is introduced.

- Vitamin B-12 deficiency is found to cause pernicious anemia.

- Chlorpromazine, marketed as Thorazine, is approved by the Food and Drug Administration for use as a tranquilizer to suppress flagrant symptoms of disturbed behavior.

23 Feb. Mass trials of Jonas Salk's polio vaccine begin.

1955

- The antiarthritis steroid drug prednisone is introduced.

12 Apr. The success of the Salk polio vaccine is announced; large-scale vaccination ensues in the U.S.

12 May A surgical procedure for victims of cerebral palsy is developed.

24 Sept. President Dwight D. Eisenhower suffers a heart attack.

2 Nov. The first successful kidney transplant is announced.

1956

- The kidney dialysis machine is developed.

15 July The U.S. Food and Drug Administration reports that some cancers may be caused by commonly used coal-tar dyes.

15 Oct. The development of a live-virus orally administered polio vaccine is announced.

9 Oct. A cancer-immunity mechanism in human cells is discovered through research on prison volunteers.

22 Nov. Researchers announce finding no benefit in the use of citrus-fruit extracts high in vitamin C to fight the common cold.

25 Nov. The American Cancer Society announces that cigarette smoking and lung cancer are clearly related.

1957

- The pain-killing drug Darvon is introduced.
- A one-minute blood test for syphilis is introduced.
- Synthetic arteries of rubberized nylon are used as surgical replacements.

9 Mar. Synthetic penicillin is developed.

1958

- The first measles vaccine is tested.
- Ultrasound examination of fetuses is introduced.
- The first catheterization of coronary arteries occurs.

5 June Athletes' use of stimulating drugs to enhance performance is investigated.

3 Oct. A drug is developed to counteract the side effects of penicillin.

29 Oct. A blind woman reports seeing flashes of light after photocells are implanted in the sight centers of her brain.

12 Nov. The U.S. ban on the sale of antibiotics to Communist countries is lifted.

18–20 Nov. The first National Conference on Air Pollution is held.

1959

- A combined vaccine for whooping cough, diptheria, and polio is released.
- A resuscitator small enough to be used on infants is developed.
- Approximately 123 million Americans have health insurance.

25 Nov. The pressure test for glaucoma is developed.

OVERVIEW

The Doctor's Office. A typical doctor's office may not have looked much different to patients of the 1950s than it looked to their parents, but a new generation of physicians was inside providing care. Sick patients received the best treatment that had ever been available, and they complained as they never had before. Using newly available medicines and fresh knowledge based on recent research, doctors were, for the first time, able to cure a variety of maladies that they previously had treated only with kind words and tender care. The doctor had access to more knowledge about the nature of disease than ever before, and he (women doctors were rare in the 1950s) was likely to take a more professional, if less kindly, attitude toward his work than older patients were used to. But the patients missed the attentive personal care they had come to associate with doctors. Many patients found comforting words more attactive than sure cures.

The Family Doctor's Job. After World War II the family doctor's role changed. For many patients he was no longer the sole provider of medical care. In 1954 the president of the American Medical Association referred to the family doctor as "the quarterback of the modern medicine medical team. He must be a health adviser who not only diagnoses and treats, but who calls upon other available medical services and specialists when necessary."

An Office Visit. The average family doctor was a busy man in his late forties. He worked about sixty hours a week and was on call twenty-four hours a day, seven days a week. If you were too ill to come to him, he would most likely agree to come to your home. Only one out of fourteen family doctors refused to make house calls in 1958. Otherwise, you went to the doctor's office between about 9 or 10 A.M. and 4:30 or 5 P.M. On a typical day most doctors treated an average of twenty-six patients in their offices (in addition to those in the hospital, whom the doctor visited before and after office hours). You would expect to wait between one and two hours in the office before seeing the doctor. Your doctor would be likely to work on a first-come, first-served basis, rather than by appointment.

The Patient's View. If you were an average patient in the 1950s, you visited your family doctor five times a

year, and you would grudgingly admit that he earned the three dollars to four dollars he charged for an office visit (though you may have felt differently if you lived in a large city, where the cost was as high as fourteen dollars). You would have grumbled nonetheless about the impersonal quality of the care and would have felt that for as much as he charged, the doctor might have spent more time treating you. It seemed to many patients in the 1950s that their doctors showed insufficient interest in their welfare, asked too few questions, and rushed treatment in an effort to see as many patients as possible.

Cure or Care? Lindsay Beaton, a doctor in Tucson, Arizona, explained the problem in the October 1960 supplement magazine on what was called the crisis in American medicine. If a child came to him with pneumonia, he wrote, the treatment would be four hundred thousand units of penicillin (widely available by the early 1950s) administered by a shot in the rump, and the patient would get well. Before the shot was available, treatment was administered at the child's bedside and consisted of hovering attention from a doctor perceived by anxious parents as being knowing and concerned. Without the shot the patient was sicker longer and faced life-threatening danger. But which family had a better feeling about its doctor? The one that received the personal treatment. The cost of modern medicine that many people found hardest to bear was the loss of the doctor's attention.

The Hospital. If you were sick enough to require hospitalization, as twenty million people a year were by 1957, you would have been exposed to another level of new medical sophistication. X-ray technology progressed rapidly during the decade, beginning with the development of the first full-body X ray in 1951. Complex tests using radioactive materials to identify malignant tumors in cancer patients were developed. Surgery more radical than ever before became routine, and stories of surgeons literally bringing patients whose hearts had stopped beating back to life had become commonplace by the end of the decade.

The Hospital Stay. Your hospital stay would likely have been surprisingly short. Childbirth, which had hospitalized women for up to two weeks in the 1940s, now required only a four-day stay on average. Even major surgery kept patients hospitalized for as little as ten days to two weeks, as doctors came to the view that patients recovered more quickly and more cheaply at home.

Cost and Conditions. Most patients were grateful for their early releases when they received their hospital bills. By the middle of the decade, a semiprivate room cost as much as thirty dollars a day, and in large cities the average per-day cost was nearly fifty dollars. Wards of eight or more patients were still common during the decade, but middle-class patients increasingly expected a semiprivate room. Hospital rooms were very different then. There were no televisions, nor were there phones. In 1952 Bell Telephone announced with great pride the introduction of a new portable pay phone that could be wheeled from bed to bed so that patients could make calls.

The Golden Age. Patients may have complained, but they still accepted without argument the claims of the medical community that in America we had entered the Golden Age of medicine. It seemed during the 1950s that medical science had an unlimited potential to cure disease and to ensure a full and healthful life for every American. The accomplishments of medical researchers in the first half of the twentieth century had been truly remarkable, and now it was time for the common man to enjoy the benefits.

Life Expectancy. A person born in 1950 could expect to live a full twenty years longer than one born in 1900.

DESEGREGATING MEDICAL ASSOCIATIONS IN THE SOUTH

Desegregation of the health-care system in the South began gradually in the late 1940s and early 1950s. Through the work of Arican-American physicians such as Montague Cobb, who taught at the Howard University Medical School and edited the *Journal of the Negro Medical Association* beginning in 1947, the American Medical Association issued a resolution in 1950 requesting segregated state and local medical associations to admit black members. That year the Florida state association desegregated. In 1952 and 1953 state and county associations in South Carolina, Georgia, Arkansas, and Alabama followed, and the other states soon fell into line. Desegregation in the white medical schools of the South was slower. By 1957 only fourteen of the twenty-six southern medical schools admitted blacks.

Source: Edward H. Beardsley, *A History of Neglect: Health Care for Blacks and Mill Workers in the Twentieth-Century South*, (Knoxville: University of Tennessee Press, 1966), pp. 245–254.

The so-called white plague of tuberculosis that afflicted the nation in the late nineteenth century was beginning to seem controllable in 1950. The most feared viral disease of the time was polio, and people assured themselves early in the decade that it was only a matter of time and money before it, too, was brought under control. They were right.

Miraculous Medicine. Heart disease, cancer, venereal disease, madness, and tooth decay were all the subjects of intensive research during the decade, and clear progress was made in treating them successfully. Surgeons lifted defective hearts from people's bodies and made repairs; they reattached severed limbs; researchers identified environmental and behavioral causes of many types of cancer; physicians slowed the alarming spread of syphilis and gonorrhea; scientists discovered drugs that controlled mental ilness; and public-health officials began fluoridating water, thus diminishing for future generations the fear and pain associated with a visit to the dentist.

Social Conscience. During the 1950s many Americans criticized the medical community for its faulty social consciousness. The cures people read about in their daily newspapers were often unavailable at the local doctor's office, especially in rural areas and poor neighborhoods, which frequently had no physician service. Critics charged that physicians failed to serve the poor with the same energy and expertise reserved for privileged patients. Medical practitioners were accused of racial discrimination and of denying women professional opportunity and respect. In 1955 less than 5 percent of all medical students were women, and less than 3 percent were black.

A New Focus. More so than at any time in the past, the public took an interest in health issues and demanded information about the care being delivered by physicians. A cabinet-level Department of Health, Education, and Welfare was established to guarantee governmental attention to the nation's health-care needs, and a presidential commission demanded that American physicians and medical researchers realign their priorities to focus on direct patient care rather than laboratory experiments. It was undeniably the golden age of American medicine. What took many people by surprise was the fact that with increased knowledge and skill came increased responsibilities and demands.

Sources:

"Doctors' Pay," *Time* (30 July 1951): 70;

"How Good Is Your Family Doctor?," *Atlantic Monthly*, 186 (August 1950): 43-47;

"Portrait of the Physician," *Science Digest* (December 1958): 68.

TOPICS IN THE NEWS

ASIAN FLU

Fearing a repeat of the 1918 worldwide flu epidemic that killed more people than military action during World War I, Americans anxiously braced themselves for an onslaught of the Asian flu in 1957. This mutant, vaccine resistant form of Type-A influenza, the most threatening of the flu viruses, began appearing in northern China early in the year and threatened to be the deadliest epidemic of the century. It was estimated that a wave of Asian flu could spread from coast to coast in a month and that as many as twenty-six million Americans might fall ill as a result.

Preparations. The World Health Organization identified the epidemic in Asia early in the year and alerted national health agencies to prepare for the worst. Before the virus made its way to America, the word had been spread to the public about its virulent potential, and medical researchers had begun to search for an effective vaccine. At a meeting called by the U.S. surgeon general, 130 members of the Association of State and Territorial Health Officers of the United States were advised to provide weekly "flu-situation bulletins" to the Public Health Service. Drug companies were mobilized for emergency preparation of a flu vaccine.

Vaccine Production. A flu vaccine was not approved until July 1957. It was tested on fifty-five volunteers at the Maryland State Correctional Institute in Patuxent and found to be 70 percent effective. At first it was feared that there would be time to produce only enough vaccine for the military serving abroad and perhaps for medical personnel, but the six drug companies chosen to manufacture the serum worked overtime. By mid September there were eight million doses available, one-third more than had been forecast, and it was estimated that by the end of the year there would be eighty-five million doses, enough to vaccinate half of the U.S. population. The vaccination required two shots to the arm, two weeks apart, each consisting of one-tenth of a cubic centimeter of vaccine. The cost was one dollar per shot, plus doctor's fees. Many people reported a mild case of the flu—fever and achiness—after taking their shots, but they were assured that the real Asian flu was much worse.

The Attack. In June 1957 Asian flu invaded America, carried by intercontinental travelers to San Francisco. By September there were thirty thousand cases reported. But by then many people in the most vulnerable occupations—hospital workers, for example—had been vaccinated. As a result of the diligent work of the medical community, the effects of the Asian flu in America were, for the most part, restricted to aches and pains. Even though one-fifth of the one hundred million respiratory infections suffered by Americans in the winter of 1957–1958 were attributed to the Asian flu, the substantial death toll that had been anticipated was avoided.

Source:
"Asian Flu: The Outlook" *Time*, 70 (12 August 1957): 74.

THE BUSINESS OF HEALTH CARE

How Much is Good Health Worth? The cliché that you cannot put a price on good health was vigorously challenged in the 1950s. People's astonishment at the accomplishments of medical science turned into shock when they found out the cost. Billions of dollars were spent on health care during the 1950s, and it was not enough. There were still sick people and dreaded diseases. There was also optimism that a disease-free society was within reach, if only Americans could afford it.

The Government and Health Care. The government became a major force in the medical field after World

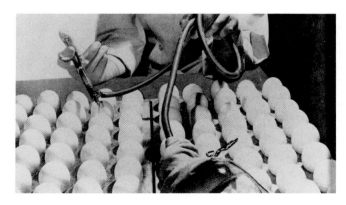

Technician injecting eggs with the Asian flu virus, part of the process of manufacturing the vaccine

As television advertising reached more homes in the 1950s, the medical community grew concerned about the promises drug manufacturers made for the effectiveness of their products. After several years of wrangling, in 1953 the American Medical Association and the National Association of Radio and TV Broadcasters established a code which prohibited actors from playing doctors without being identified as actors; overly free use of words such as "safe" or "harmless"; and "advertising material which describes or dramatizes distress."

Advertisers, however, continued to test the limits, and in 1956 the Federal Trade Commission announced that it would begin monitoring all radio and television commercials for "false or misleading" information.

Some of the more dubious claims made by broadcasters during the 1950s:

"Infra-Rub speeds up the flow of fresh, rich blood, thus helps drive away pain-causing pressure";

"This doctor's discovery is called Sustamin 2–12. Doctors of three leading hospitals personally witnessed amazing results. They saw agonizing, crippling pains relieved day and night"; and

"Javitol contains 85% choice coffee blends, combined with a vegetable extract that lets you literally drink that extra weight right off your body. Can you imagine?"

Source: "The Great Medicine Show," *Time* (22 October 1956): 87–88.

War II. Both Presidents Harry S Truman and Dwight D. Eisenhower were outspoken supporters of federally sponsored medical research. Under their administrations the National Institutes of Health, which became the umbrella agency for federally sponsored research projects, flourished. Its support for medical science grew from $180,000 in 1945 to $100 million in 1956, which was still a modest sum relative to total health costs. In 1954 various public-health agencies were consolidated into the Department of Health, Education, and Welfare (which grew large enough to be split into the Department of

Education and the Department of Health and Human Services in 1979). Public health has commanded a significant share of the national budget ever since. But that was just the beginning. Most health costs were finally passed on more directly to the people.

The Threat of Socialized Medicine. In 1950 total health-care costs in America were $8.4 billion. By the end of the decade, they had soared to $17.2 billion — $115 for every man, woman, and child in the country — and President Eisenhower (who was elected in 1952) had warned that socialized medicine would result if the problem were not solved. During the early years of the cold war, when socialism was identified with communism, that threat was dire enough to mobilize those who passionately believed in the private medical-care system. They argued that to take the profit out of medicine would remove the incentive for physicians and researchers to continue their good work. But they had to contend with those who could show that between 1950 and 1957 medical care costs rose 250 percent more than food costs, 160 percent more than housing costs, and more than 175 percent more than the total cost of living.

Who Paid and How Much. In 1959 the average family earned just over $6,600 and had medical expenses of $394, or about 6 percent of their income. At the same time, the average doctor made $16,000 and the average surgeon earned about $25,000 per year. Between 1950 and 1960 the average cost of a hospital room more than doubled to over $30, and the average cost of a day of care in the hospital was nearly $200. To Americans in poor health, the fact that there were some five hundred medicinal substances being distributed by pharmacists in over twenty thousand forms in 1959 was of little consolation.

Chest X ray, 1954

George Papanicolaou

Most of them cost too much, and some of them did not work anyway. In 1958 Americans spent $344 million on antibiotics that did not exist a decade earlier and that were often prescribed for the wrong illness by overextended physicians who used prescription medicines as easy cures.

The Insurance Industry. Health insurance promised to insulate people from the risk of financial ruin due to runaway medical costs through what amounted to an easy-pay system for health care. While large businesses provided health insurance to employees, it was not free. The cost of health services determined the cost of insurance, and insured employees' salaries were reduced accordingly. In 1950 about half of all Americans were covered by health insurance; by 1959, 71 percent were covered. That still left about fifty million people uninsured at the end of the decade and a booming insurance industry standing ready to serve them when they could scrape together the premiums. Physicians rebelled against the paperwork insurance companies required before they would pay. Busy practices had to hire employees to do nothing but file insurance forms, which were not standardized. The Health Insurance Council conducted a survey in 1957 that found forty-six different forms were required from physicians by as many insurance companies to report treatment performed on insured patients. Many physicians responded by charging an insurance-filing fee, usually three dollars.

Sources:
"The Crisis in American Medicine," *Harper's,* special October 1960;

O. D. Dickerson, *Health Insurance* (Homewood, Ill.: Richard D. Irwin, 1959).

The Most Dreaded Disease. For Americans in the 1950s, there was no diagnosis of illness more feared than cancer. Heart disease killed twice as many people annually, but it did not cause the pain or fear of malignant tumors. In 1958 *Science Digest* reported that there were 450,000 new cases of cancer diagnosed each year and that at any one time about seven hundred thousand cases of cancer were being treated in America. In 1958, according to *Patterns of Disease,* a publication by Parke, Davis, one woman in four under the age of thirty-five could expect to get cancer, and one in seven would die from it; one man in five under the age of fifty would be afflicted, and one in eight would die.

Focusing Attention. At the beginning of the 1950s some physicians considered cancer to be incurable, and many hospitals considered it their duty to guard their cancer patients from intrusions by researchers. Two groups changed that attitude and focused health attention during the decade on cancer. The American Cancer Society devoted enormous energy to the fight against the disease. Its high-visibility fund-raising campaign heightened public optimism that cancer was curable, concentrated the attention of the public on early detection, and provided much-needed money for research.

The Government Response. The government, through the National Cancer Institute, made a commitment to eradicate the disease as well. In 1953 a cancer research hospital was opened at the National Institutes of Health Complex in Bethesda, Maryland. That same year the National Institutes of Health, acting on the instructions of Congress, began a concentrated effort to find a cure for leukemia, a malignancy of blood cells that often strikes children. With the active lobbying support of the private American Cancer Society, the National Cancer Institute budget rose from $4 million in 1947 to $110 million in 1959.

Cancer Detection. On 1 January 1950 there were 134 special cancer-detection centers in the United States, approved by the American College of Surgeons (ACS), where a person could go for inexpensive cancer screening. The initial screening fee was ten dollars for tests that would cost twenty-five dollars to one hundred dollars in a doctor's office. (By the mid 1950s the screening fee had gone up in some centers to twenty dollars.) Initial screening consisted of a series of tests, sometimes with unpronounceable names—cytological smears, tests in which body fluids or cast-off cells are examined under a microscope to search for cancerous or precancerous cell formations; sigmoidoscopies, in which the colon is inspected for abnormalities; chest X-rays to search for growths; and breast examinations, especially for women. Everyone over the age of thirty-five was advised to undergo cancer screening once a year.

Cancer and Women. By 1952 women were advised to visit a gynecologist, rather than a family doctor, for a properly administered Pap smear (a cytological test named for George Papanicolaou to identify cervical cancer). The American Cancer Society prepared a film, distributed at no cost to women's groups, to demonstrate how women could examine their own breasts for suspicious lumps, which the ACS advised be done monthly.

The Cost of Cancer. In addition to its emotional cost, a diagnosis of cancer indicated the need for very expensive treatment and usually prolonged hospitalization. By 1958 cancer patients paid $300 million annually in hospital bills, and, according to the National Cancer Institute, the disease was calculated to cost the nation over $12 billion a year, including direct costs of treatment and lost productivity of workers. There were basically three types of cure: surgery, in which the malignancy was cut out; radiotherapy, in which the malignant cell growths were subjected to radiation in an attempt to kill them; and the newest treatment, chemotherapy, in which a medicine was taken to attack the malignancy.

Surgery. The most common response to cancer in the 1950s was surgical removal, but it was an expensive, imperfect cure that often debilitated patients. The surgical cure for cancer of the larynx, for example, left victims without a voice and able to communicate only by training that taught them to gulp air and belch it out to form a sound. Statistics showed in 1958 that most cancers grew for two to three years before symptoms appeared and that most people waited six months to a year before seeing a doctor when they detected symptoms. By then it was

often too late for surgery. Even when surgery was performed, there was always the question of whether all of the cancerous cells were removed. If some were missed, a recurrence could be expected.

Preventive Surgery. Cancer surgery in the 1950s was not limited to patients who had been diagnosed as having malignancies. Many surgeons in the 1950s advocated the

---

WHAT IS CANCER?

Cancer is a very general word used to indicate many malignant diseases that may have only the vaguest relationship. Generally a cancer is an invasive group of cells that grow uncontrollably. Eventually cancer cells may spread into the territory of healthy cells critical to the operation of the body and kill or disable them. Cancers strike in many different ways; they react differently to medical treatment; and they have different growth patterns. They tend to have one grim characteristic in common, though: they usually kill. Taken together cancers have long been the second most common cause of death in America after heart disease. In 1950, 204,000 people died of cancer, accounting for about 14 percent of all deaths in the country.

CANCER QUACKS

In his book *The Truth about Cancer* (Prentice-Hall, 1956) Dr. Charles Cameron identified three types of cancer quacks: the dumb quack, "who knowing nothing at all about cancer, yet believes that it will yield to the secret formula which he alone possesses"; the deluded quack, who may be educated and is sometimes even a doctor, "but his knowledge of cancer is scanty, and his understanding of research methods is strictly limited"; and the dishonest quack, "far and away the commonest type. . . . He is in the business of treating cancer for one reason only — to make a killing, which he often does, both ways."

Among the quack cures are pastes or poultices to "draw the cancer out," secret potions that destroy the cancer, and eccentric diets to starve the cancer. One quack recommended a poultice of red cabbage to entice the cancer to the surface of the skin and a diet of the same red cabbage, ostensibly to push

from the inside. One secret medicine was found to include water, vinegar, fly specks, and insect wings; another called "glyoxylide" omitted the extras — it was simply water. Quack diets included the grape-diet cure, in which the patient choked down grapes all day long; a diet of lettuce, liver, fruit juice, and vitamins to the exclusion of meat, eggs, and what Dr. Cameron calls "other staples of balanced fare." One quack raided by the Food and Drug Administration used a machine that consisted of "a senseless jumble of wires" to cure the cancer.

The tragedy, of course, is that the quacks kept patients from real doctors who could treat them as effectively as modern medicine knew how. The quacks took extorted money from terminally ill people and in return denied them whatever hope the golden age of medicine had to offer. For a portrait of the most celebrated of the cancer quacks, see the entry in this chapter on Harry Hoxsey.

---

preventive removal of women's reproductive organs after they had passed childbearing age, because the incidence of uterine and cervical cancer increased for them, but some doctors found that practice unethical, even if it was widespread. In 1953 the American Medical Association *Journal* estimated that as many as two-thirds of all hysterectomies (the surgical removal of a woman's uterus) were unnecessary.

Radiotherapy. Radiation kills cells and can be focused on a selected spot that may be unreachable by surgery without damaging vital organs. Radiotherapy was still being developed during the 1950s, but it was widely used nonetheless to attack malignant tumors. One system of exposing tumors to radiation was to implant radioactive seeds in the cancerous mass. The seed would kill the tumor in time.

Rays. The most common form of radiotherapy was administered by huge machines such as the two-million-volt X-ray machine developed by Massachusetts Institute of Technology scientists for use beginning in 1953 by cancer specialists at Massachusetts General Hospital in Boston, the 450-million volt synchrocyclotron at the Argonne Cancer Research Hospital in Chicago, and the powerful cobalt-ray machine that could produce as much energy as a $100 million chunk of radium. These machines consisted largely of imposing tubes, sheathed in lead to prevent radiation from escaping, that projected radioactive rays to a designated focal point. Often the patient sat on a turntable so that the rays concentrated on some internal spot in the body

could pass through outer tissues in diminished concentrations.

Chemotherapy. Not yet fully developed during the 1950s, chemotherapy nonetheless seemed to many spe-

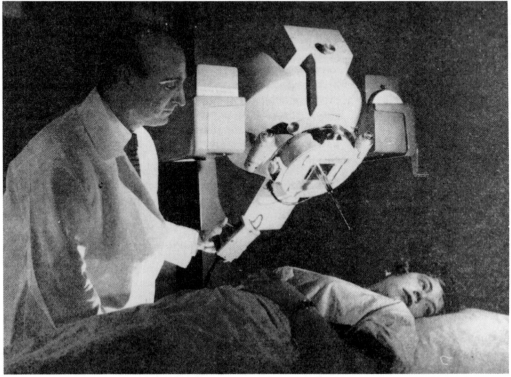

Co-60 cobalt ray machine, 1958, used in cancer therapy

PHOTO CREDIT

cialists the most promising of the available cancer treatments. At multimillion-dollar labs, such as Dr. Selman Waksman's $2.5 million Microbiology Research Center at Rutgers University in New Brunswick, New Jersey, researchers tried thousands of chemical compounds each year in the attempt to find one that would effecively cure cancer. In 1959 Dr. John R. Heller of the National Cancer Institute reported that researchers were screening compounds at the rate of forty thousand a year and had found seventy-two compounds that were promising enough to merit further testing. The trouble was that there were so many different cancers. In 1959 seventeen separate types of viruses were known to cause different types of cancer in animals, and one virus, polyoma, caused twenty-six types of cancer all by itself. At the same time, one type of virus seemed to attack cancers, and some thought was given to infecting people with a flu virus to protect them from cancer.

Cancer and the Environment. During the 1950s many people tried to dismiss the overwhelming evidence suggesting environmental causes of cancer, because the implications were so intimidating. To avoid apparent risks of cancer, people faced the prospect of changing dramatically the way they lived and of harnessing the progress and prosperity of the nation's biggest industries. Some scientists went so far as to say that cancer was the price of a middle-class American lifestyle. Tearing down the nation's industrial smokestacks and cleaning up the exhaust emissions of the seventy million registered motor vehicles in the country (as of 1959) was too radical for most Americans. People in the 1950s were not so frightened by the risk of cancer that they would radically alter their way of life to avoid it.

Cancer and Smoking. The most debated cause of cancer in the 1950s was tobacco. Researchers were able to show in 1954 that mice painted with tobacco tars developed skin cancer, and they noted that human victims of malignancies in the respiratory system were very often smokers. But the news that there is a link between smoking and cancer was not received kindly by a nation that produced over a half trillion cigarettes at the end of the decade. Smokers did not want to believe it, and manufacturers were outraged. In 1954 the American cigarette companies formed the Tobacco Industry Research Council, a high-budget, public relations organization that defended the industry against criticism from health-conscious scientists.

Results. In 1956 there were, by one report, over nine thousand original scholarly articles on cancer, and hundreds of meetings were held each year in the late 1950s to discuss the disease. The results were encouraging, but hardly as dramatic as the polio researchers could claim. By the end of the 1950s cancer specialists were beginning to understand some of the causes of malignancy, but prevention was a difficult issue. Treatment by radiotherapy and chemotherapy supplemented radical surgery, which itself became more advanced. In 1950 alone 2,500

THE ATOMIC HOSPITAL

The Argonne Cancer Research Hospital at the University of Chicago opened in March 1953. It was designed to conduct research in the use of radiation to treat cancer. The eight-floor hospital, which cost $4.2 million to build, was underwritten by the Atomic Energy Commission, which also provided $1 million a year for operating costs.

Among the cancer-fighting equipment in the hospital were a 450-million-volt synchrocyclotron; a 50-million-volt linear accelerator; the most powerful cobalt-ray emitter known; a two-million volt Van de Graaf generator; and a 250,000-volt X-ray machine. To protect against unwanted radiation, the two floors of patient rooms had eight-inch concrete walls and the floors were covered with an easily cleanable plastic. The Atomic Energy Commission specified that the hospital's facilities be available to the nearby Argonne National Laboratory, which conducted experiments in atomic energy, as well as many other research institutions.

chemicals were tested as cancer cures, and 124 of them were thought to show promise. By 1960 one patient in three was said to have been cured by surgically removing the cancerous tumor. Nonetheless, cancer was not eradicated during the 1950s, nor even close. The failure to make more headway after such a concentration of effort costing so much money was disappointing to some. But even if researchers could not cure cancer in 1959, they could sometimes treat it. Eight hundred thousand patients who had been diagnosed with cancer were alive in 1959 who would arguably not have survived the decade without the treatment modern medicine offered. Most important, these patients and their families were offered genuine hope of more effective treatment for the next generation.

Sources:

Walter C. Alvarez, "The Search for a Cure for Cancer," *Good Housekeeping,* 146 (April 1958): 92, 248–251;

Charles S. Cameron, "Cancer Quacks Can Kill You," *Science Digest,* 40 (October 1956): 26–30;

"Cancer: New Methods—and Drugs—Hold High Hope," *Newsweek,* 43 (17 May 1954): 58, 60–61.

THE COMMON COLD

False Promises of a Cure. Colds are caused by a variety of different viruses. To vaccinate a person against a cold or to cure one would require a defense against each of the possible viral culprits, an unlikely possibility. That did not stop drug companies advertising cold medications, usually consisting of antihistamines to control nasal stuffiness, from claiming they could cure or prevent colds. In March 1950 the Federal Trade Commission charged the makers of the popular medicines Resistabs, Inhiston, Kripton, and Anahist with false advertising for their exaggerated claims of effectiveness against colds. Later in the year, another federal agency showed that antihistamines are about as successful against colds as plain sugar.

A Cold Vaccine. In 1959 there was a stir of interest when Dr. Victor Haas, director of the National Institute of Allergy and Infectious Diseases, announced that a vaccine seemed imminent that would prevent at least half all of respiratory illnesses, including common colds. The breakthrough came with the identification of adenoviruses (viruses originating in the adenoids that cause respiratory illnesses), which do not cause colds. A vaccine was tested succesfully by the U.S. Navy, but it prevented only one type of cold and was soon dismissed as more trouble than it was worth. Cold sufferers during the fifties may have taken some comfort from the hope of an imminent cure, but true relief from the misery of the common cold proved elusive.

Source:
"Latest on Allergies . . . Colds . . . Heart Disease," *U.S. News and World Report,* 49 (12 December 1960): 74, 76.

GERMS

Public Awareness of Germs. If the health concerns of the average American during the 1950s had to be reduced to a single word, it would probably be germs, or disease-

---

THE ROOT OF ALL EVIL

Dr. Jonas Salk suggests that weak backs, abdominal-muscle weakness, high blood pressure and stomach ulcers may be traced to the accumulated effects of minor damage done to our brain cells and spinal nerves by the long series of virus infections we have as children.

Source: Greer Williams, "The Era of New Viruses," *Saturday Evening Post,* 16 (October 1959): 100.

---

causing microorganisms. Then as now, few people knew much about germs except that they were sometimes passed from one person to another and that they can cause many types of misery, including colds, flu, measles, mumps, herpes, syphilis and gonorrhea, tuberculosis, polio, and even, according to some researchers of the day, cancer. The public concern about germs was not to know more about how they lived but to know more about how to kill them, and thus the new miracle germ poisons—especially streptomycin, Terramycin, and synthetic penicillin—seemed to herald a disease-free society.

What are Germs? The two most feared germs are bacteria and viruses. During the 1950s microbiologists made advances in the understanding and control of these tiny enemies. But not all viruses and bacteria are harmful; on the contrary, many forms pose no threat to humans. In fact, the body depends on good bacteria to function properly.

Differences. The important difference between bacteria and viruses for the nonscientist is that while bacteria can be killed, viruses can sometimes only be disabled. Though bacteria are larger than viruses, both are invisible except through microscopes. One gram (one-twenty eighth of an ounce) of dirt contains about one hundred million bacteria, and a million viruses can fit onto the head of a pin. Both cause disease by invading cells and either killing them or disrupting their processes. Bacteria reproduce quickly, especially under unsanitary conditions. Viruses are mysterious parasites that are only half alive outside a living cell. Only after they invade a cell and use cell materials can they reproduce, but then they multiply furiously. Some scientists believe that viruses outnumber any other life form on earth.

History. Bacteria, of which there are in many types, were identified in the seventeenth century; viruses were unknown before the 1890s. In 1947 sixty viruses were thought to contribute to human disease; by 1959 seventy-six new viruses had been identified. Bacteria can be viewed through simple microscopes, but it was not until the development of the electron microscope in the 1930s and 1940s that scientists first saw viruses. In the 1950s the viruses that cause polio and measles, for example, were actually viewed for the first time. It is hard to fight

---

HOW TO CURE A COLD

In 1956 *Consumer Reports* surveyed cold remedies and reported on their usefulness:

Nose Drops and Inhalers—short-term relief only, and excessive use is habit-forming;

Cold Vaccines—of no value;

Pills—Usually a mixture of laxatives and analgesics, sometimes with antihistamines; of no greater value than aspirin, which relieves aches temporarily;

Antihistamines—Useless and potentially dangerous;

Sulfa Drugs and Antibiotics—over-the-counter medications of no value and may be harmful; prescription medications may prevent complications;

Alkalizers, Vitamins, Laxatives—of no value;

Lemon Drinks—of no value;

Ultraviolet Light and Diathermy (localized applications of heat, as with heating pads)—of no value;

Special Diets—of no value;

The most effective remedy of all?

Rest in Bed—it prevents complications and avoids infecting others.

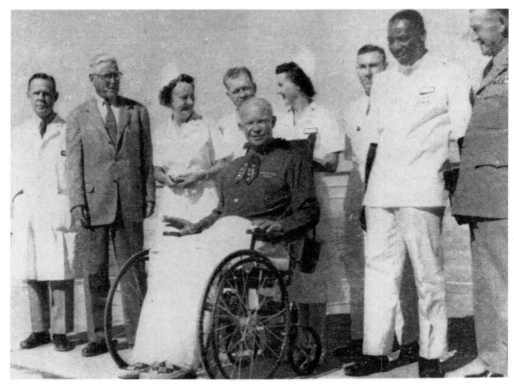

President Eisenhower in Denver after his 1955 heart attack

an enemy that cannot be seen, and now that viruses were increasingly visible, the dimensions of their destructive powers slowly became known. So did the difficulty of disarming them.

Germ Control. When disease hits, there are two ways to attack it. Doctors can treat the symptoms, or they can try to eliminate its cause. Good physicians do both. They treat symptoms to make patients feel better, and they eliminate causes to make sure that healthy people stay that way. The 1950s were a time of trying to eliminate disease, and, in the case of bacterial disease, that means killing the harmful germ—or at least making it harmless. To control a germ, you have to know what it is, how it lives, how it reproduces, how it makes people sick. That is what researchers in the 1950s concentrated on with dramatic success. Not only were they able to view isolated viruses for the first time, they learned enough about their structure to manufacture viruses from available materials in their laboratories.

Pills, Shots, and Disinfectants. There are three basic defenses against germs: avoidance, antibiotics, and vaccinations. Public-health departments had been preaching avoidance for about eighty years by the middle of the twentieth century, and their efforts had proven successful, especially against diseases such as typhus that are spread directly as a result of poor sanitation.

Antibiotics. But while cleanliness may be a virtue, it does not necessarily prevent the spread of disease. Many Americans in the 1950s thought the ultimate remedy for illness lay in pills and shots, particularly the miracle-working medicinal microbe killers called antibiotics. Penicillin, the antibiotic fungus Alexander Fleming discovered in 1928, was artificially produced for the first time in 1950. The result was that during the decade penicillin became widely available for use against bacterial infections of wounds, venereal disease, and a host of other infectious diseases. Other antibiotics with familiar names were either developed during the 1950s — streptomycin, for example—or discovered during the decade. Aureomycin was effective against Rocky Mountain spotted fever, typhus, streptoccocal pneumonia, and whooping cough. Neomycin was introduced to combat tuberculosis.

Vaccines. But as effective as antibiotics were against bacteria, they were powerless against viruses. In a series of dramatic developments during the 1950s scientists developed vaccines that provided protection against the most feared viruses. Vaccination is the process of introducing a dead or impotent live virus into the body, usually by means of a shot, to encourage the body's cells to manufacture antibodies, or defenses, against that virus. When a vaccinated person is exposed to a full-strength virus, the body has the ammunition to fight it. The trouble is that infectious viruses come in many different types, and each requires its own vaccination. Some bacteria can be controlled by vaccines as well. Successful vaccinations in the 1950s were developed against such diseases as polio, measles, and measles and rubella together (released

Heart-lung machine, 1953

in 1963). An improved method of vaccination against flu was also developed.

Summary. Medical scientists laid a solid foundation of research and technological advances during the 1950s that succeeding generations would build on. It was difficult for people without scientific training to understand the importance of the work being done by specialists and to foresee the benefits that would result, yet Americans supported unprecedented federal expenditures on health care and research and generously supported such charities as the American Heart Fund and the March of Dimes. The results were dramatic. Some of the medicines they developed are used today, and the vaccines protect us still.

Sources:
Frank Macfarlane Burnet, *Viruses and Man* (London & Baltimore: Penguin, 1953);
William Greer, *Virus Hunters* (New York: Knopf, 1959).

HEART DISEASE

The Deadliest Disease. Half of all American deaths were caused by cardiovascular disease in the 1950s. Though that statistic has not changed significantly in recent decades, it seemed during the first half of the century that every year there were more people complaining of heart ailments and more people dying from them. In fact, the increase was probably a result of better diagnosis. Doctors knew far more about the heart in 1950 than they did in 1900. Like the other major diseases, heart disease attracted unprecedented attention from medical researchers during the 1950s. When President Eisenhower was struck by a heart attack in 1955, the nation's attention was focused sharply.

Experimentation and Discovery. An American reading a newspaper in the early 1950s could only have shaken his head incredulously at the fantastic news about the work of cardiologists and heart surgeons. In Philadelphia an eleven-year-old girl was put in a freezer, like the ones people had in their kitchens, to lower her body temperature to eighty-eight degrees so doctors could stop her blood flow for five minutes while they closed a hole in the wall of her heart. In Washington, D.C., surgeons implanted an artificial, mechanical valve similar to a plumbing device in the rheumatic heart of a thirty-year-old woman, restoring her to health.

Animal Experimentation. At New York University a flap of skin from the chest wall of a dog was sewn to the surface of his heart so that the blood supply from the skin flap could revitalize a heart crippled by blocked coronary arteries. In Chicago a healthy heart transplanted from one dog to another continued to beat for forty-eight minutes, suggesting to surgeons that they could use animal hearts to keep humans alive during extensive surgery. The reporter in the January 1953 *Science Digest* explained, "Since no human heart could obviously be transplanted, the thought is to use the heart of a monkey together with the animal's lungs so that pumping and breathing would be taken over."

The Talcum-Powder Cure. In 1950 *Time* reported the case of Abell H. Bernstein, a businessman with coronary artery disease who claimed to have been cured by surgeons who cut open his heart sac, dumped in two drams of talcum powder, and sewed him back up. The powder irritated the heart and stimulated blood flow. It was sometimes hard to tell the real accomplishments of medical pioneers from science fiction. Procedures that were unthinkable before World War II became routine.

Heart Surgery. Heart surgery was introduced in the nineteenth century, but it did not become fully practical until the 1950s. By the end of the decade, open-heart surgery was commonly performed, and the University of Minnesota reported that only about 2.5 percent of the patients died as a result of the surgery. The rate had been 40 percent a few years earlier. Two innovations made the difference. Most important was the heart-lung machine, introduced in 1953, which took over the function of the heart during surgery (see Gibbon entry). This device allowed surgeons to replace heart valves and to perform other delicate procedures that required stopping the heart from beating.

Cardiac Shock. The other important innovation was the use of electrical shock to control heartbeats. Shocks could provide the stimulus to cause hearts beating out of

control to beat regularly, and they could revive lifeless hearts. In 1952 a patient who died during surgery was brought back to life by electrical shocks to her heart. By the end of the decade, this procedure was commonly used.

Pacemakers. Many heart disorders disrupt the heart's rhythm. The development of the electric pacemaker in 1952 provided a new method of treating these patients. But they had to stay near an electric outlet until the battery-operated pacemaker evolved. Initially it was about twice the size of a pack of cigarettes. Surgeons placed it just under the skin and connected it to the heart by electrical leads. The device emitted controlled electric shocks to stimulate a regular heartbeat. Batteries had to be changed periodically, but that required only minor surgery. By the end of the decade pacemakers were routinely implanted.

Heart Attacks. The heart attack was first diagnosed by a Chicago doctor in 1910 — after the patient died. That outcome was common for heart patients in succeeding decades, but in the 1950s diagnosis was surer, and effective treatment became available. Research was coordinated by the National Heart Institute of the National Institutes of Health, established in Bethesda, Maryland, in 1948. Cardiopulmonary resuscitation (CPR), was developed in 1950 and by the end of the decade was being used in conjunction with mouth-to-mouth resuscitation as a lifesaving technique to keep a heart attack victim alive until he could be hospitalized.

Prevention. Less dramatic than the innovations of the surgeons, but no less important, was research into the effects of hypertension and cholesterol levels in the blood on heart disease. The basics of the roles these factors play in hardening of the arteries were finally established by the end of the decade and determined a new era of well-patient advice.

Diet. Doctors routinely advised their patients to avoid too much salt, which causes hypertension in many people, and they prescribed newly available medicines to their otherwise healthy hypertensive patients to keep

WHAT IS HEART DISEASE?

Cardiovascular disease comprises disorders of the heart and blood vessels; it includes strokes. The disorders are varied. In 1950 the National Heart Institute considered the term heart disease to include over twenty cardiovascular maladies, and it concentrated its efforts on the three types of heart disease that caused 90 percent of the deaths—rheumatic heart, hypertension or high blood pressure, and atherosclerosis, also called hardening of the arteries. Sometimes heart disease is inherited or caused by another illness, such as rheumatic fever; other times it is caused by lifestyle, particularly poor habits regarding diet, stress, exercise, and weight control. During the 1950s researchers pointed out that smoking contributes significantly to the risk of cardiovascular disease.

A major category of cardiovascular diseases includes those that stem from the inability of vessels to deliver blood to parts of the body. When the defective vessels are in the heart, the result is a heart attack, or a myocardial infarction. When the defective vessel is in the brain or neck, the result is a stroke. Sometimes the heart itself is defective, with holes in the walls of one or more of its four chambers or defective valves in the paths between chambers. All of these disorders became more treatable during the 1950s.

them from developing heart disease. High-fat diets were identified as unhealthy, and while much of the population was not yet ready to heed doctors' advice about avoiding saturated fats and controlling weight, the danger was clear to specialists.

Sources:

P. E. Baldry, *The Battle Against Heart Disease* (Cambridge: Cambridge University Press, 1971);

Milton B. Plotz, *Coronary Heart Disease* (New York: Hoeber-Harper, 1957);

Paul Dudley White, *Heart Disease* (New York: Macmillan, 1951).

THE BENNY HOOPER INCIDENT

Boy Falls in Well. For twenty-four hours in May 1957, seven-year-old Benny Hooper was a national celebrity. He fell into a twenty-one-foot-deep, ten-inch-wide well being dug for irrigation by his father, and he was trapped. Manorville, the Long Island, New York, community where he lived rallied to his support, along with the East Coast news establishment, as construction workers, firemen, policemen, and a physician worked feverishly over a daylong period to save Benny's life. The drama was covered by over one hundred news reporters and over forty television and radio broadcasters. Both the *New York Times* and the *New York Daily News* used airplanes to get the pictures they needed. Nineteen and a half hours into the ordeal, Dr. Joseph H. Kris, attending physician, admitted that there was little hope. But he was

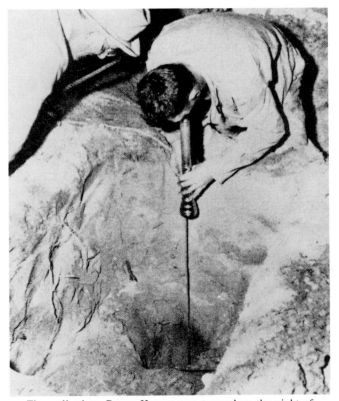

The well where Benny Hooper was trapped on the night of 17 May 1957

wrong. Five hours later a construction worker lifted Benny out of the well. Billy Graham, who was conducting a crusade in Manhattan, sent the boy a Bible telling him that prayers had saved him. Dr. Kris said Benny was saved by oxygen and continued to see the boy in the hospital during treatment for a respiratory infection.

Doctor Bills Hooper Family. When Benny was out of danger, Dr. Kris billed the Hoopers fifteen hundred dollars for his services. People were furious. When questioned, Dr. Kris claimed to have submitted a very conservative bill only after he read about donations the family received to help pay for Benny's rescue. But his protests only served to make people angrier at what was perceived as an outrageous example of the greed and lack of compassion that many Americans thought characterized the medical profession. Benny's father made sixty-two dollars a week driving a truck for the city highway department; his mother made forty-three dollars a week as a telephone operator. The family claimed that the donations came to less than five hundred dollars and that they could only pay the bill by dipping into their modest savings set aside for Benny's education. Moreover, they worried publicly about what they would do if other volunteer workers who assisted Benny decided to submit bills.

The Press and the AMA. The reporters who had paid so much attention to Benny's plight were relentless in their criticism of Dr. Kris's bill. Even the AMA was moved to comment. The chairman of the board of trustees said, "The AMA feels the physician in the Hooper case was rendering a public service and acting in the noblest tradition of medicine when he stood by while the boy's life hung in the balance. . . . The AMA feels, however, that not one doctor in a thousand would have charged a fee. We strongly disagree with the action of the doctor in this case."

Resolution. Dr. Kris was by turns perplexed and annoyed. He argued that he billed less than his normal fee because of the circumstances, but he did not receive a sympathetic hearing. Finally he withdrew the bill on the grounds that the family could not pay and he did not want to burden them with debt. But critics of the medical profession had seized the opportunity to embarrass the medical profession for its impersonal treatment and its rapidly rising fees. In his popular indictment of the medical profession, *The Doctor Business* (1958), Richard Carter recounted Benny's story in the introduction as evidence that the profession had lost sight of its moral beacon.

Sources:

"A Boy Trapped, a Big Story," *Newsweek*, 49 27 (May 1957): 94–95;

E. J. Kahn, Jr., "Billy and Benny," *New Yorker* (8 June 1957): 117, 119–123.

HOXSEY CANCER CURE

Hope for Sale. People tend to look first to the medical community for cures to their diseases. When doctors fail, desperate patients seek hope in the form of quackery. Because it was so frightening and because medical researchers were frustrated in their efforts to find a cure, cancer attracted an unusual share of fake healers.

Coal Miner's Recipe. Among the most persistent was Harry M. Hoxsey, a coal miner who began selling liquid medicines and pills in 1924, promising miracle cures to cancer victims. According to his own account, Hoxsey's cancer medicine included licorice, red clover, burdock root, stillingia root, barberis root, poke root, cascara, prickly ash bark, buckthorn bark, and potassium iodide, an old family recipe. His grandfather developed the medicine to cure horses. The Food and Drug Administration ruled that Hoxsey's pills were useless for humans and maybe even promoted the growth of cancer.

The Cost of Treatment. Hoxsey survived many local, state, and federal attempts over the years to put him out of business, producing with unflagging energy a succession of patients attesting to cures at his seventeen clinics, with main offices in Dallas, Texas, and Portage, Pennsylvania. The cost was $460 per treatment in the mid 1950s. The FDA charged that Hoxsey's cures, which numbered in the hundreds by his account, fell into three categories: 1) people who never had cancer, 2) people who were treated by legitimate doctors as well as Hoxsey, and 3) people who died of cancer despite Hoxsey's pills.

Injunction. An injunction request against Hoxsey filed in 1950 was finally granted by a federal court in Dallas in 1953, but he bragged publicly that he ignored it. While that case was in court, Hoxsey had won a highly publicized judgment of $1.05 million for libel in 1952 against Dr. Morris Fishbein, editor of the *Journal of the American Medical Association.* In 1956 Hoxsey published *You Don't Have to Die,* a book touting the benefits of his treatment, with the signed endorsement of ten doctors.

Hoxsey Undeterred. In November 1956 another federal court held that Hoxsey's pills were worthless, ordered a half million of them destroyed, and declared them illegal. Hoxsey was considered so pervasive a threat that the FDA issued a circular titled *Public Beware! Warning Against the Hoxsey Cancer Cure.* But he was not deterred. Hoxsey continued to offer cancer victims the benefit of his cure until his death in 1973 of pancreatic cancer at the age of seventy-two, and then the practice was taken over by a succession of disciples, including the self-described naturopathic physician Edward L. Carl, who republished Hoxsey's book, with his own augmentations, in 1977.

Sources:

James Cook, *Remedies and Rackets* (New York: Norton, 1958);

Harry M. Hoxsey, augmented by Edward L. Carl, *You Don't Have to Die* (Chapala, Mexico: Nature Heals, 1957).

MENTAL ILLNESS

A National Disgrace. During the 1950s it was calculated that one family in three would admit a member to a mental institution. By 1959 on an average day some eight hundred thousand Americans were in mental hospitals, and many of them would never leave. Yet in 1955 there were only some forty-seven hundred fully certified psychiatrists in the United States, and only five hundred new psychiatrists were being trained each year. In a decade of enthusiastic spending for medical research, mental health was shorted. Cancer, which afflicted about 16 percent fewer people than mental health, attracted more than 400 percent more research money. As a result, many mental institutions became little more than overcrowded warehouses where tormented people waited to die.

Columbus State Hospital. In October and November 1956 *The Saturday Evening Post* ran a six-part series on mental hospitals that focused attention on one that seemed to be typical—Columbus State Hospital, which had been called the Central Ohio Lunatic Asylum before modern sensitivity demanded that the name be changed. A sprawling complex on 333 acres of land, Columbus State Hospital was one of the eleven "prolonged care" mental hospitals in Ohio which housed altogether 35,000 patients and employed a staff of 9,000. Columbus State Hospital cared for some 2,700 patients. Of these, 117 of the patients were on shock treatment, 213 were on new tranquilizing drugs, 24 in individual psychotherapy, and 31 were in group therapy. They formed the core group of patients considered to be on active treatment; another 1,400 were judged to be candidates for active treatment if resources became available; the remaining 900 patients

Harry M. Hoxsey with Senator William Langer, who introduced a bill calling for a congressional investigation of alternative cancer treatments

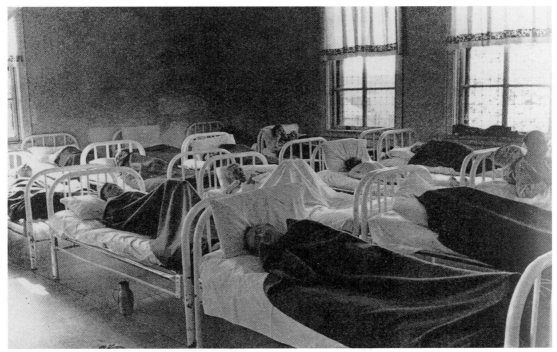

Patients' ward, Columbus State Hospital, 1956

were called "custodial," meaning they would be given minimal attention until their death in the hospital.

Patient Care. Some patients worked. The 195 considered productive workers were paid $1 per hour; 500 other patients worked for free. The hospital spent $2.60 per day on patient care, about average for mental institutions nationwide. (At the end of 1956 the Ohio legislature passed a bill that raised the per-patient expenditure to $3.19 per day, which was above the national average.) Of that amount, $0.16 was allotted per patient for each meal. Two hundred forty-eight attendants worked the three forty-four-hour shifts required to man the hospital's forty wards. They made $50 per week and were required only to be an Ohio resident, a U.S. citizen, and between the ages of eighteen and seventy. Some attendants were illiterate, and others were on parole from penal institutions.

Chance of Release. New patients got most of the attention at Columbus State Hospital. Those who failed to respond promptly were shuffled into the bowels of the institution, where they became less likely to be released with the passage of each day. Dr. Robert Felix, director of the American Institute of Mental Health, allowed that in America mental patients had a fifty-fifty chance of being released in the first year of hospitalization, a sixteen to one chance in the second year, and a ninety-nine to one chance after that.

EST. Because it was cheap, the preferred form of treatment for many new patients was electroshock therapy, or EST, in which electric current is passed through the brain to induce convulsions that have a calming effect

after the initial trauma. In the hospital superintendent's words, "EST is our mainstay." It was thought particularly useful in treating depression, manic-depression, and involuntary melancholia. The treatment itself was sometimes so violent that patients broke bones pulling against restraints, and it was administered as many as three times a week per patient, particularly to violent patients. One patient at Columbus State had undergone 427 bouts of EST.

A Doctor Shortage. Psychiatrists at Columbus State Hospital were in short supply, and when they were available, it was usually because they were in training or otherwise unemployable. A staff psychiatrist earned $7200 a year at a time when a psychiatrist in a new private practice could expect to make $20,000 annually. At the end of 1956 the legislature approved a raise to $12,000 with a ceiling of $17,000 for senior doctors. The 1957 budget stipulated a salary of $3,400 for residents, $6,000 for staff doctors who were not psychiatrists, and $18,000 – $19,000 for superintendents, which put Ohio doctors near the top of the pay scale nationwide for physicians at mental institutions, but not for doctors on the outside.

Drug Therapy and Psychoanalysis. Psychotherapists were very scarce at Columbus State Hospital—the American Psychoanalytic Association had only six hundred members in 1956—and because psychotherapy took so long, it was considered impractical in a state hospital. Drug therapy was primitive in the 1950s by today's standards. The two drugs most often used were the sedatives Thorazine and Serpasil, both of which had come into common use only recently, but they were expensive, costing ten to fifteen dollars per month per patient. As a result less than 20 percent of the nine hundred patients who, in the staff's opinion, would benefit from drugs received them, and half of those who got drugs paid the cost themselves.

Private Institutions. Private mental hospitals were far different from Columbus State. Individual psychotherapy was the preferred mode of treatment there, and patients got far more individual treatment. But the cost was also greater—as much as sixteen hundred dollars a month. As might be expected, only 2 percent of all patients in mental hospitals were in private institutions.

Sources:

Ivan Belknap, *Human Problems of a State Mental Hospital* (New York: McGraw-Hill, 1956);

John Maurice Grimes, *When Minds go Wrong: The Truth About our Mentally Ill and Their Care in Mental Hospitals* (New York: Devin-Adair, 1954);

"Inside the Asylum," Six-part series in *Saturday Evening Post* (6 October 1956–10 November 1956).

Polio victims at March of Dimes gathering, January 1954

NATIONAL FOUNDATION FOR INFANTILE PARALYSIS

The March of Dimes. The National Foundation for Infantile Paralysis was founded in 1938 by Franklin D. Roosevelt as a national successor to the Warm Springs Foundation he established in 1927. The purpose of the foundation was to provide funds for polio research, education, and patient aid. It was supported by private donations to what was throughout the 1950s an annual fund-raising drive called the March of Dimes. By the mid 1950s most large cities held televised twenty-four-hour telethons in which celebrities would urge viewers to give. The telethons were augmented by door-to-door collections performed by individuals and community groups. Between 1937 and 1957 the March of Dimes collected approximately $500 million, and 1956 alone the March of Dimes raised $52 million. In 1958, the war against polio largely won, the organization changed its name to the National Foundation and broadened its interests.

POLIO

Fear of Polio. During the early 1950s no disease attracted as much attention as polio. A Gallup poll conducted in 1954 when the Salk vaccine was being tested indicated that more people knew about the polio vaccine tests than knew the name of the president. Polio struck children far more often than adults, and there seemed to be little a parent could do to protect against it. Moreover, it struck without regard to the victim's race or social class, and so it demanded the attention of both the medical and political establishments. When Dr. Hart E. Van Riper, the director of the NFIP, announced in 1953 that more cases of polio had been reported in the past five years than in the previous twenty, many parents failed to hear that he was optimistic about a cure.

Polio Warnings. The rumor mill was pernicious as ever. Dr. Van Riper dispelled the notion that fruit, insects, animals, and bad genes cause polio. As polio tended to strike during the summer, he advised parents that they could send their children to camp if the camp had proper medical supervision, but he warned against camps where polio had been reported. He cautioned parents about letting their children mix with crowds or come into close contact with stangers in such settings as movie theaters, playgrounds, or beaches. He advised that swimming pools do not themselves cause polio, but crowds at swimming pools might increase the risk of transmission, and the fatigue of a hard day at play as well as the chill of getting out of the water might increase a child's susceptibility.

Polio Precautions. As a result of the information distributed by the NFIP, public swimming pools were closed. Children were confined to their yards during the summer, especially in warmer climates, where the virus seemed to thrive. Active boys and girls were encouraged to play quietly because sweating was thought to promote polio. Children were discouraged from playing with any but their closest friends.

How Polio Spreads. Polio is an infectious disease. It is caused by any one of three types of virus that enters the body through a patient's mouth and resides briefly in the bloodstream before taking one of two routes. The virus may make its way into the bowels, where it is expelled without more serious harm to the patient than the symptoms of a common cold. If the patient is unlucky, the virus travels into the central nervous system instead, where it irreparably damages cells in the brain stem or spinal cord and can cause severe paralysis and, sometimes, death.

Effects of Polio. According to Dr. Van Riper, about 50 percent of all polio victims recovered completely, some

Salk vaccine being distributed from Cutter Labs, 1956

30 percent suffered mild aftereffects, about 14 percent suffered severe paralysis, and about 6 percent died. These latter two categories comprise what are called acute cases, of which 28,386 were reported in 1950. In 1952 the number of acute cases had risen to 55,000.

History. Polio is thought to have existed since ancient times, and it was known to be caused by a virus since 1908. It did not become a public health threat, though, until the twentieth century, when in 1916 about twenty-seven thousand acute cases were reported in the northeast and north-central states. In 1921 it struck Franklin D. Roosevelt, who was elected president of the United States eleven years later. He founded the NFIP in 1938, a charity supported by an annual national fund-raising effort called the March of Dimes.

Early Vaccines. In 1950 the medical community responded to the rising public fear of polio with a safeguard of dubious value. Researchers discovered that injections of gamma globulin, a part of human blood that carries antibodies against infectious viruses, could temporarily prevent polio infection. The problem was that immunity lasted for only one to eight days, and gamma globulin was in short supply, because it was used in the vaccine against measles that was routinely administered to school-age children. People wanted better protection for their children.

Jonas Salk. (See Salk entry) A more encouraging alternative was offered by reports in the early 1950s of the research being directed by Dr. Jonas Salk, a young doctor at the University of Pittsburgh. He had developed a vaccine consisting of all three types of polio viruses, killed by dipping them in formaldehyde. The vaccine was injected into the bloodstream, where it caused the body to develop

POLIO MASQUERADES

In 1953 Dr. Max J. Fox and Irvin Moskowitz reported in the *Wisconsin Medical Journal* that as many as one-third of the patients admitted to hospital for treatment as polio victims only feared they had the disease. These so-called hysterical paralytics typically exhibited a morbid interest in poliomyelitis and suffered the symptoms of the disease without any physical cause. Sypmtoms usually disappeared when the patient was assured that he or she was disease-free. Often psychological care was recommended.

Even when there were clearly physical causes of polio-like symptoms, diagnosis was uncertain in the early 1950s. The Southwestern Poliomyelitis Center in Houston reported that about one in six patients diagnosed as having polio suffered instead from another, less serious disease. The reason was that doctors, who were taught in medical school that it is better to be safe than sorry in diagnoses, were reluctant to rule out polio in patients who exhibited any of the symptoms of the disease.

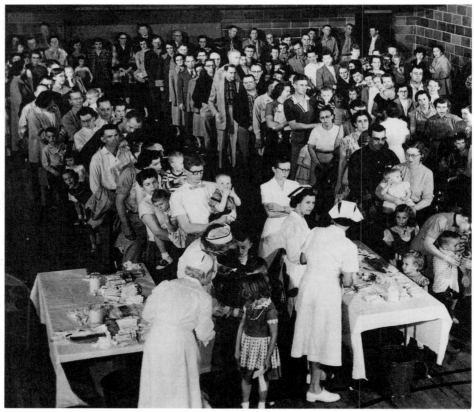

Polio vaccination center, Protection, Kansas, 1957

protective antibodies. The Salk vaccine was administered in three shots to the arm, 1 cc of pink liquid each. The second shot came two weeks after the first, and the third one month later.

Polio Pioneers. In the spring of 1954 the Salk vaccine was tested on 1.8 million schoolchildren, called Polio Pioneers. Of these, 440,000 children got the Salk vaccine; 210,000 got what were called dummy shots, or placebos; the rest were simply observed as a control group. The test results, announced in April 1955, showed that those who received the placebo contracted 3.5 times more cases of polio than those children who received the vaccine. The Salk vaccine was proven, and President Eisenhower encouraged passage of the Poliomyelitis Vaccination Act, which provided $30 million to states to buy the vaccine for the general population, children first. A consortium of four major drug companies mobilized to provide 9.8 million doses for elementary-school children in 1955. The vaccine, which cost the government about a dollar for each three-shot sequence, was administered free in the summer of 1955, first to every first grader, then to children in grades two to four, then to pregnant women past the twelfth week of pregnancy. Children got their shots at schools and other public places. By the end of 1958, 200 million shots of Salk vaccine were given.

Drawbacks to Salk Vaccine. The benefits of the Salk vaccine had limitations: it conferred polio immunity for only about thirty months, at which time a booster shot was required. It also turned out that the vaccine was difficult to mass-produce. The polio viruses were hard to kill in large quantities, and if live viruses made it into the vaccine, the serum could cause the disease it promised to prevent, as it did in 1955 when Cutter Laboratories of Berkeley, California, delivered a batch of partially live vaccine that infected forty-four children with polio within days of vaccination. Salk provided an admirable stopgap antidote to the polio epidemic, but the search continued for a better solution to the problem.

Types of Vaccines. In general, vaccines come in two types. The first consists of dead viruses, like the Salk vaccine, that cause the body to produce antibodies that will, for a short time, disable any live virus introduced into the bloodstream. The second consists of attenuated, or weakened, live viruses that are too impotent to cause the disease but strong enough to stimulate the body to produce more antibodies for a longer time. Live-virus vaccines confer a lengthier period of immunity and an increased likelihood that the virus type, which cannot reproduce itself outside the body, will be eradicated altogether.

Albert Sabin. (See Sabin entry.) The leader in the attempt to produce a live-virus vaccine was Albert Sabin, who successfully tested his vaccine on thirty prisoner-volunteers in 1955. His announcement on 6 October 1956

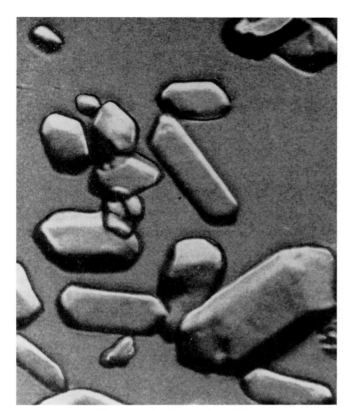
Crystallized polio vaccine, 1955

that his vaccine was ready for mass testing created only an anxious stir in America, where the principle that the only good virus is a dead virus held sway. In a gesture characteristic of the cold war, the Polish-born Sabin was allowed to accept the invitation of Soviet scientists to test his vaccine there. Only after he had successfully vaccinated millions of Soviet schoolchildren did Americans adopt his vaccine in 1961. Children were delighted, because they no longer had to take polio shots. The Sabin vaccine was administered by mouth in a 2-cc, cherry-flavored dose.

Sabin's Effects. The names Salk and Sabin have come to represent the fight against polio, but thousands of researchers devoted their talents to the search for a polio shield in the 1950s, and Americans donated hundreds of millions of dollars for polio research and patient care to the March of Dimes. As people expected, the fight was won. The incidence rate of polio fell from 37.2 cases per 100,000 Americans in 1952 to 1.8 cases per 100,000 in 1960. By the 1980s fewer than ten cases were reported each year. (See Koporowski entry).

Sources:

Alton L. Blakeslee, *Polio and the Salk Vaccine: What You Should Know About It* (New York: Grosset & Dunlap, 1956);

Richard Carter, *Breakthrough: The Saga of Jonas Salk* (New York: Pocket Books, 1967);

"O Pioneers!" *New Yorker*, 30 (8 May 1954): 24–25;

"Polio: Free Shots" *Newsweek*, 4 (1 November 1954): 62–63.

PRESIDENT'S COUNCIL ON YOUTH FITNESS

Weak Americans. In 1957 President Eisenhower acted on his dismay at the physical weakness of American youth. According to the results of a study testing "minimum muscular fitness," more than half of the American children tested could not pass. Worse, when the same test was given to a group of European students, more than 90 percent of them passed.

The President's Response. The president, a former army general, considered the country's physical fitness important to national security and a strong national character. To try to correct what he called the "fitness gap," he created the President's Council on Youth Fitness, a cabinet-level project headed by Vice-president Richard Nixon. The council advised schools and communities to provide more opportunities for organized sports and safe outdoor play.

The Price of Progress. Behaviorial experts of the time pointed out the irony of the situation: much of the decline in American fitness was a result of the country's progress. Thanks to the labor-saving devices in almost every American home, children had fewer, and less-strenuous, chores. More roads and more traffic often made walking or bicycling to school too dangerous. The growth of cities and suburbs took away space outside for children to play; and because of television, they too rarely wanted to go outside anyway.

RADIATION

A New Way of Seeing. You cannot fix what you cannot see. That principle explains in large part why medical research showed such dramatic results in the 1950s. On the one hand the very powerful electron microscope was available in some labs for the first time. On the other, X-ray technology was refined so that it could be commonly used for diagnosis. The first X-ray machine that could take a picture of an entire human body without overly exposing it to radiation was announced in 1951.

Medical Radiation. Radiation therapy extended beyond the X-ray lab. A happy side effect of the nuclear research being conducted in the cause of national defense was that scientists began to understand how radiation works. They learned that controlled low-level radiation could be used for medical purposes.

Atomic Highlighter. In 1950 physicians developed a technique using radiation and X rays together. Doctors learned that cancerous tumors absorb radioactive material several times more readily than normal tissue. They asked patients to swallow capsules filled with low-level radioactive materials. After allowing time for digestion, they used a Geiger counter on the outside of the abdomen. If they found areas unusually high in radioactivity, they assumed the reaction came from a cancerous tumor. Soon similar diagnostic procedures were performed using X rays.

Radiotherapy. Radioactivity was also used to heal. In 1953 doctors unveiled on national television the cobalt-ray machine that could send the equivalent of a three-million-volt X ray to a focused spot on a patient's lung, killing the targeted cancerous tissues. It was announced as a new cancer treatment, effective on malignant tumors that could be isolated.

Fallout Shelters. But radioactivity kills healthy cells, too. A major cause of anxiety during the 1950s was the threat of exposure to radiation after an enemy attack using atomic bombs. People built fallout shelters—cellars in their backyards—and stocked them with as much non-perishable food as they could fit so they could shield themselves from radioactive fallout in the event of enemy attack.

Watch Dials and Televisions. A more immediate concern came from the very low-level radiation to which people were exposed in everyday life. Luminous watch dials, which became very popular in the 1950s, were often made from strontium 90 or some other radioactive material. Doctors warned of the health risk to watchmakers and watch wearers, suggesting that the radioactivity could cause skin or bone cancer. Watchmakers, led by Rolex, announced recalls of luminous-dial watches and scurried for an alternative glow-in-the-dark material. It was also reported that television screens emitted radiation, but the levels were very low. *Better Homes & Gardens* assured readers in April 1960 that the risk from television was minimal.

Source:
"World's First Atomic Hospital," *Today's Health* (November 1953): 22–23, 44–47.

TRANQUILIZERS

The Tranquilizer Boom. In 1957 there were seventy-three brands of tranquilizers, marketed by thirty-six drug companies, available to Americans by prescription. Most of them were derivatives of the same small group of chemicals that slow down the action of the central nervous system and thus reduce nervous tension and anxiety. In 1956 physicians and psychiatrists wrote thirty-five million prescriptions for tranquilizers—a rate of one every second—and anxious patients paid $150 million to get their pills, or about $4.30 per prescription. In the mid 1950s, when tranquilizer prescriptions could be refilled indefinitely, these new drugs gained a popularity that alarmed some doctors.

Relaxation without Aftereffects. The most popular tranquilizer, generically called meprobomate, was developed in 1950 by the drug firm Ludwig and Piech from a chemical similar to antifreeze. This medicine, called Miltown, seemed to have all the benefits and none of the side effects of the most heralded tranquilizer being tested, thorazine. Also called Equinal by the drug manufacturer

Wyeth Laboratories, meprobomate was touted as a non-habit-forming cure for anxiety and nervous tension. The drug, which came in pill form, achieved its effect about forty-five minutes after ingestion. The result was a satisfying sensation caused by muscular relaxation.

Happy Pills. When they were released for distribution as a prescription drug in 1955, Miltown and Equinal were instant successes. They were prescribed for illnesses ranging from insomnia to alcoholism, but most often to people suffering from cases of "nerves." In 1957 *Time* (March 11) reported that a woman in Beverly Hills asked her doctor to prescribe tranquilizers for her daughter, "who needed them to get through the trying first week of her honeymoon," and a lady in Boston asked her pharmacist for a bottle of "happiness pills." Dr. David B. Allman, president of the American Medical Association in 1958, cautioned that "modern man cannot solve his problems of daily living with a pill."

Sources:
"No Martinis!" *Time,* 69 (3 June 1957): 48;
"Facts about Tranquilizers," *Consumer Reports,* 23 (January 1958): 4.

TUBERCULOSIS

The White Plague. Americans had lived in fear of tuberculosis for nearly three-quarters of a century by the 1950s. Because the disease is deadly and highly infectious, victims were isolated in special hospitals called sanatoriums, where at the beginning of the century, at least, they lived out their last days with other patients. The death rate from tuberculosis in 1950 was only 11 percent of what it was in 1900; still 33,633 people died from the disease that year. By 1955 the number of deaths from tuberculosis had been halved.

Good News. In 1956 the Annual Report of the National Tuberculosis Association contained good news: deaths from tuberculosis were down to sixteen thousand a year. For the first time in history, tuberculosis had fallen from the list of the top ten diseases rated by the number of deaths they cause. (By the end of the decade the death rate was down to just over ten thousand a year.) The report also contained the alarming fact that one American in three was infected with the bacillus that causes tuberculosis. The conclusion was that everyone had to be

New York City Syphilis Detectives giving blood tests, 1953

careful of developing the disease. Schoolchildren were tested periodically, and physicians acted swiftly with effective drugs when tuberculosis was suspected. As a result, by the middle of the decade new infections were most common among the down-and-out who did not receive adequate health care. One study conducted in Philadelphia showed the tuberculosis rate among inhabitants of skid row was eighteen times higher than among the general population

New Defenses. The most common form of tuberculosis, or TB, as the disease is known, affects the lungs. It is a bacterial disease that often results from unsanitary conditions or occupational hazards in such jobs as medical treatment. In the 1950s physicians tried to find cures and attempted to isolate victims to prevent its spread. The new antibiotic Terramycin, announced in 1950, joined streptomycin as a major weapon in the fight against the disease. The availability of other new medicines that stopped the progression of TB, coupled with the development of a blood test anounced in 1952 that accurately detected the disease in its early stage, marked the beginning of the end of the TB scare.

Eradication. By the end of the 1950s, a controversial live-virus vaccine against TB, called BCG (for Bacillus developed by Albert Calmet and Camille Gudérin, scientists at the Pasteur Institute of Paris) was widely used, especially among medical personnel, in America. In a book, *BCG Vaccination against Tuberculosis* (Little, Brown, 1957) Dr. Roy Rosenthal, director of tuberculosis research at the University of Illinois, argued effectively for wider general use. A BCG shot cost fifty cents and provided long-term immunity against the disease. Sanatoriums were already being closed because people could be treated effectively at home, and the disease was considered well on its way to being eradicated.

A PREGNANCY VACCINE

In 1950 longtime birth-control advocate Margaret Sanger enlisted Gregory Pincus, a reproductive biologist at the Worcester Foundation in Massachusetts, and his associates to work on what might be called a vaccine against pregnancy. After three years of research, the team focussed their attention on the effects of a synthetic form of the hormone estrogen, which seemed to control the rabbit population in the lab. In 1957 the G. D. Searle Company began marketing the synthetic hormone, called norethynodrel, but only as a treatment for menstrual cramps. There was no mention of its effectiveness at preventing pregnancy, a very controversial issue in the 1950s. Other companies had flatly refused to market medications for the purpose of birth control. For three years norethynodrel was quietly taken for either its stated purpose or its less-publicized effect of controlling pregnancy before the U.S. Food and Drug Administration finally in 1960 licensed several hormone preparations for contraceptive use.

Source: James Bordley III and A. McGehee Harvey, *Two Centuries of American Medicine* (Philadelphia: Saunders, 1976), pp. 555–556.

Source:

Arthur J. Snider, "The Progress of Medicine," *Science Digest* (July 1955): 49;

"TB—and a Harsh Fact," *Newsweek* (7 October 1957): 100–101;

"Vaccination for TB," *Time* (26 March 1956): 69–70.

VENEREAL DISEASE

War and Sex. In the decade after World War II, reported cases of both syphilis and gonorrhea dropped dramatically. There were two reasons. First, during wartime many people tend to relax their standards of sexual behavior, with the result that venereal diseases increase. With the return to normality, there is a corresponding decrease in sexually transmitted diseases. The pattern also occurred during and after World War I.

Case Finders. The second reason for the decrease was that after World War II public health offices, bolstered by generous federal, state, and local budgets, devised a system called case finders to diagnose venereal disease in patients and then to locate and treat every person who had sexual contact with a disease carrier. The case-finder system actively sought out disease carriers and cured them, effectively controlling the spread of disease.

The Cost of Success. The system was so successful in reducing reported cases of venereal disease that the expense-conscious federal government concluded in the early 1950s that expenditures for the control of venereal disease could be sharply reduced. The decade-long decline in syphilis rates ended in 1956, and it was estimated that there were about one million cases a year of gonorrhea. In 1947 the federal government provided about $17 million for control of venereal diseases. In 1957 activists boldly requested federal funding of $5 million to begin reestablishing the case-finder program.

Source:

"Blood on the Sidewalks," *Time* (18 May 1953): 75.

HEADLINE MAKERS

THOMAS A. DOOLEY

1927-1961

MEDICAL MISSIONARY TO SOUTHEAST ASIA

A Vow to Help the Disadvantaged. To Americans in the 1950s Dr. Thomas A. Dooley was a "secular saint," risking his life to take the benefits of the Golden Age of Medicine to the neediest people in the world. During his service as a U.S. Navy ship's doctor in 1954 he treated refugees from North Vietnam to South Vietnam, tending as best he could to their cholera, leprosy, many tropical diseases, and war and torture injuries. Moved by their poverty and poor health, Dooley vowed that when his navy service was over he would return to help the people of Laos, a small neighbor of Vietnam. He provided many people in Southeast Asia with the first medical treatment they had ever received.

Medico. In the United States Dooley and several other doctors formed Medico, a nonprofit organization created to gather personnel and supplies for Dooley's planned hospital in Laos and other similar facilities projected for Asia, Africa, and South America. The profits from a best-selling book he had written about his experiences in Vietnam, *Deliver Us From Evil* (1956), helped start the group. In many of the areas in which the Medico doctors practiced, the local population or ruling government was strongly anti-American. (Dooley once refused to obey an order from the American ambassador that he leave Laos because Communists there wanted to kill him.) Dooley and his colleagues overcame hostility by dealing personally with their patients without attempting to push American or Western values. Their political neutrality often improved local attitudes toward the United States.

Treatment and Training. Dooley also believed in the importance of training local inhabitants to tend to their own medical needs. Whenever he treated anyone, he explained to his local trainees what he was doing. In this way native doctors could continue for themselves the process the Medico doctors had begun. The health care that Dooley and his followers practiced was primitive by American standards. "In the jungle, I practice nineteenth-century medicine," he explained. It's the best I can do under the conditions here. When I leave, the personnel I've trained practice eighteenth-century medicine. Good—this is progress, because most of the villagers live in the fifteenth century."

The Last Years. Dooley died in 1961 at age thirty-four after a long battle with cancer. He spent the last two years of his life traveling betweeen the United States, where he received medical treatment, and the Medico hospital in Laos. While in America he toured the country, lecturing and raising funds on Medico's behalf. Dooley was uncomfortable being a celebrity, but he was gratified by the contributions the publicity brought for Medico. To help educate the public about the disease that would eventually kill him, he allowed CBS to make a documentary, "Biography of a Cancer," about his first surgery in 1959. The Thomas Dooley Foundation, created to continue the work he had started, was established the year after he died.

Source:
Terry Morris, *Doctor America: The Story of Tom Dooley* (New York: Hawthorn, 1963).

DR. JOHN FRANKLIN ENDERS

1897-1985

DEAN OF THE AMERICAN "VIRUS HUNTERS";
DEVELOPED PROCEDURE FOR MASS
PRODUCTION OF POLIO VIRUS; DEVELOPED
VACCINE AGAINST MEASLES

Delivery of Polio Vaccine. Dr. John Franklin Enders made important contributions in the 1950s to the fight against several infectious diseases, most notably polio. The development of the Salk vaccine in the first half of the decade was a major step in controlling the disease, but even this first major victory was only half-won. The problem of immunizing

American children on a wide scale still remained. Large quantities of the polio virus were necessary to make the vaccine, which injected dead viruses into the body in order to stimulate the body's immune system. (See the section on polio in this chapter.)

Nobel Prize. At this time Enders was a professor of microbiology at Harvard Medical School and a director of research at the Children's Medical Center in Boston. His own research into polio determined that the virus could be cultivated in a variety of types of tissue. This discovery made possible mass production of the Salk vaccine. For his achievement Enders was honored by the medical community with several awards, including the 1954 Nobel Prize in medicine, which he shared with two colleagues (and former students), Drs. Thomas Weller and Frederick Robbins.

Measles Vaccine. Enders's work on viruses and tissue cultures made viral research cheaper and simpler, so that more laboratories and hospitals were able to isolate and identify viruses. Enders used his techniques to isolate the virus that causes measles in 1956, and two years later he developed a live-virus measles vaccine by cultivating the virus in a tissue sample, then isolating it and recultivating it in another sample. After seventy passes, the virus was sufficiently attenuated (weakened) for use in vaccines. The vaccine was tested over a period of several years, during which it often provoked reactions nearly as severe as an actual case of the measles. Researchers eventually determined that the vaccine worked best in conjunction with a dead-virus vaccine or an injection of gamma globulin.

Source:
William Greer, *Virus Hunters* (New York: Knopf, 1959).

DR. WALTER FREEMAN
1895-1972

CHIEF PROMOTER AND PRACTITIONER OF TRANS-ORBITAL, OR ICE-PICK, LOBOTOMY IN THE UNITED STATES

Ice-pick Wizard. Dr. Walter Jackson Freeman was a tireless missionary preaching the benefits of the lobotomy to mental-health practitioners during the 1950s. He promoted the transorbital lobotomy, which he had popularized, as such an uncomplicated procedure that psychiatrists not schooled in surgery could perform it with minimal training. Also known as the ice-pick lobotomy, because Freeman performed his earliest surgeries with that common tool before more-precise surgical instruments were designed for his use, transorbital lobotomies were performed by inserting a sharp probe into the frontal lobe of the brain through the eye socket and wiggling the probe vigorously

to dislodge portions of the brain thought to cause emotional disruptions. Throughout the 1950s Freeman traveled around the country demonstrating and teaching this procedure, sometimes performing as many as twenty-five lobotomies in a day.

Promoting the Lobotomy. Dr. Freeman was introduced to the notion of what was called psychosurgery in 1936 through a journal article by the surgeon Egas Moniz. The Portuguese doctor advocated treating extreme forms of mental illness by drilling holes in a patient's skull and digging cores of material from his brain. With a medical partner, Dr. James Watts, Freeman became the American master of the technique, personally performing 10 percent of the ten thousand lobotomies in America by 1949. Lobotomy was popular at state mental institutions because it was quick, effective, and cheap. In the days before drugs were available to quiet disruptive patients, lobotomy was viewed as an acceptable means of managing the most difficult inmates among the rapidly growing population at mental institutions. In articles with titles such as "Wizardry of Surgery Restores Sanity to Fifty Raving Maniacs" and "No Worse Than Removing Tooth," the press proclaimed the benefits of Freeman's specialty, referring to it as a miracle cure.

Critics Respond. Critics of lobotomy disputed such claims. They charged that cutting the brain without being able to observe the exact location or extent of the damage amounted to little more than mutilation. They also accused Freeman and the procedure's other supporters of exaggerating its benefits. Even when lobotomy alleviated some or all of a patient's symptoms, mental-health practitioners pointed out, it rarely enabled him to resume a normal life. Lobotomy patients were frequently listless, sloppy, bad-tempered, and childish. Often they relapsed entirely, and the process had to be repeated. And some died during the procedure. In 1951, during one of his lecture tours, four patients died as Freeman was operating on them.

Freeman's Last Years. In 1953 Freeman gave up his position at George Washington University Medical School, which he had held since the mid 1930s, to move to California. There he established a private practice, advised on hospital committees, and continued his research in lobotomy. He realized, however, that his days of influence were coming to an end. After Thorazine was approved for sale by the Food and Drug Administration in March 1954, lobotomy quickly lost ground to chemical therapy as a method of treating mental illness. Psychoanalysis and psychotherapy made the procedure seem outmoded, even barbaric. Freeman continued to champion his surgery, but to increasingly hostile audiences. By the early 1960s his colleagues regarded his ability to practice any form of medicine with open suspicion, and he was gradually retired from his few remaining residencies. He devoted his time to writing and to contacting former patients. By the time of Freeman's death in 1972, lobotomy was used almost exclusively to relieve pain in victims of terminal disease.

Source:
Elliot S. Valenstein, *Great and Desperate Cures* (New York: Basic, 1986).

JOHN H. GIBBON, JR.
1903-1973

DEVELOPER OF THE FIRST PRACTICAL HEART-LUNG MACHINE

Stimulus to Discovery. One day in 1930, while serving as a Harvard research fellow in surgery at Massachusetts General Hospital, Gibbon watched a patient undergoing heart-lung surgery suffocate on his own blood. To help such patients, he and his wife experimented with several different types of machines, until in 1935 they successfully used a heart-lung device on a dog, maintaining its life for thirty-nine minutes. But they had trouble developing an artificial lung big enough for humans.

Research Support and Success. In the late 1940s Gibbon became associated with the IBM Corporation, which provided engineers at the company's expense to aid him in the development of his oxygenator. Finally, in May 1953, Gibbon and F. F. Albritten, Jr., used the heart-lung machine during surgery to close a large opening in the heart wall of an eighteen-year-old girl, maintaining all of the patient's heart and lung functions on the machine for twenty-six minutes. The heart-lung machine paved the way for modern open-heart surgery, including procedures for the correction of congenital heart defects in infants, the repair of heart valves, coronary-bypass surgery, and heart transplants.

Contemporary Improvements. Researchers have greatly improved upon Gibbon's original design. In the 1990s heart-lung machines allow surgeons as much time as they need to operate without danger to the patient.

Source:
Ada Romaine-Davis, *John Gibbon and His Heart-Lung Machine* (Philadelphia: University of Pennsylvania Press, 1991).

HILARY KOPROWSKI
1916-

EMINENT VIROLOGIST; DEVELOPER OF THE FIRST POLIO VACCINE

Useful Failure. Hilary Koprowski developed the first polio vaccine tried on humans, but it failed, and his work in the field was overshadowed by the successes of Drs. Jonas Salk and Albert Sabin. Even so, Dr. Koprowski's polio research revealed much about the structure and operation of the virus.

He later distinguished himself for his research in cell biology as director of the Wistar Institute.

Yellow Fever. Koprowski emigrated from Poland in 1939. He took a position on the staff of the Yellow Fever Research Service of the Rockefeller Institute in Rio de Janeiro, Brazil, where he worked on the development of vaccines against a parasitic disease related to yellow fever. In Brazil he gained much experience with infectious viral disease patterns and with vaccination using attenuated, or weakened, strains of virus.

Lederle Labs. Beginning in 1946 Koprowski worked on the staff at Lederle Laboratories in Pearl River, New York, where he supervised experiments dealing with two viruses of the central nervous system, polio and rabies. After President Franklin D. Roosevelt founded the National Foundation for Infantile Paralysis, Lederle and Koprowski assumed a leading role in polio research.

Polio Vacccine. Koprowski began human experiments with his attenuated vaccine in 1950, two years before Salk and Sabin, but mass trials in Belfast, Northern Ireland, in 1956 were unsuccessful, resulting in several deaths and the end of Koprowski's association with Lederle. He resumed his research at the University of Pennsylvania in 1957 and made plans for mass vaccinations in the Congo, but a civil war frustrated his plans. The Sabin vaccine proved itself before Koprowski could regain his momentum.

ALBERT B. SABIN
1906-

VIROLOGIST WHO DEVELOPED THE UNTIMATE POLIO VACCINE

A Better Vaccine. Albert Sabin developed an orally administered attenuated-virus vaccine against polio that by the early 1960s had completely replaced the dead-virus vaccine developed by Dr. Jonas E. Salk. Sabin's vaccine provided nearly lifetime immunity and furnished the means to eradicate polio ultimately, yet his work did not attract the publicity that Salk's did. This was because Sabin did much of his research in the Soviet Union during the cold war.

Preparation. Polish-born Sabin worked at odd jobs to put himself through undergraduate and medical school. He developed his interest in virology as an intern at Bellevue Hospital in New York City, where he succeeded in isolating a strain of the pneumonia virus. In 1935 he took a position at the Rockefeller Institute and began investigating the polio virus. His early research at the University of Cincinnati College of Medicine, supported by the

National Foundation for Infantile Paralysis, established the relationship between the paralytic form of polio and indulgence in heavy exercise.

Live-Virus Experimentation. Sabin served in the U.S. Army Medical Corps during World War II, developing a vaccine against dengue fever and vaccinating sixty-five thousand American soldiers on Okinawa against encephalitis. After the war he resumed his research at the University of Cincinnati, where he cultivated the three types of polio in monkey kidney tissues, weakened the virus by allowing it to infect a series of research animals, and then recultivated the strains. He had learned how to make a solution of the virus for oral doses and began administering his vaccine to small numbers of prisoner-volunteers in 1952. When he was denied permission to begin mass innoculations in the United States, he accepted the invitation of the Soviet Union to vaccinate the millions of unprotected children there in 1957 and 1958.

Success. Sabin announced the results of his campaign at the June 1959 meeting of the International Scientific Congress on Live Virus Vaccines. In 1961 the U.S. Public Health Service licensed the Sabin vaccine for use in the United States.

JONAS E. SALK
1914-

VIROLOGIST WHO DEVELOPED THE
FIRST WIDELY ADMINISTERED POLIO VACCINE

Medical Hero. Jonas Salk was propelled into worldwide acclaim for his development of the first successful long-term vaccine against polio. Although the Salk polio vaccine achieved incomplete immunity and was completely replaced within a decade, Americans in the mid 1950s viewed Salk as a hero in the battle against a disease that had crippled a president (Franklin Delano Roosevelt) and shortened or restricted tens of thousands of young lives.

Director of Virus Research. When the University of Pittsburgh School of Medicine expanded its Virus Research Laboratory in 1947, the thirty-three-year-old Salk was named its director. During the course of a three-year project funded by the National Foundation for Infantile Paralysis, he demonstrated the existence of three types of polio virus and concluded that a vaccine must immunize against all of them to be effective.

Salk and the NFIP. Salk developed a close relationship with NFIP director Basil O'Connor, who came to regard him with almost fatherly affection. After developing a technique introduced in 1949 for cultivating polio virus in nonnervous tissues, Salk, with O'Connor's assent, began working on a vaccine against polio using dead viruses suspended in mineral oil and formaldehyde.

Success with Dead Viruses. Researchers hotly debated the virtues of a dead-virus vaccine versus a vaccine using attenuated, or weakened, virus. The consensus in the early 1950s was that an attenuated vaccine would require more time to develop and might be risky to use; therefore, O'Connor devoted the private funding of the NFIP to Salk.

Trials of the Salk vaccine in 1953 and 1954 were successful, and the mass immunization of American children began in 1955.

Source:
Richard Carter, *Breakthrough: The Saga of Jonas Salk* (New York: Pocket Books, 1967).

HELEN B. TAUSSIG
1898-1986

UNHERALDED DEVELOPER OF PROCEDURE TO
CURE "BLUE-BABY SYNDROME"

Preparation. In 1927 Helen B. Taussig graduated from Johns Hopkins Medical School, and in 1930 she assumed the directorship of the school's Pediatric Cardiac Clinic. She worked in the field of congenital heart disease, particularly the "blue-baby syndrome," in which blood left unoxygenated by a defect in the circulatory system turns the skin of babies blue.

Partnership with Alfred Blalock. In 1940 Taussig began to ponder the possibility of an operation to increase blood flow to the lungs, and she enlisted the aid of Dr. Alfred Blalock, a full professor in surgery at Johns Hopkins, in 1942. Taussig suggested to Blalock that he attempt to increase the blood flow to the lungs by joining two arteries that are naturally close to one another, the subclavian artery and the pulmonary artery.

Success. In November 1944, after more than two years of experiments performed on dogs, Blalock successfully tried the procedure on a one-year-old girl who weighed only about one pound due to the disease. He subsequently refined the operation so that the mortality rate was only 4.7 percent, and the operation became the preferred method of treating "blue babies."

Recognition Denied. In recognition of this joint achievment Blalock won election to the National Academy of Science in June 1945. Meanwhile Taussig, who originated the idea, worked in relative anonymity for the rest of her career, bitter, historians say, at being denied the recognition her male colleague received as a matter of course. She did not win promotion to full professor at Johns Hopkins until 1959.

PEOPLE IN THE NEWS

In 1950, **Walter L. Blum,** while serving as professor of biochemistry at Emory University, developed dextran, a synthetic substitute for blood plasma.

In 1958 physician **K. Brodman** formulated a computer method for medical diagnosis, feeding patient data into an IBM processor.

In 1959 Houston physician **B. S. Freeman** successfully transplanted a girl's toe to replace a thumb lost in an accident.

University of Illinois clinician **W. J. Fry** began destroying small sections of his patients' brains with radiation to reduce the tremors of Parkinson's disease in 1958.

John W. Gofman, a coronary researcher at the Donner Laboratory of the University of California, developed the Gofman test, a procedure that separated human blood parts in a centrifuge to predict atherosclerosis, or hardening of the arteries.

In 1958 **Carl Heller,** a University of Oregon clinician, administered large doses of the female hormone progesterone to twenty-one convict volunteers and reported that the subjects' potency, sperm count, and libido dropped to zero. After ceasing use of the drug normal function reappeared in all the subjects in about fourteen weeks.

From 1957 to 1959 **A. L. Higden,** a Teaneck, New Jersey, physician, studied the childbirth experiences of twenty-one thousand mothers and found very little difference in the incidence of complications or the length of pregnancy between younger mothers and mothers over forty.

Robert J. Hoagland discovered in 1950 that infectious mononucleosis can be transmitted through kissing.

In 1957 **F. L. Horsfall,** a Rockefeller Institute researcher, reported on two experimentally promising antiviral agents, which he claimed inhibited the growth of mumps and several influenza viruses.

In 1958 **Samuel L. Katz** of Harvard University Medical School announced, with Nobel Prize winner **John F. Enders,** clinical trials of what turned out to be the first effective vaccine against measles.

The physicians **S. Landreth** and **A. Gathright** in 1958 reattached a man's leg that had been almost completely severed just above the knee.

John Lawrence, a University of California, Berkeley researcher, developed in 1958 a method to "scan" the entire human body for cancer by administering a dose of radioactive iodine, which collects in abnormal tissue and can be detected by X ray.

In 1959 **H. Lemon,** a Boston University researcher, developed a blood test for bone cancer.

C. H. Li of the University of California, Berkeley announced in 1957 the isolation of a hormone from monkey pituitary glands that, he posited, would stimulate growth in children.

From 1954 to 1958 **D. C. W. Lillihei,** a University of Minnesota clinician, reduced the mortality rate from open-heart surgery performed in his clinic from 40 percent to 2.5 percent.

Hahnemann Medical College physician **M. P. Mandarino** began using an adhesive known as Ostamer to glue fractured human bones back together in 1959.

J. Martinek of the Reed Research Foundation developed an electrocardiograph in 1959 that not only recorded the heart's action but made a heart diagnosis electronically.

Mayo Clinic physician **W. F. McGuckin** developed an "autoanalyzer" in 1959 capable of determining the blood-sugar content of up to forty separate samples within one hour.

W. T. Mustard developed a surgical procedure in 1952 to transplant lungs from monkeys into human babies.

In 1959 **William Raab** and **Yvonne Starcheska,** University of Vermont researchers, coined the term "loafer's heart" to describe the "cholinergic deficiency" of the unexercised heart. In a study of 336 seemingly healthy men, Professors Raab and Starcheska demonstrated that unexercised hearts are more vulnerable to damage from stress than hearts in good condition.

In 1952 **Gustav William Rapp** of the Loyola University School of Dentistry and **Garwood Richardson** of the Northwestern University Medical School developed a saliva test they said could predict the sex of an unborn child with nearly 100 percent accuracy.

In the late 1950s **Samuel Rosen** developed a surgical treatment for otosclerosis, a deafness-producing ear disease. Called "stapes mobilization," the procedure involved loosening the chain of three middle-ear bones under local anesthesia.

In 1959 **R. H. Rosenman** and **M. Freidman**, San Francisco physicians, released the results of studies claiming that stress increased the cholesterol content of the blood.

In 1953 brothers **Mortimer, Raymond,** and **Arthur Sackler** formulated a theory that held that overactive adrenal glands produced chemicals causing the breakdown of nervous tissue, leading to schizophrenia.

E. S. Sinaiko, a Loyola University surgeon, replaced a woman's cancerous bladder with a portion of her stomach in 1957.

C. A. Smith, W. Garson, and **J. Portnoy** of the U.S. Public Health Service in 1957 developed a one-minute test for syphilis they called the Rapid Plasma Reagin Test, which they claimed to be as accurate as and cheaper than standard serum tests.

Paul Starr, a University of Southern California researcher, found in 1958 that 5 percent of males suffered from sluggish thyroid-gland secretion, which causes lethargy.

M. Teller of the Sloan-Kettering Institute for Cancer Research described in 1958 an antibiotic called actinobolin, which he claimed was effective against two human cancer tumors transplanted in rats.

In 1952 MIT researcher **John G. Trump** developed a two-million-volt X-ray device for the treatment of advanced forms of cancer.

In the September 1959 issue of *Scientific American,* **Shields Warren** published an article explaining the harmful genetic effects of X-ray radiation and recommending the avoidance of all but the most necessary X rays, especially for young children and pregnant mothers.

E. L. Wynder of the Sloan-Kettering Institute reported in 1957 that cigarette filters did little to reduce the susceptibility of smokers to lung cancer.

AWARDS

NOBEL PRIZE WINNERS IN MEDICINE OR PHYSIOLOGY

1950: Philip S. Hench (United States), **Edward C. Kendall** (United States), and **Tadeus Reichstein** (Switzerland), for work on the structural and biological effects of the adrenal cortex hormones cortisone and ACTH.

1951: Max Theiler (United States, born in South Africa), for work on the yellow fever virus and related organisms.

1952: Selman A. Waksman (United States, born in Russia), for the discovery of streptomycin and its development as a treatment for tuberculosis and other diseases not affected by penicillin.

1953: Hans A. Krebs (Great Britain, born in Germany), for the discovery of the citric-acid cycle by which the body produces energy; and **Fritz A. Lipmann** (United States, born in Germany), for the discovery of coenzyme A and its role in the metabolic system.

1954: John F. Enders (United States), **Frederick C. Robbins** (United States), and **Thomas H. Weller** (United States), for their discoveries concerning the cultivation of poliomyelitis virus in nonnervous tissues.

1955: Alex H. T. Theorell (Sweden), for work on oxidation enzymes.

1956: Andrè F. Cournand (United States, born in France), **Werner Forssmann** (Germany), and **Dickinson W. Richards, Jr.** (United States), for work on heart catheterization and changes in the circulatory system.

1957: Daniel Bovet (Italy, born in Switzerland), for work on synthetic compounds that curtail hormonal action.

1958: George W. Beadle (United States) and **Edward L. Tatum** (United States), for the discovery that genes regulate the chemical makeup of the body; and **Joshua Lederburg** (United States), for work in genetic recombination and the organization of genetic material in bacteria.

1959: **Arthur Kornbert** (United States), and **Severo Ochoa** (United States, born in Spain), for discovering the processes of synthesis of DNA and RNA.

AMERICAN MEDICAL ASSOCIATION DISTINGUISHED SERVICE AWARD RECIPIENTS

The AMA Distinguished Service Award honors a member of the association for general meritorious service.

1950: **Evarts A. Graham,** Saint Louis.

1951: **Allen C. Whipple,** New York City.

1952: **Paul Dudley White,** Boston.

1953: **Alfred Blalock,** Baltimore.

1954: **W. Wayne Babcock,** Philadelphia.

1955: **Donald C. Balfour,** Rochester, Minn.

1956: **Walter L. Bierring,** Des Moines, Iowa.

1957: **Tom Douglas Spies,** Birmingham, Ala.

1958: **Frank H. Krusen,** Rochester, Minn.

1959: **Michael De Bakey,** Houston.

ALBERT LASKER AWARDS

The Albert Lasker Awards are given in honor of medical research of a pioneering nature.

Basic Research Awards

1950: **George Wells Beadle,** for contributions to the understanding of the genetic control of metabolic processes.

1951: **Karl F. Meyer,** for bacteriological research in parasitology.

1952: **F. MacFarlane Burnet,** for fundamentally modifying knowledge of viruses and of the inheritance of characteristics by viruses.

1953: **Hans A. Krebs,** for the discovery of urea and the uric-acid cycles; **Michael Heidelberger,** for the development of the field of immunochemistry; **George Wald,** for his explanation of the physiology of human vision.

1954: **Edwin B. Astwood,** for research on endocrine function leading to the control of hyperthyroidism; **John F. Enders,** for the cultivation of the viruses of poliomyelitis, mumps, and measles.

1955: **Karl Paul Link,** for work on the mechanism of blood clotting and the development of methods of treatment for thromboembolic conditions.

1956: **Karl Meyer** and **Francis O. Schmitt,** for studies of the biochemical components of connective tissues contributing to an understanding of arthritis and rheumatic diseases.

1957: No award.

1958: **Peyton Rous,** for work on the causes of cancers, the source of antibodies, and the mechanism of blood-cell generation and destruction; **Theodore Puck,** for the development of original methods for the pure culture of living mammalian cells as a basis for research on nutrition, growth, and genetic mutation; **Alfred D. Hershey, Gerhard Schramm,** and **Heinz Fraenkel-Conrat,** for discoveries concerning the fundamental role of nucleic acid in the reproduction of viruses and the transmission of inherited characteristics.

1959: **Albert Coons,** for work in immunology; **Jules Freund,** for discoveries in immunology and allergy, strengthening immunization procedures against tuberculosis, malaria, rabies, and poliomyelitis.

Clinical Research Awards

1951: **Elise L'Esperance** and **Catherine McFarlane,** for the development of cancer-detection clinics for the discovery of early cancer or precancerous lesions; **William G. Lennox** and **Frederic A. Gibbs,** for research on epilepsy.

1952: **Conrad A. Elvehjem,** for contributions to biochemical and nutrition research; **Frederick S. McKay** and **H. Trendley Dean,** for the development of community-wide fluoridation programs.

1953: No award.

1954: **Alfred Blalock, Helen B. Taussig,** and **Robert Gross,** for contributions to cardiovascular surgery.

1955: **C. Walton Lillehei, Morley Cohen, Herbert Warden,** and **Richard L. Varco,** for advances in cardiac surgery; **Hoffman-LaRoche Research Laboratories, Squibb Institute for Medical Research; Edward H. Robitzek, Irving Selikoff, Walsh McDermott,** and **Carl Muschenheim,** for the establishment of the efficacy of isoniazid drugs to treat tuberculosis, meningitis, and generalized miliary tuberculosis.

1956: **Jonas A. Salk,** for the development of a vaccine against poliomyelitis.

1957: **Rustom Jal Vakil, Nathan Kline, Robert Noce, Henri Laborit, Pierre Deniker,** and **Heinz E. Lehmann,** for various studies.

1958: **Robert W. Wilkins,** for work on the control of heart and blood-vessel diseases through investigation of causes and the diagnosis and treatment of hypertension.

1959: **John Holmes Dingle,** for work on acute respiratory diseases; **Gilbert Dalldorf,** for demonstrating the ability of one virus to modify the course of infection by another, and for the discovery of the Coxsackie virus by a unique and broadly applicable technique.

PASSANO FOUNDATION AWARDS

Passano Foundation Awards honor distinguished work done in the United States in medical research.

1950: **Edward C. Kendall** and **Philip S. Hench,** Mayo Clinic, Rochester, Minn.

1951: **Philip Levine,** Ortho Research Foundation, Raritan, N. J., and **Alexander S. Wiener,** Jewish Hospital, Brooklyn, N.Y.

1952: **Herbert McLean Evans,** University of California.

1953: **John F. Enders,** Harvard Medical School.

1954: **Homer William Smith,** New York University College of Medicine.

1955: **Vincent du Vigneaud,** Cornell University Medical College.

1956: **George Nicholas Papanicolaou,** Cornell University Medical College.

1957: **William Mansfield Clark,** Johns Hopkins University.

1958: **George Washington Corner,** American Philosophical Society.

1959: **Stanhope Bayne-Jones,** Office of the U.S. Surgeon General.

DEATHS

Carl Beck, 88, surgeon, specialist in treating crippled hands and arms, cofounder of Saint Anthony's Hospital and North Chicago Hospital, 21 July 1952.

Nathan Thomas Beers, 76, dermatologist, 7 July 1950.

Jean Broadhurst, 80, bacteriologist who discovered a test for the measles virus, 5 September 1954.

Edward H. Cary, 81, eye specialist, former president of the American Medical Association, 11 December 1953.

Theodore L. Chase, 84, surgeon and cancer specialist, 12 February 1950.

Edwin J. Cohn, chemist, contributed to the development of gamma globulin, serum albumin, and liver extract, 1 October 1953.

Lewis A. Conner, 83, authority on heart disease, 3 December 1950.

Charles S. Danzer, 54, specialist in internal medicine, 19 January 1950.

Robert Latou Dickinson, 89, gynecologist, advocate of birth control and euthanasia, 29 November 1950.

Benjamin Duggar, 84, discoverer of the antibiotic Aureomycin, 10 September 1956.

Howard Fox, 81, skin specialist, founder and first president of the American Academy of Dermatology and Syphilology, 19 October 1954.

Annie W. Goodrich, 89, nurse, in 1918 established the first U.S. Army school for nurses, later established at Yale University the first graduate professional school of nursing, 31 December 1954.

Isaac Faust Harris, 73, biochemist who refined diphtheria antitoxin into safe form, 31 January 1953.

Charles James Hatfield, 84, cofounder and former president of the National Tuberculosis Association, 25 August 1951.

Elmer Lee Henderson, 68, former president of the American Medical Association, campaigner against national health insurance, 30 July 1953.

Edgar Erskine Hume, 62, former chief surgeon of the U.S. Far East Command and surgeon of the U.S. Command in Korea, 24 January 1952.

Robert Benjamin Irwin, 68, executive director of the American Foundation for the Blind, 12 December 1951.

Hinton D. Jonez, 63, physician, head of an internationally known multiple sclerosis clinic in Tacoma, Washington, 11 October 1953.

Adolphe Magnus Levy, 90, physician, pioneer researcher in basal metabolism, 6 February 1955.

Elmer H. Lutz, 59, Veterans Administration psychiatrist and leading brain surgeon, 24 June 1950.

Charles Frederick Menninger, 91, psychiatrist, founder of the Menninger Clinic and Foundation, 28 November 1953.

Alfred Meyer, 96, tuberculosis authority, cofounder of the National Tuberculosis Association, 14 July 1950.

Otto F. Meyerhof, 67, winner of the 1923 Nobel Prize in medicine and physiology, 6 October 1951.

George R. Minot, 64, winner of the 1934 Nobel Prize in medicine and physiology for the codiscovery of the liver treatment for pernicious anemia, 25 February 1950.

Frederick Wharton Rankin, 67, cancer specialist, president of the American College of Surgeons and former president of the American Medical Association, 22 May 1954.

William R. Redden, 71, developer of a U.S. Navy influenza pneumonia serum during World War I, 10 August 1952.

Cornelius P. Rhoads, 61, physician and pathologist, director of the Sloan-Kettering Institute for Cancer Research from 1945 to 1949, 13 August 1959.

Thurman Rice, 64, professor of public health at Indiana University, expert on marital relations and sex education, 27 December 1952.

Florence Rena Sabin, 81, medical researcher, first female member of the American Academy of Sciences, 3 October 1953.

Manfred J. Sakel, 57, psychiatrist, developer of insulin shock-therapy treatment for mental disease, 2 December 1957.

Wilbur A. Sawyer, 72, developer of the yellow fever vaccine adopted for mass production by Nobel Prize winner Max Thieler, 12 November 1951.

James Winn Sherrill, 64, physician who developed a method of treating diabetes with drugs and diet modifications, 4 January 1955.

William K. Sherwood, 41, biochemist engaged in cancer research; committed suicide after being called to testify before the U.S. House Un-American Activities Committee, 16 June 1957.

James S. Simmons, 64, dean of the Harvard School of Public Health, chief of the U.S. Army Preventive Medicine Service during World War II, 1 August 1954.

Henry Louis Smith, 91, pioneer in use of X ray, former president of Davidson College and Washington and Lee University, 27 February 1951.

Malcolm H. Soule, 54, bacteriologist, 3 August 1951.

Nathan Bristol Van Etten, 88, a founder of the Blue Cross and Blue Shield medical-insurance programs, former president of the American Medical Association, 23 July 1954.

Anna W. Williams, 91, bacteriologist known for her work on rabies and diphtheria, 20 November 1954.

Frank Norman Wilson, 61, pioneer in electrocardiography, 11 September 1952.

Francis Carter Wood, 81, cancer specialist, 5 January 1951.

John Dutton Wright, 85, developer of teaching methods for the blind, founder of the Wright Oral School, 19 January 1952.

Louis Tompkins Wright, 61, physician and surgeon, chairman of the National Association for the Advancement of Colored People, 8 October 1952.

Charles E. Ziegler, 79, obstetrician, inventor of the coffee percolator, 26 April 1950.

PUBLICATIONS

―――

General

Hank Bloomgarden, *Before We Sleep* (New York: Putnam, 1958);

Frank Macfarlane Burnet, *Viruses and Man* (London & Baltimore: Penguin, 1953);

James Bordley, III, and A. McGehee Harvey, *Two Centuries of American Medicine* (Philadelphia: Saunders, 1976);

Charlotte Carter, *Cancer, Smoking, Heart-Disease, Drinking—In Our Two World Systems Today* (Toronto: Northern Book House, 1957);

"The Crisis in American Medicine," *Harper's*, 221 (October 1960): 121–168;

Michael M. Davis, *Medical Care for Tomorrow* (New York: Harper, 1955);

Agnes Wise Dooley, *Promises to Keep* (New York: New American Library, 1964);

Rene Dubos, *Mirage of Health* (New York: Harper, 1959);

Leonard Engel, *The Operation: A Minute-by-Minute Account of a Heart Operation—and the Story of Medicine and Surgery that Led Up to It* (New York: McGraw-Hill, 1958);

William Greer, *Virus Hunters* (New York: Knopf, 1959);

"The Half-Century Mark," eleven-part series in *Today's Health*, February 1950 –December 1950;

Alfred Kinsey, *Sexual Behavior in the Human Female* (Philadelphia: Saunders, 1953);

"Medicine: What's Happening, What to Expect," *Changing Times*, 13 (April 1959): 37–42;

Terry Morris, *Doctor America: The Story of Tom Dooley* (New York: Hawthorn, 1963);

National Health Forum, *The Health of People Who Work*, ed. Albert Q. Maisel (New York: National Health Council, 1960);

Monte M. Poen, *Harry S Truman Versus the Medical Lobby: The Genesis of Medicare* (Columbia & London: University of Missouri Press, 1979);

Fred Reinfeld, *Miracle Drugs and the New Age of Medicine* (New York: Sterling, 1957);

Dietrich C. Reitzes, *Negroes and Medicine* (Cambridge, Mass.: Commonwealth Fund / Harvard University Press, 1958);

"Should Doctors Tell All?," *U.S. News & World Report*, 41 (13 July 1956): 104–105;

Steven M. Spencer, *Wonders of Modern Medicine* (New York: McGraw-Hill, 1953);

Consumer Reports Buying Guide, periodical.

Cancer

American Cancer Society annual report;

Horace Beard, *A New Approach to the Conquest of Cancer, Rheumatic, and Heart Diseases* (New York: Pageant, 1958);

Mark Boesch, *The Long Search for the Truth About Cancer* (New York: Putnam, 1960);

Charles S. Cameron, *The Truth About Cancer* (Englewood Cliffs, N. J.: Prentice-Hall, 1956);

Leonard M. Goldman, *There Is an Answer to Cancer* (New York: Harper, 1958);

Andre Voisin, *Soil, Grass, and Cancer: Health of Animals and Men is Linked to the Mineral Balance of the Soil* (New York: Philosophical Library, 1959).

Health Insurance

Odin W. Anderson, *Family Medical Costs and Voluntary Health Insurance: A Nationwide Survey* (New York: McGraw-Hill, 1956);

Oliver Donald Dickerson, *Health Insurance* (Homewood, Ill.: Irwin, 1959);

Davis Weinert Gregg, ed., *Life and Health Insurance Handbook* (Homewood, Ill.: Irwin, 1959);

Oscar N. Serbein, *Paying for Medical Care in the United States* (New York: Columbia University Press, 1953).

Heart Disease

Joyce Baldwin, *To Heal the Heart of a Child* (New York: Walker, 1992);

Joseph Eric Bittner, *Prevention of Heart Disease and Cancer* (Yakima, Wash.: Bittner Research Foundation, 1955);

Alton L. Blakeslee, *Heart Disease: What You Should Know About It* (New York: Grosset & Dunlap, 1957);

Emil G. Conason, *Eat Well and Live Longer: The Heart-Saver Cookbook* (New York: Crown, 1958);

Walter Donald Close, *Fundamentals of Heart Disease* (Indianapolis, 1954);

Charles Frederick Terence East, *The Story of Heart Disease* (London: Dawson, 1958);

Emanuel Goldberger, *Heart Disease, Its Diagnosis and Treatment* (Philadelphia: Lea & Febiger, 1955);

William Hyatt Gordon, *What is Heart Disease?* (New York: Homecrafts, 1952);

Milton B. Plotz, *Coronary Heart Disease* (New York: Hoeber-Harper, 1957);

Paul Dudley White, *Heart Disease* (New York: Macmillan, 1951).

Medical Profession

Richard Carter, *The Doctor Business* (Garden City, N.Y.: Doubleday, 1958);

"How Good Is Your Family Doctor?," *Atlantic Monthly* (August 1950): 43–47;

James Howard Means, *Doctors, People and Government* (Boston: Atlantic / Little Brown, 1953);

Walter E. and Jean K. Boek, *Society and Health* (New York: Putnam, 1956).

Mental Illness

Ivan Belknap, *Human Problems of a State Mental Hospital* (New York: McGraw-Hill, 1956);

William A. Caudill, *The Psychiatric Hospital as a Small Society* (Cambridge: Harvard University Press, 1958);

Mike Gorman, *Every Other Bed* (Cleveland: World, 1956);

John Maurice Grimes, *When Minds go Wrong: The Truth About our Mentally Ill and Their Care in Mental Hospitals* (New York: Devin-Adair, 1954);

"Inside the Asylum," six-part series in *Saturday Evening Post*, 6 October 1956–10 November 1956;

Elliot S. Valenstein, *Great and Desperate Cures* (New York: Basic, 1986).

Physical Fitness

L. Jean Bogert, *Nutrition and Physical Fitness* (Philadelphia: Saunders, 1954);

"Is American Youth Physically Fit?," *U.S. News & World Report*, 43 (2 August 1957): 66–77.

Polio

Alton L. Blakeslee, *Polio and the Salk Vaccine: What You Should Know About It* (New York: Grosset & Dunlap, 1956);

Richard Carter, *Breakthrough: The Saga of Jonas Salk* (New York: Pocket Books, 1967);

Victor Cohn, *Four Billion Dimes* (Minneapolis, 1955);

Robert Coughlan, *The Coming Victory Over Polio* (New York: Simon & Schuster, 1954);

Marjorie Curson, *Jonas Salk* (Englewood Cliffs, N. J.: Silver Burdett, 1990);

John R. Paul, M.D., *A History of Poliomyelitis* (New Haven & London: Yale University Press, 1971);

John Rowland, *The Polio Man: The Story of Dr. Jonas Salk* (New York: Roy Publishers, 1961);

John Rowan Wilson, *Margin of Safety: The Story of the Poliomyelitis Vaccine* (London: Collins, 1963).

Periodicals

Annual Review of Medicine, begun in 1950;

Alton L. Blakeslee, "Health in the Headlines," monthly feature of *Today's Health*, 1950 –1951;

Blakeslee, "Today's Health News," monthly feature of *Today's Health*, 1952–1960;

Journal of the American Medical Association;

Medical History, begun in 1957;

"Medicine," weekly report in *Newsweek*;

"Medicine," weekly report in *Time*;

Science News Letter, annual report on medicine.

Cigarette advertisement, January 16, 1950

RELIGION

by JOHN SCOTT WILSON

CONTENTS

Sidebars and tables listed in italics.

1950

- A House bill that excludes parochial schools from education funding is rejected by the Education and Labor Committee.

- Gordon W. Allport's book *The Individual and His Religion, a Psychological Interpretation* is published.

May   Two Southern Baptist seminaries are recognized, one at Berkeley, California, the other at Wake Forest, North Carolina.

22 May   The American Baptist Convention extends an invitation to all organized Baptist Conventions (including Southern Baptists and two African-American Conferences) to join the National Baptist Convention.

1951

- The Supreme Court assumes the right to review cases of state interference in religious freedom.

- The Supreme Court agrees to review the constitutional status of released-time programs for religious study in public schools in New York City.

- Because of the Korean intervention American missionaries are no longer accepted in China.

- Bombing of Jewish synagogues occurs in Miami, Florida, at the end of the year.

- The United States fails to ratify the UN Genocide Convention.

- California joins other states in granting tax exemption to parochial schools.

1952

- The Methodist church grants the right of African-American churches to transfer to white jurisdictions upon mutual agreement.

- New York State's released-time program for religious studies is upheld by the Supreme Court.

- The Supreme Court holds that states and cities may not ban movies on the grounds of being sacrilegious.

- The Eastern Orthodox church begins training American youths to become priests rather than bringing priests to America from abroad.

30 Sept.   The National Council of Churches publishes the New Revised Standard Version Bible.

23 Nov.   The dedication of a Buddhist temple for 250 Kalmucks (Russian Buddhists) takes place at Farmington, New Jersey.

1953

- Distribution of Bibles in New Jersey public schools is held unconstitutional by the state supreme court.

- The General Board of the National Council of Churches responds to attacks by various groups on the loyalty of clergy.

- President and Mrs. Dwight D. Eisenhower join the National Presbyterian Church in Washington, D.C., making him the first president to join a church while in office.

- The oldest Yiddish newspaper in the United States, the *Jewish Morning Journal,* suspends publication after fifty-two years.

4 May   The National Lutheran Council releases the full-length film *Martin Luther.*

July   Dr. J. B. S. Mathews charges the clergy as the "largest single group supporting Communist apparatus in U.S. today," in an *American Mercury* article.

1954

- A Pennsylvania court orders Amish children to attend high school.

- The Southern Baptist Convention passes a resolution supporting the Supreme Court decision outlawing segregation in public schools.

- The Revised Standard Version Bible breaks all-time publishing records, selling over three million copies.

9–11 July   The National Conference of Methodist Men holds its first conference in forty years.

1955

- California's attorney general rules that Gideon Bibles cannot be handed out inside public schools.

- Connecticut passes a law allowing Workman's Compensation Statutes to include payment for treatment by prayer or spiritual means alone.

- Delaware officially recognizes the Eastern Orthodox church.

- The evangelist Billy Graham conducts a successful series of revivals in Great Britain and France.

Oct.   An African-American minister becomes pastor at a white Methodist church in Connecticut.

27 Nov.   Three Roman Catholic women are excommunicated in Louisiana for beating a teacher who instructs African-American and white children in the same classroom.

1956

- During the Methodist General Conference women are granted full clergy rights.

- The Presbyterian Church in the U.S.A. gives final approval to the ordination of women; the Presbyterian Church in the U.S. votes to permit the ordination of women as ruling elders and deacons.

- A court ruling allows the Reverend William Howard Melish to remain as supply pastor to an Episcopal church in Brooklyn in spite of alleged left-wing loyalties.

1957

- A Florida circuit court rules that a Jewish couple can retain custody of the six-year-old daughter of a Catholic woman.

- The New York State Education Commission rules against classroom display of an interdenominational version of the Ten Commandments.

- Colorado's attorney general advises that distribution of Gideon Bibles in public schools is a violation of state laws.

25 June   The United Church of Christ is formed by the union of the Congregational Christian church with the Evangelical and Reformed church.

1958

- As a means of curbing juvenile delinquency in Michigan, a constitutional amendment making Bible reading mandatory in public schools is proposed.

28 May   The United Presbyterian Church in the U.S.A. is formed by the merger of the former Presbyterian Church in the U.S.A. and the United Presbyterian Church.

12 Oct.   President Dwight D. Eisenhower participates in the laying of the cornerstone of the Interchurch Center in New York City.

Nov.   American cardinals do not lose their citizenship by voting for a new pope because it is not a political election.

1959

- A New York Supreme Court justice holds that morning prayers in public schools should be allowed if the prayers are nondenominational and non-mandatory.

- The Interchurch Center in New York City increases opportunities for contact between Protestant and Orthodox churches.

- Most Protestant churches speak out in favor of birth-control measures in family planning.

- Many Protestant groups agree to meet only where accommodations are available without regard to the race of the participants.

- President Dwight D. Eisenhower says in a press conference that a Roman Catholic can be elected president.

Summer   The National Student Christian Federation is formed.

OVERVIEW

A New Awakening. The religious upsurge that followed World War II continued into the 1950s. By all concrete measurements — membership, contributions, media attention, films, and best-selling books — interest in religion was so high in the United States that optimists talked of a new awakening, with hopes that this one would affect American culture as deeply as those of the eighteenth and nineteenth centuries. But critics from both the right and left of the religious spectrum speculated whether religion had made its peace with the secular culture and had become just another commodity to be consumed in the American marketplace.

Surge in Affiliation. Optimists, however, pointed to concrete achievements. By 1960 an astonishing 63.6 percent of the population was affiliated with some religious group, and 60 percent of the people said they went to weekly religious services. The average annual monetary contribution to religious groups was at an all-time high.

Mergers. The decade began with the creation of the National Council of Churches of Christ in America, which brought together thirty-one million members of the main line Protestant and Orthodox churches to work on a broad range of issues. Mergers continued to bring together groups long divided by issues that had lost their relevance. The Evangelical Lutheran Church and the United Evangelical Lutheran Church merged to create the American Lutheran Church. The Northern Presbyterians and the United Presbyterians joined to create the United Presbyterian Church, U.S.A., and the Christian Congregationalist Church and the Evangelical and Reformed Church merged into the United Church of Christ, despite their differing forms of government. But old tensions remained. The Southern Presbyterian Church refused to join the northern churches, fearing the loss of their identity and more conservative beliefs by joining the larger group.

Old Quarrels. Old religious quarrels continued. Traditional Protestant suspicion of the Roman Catholic church remained and broke into the open over questions of public aid to parochial schools and attempts on the part of the Roman Catholic hierarchy to impose their standards on certain movies. While anti-Semitism declined after the revelations of the Holocaust and the establishment of the state of Israel in 1948, there were occasional outbreaks of hatred. The temple in Atlanta and other Jewish structures in the South were bombed in the course of the civil rights struggle.

Religion in Culture. While religious organizations remained a primary way to measure religious interest, the general culture reflected a deep preoccupation with religion in various forms. Books with religious themes became best-sellers throughout the decade. Hollywood competed with the small screen of television with widescreen religious spectaculars. Lloyd C. Douglas's best-selling novel, *The Robe*, was the first movie to be presented in Cinemascope, and the old warhorse, *Quo Vadis*, first filmed in 1912, again brought in movie crowds when it was remade in 1951. Ministers such as Archbishop Fulton J. Sheen, Billy Graham, and Norman Vincent Peale assured their readers that "life was worth living" in a religious fashion, and huge crowds thronged the Graham crusades in the United States and abroad.

Religion and Politics. Politicians recognized the importance of religion to many of the voters and approved the inclusion of "under God" to the Pledge of Allegiance and the adoption of "In God We Trust" as the national motto and the placement of the motto on the nation's currency. The Advertising Council assured the public that "The family that prays together stays together" and encouraged people to "Attend the Church of Your Choice on Sunday."

A New Pluralism. Perhaps the most significant religious development of the 1950s was the collapse of the old Protestant dominance of the culture. People in the 1950s began to talk of the Judeo-Christian heritage as opposed to Christian America; the Roman Catholic church lost its aura of an immigrant church and received the long-coveted acknowledgement as an American institution. Its wealth and power were factors that could no longer be scorned or ignored. At the end of the decade, Sen. John F. Kennedy began his successful campaign for the presidency, becoming in 1961 the first Catholic to hold that office. By mid century Americans freely identified themselves as Protestant, Catholic, or Jew, and many people believed that some sort of religious identification was necessary for national identification.

TOPICS IN THE NEWS

THE BILLY GRAHAM NEW YORK CRUSADE, 1957

Spectacular Revival. In the summer of 1957 the Billy Graham Crusade filled Madison Square Garden with the most spectacular revival meeting since the decline of Billy Sunday earlier in the century. After a series of highly publicized revivals in the United States, Great Britain, and Western Europe, Graham and his associates were willing to tackle the city even Billy Sunday had been unable to tame.

Planning. By 1957 the Graham team, organized as the Billy Graham Evangelistic Association, had fully polished their system. A huge budget, amounting to six hundred thousand dollars, was set and guaranteed by a group of wealthy backers. A significant percentage of the Protestant churches in the city were brought in as supporters of the crusade, as Graham's revivals were called. (The support Graham received from more-liberal Protestants brought a rift between him and more-conservative fundamentalists.) In the weeks before the crusade began, prayer teams around the world prayed for the success of the effort and ministers in the area encouraged their parishioners to support the effort. The city was saturated with pictures and flyers calling attention to the approaching event.

Media Coverage. By 15 May, when the crusade opened in Madison Square Garden, few in Protestant circles were unaware of the event. The city's newspapers, still the dominant medium of information, gave extensive coverage to the crusade. Graham was even given the opportunity to write a front-page column during the crusade for the *New York Herald Tribune*. But the growing medium of television was enlisted to broadcast a thirty-minute program scheduled for 11:30 P.M. on one of the city's stations. As the crusade built in strength, ABC, the weakest of the three national television networks, agreed to sell time to broadcast the Saturday evening services. That program proved an enormous success, and more viewers followed the crusade on television than viewed

Billy Graham preaching at a revival

DENOMINATIONS, 1951 AND 1959

1951	1959
Roman Catholic 28,635,000	Roman Catholic 39,505,000
Methodist 9,066,000	Methodist 9,815,000
Southern Baptist 7,373,000	Southern Baptist 9,485,000
Jewish 5,000,000	Jewish 5,500,000
Episcopal 2,643,000	Episcopal 3,359,000
Presbyterian 2,360,000	Presbyterian 3,210,000

Source: U.S. Bureau of the Census, *Historical Statistics of the United States* (Washington, D.C.: GPO, 1975), p. 391.

the crusade in person. Graham was quoted as saying "St. Paul didn't have television. We can reach more people by TV probably than the population of the world was then." The television programs brought in between fifty thousand and seventy-five thousand letters per week, and Graham estimated that contributions from those viewers amounted to more than $2.5 million, money which Graham's association used for future work.

Celebrities and Crowds. By mid June more than five hundred thousand people had crowded into Madison Square Garden, and Graham extended the crusade again and again until its final close Labor Day weekend. The crusade attracted many celebrities. Vice-president Richard Nixon brought greetings from President Dwight D. Eisenhower to the more than 100,000 people who filled Yankee Stadium on 20 July. The overflow crowd was the largest at Yankee Stadium up until that time and bested the previous record — 88,150 at the 1935 Max Baer–Joe Louis fight — by almost 20,000.

Appearance by King. Graham worked to include the entire mosaic of New York life. Martin Luther King, Jr., the country's best-known civil-rights leader, joined Graham on the stage on 18 July. Graham introduced King by saying, "A great social revolution is going on in the United States today. Dr. King is one of its leaders, and we appreciate his taking time out from his busy schedule to come and share this service with us." Graham did not relish the controversy that welcoming the civil-rights leader would bring among conservative whites. He downplayed King's appearance, so much so that it garnered just four lines in the *New York Times*. But his willingness to appear onstage with King brought increased acceptance from the black community. One observer estimated that by the end of the crusade almost 20 percent of the audience was black.

Closing Rally. The crusade closed 2 September with a giant rally in Times Square. It was estimated more than one hundred thousand people packed the streets in the area as Graham brought his effort to a close. Graham's association claimed that two million people had attended the services and fifty-five thousand decisions for Christ had been registered. Over 1.5 million letters were received.

Limited Effect. But Graham himself conceded that all the enthusiasm and excitement he had generated did not affect the general public life of the great city. Bible sales and new church memberships were not much increased during the months of the crusade. He consoled himself by reminding people that he was interested in changing individuals. Only that way could society itself be changed, and his crusades played a role in that battle. The Reverend Dr. John Ellis Large of the Episcopal Church of the Heavenly Rest, while not cooperating with the Graham organization, defended Graham's ministry:

> Some ministers have used bad taste in criticizing Graham, and one said the Holy Spirit couldn't exist in the Garden. But what started in the Garden of Eden and reached its finest moment in the Garden of Gethsemane should be brought out of those gardens and into the present. Madison Square Garden is as good a place as any for that.

Sources:

"Billy Graham Opens His Crusade Here," *New York Times*, 16 May 1957, pp. 1, 24;

"Crusade's Budget Totals $1,300,000," *New York Times*, 16 May 1957, p. 24;

"Crusade's Impact," *Time* (8 July 1957): 57–58;

"Held Over," *Time* (29 July 1957): 48;

E. J. Kahn, "The Wayward Press: Billy and Benny," *New Yorker* (8 June 1957): 117–123;

William Martin, *A Prophet with Honor: The Billy Graham Story* (New York: Morrow, 1991).

BLACK CHURCH LEADERS AND CIVIL RIGHTS

Struggle for Rights. The long-running efforts by black Americans to gain constitutional rights, especially in the

South, acquired national attention in the 1950s. The 1956 Supreme Court decision in *Brown* v. *Board of Education of Topeka, Kansas* ruled that legal segregation was unconstitutional, a ruling that signaled its ultimate end. But national attention was drawn to the problem of civil rights in the South in the Montgomery, Alabama, bus boycott. On 1 December 1955 Mrs. Rosa Parks was arrested when she refused to obey a city ordinance that required her to give up her seat to a white person when ordered to do so by the bus driver. The long-simmering dissatisfaction of the black community with the segregated bus system boiled over.

The Boycott. After a successful one-day boycott of the buses, a meeting at the Holt Street Baptist Church organized the Montgomery Improvement Association and elected Martin Luther King, Jr., the new pastor of the Dexter Avenue Baptist Church, as its head. In his first speech in the campaign, King struck the note of his civil rights career. "We are impatient for justice — but we will protest with love. There will be no violence on our part." When his house was bombed, King quieted the crowd of angry blacks with the admonition "if I am stopped, our work will not stop, for what we are doing is right. What we are doing is just and God is with us."

Supreme Court Victory. The boycott continued with various setbacks to blacks through the summer and fall, but on 13 November 1956 the U.S. Supreme Court affirmed a special district court order declaring Alabama's state and local laws segregating buses unconstitutional. By that time the Montgomery bus boycott had attracted national attention, and King had become a celebrity.

Leading the Battle. Even before the Montgomery boycott ended, the Reverend Charles K. Steele led bus desegregation campaigns in Tallahassee, Florida, and plans were made by other clergymen for similar efforts in Mobile and Birmingham. The civil rights movement, as it gained furious momentum, was lead in the 1950s by black church leaders.

SCLC. In response to an invitation by King, Steele, and the Reverend Fred Shuttlesworth of Birmingham, sixty black clergymen met in Atlanta 10–11 January 1957 to organize what became the Southern Christian Leadership Conference (SCLC), one of the leading civil rights organizations that helped end legal segregation in the 1960s. The black religious leaders in the South helped the civil rights movement frame the controversy over rights as a moral issue and, in some religious communities, as a Christian one.

Sources:
Taylor Branch, *Parting the Waters: America in the King Years, 1954–1963* (New York: Simon & Schuster, 1988);

John L. Eighmy, *Churches in Cultural Captivity: A History of the Social Attitudes of Southern Baptists* (Knoxville: University of Tennessee Press, 1987);

David Garrow, *Bearing the Cross: Martin Luther King, Jr., and the Southern Christian Leadership Conference* (New York: Morrow, 1986);

Andrew M. Manis, *Southern Civil Religions in Conflict: Black & White*

President Dwight D. Eisenhower gave proof that the United States was a religiously diverse nation when he attended the dedication of a $1.25 million Muslim mosque in Washington, D.C., on 28 June 1957. Financed by fifteen Islamic countries, the mosque was built to serve as the principal spiritual shrine to the 32,500 Muslims in the United States and Canada.

The news media was abuzz with speculation about how the president would observe the Muslim custom of removing shoes before entering a holy place. White House officials had prepared slippers that the president could slip over his shoes. Respectfully, Eisenhower removed his shoes and wore the slippers over his socks.

In his speech at the mosque Eisenhower forcefully defended the U.S. tradition of freedom of religion and its role in defining the character of the United States.

> And I should like to assure you, my Islamic friends, that under the American Constitution, under American tradition, and in American hearts, this Center, this place of worship, is just as welcome as could be a similar edifice of any other religion. Indeed, America would fight with her whole strength for your right to have here your own church and worship according to your own conscience.

Sources: "Minaret in Washington, *Time* (8 July 1957): 58;

"Opening of Islamic Center," *Department of State Bulletin*, 37 (15 July 1957): 102–103.

Baptists and Civil Rights, 1947–1957 (Athens: University of Georgia Press, 1987).

COMMUNISM IN THE CHURCHES

Red Religion. In the wildly anti-Communist climate of the cold war some American religious leaders, mostly Protestant, became targets of red-baiters. While some clergymen had been Communists or fellow travelers, particularly in the 1930s, few remained allied with Soviet communism after World War II. In many cases the postwar charges of Communist sympathy were made and supported by conservative Protestants, often labeled fundamentalists, who were angry with what they perceived as a liberal drift by the mainline denominations.

Senate Hearings. In 1951 the *Reader's Digest* carried an article, "Methodism's Pink Fringe," which charged that organizations within Methodism, the largest Protestant church in the United States, were filled with Communists and fellow travelers. In 1952 the House Committee on Un-American Activities extended that attack when it issued an eighty-seven- page pamphlet, *Review of the Methodist Foundation for Social Action*, charging that the organization generally followed the Communist party line.

Eisenhower's Response. These issues came to a head in March 1953 when Harold H. Velde, the Republican representative from Indiana and the new chairman of the House Committee on Un-American Activities (HUAC), remarked in a radio interview that the Protestant churches offered an area for investigation by his committee. His offhand comment triggered an uproar and charges and countercharges filled the air. On 19 March President Dwight D. Eisenhower blandly observed that an investigation into the clergy for communism was unnecessary and would do no good.

"Reds in Our Churches." The issue drifted from public attention until July, when Joseph Brown Matthews, a former member of the Communist party and the new staff director of the Senate Subcommittee on Investigations, the McCarthy Committee, published an article, "Reds in Our Churches" in the ultra right-wing magazine American Mercury. He charged that "the largest single group supporting the Communist apparatus in the United States today is composed of Protestant clergymen." He added that while the vast majority of the clergy was loyal, at least seven thousand Protestant ministers had served the Kremlin conspiracy. Once again there was an uproar. Again President Eisenhower was forced to speak out against the

Bishop G. Bromley Oxnam, left, with House Un-American Activities Committee chairman H. Velde

FLOCKING TO CHURCH, FORGETTING ABOUT CHRIST

Will Herberg's classic book *Protestant, Catholic, Jew* was published in 1956 and offered a sober response to those who hailed a rise in religious behavior in midcentury America. In his introduction Herberg cites evidence that at the time discouraged more-sanguine outlooks on the revival of religious fervor in the United States:

> In the five years from 1949 to 1953 the distribution of Scripture in the United States increased 140 per cent, reaching an all-time high of 9,726,391 volumes a year. People were apparently buying and distributing the Bible at an unprecedented rate. Furthermore, over four-fifths of adult Americans said they believed the Bible to be the "revealed word of God," rather than merely a "great piece of literature." Yet when these same Americans were asked to give the "names of the first four books of the New Testament of the Bible, that is, the first four gospels," 53 per cent could not name even one. The Bible can hardly be said to enter into the life and thought of Americans quite as much as their views on its divine inspiration and their eagerness to buy and distribute it might suggest.

> This is at least part of the picture presented by religion in contemporary America: Christians flocking to church, yet forgetting about Christ. . . .

> The religion which actually prevails among Americans today has lost much of its authentic Christian (or Jewish) content. Even when they are thinking, feeling, or acting religiously, their thinking, feeling, and acting do not bear an unequivocal relation to the faiths they profess. Americans think, feel, and act in terms quite obviously secularist at the very same time that they exhibit every sign of a widespread religious revival. It is this secularism of a religious people, this religiousness in a secularist framework, that constitutes the problem posed by the contemporary religious situation in America.

Source: Will Herberg, *Protestant, Catholic, Jew: An Essay in American Religious Sociology* (Garden City, N.Y.: Doubleday, 1956), pp. 14, 15.

excesses of the anti-Communist movement. In a vague statement the president stated that "generalized and irresponsible attacks that sweepingly condemn the whole of any group of citizens are alien to America." Matthews was forced to resign his position with the Senate committee.

Oxnam's Appearance. In the ongoing furor G.

Bromley Oxnam, Methodist bishop of Washington, D.C., asked to appear before the HUAC to defend himself against the charges he supported communism or Communist organizations, charges which had long circulated in right-wing circles and had been repeated by members of the committee. Oxnam was a pronounced liberal who had a long, distinguished career as a defender of civil liberties and of the weaker segments of society, including organized labor and blacks. One of the outstanding leaders of his denomination, he was one of the leaders of the modern ecumenical movement. He was a founder of the National Council of Churches and one of the presidents of the World Council of Churches. A longtime member of the executive board of the American Civil Liberties Union, he was a critic of HUAC and the anti-Communist excesses of Senator McCarthy. He was not a Communist.

End of the Furor. It was generally agreed that Oxnam defended himself effectively in the nearly ten hours he appeared before the committee. Liberal commentators, most newspapers, and large numbers of his fellow Methodists applauded not only his defense, but the questions he raised about the procedures and tactics of the committee. His appearance paved the way for the decline in anti-Communist hysteria in the following year. No formal investigation of communism in the churches took place.

Sources:

Richard M. Fried, *Nightmare in Red: The McCarthy Era in Perspective* (New York: Oxford University Press, 1990);

Walter Goodman, *The Committee: The Extraordinary Career of the House Committee on Un-American Activities* (New York: Farrar, Straus & Giroux, 1968);

Brooks R. Walker, *Christian Fright Peddlers* (Garden City, N.Y.: Doubleday & Company, 1964).

DEAD SEA SCROLLS

Discovery. In 1947 a Bedouin youth discovered some manuscripts in a cave at Qumran in the Dead Sea area of British-occupied Palestine. The developing tension in Palestine, the creation of the new Jewish state of Israel, and the resulting Arab-Israeli War all diverted attention from the quiet announcement in April 1948 by Millar Burrows of Yale University that the earliest known manuscript of the Book of Isaiah had been found in the Syrian monastery of Saint Mark in Jerusalem. (The Arab-Israeli War that followed the declaration of Israel's independence caused scholars interested in the manuscript fragments to disguise their source.)

Edmund Wilson. While academics in religious circles grew excited about the potential light the Dead Sea Scrolls would shed on Jewish culture and religion at the time of Jesus, the general public paid little heed until May 1955, when Edmund Wilson published a lengthy article in the *New Yorker* about the manuscripts and their implications. Later that year Wilson published *The Dead*

SABINE WEISS/RAPHO, PARIS

Scholars working on deciphering Dead Sea Scroll fragments in the Research Room of the Jerusalem Museum

In the following January 1960 statement Methodist bishop G. Bromley Oxnam presented his prediction of what the 1960s would hold for the world and the church.

The decade's most dramatic event will be the Interplanetary Conference of Religious Faith to be attended by the finest minds of all the planets of the universe. It will be the first "universal" conference on religion, made possible by scientific mastery of space travel. Teachable humility will characterize the delegates who will make known the revelation of God to all. Fundamentalist dogmatism and papal infallibility will have no place among men who love one another and seek the truth in freedom. It will be a "sharing" conference. How did God make Himself known to the inhabitants of Mars? Through incarnation in a Person, by revelation in a Book, through the thinking of a scholar or a saint? Is there evidence for immortality? The sessions will be televised, and the universe will come to know the universal truth that frees.

Source: Robert Moats Miller, *Bishop G. Bromley Oxnam, Paladin of Liberal Protestantism* (Nashville, Tenn.: Abingdon Press, 1990), p. 607.

Sea Scrolls, an expanded version of his article, and interest increased.

Clues of Historical Jesus. Early the following year a new excitement swept religious circles when John Allegro, one of the scholars working with the Dead Sea Scrolls, made a series of broadcasts in northern Great Britain in which he noted that one of the scrolls contained the assertion by the community at Qumran that their leader, called the Teacher of Righteousness, would be crucified, a seeming parallel to the crucifixion of Jesus. Allegro and others raised the question of the relation between the group at Qumran and the early Christians.

Public Interest. The issues of the Dead Sea Scrolls moved from the staid world of the academic and religious press into the popular press. *Time, Life, Newsweek,* and even *Reader's Digest* informed their readers of the controversy between Allegro and others who were willing to see the Gospels in a radical new light and the Christian scholars working on the manuscripts themselves in Jordan and Israel.

Exclusive Control. Questions were already being raised by concerned intellectuals such as Wilson about the exclusive control these scholars had over the fragments called the Dead Sea Scrolls. The refusal of those scholars to allow others to examine the fragments remained a source of controversy until the 1990s, when photocopies of the manuscripts themselves were finally released for general scholarly use.

Hopes and Fears. The Dead Sea Scrolls raised scholarly interest in biblical history to a fever pitch. The inability of scholars and intellectuals to examine the scrolls led to widespread speculation about their content. The lack of knowledge led many to theorize that the scrolls would radically revise biblical and Christian history and reverse what many considered theological mistakes.

Sources:
John Allegro, *The Dead Sea Scrolls and the Origins of Christianity* (New York: Criterion Books, 1957);

Michael Baignet and Richard Leigh, *The Dead Sea Scrolls Deception* (New York: Summit Books, 1991);

Millar Burrows, *The Dead Sea Scrolls* (New York: Viking, 1955);

"The Scrolls From The Dead Sea," *New Yorker* (14 May 1955): 45–133;

Edmund Wilson, *The Dead Sea Scrolls, 1947–1969* (New York: Oxford University Press, 1969).

SEPARATION OF CHURCH AND STATE

Spellman and Roosevelt. The issue of government aid to parochial schools remained divisive through the decade of the 1950s. Attempts to provide federal aid to education were opposed by the Roman Catholic church when the legislation that was proposed specifically prohibited any money going to church-run schools. In 1949 Eleanor Roosevelt, widow of the former president Franklin Roosevelt, supported federal aid with such restrictions. In a bitter letter Francis Cardinal Spellman, archbishop of New York, accused Mrs. Roosevelt of anti-Catholic prejudice and announced "I shall not again publicly acknowledge you."

Protestant Outrage. While the quarrel between Mrs. Roosevelt and the archbishop was publicly papered over, his letter stimulated an outcry and triggered the revitalization of the Protestants and Others Organized for the Separation of Church and State. Paul Blanshard, head of Protestants and Others, published two best-selling books in the 1950s attacking what he considered anti-democratic and dangerous tendencies in the Roman Catholic church.

Supreme Court Ruling. But the absolute separation of church and state was modified in 1952, when the U.S. Supreme Court in *Zorach* v. *Clauson* upheld a New York City law that gave students in public schools permission to leave the school for religious education. The only stipulation was that the instruction must be held in separate facilities with a separate faculty not paid with public funds. In his majority opinion Justice William O. Douglas noted that government is not required by the Constitution to be hostile to religion. Allowing public school children time during the school day for religious education did not violate the First Amendment.

New Jersey Cases. Religion in the public schools received somewhat confusing responses from the New Jersey Supreme Court. In 1950 that court upheld a forty-

The skirmish between fundamentalist and liberal conceptions of Christianity continued during the 1950s. In El Paso, Texas, in January 1953, the clash erupted into a full-scale battle. The focus of the uproar in Texas was the Reverend William Wright, rector of Saint Clements Protestant Episcopal Church. In a speech to the El Paso Bar Association, Reverend Wright addressed the issue of fundamentalist Christians.

He denounced the popular "camp meeting," an outdoor revival crusade popular in the area, as "emotional whingdings that provide a vacation from thinking." He pronounced reason equal to faith as a guide to religious belief. As an example of the need for reason in evaluating the miracle stories contained in the Bible, Wright said, "who does believe those stories that has any mind at all?"

The reaction from the fundamentalist community was quick and sharp. In a sermon at his First Church of the Nazarene, the Reverend Harold W. Morris replied that "we believe all that he makes fun of." A letter writer to the *El Paso Times* was even angrier, defending the anti-intellectualism at the heart of fundamentalism:

> I may not have as many college . . . degrees to my name as [Wright], but I have one degree, a God-conferred degree of B.A. (Born Again), which man did not give.

The anger was not aimed solely at Reverend Wright but at all Episcopalians. Camp meeting organizer Joe Evans, a Baptist layman, defended fundamentalism and attacked Wright and the Episcopal church in provocative terms. Camp meetings, Evans said, represent

> real, undefiled religion. If the Episcopal Church endorses the things Wright said in his address to the lawyers, I think they are fundamentally unsound in their belief and doctrine.

The bitter recriminations between fundamentalists and the older mainline religions in Texas hinted at slowly changing religious attitudes of Americans. The effects were not clear until the late 1960s and 1970s, when growth of the mainline denominations slowed, then stopped, and the fundamentalist denominations multiplied.

Source: "El Paso Whingding," *Time* (26 January 1953): 62.

seven-year-old law that required recitation of five verses from the Old Testament by public-school children at the start of each school day. But in 1953 that court prohibited the distribution of free Bibles in those schools, even when the children had written permission from their parents to receive one. The distribution program was held to be a violation of the separation of church and state.

A Continuing Controversy. The controversy over the government role in regulating religious activity escalated during the decade. The conflict between a secular state and a society that saw itself as generally religious and specifically Christian was an age-old problem that developed new twists in rapidly changing postwar America.

HOLLYWOOD AND RELIGIOUS FILMS

Great Religious Interest. The decade of the 1950s saw the movie industry produce several religious films which attracted large audiences and wide-spread attention. Hollywood had a long tradition of biblical and religious films set in a historical context, so these religious movies were not unique. Rather they were examples of the movie industry's long tradition of catering to the public mood. The great religious interest of the decade suggested a ready-made audience for such movies as Hollywood faced the growing competition of television. Historical spectaculars, shown on wide screens in vivid colors that the small, black-and-white television sets of the time could not match, were supposed to confirm the movie industry's slogan that "Movies Are Better Than Ever."

Quo Vadis. Most of the popular religious films of the decade were fictions set in the early Christian era. In 1951 Mervyn LeRoy directed Robert Taylor and Deborah Kerr in a version of 1905 Nobel Prize winner Henryk Sienkiewicz's novel *Quo Vadis* (1897). Peter Ustinov played Nero. In 1953 20th Century–Fox introduced its new wide-screen process, CinemaScope, with a version of Lloyd C. Douglas's best seller, *The Robe*. This popular film, directed by Harry Koster, starred Richard Burton, Jean Simmons, and Victor Mature. Mature starred in a less popular sequel the following year, *Demitrius and the Gladiators*.

Ben-Hur. The decade closed with William Wyler's sound version of *Ben-Hur*, that old warhorse from the silent era. This extravaganza starred Charlton Heston and Stephen Boyd. The chariot race scene enthralled audiences and critics, who had some reservations about the rest of the movie. The film swept the Academy Awards for 1959. Heston won the best actor award, Hugh Griffith, best supporting actor, Wyler, best director, and the film won the best picture award.

Problem of Pluralism. These movies set in the early Christian era faced significant problems. The producers had to recognize that there were a variety of religious views in the nation. Not only were there Protestants and

Catholics but there were liberals and conservatives in both these communities. In addition there were the sensibilities of the large American Jewish community to be taken into consideration. Finally the low level of biblical information in the general population raised problems even in the Christian fictions.

The Ten Commandments. These issues faced the director Cecil B. DeMille when he returned to the story of Moses in 1956 in his last movie, *The Ten Commandments.* The film had a star-filled cast with Charlton Heston playing Moses and Yul Brynner as Rameses, his competitor for the throne of Egypt. As in most of the films made in the cold war era, DeMille contrasted the freedom seeking of the captive Jews with their Egyptian slave masters. The unconscious cold war assumptions of the American public were ahistorically applied to the past.

Science and Religion. DeMille also faced the problem other directors of the period encountered, how to treat the miracles of the Bible stories in an age when some accepted them as given in the Bible and others would accept only a scientific explanation. Like other directors DeMille tried to present the burning bush and the parting of the Red Sea in ways that either camp could accept. He was not always successful for those who looked for a natural, not a miraculous, explanation of these biblical events.

Uncertain Effect. The success of films with religious themes was significant mainly in that it revealed the extent that the public was interested in spritual matters. The effect of these movies on anything other than the financial health of movie studios and theaters is pure speculation.

Churches' Role. Much of the hard work of promoting civil rights and integration during the 1950s took place in the churches of the United States. In November 1952 eight of the nine faculty of the Graduate School of Theology of the University of the South in Sewanee, Tennessee, including the dean of the school, announced their resignation effective at the end of the academic year in 1953. They were protesting a ban on admission of black students to that Episcopal university. In June 1953 the trustees of the institution voted to permit the entrance of students to that graduate program without regard to race. The Reverend John M. Moncrief, black, of Orangeburg, South Carolina, applied.

Simon Montgomery. In 1955 the Reverend Simon P. Montgomery was named pastor of the Methodist church in Old Mystic, Connecticut. A native of South Carolina and a graduate of Boston University, he was the first black minister to head an all-white Methodist congregation. His appointment was not forced on the Old Mystic congregation but was a result of a two-week visit as a guest minister. After two sermons the congregation voted to ask Montgomery to remain in Old Mystic. One worshiper commented, "It was the work of God that sent him here." In May 1956 the Quadrennial Conference of the Methodist Church, the nation's largest Protestant denomination, voted to send to its conferences a resolution to abolish the denomination's all-black Central Jurisdiction. The Central Jurisdiction, with its own bishop, was created when the Northern and Southern Methodist Churches merged in 1936. It encompassed almost all the church's 360,000 black members. When a geographic,

Rev. Simon P. Montgomery, the first black pastor of an all-white Methodist parish, preaching in Old Mystic, Connecticut

annual conference approved, a conference from the Central Jurisdiction could merge. Joint approval by a local congregation and an annual conference could move that congregation from the Central Jurisdiction. In eleven years the Central Jurisdiction came to an end.

Catholic Success. The Roman Catholic church was more successful in desegregating its congregations in the Deep South. As early as 1953 Archbishop Joseph F. Rummel of New Orleans abolished segregation in the churches of his archdiocese and said blacks could no longer be barred from parish organizations. In 1955 he suspended a mission congregation at Jesuit Bend, Louisiana, when the parishioners refused to hear a black priest say mass. Also in 1955 Bishop Jules B. Jeanmard of Lafayette, Louisiana, excommunicated three female parishoners after they attacked a white lay teacher teaching catechism in a mixed-race classroom. In February 1956 Archbishop Rummel issued a pastoral letter in which he said racial segregation is "morally wrong and sinful."

Work Remaining. But segregation was still a social fact in most American churches at the end of the decade, despite the courageous efforts of many religious leaders.

Sources:
"Guest Editorial of the Week," *Christian Century* (19 October 1955): 1196;

" 'Work of God' in Old Mystic," *Life,* 39 (31 October 1955): 65–66.

THE BANNING OF THE MIRACLE

Critical Acclaim. On 30 December 1950 the New York City License Commissioners banned the showing of Roberto Rossellini's award-winning film, *The Miracle.* The movie, shown in Italian with English subtitles, concerned a half-witted peasant girl, played by Anna Magnani, who is seduced by a man calling himself "Saint Joseph." The girl becomes convinced that she has miraculously conceived her child. Although the New York Film Critics gave *The Miracle* its award as best foreign film for 1950, the film attracted the attention of the New York archdiocese, which secured a permanent ban from the city's license commission on the grounds that the movie was "officially and personally blasphemous."

Pastoral Condemnation. A temporary injunction against the ban was secured, but in January 1951 Francis Cardinal Spellman issued a pastoral letter to the two million members of the New York archdiocese. He condemned the film and decreed that New York Catholics boycott it. Spellman also recommended a boycott to all Catholics. A month later the New York State Board of Regents issued a ban, calling the movie sacrilegious, citing a state law which made it unlawful to "treat any religion with contempt, mockery or ridicule."

Supreme Court Ruling. In the 1952 case *Burstyn v. Wilson,* the U.S. Supreme Court overturned the ruling by the regents as an unconstitutional violation of the First Amendment. In his unanimous decision Justice Tom C.

CARDINAL SPELLMAN'S DECREE ON BABY DOLL

On 16 December 1956 Francis Cardinal Spellman instructed American Catholics not to see the racy film *Baby Doll*. The steamy movie starring Carroll Baker was masterfully suggestive. Not even a kiss was exchanged in the film adapted from "27 Wagons full of Cotton" by Tennessee Williams. Cardinal Spellman decreed:

> In the performance of my duty as Archbishop of New York, in solicitude for the welfare of souls entrusted to my care and the welfare of my country, I exhort Catholic people to refrain from patronizing this film under pain of sin.
>
> It has been suggested that this action on my part will induce many people to view this picture and thus make it a material success. If this be the case, it will be a indictment of those who defy God's laws and contribute to corruption in America.

The effect was controversial. Critics called the boycott decree religious censorship while supporters hailed Spellman for his courageous moral stand. The controversy no doubt contributed to the commercial success of the movie.

Source: Robert I. Gannon, *The Cardinal Spellman Story* (Garden City, N.Y.: Doubleday, 1962), p. 335.

Clark wrote that the state could not ban a movie because it was sacrilegious. Such a level of censorship would set local censors and the courts "adrift upon a boundless sea of conflicting religious views" and might end in favoring one religion against another, a clear violation of the establishment clause. For the first time movies were recognized as being protected under the First Amendment, perhaps even as broadly as the printed word.

Sources:
"Catholics & the Movies," *Time* (22 December 1952): 66;

Walter Kerr, "Catholics and Hollywood," *Commonweal* (19 December 1952): 275–279.

NATIONAL COUNCIL OF CHURCHES

The Ecumenical Movement. The ecumenical movement gained strength during the 1950s as Christian churches joined together to attempt the formation of a single voice in support of peace and civil rights.

Founding of the NCC. On 1 January 1951 the National Council of the Churches of Christ in the United States of America (NCC) came into being. This organization brought the old Federal Council of Churches and eleven other interdenominational bodies into a coopera-

Henry K. Sherrill, first president of the National Council of Churches

tive body that included twenty-five Protestant denominations and four Eastern Orthodox churches. It was, as the *Christian Century* commented, "potentially one of the most influential bodies in American Protestantism." The following year the Greek Orthodox Archdiocese of North and South America affiliated with the National Council. The largest bodies remaining outside the council included the Roman Catholic church and the Southern Baptist Convention.

Dedication of Headquarters. In 1958 President Eisenhower laid the cornerstone for the Interchurch Center, an eighteen-story building that occupies a city block on Morningside Heights in New York City near Riverside Church, Union Seminary, and Columbia University. The first of the NCC agencies moved to the building the following year.

Controversy. The organization drew fire from conservative and fundamentalist faiths, which maintained that the NCC distorted biblical truths in the name of political goals, but it did much to engage the churches in ministering to lessen social problems.

Sources:
"Here We Stand," *Christian Century,* 75 (26 March 1958): 363–364;

Henry J. Pratt, *The Liberalization of American Protestantism* (Detroit: Wayne State University Press, 1972).

REVISED STANDARD VERSION OF THE BIBLE

Publication. On 30 September 1952 the Revised Standard Version (RSV) of the Bible was published under the sanction of the National Council of Churches of Christ. A group of thirty-two scholars worked for fifteen years to produce this contemporary translation of the Bible. The new translation was received with enthusiasm by most Protestants and immediately became a best-seller. The first printing of one million copies was sold in two days, and the translation sold an average of one million copies a year throughout the decade. That translation, along with other versions, made the Bible the continual top best-selling book. In 1955 booksellers agreed to take its status as a given and drop it from the popularity charts.

Controversy over the NCC. There were protests against the new version. Conservative Protestants were offended at what appeared to be an attempt to replace the beloved King James Version. Criticism focused on two general issues, the relation of the RSV to the National Council of Churches, which had sponsored the scholars and benefited from its sales, and some shifts of words used between the RSV and the King James Version. A particular irritant for conservatives was the RSV's use of the phrase *young woman* instead of *virgin* in Isa. 7:14 foretelling the birth of the Messiah. These complaints charged that the RSV challenged the Virgin Birth of Jesus.

Other Versions. Others versions of the Bible were published during the decade. In 1953 Hebrew University's Magnes Press issued the Jerusalem Bible, the first revision of the Hebrew text by Jewish scholars in Jerusalem. In 1956 Reginal Knox issued a new translation of the Holy Bible from the Latin Vulgate, reflecting the Hebrew and Greek originals. And in 1958 a new English edition of the Roman Catholic Bible, known as the Catholic Bible in Saint Peter's Edition, was published.

Interest in Religion. The almost continual retranslation and publishing of biblical texts was one example of the swell of religious interest during the decade. It was also the product of new knowledge and new techniques of gaining information about biblical history and languages

RELIGIOUS BEST-SELLERS

A Man Called Peter. The widespread interest in religious issues was evident in popular books with religious themes in the early part of the decade of the 1950s. In 1950 the words of the late Peter Marshall, *Mr. Jones Meet Your Maker,* continued on the best-seller list. In 1951 his widow, Catharine Marshall, published *A Man Called Peter,* a popular biography of this former chaplin of the U.S. Senate. For nearly three years the book was on the best-seller list, and more than one million copies were sold.

TILLICH ON NIETZSCHE

In the following passage from *The Courage to Be,* Paul Tillich discusses the German philosopher Friedrich Nietzsche and his relation to Tillich's ideas about existential Christian courage:

Life has many aspects, it is ambiguous. Nietzsche has described its ambiguity most typically in the last fragment of the collection of fragments which is called the *Will to Power.* Courage is the power of life to affirm itself in spite of this ambiguity, while the negation of life because of its negativity is an expression of cowardice. On this basis Nietzsche develops a prophecy and philosophy of courage in opposition to the mediocrity and decadence of life in the period whose coming he saw.

Source: Paul Tillich, *The Courage to Be* (New Haven: Yale University Press, 1952), pp. 27–28.

Peale. Other nonfiction books with religious themes attracted large numbers of readers. In 1952 the Reverend Norman Vincent Peale, pastor of the Marble Collegiate Church in New York City, continued his run of best-sellers with *The Power of Positive Thinking,* which sold 971,336 copies in the next three years.

Sheen. Bishop Fulton J. Sheen confirmed the popularity of his television program with a 1953 collection of his messages, *Life Is Worth Living.* Neither Sheen's book nor Billy Graham's collection of sermons, *Peace with God,* published that same year, had the lengthy life on the best-seller list as did Peale's work.

Cardinal Spellman. In fiction Francis Cardinal Spellman published *The Foundling* first as a serial in *Good Housekeeping* magazine and then in book form. Lloyd C. Douglas's *The Robe* returned to the best-seller list after the success of the film version of the novel, and his last book, *The Big Fisherman,* a novel about Saint Peter, continued his best-selling works.

Drama. In the theater the New York Drama Critics Circle chose T. S. Eliot's *Cocktail Party* as the best foreign play for 1950, and in 1959 Archibald Macleish's *J. B.,* a version of the Book of Job, won the Antoinette Perry (Tony) Award for best play. Elia Kazan won the Tony for his direction of the play, which went on to win the Pulitzer Prize for 1958.

HEADLINE MAKERS

BILLY GRAHAM

1918-

EVANGELIST

GALE PORTRAIT GALLERY

Famous for Crusades. By the end of the 1950s William Franklin Graham, better known as Billy, had become the most famous revivalist in the world. His effective presentation of evangelical Christianity in his "crusades" made him one of the leading figures in the revival of religious fervor in the postwar period.

Early Life. Born in North Carolina to a family of dairy farmers, Graham first began preaching in 1938 in Florida. He was ordained in 1939 as a Southern Baptist minister and spent the next few years studying at Wheaton Bible College in Illinois and ministering at the First Baptist Church in Western Springs, Illinois. From 1944 through 1947 he was chief preacher at a series of "Youth for Christ" rallies conceived by Minneapolis, Minnesota, bookshop owner George W. Wilson.

Cold War Preaching. Graham burst onto the national stage when his Los Angeles revival of 1948 received the attention of the Hearst newspaper chain. In the coming years he refined his presentations, honed his skills, but kept the familiar message that faith in Jesus brought salvation. In those tense days of the cold war, he also warned of the dangers that communism presented to Christians and Americans. At times he seemed to indicate that Christianity and Americanism were the same.

Good Planning and Organization. One of the causes of Graham's success was the team he brought into his organization, the Billy Graham Evangelistic Association.

His association was guided by three principles that helped to create the success of the crusades: he would crusade only in a city where local churches had invited him; all financial proceeds would go to the Graham's association, which would pay Graham only a reasonable annual salary; and the crusade would concentrate on telling the audience to attend a local church. In the 1950s Graham and his associates moved from city to city and demonstrated that large numbers of people, mostly members of evangelical churches, were eager to hear the old-time message. By middecade he had become famous and a leading figure in the renewal and growing self-confidence of conservative Protestantism. In 1955 he helped found *Christianity Today*, a self-conscious magazine voice for evangelicals, as they called themselves

London Crusade. In 1954 Graham took his crusade to Harringay Arena in London for a twelve-week Billy Graham Greater London Crusade. Not since the triumph of Dwight L. Moody nearly a hundred years earlier had an American evangelist attracted the crowds and attention of the British public. The press attention in London spread Graham's name throughout the English-speaking world. The crowds he attracted later that summer as he moved from one European city to another extended his fame. Graham returned to the United States as the most famous evangelist in the world. As Graham's fame grew, he became friends with other national figures. He was especially close to President Eisenhower, and Vice-president Richard Nixon appeared at his New York Crusade in 1957.

Appealing Across the Spectrum. Graham came out of the conservative evangelical community, but his generosity of spirit and focus on a general Christian message made him acceptable to most mainline Protestants. By the end of the decade some conservatives distanced themselves from Graham because of the support he received from denominations and churches they perceived as too liberal.

Civil Rights. Graham came somewhat late to the civil rights movement, but by 1957 he was willing to have the Reverend Martin Luther King, Jr., appear with him in New York, and he joined the condemnation of racism as un-Christian.

Newspaper Work. Graham developed a widely syndicated newspaper column, "My Answer," in which he addressed religious and moral issues. His sermons were collected in a widely read book, *Peace with God*, published in 1953. The success of televising his sermons enabled him to reach an unprecedented number of people, and his efforts to turn men and women back to God continued.

Sources:
William Martin, *A Prophet with Honor: The Billy Graham Story* (New York: Morrow, 1991).

MARTIN LUTHER KING, JR.

1929-1968

MINISTER AND CIVIL RIGHTS LEADER

BETTMANN

New Pastor. Martin Luther King, Jr., first attracted national attention as the president of the Montgomery Improvement Agency, which successfully conducted a bus boycott in Montgomery, Alabama, from 1955 to 1956. This role began when, as the new pastor of the Dexter Avenue Baptist Church, he was elected president of the ad hoc group organized in December 1955 to coordinate a one-day boycott of the Montgomery bus system to protest the arrest of Mrs. Rosa Parks. Parks had violated a city ordinance by refusing to give up her seat for a white man.

Success of the Boycott. The success of the one-day boycott was such that it was continued for over a year as blacks refused to ride the buses until the Jim Crow restrictions were lifted. In time the bus company went into bankruptcy, and the city ordinance segregating blacks was struck down as unconstitutional. On 20 December 1956 King was one of the first to board the bus when the Montgomery bus company allowed its riders to occupy seats of their choice.

National Attention. King, who was completing his Ph.D. at Boston University during this time, solidified his support in the black community of Montgomery and gained national attention when his house was bombed 30 January 1956. The threat to the lives of his wife and small children garnered much sympathy. His appeal for calm and his insistence that the boycotters would face their opponents with Christian love gave a special character to

the demonstration and the southern civil rights movement that followed. King was noted for his adoption of the Gandhian strategy of nonviolence, in which protesters rejected violence as a means of political and social change.

SCLC. In 1957 King joined a group of Baptist ministers in forming what became the Southern Christian Leadership Conference (SCLC). He was elected the first president of what became one of the leading civil rights organizations. His leadership helped form the nonviolent character of much of the civil rights movement. As the leader of the SCLC, King made 208 speeches and traveled more than 780,000 miles during 1957.

Influence of India. In 1958 King published *Stride Toward Freedom: The Montgomery Story*, his first book. At a book signing in Harlem King was nearly killed when a deranged woman stabbed him in the chest. King's reaction was to see this act of violence as a product of "the climate of hate and bitterness" that permeated the United States. In 1959 King traveled to India to visit the land of Gandhi. He spent the rest of the year demonstrating against segregation.

Effect on Religious Leaders. The religious content of the civil rights movement, due in large part to the influence of King, helped develop the social conscience of American churches. Many U.S. religious leaders and preachers came of age during the struggles of the 1950s and 1960s, and King's influence on them was hard to underestimate.

Sources:
Taylor Branch, *Parting the Waters: America in the King Years, 1954–1963* (New York: Simon & Schuster, 1988);

David Garrow, *Bearing the Cross: Martin Luther King, Jr., and the Southern Christian Leadership Conference* (New York: Morrow, 1986).

REINHOLD NIEBUHR

1892-1971

THEOLOGIAN

ALFRED EISENSTADT

Neo-orthodoxy. In 1950 *Time* magazine called Reinhold Niebuhr the "number one theologian of United States Protestantism." Although a stroke affected his work to some extent Niebuhr remained an influential figure in American religious thought and political affairs throughout the 1950s. He resisted being classified as part of the European movement called Neo-orthodoxy, but his insistence on man's sinful nature and distance from God and the need for the mediating presence of Jesus gave some support to those who saw him as representing an American version of the movement. His theology, which greatly affected religious thought during the following decade, was best expressed in *The Nature and Destiny of Man: A Christian Interpretation*, a work of two volumes published in 1941 and 1943.

Political Views. The secular world paid more attention to Niebuhr the political thinker than Niebuhr the theologian. But his political views were shaped and developed in a religious context. In his first major book, *Moral Man and Immoral Society* (1932), he attacked the utopian ideas of Marxism and the liberal belief that education could alleviate human suffering. Niebuhr left the Socialist party in 1940 in protest over its pacifistic views of World War II. He increasingly turned to liberal democracy as the system best able to maximize justice and minimize oppression.

Defending the Democratic System. In *The Children of Light and the Children of Darkness: A Vindication of Democracy and a Critique of the Traditional Defense* (1944), he attempted to find a religious defense for the democratic system. As he said in *The Nature and Destiny of Man*, "Man's capacity for justice makes democracy possible, but man's inclination for injustice makes democracy necessary."

Countervailing Power. With other liberal defenders of democracy, Niebuhr contributed to the liberal concept of countervailing power to show how democracy could work, if not smoothly. Competition among various interests in the nation, such as big business, labor, and the federal government, would contribute to the general good. Democracy is "a method of finding proximate solutions for insoluble problems."

ADA. In 1947 Niebuhr joined the organizing Americans for Democratic Action (ADA) in an effort to counter Henry Wallace's Progressive Citizens of America. As the Progressive party, this Communist-infiltrated group supported Wallace in the presidential campaign of 1948. With the collapse of the Progressive movement, the liberal ADA was the dominant force on the left in American politics in the cold war era.

Irony and Paradox. In his last major book, *The Irony of American History* (1952), Niebuhr displayed his use of irony and love of paradox to discuss the problems faced by a nation that believed in a special destiny, whose actions tended to achieve results contrary to their original aims.

Christianity and Crisis. Niebuhr served as editor of *Christianity and Crisis*, a political journal he founded in 1941. In this journal he maintained a running commentary on the current political scene. His influence was more public than Paul Tillich's, though each contributed to the moral tenor of the times. Both were important underpinnings to the moral arguments sustaining the cold war.

Sources:

Charles C. Brown, *Niebuhr and His Age: Reinhold Niebuhr's Prophetic Role in the Twentieth Century* (Philadelphia: Trinity Press International, 1992);

Ronald H. Stone, *Reinhold Niebuhr: Prophet to Politicians* (Nashville: Abingdon Press, 1972).

G. BROMLEY OXNAM
1891-1963

METHODIST BISHOP OF WASHINGTON, D.C.

Ecumenical Leader. G. Bromley Oxnam, Methodist bishop of Washington, D.C., was one of the six founding presidents of the World Council of Churches. He served as president of the Federal Council of Churches of Christ in America and was the presiding officer at the founding meeting of the National Council of Churches in 1950.

Opposed to Catholic Church. He was an opponent of many policies of the Roman Catholic church and clashed with Francis Cardinal Spellman over international affairs, questions of public aid to parochial education, and the appointing of an American ambassador to the Vatican. In 1948 he helped found Protestants and Others Organized for the Separation of Church and State, an organization that attempted to limit the influence of the Roman Catholic church in American politics.

Liberalism. An active liberal, he abolished the ROTC and military training at DePauw University when he was president of that college from 1928 to 1936. He was popular with students there because he permitted dancing. Oxnam traveled in the Soviet Union in the 1920s and became a target of red-baiters in the 1930s as they agitated about the supposed infiltration of Communists into American life.

Accused as Fellow Traveler. Oxnam's willingness to join groups whose goals he approved gave him the appearance of being a fellow traveler as he associated himself with organizations that were influenced by Communists. While never in the Communist orbit, he was widely regarded as too uncritical of some front organizations and continued to be a target for religious and political conservatives in his denomination.

Senate Hearings. When Harold H. Velde, (R.-Indiana), chair of the House Committee on Un-American Activities and a fellow Methodist, remarked that the Protestant church was subject to investigation for Communist infiltration, Oxnam volunteered to appear before the committee. His defense of his record attracted wide attention, and his friends believed he fully vindicated himself. In 1954 he published *I Protest*. In 1958 he published his last book, *A Testament of Faith*.

Untroubled by Despair. Oxnam's importance was in his service in the ecumenical organizations the National Council of Churches and the World Council of Churches. He was a modern thinker and believed the future would bring great progress. Christianity would have its place in that progress. Oxnam seemed not to be troubled, as were Tillich and Niebuhr, with the philosophical despair so evident in the post-atomic-bomb world of the 1950s.

Sources:
Robert Moats Miller, *Bishop G. Bromley Oxnam: Paladin of Liberal Protestantism* (Nashville: Abingdon Press, 1990).

NORMAN VINCENT PEALE

1898-1993

AUTHOR AND MINISTER

Marble Collegiate. Norman Vincent Peale came to the Marble Collegiate Church in New York City in 1932, leaving his Methodist background for this Reformed Church in America congregation. He revitalized that congregation, turning it into one of the largest congregations in the city. One of Peale's most important innovations for Marble Collegiate was what became the American Foundation for Religion and Psychiatry, a psychological counseling program affiliated with his congregation. Another aspect of his ministry was the creation of the magazine *Guideposts*, a periodical that focused on stories of religious faith in action.

Best-Seller. In 1948 Peale published *The Power of Confident Living* and followed it with *The Power of Positive Thinking* (1952), which stayed on the best-seller list for years. He revised his sermons into other books assuring his readers that religion would improve their personal lives, *Stay Alive All Your Life* (1957) and *Amazing Results of Positive Thinking* (1959).

Stevenson's Put Down. While Peale was one of the most beloved ministers of the postwar world many people, particularly intellectuals, found his piety shallow and his religiosity offensive. Adlai Stevenson, the Democratic candidate for president in 1952 and 1956, remarked that while he found Saint Paul appealing, he found Peale appalling.

Sources:
Carol V. George, *God's Salesman: Norman Vincent Peale and the Power of Positive Thinking* (New York: Oxford University Press, 1992).

JOSEPH FRANCIS RUMMEL

1876-1964

ARCHBISHOP OF NEW ORLEANS

Role in Integration. Archbishop Joseph Francis Rummel was one of the most forthright white supporters of integration in the American Christian churches. His efforts to accomplish integration in the Catholic schools in his New Orleans archdioscese made him a much-admired and much-hated figure.

Knowledge of Racial Tension. Rummel served as archbishop of New Orleans, the largest archdiocese in the South from 1935 to 1964. He served as pastor of a parish in Harlem in New York City from 1924 to 1928. The neighborhood was still predominantly white, but it had begun to experience the influx of black residents that soon made it the leading black urban area in the nation. The experience made Rummel sensitive to the issues of race and prejudice. In New Orleans one-fifth of the nearly 550,000 members of his archdiocese were black. The Roman Catholic church ran the largest school district in the state of Louisiana, with 184 elementary schools and high schools. Forty of those schools served only black students.

Integrating His Dioscese. In 1953 Archbishop Rummel began the process of integrating the Catholic church in his dioscese. He ordered the desegregation of his parishes, including parish organizations from which blacks had been banned from joining. He demonstrated his commitment in 1955 by suspending the Mission of Saint Cecilia at Jesuit Bend, Louisiana, when the congregation refused to hear a black priest say mass. Rummel called the congregation's refusal "a violation of the obligation of reverence and devotion which Catholics owe every priest of God, regardless of race, color, or nationality."

Threatening Excommunication. In 1956, four days after a federal court declared all Louisiana school segregation laws unconstitutional, Archbishop Rummel issued a pastoral letter, read in each of the churches of the archdiocese, denouncing racial segregation as "morally wrong and sinful." He announced he would desegregate the church's schools on a year by year basis, beginning at the first grade. The Louisiana legislature reacted to the federal court ruling by passing laws which gave the state police powers to continue to enforce segregation. Three Catholic legislators proposed extending the same powers to the parochial schools. Rummel responded by threatening the legislators with excommunication if they continued to work for state intervention in church affairs.

Opposition. Rummel's stance brought opposition from the White Citizens' Council and the Association of

Catholic Laymen. His stoutly moral position aided in the church being a positive force in the civil rights struggle in Louisiana.

Sources:

"Archbishop's Way," *Time*, 67 (5 March 1956): 80;

"Catholic Discipline at Its Finest," *Christian Century*, 72 (2 November 1955): 1260;

"Integration in New Orleans," *Commonweal*, 63 (2 March 1956): 562.

FULTON J. SHEEN

1895-1979

ROMAN CATHOLIC PRIEST; TELEVISION PERSONALITY

NAT FEIN

Religious Decade. The idea of the 1950s as a religious decade is given credence by the fact that a religious show was one of the most popular programs on television.

Man of the Year. Bishop Fulton J. Sheen was probably the best-known Roman Catholic clergyman of the 1950s because of his widely popular television show, "Life Is Worth Living." Sheen, who had attracted attention by his writings and his conversions of celebrities such as Clare Booth Luce, took his radio show to the new medium of television and excelled. He became one of the first television celebrities. In 1953 a *Radio-Television Daily* poll named him Television Man of the Year, and that same year the Academy of Television Arts and Sciences presented him with one of the first Emmy Awards as most outstanding personality.

Sermons. That same year his television sermons, published under the title of his show, were eagerly purchased, and a series of those sermons were issued each year. He served as director of the Society for the Propagation of the Faith and was named auxiliary bishop of New York in 1951.

FRANCIS CARDINAL SPELLMAN

1889-1967

ARCHBISHOP OF NEW YORK

The American Pope. Francis Cardinal Spellman, named to the Papal Curia in 1946, was America's leading Roman Catholic clergyman in the mid twentieth century. His enemies sometimes called him "the American Pope," and the cardinal's residence and office on Fifth Avenue was openly referred to as "The Powerhouse." A staunch defender of the interests of his church as he

saw them, he had few compunctions in engaging in public quarrels with those he opposed. As in his quarrel with Eleanor Roosevelt in the late 1940s over government aid to parochial schools, he frequently accused his opponents of being prejudiced against Catholics.

Ambassador Controversy. One of his tactics was to create controversy in 1951, when President Harry S Truman nominated Gen. Mark Clark ambassador to the Vatican. Cardinal Spellman defended this appointment and its usefulness but weakened his case by implying those who opposed diplomatic relations with the papacy were anti-Catholic. In spite of extensive Catholic support for the appointment, Clark withdrew his nomination in early 1952. The resistance from Protestants and other people concerned about direct political relations with what they saw as a religion was too great. No ambassador was named.

Protestant Suspicion. Protestants, alarmed by the thought of a direct connection between the United States government and the Vatican, continued to express their concern, directing much of it at the cardinal. But Cardinal Spellman continued to support diplomatic relations and made it clear that he disapproved of Sen. John F. Kennedy's promise that he would not appoint an ambassador to the Vatican when in 1958 the Roman Catholic senator began his campaign for the presidency.

Movie Censorship. Cardinal Spellman further angered non-Catholics and civil libertarians by his attempts to block presentations of films he considered morally offensive. The controversy over *The Miracle* in 1950 led to the 1952 Supreme Court ruling in *Burstyn* v. *Wilson* that extended First Amendment protection to movies, thereby making regulation and censorship more difficult. In spite of this loss Cardinal Spellman attacked the movie *Baby Doll* from his pulpit in 1956, condemning it for sexual immorality. The resulting uproar probably contributed to the film's financial success.

Political Power. The cardinal used his power in church, city, state, and government affairs. He linked his religion and his patriotism, as did many other religious figures during these early years of the cold war. As military vicar for the United States, the cardinal endeared himself to soldiers and their families, as well as to his fellow Catholics, by his frequent appearances before the military. This was particularly true in the bitter years of the Korean War, when he made several trips to the battle field.

End of an Era. Spellman's significance was more telling in the years and decades that followed the 1950s. Spellman wielded power when the public perception of American Catholicism was that it was unified and of one mind. With the crisis of Vatican II during the early 1960s and the turmoil of the Vietnam War, Catholics came to be seen as one more group rent by divisive disagreements over substantive matters. He was probably the last American Catholic clergyman to seem to speak for a unified religious body.

Sources:

John Cooney, *The American Pope: The Life and Times of Francis Cardinal Spellman* (New York: Times Books, 1984);

Robert I. Gannon, S.J., *The Cardinal Spellman Story* (Garden City, N.Y.: Doubleday, 1962);

Langdon B. Gilkey, *Catholicism Confronts Modernism: A Protestant View* (New York: Seabury Press, 1975).

PAUL TILLICH

1886-1965

THEOLOGIAN

Responding to Modernity. Paul Tillich was the most influential Protestant theologian in the United States in the 1950s. His program was to meld traditional Christianity with modern sensibilies regarding science, psychology, sociology, and ethics. His influence was immense, and along with Niebuhr he was instrumental in developing a Christian realism which many religious people felt necessary in the modern scientific and technological world of the 1950s.

Against the Nazis. A professor of philosophy at the University of Frankfurt, the Prussian-born Tillich was suspended from that position by the National Socialist government in early 1933 and immigrated to the United States later that year. He took pride in asserting that he was "about the first non-Jewish professor dismissed from a German university." When he arrived he was given a visiting professorship at Union Theological Seminary in New York City. Tillich became an American citizen in 1940. The post at Union became permanent, and he stayed there until summer 1954, a span of twenty-two years. On 1 July 1954 he was appointed University Professor at Harvard University Divinity School, a position he held for six years.

Culture and Religion. Tillich's work connected a variety of fields to theology and philosophy. He was always on the border. He was concerned with linking culture in its widest sense to religion. He did extensive work in art and depth psychology. But always he was concerned with what he called the Protestant principle, "the protesting voice of the prophet outside the temple calling the people back to God. . . ." In 1951 he published the first volume of his major work *Systemic Theology*. He said he had been preparing for thirty years to write it. The second volume was published in 1957 and the concluding volume in 1963.

Existentialism. A more accessible work and one which brought him much attention among the general public was *The Courage to Be* (1952), which approached existen-tialism from a religious perspective. His influence was also felt in the Christian response to the cold war arms buildup. A Federal Council of Churches of Christ in America task force, on which Tillich served, concluded that Christian teaching must oppose all unnecessary killing and destruction without surrendering to tyranny. The important caveats, "unnecessary" and "without surrendering to tyranny," were crucial moral underpinnings for U.S. policy in the cold war.

Sources:

Langdon B. Gilkey, *Gilkey on Tillich* (New York: Crossroad, 1990);

Wayne W. Mahan, *Tillich's System* (San Antonio: Trinity University Press, 1974);

Bernard Martin, *The Existentialist Theology of Paul Tillich* (New York: Bookman Associates, 1963);

Wilhelm and Marion Pauck, *Paul Tillich: His Life and Thought* (New York: Harper & Row, 1976).

ALAN WATTS

1915-1973

WRITER AND THINKER

Lucidity. During his career Alan Watts became known as the most lucid Western interpreter of Zen Buddhism. His blend of Eastern religion and drug exploration had great influence in the Beat movement and nascent counterculture movement which flowered in the 1960s.

Leaving the Episcopals. Watts was born in Great Britain and came to the United States in 1939. He was ordained in the Episcopal priesthood in 1944 and served as chaplain at Northwestern University in Chicago until 1947. Watts left the church in 1950 and married Dorothy De Witt shortly afterward. He was quoted as saying that he left the Episcopal church "not because it doesn't practice what it preaches but because it preaches."

Success. He taught at the American Academy of Asia Studies, a graduate school of the College of the Pacific, in San Francisco from 1951 to 1957, serving as dean of the school from 1953 to 1956. He left the school when the success of his *The Way of Zen* (1957) gave him the financial and intellectual independence to leave the academic world.

Voice for Asian Religions. Watts was a leading voice for Asian religions, particularly the Zen form of Buddhism. His first book, *The Spirit of Zen*, was published in 1936. He published extensively during the 1950s. His *The Way of Zen* and *Beat Zen, Square Zen, and Zen* (1959) appeared during the excitement brought about by the attention given to the Beat movement. Several of the Beatniks, including Allen Ginsberg and Jack Kerouac, became involved in practicing Zen and triggered an interest in Zen and other Eastern religions. In 1959 and 1960 he hosted a television program, "Eastern Wisdom and Modern Life," which ran for twenty-six episodes on National Educational Television.

Counterculture. Watts's influence on the culture and counterculture of the 1950s and later that of the 1960s is difficult to measure. He was the most public exponent of Eastern religions in general, and Zen in particular, and as such received much of the credit for Zen's sudden popularity in the 1950s. Watts's popular success was in ex-ploiting the unfocused spiritual hunger that was evident in the United States of the 1950s.

Sources:

Bruce Cook, *The Beat Generation* (New York: Scribners, 1971);

Harvey Cox, *Turning East: The Promise and Peril of the New Orientalism* (New York: Simon & Schuster, 1977);

Monica Furlong, *Zen Effects: The Life of Alan Watts* (Boston: Houghton Mifflin, 1986);

Alan Watts, *In My Own Way: An Autobiography* (New York: Pantheon, 1972).

PEOPLE IN THE NEWS

In February 1950 **Dr. Bernard Beskamp** was installed as chaplain of the U.S. House of Representatives. His predecessor, **Dr. James Shera Montgomery,** served in the post for almost thirty years.

On 10 September 1958 **Rev. Dr. Eugene Carson Blake,** stated clerk of the United Presbyterian Church, U.S.A, issued a statement saying that desegregation in the South should be enforced "with troops and tanks if necessary."

On 3 March 1950 **Rev. Dr. Osmond H. Brown** was appointed honorary canon of the Protestant Episcopal church. He was the first black to hold that position.

In January 1953 President-elect **Dwight D. Eisenhower** selected National Presbyterian Church in Washington, D.C., as his presidential place of worship. National Presbyterian was pastored by **Dr. Edward L. R. Elson.**

In January 1950 **Donald D. Foster,** a San Francisco businessman and state of California tax official, resigned his positions and made preparations to enter the Benedictine monastery of Saint Johns Abbey in Collegeville, Minnesota.

On 9 December 1958 **Clara French,** Methodist missionary secretary for China and Southeast Asia, was elected as the first female chairman of the National Council of Churches Foreign Missions Division.

Dr. Arthur D. Gray was elected chairman of the executive committee of the Congregational Christian Churches on 26 June 1950. He was the first black to hold that position.

Rev. Theodore Hesburg was named president of Notre Dame University on 28 June 1952.

On 30 November 1952 **Rev. Martin Luther Hux** of Temple Baptist Church in Rocky Mount, North Carolina, burned a page of the Revised Standard Version (RSV) of the Bible, saying the RSV was the "master stroke of Satan."

On 31 December 1952 **Prophet Jones,** founder and minister of the Universal Triumph, the Dominion of God Church in Detroit, Michigan, celebrated in a special service the election as president of Dwight Eisenhower, whose victory he had predicted.

Rev. Maurice McCrakin of Saint Barnabus Presbyterian and Episcopal Church in Cincinnati, Ohio, was sentenced to six months in prison on 12 December 1958 for refusing to answer an Internal Revenue Service summons. He had been refusing to pay income taxes because of the amount that went for military expenditures.

On 24 January 1953 **Rev. Carl McIntire,** president of the International Council of Christian Churches, said the Revised Standard Version of the Bible was "full of contradictions" and challenged the National Council of Churches to release figures revealing how much the council was making in royalties.

Bishop James Francis McIntyre was named a cardinal of the Roman Catholic church in December 1952.

A deaf minister, **Dr. Edwin Nies,** was ordained as pastor of Saint Mark's Church-in-the-Bouwerie in sign language on 8 January 1950.

Mrs. Sheldon Robbins was appointed cantor of Temple Avodah, Reform Jewish Synagogue of Oceanside, New York, on 2 August 1955. She is believed to be the first woman ever appointed cantor.

Bishop Fulton J. Sheen was presented the Emmy Award for Most Outstanding Personality on 5 February 1953.

Myron C. Taylor resigned his post as President Harry S Truman's personal representative to the Vatican on 18 January 1950.

One hundred thousand people watched on 15 August 1950 as Mary Anna van Hoof prayed to the Virgin Mary. She claimed that the Virgin Mary appeared to her seven times and told her "to pray and pray hard" for peace. The Roman Catholic church refused to sanction the visions.

DEATHS

Mother Mary Aloysia, 84, founder and first president of the Roman Catholic College of Our Lady of Good Counsel, 29 December 1950.

Dr. Thomas W. Ayers, 95, the first Southern Baptist missionary to China, 5 January 1954.

Rev. George Bolton, director of the Christian Herald Bowery Mission in New York City and known as the "Bishop of the Bowery," 29 July 1959.

Most Rev. Hugh C. Boyle, 77, Roman Catholic bishop of Pittsburgh since 1921, 2 December 1950.

Cardinal Giuseppe Bruno, 79, chamberlain of the Vatican College of Cardinals, prefect of the Apostolic Signature, 10 November 1954.

Dr. George Albert Coe, 89, religious educator, 9 November 1951.

Rev. Dr. Henry S. Coffin, 77, president of Union Theological Seminary (1926–1945), 25 November 1954.

Archbishop Christopher Contorgeorge, 56, Turkish-born primate of the Greek Orthodox church in the United States, 30 August 1950.

Rev. James R. Cox, 65, Roman Catholic priest who led the march of the unemployed to Washington, D.C., in 1932, 20 March 1951.

Rev. Arthur Powell Davies, outspoken liberal Unitarian clergyman, 26 September 1957.

Rev. Edward Thomas Demby, 88, at the time the only black bishop of the Episcopal church, 14 October 1957.

Dennis Cardinal Dougherty, 85, archbishop of Philadelphia since 1919, named to the college of cardinals in 1921, 31 May 1951.

Most Rev. Francis J. Haas, 64, Roman Catholic bishop of Grand Rapids, Michigan, labor mediator, chairman of the Fair Employment Practices Commission under President Franklin D. Roosevelt, 29 August 1953.

Rev. Dr. Paul Jacob Hoh, 58, president of the Lutheran Theological Seminary (Philadelphia), 20 January 1952.

Mother Mary Joseph (Mary Josephine Rogers), 72, founder of the Mary Knoll Sisters, a Roman Catholic missionary order, 9 October 1955.

Massimo Cardinal Massimi, 76, prefect of the Vatican's Supreme Tribunal (court of appeals) and dean of the Rota (highest tribunal), 6 March 1954.

Israel Matz, 81, prominent Lithuanian-born Zionist and Hebrew scholar, 10 February 1950.

Most Rev. Patrick J. McCormick, 72, rector of the Catholic University of America in Washington, D.C., 8 May 1953.

Most Rev. John Timothy McNicholas, 72, Roman Catholic archbishop of Cincinnati since 1925, cofounder of the Legion of Decency (1934), 22 April 1950.

Metropolitan Theophilus (Theodore Pashkovsky), 76, primate of the Russian Orthodox church in North America, opponent of the Soviets, 27 June 1950.

Rev. James Shera Montgomery, 89, Methodist Episcopal chaplain of the U.S. House of Representatives (1921–1950), 30 June 1952.

Edward Mooney, 76, American cardinal and archbishop of Detroit, 25 October 1958.

Dr. John R. Mott, 89, evangelist and YMCA leader, winner of the 1946 Nobel Peace Prize, 31 January 1955.

Archbishop Michael (Thucydides Constantinides), 66, head of the Greek Orthodox Church of the Americas and a president of the World Council of Churches, 13 July 1958.

Oom the Omnipotent (Pierre Arnold Bernard, born Peter Coon), 80, founder of a Hindu-like mystic cult, 27 September 1955.

Archbishop John F. Noll, 81, founder of *Our Sunday Visitor* and cofounder of the Legion of Decency, 31 July 1956.

Rev. J. Frank Norris, 74, pastor of the First Baptist Church of Fort Worth, Texas, and a leader in the fundamentalist movement, 20 August 1952.

Pius XII (Eugenio Giuseppe Giovanni Pacelli), 82, supreme pontiff of the Roman Catholic church since 1939, 9 October 1958.

Herman Rodehaver, 75, hymn writer, singer, and musical director for evangelist Billy Sunday, 18 December 1955.

Effendi Shoghi, 61, head of the world Baha'i religion, 4 November 1957.

Dr. Robert Holbrook Smith, 71, a founder of Alcoholics Anonymous, 16 November 1950.

Anson Phelps Stokes, 84, Protestant Episcopal clergyman, philanthropist, and former canon residentiary of the National Cathedral in Washington, D.C., 13 August 1958.

Samuel Alphonsus Stritch, 70, cardinal and archbishop of Chicago, the first American to be appointed to the Papal Curia, 27 May 1958.

Rabbi Jonah B. Wise, 77, founder of the United Jewish Appeal, 1 February 1959.

PUBLICATIONS

John Allegro, *The Dead Sea Scrolls and the Origins of Christianity* (New York: Criterion Books, 1957);

Robert E. Bremner, ed., *Reshaping American Society and Institutions, 1945-1960* (Columbus, Ohio: Ohio State University Press, 1982);

Bruce Cook, *The Beat Generation* (New York: Scribners, 1971);

Richard M. Fried, *Nightmare in Red: The McCarthy Era in Prespective* (New York: Oxford University Press, 1990);

David Garrow, *Bearing the Cross: Martin Luther King, Jr., and the Southern Christian Leadership Conference* (New York: William Morrow, 1986);

Walter Goodman, *The Committee: The Extraordinary Career of the House Committee on Un-American Activities* (New York: Farrar, Straus and Giroux, 1968);

Arthur Gordon, *Norman Vincent Peale* (Englewood Cliffs, N.J.: Prentice Hall, 1958);

Will Herberg, *Protestant, Catholic, Jew: An Essay in American Religious Sociology* (Garden City, N.Y.: Doubleday, 1955);

Eric Hoffer, *The True Believer: Thoughts on the Nature of Mass Movements* (New York: NAL, 1951);

Martin Luther King, *Stride Toward Freedom (New York: Harper, 1958);*

Andrew M. Manis, *Southern Civil Religions in Conflict: Black And White Baptists and Civil Rights, 1947-1957* (Athens, Ga.: University of Georgia Press, 1987);

Catherine Marshall, *A Man Called Peter: The Story of Peter Marshall* (New York: McGraw-Hill, 1951);

Martin E. Marty, *The New Shape of American Religion* (New York: Harper, 1959);

William L. Miller, *Piety Along the Potomac: Notes of Politics and Morals in the Fifties* (Boston: Houghton, Mifflin, 1964);

Reinhold Niebuhr, *Christian Realism and Political Problems* (New York: Scribners, 1953);

Niebuhr, *The Irony of American History* (New York: Scribners, 1952);

Niebuhr, *Pious and Secular America* (New York: Scribners, 1958);

Niebuhr, *The Self and the Dramas of History* (New York: Scribners, 1955);

William L. O'Neill, *American High: The Years of Confidence, 1945-1960* (New York: Free Press, 1986);

Bishop G. Bromley Oxnam, *I Protest* (New York: Harper, 1954);

Oxnam, *A Testament of Faith* (Boston: Little, Brown, 1958);

Everrett C. Parker, David W. Barry, and Dallas Smythe, *The Television-Radio Audience and Religion* (New York: Harper, 1955);

Bishop Fulton J. Sheen, *Life Is Worth Living* (New York: McGraw-Hill, 1953);

Sheen, *Life of Christ* (New York: McGraw-Hill, 1958);

Homer William Smith, *Man and His Gods* (Boston: Little, Brown, 1952);

Paul Tillich, *Biblical Religion and the Search for Ultimate Reality* (Chicago: University of Chicago Press, 1955);

Tillich, *The Courage to Be* (New Haven: Yale University Press, 1952);

Tillich, *The Dynamics of Faith* (New York: Harper, 1957);

Tillich, *The New Being* (New York: Scribners, 1955);

Tillich, *Systematic Theology,* 3 volumes (Chicago: University of Chicago Press, 1951–1963);

Alan Watts, *Beat Zen, Square Zen, and Zen* (San Francisco: City Lights Books, 1959);

Watts, *The Way of Zen* (New York: Pantheon, 1957);

Watts, *The Wisdom of Insecurity* (New York: Pantheon, 1951);

Christian Century, periodical;

Christianity and Crisis, periodical;

Christianity Today, periodical founded in 1956;

Ecumenical Review, periodical;

Our Sunday Visitor, periodical;

Pastoral Life, periodical;

Theology Today, periodical.

SCIENCE AND TECHNOLOGY

by WAYNE BURROWS and LYNDY WILSON-BURROWS

CONTENTS

Sidebars and tables listed in italics.

1950

- Commercial color transmission of CBS television "Colorcast," starring Ed Sullivan and Arthur Godfrey.

- The Sulzer weaving machine begins modern commercial production of cloth using an automatic loom. Only a single-color yarn was used at first; by 1959 four colors could be used simultaneously.

- An embryo (early form of life developed from a fertilized egg) is implanted in the uterus of a cow at the University of Wisconsin.

- Eastman develops a method to use regular movie cameras to produce color movies. Before this, only Technicolor cameras produced color movies.

1951

- Computer is used by Dirk Brouwer to predict planetary orbits.

- Chrysler introduces the first production-model car with power steering.

- The first 3-D movies are produced. Viewers must wear special polarized glasses to see them. Cardboard glasses containing plastic lenses are given out at the box office. Hollywood eventually produces sixty 3-D movies.

- Du Pont produces Orlon, a synthetic acrylic fiber that can be spun into yarn and knitted. A major advantage is that it feels soft to the touch.

- The nuclear testing station at Arco, Idaho, produces electricity from nuclear power using molten metal to transfer heat from the reactor to produce steam, which drives the turbines to generate electricity.

- The first trancontinental television transmission is broadcast from the United States.

Apr.
- The Remington Rand Corporation sells the first commercially available computer, the UNIVAC I (Universal Automatic Computer). The machines are made available commercially and are based on decimal mathematics, not the binary system. The first machines use magnetic tape to store data.

1952

- Bull semen is frozen, thawed, and used to fertilize an egg and produce a calf.

- Raytheon uses the transistor, produced by Bell Laboratories, to produce a hearing aid.

- Hydrogen bomb developed.

- Former American soldier George Jorgensen undergoes the first sex change operation — becomes known as Christine after surgery.

1953

- Maser, acronym for Microwave Amplification by Stimulated Emission of Radiation, is developed by Charles Hard Townes; the search begins for the light-wave equivalent, a LASER.

- Kinsey sex-survey results shock a nation.

- American mathematician Norbert Weiner introduces the new field of "cybernetics," the study of control and communication in the animal and the machine.

- A Pratt-Whitney J57 engine fitted onto an F-100 propels the plane to a speed of Mach 1.3, or 850 miles per hour (1.3 times the speed of sound). The first surface-to-air missile (Nike-Ajax) is deployed. In Nevada, "Atomic Annie," the first atomic heavy-artillery shell, is fired.

- Aerosol valve is invented.

- James Watson, an American, and Francis Crick, a British physicist, publish their work on DNA. They determine the double-helix structure of DNA, leading to significant breakthroughs in the study of the genetic "code" on which all life is based.

- Graham and Wydner use tars from cigarette smoke to produce cancers in mice.

1954

- Texas Instruments produces transistorized chips made out of silicon instead of the rare germanium.

- The commercial transistor radio, the Regency, enters the U.S. market.

- Hybrid wheat is developed for drought and disease resistance

- Odeco, Inc., uses the first mobile, submersible oil-drilling unit for offshore drilling in the Gulf of Mexico.

- Using new techniques in genetics, J. H. Tijo and A. Levan show there are only forty-six human chromosones, not forty-eight as previously thought.

- The U.S. Navy's *Nautilus* is launched. The submarine has a nuclear power source enabling it to remain under water almost indefinitely.

- Bell Laboratories develops the photovoltaic cell, which converts sunlight into electricity.

1955

- Multiple-track recording, in which songs are recorded with voice on one track, music on another, is introduced, leading to the commercialization of stereophonic sound equipment and records.

- Rosalyn Yalow and Solomon Berson develop a very sensitive hormone measuring method called Radio Immuno Assay, or RIA; it uses antibodies and displacement of radioactively tagged hormones by natural ones.

- Radio astronomers Franklin and Burke detect naturally occurring radio emissions from the planet Jupiter; radio astronomy is improved by development of the interferometer that lets radio telescopes resolve different radio sources accurately.

- The Field-Ion microscope, the first microscope that can (indirectly) see individual atoms, is developed.

- A home freezer able to maintain a temperature of -27° F is introduced.

- GEC in New York produces a diamond by putting graphite under ultra-high pressure; the result retains the property of being the hardest substance in the world and is used for cutting in such applications as oil-drilling operations.

- Homological algebra, combining abstract algebra and algebraic topology, produces a uniform type of mathematics.

- Antiprotons, particles in the nucleus of atoms, are produced in laboratory proving the existence of antimatter.

1956

- Burroughs produces the E-101 desk-size computer for scientists and mathematicians; it has some capabilities of a computer and some of an adding machine.

- The "Ampex" system, developed by Alexander Poniatoff, produces taped television shows of comparable quality to live shows; it is first used by CBS in the Pacific area.

- Bell Labs produces a transistorized computer, "The Leprechaun."

25 Sept. The transatlantic telephone cable from the United States to Europe begins operations on 25 September.

- DNA is synthesized outside a cell

- Arthur Kornberg uses the common intestinal bacterium, Escherichia coli, to synthesize DNA in vitro.

- Bruce Heezen and Maurice Ewing discover the Mid-Oceanic Ridge, a formation of mountains and rifts that circles the world under the oceans.

- Birth-control pills, using female hormones to prevent pregnancy, are tested on fifteen thousand volunteers in Puerto Rico and Haiti.

- FORTRAN, a computer-software language that was developed for scientists and mathematicians, and LISP, the computer language of artificial intelligence, are introduced.

- The use of fiberglass, aluminum, and stainless steel allows the development of the B-58 Hustler, capable of reaching Mach 2.

1957

- Doppler navigation, a device for accurately determining aircraft position and airspeed, makes civil aviation safer.

- Hoover develops a spin clothes dryer applicable for home use.

- The "Airotor," a high-speed dental drill, is introduced; the small cutting blade is rotated by compressed air at a rate of 350,000 revolutions per minute and cooled by a water spray.

- An American intercontinental ballistic missile (or ICBM), the Atlas, passes government testing processes two months after the Soviet Union used a similar rocket to launch the first artificial satellite, the *Sputnik I*.

- Fifty-six countries participate in the International Geophysical Year, 1957–1958, sponsored by the International Council of Scientific Unions.

- The first American nuclear power generator is operational.

Dec. The Shippingport, Pennsylvania, nuclear-power plant, a "pressurized water" reactor built by Westinghouse and run by Duquesne Power and Light for the Atomic Energy Commission, opens.

1958

- Eugene Parker proves that a stream of particles he calls the solar wind is given off by the sun.

- The first U.S. artificial satellite orbits earth.

- Bifocal contact lenses are developed.

- After the Navy *Vanguard* satellite blows up on the launchpad in December 1957, NASA (National Aeronautics and Space Administration) is formed to coordinate space projects; it immediatedly approves of the Mercury space project.

- A *Nautilus* submarine goes under ice cap at North Pole.

- Pan American Airlines flies the first commercial transatlantic route in in a jet.

Jan. The United States launches *Explorer I* from a Jupiter rocket at the Redstone Arsenal, an army facility.

July The *Explorer IV* satellite verifies that there is a radiation belt around earth; it is named the Van Allen Radiation Belt after the discoverer, James Van Allen.

1959

- Temperature-Humidity Index developed by U.S. Weather Bureau.

- First commercial copier is introduced by Xerox.

- The Saint Lawrence Seaway connecting the Saint Lawrence River to the Great Lakes opens.

- COBOL, a computer software language for business use, is introduced.

- Transistors are placed on silicon-chip surfaces for the first time.

- Thermofax (3M) makes large copies from microfilm.

- Sony produces the first transistorized (black and white) television for sale in the United States.

OVERVIEW

Giant Steps. Great strides were made in American science during the 1950s. Major inventions and discoveries were almost daily events, and previously ignored technology improved upon and made commercially applicable. The field of science seemed to change overnight. Previously, the scientist generally worked alone or, perhaps, with a student assistant or two. He (most scientists were men in the 1950s) worked with minimal equipment and funding to find answers to questions that interested him. The questions changed over time as scientific interests — and budgets — changed. During the 1950s people turned to scientists to solve their problems more often than ever before.

Practical Science. The massive military projects of World War II demonstrated that large groups of scientists could be brought together to work with each other toward a specified research goal. The most significant example is the production of the atomic bomb. Because of the urgency of the project, the government provided expensive equipment and huge research budgets, both of which shortened the time between the idea and its practical application. The need to convince people who controlled the money for scientific projects to provide funding made science a more disciplined pursuit: scientists were forced to state their goals in advance and to conduct specific experiments to reach those goals. This procedure seemed to promote efficiency, which pleased the funders. It was decades until the scientific community realized that this prescription for success sometimes had unpleasant side effects.

Science in People's Lives. It is difficult to separate the achievements of science and technology in the 1950s from other aspects of life. Credit cards, which repre-sented several scientific and technological advances, became widespread during the decade. But before they could be used a large number of people had to be able to afford to buy things with them, so the growth of credit cards was directly related to the growth of the economy. The development and testing on a large scale of birth control pills required social change making their availability acceptable. The first effective birth control pill was made available late in 1957, but it had to be prescribed for menstrual cramps only until the Food and Drug Administration formally licensed drugs for sale as contraceptives in 1960. Even the development of TV dinners, which applied freeze-drying of food to increase its shelf life, required an appropriate social setting, which was provided by the introduction of television sets into homes. What good is a TV dinner if nobody watches television?

A Time of Wonder. In science and technology the 1950s were a time of wonder. It seemed that the newly applied methods of science were improving life on a daily basis. Polio was a killer, and scientists found a vaccine for it. Dental drills hurt, so scientists improved them. Movies had to compete with television, so scientists invented the gimmick of three-dimensional films. In many ways Americans demanded that the 1950s be the decade of science and technology.

Sources:
Patrick Harpur, and others, eds. *The Timetable of Technology* (New York: Hearst Books, 1982);

Trevor Illtyd Williams, *A History of Discovery in the Twentieth Century* (Oxford and New York: Oxford University Press, 1990);

Alexander Hellemans and Bryan Bunch, *The Timetable of Science* (New York: Simon & Schuster, 1988).

TOPICS IN THE NEWS

CHROMOSOME NUMBER IN HUMANS

The Purpose of Sex. Scientifically, sex has a single purpose: to pass on one's genes to a new generation. The genes are part of the DNA molecules, the basis of heredity within each cell. In turn, the DNA is packaged into structures called chromosomes. Every species of animal and plant has a certain number of such chromosomes within each of its cells. Remarkably, it was not until 1956 that the number of human chromosomes was correctly determined.

Background. In 1865 Gregor Mendel published his famous work on genetics in which he used garden peas in his experiments. Mendel showed that certain characteristics of the peas were inherited in predictable ways. Some traits were dominant and others recessive. If two pea plants are crossed, for example, one might have a dominant trait that determines the shape of the pea while the other might have a recessive trait that calls for a different shape. When these two are crossed, all their offspring will have the dominant-type pea shape. Only if the recessive gene is inherited from both parents will the pea have the recessive-type shape.

Sperm + Egg = ? Mendel had no idea that the genes he was studying were located in the chromosomes. In the 1880s, Pierre-Joseph von Beneden found that the germ cells, or seeds, contain half as many chromosomes as other cells of an organism. Germ cells are called the sperm and egg in mammals. When a sperm and egg combine, the resulting cell has the normal number of chromosomes in it for that particular organism.

Forty-seven or Forty-eight? In 1912 it was suggested that the normal number of human chromosomes was forty-seven. This theory was revised in 1923, when it was decided that in fact humans have forty-eight chromosomes, a notion that stood for a third of a century.

No, Forty-six. In 1956 two researchers proved that the actual human chromosome number is forty-six. J. Hin Tjio and Albert Levan studied human embryo cells. They took painstakingly careful photographs of many cells to prove that humans have forty-six chromosomes per cell (except for germ cells, which have twenty-three chromosomes per cell). In 1959 Jerome Lejeune reported a new finding after studying mongolism, now called Down's Syndrome. Lejeune found that children with mongolism had forty-seven chromosomes instead of forty-six.

Source:
Edgardo Macorini, ed. *The History of Science & Technology: A Narrative Chronology* (New York: Facts-on-File, 1988)

COMMUNICATION

Anthropological View. Communication skills are the key to advancing civilization. Until the earliest humans developed a way to communicate effectively, they were little different from the other animals around them. Civilizations that developed written communication methods tended to be much more successful than those that did not. Mathematical skills developed written communication even further. There were distinct limits to the engineering capabilities of ancient cultures without a mathematical system that was easy to use and understand.

Improvements. During the 1950s communication was rapidly improved by several highly technical innovations. Advancements in electronics made television available to almost everyone. Then electronic engineers developed systems of broadcasting and receiving broadcast signals in color. Eventually shows could even be taped for high-quality broadcast at the convenience of the television studio. The result of these technological capabilities was a reshaped society that spent its leisure time differently and was better informed than ever before. Americans who rarely read newspapers were, by the end of the decade, faithful viewers of the evening news and thus had daily exposure to world events that could frequently be viewed as they happened.

Long Distance. Telephone communication was also improved drastically during the decade. By 1960 it was possible to call Europe using a transatlantic cable system. In 1950 the Aircall Corporation of New York marketed a radio pager (beeper). The first person to be paged was a physician — on a golf course. The development of one small item, the transistor, was the key to an entire universe of electronic advances, which gave people the capacity to program machines to do their bidding in ways that were previously unthinkable. The transistor was

Grace Hopper teaching COBOL

probably the greatest single force for change in communication in the twentieth century.

New Forms of Language. The communications changes of the 1950s involved a new way of writing called computer language. Various computer languages were based on a system of logic and mathematics, called Boolean algebra. The binary mathematical system had been known for centuries, and the logic system that utilizes it was devised by an Irish mathematician named George Boole in the 1850s. Using a simple two-value numbering system, Boolean algebra allows computer programmers to talk to their machines in terms the machine understands — all communication is expressed in the form of a set of switches, which are either open or closed to control the electrical current running to them. FORTRAN, an acronym for formula translation language, is a computer language introduced in 1956 that allows scientists to program computers in a form much like algebraic notation most suitable for mathematical applications. A nonscientific language, COBOL, an acronym for common business-oriented language, was, as the name suggests, developed to control computers used in businesses. A language called LISP was used by scientists at the Massachusetts Institute of Technology in the late 1950s to develop computers that would respond intelligently to commands. These languages were made possible by computer scientist Grace Murray Hopper, who devised a language compiler, a translation system that converts computer languages into commands understood by computers.

Language of Tomorrow. As with any language, computer languages allowed people in a closed group to communicate, and people who did not know the language were at the mercy of those who did for translations. At the same time, such communications aids as computers, advanced telephones, television, and pagers brought people into closer contact with one another. These were the basic tools with which a new world society was being built

Source:
Patrick Harpur, et al, eds. *The Timetable of Technology.* (New York: Hearst Books, 1982): 138.

THE COMPUTER COMES OF AGE

Efficient Calculations. The computer is a tool whose power is almost beyond comprehension. It developed as an enhancement of adding machines, made possible by electronic innovations. Precursors of the modern computer were required by scientists for their increasingly intricate and detailed calculations. After World War II these machines developed almost naturally to serve the needs of people for a reliable method to perform more-mundane calculations.

Digital Business. The business potential for computers is obvious today, when they are the operations centers for even small businesses. Computers have made it possible to run businesses more efficiently by performing reliably certain tasks that formerly required people whose work had to be checked for accuracy. Still, there was great opposition to computers when they were first developed.

UNIVAC I, March 1951

The first commercial computers went on sale in the United States in the early 1950s. Social observers suggested that by the year 2000 perhaps fifty of the huge, expensive machines would be in use. It was thought that only governments of prosperous nations and a few nationally sponsored scientific endeavors could afford to use computers.

Fears. Computers inspired fear in some, anxiety in others. Paranoid opponents saw them as machine invaders that had the potential to run amok and take power over their creators. Others faced with computer technology were paralyzed with dread about their inability to learn the language to communicate in a computerized world. More-rational people saw a practical drawback to these remarkable machines. When one hundred typists, clerks, and bookkeepers could be replaced by five or ten people using computers, where would the other ninety or ninety-five people find jobs?

Computer Potential. Computers had potential consequences their inventors did not expect. The accurate prediction of the presidential election results soon after the polls closed in 1952 was the beginning of the American fascination with these machines. By the end of the decade the computer was more than a curiosity. The development and availability of the transistor made it possible to produce compact and affordable computers. With the advancement of computer languages it became possible to program computers easily with what is called software,

so that computer functions became varied enough to appeal to a broad range of users. These changes all occurred or began to occur during the 1950s.

Calculators vs. Computers. Computers were initially designed as powerful calculators. The adding machine was in every office in 1950. It could efficiently add or subtract columns of numbers and perform other everyday calculations. The only mistakes made on machines in good working order were the result of human error. Still, they were mechanical devices and subject to occasional breakdown. They were also limited. One could enter numbers into a calculation only as fast as a human being could accurately type them in — not fast enough for some of the applications of the technological age. Calculators were not generally capable of any higher mathematical functions, and they had no memory.

Slide Rule. Higher mathematics was calculated with a slide rule or pen and paper. The slide rule was every engineer's friend. It was a modified ruler with a sliding middle portion. Different mathematical functions were on different scales printed on one or another of the wooden rule's parts. Mathematical functions were simplified by converting them to logarithmic scales. A sliding piece across the front of the rule usually had a glass or clear plastic viewer with a hairline inscribed for lining up the scales on different parts of the sliding rule.

Tedious Calculations. Two of the most tedious forms of mathematics are statistics and probability determinations. Using the mathematics of probability, predictions can be made about future events. Probability calculations require repetitive mathematics and take a very long time to perform by hand. Probability is a standard calculation required of mathematicians, and it also has business applications. A manufacturer has to know how much to produce, and that decision affects hiring, purchasing, scheduling, and advertising. Accurate predictions based on past sales can be the difference between huge profit and bankruptcy. Similarly, engineers who know that a building material has a certain strength under given conditions use mathematical calculations to predict how long a product will last. If the material used to make the product is stronger than it needs to be, it probably costs more than is necessary; if the material is too weak, the product — a bridge, perhaps — will collapse. Computers easily performed those calculations

UNIVAC. The U.S. Census Bureau is logically another user of fast, accurate tallying machines. The census is taken every ten years, and it is the basis for important decisions about such matters as federal funding, resource development, and business location. There are compelling reasons to compile the census as quickly and accurately as possible. The U.S. Census Bureau was the first purchaser of a UNIVAC, the first commercially available digital computer. Delivery was accepted in April 1951. The UNIVAC could perform 2,000 addition functions or 450 multiplication functions per second, and it had an internal memory of 1,000 "words," defined as twelve alphabetic or decimal quantities.

A Slow Start. It is not surprising that the early history of computers includes predictions that nobody would use the new machines. They were expensive and large, required special operators, and could be programmed (and thus used) only by a few highly trained individuals. The pioneers in the field had extreme difficulty getting financial backing for their products. By 1958 only about fifty of the impressive UNIVACs had been sold by Sperry-Rand. Nobody could predict how quickly the transistor and microchip would change the computer industry. Still, even the old UNIVAC was so much better than no computer at all.

COMPUTER PREDICTS ELECTION

Power of UNIVAC. The 1952 presidential election between Dwight D. Eisenhower and Adlai E. Stevenson demonstrated the power of the computer in the living rooms of millions of Americans. Even the programmers did not believe in the ability of their computers to make predictions.

UNIVAC vs. Cronkite. Before 1952 the networks had to broadcast election results as they were returned, precinct by precinct, all over the United States. This was a long and tedious process for the networks and the viewers alike that sometimes took days. Election predictions were unsystematic and untrustworthy. In April 1952 CBS rep-

resentatives approached Remington-Rand about using their adding machines and typewriters in the election coverage in exchange for free television advertising. One of the Remington-Rand employees suggested a new twist: use their UNIVAC computer to predict the election results, and viewers would be "glued to the tube" through the tedious precinct-by-precinct results just to see if the computer was correct. The deal was made even though newscasters had their doubts. Walter Cronkite, the well-known CBS newscaster, said, "Actually, we're not depending too much on this machine. It may turn out to be just a sideshow. . . ."

Fail-safe. Since computers were so new, no one had ever tried to enter the massive amounts of data involved in predicting a national election. Also, the statistical methods needed for prediction had to be redeveloped. Just to be safe, three computers were used. One was to be seen on the television itself and acted as the primary machine. Another checked the results from the first, and a third was ready for use just in case.

The Prediction. At 9:00 P.M., after tallying and analyzing 3 million votes (7 percent of the total vote), UNIVAC predicted Eisenhower would win by a landslide. Having such a prediction so early in the election was considered impossible. Television viewers noticed the reaction among newscasters as the computer prediction was received, but CBS decided to keep the information quiet to avoid embarrassment if the computer had made a mistake. Viewers were told the computer was not ready to predict yet, while programmers and analysts were busy trying to find out what had gone wrong with UNIVAC.

The Winner. UNIVAC's mathematical formulas were revised and rerevised. The original prediction was that Eisenhower would win in forty-three states for a total of 438 electoral votes. After multiple revisions of the formula for prediction, UNIVAC declared at 10 P.M. an Eisenhower victory of 270 electoral votes to 261 for Stevenson, each winning twenty-four states. (There were only forty-eight states at the time.) CBS broadcast these figures. By 11 P.M. it was obvious that UNIVAC's first prediction was closer to the truth, as election returns came pouring in favoring Eisenhower. The network finally admitted that UNIVAC had made the prediction earlier, but it was not considered credible. The final count? Eisenhower won 442 electoral votes (UNIVAC predicted 438), and Stevenson won 89 (versus a predicted 93).

Sources:

Patrick Harpur, et al, eds. *The Timetable of Technology* (New York: Hearst Books, 1982);

Trevor Illtyd Williams, *Science: A History of Discovery in the Twentieth Century* (Oxford and New York: Oxford University Press, 1990);

John Diebold, *The Innovators: The Discoveries, Inventions, and Breakthroughs of Our Time* (New York: Dutton, 1990);

Alexander Bryan Hellemans and Bryan Bunch, *The Timetable of Science* (New York: Simon & Schuster, 1988;

Harry Wulforst, *Breakthrough to the Computer Age* (New York: Charles Scribner's Sons, 1982).

Before the introduction of word processors and copying machines, offices were far more labor-intensive places because scientists and technology experts had not yet found a way to automate certain jobs of secretaries and clerks. The simple task of typing a letter was demanding because if the typist made a mistake, correcting it was difficult. There were a few innovations provided by practical scientists that addressed this problem. One was called Liquid Paper, is sometimes referred to as "whiteout." Liquid Paper allowed the secretary to paint over mistakes and, after painstakingly realigning the paper in the typewriter, retype corrections. The other was correction paper, which functioned like white carbon paper. When a mistake was made, the typist backed up, inserted correction paper, and retyped the mistake so that the struck letters were white and, therefore, difficult to see. Then the secretary typed again, correcting the error this time. Liquid Paper and correction paper were preferable to retyping an entire page to correct an error, but they were still messy methods of correction, especially when there were several errors that had to be corrected.

Another innovation was the copier. Most businesses require copies of important letters and other documents they generate. In the 1950s carbon paper was the copying method of choice. By inserting a piece of carbon paper and a blank sheet of paper behind an original, a typist could make two or, by inserting more carbon paper and blank sheets, as many as five copies of an original. The process was messy because the carbon copies smeared and inefficient if more than a couple of copies were required. (The more carbon copies made at once, the lighter the copies near the bottom of the stack would get.) When several copies were required, businesses used mimeograph machines, which were really desktop printing presses: a master copy was prepared on special paper; it was attached to a roller, and by the process of ink transfer, the image of the original was transferred to blank sheets of paper.

Then came the copying machine. Two types of copiers were introduced in the 1950s, both operating on simple scientific principles: the thermofax, which copied on coated paper; and xerography, which copied on plain paper. Large offices frequently needed to produce several copies of documents. The secretary's job was made far easier, and the cost of running an office was reduced. Copiers made duplicating a quick and inexpensive process, and the demand for them gave rise to a major industry in America.

Source: Ethlie Ann Vare, G. Ptacek, *Mothers of Invention: From the Bra to the Bomb: Forgotten Women & Their Unforgettable Ideas* (New York: Morrow, 1988);

John Diebold, *The Innovators: The Discoveries, Inventions, and Breakthroughs of Our Time* (New York: Dutton, 1990).

COMPUTER TECHNOLOGY: EVOLVING SCIENCE

Room-sized Computer. The UNIVAC of 1950 was far different from microcomputers. It was fourteen-by-seven-by-nine feet, the size of a small bedroom. A set of five thousand vacuum tubes made it work. It worked on a decimal (ten-digit) system rather than a binary (two-digit) system. The internal memory was one thousand words, which was the memory unit and each word consisted of twelve digits or letters (although it could process multiple magnetic tapes simultaneously with millions of bits of information on them). Software, a term that means stored programs, existed only in a primitive form, but it hardly resembled the software that was commonplace by the end of the decade as internal memory systems in computers improved.

Innovations. Major changes were made in the computer between 1950 and 1959. The transistor revolutionized the industry by replacing vacuum tubes in the computer's processing unit. Transistors also made the computer easy to miniaturize, allowing its imposing size to be reduced without any loss of function. One of the most important features of transistors is their ability to calculate in the binary numbering system. The decimal system uses ten digits (from 0 to 9) to express numbers. The binary system uses only the digits 0 and 1. All the numbers with which we are familiar in the decimal system can be expressed by a string of zeros and ones in the binary system or in a computer by running electrical current through a tiny switch (1) or not running the current (0). It did not take long for computer programmers to begin exploiting the binary system, particularly when transistors made it possible to link together many switches in a limited space, thus increasing the number of possible communications to the computer and increasing the computer's ability to respond to instructions.

What Memory Leads To. Another major change in the 1950s was the development of software, made possible by the introduction of magnetic-core memory that increased the internal information-storage capacity of a

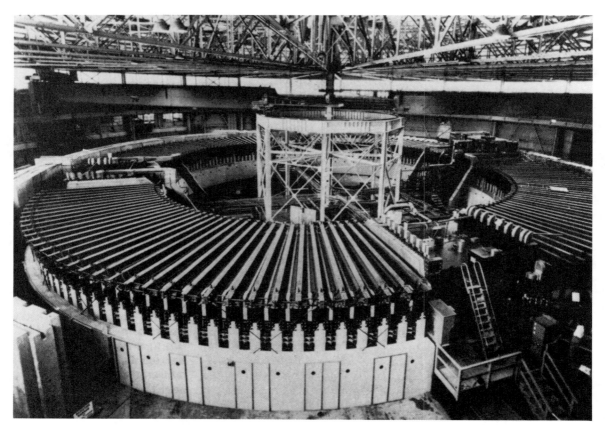

The Bevatron at the University of California radiation laboratory

computer about eightfold. As a result, computers could remember more-complicated routines of calculation. At first, giving instructions to the computers required speaking the language of numbers — what is called machine language. A translation routine, called a compiler, was developed to translate between programming language, which consisted of formulas and various types of mathematical and linguistic shorthand (still extremely obscure to most people) into machine language. Programming languages were complex, with many grammatical rules. The earliest was called FORTRAN, and it bridged the gap between English (or any language) and the machine's language of mathematics. Mastery of FORTRAN takes considerable effort. Still, it was far better than communicating in numbers alone. FORTRAN lends itself to scientific and mathematical uses. An accounting ledger could be incorporated into FORTRAN, but it would be cumbersome. In the mid 1950s another programming language, COBOL, was developed for business uses. Still, a highly trained computer programmer had to translate from English to the software language. The phrase *user friendly* had not been coined yet.

CYCLOTRON/BEVATRON

High-Speed Crash. In atomic physics an accelerator is an atom smasher. It takes a subatomic particle, speeds it up, and smashes it into a group of atoms. The result is a new set of subatomic particles that have new properties to be studied. The faster the original particles move before smashing into atoms, the more subatomic particles result.

Boost. Accelerators were first built in the early twentieth century with direct current. Electrons were used to smash atoms, but the process was very slow by 1950s standards. The original cyclotrons were developed in the 1930s. They moved particles in a circular path using magnetic fields before bombardment. Acceleration of the particles was accomplished with a series of electrical-field "boosts" or "kicks" in the pathway.

Synchrocyclotrons. The 1940s saw the birth of synchrocyclotrons, which increased the speed of particles even more by synchronizing the kicks with the movement of the particles. By this time the particles, now much larger and heavier protons instead of electrons, were accelerated to speeds approaching the speed of light. As Albert Einstein had predicted, the protons' mass increased at such speeds.

Faster Particles. In the 1950s physicists needed to produce even faster particles. The result was a bevatron, a synchrocyclotron (or synchrotron) that got its name because it produces a billion electron volts. These synchrotrons adjust the magnetic field as well as the electrical field as the particles speed up. The first regularly operational bevatron was built in Berkeley, California, by the Atomic Energy Commission and the University of California. (A prototype at Brookhaven National Laboratory was the first billion-volt accelerator, but it was not designed for regular use.) It included a ten-thousand-ton steel doughnut, a giant electromagnet that provided a circular path 135 feet in diameter. When it was first turned on in 1954, iron objects around the housing shook the structure as they aligned themselves with the powerful magnetic field.

Six Billion Volts. The speed of the particles in the bevatron was astonishing. They circled the giant doughnut over two million times a second. It had a capacity to produce more than six billion electron volts of energy in the racing particles. The smashing force it produced went deep into the nucleus of the atoms being bombarded and changed scientists' perception of molecular physics. The results revealed such previously unknown atomic particles as mesons, antiprotons, and antielectrons.

DNA

Combining Cells. The purpose of sex is to create a new generation. Its methodology is the transmitting of genetic material. This genetic material is contained within the deoxyribonucleic acid (DNA) in the nucleus of our cells. Within DNA are regions called genes. These genes carry the code for manufacturing the various proteins that allow the cells to function and make us what we are. The sex cells, sperm and ova, contain only one copy of the DNA (some of which was from the mother and some from the father in each sex cell). When these cells combine, they provide the double strand of DNA required to make new cells with a unique genetic code.

Learning the Process. In the early 1950s very little was known about genes and how they function. The major achievement of the decade was determining the structure of DNA. With that knowledge, scientists determined that DNA contained the code for genes. Three molecular biologists made discoveries in the 1950s that permanently altered scientists' perception of life.

DNA Structure. DNA was first isolated in 1869, but its significance was unknown. In the early 1950s Rosalind Franklin, working in the lab of Irish scientist M. H. F. Wilkins (who had studied uranium isotopes for use in the atomic bomb during the Manhattan Project), used X-ray diffraction to study DNA in its pure form. In this technique X-rays are bombarded into the molecule and reflected onto a photographic screen (see Women in Science). The Wilkins group discovered that DNA was helical and that the molecule had a constant width down its backbone. The American biochemist James D. Watson was working in England with English biophysicist Francis H. C. Crick when they learned about these findings. They tried various models, but found only one that would agree with the Wilkins data: the double helix. They posited that DNA is formed by two helixes wound around each other.

James D. Watson and Francis H. C. Crick with model of DNA

Complementarity. Together these scientists found that DNA is composed of four bases (adenine, thymidine, guanine, and cytosine) attached to a sugar-phosphate backbone. The two strands of DNA interact so that an adenine always bonds to a thymidine, and a guanine to a cytosine; this assures that the two strands always have what in scientific jargon is called the property of complementarity. It was found that the double helix could unwind to allow the structure to duplicate itself exactly. An adenine on one side will only bind to a thymidine and vice versa. Similarly, a guanine on one side of the molecule will only bind to a cytosine. The cytosine on the other side will only bond a guanine. As a result of the property of complementarity the molecule can reproduce itself with the accuracy required for reproduction.

Nobel Prize. These discoveries gave birth to the field of molecular biology, in which it can be determined exactly what genes cause certain characteristics in living organisms, including humans. Wilkins, Watson, and Crick were awarded the Nobel Prize in 1962 for their pioneering work on DNA.

Source:
Trevor Illtyd Williams, *Science: A History of Discovery in the Twentieth Century* (Oxford and New York: Oxford University Press, 1990).

DENTAL DRILLS: HIGH SPEED AND PAINLESS (MORE OR LESS)

Slow Pain. Before 1950 dental drills were available, but they were slow and required a series of belts and pulleys. Having teeth drilled was a long and tedious process. Dentists could treat only a few patients each day.

The process of drilling teeth was so painful, though, that patients did not complain about the wait: they wanted as many days between treatments as possible.

Nelson-Kampula. In 1951 a Swedish dentist made an air-powered, high-speed drill. This tool was a significant advance, but it had technical problems. It produced heat and could only be run for a short while before it burned the dentist's hand. In 1953 American dentist Robert Nelson and engineer John Kampula, funded by the American Dental Association, developed a water-powered drill. It ran at high speed, stayed cool, and did not require belts and pulleys. It had other technical drawbacks, though, including a slight drip of oil in the patient's mouth during use.

Airotor. In 1957 Washington, D.C., dentist John Borden designed an air-powered drill called the Airotor, the hit of the Rome International Dental Congress that year, which used ball bearings to increase its efficiency. The water-cooled Airotor was five times faster than the fastest drill then available. It operated at 350,000 revolutions per minute, compared to 61,000 RPM for the Nelson-Kampula device.

FOSSIL DATING

A Better Test. In the 1950s important advances were made in scientists' ability to date fossils accurately. While radioactive dating techniques had been developed before 1950, the new radioactive-potassium dating system devised during the decade was much more reliable.

Decaying Isotopes. Radioactive dating is possible because all naturally occurring material contains small amounts of radioactive isotopes, which are maintained at a predictable ratio to nonradioactive elements in the same material. When an animal dies, the nonradioactive traces remain stable during decay, but the radioactive traces diminish at a steady rate over a very long period of time. Long after an organism's death, the amount of radioactive element remaining in dead tissue can be carefully measured and compared to nonradioactive material to determine how long it has been since the organism's death.

Carbon Dating. Standard radioactive dating processes such as carbon dating, discovered in 1948, will not work for most fossils, though. Fossilized remains contain very little carbon, if any, from the original organism. The only methods of dating fossils in the early 1950s were crude. A scientist might date a new specimen based on knowledge of the age of other specimens in the area. Or the scientist might know how deep the new fossil was when recovered and make an estimate about the age of the remains by guessing how long it took layers of earth to form over it. Such estimates were known not to be very accurate.

Uranium Dating. A group of geologists and physicists at Berkeley were using radioactive dating to measure uranium traces so they could determine the age of ancient

rocks and fossils. The half-life of the uranium isotope (the time it takes to lose half its radioactivity by conversion to lead) being measured is 4.5 billion years. This system works well for dating ancient rock, but a method based on a quicker rate of disintegration had to be found for dating more-recent formations, such as animal fossils, which are unlikely to be old enough for the the uranium disintegration to be measurable.

Potassium Dating. The Berkeley group turned to radioactive potassium as a dating measure. Like radioactive uranium, radioactive potassium is found in small amounts in rock. It forms argon (a gas) and has a half-life of only 1.31 billion years. So it was theoretically possible to measure the small amounts of radioactive potassium converted to argon over a period of a few million years. The measurements were still difficult, but by using very laborious extraction methods and a highly sensitive monitoring device called a mass spectrometer, the Berkeley group succeeded in developing an acceptable method.

Recent Developments. Not every fossil bed contains enough naturally occurring radioactive potassium to make the technique useful. After the Berkeley method was announced, similar methods of accurate dating have been developed. Since the pioneering work by the Berke-

Professor Libby at the University of Chicago with a carbon clock for fossil dating

ley group, dating by radioactive decay has become the standard in anthropology and archaeology.

Source:
John Reader, *Missing Links: The Hunt for Earliest Man* (Boston: Little, Brown, 1981).

H-Bomb

A Time of War. The H-bomb, or hydrogen bomb, resulted from scientific research that developed from the atomic bomb, which was dropped on Nagasaki and Hiroshima in Japan to end World War II. The H-bomb technology follows from that required for the A-bomb, so H-bomb development did not begin in earnest until the 1950s.

Fission. The A-bomb is based on nuclear fission. The nuclei of uranium atoms are bombarded with neutrons propelled from a magnetized coil. As a result, the uranium atoms are split (fission), releasing enormous amounts of energy. In addition, during the process neutrons are released, which can interact with even more uranium nuclei. The final product is a self-sustaining nuclear reaction that releases enormous amounts of energy. When this energy release is contained in a small area, it produces a bomb.

Fusion. The H-bomb is based on nuclear fusion. Instead of splitting atoms, it combines atoms. As a result, there is a small amount of matter converted into a massive amount of energy. Atoms of deuterium were found to be good candidates for fusion. Deuterium is an atomi-

cally heavy form of hydrogen that occurs naturally in small amounts. The H-bomb can release even more energy than the A-bomb, but it requires considerable energy to detonate. The easiest way to reach the energy level necessary for the H-bomb is with an A-bomb. That is why *A* comes before *H* in the alphabet of nuclear destruction.

Responsibility of Power. Social attitudes in America caused work on the H-bomb to be temporarily interrupted. The awesome power of the A-bomb shocked the world, and there was a heated debate about the morality of its use. The thought of an even more powerful weapon was repellent to many people, suggesting the possibility that some day a bomb capable of destroying all civilization might be developed. Nuclear scientists divided into two camps. Those who opposed the development of nuclear power for destructive use were led by J. Robert Oppenheimer. Those who favored development of weapons such as the H-bomb were led by Edward Teller. The debate was fueled by fear of the Soviet enemy. In 1948 the Soviets successfully tested an A-bomb, and in 1949 reports of their substantial progress toward an H-bomb reached the United States.

Testing. The buck stopped with President Harry S Truman, who, after having suspended nuclear-weapons research temporarily after the war, sided with Teller's group and ordered the bomb makers to continue their work. In November 1952 a crude version of the H-bomb was exploded by the United States on Elugelab Island in the Pacific. The Soviets followed with a more sophisti-

First full-scale H-bomb explosion on Elugelab Island, 1 November 1952

cated device in August 1953. In March 1954 the United States exploded the first H-bomb capable of being dropped from an airplane onto an enemy. The result was that both superpower enemies could credibly threaten to shower each other with awesomely destructive bombs. The scientists had done their work, leaving diplomats to argue over how the power to destroy would be used.

Sources:

Saturday Evening Post (25 October 1952): 29;

Time (November 1952);

Time (August 1953);

Time (8 November 1954): 25.

ICBM

Need. ICBM stands for intercontinental ballistic missile — a long-range missile that takes advantage of the scientific laws of flight trajectory. The concept was born in the cold war, when new atomic bombs, or warheads, were developed in an attempt to maintain military superiority over the Soviet Union. As the arms race progressed, it became clear that a new delivery system for warheads had to be developed. Atomic weaponry could be placed on bombers, as it had been in World War II, but the bombers had to be kept on constant alert, which meant that some planes were flying all the time. The bombers were vulnerable to attack by antiaircraft defense systems, and the effectiveness of the warheads was limited by the number of planes carrying them that could reach their targets. A more effective delivery system had to be developed.

Rocketry. The science of rocketry became a military priority during World War II. Some early rockets were used as terrorist weapons late in the war. After the war ended, scientists working in the Nazi rocketry program were recruited by both the United States and the Soviet Union. From the late 1940s onward both countries engaged in a frantic race to be the first to develop rockets capable of delivering atomic weaponry from domestic launchpads to strategic enemy sites.

Short-Range Rockets. Both sides were quick to develop short-range rockets. These were useful as tactical weapons on battlefields but not for delivering a payload on an enemy half a globe away. The Soviets produced the first ICBM, with a six-thousand-mile range. This "Sapwood" rocket was operational in 1957. The Americans were already testing their "Thor" and "Atlas" ICBMs at the time and developing the "Minuteman" rocket, which was in the design stage.

Staging. The technological breakthrough was the new application to rockets of the old concept of staging. Rockets require massive fuel supplies and engines to be capable of liftoff. Once in flight, however, they require much less fuel and motor capability. Without staging, the fuel tanks and engines required for liftoff are simply added deadweight that limits the rocket's range. Staging eliminated the deadweight. At liftoff, all the heavy fuel and engine parts are attached to the rocket. Once liftoff is completed, these are jettisoned. Another stage might have some fuel and motor capabilities for steering and speed adjustment. When the warhead is on course, directed at the target, this stage can be jettisoned also. What is left is a rapidly moving warhead, assisted in its descent by gravity and without the weight of the machinery and fuel that got it to that point. This was the concept that allowed ICBMs to be developed. The same technology led to manned and unmanned rockets sent into space for peaceful purposes.

Boeing 707 jet tanker transport demonstrator introduced in May 1954

Source:
Trevor Illtyd Williams, *Science: A History of Discovery in the Twentieth Century* (Oxford and New York: Oxford University Press, 1990).

JETS

Development. During the 1950s jet aircraft replaced slower, propeller-driven planes. In the military the change was swift; in civilian aviation it took place more slowly. World War II forced the United States government to accelerate research and development of high-performance jet aircraft in order to counter the German air force's jet fighters. While American pilots never flew jets during the war, the air force tested a number of jet- and rocket-powered planes from 1942 onward.

Background. The jet age arrived on 27 August 1939 when Erich Warsitz flew a turbojet-powered Heinkel 178 aircraft at Marienehe airfield in Nazi Germany. German officials shrugged indifferently. In the United States, Bell Aircraft's XP-59 Airacomet jet made its debut on 1 October 1942 over Muroc, California. Neither plane was substantially faster than its piston-engine counterpart, and while both aircraft served as prototypes and training models for later, more-advanced jet aircraft, early jet engines only hinted at the possibilities of supersonic flight.

Mach-1. Attitudes changed on 14 October 1947 when a Bell X-1 rocket plane, piloted by Capt. Charles ("Chuck") Yeager, reached a speed of 964 miles per hour (Mach 1.06) in level flight at an altitude of 42,000 feet over California's Muroc Air Base. The Bell X-1 demonstrated that aircraft could fly faster than the speed of sound (760 miles per hour at sea level) without disintegrating. But jet aircraft still lacked the range and engine life of propeller aircraft. Although the United States Air Force and the National Advisory Council on Aeronautics (the forerunner to the National Aeronautics and Space Administration) successfully tested and operated American jet-fighter aircraft early in the decade.

Korean War. During the Korean War the United States Air Force and Navy employed large numbers of both jet and propeller aircraft. Most American fighters were jets, but none of them, including the Lockheed P-80 "Shooting Star," the North American F-86A "Sabre," or the Grumman F9F-2 "Panther," could fly at the speed of sound in level flight. American bombers were either piston engine or turboprop (basically a jet turbine driving a high speed propeller). The only American multiengine jet bomber of the Korean War was the B-45 "Tornado." The large strategic jet bombers, the Boeing B-47 and B-52, became operational in 1951 and 1952 but did not see combat in Korea. These huge bombers provided research information vital to the design of the American passenger jets.

Early Misgivings. Despite Boeing's technical advancements in jet bombers, airline companies in the United States did not have a great deal of faith in the reliability of jet-powered aircraft. C. R. Smith, president of American Airlines, stated that America would be ready for high-speed commercial jet transport after the British Rolls-Royce Nene jet engine proved it could operate for five hundred hours. There was the further complication of negative publicity generated by Great Britain's de Havilland aircraft company, which operated the first commercial jet passenger aircraft, the DH.106 "Comet I." Early models suffered from structural problems involving stress fractures in the fuselage from the pressurized passenger cabin. The "Comet I" first flew successfully on 27 July 1949 after the disastrous midair crack-up of an earlier prototype research plane, the de Havilland DH.108. Two "Comet I's" crashed into the Mediterranean Sea on 10 January and 8 April 1954, forcing de Havilland to ground the plane temporarily so that diagnostic technicians could discover the flaws.

Boeing and Douglas. In the United States the Boeing and Douglas aircraft companies tried to sell their respective jet-transport aircraft designs to the air force before approaching the commercial airline industry. Like other defense contractors, these two aircraft-design firms minimized their financial risk when they competed for military contracts since the air force subsidized a significant portion of the research and production.

Boeing 707. But Boeing invested its own money in developing what would eventually become the first American passenger jet, the Model 707. The Boeing 367-80, the first variant of the 707, and the Air Force's KC-135 airborne refueling aircraft flew on 15 July 1954. During its October nonstop flight from Seattle to Washington, D.C., the Boeing 367-80 flew at an average speed of 592 miles per hour. On the return trip the aircraft averaged 567 miles per hour for four hours and eight minutes. The commercial airline industry signaled its confidence in the plane when Pan American Airways purchased thirty 707s on 8 November 1955.

DC-8. The earliest jet competitor to the 707, the Douglas DC-8, competed for commercial contracts in 1955. On 13 October 1955 Pan Am ordered twenty DC-8s and twenty Boeing 707s. On 25 October 1955 United Airlines ordered thirty DC-8s for their new nonstop transatlantic flights. Although the Boeing 707 was available, it was not yet capable of flying the Atlantic nonstop. The DC-8 it did not make its first flight until 30 May 1958. In the interim Boeing continued to improve and modify the 707 with numerous variants for the air force and civilian airlines.

Decade's End. By the end of the decade jet transports, supersonic fighters and bombers, and transcontinental jet passenger aircraft were the norm in aviation. Scientists, designers, technicians, and pilots worked together to improve the reliability, fuel efficiency, power, and overall flying performance of all types of jet aircraft. During the 1950s jet aircraft carried out numerous military missions as well as civilian transport of people and goods on a scale not previously imagined.

Sources:

Enzo Angelucci, *Airplanes: From the Dawn of Flight to the Present Day* (New York: McGraw-Hill, 1973);

Walter J. Boyne and Donald S. Lopez, eds, *The Jet Age: Forty Years of Jet Aviation* (Washington, D.C.: Smithsonian Institution Press, 1979);

Michael J. H. Taylor and David Mondey, eds., *Milestones of Flight* (London: Jane's, 1983).

MAPPING THE OCEAN FLOOR

Early Mapping. With the development of sonar in World War II, a means was provided for studying the contour of the land underneath the oceans. Before sonar, the configuration of the ocean floor was mapped by a crude tracing method. A weight on a long chain or cable was lowered from a ship until the weight hit bottom. The depth of water at that point was determined. Then the weight was dragged slowly to show how the depths changed from place to place. Very deep oceans, strong

---

INTERNATIONAL GEOPHYSICAL YEAR

The International Council of Scientific Unions declared July 1957–December 1958 the International Geophysical Year (IGY). The council acted on the suggestion of American physicist Lloyd V. Berkner, who made a more modest proposal that the period be designated the third International Polar Year (the previous two had been 1882–1883 and 1932–1933). Timing was appropriate because IGY coincided with a time of unusual solar activity that could be observed with unprecedented accuracy.

U.S. scientists cooperated with colleagues worldwide to establish observation stations that collected and shared data in the fields of meteorology, geomagnetism, the aurora, the airglow, cosmic rays, ionospheric physics, latitude and longtitude determination, glaciology, and oceanography. An innovation of IGY data collection was the use of satellites and high-altitude weather balloons to collect data in the upper atmosphere. The Soviet *Sputnik I* was launched in October 1957 during IGY. By August 1958 the U.S. had four satellites in orbit and the U.S.S.R. had three. IGY projects showed that Earth's atmosphere extended further out into space than scientists had suspected and that there is a layer of atmosphere that contains high-energy electrons.

Source: Trevor Illytd Williams, *Science: A History of Discovery in the Twentieth Century* (Oxford & New York: Oxford University Press, 1990).

currents, and turbulent seas limited the usefulness of this method.

Sonar. With sonar the picture is much clearer. As a ship moves along it can bounce sound waves down to the ocean floor. The reflection of the sound waves indicates the depth of the water and the shape of the bottom. Ships using sonar can move continuously, covering larger and deeper areas than with the tracing method.

Discoveries. Oceanographers were astonished by the immense volcanoes and canyons they found in the Pacific Ocean. East of the Tonga Islands (where Captain Bligh and Fletcher Christian parted company in *Mutiny on the Bounty*) lies a canyon seven miles deep — seven times the depth of the Grand Canyon. This Tonga-Kermadec Trench is but one of several canyons in the central Pacific Ocean. Some are two thousand miles in length, two-thirds the length of the United States; many are very narrow but extremely long and deep.

Volcanoes. There are also underwater volcanoes surrounding the Tonga-Kermadec Trench, one of which rises twenty-seven thousand feet above the sea floor (but still the tip is twelve hundred feet below the surface of the water). This underwater volcano is one of the highest mountains on earth.

Underwater World. The many deep trenches in the Pacific have common characteristics: they are about the same maximum depth (thirty-five thousand to forty thousand feet); they seem to have a V shape, with one side of the V more gently sloping and the other side more abrupt. Shallower trenches tend to have a U shape. Another characteristic of the trench regions is earthquake activity. Some of the most powerful earthquakes on the planet occur under water. Along with the quakes come the volcanoes. Many of the volcanoes have flattened tops, suggesting that they once rose above water and had their tops flattened by the action of pounding surf.

MASER/LASER

Daydreaming Townes. In spring 1951 Charles H. Townes was in Washington, D.C., to attend a conference at the Office of Naval Research. He was trying to develop ways to produce extremely high frequency radio waves. The applicable technology of the day was vacuum tubes, and there was simply no way to make them so that they could produce waves high enough in frequency to satisfy Townes. While sitting on a park bench Townes realized how he could produce the radio waves he wanted using atoms and molecules instead of vacuum tubes.

Quantum Theory. Townes's concept used Einstein's theory of "stimulated emission of radiation." Einstein suggested that forcing radiation (light or microwave, for example) past a group of atoms stimulates them to release energy. This energy will travel in the direction of the stimulating source and be of the same frequency as the source. Einstein theorized that energy is released in what

he called quanta — certain specific amounts, not randomly. Townes returned home to Columbia University to work on the idea after the conference.

Maser. Townes worked with J. Weber to find just the right stimulating force for his microwaves. Then they had to couple it with an atomic structure that would respond with the correct wavelength of energy. In 1954 they developed a device using ammonia gas to amplify microwave energy. The point was that they showed that waves could be amplified to produce a powerful tool, which they called a maser. The real discovery, however, was that light energy could be amplified as well. They called this phenomenon a laser. The race was on to produce a laser device.

Laser. Townes and his brother-in-law, Arthur Schawlow of Bell Laboratories, published a paper in 1958 describing the "optical maser," and Bell Labs filed a patent application. When he saw Townes and Schawlow's paper, physicist Gordon Gould of Columbia University claimed he had the idea for a laser in 1957 did not file a patent. His proof was an affidavit he prepared in November 1957 and had notarized in a candy store. Gould fought the legitimacy of Bell Labs' patent in the courts. In October 1977, after the Bell Labs patent had expired, the court ruled in his favor. In 1982 Gould's legal victory was upheld on appeal, and he collected a small fortune from Bell. Neither Townes and Schawlow nor Gould ever made a working laser, though. The first one was made in 1960 by Theodore Maiman.

THE MICROWAVE OVEN

Melting Chocolate. The microwave oven was born in 1946 by accident. Percy Spencer was in one of his Raytheon Company laboratories standing next to a magnetron, which is the operational part of radar equipment, with a chocolate bar in his pocket. The candy melted. Possessed of a scientist's inquisitiveness, Spencer sent for unpopped popcorn. When he put it next to the magnetron, the popcorn popped. After Spencer conducted careful experiments, Raytheon patented the "high frequency dielectric heating apparatus" in 1953.

After Magnetrons, What? After the war Raytheon was in a quandary. The need for its radar equipment had dropped sharply. Raytheon hoped to continue to supply the government with magnetrons, but who knew when the government would want thousands of magnetrons a week again? The new heating apparatus seemed the answer to a corporate prayer.

Radarange. The first "Radarange" weighed 750 pounds and cost three thousand dollars. It was a commercial product, attractive to restaurants, but not suitable for home use. Then Tappan formed an alliance with Raytheon. Skilled engineers were able to reduce the size of the magnetron and make a version marketable in 1955 as a home appliance. They were still expensive and bulky,

Baker and Able, the first American monkeys in space, aboard the *Kiowa*, after their return from orbit in 1959

had a military significance. Both the U.S. and the U.S.S.R. had a moon fixation: they wanted to launch a satellite into lunar orbit in order to study the moon's surface close up. Both the Soviet *Metcha*, called *Lunik* in the U.S., and the American *Pioneer IV* missed the moon and went into solar orbit, where they soon turned into cinders. In 1959 the Soviets achieved moon orbit with their *Lunik III*.

Animals in Space. Animals served nobly to test the effects of outer space on living organisms. The Soviets, without publicizing the fact, sent animals into space without hope of returning them to Earth. When reentry and landing systems were developed to bring satellites back to Earth, the animal visitors to outer space were not only named but celebrated. In 1958 the Soviets launched a dog named Laika, and in 1959 the U.S. sent two monkeys, Able and Baker, into space. Able represented the army, Baker the navy.

though, because of the cost and size of components. Microwave ovens were not widely accepted for household use until the development of transistors made them compact and cheap to build in the 1960s.

THE NEW FRONTIER

Sputnik I. The Soviet Union was the first nation to enter space. On 4 October 1957 it launched the first artificial satellite, called *Sputnik I*. The Soviet satellite was a small metal ball that did not do much of anything. It weighed 185 pounds, was 23 inches in diameter, and orbited Earth every 90 minutes. It carried two tiny radio transmitters that produced a repetitive beeping noise as it traveled. *Sputnik I* seemed to demonstrate that the Soviets were capable of producing rockets that could also send nuclear weapons to land on American soil.

American Response. America responded energetically. In 1958 the National Aeronautics and Space Administration (NASA) was created to meet the challenge. During 1958–1959 America launched nineteen satellites. These included the communications satellite *Score*, which

---

ANIMALS IN SPACE

Late in 1952 the U.S. Air Force launched an Aerobee. The Aerobee was a rocket capable of reaching altitudes between fifty-five and seventy-five miles. The Aerobee had several purposes. Its most publicized goal was to gather weather data by releasing an inflatable nylon baloon called the Sphere, which held electronic equipment to send data back to ground station receivers. In its nose, the Aerobee also contained two capsules, one holding two mice and one holding two monkeys. At the crest of the rocket's path, which occurred at a forty miles above ground level, the nose capsule was ejected and the animals parachuted to earth.

One of the points of the animal experiments was to determine a body's tolerance of weightlessness. Cameras mounted in the rocket filmed the animals during a period of zero gravity so that they could be observed floating in their capsule cages. Examinations after the mice and monkeys returned to land showed them to be fit. Scientists were encouraged that man would tolerate weightlessness well.

In 1956 a Navy Aerobee-Hi earned a distinction of another type: it set the altitude record for a single-stage rocket. The Aerobee rose 163 miles above sea level. The rocket was being developed to explore the upper atmosphere during the International Geophysical Year, 1957–1958.

Sources: "Rocket Record," *Time*, 68 (9 July 1956): 48;

1953 Collier's Year Book (New York: Collier's, 1953);

Year 1953 (New York: Simon & Schuster, 1953).

The U.S.S. *Nautilus*

Sources:

Patrick Harpur, et al, eds. *The Timetable of Technology* (New York: Hearst Books, 1982);

Trevor Illtyd Williams, *A History of Discovery in the Twentieth Century* (Oxford and New York: Oxford University Press, 1990);

Alexander Hellemans and Bryan Bunch, *The Timetable of Science* (New York: Simon & Schuster, 1988).

NUCLEAR SUBMARINES

New Submarine Needed. During World War II the Germans had proven the effectiveness of submarines by using them to devastate Allied shipping early in the war. With the development of sonar and the use of depth charges, submarines became less of a threat, but they still could not be ignored.

Coming Up for Air. World War II– era submarines had to surface at least once a week and stay on the surface for a while, and thus their effectiveness was diminished. Diesel or gasoline engines require oxygen for combustion. Submarines with these engines had to replenish their oxygen supplies with fresh air to keep the engines running and to freshen the atmosphere so the crew would have breathable air.

Rickover's Idea. Capt. (later Adm.) Hyman Rickover realized the potential for a nuclear-powered submarine. The nuclear reactor would heat a fluid. The fluid would pass through a heat exchanger (like a radiator) and convert water to steam. The steam would run a turbine that powered the sub, leaving stored oxygen to be used solely to replenish the air supply for the crew. The result was a submarine that could stay submerged for a month or more. Rickover convinced Adm. Chester Nimitz of the need for such a sub in 1947.

Nautilus. The Electric Boat Company of Groton, Connecticut, contracted to produce the submarine. The resulting *Nautilus* was commissioned in October 1954, the start of an atomic fleet. It made its first dive in January 1955 in Long Island Sound. The first dive lasted only an hour, but the submarine was designed to stay submerged for a month. The atomic-powered submarine became a basic element in the nuclear military strategy developed during the 1960s.

Sources:

Newsweek (31 January 1955): 23;

Newsweek (11 October 1954): 32.

MOO-TERNITY

The bulk of the feat aside, it may seem simple to transplant an embryo from one cow to another, but it is a very complex procedure. When the operation was first performed in 1953, it was hailed as a remarkable achievement both in veterinary medicine and in the larger field of reproductive science. In the 1953 experiment, the embryo was removed from one cow that had conceived in the normal way and was then transplanted into another cow, where the embryo matured and was delivered in good health. The advantage to veterinarians and breeders was that high-quality cattle could be used for conception and spared the rigors of pregnancy by having their burden transferred to cows genetically unsuitable for breeding.

For researchers in the field of human reproduction, the cow-embryo transplant was a major step in the development of in-vitro fertilization (in vitro meaning "in glass"; i.e., in a test tube) in 1978. By in-vitro fertilization an egg could be removed from a woman unable to carry a fetus to term, fertilized in a test tube with her mate's sperm, and then transplanted to a living surrogate mother, who would carry the fetus in her womb until it was ready to deliver.

John Rock

M. C. Chang

Gregory Pincus

ORAL CONTRACEPTIVES

Hormone Manipulation. The concept behind oral contraceptive pills is fairly simple. Every month, women have a cycle of hormones produced by their ovaries. This cycle leads to ovulation, or the production of an egg that can become fertilized to result in pregnancy. The two main hormones produced by the body in this cycle are estrogen and progesterone. If their levels do not rise and fall in accordance with the body's requirements during the monthly cycle, ovulation normally does not occur, and even if it does, unbalanced hormone levels could prevent the uterus from accepting the resultant pregnancy. The oral contraceptive pill was designed to manipulate levels of these two hormones to prevent unwanted pregnancy effectively.

The Team. An interesting group of people was involved in the development of oral contraceptives. Margaret Sanger was a pioneer of women's rights and founded the organization Planned Parenthood. Her friend Katherine McCormick was an heiress (McCormick farm machinery) who funded much of the project. Gregory Pincus and M. C. Chang were Massachusetts biologists. John Rock was a Boston gynecologist willing to try the new method on women volunteers. Russell Marker was a

chemist and entrepreneur who made it all possible because of his work with Mexican yams.

A Marriage of Interests. Pincus approached Sanger with a report about his research on oral contraceptives in 1951. Sanger was impressed with his work and introduced him to McCormick, who eventually gave more than $2 million to the project. Synthetic estrogens were developed in the 1950s by Syntex chemists G. Rosenkranz, C. Djerassi and F. Sondheimer. Their synthetic hormones could be taken orally to control the body's estrogen level, but the progesterone component had to be controlled as well for effective birth control. That is where yams came in.

The Pill. Marker was able to produce progesterone in large amounts at a very low cost from the yams. Pincus recognized that Marker's research had identified a source for the previously rare and costly hormone, and he engaged Rock to help set up human testing when the time was right. After initial development and testing to develop the final product, the G. D. Searle Company announced its sponsorship of the Pincus and Rock tests in 1955 at a Planned Parenthood meeting in Tokyo. In 1956 fifteen thousand women in Puerto Rico and in Haiti volunteered to test the effectiveness and safety of the contraceptive. The results were positive, and for the first time women had access to a highly effective, safe, inexpensive, convenient form of totally reversible temporary birth control. Although thousands of types of pills are produced annually by American pharmaceutical companies, the oral contraceptive had such a dramatic social

EXPANDING UNIVERSE

In September 1952 Dr. Walter Beade of Mount Wilson-Palomar Observatories made an announcement to the International Astronomical Union that shocked astronomers. Observations with the two hundred-inch Hale telescope at his observatoy had revealed that all objects beyond the Milky Way were twice as far from Earth as previously believed. By the new calculations the Andromeda Nebula was shown to be 1.7 million light-years from Earth, meaning that whatever light from the nebula might reach us would have begun its travel 1.7 million years ago.

Dr. Beade's discovery affected calculations of the age as well as the size of the universe. His best estimate was that the universe was 3.9 billion years old, not 1.8 billion years, as astronomers had previously believed. The new calculation corresponded to radioactive dating of the Earth's crust.

Source: William T. Couch, *Collier's 1954 Year Book* (New York: Collier's, 1954).

impact that it is known as the Pill. In 1960 it was approved for use throughout the United States.

Sources:

Kenneth Morris, Marc Robinson and Richard Kroll, *American Dreams: One Hundred Years of Business Ideas and Innovation From the Wall Street Journal* (New York: Abrams, 1990);

Trevor Illtyd Williams, *Science: A History of Discovery in the Twentieth Century* (Oxford & New York: Oxford University Press, 1990);

Lawrence Lader and Milton Meltzer, *Marganet Sanger: Pioneer of Birth Control* (New York: Crowell, 1969).

RADIO ASTRONOMY

Light Astronomy. In the 1950s light astronomy, that is, scientific advancement based on what one could see through various telescopes that magnified images, was nearing its technological limit. The giant telescope at Mount Palomar was producing sharp, clear views of celestial bodies, including the planets. These images would not be greatly improved until satellites began transmitting pictures of the planets from close range decades later. The next big technological breakthrough in astronomy during the 1950s was the radio telescope.

Celestial Static. Radio astronomy was born in 1932, when K. G. Jansky noted that radios picked up static from some source. He traced this to radio waves emitted by celestial bodies, especially certain stars. This curious finding became the field of radio astronomy. It was subsequently discovered that all stars emit various waves: light is one form of electromagnetic wave; radio is a

A radio telescope

nother, with a longer wavelength. Using a telescope with a special antenna, an observer can detect these radio waves on ground stations. These receivers are usually made of a large wire-mesh concave dish with a central antenna. They can be grouped to scan wider areas of the sky.

Versatility. Radio telescopes are versatile. They can be mounted on pivots so that they can be pointed accurately in a particular direction. They can also have their pivots mounted. If the pivots are mounted on a circular track, the telescope can detect waves from three dimensions at any point above the horizon.

The Sounds of Jupiter. Just as each star has a characteristic light signature on a spectrograph, it also has a characteristic radio signature. Some stars are very strong emitters (radio stars). Their emissions may change over time, as our own sun does when it has a solar storm. Even planets may have radio emissions. Jupiter was first heard in 1955. By the end of the decade, radio telescopes outnumbered light telescopes in use in America for academic astronomy.

Sources:

Trevor Illtyd Williams, *Science: A History of Discovery in the Twentieth Century* (New York and Oxford: Oxford University Press, 1990);

Life (17 November 1952): 130;

Popular Mechanics (November 1952): 148.

RADIOIMMUNOASSAY

Minute Measures. Critical to any scientific research is the ability to measure. Various measuring methods have been used in biochemistry over the years — some crude, some sophisticated. Most assay systems for materials in the body have limited use because they require a greater quantity of what is to be measured than is available. The body can spare only small amounts of hormones and other biological molecules for testing purposes.

The Researchers. Rosalind Yalow and Solomon Berson were well prepared as a research team to tackle the problem of measurement testing. Yalow had a Ph.D. in physics and expertise in radioactive materials. Berson was a physician and researcher. Together they developed the radioimmunoassay (RIA) technique, which has been applied not only in medical science but also in a wide range of fields.

The Procedure. The concept of RIA is simple, but it requires some background knowledge. Part of the immune system functions by producing antibodies to foreign substances. With various manipulations, the immune systems of mammals can be forced to make antibodies to almost anything. Antibodies are very specific. An antibody recognizes a chemical structure, and it will bind only to that one structure. Even similar structures will not be recognized by the antibody. But antibodies are also sensitive: they will find and bind to even tiny amounts of the substances they recognize. If a researcher wants an exact measure of hormone X, which is present

Rosalyn Yalow

in small amounts in the blood, RIA is the best method to use. First the researcher needs some pure hormone X that has a radioactive atom in its structure. This can often be produced by a chemical reaction of a small molecule with a radioactive atom and nonradioactive X. Then the researcher needs an antibody that recognizes X.

Measuring Leftovers. To perform the RIA, the researcher puts carefully measured amounts of radioactive X and its antibody into a test tube. Next, a carefully measured amount of blood is added. When hormone X in the blood goes into the test tube, it displaces some of the radioactive X from the antibody. The more X in the blood, the more radioactive X it displaces. Now everything except the antibody and the molecules to which it is bound is removed. The amount of radioactive X left in the tube indicates how much X was in the blood.

The Prize. Yalow and two other physicians, Roger C. L. Guillemin and Andrew V. Schally, received the Nobel Prize for physiology in 1977 for their research into the role of hormones in the chemistry of the body — work made possible by RIA.

Source:
Ira Flatow, *They All Laughed-From Light Bulbs to Lasers, the Fascinating Stories Behind the Great Inventions That Have Changed Our Lives* (New York: Harper Collins, 1992).

THE SAINT LAWRENCE SEAWAY

A Binational Waterway. One of the engineering marvels of the twentieth century is the Saint Lawrence Seaway, which provides sea access from the Atlantic Ocean to the Great Lakes along the northern border of the United States. The Saint Lawrence River provides the natural outlet for the Great Lakes to the Atlantic, but small channels and rapids prevented navigation by vessels much larger than a canoe, and so the river was closed to commercial use. The demands of commerce required a waterway accessible to large oceangoing vessels. That required redigging a long stretch of the river.

Early Chicanery. The idea of opening up the Saint Lawrence originated in 1895. In 1907–1910 three powerful American congressmen proposed a plan to build a plant to use water flow to produce electricity — hydroelectric power — and dig part of the seaway in the process. When the Alcoa Aluminum Company applied to the Canadian Parliament for permission to export power to America without a license in 1910, it was alleged that the company attempted to bribe members of the Parliament. The American congressmen who proposed the scheme all had personal financial interests in it as well. Parliament rejected the plan.

Cooperative Effort. After that the seaway project was postponed for decades as the United States and Canada negotiated a cooperative plan and each nation worked independently to open up parts of the river. Over the years political and financial controversy continued. Parts of the seaway were built at different times by Canadian and American interests. Then, in May 1954 the Wiley-Donder Act authorized the American government to enter into a cooperative effort with the Canadians to dig a twenty-seven-foot-deep canal between Montreal and Lake Ontario. This massive project involved fifty-nine

Saint Lambert lock on the Saint Lawrence Seaway, July 1952

Christine Jorgensen on her return to the United States, 12 February 1953

thousand workers and $80 million worth of heavy equipment. Tons of heavy rocks, gravel, and slimy marine clay had to be moved to connect the Great Lakes to the sea.

Minnesota to the Ocean. Surprisingly, the work was completed more or less on schedule. In July 1958 thirty-eight thousand acres of land along forty miles of the seaway were flooded, providing access for deep-sea ships from the tip of Lake Superior in northern Minnesota to the Atlantic. This access was particularly important to midwestern steel producers, who now had an efficient means of shipping their products abroad. On 25 April 1959 the seaway was opened to shipping in a ceremony presided over by Queen Elizabeth II of England and President Dwight D. Eisenhower of the United States.

Sources:
Helen Leavitt, *Superhighway-Superhoax* (Garden City, New York: Doubleday, 1970);

Jacques LesStrang, *Seaway: The Untold Story of North America's Fourth Seacoast* (Seattle: Superior Publishing, 1976).

SEX CHANGE

Not Cut Out for the Army. In 1952 Americans were shocked by the news that George Jorgensen, a twenty-six-year-old private in the U.S. Army Service Command at Fort Dix, New Jersey, had an operation to change his sex. Jorgensen was unhappy as a man and wanted to change his body to that of a woman. He went to Denmark for the surgery to make the transformation.

A Quiet History. Jorgensen's was not the first sex-change operation. In a highly publicized case, a woman in Great Britain was converted to a man by similar means in order to be able to inherit a title and land available only to a man. In fact, Jorgensen might not have been even the first American to have undergone a sex-change procedure. His notoriety was based on the fact that his case was publicized.

The Transformation. At the Rigs Hospital in Copenhagen, Jorgensen was subjected to slow changes in his hormone levels as surgical procedures were used to remove his male organs and produce female genitals. The hormonal therapy produced breasts and other necessary physical changes.

A Curious Nation Awaits News. While Jorgensen was undergoing therapy at Rigs, someone who knew him informed an American news reporter of the procedure. The reporter convinced Jorgensen's parents to divulge the story. When Jorgensen, now named Christine, arrived back in New York, she was met by a throng of reporters at the airport. They asked such questions as whether she could have a baby (only by adoption; she had no uterus). They also asked her to confirm rumors that she had been dating an American GI while in Europe. She moved into a suite at the Carlyle Hotel and started on the first chapter of her memoirs for *American* magazine. Privacy would never be easy for her again.

Sources:
Time (23 February 1953): 28;
Newsweek, 40 (15 December 1952): 64.

TELEPHONES IN THE AGE OF TECHNOLOGY

TV on the Front. The TV phone was first described in the popular press in 1950. The U.S. Army saw a need for a voice communicator that could cover long distances and include the capability of sending pictures at the same time. For example, an infantry commander near the front lines might want to call headquarters and point on a map to show where enemy positions were located to request artillery assistance. Such a capability would require the ability to link a telephone and a television video screen. Producing a live television show required lots of fancy gadgetry that was not applicable for field use. Moreover, the telephone lines used by the military could be secured, but live television broadcasts could not. Thus, a telephone TV was superior to a field TV transmitter.

A Soundproof Booth. The army solved this problem by developing a TV phone booth. It was first displayed at the U.S. Army Signal Corps in Fort Monmouth, New Jersey. A person could enter the booth and sit in a specific location. The receiving party would enter a similar booth at another location. The booth included an overhead TV screen, a telephone, and a TV camera pointed at the seat. Special lamps were required for the video image. Maps, charts, and the like could be held in front of the camera while the parties conversed on the phone about them.

World's Fair. The TV phone never became widely used, probably because of the expense and the need to have a special booth during the operation of the equipment. At the 1964 World's Fair in New York, one of the most popular exhibits was a series of AT&T booths on the fairground. People could sit in a booth, call another booth at the fair, and watch each other while they talked — the TV phone.

Radio Phone. In an age of cellular phones when people routinely place calls from their cars, it is difficult to imagine that the radio telephone was considered a radical concept in the 1950s. In fact, it was developed because of a pressing need. Many people lived in rural areas where phone lines did not yet extend, and they wanted telephone service. Building the poles and wires required to provide phone service to these areas was an expensive prospect.

REA. In 1952 the Rural Electrification Administration proposed a radio telephone. Their Technical Standards Division worked with the General Electric Company to build such a system on a small scale and test it for efficiency and economy. The radio telephone connected Chancellor and Alsop, Virginia, about ten miles apart. The voice was converted to a radio signal at the exchange in one town and was received at the exchange in the other. The signal was then converted back to phone cir-cuitry and sent to the receiver (earpiece) of the second caller.

Answering Machine. In 1951 Assen Jordanoff and Norman Robin of New York City developed a special phone attachment. It could receive calls and record them even if no one answered the phone. It could also record an entire phone conversation by both parties. Today, we call the device a telephone answering machine — or a wiretap.

Sources:
Science Digest (April 1951): 96;
Popular Science, 157 (August 1950): 81;
Popular Mechanics, 98 (August 1952): 207.

TELEVISION

Just a Quiet Evening. After World War II Americans wanted peace, Korea and the cold war notwithstanding, and they found it at night in their living rooms where a few hours of escapism were delivered for free by a new gadget, the television. Television technology allowed transmission of high-quality images, and mass-production techniques meant that sets were available and affordable. But the pictures on those televisions were black-and-white, and industry leaders hoped for more.

Goldmark. In 1951 a CBS engineer named Peter Goldmark devised a method of color television broad-

Fifty-five pound "Man-Pack Television System" tested by the U. S. Army in 1957

casting. The concept of color television is simple. All pictures are transmitted and received as combinations of red, green, and blue. Goldmark's system required a set of whirling red, green, and blue filters placed in front of the camera lens; a similar set of filters inside the television set decoded the color signals. A black-and-white television set could not receive the pictures transmitted by a Goldmark-equipped camera. Not only could it not receive color pictures, it could not receive pictures at all. Since ten million people in the United States already owned black-and-white sets, there was what businessmen call sales resistance to the introduction of the Goldmark system in the United States.

Sarnoff. Meanwhile, David Sarnoff of the NBC network was working on an all-electronic system to send color pictures over channels carrying black-and-white images. With this system a television equipped for color could receive color images when the transmitter sent them. Black-and-white sets received the same show, but without the color. The Sarnoff system worked by splitting images into red, blue, and green components. If a television had a screen with tiny color dots and the electronics to activate them, it could receive color broadcasts. Otherwise, the television simply showed black-and-white images.

FCC's First Decision. Because the size of the potential market for color television was huge, the Federal Communications Commission (FCC), which regulated the television industry, felt there had to be some uniform broadcast standard. A lawsuit ensued. The FCC chose the Goldmark system in 1951, but due to material shortages resulting from the Korean War, CBS decided to postpone starting its color system.

Sarnoff Undeterred. Meanwhile, Sarnoff continued to improve his all-electronic system. In 1953 the National Television Standards Committee reassessed the situation and reversed the FCC ruling. The NBC system was designated the standard for transmission of color television broadcasts.

Videotape. Another major advance during the decade came with the development of taped television broadcasts in the mid 1950s. Previously, television shows could be taped, but the quality of broadcast transmission was poor. As a result, almost all television shows were live, creating a problem for people living on the West Coast. Most television shows originated in New York. If a show was broadcast live at 8:30 P.M. in New York, because of the differences in time zones it was received in California at 5:30 P.M. — before many working people arrived home.

Ampex System. Alexander Poniatoff developed a videotape recorder that drastically changed the television industry. First demonstrated in Chicago, his Ampex system was able to broadcast a taped show with the same quality as live television programs. The Ampex system was first used in November 1956 for the Pacific Coast television region. It quickly became standard practice to

tape shows for later broadcast. One important result was that news could be broadcast using taped sequences from various sites, providing audiences with nightly views of the world.

Transistors. The inside of the television set also changed during the decade. In the early 1950s television sets consisted of numerous vacuum tubes, the electronic workhorses of the day. Sets were large, although the screens were often small, and they required periodic repairs as tubes failed. When the transistor became inexpensive, it began replacing the vacuum tube. By 1959 the first all-electronic television set was produced and available in the United States. It contained no vacuum tubes except the picture tube, and it was far more reliable than its predecessor.

Sources:

Trevor Illtyd Williams, *Science: A History of Discovery in the Twentieth Century* (Oxford and New York: Oxford University Press, 1990);

Carl Dreher, *Sarnoff: An American Success* (New York: Quadrangle / New York Times Book Co., 1977).

Extension of transatlantic cable being pulled ashore in Newfoundland, 1957

Transatlantic Telegraph. While radio telephone was being considered for the continental United States, it was the only option available for transatlantic voice communication. Such telephone links were at the mercy of storms and assured a great deal of static in connections at the best of times. The only transatlantic communication option was the telegraph, via a transoceanic telegraph cable the first one of which was laid in 1866. Since 1928 consideration had been given to linking the continents with a cable system for direct telephone communication.

The Cable. The transatlantic cable was actually just two big specially coated and insulated wire bundles laid along the ocean floor: one eastbound, one westbound. The cable required a series of more than one hundred tiny "repeaters," electronic components (made of vacuum tubes) which amplified the sound carried along the cable and made up for volume lost in the long trip as sound traveled across the Atlantic. The coatings and insulation had to be able to withstand pressures of 6,800 pounds per square inch and a 26,000 pound pull.

Engineering. The cable was an engineering masterpiece. It was designed to carry thirty-six conversations at a time and up to twelve hundred calls a day. The cable itself cost $40 million. It had to be more than twenty-five hundred miles long in each direction. Near the shores the cable also had to be specially reinforced. Unlike in mid ocean, the area near the shore exposed the cable to stresses such as anchors and even icebergs.

Planning. American Telephone and Telegraph (AT&T) sponsored the operation in conjunction with the British Post Office (which ran the British telephone system) and the Canadian Overseas Telecommunication Corporation. They decided on a route to avoid the twenty-one telegraph cables already on the floor of the Atlantic. Simplex Wire & Cable Company (Newington, New Hampshire) produced the extra-heavy cable, while Western Electric (an AT&T subsidiary) built a factory at Hillside, New Jersey, to make the repeaters, which were flown to England and incorporated into the entire cable length.

Laying the Cable. The British ship *Monarch*, the world's largest cable-laying ship, was chosen to lay the cable. The difficulties in laying it were enormous. Rain, shine, or storm, the cable laying had to continue at a steady pace. Stopping could kink or break the cable. The ocean floor has deep caverns. Laying the cable across the top of two opposing cliffs under water would expose it to potentially destructive hazards, so the *Monarch* had to map the ocean as it went along and bypass these areas. The actual cable-laying began in June 1955. At one point, Hurricane Ione caused the buoy marking the cable route to be lost, and the ship had to grapple the ocean floor to find the cable end for splicing. But the job was, at length, completed. On 27 September 1955 AT&T's William Thompson first used the completed eastbound cable

William Shockley, Walter Brattain, and John Bardeen, who won the Nobel Prize for developing the transistor

for a transatlantic phone call. By 1956 the full system was operational. Not many people were expected to use the local pay phone for transatlantic calls, though. Calls via the cable cost twelve dollars during the day or nine dollars at night for three minutes' time.

Sources:
Popular Science, 132 (May 1956): 168.

THE TRANSISTOR

Vacuum Tubes. Before transistors, electronic equipment consisted of glass tubes containing electronic components. The inside of the tubes was kept in a vacuum to avoid air interference with their function. The concept of replacing these tubes with simpler devices started in the late 1930s at Bell Labs, the research arm of the old national AT&T telecommunications monopoly. The idea was shelved during World War II.

Germanium. Using semiconductor materials made out of the metal germanium, a crude device was developed in late 1947. William Shockley, John Bardeen, and Walter Brattain are credited with developing the transistor, but they worked with a large number of people at Bell Labs in the process. There were two problems with the original transistor. One was obtaining enough germanium to produce meaningful quantities of transistors. The other was purifying germanium adequately. Gordon Teal and J. B. Little at Bell Labs worked out a new purification method later improved upon by William Pfann, who developed what was called the zone refining technique, also developed at Bell Labs.

Silicon. In 1950 only about thirteen pounds of germanium were produced each year in the whole world. Because it was so scarce, it was also expensive to obtain, so the transistors produced at the time were much more costly than the vacuum tubes they were designed to replace. Various Bell Labs scientists, including Henry Theurer, then discovered ways to substitute silicon for germanium to produce a cheaper, more marketable transistor. Silicon was much more plentiful but harder to work with. Teal moved from Bell Labs to Texas Instruments and produced the first commercially practical silicon transistor in 1954. Its cost-lowering effects led to the transistor revolution.

The Bell Monopoly. Bell Labs spent well over $1 million in developing the transistor. Various manufacturers and trade groups, recognizing that the profit potential was enormous, began pointing out the monopoly position of AT&T, the Bell parent company, in holding all rights to transistor technology. In April 1952 Bell Labs took an unprecedented step. They invited thirty-five representatives of various companies to come and learn transistor technology. Each invitee paid Bell Labs only twenty-five thousand dollars and had to prove an interest in developing products using transistors. One of these representatives was from Raytheon Corporation. In 1953 Raytheon was the first company outside the Bell system to produce a product using transistors. The hearing aid they produced was more expensive than its pretransistor counterpart, but smaller and lighter.

Microchips. In 1958–1959 the silicon microchip was developed. A microchip is a small wafer of silicon. Innovators at Texas Instruments and Fairchild Semiconductor developed techniques to use microchips in electronic circuits. Jack Kilby at Texas Instruments conceived the idea of placing circuits onto microchips. Robert Noyce at Fairchild developed a way to connect microchip circuits. The result was the age of miniaturization. The UNIVAC computer of the early 1950s took up a whole room that required its own air-conditioning system. Hand-held computers today have superior capabilities to those of the old UNIVAC. The difference is transistors and microchip circuitry.

The Prize. Today every television, radio, and computer, as well as most household appliances and key parts of cars, depend on transistorized components. The transistor lends itself to miniaturization, and electronic components get smaller and smaller. The pioneers in this field had an enormous impact on people's lives. In 1956 Shockley, Bardeen, and Brattain won the Nobel Prize in physics for their discovery.

Sources:

John Diebold, *The Innovators: The Discoveries, Inventions, and Breakthroughs of Our Time* (New York: Dutton, 1990);

Rosalind Franklin

Patrick Harpur, and others, eds. *The Timetable of Technology* (New York: Hearst Books, 1982);

Alexander Bryan Hellemans, *The Timetable of Science* (New York: Simon & Schuster, 1988);

Trevor Illtyd Williams, *Science: A History of Discovery in the Twentieth Century* (Oxford & New York: Oxford University Press, 1990).

WOMEN IN SCIENCE AND TECHNOLOGY

Marion Donovan. In 1951 Marion Donovan had a problem. The diapers of the day were made of cloth. As a young mother, she had to wash her baby's diapers by hand in hot water, then bleach and boil them. The only alternative was an expensive diaper service. Marion Donovan's solution was "The Boater." Made of an absorbent layer coated with a piece of shower curtain, The Boater was a disposable diaper held in place by snaps (instead of the usual safety pins). Remarkably, manufacturers were not interested in the product. Donovan manufactured her product herself and was quite successful.

Rosalyn Yalow. The term *supermom* refers to a woman with a career who also successfully raises a family. A prime example is Rosalyn Yalow. After graduating from college, she was denied positions in graduate school on the grounds that a Jewish woman did not belong in science. She persevered and received her Ph.D. in physics from the University of Illinois in 1945. She worked at a Veterans Administration hospital in New York with a physician, Dr. Solomon Berson. With Berson's medical knowledge and Yalow's knowledge of radioactive materials, they developed the technique known as radioimmunoassay (RIA), used to measure accurately the presence of various substances (such as hormones and viruses, for example) in the body, even if they are only present in very small amounts. RIA is used in numerous medical and nonmedical fields today. Yalow raised two children successfully. She also won the Nobel Prize for her work on RIA.

Chien-Shiung Wu. Dr. Chien-Shiung Wu of the U.S. National Bureau of Standards did a remarkable bit of experimental work in pure theoretical physics. She disproved the theory of conservation of parity — the molecular equivalent of handedness (like left-handedness or right-handedness). The theory held that nature is always symmetrical. Whatever happens on a left-handed molecule will happen as a mirror image on a right-handed molecule. Wu worked with electrons at ultralow temperatures and proved that atomic parity was wrong. Her two male colleagues received the Nobel Prize for their theoretical work in the field. Wu did the experimental work that proved their ideas, but the Nobel committee failed to recognize her role.

Barbara McClintock. Another innovator was Barbara McClintock. She, too, was rejected by various graduate school programs before she earned a Ph.D. in botany and studied plant genetics using corn. In 1951 she published her work proving that genes do not always behave in the predictable ways described by Gregor Mendel many years earlier. The chromosomes in every cell contain DNA, which includes genes — regions of DNA that determine the structure of proteins using a special molecular code. In 1866 Mendel had concluded that the inheritance of genes is perfectly predictable, and his theory of genetics was accepted until McClintock stunned the scientific world by proving that genes could jump around in ways that were totally unpredictable and almost random. She showed that genes can shift within chromosomes and even between different cells. Her studies were ridiculed, and she continued her work through the Carnegie Institute for decades without publishing or gaining any recognition from colleagues. Eventually, the value of her work was recognized and she won the Nobel Prize in 1983.

Rosalind Franklin. One of the saddest stories of women scientists of the 1950s was that of Rosalind Franklin. She experienced repeated scorn by male supervisors and colleagues throughout her career. Her work was in X-ray studies of the structure of complex molecules. In 1951 she deduced the complex helical structure of DNA. Her colleague at King's College (London), Maurice Wilkins, resented her. Without her permission, he gave Franklin's research findings on DNA structure to two of his friends, Watson and Crick. Franklin never received credit for her efforts. She developed cancer and died a bitter and lonely person at age thirty-seven in 1958. In 1962 Wilkins, Watson, and Crick received the Nobel Prize for discovering the structure of DNA.

HEADLINE MAKERS

CHESTER CARLSON

1906-1968

INVENTOR OF XEROGRAPHY

The Need. Chester Carlson was an ingenious and determined man who saw a problem and solved it. After graduating from college, he worked briefly for Bell Laboratories. He lost this position during the Depression of the 1930s and went to law school. He eventually became a patent attorney. To copy the information from various sources required for his job, he had to write it out tediously by hand. Carlson saw the need for a copying machine and set about making one. He used the kitchen of his apartment as a laboratory. His landlord's daughter came to his door to investigate a foul odor one day. She was intrigued enough by his activities to marry him.

The Principle. He began from a basic scientific principle: some charged particles (positive or negative), when exposed to light, will attach themselves to a surface that has the opposite charge. After some experimentation, he placed an image on a charged metal plate and shone a light on it. The light hit the plate, and the charged particles lightened or disappeared where light hits the plate (depending on how much light hits it). So he used a powder of the opposite charge to stick to the charged areas of the plate. By heating the plate, he found he could transfer the image into a piece of plain paper.

The First Copy. In 1937, Carlson patented his copying process, though he still had not made a copy without using wet chemicals. In 1938 he and an assistant made the first dry copy of words he had written, "10-22-38 ASTORIA." The process worked, but he could not find an investor to develop a commercial application.

Battelle Institute. In 1944 Carlson had run out of money trying to develop a machine for his process. When the nonprofit Battelle Memorial Institute sent a representative to Mallory & Co., one of his patent clients, Carlson began talking about his idea. Battelle gave Carlson money for research in return for a share of any profits he would make from his new process.

Haloid Corp. In 1945 Carlson's wife, apparently sick of the smell of chemicals, divorced him, and in 1946 Battelle was running out of money to support his research. Carlson found a new source of support — John Dessauer of the Haloid Company in Rochester, New York. Haloid made photographic supplies; but business was not good, and they needed a new product. Dessauer joined Battelle in backing Carlson in his work. Haloid coined the name "xerography" for the new process (*xeros* is Greek for "dry," *graphos* is Greek for "writing").

Xerox. Still most people thought the new product was worthless. In 1949–1950, the Xerox Model A machine was produced for commercial sale. Large and complex to operate, it was a resounding failure. In 1955 Haloid produced the CopyFlo, which produced dry prints from microfilm. The company changed its name to Haloid Xerox. Then the Xerox 914 copier was developed in 1959. Dry copies were made on plain paper with a convenient machine using dried ink powder. The machine was a spectacular success. In 1961 the company changed its name to Xerox Corporation.

The Reward. Carlson became a wealthy man. He gave away more than $100 million, often anonymously, to private citizens and charities before his death in 1968. Most of the time, Carlson asked to remain anonymous when making his donations. After decades of work and hardship, his reward was seeing the success of his idea for the dry copier.

WILLY HIGGINBOTHAM

?-?

INVENTOR OF FIRST VIDEO GAME

Background. Willy Higginbotham was a physicist. During World War II he joined the Massachusetts Institute of Technology Radiation Laboratory to work on radar display. He contributed to research on the atomic bomb at Los Alamos, New Mexico, and helped develop a radar system associated with the B-29 bomber. After the war, Higginbotham worked for the U.S. government at

Brookhaven National Laboratory, where every year there was an open house. People could come in and tour the nuclear research lab and see the equipment used and displays of work in progress. Higginbotham feared that visitors to the open house were bored.

A Visitors' Game. As director of the instrumentation division of the lab, he decided to make something interesting for the public in 1958. He took spare parts from an oscilloscope and some other equipment around the lab, hooked it together, and created a game for his visitors to play. On a five-inch screen, Higginbotham electronically drew a tennis court. A bouncing dot of light represented the ball. Two controls (one on either side) included a button and a knob. When the button was pushed it caused the ball to move across the court; the knob controlled the ball's speed. The tennis game was an instant success with Brookhaven guests. While their eyes may have glazed over at descriptions of sophisticated electronic equipment and its scientific use, they were endlessly fascinated by watching a dot they could control bounce back and forth on an oscilloscope.

Remembered for a Game. Higginbotham saw no commercial application for his idea, and even if he had, he could not patent it because he worked for the government and created his game on government time. A patent lawyer for Magnavox, which had bought Sanders Associates, the company that in 1964 applied for the first video game patent found out about Higginbotham and called him to testify in one of the suits Magnavox filed against video game tyros. As a result of his testimony, Higginbotham achieved a certain celebrity, though he would have preferred that it were for his nuclear-safety engineering skills and his work in arms control.

GRACE MURRAY HOPPER

1906-1992

Computer Engineer

Background. Grace Hopper graduated from Vassar College in 1928 and entered Yale University, where she earned a Ph.D. in mathematics and physics in 1934. She returned to Vassar to teach, but World War II changed her career path.

UNIVAC. In 1943 she joined the WAVES, (Women Accepted for Volunteer Emergency Service) as a lieutenant and was sent to the Bureau of Ordnance Computation Project. There she learned to program the Mark I, the world's first large digital computer. After the war she was a research fellow at Harvard for three years before she joined the Eckert-Mauchly Computer Corporation, which became a division of Remington Rand. By 1959 she was director of automatic program development for the UNIVAC division at Remington Rand, the first commercial computer. At Remington Rand, Hopper changed the computer forever.

Compiler. Prior to her work computers were programmed in machine language, a purely digital, very complex coding structure that required a precise knowledge of how computers actually performed the operations they were given. This language of mathematics bore no resemblance to English or any other spoken tongue. Hopper created a compiler for programmers that amounted to a translator and a shorthand system. The compiler provided the bridge between such simple commands as GOTO, which tells the machine to link one instruction with another, and the intricate set of purely electronic, machine-language commands that speak directly to parts of the computer. When a program is written, it uses English-lanuage (or any other language) terms and mathematical symbols and formulas, written according to precise rules of grammar. The compiler recognizes these and converts them into forms the computer can use.

COBOL. The earliest generally accepted computer programming language not in machine language was FORTRAN, which was used primarily by mathematicians. Hopper developed a programming language called COBOL that made business applications on computers practical. While trained programmers were required in order to talk to computers in COBOL, the language was simple, flexible, and practical enough to make it usable in various settings and to demonstrate the capacity of computers to perform difficult business-related functions. Hopper expanded the universe of computer users.

ALFRED C. KINSEY

1897-1956

Sex Researcher

Childhood. Alfred Kinsey was born in Hoboken, New Jersey, and his family moved to South Orange, New Jersey, when he was ten years old. He was ill during much of his childhood, suffering rickets (bone deformity from lack of vitamin D), rheumatic fever (which affected his heart), and typhoid fever. His deeply religious family was very protective. While other boys played baseball, Kinsey collected plant specimens and wrote poetry. Even in high school he avoided female companionship rather than upset his religious parents, who disapproved of dating.

Education. Kinsey's father wanted him to become a mechanical engineer, and he initially tried this field at Stevens Institute, where his father worked. After a stunning failure, he decided to become a biologist. His father gave him one suit of clothes for support, and Kinsey enrolled in Bowdoin College in Brunswick, Maine, to study biology. After graduation he won a scholarship for graduate studies in applied biology at Harvard University.

Gall Study. Kinsey chose to study gall wasps. These insects lay their eggs in "galls" — round growths — on plants. He continued this study for twenty years. Kinsey also wrote *Edible Wild Plants of Eastern North America*, published in 1943. He was a naturalist who enjoyed the outdoors.

A Teacher's Responsibility. In 1920 Kinsey accepted a position in the zoology department at Indiana University. By 1929 he was a full professor. Early in his career at Indiana, he met Clara McMillen, whom he married in June 1921. His career continued as uneventfully as that of any other midwestern academic at a midwestern university until 1938. That year Indiana University started a marriage course, a radical move for the times. Kinsey became chairman of a committee comprised of seven faculty members to decide what was to be taught in the course and how to teach it. He began collecting individual case histories as part of a student questionnaire about the course. His scientific curiosity was aroused by the responses. He saw the need for an objective study of human sexuality.

Sex Tapes. Kinsey soon switched from questionnaires to face-to-face interviews to collect data. By 1939 he had committed himself to large-scale data collection by the interview technique. In that year he began making weekend trips to Chicago to expand the size and diversity of his research population. He eventually began to interview prisoners for their sexual histories.

Publication. Kinsey's sexual histories became an obsession. He was dealing with a major aspect of human biology that had never been given scientific scrutiny before. He obtained financial backing from the National Research Council and the Committee on Sex Research of the Rockefeller Foundation. In the early to mid 1940s, he began the painstaking statistical analyses that were the main focus of his research. On 5 January 1948 *Sexual Behavior in the Human Male* was published, including numerous exacting tables of statistical results from his interviews. In 1953 his *Sexual Behavior in the Human Female* followed. Magazine accounts of the day were strongly critical on an emotional level. Kinsey was accused of threatening the moral fiber of the nation by indulging prurient interests in the name of scientific research.

Aftermath. In 1955 the Kinseys took a vacation to Europe. He was warmly received for his scientific accomplishments and invited all over the continent to speak to professional groups. In 1956 he completed the last of 7,985 interviews. Kinsey died at sixty-two years of age in 1956.

Sources:

Cornelia V. Christenson, *Kinsey, a Biography* (Bloomington: Indiana University Press, 1971);

Reader's Digest, 63 (October 1953): 5.

ARTHUR KORNBERG

1918-

MEDICAL RESEARCHER

Background. The son of Jewish immigrants, Arthur Kornberg grew up in New York and attended Abraham Lincoln High School in Brooklyn, graduating three years ahead of schedule. His favorite course was chemistry. He went to the City College of New York and then, in 1937, to medical school at the University of Rochester. Biochemistry is the main chemistry course during medical school. In Kornberg's day it was a dull course describing the chemical contents of body fluids.

Bilirubin Research. Kornberg's main interest was in internal medicine, but that interest soon led him to research. He had always had a mild jaundice, or yellowing of the white parts of his eyes caused by an excess of the chemical bilirubin in the blood. Bilirubin is formed as old red blood cells break down to be replaced, and normally it is removed rapidly by the liver. He found other medical students with similar jaundice and compared them to controls (people without jaundice) and to people recovering from hepatitis. His first paper, based on this research, was published in the prestigious *Journal of Clinical Investigation*.

Jaundice Expert. Kornberg continued his bilirubin research in internship, and then on a navy ship. As the army and navy were expanding for World War II, they had a problem: the vaccine for yellow fever given to recruits often caused severe jaundice. The director of the small National Institute of Health (NIH) came to the University of Rochester to see the famous researcher Dr. George H. Whipple, a Nobel Prize winner. He also wanted to see the expert on jaundice from Rochester, Dr. Kornberg. Kornberg was promptly appointed to the Public Health Service and was sent to the NIH Nutrition Laboratory in 1942.

On to Enzymes. Kornberg had a long and illustrious career in biochemistry from that point forth. He first was assigned to find out why rats on a "purified" diet died if a sulfa drug (an early antibiotic) was given to them. From his work came knowledge of the role of intestinal bacteria in providing vitamins in the diet. By 1945 he grew bored with nutritional work and moved to working on enzymes.

The Prize. Enzymes are large proteins. They speed up chemical reactions and direct the chemical outcome. After training in various laboratories around the United

States in 1946–1947, he started the enzyme section of the NIH in 1947. His main interest became the enzymes associated with DNA synthesis. In 1953 he resigned as medical director of NIH to become chairman of microbiology at Washington University in Saint Louis. (His research involved using bacteria and the viruses that infect them.) There he continued work on the enzymes of DNA synthesis, for which he won the Nobel Prize in 1959. One of the products of his work was the development of the field of molecular biology.

BETTE CLAIR MCMURRAY

1924-1980

INVENTOR OF LIQUID PAPER CORRECTION FLUID

Lousy Typist. Bette Clair McMurray dropped out of school when she was seventeen because of disciplinary difficulties. In the 1940s there were very few jobs open to young women. She could not type, but she got a job as a secretary for a law firm because of her personality. The attorneys sent her to night school for her high-school diploma and secretarial training. She married Warren Nesmith in 1942, and their son (Michael) was born in 1943. After she and her husband divorced in 1946, she had to provide for her son and herself, and she attempted to do so, relying on her shaky secretarial skills.

Tempera Solution. In 1951 McMurray was an executive secretary at Texas Bank and Trust in Dallas. The typewriters used there had ribbons made with carbon film. Erasing errors made on these typewriters looked messy. As an amateur painter, McMurray knew that artists made corrections by painting over mistakes rather than erasing them. So, she began using a white tempera paint to paint over her mistakes.

Mistake Out. It did not take long for the secretaries at the Texas Bank and Trust to catch on to McMurray's idea. By 1956 she was bottling "Mistake Out" in her garage for their use. She started learning about how paints are made and experimented with changing the formula. She developed a quick-drying modification that was nearly undetectable after use. By 1957 she had patented her product with the new name "Liquid Paper." She had her son fill little bottles with Liquid Paper in a work space at her home. After she was fired for accidentally typing "The Liquid Paper Company" on a letter instead of her employer's company name, she devoted herself full-time to selling Liquid Paper.

Gillette. It was not until the late 1960s that McMurray's efforts began to pay off, and then it became very successful. Gillette bought Liquid Paper in 1979 for $47.5 million and agreed to pay royalties to McMurray

on every bottle sold until the year 2000. Her son Michael Nesmith, meanwhile, had become a rock 'n' roll star in the 1960s with the Monkees.

Source:
Ethlie Ann Vare and G. Ptacek, *Mothers of Invention: From the Bra to the Bomb, Forgotten Women and Their Unforgettable Ideas* (New York: Morrow, 1988).

MARGARET SANGER

1879-1966

BIRTH-CONTROL ADVOCATE

Accomplishments. Margaret Sanger was directly responsible for the development of the oral contraceptive pill, though that accomplishment was only a very small part of her life's work. She was convinced at an early age that women had to have control of their reproduction as a matter of health and well-being. Also, she predicted the horrible consequences of unchecked population growth. Thomas Malthus had done this first a century before, but his work was flawed by a failure to realize the potential of new technologies in farming to feed more mouths. Sanger predicted World War II as a consequence of over-population.

Childhood. She was born in 1879, the sixth of eleven children of Michael and Anne (Purcell) Higgins. Her father encouraged his children to think freely. When an insulting teacher drove Margaret Higgins from public school in the eighth grade, the family pooled their money to send her to the private Hudson River Institute in New York, where her ability to think for herself was fostered.

Early Years. She had planned to become an actress but changed her mind because drama schools seemed to her more interested in personal measurements than talent. After helping her mother during a terminal case of tuberculosis, she decided on a nursing career. She really wanted to be a physician but lacked the money for her studies. At one hospital she met architect William Sanger, and they were soon married.

Midwifery. The Sangers had three children in rather rapid order even though Margaret had contracted tuberculosis from her mother and the strain of repeated childbirth almost killed her. Her nursing skills came to focus on helping women through childbirth. Most women did not deliver at hospitals in those days but rather at home. The poor would often hire midwives, such as Sanger, to attend to the births of their children. After delivery, women often asked her for the secret to preventing pregnancy. She knew of no secrets but watched in horror as these women produced one child after another, sometimes at personal risk. She became convinced that women needed contraception information.

Sanger vs. Comstock. The Comstock law in New York, named for a postal inspector who crusaded against "obscene" materials, essentially made it illegal to send anything through the mail regarding birth control. Physicians were not taught contraception in medical school. When Sanger opened her first clinic in Brooklyn in 1916, Comstock and his New York Society for the Suppression of Vice took it as a direct challenge. The Roman Catholic church also opposed her since they opposed any birth control on religious grounds. This clinic opening started a series of legal battles with the church and Comstock that lasted for decades before Sanger finally won.

Birth Control. Physicians knew little about contraception and feared the law so much that they were afraid to back Sanger. She had to go to Europe to get information on contraception. She returned with the contraceptive diaphragm and spermicidal jellies, battling the law all the way to introduce them in America. She coined the term *birth control* and formed the Birth Control League, which grew into the International Planned Parenthood Federation by 1952. Sanger was its first director.

The Pill. In the 1950s Sanger was still searching for the ultimate birth-control method, which would have to be controlled, in her view, by the woman. It would also have to be safe, cheap, and in the form of either a pill or a long-term injection. Finally, it had to be nonpermanent so a woman could have children when she wanted. In 1950 she met Dr. Gregory Pincus. Their collaboration eventually led to the development of the oral birth-control pill by the end of the decade. Sanger died peacefully in September of 1966. She had accomplished most of what she started to do in 1916. Birth control was available, laws were changed to allow contraception to be discussed (in the mail and in the medical setting), and women had hopes of controlling their own futures.

WERNHER VON BRAUN

1912-1977

ROCKET SCIENTIST

Early Interest in Rocketry. Wernher von Braun was born in Prussia in 1912. His father, a baron, was minister of food and agriculture during the Weimar Republic before Hitler came to power in Germany, and his work caused him to move frequently. Baroness von Braun had broad interests, including astronomy, which she passed to her son. In school, von Braun was particularly poor at math and science. His father moved him to a more practical school that taught farming and land management. He did well there, and his mother encouraged his interest in astronomy by buying him a telescope as a reward. He later recalled that his interest in space travel was further excited by an article on flight to the moon that he read when he was eighteen. For whatever reason, he became involved with astronomy and rocketry, interests that led him to study engineering at institutes in Berlin and Zurich, where he assisted the famous scientist Hermann Oberth in his studies of rocket-propulsion systems.

Rocket Club. Von Braun joined a rocketry club in Berlin that leased an abandoned field for test launches. In the early 1930s the club generated operating revenue by charging admission to its impressive blastoffs. By the time he earned his B.S. in engineering in 1932, von Braun had staged eighty-five tests, and his rocketeering abilities had come to the attention of German army ordnance officers. The German army sought a weapon, like von Braun's rockets, not prohibited by the restrictive Versailles treaty, which had ended World War I, disarming Germany to prevent further militarism. By 1934 von Braun had earned his Ph.D. in physics at the University of Berlin while serving as director of an army rocket-testing station.

V-2. Adolf Hitler came to power in 1933. It was not long before he saw the military implications of von Braun's experiments in space rocketry. He set up a generously funded rocket-research center on the Baltic Sea with von Braun as its chief. Von Braun's orders were to develop a rocket for use in the field to deliver warheads beyond the range of artillery. His team responded with the V-2 "Revenge Weapon" in 1938 (which was developed for military use in 1944). It carried a ton of explosives 190 miles and could be launched from any twenty-five-square-foot flat surface. During the war thirty-six hundred V-2s were fired on England and Belgium. The rocket program was so successful that Hitler's Gestapo chief, Heinrich Himmler, attempted to take over its control. When von Braun refused to step down, he was imprisoned briefly before Hitler ordered his release. Near the end of the war, both Russian and American forces were closing in on his rocket research center, which was by then developing a rocket that could carry twenty tons of explosives three thousand miles — far enough to reach the United States. Von Braun feared he would be captured by enemy forces, so he decided to defect, choosing to join the Americans over the Soviets.

American Defection. He was welcomed by the American army, which was actively promoting the defection of highly skilled German scientists. In the United States the branches of the military competed for support funds to develop rocket weaponry, and thus each developed a specialty. The army concentrated on short- to medium-range missiles, and von Braun's efforts during the first half of the decade were on such systems. In 1950 he became chief of guided-missile development at the Redstone Arsenal in Huntington, Alabama, and in 1956 he became director of the development operations division of the Army Ballistic Missile Agency. In 1955 he became a U.S. citizen.

Jupiter-C. After the Soviets launched *Sputnik I* in 1957, there was enormous pressure on the Americans to demonstrate that they had the technology to do likewise. The navy had concentrated on space rocketry, and its *Vanguard* rocket was chosen as the best candidate for success. That program seemed doomed to fail, however, and von Braun's *Jupiter* project took precedence. In January 1958, a *Jupiter-C* was the first U.S. rocket to carry a satellite into orbit. His subsequent work was focused on launching a manned lunar flight, developed under the auspices of the newly formed National Aeronautics and Space Administration (NASA). He received primary credit for the *Saturn V* rocket that carried three American astronauts on the first lunar landing in July 1969. Von Braun served as deputy associate administrator of NASA from 1970 to 1972, when he left government service to take a position as vice-president of engineering and development for Fairchild Industries, where he worked until just before his death.

Books. For much of his adult life, von Braun was the foremost rocket scientist in the world. He also promoted the science of rocketry in popular books, including: *Across the Space Frontier*, edited with C. Ryan (1952); *The Exploration of Mars*, with Willy Ley (1956); *First Men to the Moon*, with C. C. Adams and F. Il. Ordway III (1960); *The Rocket's Red Glare*, with Ordway; and *New Worlds: Discoveries from Our Solar System* (1979).

Source:
Erik Bergaust, *Wernher von Braun: The Authoritative and Definitive Biographical Profile of the Father of Modern Space Flight* (Washington, D.C.: National Space Institute, 1976).

PEOPLE IN THE NEWS

Jim Backus and his team at IBM introduced the computer language FORTRAN in 1956.

In 1955 C. J. Balentine and Earl B. Reitz described the first 330,000-volt circuit breaker for use in the new Muskingum River Plant of the Ohio Power Company, which operated at the highest transmission voltage in the United States.

John Bardeen, Leon N. Cooper, and John R. Schrieffer explained superconductivity by supposing the existence of coupled electrons that cannot be split in 1957.

William and Lyle Boyd identified thirteen separate human races in 1956 after studying blood groups.

Owen Chamberlain, working in 1955 with Emilio Segre, succeeded in producing antiprotons.

In 1959 Dr. William M. Chardack, a physician, and Wilson Greatbatch, an electronics engineer, developed the first heart pacemaker, which could be implanted in a human's chest for up to five years.

In 1957 Scovil G. Feher and H. Seidel introduced the first solid-state maser, which was used in radio astronomy and timekeeping. It could emit a signal whose frequency was constant within a variation of one second every 300,000 years.

Kenneth Lynn Franklin, using a radio telescope, detected radio waves from Jupiter in 1955.

J. Willard Gibbs, a thermodynamicist, in 1950 became the first chemist named to the New York University Hall of Fame.

Using his bubble chamber, a glass bulb filled with ether, Donald Glaser observed cosmic-ray tracks in 1952.

Gordon Gould conceived of the laser in 1957, but failed to patent the idea.

Bruce Charles Hazeen and Maurice Ewing discovered the Mid-Oceanic Ridge in 1956.

Mahlon Bush Hoagland in 1955 showed the workings of transfer and messenger RNA in the manufacture of DNA.

Arthur Kornberg synthesized DNA in 1956.

In 1954 Paul Kotin of the University of Southern California reported that Los Angeles smog contained carcinogens.

In 1950 William Lear won the Collier Trophy, the highest award in aviation, for developing the automatic pilot, a thirty-six-pound device adopted for use in jet fighter planes by the U.S. military.

Joshua Lederberg in 1952 discovered that viruses that attack bacteria can transmit genetic material in the process.

In 1954 Willard F. Libby became the first chemist to be named to the Atomic Energy Commission.

John McCarthy introduces LISP, a computer language designed to aid in development of artificial intelligence.

John William Mauchly and John Prosper Eckert, computer engineers at Remington Rand, built the UNIVAC I in 1950, the first commercially available computer.

Ben Roy Mottleson, working with Niels Bohr in 1950, showed that the nucleus of an atom is not necessarily spherical.

In 1959 Dr. Erwin Mueller of Pennsylvania State University invented the ion microscope, which magnifies objects up to two million times, allowing scientists to view individual atoms.

Eugene Norman Parker proved the existence of solar winds in 1958.

In 1954 Paul Rapaport of the RCA Research Center developed a usable, tiny, low-power atomic battery.

In 1955 William Spindel and T. Ivan Taylor produced a 95 percent concentration of a nitrogen isotope significant in the development of nuclear reactors which sold for $500 a pound. Previously only a 65 percent concentration was available at $175,000 a pound.

Belso Sterrenberg and Stanley A. Talyor discovered fossils in Canada that were 1.5 billion years old in 1954.

In 1954 M. A. Tuve of the Carnegie Institute was appointed chairman of the first National Science Foundation advisory panel on radio astronomy.

James Alfred Van Allen in 1952 invented a balloon that could launch a rocket to gather data for study of the upper atmosphere; and in 1958, when electronic equipment aboard the Explorer I and III satellites failed during ascent, he discovered that the disturbance was caused by a band of high radiation six hundred miles above the Earth. This band is called the Van Allen Radiation Belt.

Dr. John A. Van Horn of the Hamilton Watch Company introduced the world's first electric wristwatch, which retailed for $175, in January 1957.

John Von Neumann, using ENIAC, and a team of meteorologists made the first twenty-four-hour weather predictions in 1950.

Robert Burns Woodward synthesized cortisone and cholesterol in 1951.

AWARDS

NOBEL PRIZE WINNERS

During the 1950s there were thirty Nobel Prizes awarded in the sciences. Of those, fourteen were won or shared by twenty-seven Americans. The Nobel Prize is widely considered to be the highest honor bestowed upon scientists and signifies worldwide recognition of their work.

1950: Physiology and/or Medicine, P. S. Hench and E. C. Kendall

1951: Chemistry, E. M. McMillan and G. T. Seaborg

1952: Physics, F. Bloch and E. M. Purcell; Medicine and/or Physiology, S. A. Waksman

1953: Medicine and/or Physiology, F. A. Lipmann

1954: Chemistry, L. C. Pauling; Physiology and/or Medicine, J. F. Enders, F. C. Robbins, and T. H. Weller

1955: Chemistry, V. du Vigneaud; Physics, W. E. Lamb, Jr., and P. Kusch

1956: Physics, W. B. Shockley, W. H. Brattain, and J. Bardeen; Physiology and/or Medicine, D. W. Richards, Jr., and A. F. Cournand

1957

1958: Physiology and/or Medicine, J. Lederberg, G. W. Beadle, and E. L. Tatum

1959: Physics, E. Segré and O. Chamberlain; Physiology and/or Medicine, S. Ochoa and A. Kornberg

DEATHS

Walter Sydney Adams, astronomer, former director of the Mount Wilson Observatory whose observations proved Albert Einstein's theory of relativity, 10 May 1956.

Dr. Robert Grant Aitken, 87, leading astronomer, 29 October 1951.

Dr. Oakes Ames, 75, botanist, 28 April 1950.

Maj. Edwin H. Armstrong, 63, inventor of FM radio, 1 February 1954.

Liberty Hyde Bailey, 96, renowned botanist and agricultural educator, 26 December 1954.

Dr. Francis M. Baldwin, 66, leading biologist, 2 February 1951.

Lawrence Dale Bell, founder of Bell Aircraft Corporation, codesigner of experimental jet-powered Bell X-1 and X-2 aircraft, 20 October 1956.

Dr. Charles F. Berkey, 88, former head of the geology department at Columbia University, a leader in applying geology to engineering, 22 August 1955.

Clarence Frank Birdseye, inventor and industrialist, developed methods of freezing and dehydrating foods, held more than five hundred patents, 7 October 1956.

Dr. Isaiah Bowman, 71, internationally famous geographer, 6 January 1950.

William H. Buell, 72, chemical engineer who developed the tracer bullet, 24 December 1950.

George Ashley Campbell, 83, physicist and research scientist, 10 November 1954.

Alfred Clark, 76, American-British inventor, associate of Thomas A. Edison, 16 June 1950.

Edwin J. Cohn, 60, Harvard University chemist who contributed to the development of gamma globulin, serum albumin, and liver extract, 1 October 1953.

Dr. Karl Taylor Compton, 66, physicist who helped to develop the atom bomb, president of Massachusetts Institute of Technology (1930–1949), 22 June 1954.

Charles Gordon Curtis, 92, inventor of steam and gas turbines, 10 March 1953.

Allston Dana, 67, civil engineer, designer of George Washington and Triborough bridges in New York, 12 May 1952.

Clinton Davisson, 76, cowinner of the 1937 Nobel Prize in physics for work on the wave-particle character of electrons, 1 February 1958.

Dr. Arthur J. Dempster, 63, physicist, discoverer in 1935 of uranium-235 and principal authority on positive rays, 11 March 1950.

Robert E. Doherty, 65, president of Carnegie Institute of Technology (1936–1950), 19 October 1950.

Caston F. DuBois, 73, chemical engineer who developed processes for making synthetics and plastics, 1 November 1953.

Dr. Enrico Fermi, 53, famed Italian-American nuclear scientist and a leading architect of the atomic age, 28 November 1954.

Colin G. Fink, 71, scientist, discoverer of tungsten filaments for lightbulbs, 17 September 1953.

Dr. Eugene Gardner, 37, nuclear scientist, 26 November 1950.

Dr. Ronald W. Gurney, 54, electronics physicist, pioneer in the use of semiconductive solid materials to control electric current, 14 April 1953.

Edwin Wesley Hammer, 83, pioneer in development of electricity, associate of Thomas A. Edison, 11 October 1951.

Dr. William D. Harkins, 77, pioneer in hydrogen-bomb theory, 7 March 1951.

Dr. Isaac Faust Harris, 73, biochemist who refined diphtheria antitoxin into safe form, 31 January 1953.

Vladimir N. Ipatieff, 85, Soviet-born chemist, discoveries aided the production of high-octane gasoline and other petroleum products, 29 November 1952.

Charles F. Kettering, 82, engineer, inventor of the automobile self-starter and some 140 other improvements in various industries, former head of General Motors research division, 25 November 1958.

Count Alfred Habdank Korzybski, 70, scientist and philosopher, founder of the Institute of General Semantics, 1 March 1950.

Hendrick Anthony Kramers, 57, atomic scientist, chairman of the Atomic Energy Commission in 1946, 24 April 1952.

Dr. Carol O. Lampland, 78, astronomer, filmed Mars canals and discovered that Jupiter was cold, 14 December 1951.

Dr. Irving Langmuir, 76, chemist and 1932 Nobel Prize winner, 16 August 1957.

Charles Lanier Lawrence, 67, inventor of the air-cooled airplane engine, 23 June 1950.

Ernest O. Lawrence, 57, winner of the 1939 Nobel Prize in physics for work on the cyclotron, 27 August 1958.

Andrew Cowper Lawson, 90, geologist, earthquake authority, 16 June 1952.

Dr. Robert Andrews Millikan, 85, physicist, winner of the 1923 Nobel Prize in physics for isolation and measurement of electrons, a leader in research on cosmic rays, chairman of the executive council of the California Institute of Technology (1921–1945), 19 December 1953.

Mark M. Mills, 40, physicist and atomic-weapons developer, 7 April 1958.

Eugene A. Nahm, 62, inventor of the coin machine, 3 March 1954.

Grady Norton, 60, Miami Weather Bureau forecaster, authority on hurricanes, 9 October 1954.

Charles Lathrop Parsons, 86, chemist who discovered a method for converting nitrogen from the air into ammonia, 14 February 1954.

Rear Adm. William Parsons, 52, atom-bomb expert who armed the first bomb dropped on Hiroshima, Japan, 5 December 1953.

Dr. Henry Louis Smith, 91, pioneer in X-ray photography, 27 February 1951.

O. L. Sponsler, 73, botanist at the University of California, Los Angeles, discoverer of molecular structure of cellulose, 14 March 1953.

Josiah Edward Spurr, 80, geologist and explorer for whom Alaska's Mount Spurr was named, 12 January 1950.

James Batcheller Sumner, 67, biochemist, winner of the 1946 Nobel Prize in chemistry for isolating an enzyme, 12 August 1955.

Donald F. Warner, 56, Canadian-born mechanical engineer who developed the first American jet engine, 12 February 1952.

John Wilkinson, 83, inventor of the air-cooled automobile engine, 25 June 1951.

Dr. Herbert Eustis Winlock, 65, noted archaeologist and Egyptologist, 26 January 1950.

Dr. Albert F. Zahm, 92, aeronautical engineer who built a wind tunnel for aeronautical experiments in 1882 and later became director of the U.S. Navy aerodynamic laboratory, 23 July 1954.

PUBLICATIONS

Hannah Arendt, *The Human Condition* (Chicago: University of Chicago Press, 1958);

Atomic Power (New York: Simon & Schuster, 1955);

David R. Bates, *Space Research and Exploration* (New York: W. Sloane, 1958);

The Book of Popular Science (New York: Grolier Society, 1959);

Erik Bergaust, *Satellite!* (Garden City, N.Y.: Hanover House, 1956);

Edward Callis Berkeley, *Computers, Their Operations and Applications* (New York: Reinhold, 1956);

Berkeley, *Symbolic Logic and Intelligent Machines* (New York: Reinhold, 1959);

Franklyn Mansfield Branley, *Experiments in Sky Watching* (New York: Crowell, 1959);

Andrew Donald Booth, *Automation and Computing* (New York: Macmillan, 1958);

Otis W. Caldwell, *Everyday Science* (Boston: Ginn, 1952);

Groff Conklin, ed., *Science Fiction Thinking Machines* (New York: Vanguard, 1954);

Robert Alan Dahl, *Domestic Control of Atomic Energy* (New York, 1951);

William H. Desmonde, *Computers and Their Uses* (Englewood Cliffs, N.J.: Prentice-Hall, 1964);

The Effects of Atomic Weapons (Washington, D.C.: Government Printing Office, 1950);

James D. Fahnestock, *Computers and How They Work* (New York: Ziff-Davis, 1959);

Heinz Gartmann, *Man Unlimited: Technology's Challenge to Human Endurance* (London: Cape, 1957);

Gartmann, *The Men Behind the Space Rockets* (New York: D. McKay, 1956);

Kenneth William Gatland, *Project Satellite* (New York: British Book Centre, 1958);

Samuel Glasstone, *Sourcebook on Atomic Energy* (New York: Van Nostrand, 1950);

Isabel S. Gordon, *Armchair Science Reader* (New York: Simon & Schuster, 1959);

C. C. Gotlieb, *High-Speed Date Processing* (New York: McGraw-Hill, 1958);

Gaylord Probasco Harnwell, *Atomic Physics: An Atomic Description of Physical Phenomena* (New York: McGraw-Hill, 1955);

George Russell Harrison, *What Man May Be: The Human Side of Science* (New York: William Morrow, 1956);

Selig Hecht, *Explaining the Atom* (New York: Viking, 1954);

Werner Heisenberg, *Nuclear Physics* (New York: Philosophical Library, 1953);

Edward Hutchings, *Frontiers in Science, A Survey* (New York: Basic, 1958);

Margaret O. Hyde, *Atoms Today & Tomorrow* (New York: Whittelsey House, 1955);

Bernard Jaffe, *Chemistry Creates a New World* (New York: Crowell, 1957);

Robert Jung, *Brighter than a Thousand Suns: The Story of the Men Who Made the Bomb* (New York: Grove Press, 1958);

Fritz Kahn, *Design of the Universe: The Heavans and the Earth* (New York: Crown, 1954);

Waldenar Kaempffert, *Explorations in Science* (New York: Viking, 1953);

Jonathan Norton Leonard, *Flight into Space* (New York: Random House, 1953);

Burr Watkins Leyson, *Marvels of Industrial Science* (New York: Dutton, 1955);

Jack McCormick, *Atoms, Energy, and Machines* (Mankato, Minn.: Creative Educational Society, 1957);

Lorus Johnson Milne, *The Biotic World and Man* (New York: Prentice-Hall, 1952);

Robert A. Nisbet, *Man and Technics* (Tuscon: University of Arizona Press, 1956);

Rudolf Ernst Peierls, *The Laws of Nature* (New York: Scribners, 1956);

David Pietz, *Atomic Science, Bombs and Power* (New York: Dodd, Mead, 1954);

Palmer C. Putnam, *Energy in the Future* (New York: Van Nostrand, 1954);

Resources for the Future, *Science and Resources: Prospects and Implications of Technological Advance* (Baltimore: Johns Hopkins University Press, 1959);

James Speed Rogers, *Man and the Biological World* (New York: McGraw-Hill, 1952);

Francis Xavier Ross, *Modern Miracles of the Laboratory* (New York: Lothrop, Lee & Shepard, 1957);

Jean Rostand, *Can Man Be Modified?* (New York: Basic Books, 1959);

Edward J. Russell, *Science and Modern Life* (London: Epwoth Press, 1955);

Eric Frank Russell, ed., *Men, Mountains and Machines* (New York: Dobson, 1955);

Cornelius Ryan, ed., *Across the Space Frontier* (New York: Viking, 1952);

Mortimer A. Schultz, *Control of Nuclear Reactors and Power Plants* (New York: McGraw-Hill, 1955);

Herman Augustus Spoehr, *Essays on Science* (Stanford, Cal.: Stanford University Press, 1956);

George R. Stibitz, *Mathematics and Computers* (New York: McGraw-Hill, 1957);

Otto Struve, *The Astronomical Universe* (Eugene: Oregon State System of Higher Education, 1958);

Technology and Social Change (New York: Appleton-Century-Crofts, 1957);

David Shea Temple, *Atomic Energy: A Constructive Proposal* (New York: Duell, Sloan, & Pearce, 1955);

G. P. Thomson, *The Foreseeable Future* (Cambridge: Cambridge University Press, 1955);

John Von Neumann, *The Computer and the Brain* (New Haven: Yale University Press, 1958);

N. Weiner, *The Human Use of Human Beings* (New York: Avon, 1950);

Helen Wright, *Great Adventures in Science* (New York: Harper, 1956);

J. Z. Young, *Doubt and Certainty in Science: A Biologist's Reflection on the Brain* (Oxford: Clarendon Press, 1951);

Popular Science, periodical;

Popular Mechanics, periodical;

Science Digest, periodical;

Science News, periodical;

Scientific American, periodical.

CHAPTER THIRTEEN

SPORTS

by STEPHEN MOSHER and DENNIS LYNCH

CONTENTS

Sidebars and tables are listed in italics.

1950

7 Feb.   Ted Williams of the Boston Red Sox enters spring training as baseball's highest-paid player, with a $125,000 contract.

Apr.–May   The desegregation move in American sports continues when the Boston Celtics of the NBA draft the league's first black player, Charles Cooper, and the American Bowling Congress ends its white-male-only policy.

11 June   Ben Hogan completes a courageous comeback from a near-fatal auto accident to win the U.S. Open and earns "golfer of the year" honors.

8 Aug.   Florence Chadwick swims the English Channel in thirteen hours and twenty minutes, a women's record.

29 Aug.   Althea Gibson becomes the first black woman to compete in a national tennis tournament.

1951

Jan.   College basketball fans are shocked by a point-shaving scandal involving players from City College of New York (CCNY), Long Island University (LIU), and New York University (NYU).

2 Mar.   The National Basketball Association (NBA) holds its first All-Star game at the Boston Garden; the East beats the West, 111–94.

12 Mar.   Major League Baseball dismisses its second commissioner A. B. Chandler. In 1947 Chandler overrode the baseball owner's vote against signing Jackie Robinson.

18 July   Jersey Joe Wolcott wins the heavyweight championship of the world by knocking out Ezzard Charles in the seventh round. Wolcott becomes, at age thirty-seven, the oldest man ever to hold the title.

19 Aug.   One of the greatest stunts in American sports promotion occurs in Saint Louis, when three feet, seven inches, Eddie Gaedel earns a base on balls for the last place Browns. Owner Bill Veeck's ploy results in midgets being banned from participation in Major League Baseball games.

20 Sept.   Ford C. Frick is chosen Major League Baseball's commissioner.

3 Oct.   Bobby Thomson hits the "shot heard round the world" off Ralph Branca and the New York Giants beat the Brooklyn Dodgers for the National League pennant to complete one of the greatest comebacks in baseball history.

10 Oct.   Joe DiMaggio plays in his last game as a New York Yankee, ending one of the greatest careers in American sports.

1952

• *The Natural*, by Bernard Malmud, is published. It is the first serious American novel to employ a sports (baseball) setting, and it is followed in this decade by Mark Harris's *The Southpaw* and *Bang the Drum Slowly* and Douglas Wallop's *The Year the Yankees Lost the Pennant.*

1953

Feb.	At the winter Olympic games in Oslo, Norway, gold medals are won by Andrea Mead (Lawrence) in slalom and giant slalom skiing, and Dick button in figure skating. Button is the first figure skater to execute a triple jump in competition.
16 July	The International Olympic Committee (IOC) elects American Avery Brundage its president. Brundage, who has been the USOC president since 1929 will continue as IOC president until 1972.
July–Aug.	At the summer Olympic games in Helsinki, Finland, Bob Mathias wins the decathlon and the unofficial title "world's greatest athlete" for the second straight time.
23 Sept.	Rocky Marciano knocks out Jersey Joe Walcott in the thirteenth round to earn boxing's heavyweight championship. Marciano defends his title successfully throughout the decade and retires as the only undefeated heavyweight champion.

1954

11 Jan.	The first professional sports franchise move of the decade ushers in the great western expansion as the National Football League (NFL) Dallas Texans become the Baltimore Colts.
15 Feb.	Tenley Albright becomes the first American to win the World Figure Skating Championship.
17 Mar.	The Boston Braves move to Milwaukee and proceed to set a National League attendance record of 1,826,397. At the conclusion of the season, the Saint Louis Browns move to Baltimore and become the Orioles.
10 July	Ben Hogan wins the British Open, which along with his wins in the Masters and the U.S. Open make him the first golfer to win all three major championships in the same year.
7 Sept.	Maureen Connolly becomes the first woman, and only the second player, ever to win the tennis Grand Slam and the U.S. National Championship. Connolly had previously won the Australian and French Opens and Wimbeldon.
5 Oct.	The New York Yankees become the first team in baseball history to win five consecutive World Series when they defeat the Brooklyn Dodgers in six games.
9 Nov.	The U.S. Supreme Court upholds baseball's exemption from antitrust laws by ruling 7–2 against George Toolson, Walter Kowalski, and Jack Corbett. The court rules that any changes in baseball's monopoly would have to be made by Congress.

13 Feb.	Frank Selvy (Furman) breaks the NCAA single-game scoring record by making 100 points in a basketball game with Newberry.

1955

6 May	Roger Bannister of England becomes the first sub-four-minute miler in history by running 3:58.8 at the Empire Games in Vancouver, B.C.
12 July	In response to the Supreme Court's ruling in the Toolson case (1953) the Major League Baseball Players' Association is formed and becomes the first truly effective professional sports union.
20 July	Maureen Connoly, America's greatest tennis player, is seriously injured in a truck-horse accident. at 20. Connolly's remarkable career is over.
Sept.	The All-American Girls Professional Baseball League folds after the 1954 season and dies a quiet death.
Oct.	The National Basketball Association introduces the 24-second shot clock, which will revolutionize the game.

1956

•	Baseball's Western Expansion begins in full force as the Philadelphia Athletics move to Kansas City.
30 May	Bill Vukovich, winner of the 1953 and 1954 Indianapolis 500s, dies in a crash in this year's race. He is one of the first racers to die in a major auto race.
21 Sept.	Over 400,000 fans (at Yankee Stadium and through closed circuit television) see Rocky Marciano win the 49th consecutive time by knocking out Archie Moore. It is Marciano's last professional fight.

1957

26 Jan.–5 Feb.	American figure skaters Tenley Albright and Hayes Alan Jenkins win gold medals at Cortina d'Ampezzo, Italy.
27 Apr.	Rocky Marciano retires as boxing's only undefeated heavyweight champion.
29 June	Charles Dumas becomes the first person to high jump over 7 feet.
8 Oct.	New York Yankee pitcher Don Larson throws the only perfect game in World Series history. The Dodgers move to Los Angeles following their defeat.
22 Nov.–8 Dec.	The first ever Summer Olympics in the autumn are held in Melbourne, Australia. Bobby Morrow becomes the first runner since Jesse Owens (1936, Berlin) to win both the 100- and 200-meter races. Diver Pat McCormick wins both the platform and springboard events for the second consecutive Olympics.
30 Nov.	Floyd Patterson knocks out Archie Moore to win the heavyweight championship of the world.

25 Feb.	The Supreme Court rules that the National Football League is not similar to Major League Baseball and must comply with antitrust laws.
4 May	Iron Leige wins the Kentucky Derby when Willie Shoemaker, riding Gallant Man, misjudges the finish line.
6 July	Althea Gibson becomes the first black American to win a Wimbledon tennis Championship. Gibson also wins the U.S. National in September.

9 July The Major League Baseball All-Star Game is a fiasco when Cincinnati fans stuff the ballot box and seven Reds are voted to the National League team. Commissioner Frick intervenes, and fans lose the voting privilege.

1 Aug. The National Football League Player's Association becomes a recognized labor union.

29 Sept. The New York Giants play their last game at the Polo Grounds and move to San Francisco. The Brooklyn Dodgers make their move to Los Angeles official a week later.

10 Nov. Charles Sifford becomes the first black golfer to win a PGA-sponsored event at the Long Beach Open.

16 Nov. Notre Dame beats Oklahoma 7-0. It is Oklahoma's first loss since 1953, ending a streak of 47 games.

1958

- The broadway version of baseball's *Faust* becomes a Hollywood film. *Damn Yankees* stars Tab Hunter as Joe Hardy, who sells his soul to the devil, Ray Walston. Gwen Verdon recreates her Broadway role as the temptress with "Whatever Lola Wants."

12 Jan. NCAA football adopts the two-point conversion. It is the first substantive rule change in forty-five years.

28 Jan. Los Angeles Dodger catcher Roy Campanella is paralyzed in an automobile accident. Campanella was baseball's first black catcher after desegregation and a three-time winner of the Most Valuable Player Award.

6 Apr. Arnold Palmer wins the Masters, his first major golf-tournament victory, and begins a career that will make him sport's first great television hero.

Apr. The Boston Celtics, with Bill Russell injured, lose to the St. Louis Hawks in the National Basketball Association Championships.

26 Sept. For the first time in twenty years there is a challenge for the America's Cup, yachting's most prized trophy. The United States boat wins again.

28 Dec. In overtime at Yankee Stadium, the Baltimore Colts win the National Football League Championship 23–17 over the New York Giants. It becomes known as the "greatest game ever played" overnight and speaks to the power of television in determining America's sporting spectating habits.

1959

Jan. The National Basketball Association adopts a policy to protect its black players (the league is now 25% minority) from discrimination at hotels. In May the Supreme Court rules that interracial boxing matches are legally protected. In August the Boston Red Sox become the last Major League Baseball team to sign a black player.

26 June Ingemar Johansson becomes the first non-American to win the heavyweight championship of the world in twenty-five years by knocking out Floyd Patterson in the third round.

OVERVIEW

More than a Game. "He who would know the heart and mind of America had better learn baseball," observed culturist Jacques Barzun. To look at baseball and other sports to see how they wove themselves into the fabric of American life in that crazy time when the baby boomers were growing up is more than an exercise in nostalgia. It reveals an important aspect of the American character and suggests the seriousness of sports to Americans — the extent to which spectators involve themselves in sporting contests, and the way in which sports become, for the enthusiast, a metaphor for life.

Land of Confusion. The 1950s exploded in a display of cultural expression. During the 1950s almost all sports became desegregated; several sports endured scandals; the standards of professionals were imposed on amateurs and even children; antitrust exemptions were challenged; franchises moved with the population to the West Coast; new sports challenged old for an audience; and, most important, sports and television discovered they were made for each other.

Broadening Interests. At the beginning of the decade the most significant sports in American life were Major League Baseball and intercollegiate football. By the end of the decade the National Football League (NFL) dominated the airways in the fall, the National Basketball Association (NBA) filled the winter months with frenetic sports action, and the Professional Golf Association (PGA) and Professional Bowling Association were inspiring weekend athletes to join "Arnie's Army" and to emulate Don Carter.

Threat of Communism. Postwar America was in a giddy mood when it came to its sports. The lust for entertainment was never greater. Like most institutions, sports responded slowly. There was a pervading realization that athletes were citizens first, and they had a duty to their country and to their fans to act as role models. Many athletes demonstrated their patriotism by serving in the armed forces. Ted Williams, the tremendous Boston Red Sox slugger, had spent time in the military in World War II and saw action in Korea as a fighter pilot. Williams missed more than three seasons during the most productive time in his career. He was not alone among the professional athletes in the military.

Problem with Professionalization. During the economic boom of the 1950s, few citizens were interested in hearing that professional athletes might be underpaid. Most major-league athletes earned between four and six times the average earnings of the general population, but minor-league athletes were barely making a minimum wage. The Major League Baseball and NFL players' attempts to put an end to the club owners' exemptions to antitrust laws largely fell on deaf ears in the courts. The reserve systems, in which athletes endured something like indentured servitude, continued to operate, even as athletic unions were finally being organized in ways that would eventually bring on free agency so that athletes could play for the team of their choice.

Dynasties. Growing out of the fact that teams had absolute control over the movement of their players and were located in large cities with a broad economic base (especially through local television), several teams were able to establish championship dynasties unrivaled in American sports history. The New York Yankees had purchased their pennants of the 1930s from the Boston Red Sox by acquiring Babe Ruth in the 1920s. From 1949 to 1953 the Yankees won five straight World Series. In 1956, with the arrival of Bill Russell, the Boston Celtics went on a run of eleven NBA titles in thirteen years, including eight in a row.

Sport for Children. Sports were not exempt from the effects of the cold war. As the threat of a real war being waged on American soil grew with every passing day, the nation's leaders recognized that the youth of the country needed to be physically fit. The establishment of the President's Council on Youth Fitness was the result. The Communist threat included godlessness, and through sport America responded by reviving the concept of muscular Christianity. Little League Baseball, Pop Warner Football, and Biddy Basketball became tools with which American society could inculcate the moral values deemed necessary for young boys and teenagers. The notion that "sport builds character" grew increasingly more powerful as the decade wore on. Appropriately so, because while sport may do a lot of good things for children, it is a poor way to achieve physical fitness.

Girls and Women. In the 1950s the moral fiber of America's youth was considered far more important than its physical well-being, at least for males. If the men were strong, women need not worry, people believed. The gains women made during the war were quickly lost in the 1950s. Jobs women had performed admirably in factories were given back to their "rightful" owners — the returning soldiers. The All-American Girls Professional Baseball League, started in 1943, quickly turned from a moneymaking, midwestern phenomenon into a money loser abandoned by the general public. By 1954 the league, which had attracted more than a million fans a year, folded. Pockets of girls' sports remained, however. In Iowa, for instance, girls' high-school basketball had a large following even if the game was played by archaic rules to protect the fragile females. The girl's Iowa state basketball playoffs always sold out and outdrew the boys' tournament. In most towns and cities, however, girls were limited in their sports participation to softball, play days, and cheerleading. The belief that girls could not directly benefit from sports participation was powerful.

Western Expansion and Mergers. As the decade opened there were no major league baseball teams west of the Mississippi River. By the end of the decade, there were franchises of all three important professional leagues in California. Los Angeles had the Dodgers (baseball), Rams (football), and Lakers (basketball). San Francisco had the Giants (baseball) and 49ers (football). Even Kansas City had a baseball team. The NFL had swallowed up the All-American Football Conference at the end of the 1949 season, but by 1960 was threatened by the American Football League, which would take on the NFL in the very same large cities. The NBA, the National Basketball League, and the Basketball Association of America merged in the 1949 and 1950 seasons, and by 1955 the league had shrunk from thirteen unstable franchises to eight teams that stayed in the same cities for the decade. Minor league baseball shrunk and shrunk some more during the 1940s until it was barely half its prewar size at the beginning of the decade.

Television, Air Travel, and Corruption. The most profound technological influence in sports and all of society during the 1950s was television. The electronic medium allowed sports teams immediate access to any living room in the country. Regional differences, loyalties, and rivalries broke down as America became a transcontinental nation. With cheap air transportation, people could easily visit the places they saw on television. Television money flowed freely, enriching athletes who had previously played for the love of the game. Scandals in college basketball, professional boxing, professional wrestling, and even television quiz shows punctuated the era.

Desegregation. The most profound development in sports and all of society was desegregation. In an odd way, sports both led and followed the national trend. The breaking of the color line in Major League Baseball by Jackie Robinson was truly a milestone, and virtually all sports were desegregated by the end of the decade. Sports were viewed as the finest example of the American system of freedom for all, a true meritocracy in which a man could earn exactly what he was worth. Yet there remained a quota system in baseball with the unwritten rule being that no more than 49 percent of any team could be black. Blacks also had to hit for higher averages, slam more home runs, and catch more balls in a more spectacular way to earn the same money as an average white player. It was extremely difficult for a black man to be a baseball pitcher or catcher (even with the notable exceptions of Roy Campanella and Don Newcombe) or a football quarterback, or a manager or head coach. Yet black sports stars were used by the system to demonstrate how truly wonderful it was: Althea Gibson made tennis trips for the State Department, Sugar Ray Robinson testified against Paul Robeson at the House Un-American Activities Committee, and Jesse Owens became a hustler for the United States Olympic Committee. For all the gains of the 1950s and claims of sports integration, it can only be said that the process of desegregation had begun.

TOPICS IN THE NEWS

ANTITRUST, UNIONS AND DYNASTIES

Organizing to Fight the Man. On 9 November 1953 the Supreme Court ruled 7–2 against George Toolson, Walter Kowalski, and Jack Corbett, three baseball players who challenged baseball's exemption from antitrust laws. In reaching their surprising decision, the court let stand its ruling in the famous 1922 case, *Federal Baseball Club of Baltimore* v. *National League of Professional Clubs,* declaring that organized baseball did not constitute interstate commerce and was therefore outside the scope of antitrust laws. On 12 July 1964 the players formed the Major League Baseball Players Association (MLBPA), the first truly effective sports union in America. The MLBPA would spend the next twenty-five years struggling to overturn baseball's "reserve system" that perpetually bound a player to one club. The ultimate goal of the players was "free agency," which would let them, like any other worker in America, work for whoever might hire them.

Player Movement. The reserve clause was simple. A club that wanted to trade a player could do so without notice. A player who wanted to move to another team could play for a year without a contract, but he could only sign with his original team, because the other teams in the league respected the right of the original team to make the first offer. This offer was also the only offer. In effect, then, the reserve system served to bind players to clubs indefinitely, and it also served to keep salaries down.

Dynasties. The owners claimed that free agency would upset competitive balance and thus allow the wealthiest teams to buy their ways to pennants. Throughout the 1950s, before free agency, professional leagues were dominated by dynasties, but none more so than in Major League Baseball. In the American league the New York Yankees won eight pennants in the 1950s; and the Cleveland Indians (1954) and Chicago White Sox (1959), one each. In the National League, the Brooklyn/Los Angeles Dodgers won five pennants; the New York/San Francisco Giants, two (1951, 1954); the Milwaukee Braves, two (1957, 1958); and the Philadelphia Phillies (1950), one. The Yankees also won six World Series.

Source:
Marvin Miller, *A Whole Different Ball Game: The Sport and Business of Baseball* (New York: Simon & Schuster, 1992);
Branch Rickey, *The American Diamond: A Documentary of the Game of Baseball* (New York: Simon & Schuster, 1965).

BASEBALL

Yankees Dominance. If box scores were the only clue to what happened in Major League Baseball during the 1950s, then one would have to conclude that baseball had changed little. The American League's New York Yankees remained the class outfit of the big leagues and continued their winning ways. Although by the beginning of the decade it was clear to all who followed the sport that the career of the great Joe DiMaggio, whose brilliant hitting and fielding had dazzled fans at Yankee Stadium in the Bronx, was coming to an end, the team had an abundance of pinstriped talent to pick up where he left off. But, despite the Yankees' continued tradition of winning, America's favorite pastime was changing in the 1950s, and the changes were drastic in their social and cultural impact.

Baseball's Watershed Decade. Baseball had begun to integrate in 1947, and fans in the 1950s witnessed a migration of black players from the Negro leagues and toward the big-league cities. Baseball itself migrated: in 1957 the Brooklyn Dodgers, the pride of Flatbush, did the unthinkable and headed west to Los Angeles; the New York Giants followed the Dodgers west and landed in San Francisco. Other teams had already abandoned their tired-looking East Coast ballparks, where attendance was falling, and had gone to faraway places such as Kansas City and Milwaukee, where there were many more fans who craved professional baseball — and much more money to be made. The increasing number of televised games meant potentially lucrative television contracts for baseball owners, but baseball players were still owned, bought, and sold by their bosses and began looking into ways to change the system.

The Shot Heard 'Round the World — and the Few Who Heard It. The third game, played on 3 October, in the 1951 best-of-three National League playoff between the Dodgers and the Giants is considered one of

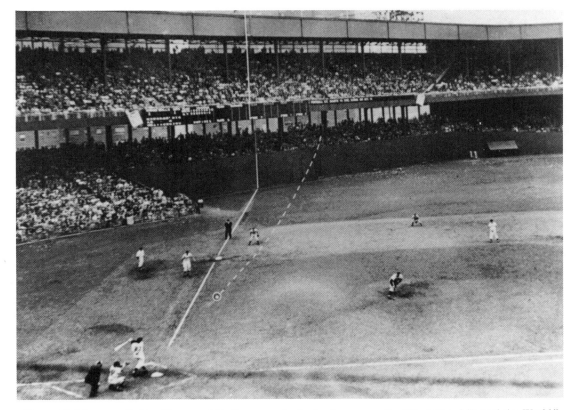

Giants third baseman Bobby Thomson hits the pennant-winning home run, the "Shot Heard 'Round the World," against the Dodgers on 3 October 1951.

baseball's greatest games; at the time it also seemed to confirm what even Dodgers fans believed in their hearts: "da Brooklyn Bums couldn't win the big one." Holding a three-run lead going into the bottom of the ninth inning, the Dodgers appeared to have a lock on the National League pennant. Before Giants third baseman Bobby Thomson stepped to the plate, his teammates had managed to cut into the Dodgers' lead by a run and put two men on base. Needing two more outs to escape the inning and holding one strike on Thomson, Dodgers pitcher Ralph Branca threw a fastball up and in, and Thomson connected, driving the ball over the Polo Grounds left-field fence to score the winning run. Across the country, baseball fans following the game on television and radio roared, as did the fans in the bleachers who numbered 34,320 — nearly fifteen thousand short of Polo Grounds capacity.

Baseball Attendance and the Dawn of the Television Era. The relatively small crowd on hand to witness Thomson's "Shot Heard 'Round the World," reflected a trend continued throughout the decade: fewer people were making the trip to the ballpark. Dwindling attendance, however, did not mean that baseball's popularity was fading during the decade. Baseball was as popular as ever — if not more so, since the entrance of black ballplayers into the majors meant an increasing number of black fans. Many people simply preferred staying home

and watching the game for free. In New York, for instance, all home games played by the city's three big-league ball clubs were being televised by 1950. Television was still a new and exotic medium at the beginning of the decade, and knowing that fans would be increasingly drawn to the flickering black-and-white images of baseball being played, many club owners were quick to cash in. By 1955 the Dodgers organization had raked in $787,155 for local television and radio rights — a hand-

---

DODGERS SMASH ATTENDANCE RECORDS

Until 1959 the Cleveland Indians, playing in their huge stadium, held Major League attendance records, but in 1959 things changed. The Los Angeles Dodgers, while waiting for their new stadium to be built, played some of their games in the Los Angeles Coliseum. For their home games in the 1959 World Series against the Chicago White Sox, the Dodgers drew crowds of 92,394; 92,560; and 92,706. Gate receipts totaled $277,600, a three-game record.

MAJOR LEAGUE SALARIES

Big Money. Baseball fans nationwide were stunned when in 1949 Ted Williams of the Boston Red Sox became the first major leaguer to earn $125,000 for a season. During the 1950s three players would join him in topping the $100,000 mark: Stan Musial of Saint Louis and two Yankees, Joe DiMaggio and Micky Mantle. Although a 1957 survey revealed that 75 percent of major-league ballplayers earned between $10,000 and $25,000, the decade witnessed the dawning of the big-money era in baseball. Many of the prewar players had reached retirement, and team owners scrambling to snatch up young talent often gave fat signing bonuses as an incentive. Braves $15,000-a-year pitching great Johnny Sain looked on with dismay as his team shelled out a $75,000 bonus to benchwarmer Johnny Antonelli. Sportswriters worried in their columns that all the money would turn the new generation of major leaguers soft. Dodgers star Duke Snider shocked and angered many of his fans when he admitted that he played for money.

Players Demand More. Although the DiMaggios and the Mantles—and the young Antonellis—of the baseball world were enjoying fat paychecks, there were many players who were fighting to keep above the game's minimum salary of $5,000. In 1951 Brooklyn Democratic congressman Emanuel Cellar, chairman of the congressional sub-committee investigating monopolies, convened hearings to investigate accusations that baseball owners were conspiring in fixing salaries. Although the hearing did reveal collusion among owners, the $5,000 minimum remained unchanged. In 1953 the Major League Baseball Players Association, still in its infancy, requested a minimum salary of $8,000. In 1955 the owners grudgingly raised it to $6,000; however, in real dollars the salary was actually less than what it had been in the late 1940s.

Sources:

Lee Lowenfish, *The Imperfect Diamond : The Story of Baseball's Reserve System and the Men Who Fought to Change It* (New York: Stein & Day, 1980);

David Quentin Voigt, *American Baseball: From Postwar Expansion to the Electronic Age* (University Park: Pennsylvania State University Press, 1983).

Dodgers and Yankees again met in the World Series, and in the fifth game played on 8 October, with the series tied at two games each, the Yankees' Don Larsen pitched a perfect game, allowing no hits or runs scored and no man to reach first base — the ultimate pitching feat in baseball and the only one thrown in World Series play. Larsen's perfect game was especially extraordinary considering that he was a relatively obscure figure in baseball who had a poor World Series record, had won only eleven games during the 1956 season, and had been out drinking until four o'clock in the morning the night before the fifth game. The Yankees went on to win the series for the seventh time in eight years, but the era in which New York's crosstown rivalries dominated headlines in baseball news was coming to an end.

Baseball Moves West. Prior to the 1950s Saint Louis was the only city west of the Mississippi River with major league baseball. Establishing a big-league team any further west was unfeasible and uneconomical because of the time and cost of railroad travel. As commercial airlines proliferated and began to expand their travel routes, however, club owners began to set their sights on potential western markets. In 1953 the Boston Braves moved to Milwaukee and set a National League attendance record of 1,826,397 in their new home — an increase of 1.5 million over their 1952 attendance. In 1955 the Philadelphia Athletics followed suit and moved to Kansas City and drew 1,393,054 fans, approximately a million more than the ball club had attracted in Philadelphia in 1954. The rest of the American League showed a combined attendance loss of 64,000; the National League losses for 1955 were even steeper, having dropped off by 340,000. Dodgers president Walter O'Malley and Giants president Horace Stoneham took notice. Both men presided over aging ballparks. At the end of the 1957 season New York's two National League teams headed west — the Giants to San Francisco and the Dodgers to Los Angeles — in search of bigger stadiums and fatter television contracts. The end of an era had arrived: Jackie Robinson had retired after being traded to the Giants, the rivals he had learned to hate; an aging Yankees team was beaten by the Milwaukee Braves in the 1957 World Series; and baseball, with teams on both coasts, truly became the nation's pastime.

Sources:

The Baseball Encyclopedia: The Complete and Official Record of Major League Baseball, revised edition (New York: Macmillan, 1974);

Roger Kahn, *The Era, 1947–1957: When the Yankees, the Giants, and the Dodgers Ruled the World* (New York: Ticknor & Fields, 1993);

David Quentin Voigt, *American Baseball: From Postwar Expansion to the Electronic Age* (University Park: Pennsylvania State University Press, 1983).

some amount that was $250,000 more than the Dodgers' player payroll.

The Perfect Game. In 1955 the Dodgers finally managed to beat the Yankees in the World Series. In 1956 the

BASKETBALL: FROM NCAA FAST TIMES TO NBA FAST BREAKS

Limited Popularity. At the start of the 1950s basketball was a local and regional spectator sport in America. While it is true that this distinctly American game (in-

Bobby Cousy of the Boston Celtics passing to Tom Heinsohn during 1957 NBA finals against Saint Louis Hawks.

vented by James Naismith, a Canadian at the Springfield, Massachusetts, YMCA Training College) had gained favor throughout the world, basketball remained a game that, for sports fans at least, simply filled the space in the winter between football and baseball seasons. National interest in basketball was restricted to the late spring, when both the National Invitational Tournament (NIT) and the National Collegiate Athletic Association (NCAA) Tournament were played.

Crooked Collegians. College basketball saw perhaps both its finest and its worst hour of the decade in 1950. In the spring City College of New York (CCNY), which had gone 17–5 during the regular season pulled off the singular feat of winning both the National Invitational Tournament (NIT) — CCNY 69, Bradley 61 — and the National Collegiate Athletics Association (NCAA) — CCNY 71, Bradley 68. Both final games were played in the mecca of basketball, Madison Square Garden in New York City, and both were intense games, hard fought to the final buzzer. CCNY's triumph was tarnished when it was learned that the team had on several occasions shaved points and controlled point spreads, which was the basis for betting. They were not alone. Before the dust had settled on the basketball scandals, CCNY, New York University (NYU), Long Island University (LIU), Manhattan, and — all in New York City — Toledo, Kentucky, and Bradley were implicated. Clair Bee, LIU's coach and author of the "Chip Hilton" adolescent sports novels was put in the position of having to admit that, at least at the college level, sports do not always build char-

acter. Even Hollywood got into the act by rushing through production of the B movie *The Basketball Fix* (1951).

Sources of Corruption. There is a variety of explanations for what went wrong in college basketball: the decay in the quality of life in urban areas; the loosening of moral standards throughout society after World War II; the hustling of naive college boys by smooth city gambling sharks; the growing number of college athletes from impoverished families; and some observers even blamed the influence of desegregation and a distinctly "black" morality. The most reasonable explanation is that college basketball had become commercialized, and gamblers seized the opportunity to exploit the national interest. The financial temptation to a corruptible coach was hard to resist. The coaches escaped any significant scrutiny though, and they were absolved of responsibility for cheating. The players took the blame and were banned from playing in the professional leagues.

The Birth of the NBA. The sudden loss of interest in college basketball finally had presented a great opportunity for professional basketball to seize the center stage, and by the end of the decade the pros had captured the attentions of basketball fans. But in 1950 professional basketball was in crisis, the National Basketball League (NBL, 1937–1949) and Basketball Association of American (BAA, 1946–1949), had folded and a new seventeen-team league NBA was formed. The next year the NBA started with eleven teams but ended with ten when Washington disbanded in mid season. In 1954 the NBA

Red Auerbach's 1956 Boston Celtics; from right; Tom Heinsohn, Bill Russell, Bob Cousy, Bill Sharman, and Frank Ramsey

was reduced to eight teams located in Syracuse, New York, Boston, Philadelphia, Fort Wayne, Minneapolis, Rochester, and Milwaukee. By 1959 the Fort Wayne franchise had moved to Detroit, and the Rochester and Milwaukee franchises had been replaced by Cincinnati and Saint Louis. Franchise stability was hardly the hallmark of the early NBA. There were, however, extremely important developments in professional basketball that assured continued growth and interest.

Integration. The first important commitment made by the NBA was to integration. From the first season, when the Boston Celtics drafted Duquesne's Chuck Cooper, several franchises actively pursued black basketball stars. Before the end of the decade the league's most heralded players were black.

Fast Breaks and Defense Make Dynasties. The second important commitment made by the NBA was to changing the style of the game. During the early part of the decade, when the league was still searching for an identity, Bob Cousy of the Boston Celtics redefined offense with behind-the-back and "no-look" passes that befuddled opponents and sent fans into a frenzy. Cousy's and the Celtics' philosophy (outlined in his 1975 memoir, *The Killer Instinct*) was to get the ball up the floor as quickly as possible and intimidate the opposition. The success of this style of play was assured when the Celtics acquired the rights to draft Bill Russell.

Bill Russell. Russell had led San Francisco to two straight NCAA titles (1955 and 1956) and had dominated the U.S. Olympic team in Melbourne. When he joined the Celtics, the impact was immediate. Russell's style of assertive defense and rebounding allowed him to get the ball to Cousy in the open court before the opposition could prepare to defend. The Boston Celtics won the 1957 NBA title in Russell's rookie year, lost it the next year (when Russell was injured), and then proceeded to win ten more championships over the next eleven years, including eight in a row (1959–1966). In a decade of professional sports dynasties, the Boston Celtics were simply the best.

Time Races On: The Advent of the Shot Clock. While the Boston Celtics were always an exciting team to watch, the rest of the teams in the NBA needed help attracting fans. A simple rule change provided the levels of excitement fans craved. It added speed and action to the game. On 22 November 1950 Fort Wayne beat Minneapolis 19–18. In another game that season, Indianapolis beat Rochester 75–73 in six overtimes. These games may have been close, but they were boring. The fans who came to watch NBA basketball were not excited by the tactic of stalling. They were also not excited by purposeful fouling and rough play. They wanted action. It was not until 1954, however, that the league finally took the advice of Syracuse Nationals owner Danny Biasone and adopted the twenty-four-second shot clock. Biasone reasoned that since NBA teams averaged a shot about once every eighteen seconds anyway, a rule that forced this pace would eliminate stalling at the end of games. The league also adopted the policy of limiting each team to six fouls in each quarter.

Results. The result of these two changes was immediate and lasting. In the first year of the new rules the average score per team per game jumped more than thirteen points and by the end of the decade all teams were averaging more than one hundred points a game. On 27 February 1959 the Russell-Cousy Celtics beat the Minneapolis Lakers 173–139.

Source:
Stanley Cohen, *The Game They Played* (New York: Farrar, Straus & Giroux, 1977).

THE BIRTH OF SPORTS ILLUSTRATED

A Sports Magazine. On 16 August 1954 sports journalism in America was changed forever when *Sports Illustrated* hit the newsstands. The first issue's cover showed Milwaukee Braves slugger Eddie Matthews taking one of his enviable home-run swings. Two major differences would separate this magazine from all the other sports journals. First, *Sports Illustrated* was directly aimed at the American middle-class consumer and budding television-sports spectator; second, and perhaps more important, *SI* was a property of the Henry Luce

---

FILM SPORTS BIOGRAPHIES

During the 1950s Americans craved heroes, and to fill the need Hollywood provided the public with a slew of sports biographies on film.

1950 *The Jackie Robinson Story*
Robinson as himself

1951 *Follow the Sun*
Glenn Ford as Ben Hogan

Jim Thorpe: All American
Burt Lancaster as the country's greatest athlete.

1952 *The Pride of St. Louis*
Dan Dailey as Dizzy Dean

The Winning Team
Ronald Reagan as Grover Cleveland Alexander

1953 *The Joe Louis Story*
Coley Wallace as Joe Louis

1954 *The Bob Mathias Story*
Mathias as himself

1956 *Somebody Up There Likes Me*
Paul Newman as Rocky Graciano

1957 *Fear Strikes Out*
Anthony Perkins as Jimmy Pearsall

---

media empire that included *Time* and *Life,* and so *SI* was guaranteed the financial backing and time required to find its audience.

Readership. During the 1950s *Sports Illustrated* was casting about for its readership; and at the end of the decade it was still sorting out exactly what sports to cover. For the first five years just about anything could and would appear in its pages: women's sports and rodeo, hunting and fishing, travel, track and field, yachting, and badminton. By the end of the decade, however, at least half of the magazine's covers showcased mainstream male spectator sports. More and more, baseball, football, basketball, boxing, golf, tennis, auto and horse racing, and (every four years) Olympic Games grew to dominate the magazine's pages.

Cultural Influence. *Sports Illustrated* did more than reflect the society's changing interests in sport. It helped shape and influence attitudes as Americans moved away from active participation in sports to the role of spectators. *Sports Illustrated* became the leader in investigative and serious reporting in sports. In 1957 it ran a feature on physical fitness in the Soviet Union, promoting in its own way the President's Council on Youth Fitness. It was followed in 1959 by a special report on the growing influence of gambling in sports and in 1960 by an examination of violence in professional football.

Sports Illustrated "Sportsman of the Year" honorees for the 1950s were:

1955	Johnny Podres
1956	Bobby Morrow
1957	Stan Musial
1958	Rafer Johnson
1959	Ingemar Johanson

BOWLING

King and Queen. Marion Ladewig and Don Carter were queen and king of the country's most popular participation sport. With the advent of automatic pinsetters and more-predictable wood oils, bowling became a game that was fun, accessible to all, and fairly easy to master. It was not surprising then that champions came from common origins. A truly middle-class sport for middle-class people, bowling was, in its own way, the greatest success story of the decade.

The Handicap. Bowling tournaments were televised locally all across the country. Handicap tournaments which allowed lesser bowlers an advantage calculated on the basis of previous performances, were popular in bowling alleys all over the country. Ordinary Joes could battle professionals such as the great Don Carter, with a reasonable expectation to make the pros at least sweat. By the end of the decade, the ABC television network was preparing to begin its long and profitable relationship with bowling.

Bowling Proprietors' Association of America (BPAA) Championship (Men's Division)

1950 — Junie McMahon

1951 — Dick Hoover

1952 — Junie McMahon

1953 — Don Carter

1954 — Don Carter

1955 — Steve Nagy

1956 — Bill Lillard

1957 — Don Carter

1958 — Don Carter

1959 — Billy Welu

Bowling Writers Association of America (BWAA) Bowler of the Year (Men's Division)

1950 — Junie McMahon

1951 — Lee Jouglard

1952 — Steve Nagy

Don Carter

BOWLING: BLACK AMERICA'S MOST POPULAR SPORT

According to *Ebony* magazine, the most popular participatory sport for black urban Americans was bowling. Yet, like most institutions, bowling was segregated. The American Bowling Congress (ABC), governing body for most bowling leagues, did not allow black membership. Blacks founded the National Negro Bowling Association (NNBA) in 1939, and in 1944 its name was changed to the National Bowling Association (NBA).

In 1948 the National Committee for Fair Play in Bowling, chaired by Minneapolis mayor Hubert Humphrey, began to pressure the ABC and the Womens' International Bowling Congress (WIBC) to change their "whites only" policy. In 1951 the ABC and the WIBC changed their rules to allow any qualified bowler into their tournaments; but the rule change did not result immediately in integration.

In the 1950s four NBA bowlers won both national singles and all-around titles. Ben Harding (1950) and William Rhodman (1953) won men's titles, while Ruth Coburn (1952) and Beverly Adams (1956) won women's crowns.

Source: Arthur Ashe, *A Hard Road to Glory: A History of the African–American Athlete Since 1946* (New York: Amistad, 1988).

1953 — Don Carter

1954 — Don Carter

1955 — Steve Nagy

1956 — Bill Lillard

1957 — Don Carter

1958 — Don Carter

1959 — Ed Lubanski

Bowling Proprietors' Association of America (BPAA) Championship (Women's Division)

1950 — Marion Ladewig

1951 — Marion Ladewig

1952 — Marion Ladewig

1953 — (Not Held)

1954 — Marion Ladewig

1955 — Sylvia Wene

1956 — Anita Cantaline

1957 — (Not Held)

1958 — Merle Matthews

1959 — Marion Ladewig

**Bowling Writers Association of America (BWAA)
Bowler of the Year** (Women's Division)

1950 — Marion Ladewig

1951 — Marion Ladewig

1952 — Marion Ladewig

1953 — Marion Ladewig

1954 — Marion Ladewig

1955 — Marion Ladewig

1956 — Sylvia Wene

1957 — Anita Cantaline

1958 — Marion Ladewig

1959 — Marion Ladewig

Source:
Herm Weiskopf, *The Perfect Game* (Englewood Cliffs, N.J.: Prentice-Hall, 1978).

BOXING

Boxing's Allure. In many ways boxing in the 1950s had changed little since the era of John L. Sullivan: it was a sport that drew its participants from mostly urban lower-class black, Italian, and Irish neighborhoods—yet was avidly followed by both the poor and the blue bloods. The American public celebrated boxing's champs as the true sports kings, the ultimate athletes competing in the most violent sport. Yet sportswriters and fight fans, who looked to the heavyweight division to determine boxing's king of kings, feared that there was no one fighter among the ranks to assume the lofty place that Joe "The Brown Bomber" Louis had held in the 1940s.

After Joe Louis. In the immediate post–Louis years Ezzard Charles and Jersey Joe Walcott fought three times for the heavyweight championship, with Walcott taking the crown from Charles in their third fight in June 1952. The public was unimpressed. Neither man had the punching power and ring savvy that had made Louis in his prime the greatest ringmaster since Jack Dempsey. Jersey Joe held on to his title for only three months before being knocked out in Philadelphia's Municipal Stadium on 23 September by the Brockton Blockbuster, Rocky Marciano. But boxing pundits were quick to point out that Rocky was no Joe Louis, either. Marciano was slow and clumsy looking. His punches were powerfully thrown, but without finesse—or accuracy—to speak of. He had a short reach and often would have to lunge at his opponent in order to score. He led with his face. As if sensing that his absence had created a void that no other fighter could hope to fill, Joe Louis attempted a comeback, and on 26 October 1951 in Madison Square Garden was knocked out by the Rock in the eighth round. The victory did not win Marciano any more respect from the fans, who felt only pity for the aged Louis. The Rock would go on to compile a 49–0 record and retire an

Rocky Marciano winning the heavyweight championship against Jersey Joe Walcott in 1953

undefeated champ. But fight fans began to look to other weight divisions in their search for the new king of kings.

Sugar Ray and Those Fabulous Middleweights. The most talked-about fighter during the decade was a middleweight. Sugar Ray Robinson, in his time called "pound for pound the greatest fighter who ever lived," had it all: speed, toughness, devastating punching power, ring smarts. On 14 February 1951 Robinson took the middleweight championship from Jake "The Bronx Bull" LaMotta. The last fight in a series of six classics fought between the two hard hitters, it lasted thirteen rounds before the referee stopped it, Robinson having left a bloodied, swollen-faced LaMotta hanging on the ropes. During the decade, Robinson lost and regained the middleweight crown four times, winning the crown five times in all. Talent and fan attention flocked to the middleweight division. Robinson, Rocky Graziano, Gene Fullmer, Randy Turpin, Bobo Olson, and Carmen Basilio generated millions fighting in what was the decade's premier weight division.

Televised Fights. Not every fan, however, could make it to Madison Square Garden to watch the fights, so companies looking to cash in on boxing's popularity brought the fight to the fans. In 1944 the Gillette Company had signed a contract with Madison Square Garden to sponsor weekly televised matches. By the mid 1950s in many viewing areas a fight fan could find a match on the television set any night of the week except Sunday. Tele-

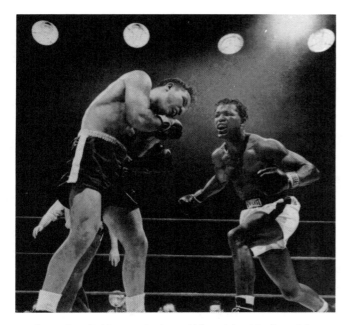

Sugar Ray Robinson winning middleweight title from Jake LaMotta in 1951

nals, Russ Hodges for the Giants, Mel Allen for the New York Yankees, and Red Barber for the Brooklyn Dodgers. They were celebrities and they were paid well. Red Barber earned $50,000 per year from the New York Yankees in 1954 after the Dodgers left Brooklyn.

Sports for Television. At the beginning of the decade, television was best equipped to handle sports that required little space and delivered plenty of action—wrestling, boxing, and roller derby, for example. Early in the decade, more than two hundred television stations carried at least one wrestling match per week. They were easy to stage, because the matches were really performances rather than legitimate sports contests. Wrestling could be shaped to fit into prearranged time slots, and spectators enjoyed the emotional involvement that the matches invited. Boxing was legitimate, but there was no shortage of matches to televise and there was a convenient pause for commercials after each three minutes of action.

Boring Productions. The first televised baseball game in 1939 was viewed critically. There were no instant replays, no color, few close-ups, limited camera coverage, and transmission was frequently interrupted due to technical difficulties. Football and tennis were equally boring on the tube. They were sports that took place over a broad playing surface, and television broadcast capabili-

vised bouts also meant better guaranteed pay for the fighters. Even the journeymen and stiffs who landed a spot in Gillette Friday night boxing's main event were paid $4,000 minimum. Phillies Cigars' Saturday night fights and Pabst Blue Ribbon's Wednesday night bouts also paid well. Before television cameras were brought into the smoke-filled fight clubs, a $40 bout, as one fighter put it, "was hitting the real jackpot." Many boxing purists, however, feared that television would ruin the sport. Television money, they argued, drew too many with too little talent into the ring. Small-time local fight promoters who had once made a comfortable living matching up bums and has-beens also took it on the chin, as many fans stayed home to watch big-name bouts.

Sources:

Sam Andre and Nat Fleischer, *A Pictorial History of Boxing,* revised edition (Secaucus, N.J.: Citadel Press, 1987);

"Buildup to a Fight — TV Makes a Difference," *Business Week* (27 February 1954): 113–119.

BROADCASTING SPORTS

Making New Fans. Television brought sports to millions of new fans in the 1950s. Since 1921, when the first baseball game was broadcast on radio, avid sports fans had become accustomed to following the fortunes of their teams as play-by-play announcers vividly described the action. Baseball lent itself particularly well to radio reporting, and fans became as attached to their team's announcer as to the team itself. The announcer was the voice of the team, the narrator of the sports drama: as the decade began, Curt Gowdy announced for the Boston Red Sox, By Samm for the Philadelphia Phillies, Bob Prince for the Pittsburgh Pirates, Waite Hoyt for the Cincinnati Reds, Harry Caray for the Saint Louis Cardi-

Mid 1950s CBS television baseball announcers Dizzy Dean and Buddy Blattner

ties were not yet advanced enough for full-field coverage comprehensive enough to satisfy serious sports spectators. Those advances came during the 1950s at roughly the same time as owners were learning how to negotiate broadcasting contracts with the networks and independent stations.

Baseball. Many baseball fans contented themselves with print coverage and radio broadcasts of baseball games until well into the 1950s. At the beginning of the decade teams averaged $200,000 in annual income from radio rights, and enterprising owners were able to line up full-season corporate sponsorship. Radio station owners, on the other hand, often looked to baseball broadcasts to fill air time. The Mutual Broadcasting Company sent its "Game of the Day" to more than 500 radio stations nationwide in the early 1950s, for example. National television coverage was slow to develop, partly because owners were unable to agree on a format for national coverage within the bounds of federal antitrust law. Not until 1961 did Congress grant sports broadcasters exemption from the law to allow owners to act jointly in negotiations with networks. The baseball game of the week followed promptly. Previously, individual teams negotiated their own deals with chaotic results. Nonetheless, in 1958 there were some eight hundred telecasts of major league games.

Overcoming Difficulties. Technical shortcomings were quickly solved, and early in the decade weekend daytime programming was dominated by sports coverage, both collegiate and professional. New York led the country. In 1950 during football season fans could watch as many as eight games each Saturday. Television provided a windfall for teams. In 1953 college teams playing on television split about $100,000 per game, and by 1960 NBC budgeted $3 million for television rights to college football games. Pro games were a bit cheaper. In the early 1950s DuMont paid $95,000 to televise the NFL championship, and CBS paid just over $1 million in 1956 for rights to professional games. Many fans insisted that a televised football game was preferable to a live one. The climate was almost always better in the fan's living room than at the football stadium, and people enjoyed the announcers' commentary, which explained elements of the game that had gone largely unappreciated before.

Attendance. Meanwhile, attendance, and thus revenues, at sporting events covered on television dropped dramatically. Early in the 1950s the practice of blacking out television coverage in the area where the event was being held became common. Television all but killed minor-league baseball, which had been protected from competition by a rule blacking out television and radio broadcasts of major-league games in minor-league cities. The rule was repealed in 1951 after baseball owners were threatened with an antitrust suit, and the effect was disastrous for minor-league baseball. Attendance at minor-league games was 42 million in 1949; 15 million in 1957 after national broadcast of baseball began. Attendance at

the Friday night fights at Madison Square Garden dropped from about ten thousand fans each week to just over a thousand in 1958 after the fights were televised.

Setting the Stage. By the end of the 1950s the consolidation of television sports was about to occur. The Sports Broadcasting Act provided for an organized format for telecast of professional sports. Collegiate sports had evolved into an entertainment business, well equipped to deliver a well-packaged program of games to national viewers. Television sports divisions had developed the technical facilities and the resources to produce superior coverage of events all over the country and the world.

Source:
Benjamin G. Rader, *In Its Own Image: How Television Has Transformed Sports* (New York: Free Press, 1984).

COLD WAR OLYMPICS

The Pride of Nations. The leaders of the Olympic Games have always insisted that the Olympics are above politics, that the nations of the world can meet on the field of sport and allow political differences to be overshadowed by the spirit of competition and fair play. Unfortunately it has never happened. When matters of national pride are displayed on a public stage for the whole

Soviet training camp, 1952 Olympics in Helsinki

world to see, even athletes become political tools. Avery Brundage himself, in the 1950s the president of the International Olympic Committee, had outraged many Americans when he chose to replace several talented Jewish sprinters in 1936, so as not to further embarrass the leader of the host German state, Adolf Hitler, when black American athletes, led by Jesse Owens, dominated the Munich Games.

Turned Away at the Gates. In 1952 the world was facing the possibility of full-scale nuclear war. The United States and the Soviet Union were bitterly competing for world domination, at least ideologically, in Europe, Asia, and Africa. The Soviet Union participated on the field in Helsinki, but the team refused quarters with other nations in the Olympic Village. In fact, the Soviet Union and its satellite nations housed their athletes in their own quarters and enclosed the quarters with barbed wire. No outsider was welcome at the Otaniemi camp. Even news reporters, no matter their nationality, were turned away.

Divided Nations. In addition to the Soviet problem, Helsinki faced other political crises. Nationalist China claimed to be the only official Chinese team. At first the IOC stated that neither Formosa nor the People's Republic could compete but then invited both. Formosa then boycotted the games. East Germany was not allowed to compete. Many athletes from nations fragmented by World War II officially had no citizenship, so they petitioned the IOC to compete under the Olympic, Swiss, Greek, or Red Cross flag. The IOC ignored the requests.

Medal Counts and "Unofficial" Records. The Soviet Union claimed that the results of the games would demonstrate quite clearly the superiority of the Communist system. Medal counts and points scored, while not official, became all-important. For the record, the United States won forty-one gold medals and the Soviet Union twenty-three; and the points-scored system showed a 614–553 1/2 victory for the American team. The Soviets went home licking their wounds and plotting their return in Melbourne. For the next three decades the U.S.S.R. would dominate the Olympic Games in a way never before seen or imagined.

Boycotts. The amount of attention paid to Nationalist China's boycott of the 1952 Olympics inspired several nations in 1956 to use the Olympics as a forum to air their political grievances. The Netherlands, Spain, and Switzerland boycotted in protest of the Soviet Union's invasion of Hungary, which had declared its intention to become a neutral state. Communist China withdrew because Nationalist China had been invited; Egypt withdrew because it was at war with Israel; and Iraq withdrew to protest the military action by France, Britain, and Israel against Egypt in the struggle for control of the Suez Canal. The Norwegians asked the IOC to ban South Africa from the Olympics because of that country's racial policy of apartheid.

Favoritism and Defections. For the first time in the Olympic Games, judges were accused of blatantly favoring athletes from politically allied nations and penalizing athletes from enemy states. The United States even went so far as to file a formal protest against Soviet and Eastern-bloc judges. Not only did the Olympic officials reject the protest, but Brundage claimed that the IOC deserved to be awarded the Nobel Peace Prize. Meanwhile, in the sport of water polo, in which the Hungarian team was among the favorites to win the gold, the match between the Soviets and Hungarians ended in a brutal and bloody fight among players that made international headlines. Many athletes from Eastern-bloc countries tried and failed to escape the Olympic Village in order to defect. Forty-five Hungarians, however, perhaps more strongly motivated than others, succeeded in reaching the Australian or American embassies and were successful in their defections.

Sources:
Christopher R. Hill, *Olympic Politics* (Manchester, U.K.: Manchester University Press, 1992);

Martin Barry Vinokur, *More than a Game: Sports and Politics* (New York: Greenwood Press, 1988).

FOOTBALL: THE FIELDS OF FRIENDLY STRIFE

Professional Football's Increasing Popularity. During the 1950s college football was surpassed in popularity by professional football. With the increased number of games on television and the growing efficiency of air transportation, regionalism became less of a factor in attracting fans. Pro teams could play throughout the country and fans could follow the fortunes of their favorite teams on television; like most pro sports, football promoted individual sports heroes. College athletes had a maximum of four years' exposure to a team's fans. Pro athletes could attract the fans' attention for their entire careers.

Symbolic Battles. Colleges had always been able to maintain the interest of alumni, but they had to rely on other, largely symbolic attractions for other fans. Colleges often battled for prestige and superiority, based on team rivalries between states and regions, and among ethnic groups, religious and political beliefs, and ways of life. Of all the teams in college football, it was the "Fighting Irish" of Notre Dame that during the 1920s and 1930s built a fame based on winning football and a spirit of Roman Catholicism that transcended even ethnicity. This small, midwestern, Catholic liberal-arts college became the focal point of the lives of sports fans who had never left the city or even graduated from high school. Notre Dame was truly the first collegiate team with a national following, traveling all over the country on its football crusade. For the most part, all challengers fell by

Oklahoma football coach Bud Wilkinson

the wayside until there arose from the Southwest a team and a coach of unparalleled quality.

The Dominance of the Coach. The only source of continuity from which the morality plays on the football field could draw their spirit was the coach. Knute Rockne (1918–1930; 105 wins, 12 losses, 5 ties) was the legendary Notre Dame coach who laid the foundation for the team's extraordinary winning reputation, and he was followed by Elmer Layden (1934–1940; 47 wins, 13 losses, 3 ties) and Frank Leahy (1941–1943, 1946–1953; 87 wins, 11 losses, 9 ties). As the 1950s opened, Leahy was already legendary and would go on to have the second-best winning percentage of all time (.864, behind only Rockne at .881); but in 1950 one coach surpassed all others — Bud Wilkinson of Oklahoma. Immersed as he was in a game often brutal and always violent and emotional, Wilkinson remained a paragon of virtue. For all the suspicion (perhaps born of envy) that surrounded Oklahoma during the 1950s, none of it ever made its way to the coach. Wilkinson's Oklahoma teams blended su-

perb physical conditioning with clean play and a commitment to enthusiastic play. As a result they often won games in which they seemed, on paper, outclassed. In 1948 the Sooners lost their season opening game to Santa Clara, but they did not lose another game for three years. When they finally lost to Kentucky, 13–7, in the Sugar Bowl to end the 1950 season, Oklahoma had won 31 straight games.

Streaks are Forever. In 1951 Oklahoma had a record of 8–2; in 1952, 8–1–1 — certainly not a significant drop in quality from the previous three season. Still, as 1953 started, Oklahoma was predicted to be beatable and Notre Dame proved the point; but that was the end of the losses in 1953. Oklahoma finished 1953 at 9–1–1 (the tie was with Pittsburgh) and fourth in the country (Notre Dame was second to Maryland). In 1954 Oklahoma did not lose, finishing 10–0 but third in the polls behind Ohio State and UCLA, also undefeated. Ohio State got the edge in the final results because it won the Rose Bowl and the others did not play. In the 1950s a variety of rules prevented teams from appearing in bowls in consecutive years. In 1955 Oklahoma went 10–0 again and beat number three Maryland 20–6 in the Orange Bowl to finish number one in the country; and in 1956 the Sooners went 10–0, undefeated for the third straight year. The winning streak was now more than 40, the longest in NCAA history. In 1957 the Sooners finally lost a game, the only game they would lose all year, and it was to a mediocre Notre Dame team that went 6–3. The score was 7–0, Oklahoma's first loss in 47 games. In a span of eleven years, from 1948 to 1958, the Oklahoma Sooners won 107 games, lost 8, and tied 2.

From Moral Wars to Making Money. In the 1950s collegiate football was a game for the fans run by the coaches. The players were pawns who found little market for their talents after four years. In the early part of the century college football came close to being outlawed by President Theodore Roosevelt. The game was violent, deaths occurred, and the players often were not even college students but paid, blue-collar workers looking to make some easy money. Under Roosevelt's threat, the colleges formed the National Collegiate Athletic association and began to regulate the college game. Still, when he played football, Knute Rockne played for six different teams in one season. In 1920, however, with the formation of the American Professional Football Association (named the National Football League [NFL] in 1922), the "student" professionals could now make their money above the table. Throughout the next three decades professional football struggled in midsize cities in the East and Midwest, constantly shifting franchises and enduring challenges from new leagues.

Television Saves the Day. In 1939 the NFL began to telecast some of its games on an experimental basis. Soon it became clear that the game was remarkably well suited to the medium. After every play, football would allow for twenty to thirty seconds in which to review the previous

Oklahoma halfback and Heisman Trophy winner Billy Vessels running sixty-two yards for a touchdown against Notre Dame in 1952

play and plot the strategy for the next. Unlike baseball, which could go on for an hour with little happening, football was a game of constant planning punctuated by bursts of energy twice in every minute. In a typical football game that lasted two and a half hours there would be only about twelve minutes of actual play — all the better to sell commercials — and since no organized collegiate sports were played on Sundays in the fall, and since the college games on Saturday had whetted fans' appetites, all the NFL had to do was wait for television technology to develop and to reach America's homes.

An Transcontinental Game. After World War II the NFL immediately geared its product for all of the country. In 1946 Cleveland's team moved to Los Angeles, became the Rams, and led the league in attendance. In 1949 the rival All-America Conference (AAC) disbanded, and the NFL assumed three franchises — Baltimore, San Francisco, and the league champion Cleveland Browns. Also in 1949 the NFL had established its draft well enough to be able to tap into the proven talent pool in the colleges. The best part of this arrangement was that even rookies in the NFL were already well known, and the NFL could market them as stars from their very first game.

Blackouts. Bert Bell, former owner-coach of the Philadelphia Eagles, was appointed NFL commissioner in 1946 and successfully destroyed the AAC. He also directed the league toward its first television contracts that assured regular transcontinental broadcasts. Having two

franchises located in California's largest cities guaranteed that fans in New York could watch the Giants play the Rams or the 49ers, but it also presented significant problems. In 1950 the Rams telecast all their home games, and attendance dropped by 50 percent; in 1951 the Rams blacked out their home games and attendance doubled. This convinced Bell that the league had to adopt a television policy different from baseball and act as a single negotiating unit. In 1952 Bell convinced the owners to make him the director of NFL television, and he promptly instituted the "blackout of home games" rule leaguewide.

The Courts Decide. Bell's tactic caused the Department of Justice to invoke the Sherman Anti-Trust Act to stop the NFL plan, and the NFL fought the injunction in court. The courts decided that football was a "unique kind of business" and that anything other than allowing an exception to antitrust law would mean financial ruin for the sport. During the rest of the decade Bell worked behind the scenes with Congress so that in 1961 the Sports Broadcasting Act became the law of the land.

Sources:

Ivan N. Kaye, *Good Clean Violence: A History of College Football* (Philadelphia: Lippincott, 1973);

David J. Miller, *The Super Book of Football* (Boston: Little, Brown, 1990);

Robert Smith, *Pro Football: The History of the Game and the Great Players* (Garden City, N.Y.: Doubleday, 1963).

GOLF

A Game with an Elitist Reputation. Like tennis, golf in America was a game that had grown around the nation's country clubs. Its participants were white and affluent — men and women of leisure who could afford to spend four hours of their day touring the lush, rolling links that were cared for by those who could not afford to play the game.

The Hogan Era. In the 1950s, however, golf was no longer just a *game* for the idle rich: the game became a *sport*. This transformation had much to do with a wiry, poker-faced Texan — Ben Hogan. Hogan attacked the golf course with a single-minded ferocity that came closer to evoking an image of a linebacker than that of a golfer. His mental and physical toughness were beyond question. After suffering serious injuries in a 1949 car crash, he came back to win the 1951 Masters. His win at the 1951 U.S. Open, however, was the one that stunned sports fans. That year the Open was held at long and treacherous Oakland Hills in Birmingham, Michigan. After shooting an unheard-of final-round score of three-under-par sixty-seven, Hogan announced with the grim arrogance of a pugilist, "I'm glad that I brought this course, this monster, to its knees."

Changing of the Guard. By the mid 1950s it had become clear that the era of Hogan was approaching an end. With the old guard, consisting of Hogan, Jimmy Demaret, and Sam Snead, no longer golf's dominant

Babe Zaharias, 1954

OUR GOLFING PRESIDENT

Although his score for a round of eighteen rarely broke ninety, President Dwight D. Eisenhower had much to do with the increasing popularity of golf. By the time he entered the White House in 1953, he had already gained a reputation as a golf addict, and during his two-term presidency he took great delight in playing highly publicized rounds with golfing greats such as Bobby Jones and Ben Hogan. In February 1953 the Public Golf Association offered to build a putting green on the south lawn of the White House. The green was placed just outside his office window, and on his way to and from work he would stop to practice his approach shots and putts. The many squirrels that populated the White House lawn, however, found the green an ideal site for burying acorns and walnuts. Furious, Eisenhower told the Secret Service, "The next time you see one of those squirrels go near my putting green, take a gun and shoot it." Secret Service men convinced the president that deadly force did not have to be used: traps were set and the squirrels were relocated.

Source: Stephen E. Ambrose, *Eisenhower: The President* (New York: Simon & Schuster, 1984).

force, many wondered if the sport would return to being a game. By the close of the decade, however, a new generation of stars was on the rise. In 1958 Arnold Palmer of Latrobe, Pennsylvania, won the Masters with a game and a swing seemingly more suited for a public course than for Augusta National — one of golf's sternest tests. He gripped his club as if he were attempting to choke the shaft to death and would beat down on the ball with all his might. In the 1960s Palmer and his blue-collar style of play were responsible for golf's unprecedented popularity. Middle America began to take to the links in droves.

Women Turn Professional. Women's golf came of age in the 1950s. Not only did Babe Zaharias-Didrikson help found the Ladies' Professional Golf Tour in 1949, she won all three major tournaments (U.S. Open, Titleholders, and Western Open) in 1950. It is hard to imagine just how good an athlete she was: winning Olympic medals in 1932 and leading national championship teams in softball. Zaharias won nine major championships in her all-too-brief career, dying of cancer at the age of forty-two on 27 September 1956. As founding mother of women's professional golf, however, she made it possible for talented golfers to prosper playing the game.

Darkstar beating Native Dancer at 1953 Preakness

Source:
Tom Flaherty, *The U.S. Open [1895–1965]* (New York: E. P. Dutton, 1966).

HORSE RACING NEAR MISSES

Horse as Symbol. Easily the most popular spectator sport in the United States during the 1950s was horse racing. Perhaps as a result of attention directed to the war effort, the quality of race horses declined sharply in the 1950s. But then the great horses of the 1940s had set a standard difficult to match. Horses of the 1950s were measured against four Triple Crown winners from the 1940s: Whirlaway (1941), Count Fleet (1943), Assault (1946), and the magnificent Citation (1948), who in 1951 became the first horse in racing history to earn $1 million.

Near Misses. The 1950s was a decade of near misses in horse racing. The most famous miss was when Willie Shoemaker misjudged the finish line of the 1957 Kentucky Derby to allow Iron Liege to nose out Gallant Man. The result of Shoemaker's miscalculation is the universal bull's-eye symbol that now marks the finish line.

More Near Misses. The Triple Crown — the designation reserved for winners of the Kentucky Derby, the Preakness, and the Belmont Stakes — was nearly won — which is to say was nearly missed — five times in the decade. Middleground (1950), Native Dancer (1953), Nashua (1955), and Needles (1956) all lost either the Kentucky Derby or the Preakness. Tim Tam in 1958 won the first two legs, only to lose the Belmont Stakes. All five horses finished second in the only Triple Crown race they did not win.

Sources:
Barry Gifford, *A Day at the Races: The Education of a Racetracker* (New York: Atlantic Monthly Press, 1988);
Marvin B. Scott, *The Racing Game* (Chicago: Aldine Publishing, 1968).

ICE HOCKEY

Canada's National Sport. In the 1950s the National Hockey League (NHL) simply stayed put. There were no franchise changes, few television contracts, and for most people in the United States the NHL remained invisible. There were only six franchises, with four in the United States: Boston, New York, Detroit, and Chicago. The only Canadian teams were Toronto and Montreal. Americans outside of the Northeast paid little attention to hockey.

American Domination. To the dismay of Canadians an American team, the Detroit Red Wings, dominated the sport from the late 1940s through the middle of the 1950s, and Red Wing offensive star Gordie Howe was the league's preeminent player. Howe may have played for an American team, but he was, like every other player in the NHL, a Canadian. Tommy Williams of Minnesota joined the Boston Bruins in the later part of the decade and was, for a long time, the only American in the league. During the later part of the decade the Montreal Canadiens led by the incomparable Maurice Richard began a run of five straight Stanley Cups. When Richard scored his four hundredth goal, he became a sports hero comparable in America to Babe Ruth.

Source:
Richard Beddoes, *Hockey! The Story of the World's Fastest Sport*, revised edition (New York: Macmillan, 1971).

Stanley Cup Champions

1950 — Detroit

1951 — Toronto

1952 — Detroit

1953 — Montreal

1954 — Detroit

1955 — Detroit

1956 — Montreal

1957 — Montreal

1958 — Montreal

1959 — Montreal

INTEGRATION AT WHAT COST?

The Breakthrough. On 9 April 1947 the Brooklyn Dodgers became the first modern team in Major League Baseball to employ a black man as a player. When Branch Rickey hired Jackie Robinson, it was trumpeted as a major breakthrough in the integration of the "separate but equal" world of sports and as a signal that all of America was ready to move toward integration. Jackie Robinson would become a hero for black Americans even more important than Jesse Owens or Joe Louis. The National League teams seemed to see the direct impact of signing black stars. Roy Campanella won the 1951 NL MVP and a black won the MVP award every other year in the decade except 1952: Campanella won two more (1953 and 1955), Willie Mays won in 1954, Don Newcombe in 1955, Hank Aaron in 1957, and Ernie Banks won in 1958 and 1959.

Brother Against Brother. The decade of race relations in America was exemplified by what Jackie Robinson was called on to do in the name of patriotism. In 1950 the House Un-American Activities Committee was at the peak of its power, holding hearings to investigate the infiltration of communism into American institutions. Paul Robeson, a former black college football and track star for Rutgers and in 1950 an actor living in Europe, had denounced the racist society of America in 1949 and had defected to the Soviet Union. In 1950 Robinson, at the urging of Branch Rickey, appeared before the HUAC to repudiate Robeson. Robinson was placed in a no-win situation. Even if he supported Robeson's freedom of political expression, Robinson had to dissociate himself from Robeson's anti-Americanism.

The following are some important events in race relations in sports for the 1950s:

Jackie Robinson, 42, congratulating Roy Campanella, 39, after a Campanella home run

1950

Apr.–May: The Boston Celtics of the NBA draft the league's first black player, Charles Cooper, and the American Bowling Congress ends its white-male-only policy.

29 Aug.: Althea Gibson becomes the first black woman to compete in a national tennis tournament.

1951

12 Mar.: Major League Baseball dismisses its second commissioner, A. B. "Happy" Chandler. In 1947 Chandler overrode the baseball owner's vote against signing Jackie Robinson. Chandler's role in the desegregation of baseball contributed to his dismissal.

1954

Male Athlete of the Year — Willie Mays (baseball)

1957

Female Athlete of the Year — Althea Gibson (tennis)

6 July: Althea Gibson becomes the first black American to win a Wimbledon tennis championship. Gibson also wins the U.S. National in September.

10 Nov.: Charles Sifford becomes the first black golfer to win a PGA-sponsored event at the Long Beach Open.

Chuck Cooper, the first black professional basketball player

1958

Summer: The ratio of black and white baseball players in the major leagues is the same as the ratio in the general population. Owners still maintain quotas.

1959

Jan.: The NBA adopts a policy to protect its black players (the league is now 25 percent minority) from discrimination at hotels. In May the Supreme Court rules that it is illegal to prohibit blacks and whites from participating in the same athletic contest.

Aug.: The Boston Red Sox are the last Major League Baseball team to sign a black player.

1960

Oct.: The Negro American League, now down to four baseball teams, disbands after the season. The decade of sports desegregation ends as contentiously as it began.

Sources:
Edwin Bancroft Henderson, *The Black Athlete: Emergence and Arrival,* revised edition (Cornwells Heights, Pa.: Publishers Agency, 1978);

Jules Tygiel, *Baseball's Great Experiment: Jackie Robinson and His Legacy* (New York: Oxford University Press, 1983).

LITTLE LEAGUE BIG MEN

Boy Soldiers. The President's Council on Youth Fitness (PCYF) was established in 1957 because Eisenhower was shocked to learn that American youth fared miserably in fitness tests when compared to youth in Europe. The council was hastily established so that the government could demonstrate support for preparing its children, especially boys. Vice-president Nixon was the first chairman of the council, but soon this largely symbolic role was given over to sports leaders. Bud Wilkinson, Oklahoma's football coach, took over leadership. The PCYF was another way to fight the cold war. Its impact was negligible largely because America was quickly moving toward being a sedentary society and because the focus of the movement fell not on fitness but sports. The PCYF was more intent on moral character than physical fitness, and it was during the 1950s that

Destiny's Darlings

Gold medalist Decathlete Bob Richards at the 1952 Olympics in Helsinki

youth sports, particularly Little League Baseball and Pop Warner Football, taught boys how to become men.

Rise of Little League. The original intentions of Little League Baseball were local, grass roots, and good. It started in Williamsport, Pennsylvania, to provide boys with something clean and fun to do after school. Little League, however, quickly became an institution that rivaled the Boy Scouts for fostering political ideology. Little boys were not just playing baseball, they were becoming good Americans. Little Leaguers had their own pledge, salute, and motto (Character, Courage, Loyalty). Most of America supported Little League's ideological goals without question.

Destiny's Darlings. In 1954 a team from Schenectady, New York, won the Little League World Series. A New York Yankee announcer called them "destiny's darlings." Twenty years later reporter Martin Ralbovsky interviewed all the players to see how their experience and their coach, Michael Maietta, had shaped their character. Several players claimed that Little League was the best thing that ever happened to them and that Maietta, a notorious taskmaster, had taught them how to win in baseball and life. The team had both a black and a Jew on its roster, and both these boys felt they had been treated as equals. Maietta used the racial taunts directed at the black players by a team from the South as a means to encourage the team to win one for race relations. Schenectady won 17–0. On the other hand, one player recalled that Maietta had promoted a killer instinct in them so that they were the meanest kids in the tournament and everyone else was afraid of them. Another player claimed that he was simply a twelve-year-old professional; and still another, that he was a pawn in a chess game.

Source:
Martin Ralbovsky, *Destiny's Darlings* (New York: Hawthorne, 1974).

THE OLYMPICS FOR ALL

The Olympic Spirit Reclaimed. After the end of World War II the International Olympic Committee (IOC) consciously attempted to return to the principles upon which the modern Olympic Games were based: "To the Glory and Honor of Youth"; "Higher, Faster, Stronger"; "It's not the winning, but the taking part." The IOC entered the 1950s with genuine eagerness to celebrate the spirit of amateurism.

A Self-Made Leader. Avery Brundage, long-time leader of the Olympic movement in America, became president of the IOC in 1952. Brundage had himself been on the 1912 U.S. Olympic team and participated in Stockholm in the decathlon and pentathlon, only to be overshadowed by Jim Thorpe. Later in life, having earned a fortune in construction, Brundage had the resources to retire from his business and lead the Amateur Athletic Union (AAU) from 1928 to 1935 and the U. S. Olympic Committee from 1929 to 1953. Brundage always approached sports as he had his business career, with a firm belief in self-determination and the positive effect of hard work. The success of the Olympic Games of the 1950s allowed him to lead the movement into the age of television and worldwide audiences in the billions.

1952 Winter Games — Oslo, Norway. An unheralded American, Andrea Mead Lawrence, surprised observers by winning two gold medals in the slalom and giant slalom. She was the first American athlete to win a medal of any kind in Alpine events. Less surprising but no less pleasant was the performance of the U.S. figure skaters. Dick Button, five-time world men's figure-skating champion (1948–1952) and winner in 1948 at Saint Moritz, capped a four-year period of domination by winning the Olympic gold medal for the second time and then announcing his immediate retirement. Figure

Gold medalist shot-putter Parry O'Brien at the 1956 Olympics in Melbourne

skater Tenley Albright, on the other hand, was at the beginning of her run to world championship status. At Oslo, Albright achieved a silver medal. A surprising performance by Ken Henry earned him a gold medal in the 500-meter speed skating. The U.S. men's ice-hockey team finished second to Canada. It was the fifth ice hockey medal for America in seven Olympics (four silvers, one bronze).

1952 Summer Games — Helsinki, Finland. Among all the modern Games before or since, Helsinki remains among the most successful sporting festivals of all. The amazing three-gold-medal performance by Czechoslovakian distance runner Emil Zatopek in the 5,000 meters, 10,000 meters, and marathon overshadowed every other achievement. Among the outstanding American performances were the five gold medals earned by the boxing team; future heavyweight champion of the world Floyd Patterson won the gold medal in the middleweight division. David Browning and Sammy Lee swept the diving events and Americans won four more golds in swimming.

American sprinters once again dominated, but it was Mal Whittfield's Olympic record (1:49.2) repeat gold-medal performance in the 800 meter that was most impressive. Walt Davis (high jump), Bob Richards (pole vault), Parry O'Brien (shot put), Sam Iness (discus), and Cy Young (javelin) won their gold medals with Olympic record performances. In their first significant basketball showdown the U.S. team beat the Soviet Union for the gold, 36–25. The outstanding American performance of the games, however, was Bob Mathias's repeat gold medal in the decathlon — this time a world record. In 1948, at the age of seventeen, Mathias had become the youngest gold-medal winner of the decathlon; in 1952 he became the first athlete to lay claim to the title "world's greatest athlete" in two Olympiads. American women won three gold medals; Pat MacCormick won both the springboard and platform diving events; and the 4x100-meter relay team also finished first.

1956 Winter Games — Cortina, Italy. The 1956 games were an Olympics of few surprises and fewer successes for the United States. The men's ice-hockey team finished second again, this time to the Soviet Union. Tenley Albright had won the women's world title in figure skating in 1953 and 1955 and easily won the gold medal. Dick Button had retired, and Hayes Alan Jenkins had won the men's figure skating title for four straight years. He glided to an overwhelming victory to earn the gold medal in the Olympics.

1956 Summer Games — Melbourne, Australia. Even though the American team was larger than ever and there were far fewer participants from throughout the world in this Olympics down under, the American medal count was not impressive. The boxing team won just two gold medals; the divers won the springboard (Bob Clotworthy) but lost the platform for the first time since 1912; and Bill Yorzyk's 200-meter butterfly gold was the only win for the swimmers. In track and field the U.S. athletes continued their domination in sprinting and field events. On the track Bobby Morrow swept to victory in both the 100 and 200 meters; Charley Jenkins won the 400 meters; and Tom Courtney set an Olympic record in the 800 meters. Lee Calhoun (100 meters) and Glenn Davis (400 meters) dominated the hurdles with Olympic records, and the U.S. relay teams won both races, setting a world record by smashing the forty-second barrier with a time of 39.5 seconds in the 4x100-meter race. In the field Charley Dumas won the high jump, and Bob Richards, for the second time, won the pole vault, both at Olympic record heights. Greg Bell won the long jump and Parry O'Brien won his second straight shot-put gold, setting an Olympic record and smashing the sixty-foot barrier.

Al Oerter. In retrospect, however, Al Oerter's Olympic record toss of 184 feet 11 inches in the discus was most remarkable because it was just a hint of what was to come. Oerter proceeded to dominate his event in a way never seen before or since in the Olympic Games. For the next four Olympic Games, Oerter won the gold and set Olympic records. In 1968 his toss was 212 feet 6 inches. Even in 1984, after over a decade in retirement, Oerter was trying to make the U.S. Olympic team and failed only because of an injury.

Women's Gold. American women won three gold medals. For the second consecutive games Pat MacCormick won both the springboard and platform diving events, and Mildred McDaniel set a world record (5 feet 9 1/4 inches) in the high jump. The relatively poor performances of American women in the Olympics during the decade can largely be attributed to social conditions that discouraged women from active participation in sports.

Source:
Allen Guttman, *The Olympics, a History of the Modern Games* (Urbana: University of Illinois Press, 1992).

TENNIS

Its Stuffy Reputation. To many Americans at the beginning of the decade, tennis was still a sport for rich people and sissies. Most tennis courts were reserved for the country-club set, and the sport's professionals and competitive amateurs were well-to-do and white — as were their tennis outfits, if they were dressed in keeping with tennis etiquette. Many tennis players and tournament officials had fought hard to change the sport's image, and the professional circuit experimented with

---

TENNIS AND THE COLD WAR

With Americans and Communists each attempting to exert influence on the Third World, the cold war was heating up. In an effort to win the trust and respect of the Third World governments, the State Department hit upon the idea of sending American athletes on goodwill tours abroad to display U.S. athletic excellence and spread the message of democracy. In 1955 the State Department found in Althea Gibson the perfect ambassador-athlete. Racial tensions in the United States had fed the Soviet propaganda machine, and U.S. government officials were anxious to show off to the world a successful black in order to prove that American democracy was moving toward racial equality. Although Gibson understood that the government aimed to exploit the color of her skin, she agreed to take part in the goodwill tour. She never regretted her decision: while in Asia she made friends with the white tennis players traveling with her, and her love for tennis was rekindled.

Source: Tom Biracree, *American Women of Achievement: Althea Gibson* (New York: Chelsea House, 1989).

Maureen "Little Mo" Connelly, 1953

various tournament formats and venues — including holding night matches under arc lights at the 1951 national professional championship at Forest Hills, New York — in an attempt to draw fans. But few were interested, and with professional tennis still in its infancy the amateurs continued to attract the larger upper-class crowds.

Vice-president Richard Nixon awarding winner's trophy to Althea Gibson at the 1957 U.S. National Tennis Championship

Tony Trabert (on back) and Vic Seixas defeating Australian Ken Rosewall and Lewis Hoad in 1954 to win the Davis Cup for the United States for the first time since 1949

A New Image for Tennis. By the end of the decade, however, the image of tennis had undergone a change as more and more Americans who could not afford a tennis court in their backyard or a country-club membership took interest in the sport and in its athletes. Women's tennis players — particularly Maureen Connolly and Althea Gibson, a black athlete from Harlem — were mostly responsible for the increasing amount of attention paid to the sport. The Davis Cup rivalry between the United States and Australia also sparked interest, as the team competition evoked nationalistic pride.

The Era of Little Mo. Dubbed "Little Mo" by the newspapers, Maureen Connolly, at the age of sixteen, burst on the tennis scene in 1951 and became the youngest player in twenty-eight years to win the U.S. National championship. She overpowered opponents with her hard-hitting groundstrokes and in so doing brought women's tennis to a new level of skill. Her youth, vivaciousness, and extraordinary athleticism also attracted new fans to the game. Grandstands were filled beyond capacity by many who had never picked up a tennis racket to catch a glimpse of Little Mo dominating the sport in unprecedented fashion. She continued to add major championships to her impressive list of wins and in 1953 achieved tennis's ultimate feat by winning all four major tournaments (the Australian, French, British, and U.S. championships) in a single year. A horse-riding accident in 1954 forced her early retirement, but her brash and hard swinging style of play had forever changed the sport.

Althea Ignites Interest. In 1957 Althea Gibson, whose style of play sportswriters described as "mannish," rose to the top rank of women's tennis. In that year she received the trophy from Queen Elizabeth after winning England's grass court title at Wimbledon, the first black to do so. Upon her return to New York she was greeted with a ticker-tape parade and later that year went on to win the U.S. championship trophy, presented to her by Vice-president Richard M. Nixon. She repeated her win-

ning performances at the 1958 British and American championships and received the Babe Didrikson Zaharias and Frederick C. Miller trophies as Woman Athlete of the Year. Her rise from the streets of Harlem, where she had learned to play paddle tennis, to the top ranks of the previously "white only" world of tennis was an extraordinary one. She became a symbol to young black athletes who sought to achieve the same kind of success in white-dominated athletics, and as a result many became interested in the urban tennis programs sponsored by the various city-park services.

Davis Cup Play and Nationalistic Enthusiasm. There was considerable interest in Davis Cup play, in which national teams competed, as the Americans and Australians fought on the court to determine who had the best tennis players in the world. Much like the Brooklyn Dodgers of baseball, however, the American team year after year would reach the final round of play only to be soundly thrashed. In men's tennis during the 1950s no country could match Australia's talent. Furthermore, tennis enjoyed immense popularity down under, and thousand of rabid Australian tennis fans would turn out to watch their players run the Americans all over the court. In 1954 the Americans, headed by perennial Davis Cup stars Tony Trabert and Victor Seixas, finally ended Australia's four years of dominance and took the cup back with them to the United States. The Americans lost the cup eight months later, but the entire nation had received a taste of victory in finally having beaten the Aussies. The U.S. Davis Cup victory made for a new kind of tennis fan: at the 1958 U.S. doubles championship partisan fans lustily booed Aussie players and applauded their mistakes — a serious breach of tennis-fan protocol. For better or worse, the era of modern tennis had been ushered in.

Sources:
Allison Danzig and Peter Schwed, eds., *The Fireside Book of Tennis* (New York: Simon & Schuster, 1972);

John Feinstein, *Hard Courts* (New York: Villard Books, 1991).

HEADLINE MAKERS

ALTHEA GIBSON

1927-

TENNIS CHAMPION

UPI/BETTMANN

Superb Athlete. Born in Silver, South Carolina, in 1927, Althea Gibson became the dominant female athlete of the late 1950s in a sport well known for its custom of racial segregation. Tennis was not Gibson's first sport; instead, she shot pool, bowled, and played basketball. She even boxed a little.

Childhood in Harlem. During the Depression the Gibson family moved north to Harlem. When she was ten years old, Gibson became involved with the Police Athletic League (PAL) movement known as "play streets." Essentially, PAL was an attempt to help troubled children establish work habits they would use later in life. In 1940 in Harlem, PAL promoted paddleball. After three summers of paddleball competition Gibson was so good that the Cosmopolitan Tennis Club sponsored her to learn the game of tennis and proper social behavior.

Early Successes. In 1942 Gibson began winning tournaments sponsored by the American Tennis Association (ATA), the black counterpart to the United States Lawn Tennis Association (USLTA). In 1944 and 1945 Gibson won the ATA National Junior Championships. In 1946 Gibson was recognized by politically astute blacks as a player who could help break down institutionalized racism in the United States. Sponsored by Hubert Eaton and Walter Johnson and inspired by Sugar Ray Robinson, Gibson soon dominated every event on the ATA schedule. By the beginning of the 1950s she was ready to endure the hardship of breaking the color barrier in tennis.

Breaking the Color Barrier. Gibson had a powerful ally: four-time U.S. singles and doubles champion Alice Marble. The USLTA finally allowed Gibson to play in the 1950 Nationals when Marble intervened on her behalf. Gibson lost her first match of the tournament, but

the entrance had been made. Over the next several years Gibson rose in the USLTA rankings (ninth in 1952, seventh in 1953). After a year of touring the world, playing special events for the U.S. State Department, Gibson staged a full-scale assault on the tennis world in 1956. That year she won the French Open in both singles and doubles.

Tennis Dominance. Over the next two years Gibson was the dominant women's tennis player in the world. In 1957 and 1958 she won both Wimbledon and the U.S. Nationals. In 1958 she wrote a book about her life called *I Always Wanted to Be Somebody.*

Sources:
Tom Biracree, *Althea Gibson* (New York: Chelsea House, 1989);

Betty Millsaps Jones, *Wonder Women of Sports* (New York: Random House, 1981);

Pat Ross, ed., *Young and Female: Turning Points in the Lives of Eight American Women, Personal Accounts* (New York: Random House, 1972).

BEN HOGAN

1912-

GOLF CHAMPION

WIDE WORLD

The Greatest Golfer? It is impossible to certify the claim that Ben Hogan is the greatest golfer who ever lived. Certainly there have been others who have won more money and titles, others who have greater natural ability, and others who have more charisma. Yet none worked as hard, has overcome greater obstacles, or has been as dominant during his hey day as Ben Hogan.

Career in Jeopardy. In 1949, while driving to a golf appointment, Hogan's car was hit head on by a bus. Remarkably, Hogan lived, but he suffered fractures of his left collarbone, pelvis, left ankle, and a rib. Doctors were certain that Hogan would never be able to play world-class golf again; they questioned whether he would ever walk. Amazingly, less than a year and a half later, in great pain and his legs wrapped in bandages, Hogan again won the U.S. National Open.

His Greatest Year. In his career Hogan won over sixty tournaments, including the U.S. Open four times (1948, 1950, 1951, 1953), the Professional Golf Association (PGA) tournament twice (1946, 1948), the Masters twice (1951, 1953), and the British Open once (1953). The most incredible performance of Hogan's career, however, was in 1953, when he almost became the first golfer to win the "new" Grand Slam of golf. Hogan started out the year with victories in the Masters, U.S. Open, and British Open; and although he failed to win the PGA tournament, he established a mark that no golfer before or since has been able to approach. (It should be noted that in 1930 Bobby Jones won a grand slam of the U.S. and British Amateur and Open Tournaments; but it could easily be argued that Hogan faced much stiffer competition.)

The Perfect Swing. Hogan, weighing barely 135 pounds, needed a perfect swing to be able to compete with larger players. His practice sessions were legendary and he was one of the first great golfers to break down the golf swing systematically. After his playing career started to wane, Hogan turned to writing magazine articles and books about the mechanics of golf, some of which have become classics. Hogan also established himself as a maker of great golf clubs.

MICKEY MANTLE

1931-

BASEBALL PLAYER

Career Summary. A brief summary of Mickey Mantle's record would read something like this: New York Yankee outfielder who was one of the dominant power hitters of the 1950s and early 1960s. Blended a rare combination of speed and switch-hitting power. Won the American League Triple Crown in 1956, was three-time American League Most Valuable Player (1956, 1957, 1962), led the league in home runs four times, and played on seven World Series winning teams.

The Best. This summary, however, would not tell the whole story. The truth is that Mantle may have been, during the 1950s, better than any player in history. At this time Mantle was a far better performer than his great National League contemporary, Willie Mays.

Sabermetricians. Researchers who study baseball are known as sabermetricians. These researchers have more mathematical means available to compare performances among baseball players than in any other sport. By virtually every conceivable measure, Mantle's performances in

1956 and 1957 amount to the greatest back-to-back years in baseball history.

What a Season! In 1956 Mantle won the Triple Crown, leading the league with a .353 batting average, 130 runs batted in (RBIs), and 52 home runs. Even more impressive was Mantle's slugging percentage (measuring the base-production of his hits) of .705 (anything over .500 is considered excellent). Mantle would smash doubles, but he would also use his blinding speed to turn singles into doubles. In 1957 Mantle spent part of September in the hospital for shinsplints, but for a season played hurt, his .365 batting average, 94 RBIs, and 34 home runs are quite extraordinary.

What a Decade. Between 1955 and 1964 Mantle finished first or second in the race for Most Valuable Player six times. During his career the Yankees won more pennants and World Series than they did in the careers of any of the other great players — Joe DiMaggio, Lou Gehrig, or Babe Ruth. Mickey Mantle's most significant contribution to his team, however, was his leadership. On a great team this great player often played injured and in pain; in fact, Mantle's ability to play hurt is legendary. In a decade that saw some of the finest offensive players in baseball history have their best years — Willie Mays, Ted Williams, Ernie Banks, Roy Campanella, Don Newcombe, Stan Musial — Mickey Mantle outperformed them all.

Sources:
Mickey Mantle, *The Mick* (Garden City, N.Y.: Doubleday, 1985);
Gene Schoor, *Mickey Mantle of the Yankees* (New York: Putnam, 1959).

ROCKY MARCIANO

1923-1969

HEAVYWEIGHT BOXING CHAMPION

Holding the Throne. In 1951 Jersey Joe Walcott knocked out Ezzard Charles to become the oldest heavyweight boxing champion of the world. But the real story of the year was that he was simply holding onto the crown until Rocco F. ("Rocky") Marciano assumed his rightful place as king of boxing. After three years of obligatory tuneup fights, Marciano, then an old rookie at twenty-nine, sent the boxing world a message with his cold-blooded and efficient pummeling of Joe Louis in 1951. If Marciano could render the former-best helpless, it was clear that he was only marking time before he took Walcott out.

Championship. On 23 September 1952 Marciano got to meet Walcott, and knocked him out in the thirteenth round. On 15 May 1953, in his first title defense, a rematch, Marciano knocked out Walcott in the first round. For the next three years Marciano fought and won twice a year; only his 17 June 1954 victory over Charles was difficult — a fifteen-round unanimous decision. As if to show Charles the first fight was a fluke, Marciano fought a rematch just three months later; on 17 September 1954 he knocked out Charles in the eighth round.

Undefeated. Marciano's final fight was his third Yankee Stadium defense. He knocked out Archie Moore in the ninth round. The unofficial attendance through closed-circuit television across the great cities of North America was over four hundred thousand. After this fight he retired. By not going back into the ring, he became the only boxer in history ever to retire undefeated.

The Legend. Rocky Marciano may not rank in the top five boxers of all time in terms of skill, speed, or power, but he was tough enough to compensate, and his fans recognized his grit. A sports writer commented that if all the heavyweight champions of all time were locked together in a room, Marciano would be the one to walk out. His tragic death in a 1969 plane crash contributed to his legend.

Source:
Everett M. Skehan, *Rocky Marciano: The Biography of a First Son* (Boston: Houghton Mifflin, 1977).

WILLIE MAYS

1931-

BASEBALL PLAYER

The Rookie Year. When Willie Mays reported to the New York Giants in 1951 to play centerfield, it was his good fortune that there were two black outfielders, Monte Irvin and Hank Thompson, already on the team. The Giants were, along with the Brooklyn Dodgers, the only team really serious about desegregation. Perhaps because he felt relatively safe or because he had Irvin to mentor him, Mays's impact on the Giants was tremendous. His first and only hit in his first twenty-seven at bats was a home run that many claimed traveled six hundred feet; seven of his first ten hits were home runs. In Mays's rookie year the Giants made their remarkable comeback against the Dodgers; Mays was on deck when Bobby Thomson hit his famous home run, called "The shot heard 'round the world."

Brilliant Play. Mays's career was put on hold in 1952 when he went into the army. Without him the Giants fell to second in 1952 and fifth in 1953; when Mays returned in 1954, the Giants won the pennant again. In the eighth inning of game one of the 1954 World Series against Cleveland with the score tied, Mays made his famous back-to-the-plate catch of Vic Wertz's 440-yard blast with two men out. After the Giants won the World Series, Mays was featured on the cover of *Time* magazine. Mays was the first player to hit 30 home runs and steal 30

bases in the same season; he hit 660 home runs in his career. Mays was the first black captain of the Giants (1964) and the highest-paid player in the major leagues in 1963.

Enduring Racial Hatred. Mays was resented by many in society and some in baseball. He endured an unusually high number of "bean-balls" that appeared to be thrown with racial hatred in mind. He also posed the threat of undercutting Joe DiMaggio's reputation as the finest all-around player in the game and the reputation of his only serious rival among his contemporaries — Mickey Mantle. Mays's experience allowed him to counsel Hank Aaron in the mid 1970s as Aaron closed in, under the constant wave of death threats, on the home-run record of Babe Ruth. Perhaps it was Mays's good fortune never to have threatened white players' single-season or life-time records. On the way to just winning ball games, however, he worked his way into the top ten of almost every offensive list and he easily gained entrance into the Baseball Hall of Fame.

Sources:
Charles Einstein, *Willie's Time: A Memoir* (Philadelphia: Lippincott, 1979);
Willie Mays, *Say Hey: The Autobiography of Willie Mays* (New York: Simon & Schuster, 1988).

SUGAR RAY ROBINSON

1921-1989

BOXING CHAMPION

The Greatest Ever. Sugar Ray Robinson is said to be pound for pound the greatest boxer who ever lived. In the world of professional boxing, although hardly anyone can agree on anything, there is general agreement among those who know the sport that Sugar Ray Robinson was the greatest ever. His boxing record is not spotless. He lost nineteen times and had six draws. He was briefly suspended from boxing in 1947 when he failed to report a bribery attempt. He also had trouble holding onto his money outside the ring, blowing most of his fortune several times.

A Hero. Yet Robinson dominated boxing for over twenty years, an eternity in a sport that rewards a young man's legs and reflexes. He started his professional career in 1940 and ended it in 1965. During this quarter century Robinson rose in the black community to the status of Jesse Owens and Joe Louis; he was a genuine hero.

Struggle to the Top. Robinson was, in effect, denied the opportunity to fight for the title contention for over a decade. James Norris, the president of the International Boxing Club, prevented Robinson from a shot at the championship until Valentine's Day, 1951, when Robinson beat Jake LaMotta with a TKO in the thirteenth round to win the middleweight championship; but, over-confident and undertrained, he lost it to Randy Turpin four months later. In front of 61,370 fans at the Polo Grounds, Robinson regained the title from Turpin on 12 September 1951. The gate receipts of nearly eight hundred thousand dollars was a record for a nonheavyweight fight.

Pushing the Edge. Robinson defended his title until the summer of 1952, when he tried to move up a weight class and faced Joey Maxim for the light-heavyweight title on 25 June. On an oppressively hot night Robinson collapsed in his corner at the end of the thirteenth round and lost, even though he was decisively ahead on all scoring cards. Robinson decided to retire and enter show business, a career he pursued for almost three years without notable success, until he decided to return to boxing.

Comeback. In 1956, at the age of thirty-four, Sugar Ray Robinson beat Carl "Bobo" Olson to earn his third middleweight title; he lost it to Gene Fullmer on 2 January 1957 but then beat Fullmer in a rematch on 1 May 1957. Robinson thus became the first man ever to win a boxing title four times.

Financial Ruin. Because of his carelessness with money and his failure to pay income taxes, Robinson faced huge debts during most of the 1950s. In his career he earned close to $4 million, but he was still fighting in the 1960s, at considerable personal risk, in order to pay his debts. Despite the embarrassing last years of his boxing career, Robinson was known the world over for a rare combination of boxing strength, brains, and grace.

Sources:
Sam Andre and Nat Fleischer, *A Pictorial History of Boxing*, revised edition (Secaucus, N.J.: Citadel Press, 1987);

Ray Robinson, *Sugar Ray* (New York: Viking Press, 1970).

BILL RUSSELL

1934-

BASKETBALL PLAYER

A Collegiate Winner. Bill Russell came into the National Basketball Association (NBA) as a proven winner. He had played in just one losing game in his entire career at the University of San Francisco (USF). His team had won two National Collegiate Athletic Association (NCAA) championships in 1955 and 1956. After his sophomore year (his first as a varsity basketball player) at USF, the NCAA widened the foul lane from six to twelve feet. This rule change was widely assumed to be as a direct result of Russell's overwhelming rebounding skill: the narrow lane allowed him to control the boards completely. Russell also led the 1956 U.S. Olympic team to a gold medal in Melbourne.

Dominance in the NBA. Throughout his NBA career Russell dominated the game and pioneered advances in rebounding and defense. His Boston Celtics team won eleven championships in his thirteen years as a player, a basketball dynasty unmatched in American professional basketball. Yet Russell encountered resentment. He was perceived by many in the basketball world to be too cocky and arrogant — especially for a black man.

The Sport's Racist Elements. In 1958, even though he was the NBA's Most Valuable Player, Russell was not named to the All-NBA team by sportswriters. Russell denounced this insult as overt racism. Life in Boston was also difficult for Russell. He found Boston, a city of ethnic neighborhoods, utterly racist. Nonetheless, in 1966 Russell, while still a player, became the head coach of the Celtics — the first black head coach of a professional sports team since World War II.

His Memoirs. Russell wrote two books about his life: *Go Up for Glory* (1966) and *Second Wind: The Memoirs of an Opinionated Man* (1979). In both these books, Russell remembers what it was like when he first became a professional basketball player. The informal quota system with which he lived was "Put two black players in the game at home, put in three on the road, and when you have to win, put in five."

Source:
Miles Shapiro, *Bill Russell* (New York: Chelsea House Publishers, 1991).

PEOPLE IN THE NEWS

Henry ("Hank") Aaron (baseball) Played entire career for Braves (Milwaukee/Atlanta); National League Most Valuable Player in 1957; league leader in hitting, 1959.

Tenley Albright (Olympic sport) Two-time world ladies' figure-skating champion (1953, 1955); won Olympic silver medal in 1952 and gold medal in 1956.

Forrest ("Phog") Allen (basketball) One of the great college-basketball coaches, coaching for forty-eight years; his Kansas team won the National Collegiate Athletic Association (NCAA) championship in 1952.

Red Auerbach (basketball) Coach of the Boston Celtics (1950–1966); his Celtics teams won nine National Basketball Association (NBA) titles in ten years, including eight in a row (1959–1966); NBA Coach of the Year Award is named after him.

Ernie Banks (baseball) Hall of Fame second baseman who played entire NL career with the Chicago Cubs; NL MVP in 1958 and 1959.

Chuck Bednarik (football) Two-time All-American college player at University of Pennsylvania and seven-time All-Pro in National Football League (NFL); led Philadelphia Eagles to NFL title in 1959.

Bert Bell (football) NFL team owner and second commissioner (1946–1959) who oversaw the league's entrance into national television; his most significant contributions were to institute the television blackout policy that drew fans to NFL games; he handpicked Pete Rozelle to be his successor.

Patty Berg (golf) Associated Press Athlete of the Year in three different decades (1938, 1943, 1955); won fifty-seven professional golf titles and fifteen majors; helped found the Ladies Professional Golf Association (LPGA).

Yogi Berra (baseball) Hall of Fame catcher with the New York Yankees, played on ten World Series–winning teams, and was a three-time American League (AL) MVP (1951, 1954, 1955).

Jim Brown (football) Arguably the greatest fullback in football history; All-American at Syracuse University; eight-time rushing leader (including 1957–1961) and All-Pro with Cleveland Browns (1957–1963); three-time NFL MVP (1958).

Avery Brundage (Olympic sport) Leader of amateur and Olympic sport in America for over forty years; president of U.S. Olympic Committee (1929–1953) and International Olympic Committee (1952–1972); led Olympic movement through the cold war and into the world of television to make the games the most-watched sports events in history.

Dick Button (Olympic sport) Five-time world men's figure-skating champion (1948–1952) and two-time Olympic gold medalist (1948 and 1952).

Roy Campanella (baseball) First great black catcher; NL MVP three times (1951, 1953, 1955); played on five NL pennant winners and 1955 World Series Champion Brooklyn Dodgers.

Don Carter (bowling) Voted (1970) by his peers to be the greatest bowler of all time; was PBA Bowler of the Year six times (1953, 1954, 1957, 1958, 1960, and 1961) and led bowling to become the only televised sport that has always made a profit.

Florence Chadwick (Olympic sport) Dominated ocean distance swimming in the 1950s; set English Channel records three times — France to England (1950) and England to France (1951 and 1955).

A. B. Chandler (baseball) Second MLB commissioner from 1945 to 1951; supported Branch Rickey's decision to desegregate Brooklyn Dodgers (NL) in 1947; during his tenure he consistently supported the integration of MLB, and in 1951 the owners removed him from his position for his proplayer decisions.

Maureen ("Little Mo") Connolly (tennis) The dominant player in women's tennis in the beginning of the decade, Connolly's career was cut short in 1954 in a riding accident. In 1953, at the age of nineteen, became the first woman to win the Grand Slam of tennis (Wimbeldon, Australian, French, and U.S. Nationals); Associated Press Female Athlete of the Year in 1951, 1952, and 1953; won Wimbeldon and U.S. National in those three years.

Bob Cousy (basketball) Gifted sleight-of-hand passer who revolutionized the passing game in basketball; led the Boston Celtics to six NBA titles; led the league in assists eight times; made All-Star first team ten times (1952–1961); league MVP in 1957.

Leo Durocher (baseball) As manager of the New York Giants, won National League pennant (1951) and the World Series in 1954.

Weeb Ewbank (football) Coached the Baltimore Colts to NFL titles in 1958 and 1959.

Bob Feller (baseball) Hall of Fame member and one of the dominant fastball pitchers of the 1940s and 1950s in the AL with the Cleveland Indians; AL leader in wins (six times) and strikeouts (seven times); three no-hitters, twelve one-hitters, and 266 wins.

Ford Frick (baseball) Sportswriter and radio announcer who replaced A. B. Chandler as MLB commissioner in 1951 and served until 1965; during the 1950s oversaw MLB western migration and expansion from sixteen to twenty teams; also negotiated first significant national-television contracts.

Eddie Gaedel (baseball) Saint Louis Browns pinch-hitting midget whose career consisted of one publicity-stunt plate appearance (19 August 1951) at which he walked.

Althea Gibson (tennis) The first black tennis player of world stature; broke the color-line in virtually every tournament she entered; enjoyed a two-year peak in 1957 and 1958 when she won both Wimbeldon and U.S. National.

Frank Gifford (football) One of the first athlete television stars, Gifford had a remarkable career as a half-back for the New York Giants; NFL MVP in 1956; led Giants to three championship games; NFL All-Pro four times (1955, 1956, 1957, 1959); turned his talent for the game into a television-sportscasting career in 1958.

Tom Gola (basketball) One of the great forwards of the 1950s to lead college basketball back to respectability; four-time All-American at LaSalle; college Player of the Year in 1955; MVP in National Invitational Tournament (NIT) (1952) and NCAA tournament (1954); played for Philadelphia Warriors in NBA.

Otto Graham (football) Spectacular college and professional quarterback; won seven league titles in ten years with the Cleveland Browns; two-time NFL MVP (1953, 1955).

Harvey Haddix (baseball) NL pitcher who, on 26 May 1959, pitched twelve perfect innings for Pittsburgh vs. Milwaukee; lost the game 1–0 in the thirteenth inning.

George Halas (football) The single most important personality in NFL history; played for, coached, and owned the Chicago Bears during sixty-three years

with the team; as a coach won seven titles in three different decades; all-time career leader in wins, with 325.

Leon Hart (football) Heisman Trophy winner with Notre Dame (1949); played on three national collegiate championship teams; NFL All-Pro on both offense and defense in 1951; won three NFL championships with the Detroit Lions (1952, 1953, 1957).

Ben Hogan (golf) Golfing legend who between 1946 and 1953 won nine Grand Slam events and four PGA Player of the Year awards; won sixty-two times in PGA career; made a stirring comeback from a near-fatal car crash; the film *Follow the Sun* chronicles his life.

Paul Hornung (football) Known as the "golden boy"; as a halfback earned the 1956 Heisman Trophy at Notre Dame; ran the ball and placekicked for the Green Bay Packers and led the league three times in scoring.

Gordie Howe (ice hockey) One of the most talented and durable professional athletes in North American history; played thirty-two seasons in the National Hockey League (NHL) and World Hockey Association (WHA); won NHL most valuable player six times for Detroit Red Wings (four times in the 1950s); and once for Houston in WHA (1974); scored a record 801 goals in his career; only player to be teammate with sons (Marty and Mark from 1973–1980).

Hayes Jenkins (Olympic sport) Four-time world figure-skating champion (1953–1956); gold-medal winner at the 1956 Olympic Games.

Al Kaline (baseball) Hall of Fame outfielder who played his entire twenty-two-year AL career with Detroit Tigers; in the 1955 season, at age twenty, became the youngest Major League Baseball batting champ with a .340 average.

Don Larson (baseball) On 8 October 1956 pitched the only perfect game in World Series history for the New York Yankees (AL), beating Brooklyn 2–0.

Andrea Mead Lawrence (Olympic sport) Won two gold medals in Alpine skiing at the 1952 Olympic Games; first American athlete to win a medal of any kind in Alpine events.

Bobby Layne (football) Premier NFL quarterback in the early 1950s; won two league titles with Detroit Lions in 1952 and 1953; played college football for the University of Texas.

Rocky Marciano (boxing) The only undefeated heavyweight champion in professional boxing history; held the title from 1952 through 1956; career record was 49–0 with forty-three KOs; defended his title seven times.

Bob Mathias (Olympic sport) In 1948, at age seventeen, became the youngest Olympic gold-medal winner of the decathlon; won the gold medal again in the 1952 Games.

Pat McCormick (Olympic sport) Achieved a remarkable Olympic double-double, winning both women's platform and springboard diving gold medals at both 1952 and 1956 Games.

George Mikan (basketball) First great center of the NBA; led Minneapolis Lakers to five championships (1949–1954).

Willie Mosconi (pocket billiards) His remarkable fifty-year career reached its peak from 1941 to 1957 when he won fourteen world championships.

James Norris (boxing) President of the International Boxing Club (IBC) (1949–1958); the IBC was deemed unconstitutional by the U.S. Supreme Court in 1958 because it effectively violated antitrust laws and restricted boxers' ability to make a living.

Al Oerter (Olympic sport) The only Olympic athlete to win a gold medal in the same event four consecutive times; won his first gold medal in the discus throw in 1956.

Satchel Paige (baseball) One of the greatest pitchers in Negro League baseball; entered Major League Baseball at age forty-two with the Cleveland Indians (AL) in 1948; pitched fifty-five no-hitters in Negro League career.

Arnold Palmer (golf) The first great golfer of the television era; broke through to fame in 1959 and dominated PGA golf for the next decade.

Floyd Patterson (boxing) In 1952 won the Olympic gold medal in the middleweight division; became the world heavyweight champion in 1956 and held the crown until 1959; later became the first boxer to regain the heavyweight title in 1960; professional career record was 55–8–1 with forty KOs.

Bob Pettit (basketball) The dominant scoring forward of the Saint Louis Hawks in the early NBA; won league MVP twice (1956, 1959); All-NBA first team ten times (1955–1964); first NBA player to score twenty thousand points.

Bob Richards (Olympic sport) Only man to win the gold medal in the pole vault in the Olympic Games twice (1952, 1956).

Eddie Robinson (football) The winningest coach in college-football history; has directed the Grambling Tigers (Division I-AA) since 1942; his teams have won eight national black-college titles.

Jackie Robinson (baseball) First black to play in modern MLB with Brooklyn Dodgers in 1947; batted more than .300 for 1949–1954; retired after 1956 season.

Sam Snead (golf) Won more golf tournaments on the PGA Tour (eighty-four) than any other man; tri-

umphed in seven Grand Slam events; PGA Player of the Year in 1949.

Warren Spahn (baseball) MLB leader in career wins for left-handed pitcher (363); pitched for Milwaukee Braves (NL); won twenty games in thirteen seasons including 1950, 1951, 1953, 1954, and 1956–1961; led NL in wins eight times and won Cy Young Award in 1957.

Bobby Thomson (baseball) Hitter of the "Shot Heard Round the World" on 3 October 1951 that won the NL play-off and the pennant for the New York Giants; with the Dodgers ahead 4–2, one out in the bottom of the ninth inning, Ralph Branca made a 1–1 pitch to Thompson, who lined his three-run homer to left field; the homer climaxed one of the greatest comebacks in Major League Baseball history for the Giants, who trailed the Dodgers by thirteen and a half games on 11 August.

Y. A. Tittle (football) One of the dominant NFL quarterbacks of the decade; was the league MVP in 1957 for San Francisco 49ers.

Norm Van Brocklin (football) NFL quarterback who directed his teams to two NFL titles (Los Angeles Rams in 1951 and Philadelphia Eagles in 1960); led league in passing three times.

Bill Veeck (football) Owner of three MLB franchises, Cleveland, Saint Louis, and Chicago, from 1946 to 1980; perhaps the greatest innovator of the marketing of spectator sports; introduced ballpark giveaways and exploding scoreboards; earned the ire of other owners when he made a "travesty" of the game by sending midget Eddie Gaedel in as a pinch hitter for the Saint Louis Browns in 1951.

Doak Walker (football) Heisman Trophy winner for Southern Methodist University (as a junior) in 1948; played halfback on the Detroit Lions team that won NFL championships in 1952 and 1953.

Bud Wilkinson (football) During his tenure as head coach of Oklahoma, Wilkinson's teams had winning streaks of thirty-one games (1948–1950) and the NCAA record forty-seven games (1953–1957); during the decade Oklahoma won three national titles, in 1950, 1955 and 1956, and won four Orange and two Sugar Bowls.

Ted Williams (baseball) Hall of Fame outfielder for Boston Red Sox (AL) for nineteen years; considered by many to be the best hitter of a baseball in history; perhaps his greatest achievement was leading the AL in hitting with a .388 average in 1957 when he was thirty-nine years old.

Mildred ("Babe") Zaharias (golf) Voted the greatest female athlete of the half-century by the Associated Press; won three medals in track and field in the 1932 Olympics; helped found the LPGA in 1949; won ten major tournaments and fifty-five overall.

AWARDS

1950

Major League Baseball World Series — New York Yankees (American League), 4 vs. Philadelphia Phillies (National League), 0

National Football League Championship — Cleveland Browns, 30 vs. Los Angeles Rams, 28

Heisman Trophy, Collegiate Football — Vic Janowicz (Ohio State)

National Basketball Association Championship — Minneapolis Lakers, 4 vs. Syracuse Nationals, 3

National Collegiate Athletic Association Basketball — City College of New York, 71 vs. Bradley, 68

National Hockey League Stanley Cup — Detroit Red Wings, 4 vs. New York Rangers, 3

Kentucky Derby, Horse Racing — Middleground (Bill Boland, jockey)

Masters Golf Tournament — Jimmy Demaret

U.S. National Tennis Tournament — Art Larsen; Margaret du Pont

Athletes of the Year — Jim Kostanty (Baseball) — Mildred ("Babe") Didrikson Zaharias (Golf)

1951

Major League Baseball World Series — New York Yankees (American League), 4 vs. New York Giants (National League), 2

National Football League Championship — Los Angeles Rams, 24 vs. Cleveland Browns, 17

Heisman Trophy, Collegiate Football — Dick Kazmaier (Princeton)

National Basketball Association Championship — Rochester Royals, 4 vs. New York Knicks, 3

National Collegiate Athletic Association Basketball — Kentucky, 68 vs. Kansas State, 58

National Hockey League Stanley Cup — Toronto Maple Leafs, 4 vs. Montreal Canadiens, 1

Kentucky Derby, Horse Racing — Country Turf (Conn McCreary, jockey)

Masters Golf Tournament — Ben Hogan

U.S. National Tennis Tournament — Frank Sedgman; Maureen Connolly

Athletes of the Year — Dick Kazmaier (Football) — Maureen Connolly (Tennis)

1952

Major League Baseball World Series — New York Yankees (American League), 4 vs. Brooklyn Dodgers (National League), 3

National Football League Championship — Detroit Lions, 17 vs. Cleveland Browns, 7

Heisman Trophy, Collegiate Football — Billy Vessels (Oklahoma)

National Basketball Association Championship — Minneapolis Lakers, 4 vs. New York Knicks, 3

National Collegiate Athletic Association Basketball — Kansas, 80 vs. St. John, 63

National Hockey League Stanley Cup — Detroit Red Wings, 4 vs. Montreal Canadiens, 0

Kentucky Derby, Horse Racing — Hill Gail (Eddie Arcaro, jockey)

Masters Golf Tournament — Sam Snead

U.S. National Tennis Tournament — Frank Sedgman; Maureen Connolly

Athletes of the Year — Bob Mathias (Track and Field) — Maureen Connolly (Tennis)

1953

Major League Baseball World Series — New York Yankees (American League), 4 vs. Brooklyn Dodgers (National League), 2

National Football League Championship — Detroit Lions, 17 vs. Cleveland Browns, 16

Heisman Trophy, Collegiate Football — John Lattner (Notre Dame)

National Basketball Association Championship — Minneapolis Lakers, 4 vs. New York Knicks, 1

National Collegiate Athletic Association Basketball — Indiana, 69 vs. Kansas, 68

National Hockey League Stanley Cup — Montreal Canadiens, 4 vs. Boston Bruins, 1

Kentucky Derby, Horse Racing — Dark Star (Henry Moreno, jockey)

Masters Golf Tournament — Ben Hogan

U.S. National Tennis Tournament — Tony Trabert; Maureen Connolly

Athletes of the Year — Ben Hogan (Golf) — Maureen Connolly (Tennis)

1954

Major League Baseball World Series — New York Giants (National League), 4 vs. Cleveland Indians (American League), 0

National Football League Championship — Cleveland Browns, 46 vs. Detroit Lions, 10

Heisman Trophy, Collegiate Football — Alan Ameche (Wisconsin)

National Basketball Association Championship — Minneapolis Lakers, 4 vs. Syracuse Nationals, 3

National Collegiate Athletic Association Basketball — LaSalle, 92 vs. Bradley, 76

National Hockey League Stanley Cup — Detroit Red Wings, 4 vs. Montreal Canadiens, 3

Kentucky Derby, Horse Racing — Determine (Ray York, jockey)

Masters Golf Tournament — Sam Snead

U.S. National Tennis Tournament — Vic Seixus; Doris Hart

Athletes of the Year — Willie Mays (Baseball) — Mildred ("Babe") Didrickson Zaharias (Golf)

1955

Major League Baseball World Series — Brooklyn Dodgers (National League), 4 vs. New York Yankees (American League), 3

National Football League Championship — Cleveland Browns, 28 vs. Los Angeles Rams, 14

Heisman Trophy, Collegiate Football — Howard ("Hopalong") Cassidy (Ohio State)

National Basketball Association Championship — Syracuse Nationals, 4 vs. Fort Wayne Zollner Pistons, 3

National Collegiate Athletic Association Basketball — San Francisco, 77 vs. LaSalle, 63

National Hockey League Stanley Cup — Detroit Red Wings, 4 vs. Montreal Canadiens, 3

Kentucky Derby, Horse Racing — Swaps (Willie Shoemaker, jockey)

Masters Golf Tournament — Cary Middlecoff

U.S. National Tennis Tournament — Tony Trabert; Louise Brough

Athletes of the Year — Howard Cassidy (Football) — Patty Berg (Golf)

1956

Major League Baseball World Series — New York Yankees (American League), 4 vs. Brooklyn Dodgers (National League), 3

National Football League Championship — New York Giants, 47 vs. Chicago Bears, 7

Heisman Trophy, Collegiate Football — Paul Horning (Notre Dame)

National Basketball Association Championship — Philadelphia Warriors, 4 vs. Fort Wayne Pistons, 1

National Collegiate Athletic Association Basketball — San Francisco, 83 vs. Iowa, 71

National Hockey League Stanley Cup — Montreal Canadiens, 4 vs. Detroit Red Wings, 1

Kentucky Derby, Horse Racing — Needles (Dave Erb, jockey)

Masters Golf Tournament — Jack Burke

U.S. National Tennis Tournament — Ken Rosewall; Shirley Fry

Athletes of the Year — Mickey Mantle (Baseball) — Pat McCormick (Diving)

1957

Major League Baseball World Series — Milwaukee Braves (National League), 4 vs. New York Yankees (American League), 3

National Football League Championship — Detroit Lions, 59 vs. Cleveland Browns, 14

Heisman Trophy, Collegiate Football — John Crowe (Texas A&M)

National Basketball Association Championship — Boston Celtics, 4 vs. Saint Louis Hawks, 3

National Collegiate Athletic Association Basketball — North Carolina, 54 vs. Kansas, 53

National Hockey League Stanley Cup — Montreal Canadiens, 4 vs. Boston Bruins, 1

Kentucky Derby, Horse Racing — Iron Liege (Bill Hartack, jockey)

Masters Golf Tournament — Doug Ford

U.S. National Tennis Tournament — Malcolm Anderson; Althea Gibson

Athletes of the Year — Ted Williams (Baseball) — Althea Gibson (Tennis)

1958

Major League Baseball World Series — New York Yankees (American League), 4 vs. Milwaukee Braves (National League), 3

National Football League Championship — Baltimore Colts, 23 vs. New York Giants, 17

Heisman Trophy, Collegiate Football — Pete Dawkins (Army)

National Basketball Association Championship — Saint Louis Hawks, 4 vs. Boston Celtics, 2

National Collegiate Athletic Association Basketball — Kentucky, 84 vs. Seattle, 72

National Hockey League Stanley Cup — Montreal Canadiens, 4 vs. Boston Bruins, 2

Kentucky Derby, Horse Racing — Tim Tam (Ismael Valenzuela, jockey)

Masters Golf Tournament — Arnold Palmer

U.S. National Tennis Tournament — Ashley Cooper; Althea Gibson

Athletes of the Year — Herb Elliot (Track and Field) — Althea Gibson (Tennis)

1959

Major League Baseball World Series — Los Angeles Dodgers (National League), 4 vs. Chicago White Sox (American League), 2

National Football League Championship — Baltimore Colts, 31 vs. New York Giants, 16

Heisman Trophy, Collegiate Football — Billy Cannon (Louisiana State University)

National Basketball Association Championship — Boston Celtics, 4 vs. Minneapolis Lakers, 0

National Collegiate Athletic Association Basketball — California, 71 vs. West Virginia, 70

National Hockey League Stanley Cup — Montreal Canadiens, 4 vs. Toronto Maple Leafs, 1

Kentucky Derby, Horse Racing — Tommy Lee (Willie Shoemaker, jockey)

Masters Golf Tournament — Art Wall

U.S. National Tennis Tournament — Alejandro Olmedo; Maria Bueno

Athletes of the Year — Ingemar Johansson (Boxing) — Maria Bueno (Tennis)

DEARTHS

Grover Cleveland Alexander, 63, Major League Baseball Hall of Fame pitcher, won thirty games for three straight years, 4 November 1950.

Max Baer, 50, won heavyweight championship of the world in 1934 from Primo Carnera, 21 November 1959.

Bert Bell, 65, commissioner of NFL from 1946 to 1959, largely responsible for reshaping professional football to the medium of television, 11 October 1959.

Edward Trowbridge Collins, 63, Major League Baseball Hall of Fame second baseman, lifetime batting average of .333, coach, manager, general manager, vice-president of the Boston Red Sox, 25 March 1951.

Hugh Duffy, 87, won first-ever Major League Baseball Triple Crown (.438 batting average, eighteen home

runs), his .438 batting average is the highest in baseball history, 19 October 1954.

Clark Calvin Griffith, 85, Major League Baseball player, union leader, general manager and owner of the Washington Senators (1921–1955), largely responsible for the formation of the American League, 27 October 1955.

James Jeffries, 77, heavyweight champion of the world (1899–1905), only loss to Jack Johnson, 3 March 1953.

Napoleon Lajoie, 83, Major League Baseball Hall of Famer (1937), player-manager for Cleveland Indians, considered the greatest fielding second baseman, 7 February 1959.

Connie Mack, 93, managed the Philadelphia Athletics (1901–1950), played Major League Baseball for ten years, inducted into the Major League Baseball Hall of Fame, considered one of the greatest tacticians, 8 February 1956.

Mel Ott, 49, Baseball Hall of Fame home-run hitter (511), played twenty-two seasons for the New York Giants, 21 November 1958.

Tris Speaker, 70, one of the best center fielders in baseball history, Hall of Famer with a lifetime .344 batting average, 8 December 1958.

Jim Thorpe, 64, native American, considered by many to be the greatest all-around athlete, gained fame in college football, won pentathlon and decathlon in 1912 Stockholm Olympics, played Major League Baseball, played in National Football League, 28 March 1953.

Bill Tilden, 60, considered the greatest male tennis player of the first half of the century, won U.S. National seven times, one of the first great tennis professionals, 5 June 1953.

Bill Vukovich, 36, the winner of 1953 and 1954 Indianapolis 500, died in an accident in the Memorial Day race, 30 May 1955.

Honus Wagner, 80, a member of the first group of inductees to the Baseball Hall of Fame in 1936, 6 December 1955.

Glen ("Pop") Warner, 83, legendary football coach responsible for many innovations that influenced the development of the modern game, lent his name to the largest youth-football league in America, 7 September 1954.

Denton True ("Cy") Young, 88, considered baseball's greatest pitcher, established record for victories (511), baseball's yearly award for the finest performance by a pitcher is named for him, 4 November 1955.

Mildred ("Babe") Didrickson Zaharias, 42, considered the greatest female athlete of all time, won two gold medals (80-meter hurdles, javelin) at the 1932 Los Angeles Olympics, All-American basketball star, and cofounder and player in the LPGA, 27 September 1956.

PUBLICATIONS

Ethan Allen, *Winning Baseball* (New York: Ronals, 1956);

Lee Allen, *The Hot Stove League* (New York: Barnes, 1955);

Mel Allen, *It Takes Heart* (New York: Harper, 1959);

Tommy Armour, *A Round of Golf with Tommy Armour* (New York: Simon & Schuster, 1959);

Armour, *How to Play Your Best Golf All the Time* (New York: Simon & Schuster, 1953);

Edward Barrow with James M. Kahn, *My 50 Years in Baseball* (New York: Coward-McCann, 1951);

C. W. Caldwell, *Modern Football for the Spectator* (Philadelphia: Lippincott, 1953);

Bob Cousy, *Basketball Is My Life* (Englewood Cliffs, N.J.: Prentice-Hall, 1958);

Parke Cummings, *American Tennis: The Story of a Game and Its People* (Boston: Little, Brown, 1957);

Arthur Daley, *Times at Bat: A Half Century of Baseball* (New York: Random House, 1950);

Everett Sterling Dean, *Progressive Basketball: Philosophy and Methods* (New York: Prentice-Hall, 1950);

Jerome H. (Dizzy) Dean, *Dizzy Baseball: A Gay and Amusing Glossary of Baseball Terms Used by Radio Broadcasters, with Explanations to Aid the Uninitiated* (New York: Greenberg, 1952);

Joe DiMaggio, *Lucky to be a Yankee* (New York: Grosset & Dunlap, 1951);

Jaroslav Drobney, *Champion in Exile: The Autobiography of Jaroslav Drobney* (London: Sportsman's Book Club, 1957);

James T. Farrell, *My Baseball Diary: A Famed American Author Recalls the Wonderful World of Baseball, Yesterday and Today* (New York: A. S. Barnes, 1957);

Buzz Fazio, *Bowling to Win* (New York: Grosset & Dunlap, 1955);

Althea Gibson, *I Always Wanted to Be Somebody* (New York: Harper, 1958);

Hy Gittlitz, *Don't Kill the Umpire* (New York: Grosby, 1957);

Louis Golding, *The Bare-Knuckle Breed* (New York: A.S. Barnes, 1954);

Frank Graham, *The New York Giants: An Informal History* (New York: Putnam, 1952);

Otto Graham, *Otto Graham—"T" Quarterback* (New York: Pultall, 1953);

Milton Gross, *Eighteen Holes in My Head* (New York: McGraw-Hill, 1959);

Herman Hickman, *The Herman Hickman Reader* (New York: Simon & Schuster, 1953);

James M. Kahn, *The Umpire Story* (Putnam, 1953);

Jack Kieran, *The Story of the Olympic Games, 776 B.C.– 1956 A.D.* (Philadelphia: Lippincott, 1951);

John Lardner, *White Hopes and Other Tigers* (Philadelphia: Lippincott, 1951);

Abbott Joseph Liebling, *The Sweet Science* (New York: viking, 1956);

Arthur Mann, *Branch Rickey: American in Action* (Boston: Houghton Mifflin, 1957);

Thomas Meany, *Mostly Baseball* (New York: A. S. Barnes, 1958);

Edwin Pope, *Football's Greatest Coaches* (Atlanta: Tupper & Love, 1955);

Harold Uriel Ribalom, *The World's Greatest Boxing Stories* (New York: Twayne, 1952);

Grantland Rice, *The Tumult and the Shouting: My Life in Sport* (New York: Barnes, 1954);

Rube Samuelson, *The Rose Bowl Game* (Garden City, N.Y.: Doubleday, 1951);

Fred Schwed, *How To Watch a Baseball Game,* drawings by Leo Hershfield (New York: Harper, 1957);

Red Smith, *Out of the Red* (New York: Knopf, 1950);

Smith, *Views of Sport* (New York: Knopf, 1954);

Alexander Weyand, *The Olympic Pageant* (New York: Macmillan, 1952);

Mildred Babe Zaharias with Harry Paxton, *This Life I've Led: My Autobiography* (New York: A. S. Barnes, 1955);

Baseball Digest, periodical;

Bowling Magazine, periodical;

Football News, periodical;

Golf, periodical founded in 1959;

Golf Digest, periodical founded in 1950;

Ring, periodical;

Sport, periodical;

Sporting News, periodical;

Sports Illustrated, periodical founded in 1954.

GENERAL REFERENCES

GENERAL

John Brooks, *The Great Leap: The Past Twenty-five Years in America* (New York: Harper & Row, 1966);

Paul Allen Carter, *Another Part of the Fifties* (New York: Columbia University Press, 1983);

Chronicle of the 20th Century (Mount Kisco, N.Y.: Chronicle Publications, 1987);

Collier's Encyclopedia Yearbook (New York: Crowell-Collier, 1950–1959);

Current Biography Yearbook (New York: Wilson, [various years]);

John Patrick Diggins, *The Proud Decades* (New York: Norton, 1988);

John W. Dodds, *Everyday Life in Twentieth Century America* (New York: Putnam, 1965);

Jane Duden, *1950s* (New York: Crestwood House, 1989);

David Halberstam, *The Fifties* (New York: Villard Books, 1993);

Jeffrey Peter Hart, *When the Going Was Good: American Life in the Fifties* (New York: Crown, 1982);

Brett Harvey, *The Fifties: A Women's Oral History* (New York: HarperCollins, 1993);

Paul Johnson, *Modern Times: From the Twenties to the Nineties,* revised edition (New York: HarperCollins, 1991);

Peter Lewis, *The Fifties* (New York: Lippincott, 1978);

Gerald McConnell, *Thirty Years of Award Winners* (New York: Hastings House, 1981);

Jeffrey Merritt, *Day by Day: The Fifties* (New York: Facts on File, 1979);

Douglas T. Miller and Marion Nowak, *The Fifties: The Way We Really Were* (Garden City, N. J.: Doubleday, 1977);

John Montgomery, *The Fifties* (London: George Allen & Unwin, 1966);

J. Ronald Oakley, *God's Country: America in the Fifties* (New York: Dembner Books, 1986);

Michael Downey Rice, *Prentice-Hall Dictionary of Business, Finance, and Law* (Englewood Cliffs, N. J.: Prentice-Hall, 1983);

This Fabulous Century, 1950–1960 (Alexandria, Va.: Time-Life Books, 1970);

Time Lines on File (New York: Facts on File, 1988);

James Trager, *The People's Chronology* (New York: Holt, Rinehart & Winston, 1979);

Dan Wakefield, *New York in the Fifties* (Boston: Houghton Mifflin/Seymour Lawrence, 1992);

Claire Walter, *Winners: The Blue Ribbon Encyclopedia of Awards* (New York: Facts on File, 1982);

Leigh Carol Yuster and others, eds., *Ulrich's International Periodicals Directory: A Classified Guide to Current Periodicals, Foreign and Domestic, 1986–1987,* twenty-fifth edition, volume 2 (New York & London: R.R. Bowker, 1986).

ARTS

Liz-Anne Bawden, *The Oxford Companion to Film* (New York: Oxford University Press, 1976);

Carl Belz, *The Story of Rock,* second edition (New York: Oxford University Press, 1972);

Gerald Bordman, *The Oxford Companion to the American Theatre* (New York: Oxford University Press, 1984);

Elston Brooks, *I've Heard Those Songs Before, Volume II: The Weekly Top Ten Hits of the Last Six Decades* (Fort Worth, Tex.: The Summit Group, 1991);

Ann Charters, ed., *Dictionary of Literary Biography 16: The Beats: Literary Bohemians in Postwar America* (Detroit: Bruccoli Clark Layman/Gale Research, 1983);

Samuel B. Charters, *The Bluesmen,* (New York: Oak, 1967);

Jim Curtis, *Rock Eras: Interpretations of Music and Society, 1954-1984* (Bowling Green, Ohio: Bowling Green University Popular Press, 1987);

Thadious M. Davis and Trudier Harris, ed., *Dictionary of Literary Biography 33: Afro-American Fiction Writers*

After 1955 (Detroit: Bruccoli Clark Layman/Gale Research, 1984);

Davis and Harris, ed., *Dictionary of Literary Biography 38: Afro-American Writers After 1955: Dramatists and Prose Writers* (Detroit: Bruccoli Clark Layman/Gale Research, 1985);

Martin Duberman, *Black Mountain: An Exploration in Community* (New York: Dutton, 1972);

J. W. Ehrlich, ed., *Howl of the Censor* (San Carlos, Cal.: Nourse Publishing, 1961);

Marc Eliot, *Rockonomics: The Money Behind the Music* (New York: Franklin Watts, 1989);

Philip H. Ennis, *The Seventh Stream: The Emergence of Rock'n'roll in American Popular Music* (Hanover, U.K.: Wesleyan University Press, 1992);

A. G. S. Enser, *Filmed Books and Plays, 1928–1983* (Aldershot, U.K.: Gower, 1985);

David Ewen, *History of Popular Music* (New York: Barnes & Noble, 1961);

Leonard Feather, *The Book of Jazz: A Guide to the Entire Field* (New York: Horizon, 1965);

Leslie Fiedler, *An End To Innocence* (Boston: Beacon, 1955);

Joseph J. Fucini and Susan Fucini, *Entrepreneurs: The Men and Women Behind Famous Brand Names and How They Made It* (Boston: G.K. Hall, 1985);

Harry F. Gaugh, *Willem de Kooning* (New York: Abbeville Press, 1983);

Louis D. Gianetti, *Understanding Movies* (Englewood Cliffs, N. J.: Prentice-Hall, 1987);

Barry K. Grant, ed., *Film Genre: Theory and Criticism* (Metuchen, N. J.: Scarecrow Press, 1977);

Jeff Greenfield, *Television: The First Fifty Years* (New York: Abrams, 1977);

Donald J. Greiner, ed., *Dictionary of Literary Biography 5: American Poets Since World War II*, 2 volumes (Detroit: Bruccoli Clark Layman/Gale Research, 1980);

Serge Guilbaut, *How New York Stole the Idea of Modern Art: Abstract Expressionism, Freedom, and the Cold War*, translated by Arthur Goldhammer (Chicago: University of Chicago Press, 1983);

Allen Guttman, *From Ritual to Record* (New York: Columbia University Press, 1978);

Mary Emma Harris, *The Arts at Black Mountain College* (Cambridge, Mass.: MIT Press, 1987);

Trudier Harris, ed., *Dictionary of Literary Biography 76: Afro-American Writers, 1940–1955* (Detroit: Bruccoli Clark Layman/Gale Research, 1988);

Jeffrey Helterman and Richard Layman, eds., *Dictionary of Literary Biography 2: American Novelists Since World War II* (Detroit: Bruccoli Clark Layman/Gale Research, 1978);

Robert Carleton Hobbs and Gail Levin, *Abstract Expressionism: The Formative Years* (Ithaca, N.Y. and New York: Herbert F. Johnson Museum of Art and Whitney Museum of American Art, 1978);

Penelope Houston, *The Emergence of Film Art: The Evolution and Development of the Motion Picture as an Art, from 1900 to the Present* (New York: Norton, 1979);

Frederick R. Karl, *American Fictions, 1940–1980: A Comprehensive History and Critical Evaluation* (New York: Harper & Row, 1983);

Alfred Kazin, *Bright Book of Life*, (Boston: Little, Brown, 1973);

James E. Kibler, Jr., ed., *Dictionary of Literary Biography 6: American Novelists Since World War II*, Second Series. (Detroit: Bruccoli Clark Layman/Gale Research, 1980);

Lawrence O. Koch, *Yardbird Suite: A Compendium of the Music and Life of Charlie Parker* (Bowling Green, Ohio: Bowling Green University Popular Press, 1988);

Mervin Lane, ed., *Black Mountain College: Sprouted Seeds: An Anthology of Personal Accounts* (Knoxville: University of Tennessee Press, 1990);

Mike Leadbitter and Neil Slaven, *Blues Records 1943–1966* (New York: Oak, 1968);

Ernest Lindgren, *The Art of the Film* (New York: Macmillan, 1963);

Herbert I. London, *Closing the Circle: A Cultural History of the Rock Revolution* (Chicago: Nelson-Hall, 1984);

John MacNicholas, ed., *Dictionary of Literary Biography 7: Twentieth-Century American Dramatists* (Detroit: Bruccoli Clark Layman/Gale Research, 1981);

Robert Myron and Abner Sundell, *Modern Art in America* (New York: Crowell-Collier, 1971);

Frank O'Hara, *Art Chronicles, 1954–1966* (New York: George Braziller, 1975);

Norman Podhoretz, *Doings and Undoings: the Fifties and After in American Writing* (New York: Farrar, Straus, 1964);

G. Howard Poteet, *Published Radio, Television, and Film Scripts* (Troy, N.Y.: Whitston, 1975);

Robert George Reisner, *Bird: The Legend of Charlie Parker* (New York: Da Capo Press, 1962);

Barney Rosset, ed., *Evergreen Review Reader, 1957–1967: A Ten-Year Anthology* (New York: Grove, 1968);

Paul Rotha, with Richard Griffith, *The Film Till Now* (London: Spring Books, 1967);

Irving Sablosky, *American Music* (Chicago: University of Chicago Press, 1969);

Irving Sandler, *The New York School: The Painters and Sculptors of the Fifties* (New York: Harper & Row, 1978);

Russell Sanjet, *From Print to Plastic: Publishing and Promoting America's Popular Music 1900–1980* (Brooklyn, N.Y.: Institute for Studies in American Music, 1983);

Eileen Southern, *The Music of Black Americans: A History*, second edition (New York: Norton, 1983);

Tony Tanner, *City of Words: American Fiction, 1950–1970* (New York: Harper & Row, 1971);

C. Robertson Trowbridge, *Yankee Publishing, Inc.: Fifty Years of Preserving New England's Culture While Extending Its Influence* (New York: Newcomen Society, 1986);

Joel Whitburn, *The Billboard Book of Top 40 Hits*, fifth edition (New York: Billboard Books, 1992).

BUSINESS AND THE ECONOMY

John Brooks, *The Autobiography of American Business* (Garden City, N.Y.: Doubleday, 1974);

Keith L. Bryant, Jr., and Henry C. Dethloff, *A History of American Business.* (Englewood Cliffs, N. J.: Prentice-Hall, 1983);

Bryant, ed., *Encyclopedia of American Business History and Biography Railroads in the Age of Regulation, 1900–1980* (Columbia, S.C.: Bruccoli Clark Layman / New York: Facts On File, 1988)

Edward F. Denison, *The Sources of Economic Growth in the United States and the Alternatives Before Us* (New York: Committee for Economic Development, 1962);

John M. Dobson, *A History of American Enterprise* (Englewood Cliffs, N. J.: Prentice-Hall, 1988);

John K. Galbraith, *Economic Development* (Cambridge, Mass.: Harvard University Press, 1964);

George Gilder, *The Spirit of Enterprise* (New York: Simon & Schuster, 1984);

Charles E. Gilland, Jr., ed., *Readings in Business Responsibility* (Braintree, Mass.: D. H. Mark Publishing, 1969);

James R. Green, *The World of the Worker: Labor in Twentieth-Century America* (New York: Hill & Wang, 1980);

William M. Leary, ed., *Encyclopedia of American Business History and Biography: The Airline Industry* (Bruccoli Clark Layman / New York: Facts On File, 1992)

Ann R. Markusen, *The Rise of the Gunbelt: The Military Remapping of Industrial America* (New York: Oxford University Press, 1991);

George S. May, ed., *Encyclopedia of American Business History and Biography: Banking and Finance, 1913–*

1989 (Bruccoli Clark Layman / New York: Facts On File, 1990)

Glenn Porter, ed., *Encyclopedia of American Economic History: Studies of the Principal Movements and Idea*, 3 volumes (New York: Scribners, 1980);

Joseph C. Pusateri, *A History of American Business* (Arlington Heights, Ill.: Harlan Davidson, 1984);

John B. Rae, *The American Automobile: A Brief History* (Chicago & London: University of Chicago Press, 1965);

Sidney Ratner, James H. Soltow, and Richard Sylla, *The Evolution of the American Economy* (New York: Basic Books, 1979);

Archie Robinson, *George Meany and His Times: A Biography* (New York: Simon & Schuster, 1981);

Graham Robinson, *Pictorial History of the Automobile* (New York: W. H. Smith, 1987);

Larry Schweikart, ed., *Encyclopedia of American Business History and Biography: Banking and Finance, 1913–1989* (Bruccoli Clark Layman / New York: Facts On File, 1990)

Bruce Seely, ed., *Encyclopedia of American Business History and Biography: Iron and Steel in the Twentieth Century* (Bruccoli Clark Layman / New York: Facts On File, 1993)

Herbert Alexander Simon, *The New Science of Management Decision* (New York: Harper & Row, 1960);

Athan G. Theoharis, *The Boss* (Philadelphia: Temple University Press, 1988).

EDUCATION

Philippe Aries, *Centuries of Childhood* (New York: Knopf, 1962);

Leslie Lee Chisholm, *The Work of the Modern High School* (New York: Macmillan, 1953);

Columbia University Teachers College, *Are Liberal Arts Colleges Becoming Professional Schools?* (New York: Columbia University Teachers College, 1958);

James B. Conant, *Citadel of Learning* (New Haven: Yale University Press, 1956);

Conant, *The Revolutionary Transformation of the American High School* (Cambridge, Mass.: Harvard University Press, 1959);

William Clyde De Vane, *The American University in the Twentieth Century* (Baton Rouge: Louisiana State University Press, 1957);

Robert M. Hutchins, *Conflict in Education in a Democratic Society* (New York: Harper, 1953);

Hutchins, *Some Observations on American Education* (Cambridge: Cambridge University Press, 1956);

Russell Kirk, *Academic Freedom* (Chicago: Regnery, 1955);

Mary Knapp and Herbert Knapp, *One Potato, Two Potato . . . The Secret Education of American Children* (New York: Norton, 1976);

John Francis Latimer, *What's Happened to Our High Schools* (Washington, D.C.: Public Affairs Press, 1958);

Gordon C. Lee, *An Introduction to Education in America* (New York: Holt, 1957);

Fritz Machlup, *The Production and Distribution of Knowledge in the United States* (Princeton, N. J.: Princeton University Press, 1962);

Iona Archibald Opie, *The Lore and Language of Schoolchildren* (Oxford: Clarendon Press, 1959);

Philip W. Perdew, *The American Secondary School in Action* (Boston: Allyn & Bacon, 1959);

Hyman G. Rickover, *Education and Freedom* (New York: Dutton, 1959);

Wilbur Schramm, J. Lyle, and I. de Sola Pool, *The People Look at Educational Television* (Stanford: Stanford University Press, 1963);

Schramm, ed., *The Eighth Art* (New York: Holt, Rinehart & Winston, 1962);

Jean Piaget, *Play, Dreams and Imitation in Childhood* (New York: Norton, 1962);

Joseph Turow, *Entertainment, Education, and the Hard Sell: Three Decades of Network Children's Television* (New York: Praeger, 1981).

FASHION

Bettina Ballard, *In My Fashion* (New York: McKay, 1960);

Michael Batterberry, *Mirror, Mirror: A Social History of Fashion* (New York: Holt, Rinehart & Winston, 1977);

Curtis F. Brown, *Star-Spangled Kitsch* (New York: Universe Books, 1975);

Garrett Davis Byrnes, *Fashion in Newspapers* (New York: Columbia University Press, 1951);

Jane Dorner, *Fashion in the Forties and Fifties* (London: Ian Allen, 1975);

The Encyclopedia of Fashion (New York: Abrams, 1986);

Beryl William Epstein, *Young Faces in Fashion* (Philadelphia: Lippincott, 1956);

Madge Garland, *The Changing Form of Fashion* (New York: Praeger, 1970);

Richard Horn, *Fifties Style: Then and Now* (New York: Beech Tree Books, 1985);

Georgina Howell, *In Vogue: Six Decades of Fashion* (London: Allen Lane, 1975);

Lesley Jackson, *The New Look: Design in the Fifties* (London: Thames & Hudson, 1991);

Udo Kultermann, *Architecture in the 20th Century* (New York: Reinhold, 1993);

Jane Mulvagh, *"Vogue" History of 20th Century Fashion* (New York: Viking, 1988);

John Peacock, *20th Century Fashion: the Complete Sourcebook* (New York: Thames & Hudson, 1993);

Mary Shaw Ryan, *Clothing: A Study in Human Behavior* (New York: Holt, Rinehart Winston, 1966);

Anne Stegemeyer, *Who's Who in Fashion* (New York: Fairchild, 1988);

Jane Trahey, *Harper's Bazaar: One Hundred Years of the American Female* (New York: Random House, 1967);

Randle Bond Truett, *The First Ladies in Fashion* (New York: Hastings House, 1954);

Elizabeth Wilson, *Adorned in Dreams: Fashion and Modernity* (Berkeley: University of California Press, 1987);

Tom Wolfe, *From Bauhaus to Our House* (New York: Farrar, Straus & Giroux, 1981);

Doreen Yarwood, *Fashion in the Western World, 1500–1990* (New York: Drama Book Publishing, 1992).

GOVERNMENT AND POLITICS

Michael Barone, *Our Country: The Shaping of America from Roosevelt to Reagan* (New York: Free Press, 1990);

Max Beloff, *The American Federal Government* (New York: Oxford University Press, 1959);

Ralph Barton Berry, *The Citizen Decides: A Guide to Responsible Thinking in Time of Crisis* (Bloomington: Indiana University Press, 1951);

Alexander M. Bickel, *Politics and the Warren Court* (New York: Harper & Row, 1965);

Daniel J. Boorstin, *The Genius of American Politics* Chicago: University of Chicago Press, 1953);

Chester Bowles, *American Politics in a Revolutionary World* (Cambridge, Mass.: Harvard University Press, 1956);

Taylor Branch, *Parting the Waters: America in the King Years, 1954–1963* (New York: Simon & Schuster, 1988);

Franklin L. Burdette, *Readings for Republicans* (New York: Oceana, 1960);

Noel Fairchild Busch, *Adlai E. Stevenson of Illinois: A Portrait* (New York: Farrar, Straus & Young, 1952);

Marquis William Childs, *Eisenhower for President? or, Who Will Get Us Out of the Mess We Are In?* (New York: Exposition Press, 1951);

Horace Coon, *Triumph of the Eggheads* (New York: Random House, 1955);

Elmer Holmes Davis, *But We Were Born Free* (Indianapolis: Bobbs-Merrill, 1954);

Robert J. Donovan, *Eisenhower: The Inside Story* (New York: Harper, 1956);

John Foster Dulles, *War or Peace* (New York: Macmillan, 1950);

Arthur Alphonse Ekich, *The Decline of American Liberalism* (New York: Longmans, Green, 1955);

Ralph Edward Flanders, *The American Century* (Cambridge, Mass.: Harvard University Press, 1950);

Benjamin Frankel, *The Cold War, 1945–1991: Leaders and Other Important Figures in the United States and Western Europe* (Detroit: Gale Research, 1992);

Milton Friedman and Rose Friedman, *Capitalism and Freedom* (Chicago: University of Chicago Press, 1962);

Lawrence H. Fuchs, *The Political Behaviour of American Jews* (Glencoe, Ill.: Free Press, 1956);

John Gunther, *Eisenhower, the Man and the Symbol* (New York: Harper, 1952);

Louis Harris, *Is There a Republican Majority? Political Trends, 1952–1956* (New York: Harper, 1954);

Gordon A. Harrison, *The Road to the Right: The Tradition and Hope of American Conservatism* (New York: Morrow, 1954);

Louis Hartz, *The Liberal Tradition in America* (New York: Harcourt, Brace & World, 1955);

Quincy Home and Arthur Schlesinger, *Guide to Politics, 1954* (New York: Dial, 1954);

Marinn Doris Irish, *The Politics of American Democracy* (Englewood Cliffs, N. J.: Prentice-Hall, 1959);

Walter Johnson, *How We Drafted Stevenson* (New York: Knopf, 1955);

James Keogh, *This Is Nixon* (New York: Putnam, 1956);

Russell Kirk, *The Conservative Mind* (Chicago: Regnery, 1953);

Arthur Larson, *A Republican Looks at His Party* (New York: Harper, 1956);

David Low, *The Fearful Fifties: A History of the Decade* (New York: Simon & Schuster, 1960);

Samuel Lubell, *Revolt of the Moderates* (New York: Harper, 1956);

John Lukacs, *Outgrowing Democracy: A History of the United. States in the Twentieth Century* (Garden City, N.Y.: Doubleday, 1984);

Lukacs, *Passing of the Modern Age* (New York: Harper & Row, 1970);

Robert MacNeil, *The People Machine: The Influence of Television on American Politics* (New York: Harper & Row, 1968);

Clarence Manion, *The Key to Peace: A Formula for the Perpetuation of Real Americanism* (Chicago: Heritage Foundation, 1950);

John Bartlow Martin, *Adlai Stevenson* (New York: Harper, 1952);

Martin Merson, *Private Diary of a Public Servant* (New York: Macmillan, 1955);

Raymond Moley, *How to Keep Our Liberty: A Program for Political Action* (New York: Knopf, 1952);

Judah Nadich, *Eisenhower and the Jews* (New York, 1953);

Steve Neal, *The Eisenhowers: Reluctant Dynasty* (Garden City, N.Y.: Doubleday, 1978);

Merlo John Pusey, *Eisenhower the President* (New York: Macmillan, 1956);

Benjamin F. Reading, *Democracy Can Succeed — How?* (New York: Parthenon Press, 1956);

Edward Reed, ed. *Readings for Democrats* (New York: Oceana, 1960);

Clinton Lawrence Rossiter, *Conservatism in America* (New York: Knopf, 1955);

Joseph H. Sharlitt, *Fatal Error: The Miscarriage of Justice That Sealed the Rosenbergs' Fate* (New York: Scribners, 1989);

Marty Snyder, *My Friend Ike* (New York: F. Fell, 1956);

Adlai E. Stevenson, *The New America* (New York: Harper, 1957);

Stevenson, *What I Think* (New York: Harper, 1956);

Ralph de Toledano, *Nixon* (New York: Holt, 1956);

Arthur Bernon Tourtellot, *An Anatomy of American Politics: Innovation versus Conservatism* (Indianapolis: Bobbs-Merrill, 1950);

Francis Graham Wilson, *The Case for Conservatism* (Seattle: University of Washington Press, 1951);

William Frank Zornow, *America at Mid-Century: the Truman Administration, the Eisenhower Administration* (Cleveland: H. Allen, 1959).

LAW

Howard Ball, *The Warren Court's Conceptions of Democracy* (Cranbury: Associated University Presses, 1971);

R. Stephen Browning, ed., *From Brown to Bradley* (Cincinnati: Jefferson Law Book, 1975);

John Denton Carter, *The Warren Court and the Constitution* (Gretna, U.K.: Pelican, 1973);

Mildred Houghton Comfort, *J. Edgar Hoover, Modern Knight Errant* (Minneapolis: Denison, 1959);

David P. Currie, *The Constitution in the Supreme Court: The Second Century* (Chicago: University of Chicago Press, 1990);

Warren Freedman, *Society on Trial: Current Court Decisions and Social Change* (Springfield, Ill.: Thomas, 1965);

Alvin H. Goldstein, *The Unquiet Death of Julius and Ethel Rosenberg* (New York: Hill, 1975);

William W. Keller, *The Liberals and J. Edgar Hoover* (Princeton, N. J.: Princeton University Press, 1989);

Robert G. McCloskey, *The Modern Supreme Court* (Cambridge, Mass.: Harvard University Press, 1972);

Kenneth O'Reilly, *Hoover and the Un-Americans* (Philadelphia: Temple University Press, 1983);

Richard Gid Powers, *G-Men: Hoover's FBI in American Popular Culture* (Carbondale: Southern Illinois University Press, 1983);

Ronald Radosh and Joyce Milton, *The Rosenberg File: A Search for Truth* (New York: Holt, Rinehart & Winston, 1983);

Arnold S. Rice, *The Warren Court, 1953–1969* (Millwood, N.Y.: Associated Faculty Press, 1987);

Richard H. Sayler, Barry B. Boyer, and Robert E. Gooding, Jr., eds., *The Warren Court* (New York: Chelsea House, 1969);

Bernard Schwartz, *The Law in America* (New York: American Heritage, 1974);

Schwartz, *Super Chief: Earl Warren and His Supreme Court* (New York: New York University Press, 1983);

Robert Shnayerson, *The Illustrated History of the Supreme Court of the United States* (New York: Abrams, 1986);

Burton B. Turkus, *Murder, Inc.* (New York: Da Capo Press, 1992);

G. Edward White, *Earl Warren* (New York: Oxford University Press, 1982);

Stephen J. Whitfield, *A Death in the Delta* (Baltimore: Johns Hopkins University Press, 1991);

LIFESTYLES AND SOCIAL TRENDS

Beth L. Bailey, *From Front Porch to Back Seat: Courtship in Twentieth-Century America* (Baltimore: Johns Hopkins University Press, 1988);

Roger G. Barker and Herbert F. Wright, *One Boy's Day: A Specific Record of Behavior* (New York: Harper, 1951);

Winni Breines, *Young, White, and Miserable: Growing Up Female in the Fifties* (Boston: Beacon, 1992);

Robert H. Bremner, et al., eds., *Children and Youth in America: A Documentary History*, 3 volumes (Cambridge, Mass.: Harvard University Press, 1970);

The Culture of Consumption: Critical Essays in American History, 1880–1980 (New York: Pantheon, 1983);

Benita Eisler, *Private Lives: Men and Women of the Fifties* (New York: Franklin Watts, 1986);

Jacques Ellul, *The Technological Society*, translated by John Wilkinson (New York: Knopf, 1964);

Betty Friedan, *The Feminine Mystique* (New York: Norton, 1963);

John K. Galbraith, *A Life in Our Times* (Boston: Houghton Mifflin, 1981);

Galbraith, *The New Industrial State* (Boston: Houghton Mifflin, 1967);

Park Dixon Goist, *From Main Street to State Street: Town, City, and Community in America* (Port Washington, N.Y.: Kennikat, 1977);

Kenneth T. Jackson, *Crabgrass Frontier: The Suburbanization of America* (New York: Oxford University Press, 1985);

Carl Kaufmann, *Man Incorporate: The Individual and His Work in an Organized Society* (Garden City, N.Y.: Doubleday, 1967);

William Kowinski, *The Malling of America: An Inside Look at the Great Consumer Paradise* (New York: Morrow, 1985);

Bart Landry, *The New Black Middle Class* (Berkeley: University of California Press, 1987);

John K. M. McCaffery, ed., *The American Dream: A Half-Century View from "American Magazine"* (Garden City, N.Y.: Doubleday, 1964);

Daniel O. Price, *Changing Characteristics of the Negro Population* (Washington, D.C.: GPO, 1969);

Milton Rokeach, *The Nature of Human Values* (New York: Free Press, 1973);

Ellen K. Rothman, *Hands and Hearts: A History of Courtship in America* (New York: Basic Books, 1984);

Mary P. Ryan, *Womanhood in America: From Colonial Times to the Present* (Danbury, Conn.: Franklin Watts, 1977);

Peter L. Skolnik, *Fads: America's Crazes, Fevers, and Fancies From the 1890s to the 1970s* (New York: Crowell, 1978);

Roger H. Smith, ed., *The American Reading Public: What It Reads, Why It Reads* (New York: R. R. Bowker, 1963);

Rick Tilman, *C. Wright Mills: A Native Radical and His American Intellectual Roots* (University Park: Pennsylvania State University Press, 1984);

William F. Whyte, *The Organization Man* (New York: Simon & Schuster, 1956).

100 Years of the Automobile (Los Angeles: Petersen, 1985);

MEDIA

Bart Andrews, *Lucy & Ricky & Fred & Ethel: The Story of "I Love Lucy"* (New York: Dutton, 1976);

Irwyn Applebaum, *The World According to Beaver* (New York: Bantam, 1984);

Association of National Advertisers, *Magazine Circulation and Rate Trends: 1940–1967* (New York: ANA, 1969);

Erik Barnouw, *Tube of Plenty*, second edition (New York: Oxford University Press, 1990);

Charles O. Bennett, *Facts Without Opinion: First Fifty Years of the Audit Bureau of Circulation* (Chicago: ABC, 1965);

A. William Bluem, *Documentary in American Television* (New York: Hastings House, 1965);

Tim Brooks, *The Complete Directory to Prime Time TV Stars: 1946–Present* (New York: Ballantine, 1987);

Robert Campbell, *The Golden Years of Broadcasting: A Celebration of the First 50 Years of Radio and TV on NBC* (New York: Scribners, 1972);

Harry Castleman and Walter J. Podrazik, *Watching TV: Four Decades of American Television* (New York: McGraw-Hill, 1982);

John Dunning, *Tune in Yesterday: The Ultimate Encyclopedia of Old-Time Radio 1925–1976* (Englewood Cliffs, N. J.: Prentice-Hall, 1976);

Walter B. Emery, *National and International Systems of Broadcasting: Their History, Operation, and Control* (East Lansing: Michigan State University Press, 1969);

Jay S. Harris, ed., *TV Guide: The First 25 Years* (New York: Simon & Schuster, 1978);

Laurence W. Lichty and Malachi Topping, *American Broadcasting: A Source Book on the History of Radio and Television* (New York: Hastings House, 1975);

J. Fred MacDonald, *Don't Touch That Dial: Radio Programming in American Life from 1920 to 1960* (Chicago: Hall, 1979);

MacDonald, *Television and the Red Menace* (New York: Praeger, 1985);

MacDonald, *Understanding Media: The Extensions of Man* (New York: McGraw-Hill, 1964);

Marshall McLuhan, *Understanding Media: The Extensions of Man* (New York: McGraw-Hill, 1964);

Alexander McNeil, *Total Television: A Comprehensive Guide to Programming from 1948–1980* (New York: Penguin, 1980);

James Robert Parish, *Actor's Television Credits: 1950–1972* (Metuchen, N. J.: Scarecrow Press, 1973);

Jeb Perry, *Universal Television: The Studio and Its Programs, 1950–1980* (Metuchen, N.J.: Scarecrow Press, 1983);

Harry J. Skornia, *Television and Society: An Inquest and Agenda for Improvement* (New York: McGraw-Hill, 1965);

Gary A. Steiner, *The People Look at Television* (New York: Knopf, 1963);

Christopher Sterling, ed., *Broadcasting and Mass Media: A Survey Bibliography* (Philadelphia: Temple University Press, 1974);

Sterling, ed., *The History of Broadcasting: Radio to Television*, 32 volumes (New York: New York Times/Arno, 1972);

Sterling, ed., *Telecommunications*, 34 books (New York: New York Times/Arno, 1974);

Vincent Terrace, *The Complete Encyclopedia of Television Programs: 1947–1979*, second edition (New York: Barnes, 1980);

Antoon J. van Zuilen, *The Life Cycle of Magazines: A Historical Study of the Decline and Fall of the General Interest Mass Audience Magazine in the United States During the Period 1946–1972* (Ulthoorn, The Netherlands: Graduate Press, 1977).

MEDICINE AND HEALTH

Leonard Berkowitz, *Aggression: A Psychological Analysis* (New York: McGraw-Hill, 1962);

The Cambridge World History of Human Disease (New York: Cambridge University Press, 1993);

Rick J. Carlson, *The End of Medicine* (New York: Wiley, 1975);

Frederic Fox Cartwright, *Disease and History* (New York: Crowell, 1972);

James H. Cassedy, *Medicine in America: A Short History* (Baltimore: Johns Hopkins University Press, 1991);

Faith Clark, ed., *Symposium III: The Changing Patterns of Consumption of Food*, International Congress of Food Science and Technology, Proceedings of the Congress Symposia, 1962, vol. 5 (New York: Gordon & Breach Science, 1967);

Companion Encyclopedia of the History of Medicine (London: Routledge, 1993);

Marjorie Curson, *Jonas Salk*, Englewood Cliffs, N. J.: Silver Burdett, 1990);

Bernard Dixon, *Beyond the Magic Bullet* (New York: Harper & Row, 1978);

John Patrick Dolan, *Health and Society: A Documentary History of Medicine* (New York: Seabury, 1978);

Martin Duke, *The Development of Medical Techniques and Treatments: From Leeches to Heart Surgery* (Madison, Conn.: International Universities Press, 1991);

Esmond R. Long, *A History of Pathology* (New York: Dover, 1965);

Albert S. Lyons, *Medicine: An Illustrated History* (New York: Abrams, 1978);

William A. Nolen, *A Surgeon's World* (Mew York: Random House, 1972);

Sherwin B. Nuland, *Doctors: the Biography of Medicine* (New York: Knopf, 1988);

John R. Paul, M.D., *A History of Poliomyelitis* (New Haven & London: Yale University Press, 1971);

Stanley Joel Reiser, *Medicine and the Reign of Technology* (New York: Cambridge University Press, 1978);

Rosemary Stevens, *American Medicine and the Public Interest* (New Haven: Yale University Press, 1971);

Elliot S. Valenstein, *Great and Desperate Cures* (New York: Basic Books, 1986).

RELIGION

Nancy T. Ammerman, *Bible Believers: Fundamentalists in the Modern World* (New Brunswick, N. J.: Rutgers University Press, 1987);

Michael Baignet and Richard Leigh, *The Dead Sea Scrolls Deception* (New York: Summit, 1991);

Bernham P. Beckwith, *The Decline of U.S. Religious Faith, 1912–1984* (Palo Alto, Cal: B. P. Beckwith, 1985);

Robert N. Bellah and Frederick E. Greenspahn, eds., *Uncivil Religion: Irreligious Hostility in America* (New York: Crossroads, 1987);

Charles C. Brown, *Niebuhr and His Age: Reinhold Niebuhr's Prophetic Role in the Twentieth Century* (Philadelphia: Trinity Press International, 1992);

Jackson W. Carroll, *Beyond Establishment: Protestant Identity in a Post-Protestant Age* (Louisville, Ky.: Westminster/John Knox, 1993);

Samuel McCrea Cavert, *The American Churches in the Ecumenical Movement, 1900–1968* (New York: Association Press, 1968);

John Cooney, *The American Pope: The Life and Times of Francis Cardinal Spellman* (New York: Times Books, 1984);

Harvey Cox, *Turning East: The Promise and Peril of the New Orientalism* (New York: Simon & Schuster, 1977);

John L. Eighmy, *Churches in Cultural Captivity: A History of the Social Attitudes of Southern Baptists* (Knoxville: University of Tennessee Press, 1987);

Carol V. George, *God's Salesman: Norman Vincent Peale and the Power of Positive Thinking* (New York: Oxford University, 1992);

Langdon B. Gilkey, *Catholicism Confronts Modernism: A Protestant View* (New York: Seabury, 1975);

Gilkey, *Gilkey on Tillich* (New York: Crossroad, 1990);

Donald G. Jones and Russell, eds., *American Civil Religion* (San Francisco: Mellen Research University Press, 1990);

Wayne W. Mahan, *Tillich's System* (San Antonio: Trinity University Press, 1974);

Bernard Martin, *The Existentialist Theology of Paul Tillich* (New York: Bookman Associates, 1963);

William C. Martin, *A Prophet with Honor: The Billy Graham Story* (New York: Morrow, 1991);

Martin Marty, *Pilgrims in Their Own Land: 500 Years of Religion in America* (Boston: Houghton Mifflin, 1984);

Robert Moats Miller, *Bishop G. Bromley Oxnam: Paladin of Liberal Protestantism* (Nashville: Abingdon Press, 1990);

Wilhelm and Marion Pauck, *Paul Tillich: His Life and Thought* (New York: Harper & Row, 1976);

Ronald H. Stone, *Reinhold Niebuhr: Prophet to Politicians* (Nashville: Abingdon Press, 1972);

Brooks R. Walker, *Christian Fright Peddlers* (Garden City, N.Y.: Doubleday, 1964);

Edmund Wilson, *The Dead Sea Scrolls, 1947-1969* (New York: Oxford University Press, 1969).

SCIENCE AND TECHNOLOGY

Gary M. Abshire, ed., *The Impact of Computers on Society and Ethics: A Bibliography* (Morristown, N. J.: Creative Computing, 1980);

Jack Belzer, Albert G. Holzman, and Allen Kent, eds., *Encyclopedia of Computer Science and Technology*, 16 volumes (New York: Marcel Dekker, 1975–1981);

Herman H. Goldstein, *The Computer from Pascal to von Neumann* (Princeton, N. J.: Princeton University Press, 1972);

J. Haugelan, *Artificial Intelligence: The Very Idea* (Cambridge, Mass.: MIT Press, 1985);

Leslie Katz, ed., *Fairy Tales for Computers* (Boston: Nonpareil Books, 1969);

Anthony O. Lewis, ed., *Of Men and Machines* (London: Dutton, 1963);

McGraw-Hill Encyclopedia of Science and Technology fourth edition, 14 volumes (New York: McGraw-Hill, 1977);

Sam Mescowitz, ed., *The Coming of Robots* (New York: Collier, 1963);

N. Metropolis, ed., *A History of Computing in the Twentieth Century* (New York: Academic Press, 1980);

Lewis Mumford, *The Myth of the Machine: The Pentagon of Power* (New York: Harcourt Brace Jovanovich, 1964);

Cass Schichtle, *The National Space Program from the Fifties to the Eighties* (Washington, D.C.: GPO, 1983);

Science & Technology Desk Reference, edited by Carnegie Library of Pittsburgh, Science and Technology Department (Detroit: Gale Research, 1993);

Robert Silverberg, ed., *Men and Machines* (New York: Meredith Press, 1968);

Herbert Alexander Simon, *Sciences of the Artificial* (Cambridge, Mass.: MIT Press, 1969);

C. P. Snow, *The Two Cultures and the Scientific Revolution* (New York: Cambridge University Press, 1961).

SPORTS

Charles C. Alexander, *Our Game: An American Baseball History* (New York: Holt, 1991);

Arthur R. Ashe, Jr., *A Hard Road to Glory: A History of the African-American Athlete Since 1946* (New York: Warner, 1988);

William J. Baker and John M. Carrol, eds., *Sports in Modern America* (Saint Louis: River City Publishers, 1981);

Jim Benagh, *Incredible Olympic Feats* (New York: McGraw-Hill, 1976);

Edwin H. Cady, *The Big Game: College Sports and American Life* (Knoxville: University of Tennessee Press, 1978);

Roger Caillois, *Man, Play, and Games* (London: Thames & Hudson, 1962);

Erich Camper, *Encyclopedia of the Olympic Games* (New York: McGraw-Hill, 1972);

John Durant, *Highlights of the Olympics* (New York: Hastings House, 1965);

James B. Dworkin, *Owners Versus Players: Baseball and Collective Bargaining* (Boston: Auburn House, 1981);

Ellen W. Gerber, Jan Feshlin, Pearl Berlin, and Waneen Wyrick, *The American Woman in Sport* (Reading, Mass.: Addison-Wesley, 1974);

Elliott J. Gorn, *The Manly Art* (Ithaca, N.Y.: Cornell University Press, 1986);

Peter J. Graham and Horst Ueberhorst, editors, *The Modern Olympic Games* (Cornwall, N.Y.: Leisure Press, 1976);

Will Grimsley, *Golf: Its History, People and Events* (Englewood Cliffs, N. J.: Prentice-Hall, 1966);

Grimsley, *Tennis: Its History, People and Events* (Englewood Cliffs, N. J.: Prentice-Hall, 1971);

Allen Guttman, *A Whole New Ball Game: An Interpretation of American Sports* (Chapel Hill: The University of North Carolina Press, 1988);

Dorothy V. Harris, ed., *Women and Sport* (College Park: Pennsylvania State University Press, 1972);

Robert J. Higgs, *Sports: A Reference Guide* (Westport, Conn.: Greenwood, 1982);

Neil D. Isaacs, *All the Moves: A History of College Basketball* (Philadelphia: Lippincott, 1975);

Bill James, *The Bill James Historical Baseball Abstract* (New York: Villard Books, 1986);

William O. Johnson, *All That Glitters Is Not Gold* (New York: Putnam, 1972);

Roger Kahn, *The Boys of Summer* (New York: Harper & Row, 1972);

Kahn, *The Era: 1947–1956, When the Yankees, the Giants, and the Dodgers Ruled the World* (New York: Ticknor & Fields, 1993);

Ivan N. Kaye, *Good Clean Violence: A History of College Football* (Philadelphia: Lippincott, 1973);

Lee Lowenfish, *The Imperfect Diamond: A History of Baseball's Labor Wars* (New York: Da Capo, 1991);

Richard D. Mandel, *Sport: A Cultural History* (New York: Columbia University Press, 1984);

Robert Mechicoff and Steven Estes, *A History and Philosophy of Sport and Physical Education* (Dubuque, Iowa: William C. Brown, 1993);

James A. Michener, *Sports in America* (New York: Random House, 1976);

Jack Olsen, *The Black Athlete: A Shameful Story* (New York: Time-Life Books, 1968);

Robert W. Peterson, *Only the Ball Was White* (Englewood Cliffs, N. J.: Prentice-Hall, 1970);

Benjamin G. Rader, *American Sports: From the Age of Folk Games to the Age of Spectators* (Englewood Cliffs, N. J.: Prentice-Hall, 1983);

Martin Ralbovsky, *Destiny's Darlings* (New York: Hawthorn Books, 1974);

Steven A. Riess, ed., *The American Sporting Experience* (West Point, N.Y.: Leisure Press, 1984);

Charles Rosen, *Scandals of '51* (New York: Holt, Rinehart & Winston, 1978);

William F. Russell, *Go Up for Glory* (New York: Coward-McCann, 1966);

Leverett T. Smith, Jr., *The American Dream and the National Game* (Bowling Green: Bowling Green University Popular Press, 1975);

Betty Spears and Richard A. Swanson, *History of Sport and Physical Education,* third edition (Dubuque, Iowa: William C. Brown, 1983);

Jules Tygel, *Baseball's Great Experiment* (New York: Oxford University Press, 1983);

David Q. Voigt, *America Through Baseball* (Chicago: Nelson-Hall, 1976);

Herbert Warren Wind, *The Gilded Age of Sport* (New York: Simon & Schuster, 1961);

Wind, *The Realm of Sport* (New York: Simon & Schuster, 1966);

Earle F. Zeigler, ed., *A History of Physical Education and Sport in the United States and Canada* (Champaign, Ill.: Stipes Publishing Company, 1975).

CONTRIBUTORS

ARTS   RICHARD LAYMAN
                                  Manly, Inc.

BUSINESS AND THE ECONOMY   LARRY SCHWEIKART
                                  University of Dayton

EDUCATION   JENNIFER DAVIS
                                  University of Dayton

FASHION   JAN COLLINS STUCKER
                                  University of South Carolina

GOVERNMENT AND POLITICS   LARRY SCHWEIKART
                                  University of Dayton
                                  and
                                  DENNIS LYNCH
                                  Bruccoli Clark Layman

LAW AND JUSTICE   ROBERT DEEB
                                  Bethea, Jordan & Griffin
                                  and
                                  CHARLES D. BROWER
                                  University of South Carolina

LIFESTYLES AND TRENDS   CHARLES D. BROWER
                                  University of South Carolina

MEDIA   JAMES HIPP
                                  Bruccoli Clark Layman

MEDICINE AND HEALTH   RICHARD LAYMAN
                                  Manly, Inc.

RELIGION   JOHN SCOTT WILSON
                                  University of South Carolina

SCIENCE & TECHNOLOGY   WAYNE BURROWS, M.D.
                                  University of South Carolina
                                  and
                                  LYNDY WILSON-BURROWS, M.P.H.
                                  *South Carolina Department of Health and
                                  Environmental Control*

SPORTS   STEPHEN MOSHER
                                  Ithaca College
                                  and
                                  DENNIS LYNCH
                                  Bruccoli Clark Layman

INDEX OF PHOTOGRAPHS

INDEX

Ferlinghetti, Lawrence, 24, 31, 36, 40
Fermi, Enrico, 437–438
Fernald, Grace M., 143
Fernandez, Raymond, 226
Fiedler, Leslie, 56
Field, Marshall, III, 112
Field-Ion microscope, 402
Field of Vision (Morris), 22
Fifteenth Amendment, 226
Fifth Amendment, 240
Film industry, 78
Filter-tipped cigarettes, 259
Fink, Colin G., 437–438
First Amendment, 229, 236–237, 383, 386, 393–394
First National City Bank, 96
Fisher, Dorothy Canfield, 71
Fisk University, 116
Fission, 413
Fitch, John Andrews, 287
Fleet, Jo van, 22
Fleetwoods, 25
Fleming, Jim, 312
Flemming, Arthur, 119
Flesch, Rudolf, 139
Fletcher, John Gould, 71
Flexner, Anne Crawford, 71
Floating Opera (Barth), 23
The Fly, 43
Flying saucers. *See* Unidentified flying objects (UFOs)
Flynn, Errol, 71
Foley, Red, 18
Foley, William J., 255
Folk remedies, 258
Folsom, James, 229
Folsom, Marion B., 131
Foltz, Frederick S., 287
Fonaroff, Nina, 64
Fonda, Henry, 22, 24
Food and Drug Administration, 283
Football
    collegiate, 458–459
    dominance of coaches, 459
    impact of television, 459–460
    professional popularity, 458
    televised, 457
    two-point conversion, 445
Foote, Shelby, 19
Forbidden Planet, 43
Ford, Katherine, 287
Ford, Mary, 20
Ford, Tennessee Ernie, 22
Ford Foundation, 294
Ford Motor Company, 80, 81, 82

Foreman, Carl, 302
FORTRAN, 402, 406, 410, 435
Fortune, 322
Forty-five (45) RPM records, 37–39
Foss, Marin M., 112
Fossil dating, 412
Foster, Donald D., 395
The Four Aces, 19
Four-minute mile, 444
Fourteenth Amendment, 226, 233–235
Fourth Amendment, 226
Fox, Howard, 368
Fox, William, 71
Franchising, 107
Frank, Jerome N., 222
Frankfurter, Felix, 245
Franklin, Kenneth Lynn, 435
Franklin, Rosalind, 317–428, 411
Frasner, Lee, 31
Fraternities, 116
Frawley, William, 303
Frazer, Joseph, 97
Frederick, Pauline, 326
Freed, Alan, 23, 24, 49, 326
Freedom of speech and press, 236–237, 244
Freeman, B. S., 365
Freeman, Douglas Southall, 331
Freeman, Walter, 362–363
Freidman, M., 366
French, Clara, 395
Freng, Ragnar T., 287
Frick, Ford C., 442, 474
Friedan, Betty, 276
Frierson, William L., 255
Frisbees, 260, 262
Fromenson, Ruth Bernard, 287
From Here to Eternity (Jones), 19, 20, 29, 42, 47
From the Terrace (O'Hara), 24, 29
Frozen food, 79, 89, 402
Fry, W. J., 365
Frye, Jack, 112
Fuchs, Karl, 251
Fugate, Caril Ann, 229
Fuller, Alfred Howard, 112
Fuller, R. Buckminster, 149, 150, 168–169
Fullmer, Gene, 455
Fund for the Advancement of Education, 135
Furniture, 160
    American modern, 164–165
    Eames chairs, 168

modern designs predominate, 149
    office, 162
    organic design, 170
    plastic, 149, 150
    simplicity of, 151
    tubular, 148
    womb chair, 170
Fusion, 413
Gaedel, Eddie, 442, 474
Gaines, William M., 270, 320
Galanos, James, 155, 172
Galaxy, 50
Galbraith, John Kenneth, 81, 263, 275, 281–282
Gallagher, Michael, 112
Gallagher, Richard S. ("Skeets"), 71
Gallant Man, 444
Gallatin, Albert Eugene, 71
Gannett, Frank Ernest, 112, 331
Garbo, Greta, 65
Gardner, Eugene, 437–438
Garfield, John, 71
Garland, Judy, 21, 43, 254
Garland, Robert, 71, 331
Garment industry, 82
Garner, Erroll, 65
Garroway, Dave, 285, 312
Garson, W., 366
Gates, Eleanor, 71
Gathings, Ezekiel Candler, 39
Gathings Committee, 39–41
Gathright, A., 365
Gaugh, Harry, 55
Gein, Ed, 229
Geismar, Maxwell, 56
Geneen, Harold, 110
General Dynamics Corporation, 78, 96
General Electric, 79
General Motors Corporation, 79, 80, 89, 93, 109–110
Genetics, 317–428
Gentlemen Prefer Blondes, 43, 59
Geodesic dome, 149, 150, 168–169
Gerber, Frank, 112
Gerber Products Company, 89, 258
Germs
    control of, 348
    definition and awareness, 347
Gernreich, Rudi, 155
Gernsback, Hugo, 50
Gerry, Peter Goelet, 222
"Get a Job," 24
Getty, Jean Paul, 110
Getz, Stan, 65
Giannini, A. P., 89

Mountfort, Harry, 72, 331
Movie industry, 297
    blacklisting, 302
    box-office totals, 79
    drive-ins, 301
    the Hollywood Ten, 301–302
    independent producers, 305
    production code, 305
    theaters, 96, 304
    threat of television, 304, 305
Movies, 18, 19, 22, 24, 25
    3-D, 20, 21, 259, 400
    color, 400
    content protected, 374
    dramas, 42
    and the First Amendment, 236, 237
    musicals, 43
    and religion, 384–385, 393–394
    science fiction and horror, 43
    sexual themes, 40, 273
    spectacles, 41–42
    sports biographies, 452
    women's, 43
Mr. Jones Meet Your Maker (Marshall), 387
Mueller, Erwin, 435
Muggs, J. Fred, 312
Mulligan, Gerry, 44
Munk, Arnold H., 113
Murchie, Harold B., 222
Murray, William Henry "Alfalfa Bill," 222
Murrow, Edward R., 88, 294, 309–310, 316, 323, 326
Museum of Modern Art (MOMA), 165
Museums, 23
Musial, Stan, 450
Music, 18, 44
Music Box Theatre, NYC, 21
Muslims, 380
Mustard, W. T., 365
Mutiny on the Bounty, 54
Mutual funds, 100
"My Foolish Heart," 18
Nahm, Eugene A., 438
Naifeh, Stevan, 56
Nailor, Gerald, 72
The Naked and the Dead (Mailer), 29
The Naked Lunch (Burroughs), 25
Narcotics arrests, 229
Nash, Florence, 72
Nathan, George Jean, 72
The *Nation*, 308
National Academy of Recording Arts and Sciences, 25

National Aeronautics and Space Administration (NASA), 82, 191, 403
National Association for the Advancement of Colored People (NAACP), 124, 229, 234, 258
National Association of Electric Companies, 92
National Automobile Show, 150
National Baptist Convention, 374
National Basketball Association, 451–452
National Basketball Association Championships, 445
National Bowling Association, 454
National Broadcasting Company (NBC), 19, 191, 299, 311–313, 317, 325
National Broadcasting Company Orchestra, 21, 51–52
National Broadcasting Company Singers, 23
National Cancer Institute, 343
National Cancer Society, 344
National Catholic Educational Association, 121
National Child Labor Committee, 141
National Conference on Air Pollution, 337
National Council for Financial Aid to Education, 116
National Council of Churches, 386–387
National Defense Education Act (NDEA), 118, 129–131, 190
National Education Association (NEA), 116, 117, 118, 121, 132, 136
National Football League, 443, 444, 459, 459–460
National Football League Championship, 445
National Football League Player's Association, 445
National Foundation for Infantile Paralysis, 354, 364
National Gallery of Art, 19
National Highway Act, 98, 262, 268
National Merit Scholarshlip Corporation, 117
National Music Council, 20
The *National Review*, 309
National Science Foundation, 132, 180

National Security Council memorandum-68 (NSC-68), 187
National Student Christian Federation, 376
National Television System Committee, 104
The Natural (Malamud), 19, 29, 442
The Nature and Destiny of Man (Niebuhr), 391
Nautilus, 401, 403, 419
Neely, Mathew M., 222
Neiman, Carrie, 113
Neiman-Marcus, 96
Nelli, Herva, 52
Nelson, George, 162, 173
Nessler, Charles, 174
The New Left, 308
"New Look," 151, 152, 167–168
New Look policy, 187
Newman, Arnold, 65
Newman, Paul, 21, 24, 65
New Orleans Board of Education, 116
Newport Jazz Festival, 21, 44–45
New Republic, 32, 308
New Revised Standard Version of the Bible, 374, 375
New Rochelle, N.Y., 241
News coverage monopoly, 295
Newspapers, 306–307
    dwindling numbers, 307
    economic status of, 297
    strikes, 294, 295, 306–307
    vending machines, 295
New York Eight, 132–133
New York Giants, baseball, 442, 445, 471
New York Giants, football, 445
New York Herald Tribune, 306–307, 318
New York Philharmonic Orchestra, 25, 28, 53, 65
The New York School of Artists, 26
New York State Board of Regents, 133, 236, 237
New York Yankees, 443, 448, 450, 470
Niagara, 59
Nias, Henry, 113
Nichols, Spencer Baird, 72
Niebuhr, Reinhold, 390–391
Nielsen, A. C., 299
Nielsen Television Index, 299–300
Nies, Edwin, 395
Niles, David F., 222
Nine Stories (Salinger), 20, 63
Nineteen Eighty-Four (Orwell), 26

Philadelphia, 25
Philadelphia Orchestra, 65
Philbrick, Herbert A., 250
Philips, Thomas Wharton, Jr., 222
Phillips, Sam, 48–49, 50–51, 62
Phonics, 139
Photovoltaic cell, 401
Pick, Franz, 111
Pickett, Wilson, 49
Pickford, Mary, 19
Picnic (Inge), 21
Piggly Wiggly, 96
The Pill, 258, 402, 420, 433
Pill, Gerald, 327
Piltdown man, 412
Pincus, Gregory, 420, 433
Pino, Tony, 232
Pinza, Ezio, 73
Pitkin, Walter Boughton, 73
Pius XII, 116, 173, 397
Pizza Hut, 260
Plastics, 149
The Platters, 23, 24, 25
Playboy, 39, 263, 283, 300
"Playboy's Penthouse," 283
Player Piano (Vonnegut), 19
Pledge of Allegiance, 226
"Pledge to Children," 130
Pleis, Jack, 20, 21
Plessy v. Ferguson, 124, 234
Plimpton, George, 20
Pohl, Frederik, 50
Poitier, Sidney, 25
Polio
    fear of, 354
    incidence of, 354
    mistaken diagnoses, 355
    nature of, 354–355
    rate, 336
    vaccine, 131, 355–356
Poliomyelitis Vaccination Act, 356
Polio Pioneers, 356
Polio rate, 336
Pollock, Jackson, 23, 26, 27, 31, 32, 33, 61, 73
Poll tax, 215
Pollution, 267
Polo Grounds, 445
Poniatoff, Alexander, 402, 425
Poole, Ernest, 73
"Pop art," 25
Pope, Virginia, 173
Popular music (list), 30
Popular songs, 18, 19, 20, 21, 22, 23, 24, 25
Population
    baby boom, 264
    mobility, 267
    statistics, 262
Pornography and obscenity, attacks on, 39–41
Portnoy, J., 366
Potassium dating, 412
Poteat, Edwin NcNeill, 288
Powell, Adam Clayton, 134
Powell, William, 22
Power, Tyrone, 73
The Power Elite (Mills), 275, 284
The Power of Positive Thinking (Peale), 388, 392
Power steering, 400
Prado, Perez, 22
Preminger, Otto, 40, 302
Presidential tenure limitation, 226
Presidential Traffic Safety Commission, 259
President's Council on Youth Fitness, 357, 464–465
Presley, Elvis, 22, 23, 24, 26, 28–29, 49, 50, 51, 61–62, 150, 260
Presley, Gladys, 288
Press conferences, 209
Preston, Roger, 288
"Pretend," 20
Prevention magazine, 258
Price, Lloyd, 25, 49
Price, Vincent, 43
Price controls, 91, 110, 248
Prince, Bob, 456
Print media, 297
Prisk, Laura B., 288
Prisonaires, 50
Prison life, 242–243
Privacy, 162
Private sector incomes, 211
Proctor and Gamble, 311
Progressive education, 127
Progressive party, 391
Prosser, Charles Allen, 143
Protestant, Catholic, Jew (Herberg), 381
Protestants and Others Organized for the Separation of Church and State, 391
Psychiatrists, 353
Psychoanalysis, 353
Publications (lists)
    about the arts, 74–75
    about business, 114
    about education, 144–145
    about fashion and design, 177–178
    about government and politics, 223–224
    about law and justice, 256
    about the media, 332–333
    about medicine, 370–371
    about religion, 397–398
    about sports, 479–480
    about the sciences, 439–440
    about trendsetters and socialites, 290–291
Public law 926, 118
Publishing, 259
Puerto Rican Nationalists, 180, 181, 194
Pulitzer, Herbert, 113
Pulitzer, Joseph, 331
Pulitzer Prize, 29, 57
Pulsifer, Lawson Valentine, 113
"Pumpkin papers," 215
Purcell, Harold, 288
Purdy, Lawson, 288
Putnam, George Palmer, 73
Putnam, Samuel, 73
Quant, Mary, 157, 170
The Quiet Man, 19
Quinn, Anthony, 19, 23
Quo Vadis?, 41, 384
Raab, William, 365
Race relations, 57, 226
    Jim Crow laws, 265
    violence, 235–236
    See also Little Rock, Arkansas; Montgomery, Alabama
Racism, 260
"Radarange, 417
Radiation therapy, 357–358
Radicalism on Campus, 133
Radio, 311, 324
    and astronomy, 421
    decline, 104
    news, 315–316
    opposing views issue, 294
    transistorized, 294, 401
Radio Corporation of America (RCA), 325
Radioimmunoassay, 317–428, 401, 421–422
Radio telephone, 424
Radiotherapy, 345
Railroad industry, 78, 99–100, 183
Raisin in the Sun (Hansberry), 25
Ramo, Simon, 98, 111
Ranier, Prince, 284
Rankin, Frederick Wharton, 369
Rapaport, Paul, 435
Rapp, Gustav William, 365
Rath, John W., 113

Truman, Harry S, 91, 200, 202, 205, 221, 238, 248, 308, 413
  assassination attempt, 180, 194
  and big business, 78, 79, 192
  and the press, 209–210
Truman, Harry S Commission of Fine Arts, 19
Truman, Margaret, 308, 327
Trumbo, Dalton, 42, 226, 301
Trump, John G., 366
The Truth about Cancer (Cameron), 344
TRW Corporation, 89, 98, 111
Tubb, Ernest, 28
Tuberculosis, 336, 358–359
Tucker, Preston, 78
Turner, Ike, 50
Turner, Lana, 43, 229
Turpin, Randy, 455
Tuskegee Institute, 259
Tuve, M. A., 435
TV dinners, 79, 259, 278
TV Guide, 313–314
Twelve Angry Men, 24
Twenty-One, 254
Twenty-second amendment, 226
"Twilight Time," 24
The Twilight Zone, 50
Twombly, Florence Adele Vanderbilt, 289
Tydings, Millard, 221
Tydings committee, 216
Ultrasound, 337
Umeki, Miyoshi, 24
Umhey, Frederick F., 174
Unemployment, 82, 110
Unidentified flying objects (UFOs), 258, 259, 260
Union of Soviet Socialist Republics (USSR)
  explodes atom bomb, 188
  launches *Sputnik*, 182
  missile development, 183
Unions
  and Communist affiliation, 226
  corruption, 93, 96, 105
  purges, 93
  and racketeering, 241–242
United Artists, 19
United Auto Workers, 93, 108–109
United Church of Christ, 376
United Nations building, 148
United Nations Genocide Convention, 374
United Nations Organization, 182, 188
United Presbyterian Church, 376

United Press International (UPI), 296
United States, 78
  army reductions, 182
  budget surplus, 81
  fear of communism, 184
  impact of television, 185
  military policies, 187
  reaction to *Sputnik*, 189–191
  Republicans elected, 185
  sentimentalized, 184
United States Congress and the FBI, 181, 182, 238
United States Steel, 80
United States Supreme Court, 253
  appointments to, 245
  and Communist affiliation, 226
  court martial limits, 228
  deals with Little Rock crisis, 229
  desegregation, 228
  desertion and citizenship, 229
  equality before the law, 228
  freedom of expression, 226, 244
  jury duty, 226
  lawful searches, 226
  limits First Amendment, 228
  limits Smith Act, 228
  prosecution in two jurisdictions, 229
  protects NAACP privacy, 229
  and public worship, 226
  race and juries, 226
  race and law school admittance, 226
  security issues, 228
  seizure of steel industry, 226
  and the FBI, 238–239
  and the Hollywood Ten, 226
  unreasonable search and seizure, 226
  and voting rights, 226
  See also names of cases
United Steelworkers of America, 81
UNIVAC, 90, 109, 400, 408, 430, 435
University of California, 133
University of California School of Music, 18
University of Florida, 116
University of Iowa, 142
University of Louisville, 124
University of North Carolina, 124
University of Oklahoma, 123
University of Rochester, 116
University of Tennessee, 124
University of Texas, 142

University of Texas Law School, 123
University of Virginia, 124
The Untouchables, 230
Upshaw, William D., 223
Uranium dating, 412
Uris, Leon, 20
U.S. Armed Forces Institute, 117
U.S. Court of Appeals, 228
U.S. Loyalty Review Board, 254
Ustinov, Peter, 42
V-2 rocket bomb, 433
Vaccines, 337, 348–349, 355–356
  for common cold, 347
  for diptheria, 337
  for flu, 341
  for measles, 362
  See also under Polio
Vacuum tubes, 426
Valens, Ritchie, 25, 36, 74
VA loans, 93
VA mortgages, 276
Van Alen, William, 174
Van Allen, James Alfred, 436
Van Allen Radiation Belt, 403
Van Alstyne, Egbert, 74
Van Brocklin, Norm, 475
Vance, Vivian, 303
Vanderbilt, Arthur T., 223
Vanderbilt, Grace Wilson, 289
Van der Rohe, Mies, 148
Van Doren, Carl, 74
Van Doren, Charles, 254
Van Etten, Nathan Bristol, 369
Van Hoof, Mary Anna, 396
Van Horn, John A., 436
Van Kort, John, 173
Van Vogt, A.E., 50
Variety shows, 325
Vatican, 393–394
Vatican Sacred Congregation of Religious Studies, 118
"Vaya Con Dios," 20
Veeck, Bill, 442, 475
Velde, Harold H., 381, 391
Venereal disease, 360
Venice Biennale, 55
"Venus," 25
Verdon, Gwen, 445
Video games, 429–430
Videotape recording, 294, 425
Vinson, Fred, 226
Virginia and school integration, 126–127
Viruses, 347
Viruses and cancer, 336
VISA, 92, 274

Vitamin B-12 deficiency, 336
Vitamin C, 337
Vito, Victor, 152
Vittum, Harriet E., 289
Viva Zapata!, 19, 54
Voice of America, 181
"Volare," 25
Volcanoes, 417
Vonnegut, Kurt, Jr., 19, 50
Von Newmann, John, 436
Von Stroheim, Erich, 73
Von Tilzer, Albert (Gumm), 74
Voting rights, 229
Vukovich, Bill, 444, 479
Wadsworth, George, 223
Wages, 93, 111
Waggoner, Porter, 28
Wagner, Honus, 479
Wakefield, Dan, 59
Walcott, Jersey Joe, 443, 455
Walker, Doak, 475
Walker, J. D., 113
Walker, Robert, 19, 74
"Walkin' My Baby Back Home," 20
A Walk on the Wild Side (Algren), 23
Wallace, Henry A., 221, 308, 391
Wallop, Douglas, 442
Wall Street lawyers, 233
Walrathe, Florence Dahl, 289
Walter, Bruno, 53
Walter, Edwin, 74
"Wanted," 21
The Wapshot Chronicle (Cheever), 29
Warburg, Frieda Schiff, 289
Ward, Arch, 332
Wareham, Harry P., 289
Warner, Donald F., 438
Warner, Glen ("Pop"), 479
Warner, Harry M., 74, 113, 332
War of the Worlds, 43, 50
Warren, Charles, 255
Warren, Earl, 124, 196, 226, 229, 231, 234, 245, 246–247, 252–253
Warren, Robert Penn, 65
Warren, Shields, 366
Warsitz, Erich, 415
War Suplus Properties Board, 88
Washburn, Stanley, 332
Washington, Dinah, 60
Watkins v. United States, 244
Watson, James D., 401, 411
Watson, Thomas J., Jr., 91, 109, 114
Wattel, Harold, 277
Watts, Alan, 394–395
Watts, James, 362

Wayne, John, 19
Weaver, Pat, 312, 327
The Weavers, 19
Weber, Joan, 22
Wegg, Simon Taylor, 289
Weinberger, Peter Howard, 254
Weiner, Norbert, 401
Weiss, Robert S., 111
Welch, George S., 289
Welch, Joseph Nye, 216, 254
Welty, Eudora, 65
Wente, Carl, 111
Wertham, Frederic, 270
Western Union, 78
West Side Story, 24, 28, 53
Weyerhaeuser, John Philip, Jr., 114
Wham-O Manufacturing, 260
"Wheel of Fortune," 20
When Worlds Collide, 50
Wherry, Kenneth S., 223
White, Bouck, 289
White, Charles E., Mrs., 142
White, E.B., 19, 25
White, Harry Dexter, 253
White, Thomas J., Mrs., 142
White Collar (Mills), 275, 284
Whitehead, Don, 238
Whitehouse, William Fitzhugh, 289
White House Conference on Children and Youth, 129, 193
White House Conference on Education, 117, 131–132, 138–139, 194
White House Press Corps, 208–210
White House remodeled, 148
"White primaries," 183
Whitmore, James, 55
Whitney, John Hay, 327
Whitney Museum, 18, 21, 55
Whittaker, Charles E., 228, 247
Whittfield, Mal, 466
Whooping cough vaccine, 337
"Why Don't You Believe Me?," 20
Why Johnny Can't Read (Flesch), 139
Whyte, William, 275
Widdicombe, Ralph Hewitt, 174
Wilbur, Richard, 53
Wilde, Pamela, 285
Wilde, Percival, 74
Wilder, Thornton, 22
Wilder, Wilbur Elliott, 289
The Wild One, 42, 54
Wilfman, Inc,, 96
Wilkins, Jesse E., 255
Wilkins, M. H. F., 411

Wilkins, Roy, 221
Wilkinson, Bud, 459, 475
Wilkinson, John, 438
Williams, Anna W., 369
Williams, Ben Ames, 74
Williams, Charles Finn, 289
Williams, Frances, 74
Williams, Hank, 19, 27–28, 63–64, 74
Williams, Harrison, 290
Williams, Ted, 442, 450, 475
Williams, Tennessee, 65
Williams, Walter, 290
Williams, William Appleman, 308
Williams College, 116
Willys-Overland Motors, Inc., 97
Wilson, Charles E., 109–110, 182
Wilson, Edmund, 382–383
Wilson, Frank H., 74
Wilson, Frank Norman, 369
Wilson, Irving "Chief," 88
Wilson, J. Finley, 290
Wilson, Kemmons, 88
Wilson, Michael, 302
Wilson, Sloan, 22
Wimbleton tennis championship, 444
Winhalter, Hugo, 20
Winlock, Herbert Eustis, 438
Winterhalter, Hugo, 21
Wischmeier, Elma H., 290
Wise, Jonah H., 397
Wise Blood (O'Connor), 19, 29
"With all deliberate speed," 234
Witness (Chambers), 215
Wolcott, Jersey Joe, 442
Wolfe, Tom, 159
Wolley, Clarence Mott, 114
Woman as Landscape, 56
Woman I, 55
Women
    admitted to divinity school, 117
    and cancer, 343–344
    career fashions, 152
    census report, 260
    changing roles, 278–279
    in Congress, 181
    evening fashions, 153
    in golf, 461
    hair fashion, 152
    makeup, 153
    media view of, 278
    the "New Look," 152
    and public policy, 278
    receive law degree, 116
    rights, 263
    as scientists, 427–428

Wood, Clement, 74
Wood, Francis Carter, 369
Wood, Natalie, 24
Woodruff, Roy O., 223
Woodson, Carter Godwin, 144
Woodward, Joanne, 24
Woodward, Robert Burns, 436
Woodward, William E., 74
Wooldridge, Dean, 98, 111
Woolson, Albert, 290
Workforce, 85
Workmen's Compensation, 375
World Health Organization (WHO), 341
World Series of baseball, 443
Wouk, Herman, 19, 22
Wright, Frank Lloyd, 23, 74, 151, 157, 171–172, 174
Wright, John Dutton, 369
Wright, Lloyd, 231

Wright, Louis Tompkins, 369
Wu, Chien-Shiung, 317–428
Wylie, Philip, 264
Wyman, Jane, 43
Wynder, E. L., 366
Xerox, 78, 403, 429
X-rays, 336, 357
Yale University, 116
Yalow, Rosalyn, 401, 421–422, 427–428
Yalu River, 188
Yates v. United States, 244
Yeager, Charles ("Chuck"), 415
The Year the Yankees Lost the Pennant (Wallop), 442
Yellow fever, 363
Yorzyk, Bill, 466
"You, You, You," 20
Young, Denton True ("Cy"), 466, 479

"Young at Heart," 21
The Young Lions (Shaw), 29, 54
"Young Love," 24
Young People's Concerts, 53
Youngstown Sheet & Tube Company v. Sawyer, 248
"You Send Me," 24
Zaharias, Mildred ("Babe") Didrickson, 461, 475, 479
Zahm, Albert F., 438
Zatopek, Emil, 466
Zeckendorf, William, 81, 89
Zen Buddhism, 394
Zenith Radio Corporation, 295
Ziegler, Charles E., 369
Zook, George F., 144
Zorach v. Clauson, 383
Zwicker, Gen., 181